AI Factory

This book provides insights into how to approach and utilise data science tools, technologies, and methodologies related to artificial intelligence (AI) in industrial contexts. It explains the essence of distributed computing and AI technologies and their interconnections. It includes descriptions of various technology and methodology approaches and their purpose and benefits when developing AI solutions in industrial contexts. In addition, this book summarises experiences from AI technology deployment projects from several industrial sectors.

Features:

- Presents a compendium of methodologies and technologies in industrial AI and digitalisation.
- Illustrates the sensor-to-actuation approach showing the complete cycle, which defines and differentiates AI and digitalisation.
- Covers a broad range of academic and industrial issues within the field of asset management.
- Discusses the impact of Industry 4.0 in other sectors.
- Includes a dedicated chapter on real-time case studies.

This book is aimed at researchers and professionals in industrial and software engineering, network security, AI and machine learning (ML), engineering managers, operational and maintenance specialists, asset managers, and digital and AI manufacturing specialists.

ICT in Asset Management

Series Editor:
Diego Galar,
LTU, Lulea University of Technology

Robots, Drones, UAVs and UGVs, for Operation and Maintenance
Diego Galar, Uday Kumar and Dammika Seneviratne

AI Factory
Theories, Applications and Case Studies
Ramin Karim, Diego Galar and Uday Kumar

For more information about this series, please visit: www.routledge.com/ICT-in-Asset-Management/book-series/ICTAM

AI Factory
Theories, Applications and Case Studies

Ramin Karim, Diego Galar and Uday Kumar

CRC Press
Taylor & Francis Group
Boca Raton London New York

CRC Press is an imprint of the
Taylor & Francis Group, an **informa** business

Designed cover image: © Shutterstock

First edition published 2023
by CRC Press
6000 Broken Sound Parkway NW, Suite 300, Boca Raton, FL 33487-2742

and by CRC Press
4 Park Square, Milton Park, Abingdon, Oxon, OX14 4RN

CRC Press is an imprint of Taylor & Francis Group, LLC

© 2023 Ramin Karim, Diego Galar and Uday Kumar

ISBN: 9781032077642 (hbk)
ISBN: 9781032077659 (pbk)
ISBN: 9781003208686 (ebk)

DOI: 10.1201/9781003208686

Typeset in Times
by codeMantra

Contents

About the Authors

Ramin Karim has a PhD in Operation and Maintenance Engineering with specialisation in Industrial AI and eMaintenance. Currently, he is a Professor of Operation and Maintenance Engineering at Luleå University and Director of the Centre of Maintenance and Industrial Services. He gained more than 15 years of work experience in the IT industry after obtaining his degree in Computer Science. He is the head of the eMaintenance LAB, an applied laboratory for research and innovation in Industrial AI and eMaintenance. His research interests include AI, digitalisation, asset management, enhanced hybrid analytics (based on model-driven and data-driven approaches), and predictive technology in industrial asset management.

Professor Karim initiated and developed the concept and platform called AI Factory, a universal concept for cross-industrial data and model sharing based on digital and AI technologies. Today, the toolkit of AI Factory has been adapted to several industrial sectors, including railway, mining, construction, and aviation. With his creative thinking and innovation-driven personality, Professor Karim has demonstrated how excellence in research can lead to sustainable development in society and benefits for business. This is in the context of digitalisation, Industrial AI, and eMaintenance. With his commitment, goal-oriented action, innovative thinking, and enthusiasm, he has created a dynamic research environment that has been a model for useful research.

His research results have resulted in a number of innovations. Professor Karim is the founder of a spin-off company from LTU, Predge AB (formerly eMaintenance365 AB), which provides advanced analytics based on cloud/edge technologies and AI. The company has been listed on Swedish "33-listan", a list of the most promising start-ups in Sweden, two years in a row.

Professor Karim's research has attracted national and international attention. He is an in-demand lecturer and advisor in various contexts. Some of these are: (i) Industrial Advisory Board of IMS Center in the USA; (ii) VALE (Brazil Mining Company); (iii) Swedish-Brazilian Research and Innovation Centre; (iv) Future Committee of the National Organisation of Swedish Maintenance; and (v) Board member of the Sustainability Circle. His work has attracted the attention of the Organisation for Economic Co-operation and Development (OECD). On behalf of OCED, he produced a report for policymakers, focusing on data-driven technology and solutions in transport.

Furthermore, Professor Karim's research results with respect to AI Factory have been recognised two years in a row on IVA's 100 list in 2020 and 2021. The list includes projects with the potential to create benefits in the foreseeable future through industrial commercialisation, business and method development and societal impact.

Diego Galar is a Full Professor of Condition Monitoring in the Division of Operation and Maintenance Engineering at Luleå University of Technology where he is coordinating several H2020 projects related to different aspects of cyber physical systems, Industry 4.0, Internet of Things (IoT), Industrial AI, and Big Data. He was involved in the SKF UTC Centre located in Lulea focused on SMART bearings and has been actively involved in national projects with the Swedish industry or funded by Swedish national agencies like Vinnova.

He is the principal researcher at Tecnalia (Spain), heading the Maintenance and Reliability research group within the Division of Industry and Transport.

Professor Diego has authored more than 500 journal and conference papers, books, and technical reports in the field of maintenance, working also as a member of editorial boards and scientific committees, chairing international journals and conferences, and actively participating in national and international committees for standardisation and R&D in the topics of reliability and maintenance.

In the international arena, Professor Galar has been a visiting Professor at Polytechnic of Braganza (Portugal), University of Valencia, NIU (USA), and Universidad Pontificia Católica de Chile. Currently, he is a visiting professor at University of Sunderland (UK), University of Maryland (USA), and Chongqing University in China.

Uday Kumar is the Chair Professor of Operation and Maintenance Engineering, Director of Research and Innovation (Sustainable Transport) at Luleå University of Technology, and Director of Luleå Railway Research Center.

His teaching, research, and consulting interests are equipment maintenance, reliability and maintainability analysis, product support, lifecycle costing (LCC), risk analysis, system analysis, eMaintenance, asset management, etc.

He has been visiting faculty at the Center of Intelligent Maintenance System (IMS), a centre sponsored by National Science Foundation, Cincinnati, USA, since 2011. He is also an external examiner and program reviewer for the Reliability and Asset Management Program at University of Manchester, Distinguished Visiting Professor at Tsinghua University Beijing, and Honorary Professor at Beijing Jiaotong University, Beijing, among others. Earlier he was visiting faculty at Imperial College London, Helsinki University of Technology, Helsinki, and University of Stavanger, Norway, among others.

Professor Kuman has more than 30 years of experience in consulting and finding solutions to industrial problems directly or indirectly related to maintenance of engineering assets. He has published more than 300 papers in international journals and conference proceedings dealing with various aspects of maintenance of engineering systems, co-authored four books on maintenance engineering, and contributed to World Encyclopaedia on risk management.

He is an elected member of the Royal Swedish Academy of Engineering Sciences.

Foreword

In 1948, Norbert Wiener published his epoch-making book, *Cybernetics, or control and communication in the animal and the machine*, where he expounded his new theory on mathematical tools to control, communicate, learn, and decide under uncertainty, in the engineering context.

That book had a tremendous impact on 20th-century technology and industry. One element of it, though, the "learn" part, has taken a lot more time to mature, as it is interwoven with the concept of artificial intelligence (AI), of which Wiener was one of the pioneers, although it is more often associated with McCarthy and the 1956 Dartmouth seminar.

In the introduction to his book, Wiener remarked that, while the 17th century was the century of the mechanical clock, and the 18th and 19th centuries were epitomised by the steam engine, the 20th century was that of the computer, where information, more than energy, became the defining commodity.

He then asked: "How do living beings learn from their environment? How can we emulate them to create machines that learn?" After some very rigorous, albeit complex reasoning, he came to the conclusion that "a learning machine operates with nonlinear feedback".

Fast forward nearly 75 years: it has become commonplace to say that data are the new fuel, while AI and machine learning (the field that makes machines learn without being explicitly programmed) are essentially household words. Deep learning relies on the nonlinear feedback laws evoked by Wiener. Computers beat chess masters and GO masters at their own game, texts are translated instantaneously, the magic of image processing blurs the border between dream and reality, and "bots" play the stock market.

What is in it for industry?

The challenge of Industrial AI is to draw on all those wonderful techniques to address key industrial needs: how to design, maintain, and operate railways, mines, factories, etc. with the highest cost-efficiency while keeping the planet clean, and how to combine Big Data with human expertise harmoniously.

This book is the outcome of an unusual effort of close cooperation between academia and industry led by Luleå University of Technology's Operation and Maintenance Engineering Division in cooperation with Swedish industry, in a project called "AI Factory". The book provides a no-nonsense approach to all aspects of the problem of integrating AI into industry, from data collection to advanced analytics, data architecture, digital twins, cybersecurity management, and more, illustrated by case studies.

In the words of the authors, it can serve as a guide to those desirous of taking the difficult but promising path of applying the latest scientific advances in AI to real industrial problems.

Sweden, a country steeped in industrial tradition, and at the same time a land at the forefront of high-technology progress and environmental awareness, is an ideal place for such an endeavour.

I have been privileged, as the representative of the world's second largest railway manufacturer, to take part in the AI Factory for Railway, and I wish the readers of this book the same enjoyment reading it as I derived from that undertaking. Follow the guide...

Pierre Dersin
Ph.D., Adjunct Professor, LTU; former PHM Director, Alstom (ret.)

Preface

Artificial intelligence (AI) is transforming society and industry! AI accompanied by digital technologies and robotics enables the convergence of hardware, software, and liveware. This convergence brings numerous advantages to our society from different perspectives such as enhanced sustainability, enablement of circularity in natural resource consumption, improved global education, and better health and well-being. Simultaneously, AI, digitalisation, and robotics enable industries to strengthen global business competitiveness, achieve excellence in business, operation, and maintenance, improve safety and security, augment asset management, and extend asset life.

The next production revolution will occur because of a confluence of technologies. These will range from a variety of digital technologies (e.g. 3D printing, Internet of Things (IoT), advanced robotics) and new materials (e.g. bio- or nano-based) to new processes (e.g. data-driven production, AI, synthetic biology). As these technologies transform production, they will have far-reaching consequences for productivity, employment, skills, income distribution, trade, well-being, and the environment (OECD, 2017).

However, AI, digitalisation, and robotics also pose significant challenges, risks, and concerns when it comes to laws and regulations, education, work, ethics, equality, access, safety, and privacy, to name just a few. The European Economic and Social Committee (EESC) believes it is therefore essential to promote an informed and balanced public debate on AI involving all relevant stakeholders. A human-in-command approach to AI should be guaranteed, where the development of AI is responsible, safe, and useful, and machines remain machines and people retain control over these machines at all times (European Commission, 2018).

Hence, The EU aims to take the lead globally in establishing clear global policy frameworks for AI, in line with European values and fundamental rights. The EU emphasises the following areas (European Commission, 2018).

Laws and Regulations: The implications of AI for existing laws and regulations are considerable. A detailed evaluation of the EU laws and regulations should be carried out in the six areas identified by STOA (Scientific Foresight Unit) that may need to be revised or adapted. The EESC opposes the introduction of a form of legal personality for robots or AI. This would hollow out the preventive remedial effect of liability law; a risk of moral hazard arises in both the development and use of AI, and it creates opportunities for abuse.

Education and training: Education, skills, and training are amongst the many areas where AI poses societal challenges. The maintenance or acquisition of digital skills is necessary to give people the chance to adapt to the rapid developments in the field of AI. Stakeholders should invest in formal and informal learning, education, and training for all in order to enable people to work with AI but also to develop the skills that AI will not or should not acquire. It is also important to highlight the role of educational training programmes in protecting European workers operating in an environment that is being profoundly changed by the gradual emergence of AI. Comprehensive action plans will be needed to underpin the modernisation of education and training systems by nurturing the new skills required by the labour market of the future.

The European researchers, engineers, designers, and entrepreneurs who are involved in the development and marketing of AI systems must act in accordance with ethical and social responsibility criteria. One good response to this imperative could be to incorporate ethics and the humanities into training courses in engineering (European Commission, 2018).

AI can be defined as the ability of a machine to imitate intelligent human behaviour. AI also denotes the area of science and technology that aims to study, understand, and develop computers and software with intelligent behaviour. Research in areas that today fall under the collective term AI has been conducted since the 1950s and the term "artificial intelligence" was coined in 1956 by John McCarthy. The principles of AI are considered to have been formed by John McCarthy, Alan

Newell, Arthur Samuel, Herbert Simon, and Marvin Minsky within the context of the Dartmouth Summer Research Project, 1956. Although AI research has evolved steadily since the 1950s, many hopes have proven to be overoptimistic, leading to reduced funding for AI research in the later decades of the 20th century. In principle, AI deals with cognitive functions, while robotics primarily involves motor functions. In practice, however, these delimitations are not sharply defined, as robots require sensory ability and the capacity to analyse relevant environments. Nevertheless, the difference between AI's essentially intangible manifestations and robots' fundamentally physical manifestations is significant (Vinnova, 2018).

REFERENCES

European Commission. (2018). Artifical intelligence for Europe. Position Paper. Brussels: Publications Office of the European Union. https://doi.org/10.2864/67825

OECD. (2017). *The Next Production Revolution.* https://www.oecd.org/governance/the-next-production-revolution-9789264271036-en.htm

Vinnova. (2018). *Artifical Intelligence in Swedish Business and Society.* https://www.vinnova.se/en/publikationer/artificial-intelligence-in-swedish-business-and-society/

Acknowledgements

During the work on the book, we had many valuable discussions and exchanged ideas with students, friends, and colleagues from academia and industry. The inputs from these individuals were a valuable source of knowledge, bringing deep insight into real-world challenges and future needs and enlightening many aspects of and perspectives on digitalisation and AI in various industrial contexts. Therefore, we would like to specifically mention our sources of knowledge and inspiration.

First, we would like to convey our appreciation to Sweden's Innovation Agency (Vinnova). Our research and innovation were made possible by its financial support of the AI Factory initiative.

Second, we would like to express our gratitude to organisations that provided insight and knowledge in domain-related aspects: Alstom, Bane NOR, Boliden, Damill, Duroc Rail, GKN, LKAB, Infranord, Norut teknologi, Predge, SJ, Smurfitkappa, Scania, SSAB, SWECO, Trafikverket, Transitio, Tyréns, Tåg i Bergslagen, Vattenfall, and Vossloh.

Last but not least, we would like to express our gratitude to the AI Factory team members, for their dedicated effort in our research and innovation process and the development and materialisation of the AI Factory concept into a toolkit adapted for several industrial sectors, including railway, mining, construction, aviation, and manufacturing. Our sincere thanks to the AI Factory team: Adithya Thaduri, Amit Patwardhan, Emil Lindh, Gustav Bergström, Jaya Kumari, Kevin Karim, Manish Kumar, Martin Arenbro, Miguel Castano, Ravdeep Kour, Robin Karim, and Veronica Jägare.

Prologue

Industrial processes are information-driven! Managing, operating, and maintaining industrial assets are examples of industrial processes that must be highly information-intensive to become sustainable, effective, and efficient. Information is interpreted data adapted to a given context.

To be able to interpret data appropriately for industry, we first need a good understanding of the various industrial domains. We also need knowledge and insight to find and then process the relevant and related data. This data processing is often done using algorithms. Algorithms are a set of instructions that can be implemented in a computer software.

Artificial intelligence (AI) represents a package of algorithms with some common characteristics and capabilities aimed at extracting information out of data. In the field of AI, machine learning (ML) and deep learning (DL) refer to subsets of these algorithms.

In industry, achieving operational excellence is dependent on the availability and accessibility of information. Information can be used to augment decision-making processes and subsequently to take actions.

Industrial automation is expected to provide profit to businesses and contribute to improved sustainability in natural resource consumption. Automation is not limited to manufacturing processes. It can also benefit other processes, such as business, operation, and maintenance. The increased level of automation in industry requires appropriate information-driven governance, management, and execution strategies. An information-driven industrial process, in turn, requires a data-driven approach that facilitates knowledge discovery through information extraction.

Going from data to decision-making and then to actions is a necessary evolution for any sustainable and competitive industry, and it can be accelerated by digital technologies and AI.

But this evolution is associated with questions that need to be answered for a company to be successful. For example, how can we enable fact-based decision-making? How can we take automated actions based on data? What needs to be done? What are the prerequisites to become successful? And many others...

Our ambition with this book is to offer insights from different perspectives that your industry can use to answer these questions and succeed in the context of AI and digital technology.

1 Introduction

1.1 AI FACTORY

Based on many years of research and real-world experiences, we created a framework, an environment, and a toolkit to demonstrate capabilities relevant for the establishment of industrial artificial intelligence (AI). These digital tools have been integrated, demonstrated, validated, and verified within our platform called "AI Factory". This, in a nutshell, is what our book is all about.

The concept, architecture, and toolkit of AI Factory were developed to support an era of AI-based problem-solving in the industrial world. Our context-driven problem-solving approach emphasises the utilisation of digital technologies and AI. In the rest of this section, we explain some basic concepts that are integral to our AI factory.

1.1.1 ARTIFICIAL INTELLIGENCE

AI is intertwined with our daily lives. At a very basic level, AI refers to the use of software to give machines decision-making capabilities. With AI, they can perceive their environment (i.e. collect and integrate data), learn, and act based on what they have learned. In what follows, we explain some basic concepts of AI and their relations with industry.

1.1.2 INDUSTRIAL AUTOMATION

In industry, smart machines can transform labour-intensive tasks, increase production efficiency, improve human safety, contribute to the sustainability aspects, change the business processes, and achieve the overall operational excellence. In other words, smart machines enhance industrial automation through increased level of autonomy in various industrial processes and contexts.

As a concept, smart machines reflect a set of well-known industrial needs. But the new digital technologies, availability of data, and enhanced algorithms associated with machine learning (ML) and deep learning (DL) create new opportunities to bring smart machines into the real world.

Enhanced analytics: Smart machines are necessary for industrial automation, but other pieces of the puzzle need to be in place to achieve operational excellence in industry, by which we mean sustainable, competitive, and effective operations. One is augmented decision-making supported by facts. Fact-based decision-making based on a data-driven approach is important to improve the quality of decisions. A data-driven approach and AI are tightly connected and bring value to industry by processing a vast amount of data and offering insights into the decision-making processes.

However, the implementation of a data-driven approach to support decision-making through enhanced analytics depends on the availability and accessibility of relevant, good quality, and timely data. The level of data relevance can only be measured in the context of usage, i.e., the context of the decision-making process. A dataset might be significant in one context, but in another context, it might not have any value. This means that to assess whether a dataset is useful for analytics, we need to understand the usage context. Understanding the usage context in industry, in turn, requires knowledge in various industrial domains.

1.1.3 ENGINEERING KNOWLEDGE

A data-driven approach is an excellent tool for analytics but is not sufficient. Understanding data and data science, including ML and DL, needs to be combined with engineering knowledge to develop industrial solutions. Let's say that we aim to predict the remaining useful life of an asset by predicting its future failures. Let's assume that the analytics team has good knowledge of data-driven approaches and learning algorithms (ML and DL) and can use various regression algorithms for predictions. Let us also assume that there are several data sources and that large datasets are available and accessible. Finally, we have access to nearly unlimited computing power. We have almost all the prerequisites in place from a computer science perspective.

1.1.4 System Understanding

Relying on a data-driven approach is built upon the assumption that we have identified the problem to be solved and have a good understanding of the root causes of a real-world phenomenon and its physics. The data-driven approach also assumes that data on features that describe a phenomenon are collected and available.

A doctor needs data to make a diagnosis, but she also needs knowledge of what those data mean. The same is true in industry: when making a diagnosis, we need the right data, but we also need to understand the system.

In the healthcare example, the problem-solving process usually starts with a phase of problem description, through which the problem owner (the patient) describes the experienced problem, not the solution. The doctor selects the appropriate medical sensors to provide data and thus gain better insight into the health situation. The doctor validates the data collected through these sensors and combines them with additional data that she collects by asking additional questions. Importantly, she has to interpret the meaning of the data. If the collected data are not sufficient for a diagnosis or prognosis, then the doctor needs additional data, which will be collected by other sensors.

The same process applies in industry. To make a diagnosis or prognosis, we need the right data, but we also need to be able to "read" those data correctly. This example highlights the importance of understanding the nature of a real-world phenomenon, before developing a solution.

1.1.5 Context Adaptation

Context is fundamental, but unfortunately, it is often neglected when developing industrial solutions using digital technology and AI. Maybe this reflects our wish to develop an ultimate solution for any existing and future challenges. For example, it would be nice to have a monolithic digital twin (DT) that is able to mirror and interact with any individual item in a complex technical system in industries such as aviation, railway, or mining and provide the necessary support to any of the enterprise processes such as operations, maintenance, and business.

But technical industrial systems are extremely complex with respect to the number of inherent items, number of interfaces, and coexistence of items in various lifecycle phases. Now combine the business and technical complexities. Industrial business processes are complex because they need to be dynamic. The dynamics reflect, for example, changes in customers' needs, social changes, changes in regulations, and changes in internal and external governance models, cost efficiency, and sustainability goals.

When we put all these complexities together, we have to admit that our "one-size-fits-all" DT is not very likely.

How can we deal with this complexity? One solution is the "distribute-and-orchestrate" approach we have applied in our creation of the AI factory. Simply stated, we create a set of digital twins, instead of one monolithic DT, and these are adapted to an individual industrial context. These DTs are aware of their existence, aware of the context they are mirroring, and able to interact with other twins. This design model has helped us to distribute the complexity and break it down into smaller, more manageable pieces. Importantly, the model of AI factory described in this book can be used as a design pattern in any industrial domain.

1.1.6 CONNECTIVITY

What else do we need in our digital factory? Just like any other factory, a digital factory empowered by AI requires "raw material" to process. In a digital space, the materials are represented in bits and bytes. These bits and bytes are often generated through various types of sensing points (also called sensors), which can be any combination of liveware, hardware, and software.

In industry, sensors play a central role. They act as receptors to detect events or changes in their environment and send the data and sometimes information to other processes such as automation, operation, maintenance, and business processes. These data and information are post-processed by algorithms, for example, ML and DL algorithms, to provide an industrial context with relevant and necessary input.

Different industrial contexts might have different demands on time-to-response. Time-to-response, which also represents an acceptable delay level, is often measured through latency. In industry, latency defines the time between:

1. An event detected by a sensor and
2. The time when an action, i.e. a decision, has taken place based on the event.

This includes anything between these two timestamps, such as pre-processing, networking, and post-processing. Latency demands refer to the response characteristics of a context, and these put requirements on the connectivity architecture of an analytics solution.

How do we build a connectivity architecture? Once again, we should remind ourselves that there is no "one-size-fits-all" in the digital world. This means the architecture of connectivity has to be adapted to the industrial context, as different contexts make different demands on latency. The architecture needs to consider the characteristics of the sensor and sensed features as well. This means the feature we are trying to detect will have an impact on the "three Vs" of the generated data: volume, velocity, and verity. These three Vs, in turn, will have an impact on the required computing power for data processing, as well as the distribution of the computing power, for example, at the cloud, edge, or fog level.

So even connectivity needs to be context-aware to support various industrial contexts. This reminds us of the importance of understanding the characteristics of industrial contexts and the attributes of the physical phenomenon of interest.

1.1.7 INFORMATION LOGISTICS

So far, we have discussed some essential ingredients for the success of AI implementation and the data-driven approach, which can be summarised as:

1. *Algorithms* such as ML and DL that enable us to process data;
2. *Data* or the raw material for data processing;
3. *Sensors* that generate data to be processed.

There is still one thing missing for the successful development of a digital solution: the logistic mechanism. In a data-driven solution supported by AI, we need mechanisms that help us handle the flows of data, information, and algorithms from one node to another. We call this process "information logistics". Information logistics aims to connect processing nodes of any type, such as sensors, algorithms, users, etc.

A processing node is any combination of liveware, hardware, or software that can consume or produce a digital asset. For example, an ML algorithm implemented in Python executed as a microservice receives a digital asset (e.g., a stream of bytes) and delivers a digital asset (e.g., a digital signal) to an actuator.

In a distributed computing environment, the logistic process has to be adapted to various industrial contexts. Because the logistic process feeds a processing node with necessary input while also delivering the processing output to the next node in the computing chain, it must meet some fundamental requirements defined by individual processing node. Examples of the requirements a processing node might have include cybersecurity, fidelity, quality of data and information, quality of service, availability, accessibility, timeliness, latency, traceability, and trackability.

1.1.8 IN SUMMARY

Understanding various aspects of digitalisation and AI is an essential, fundamental, and necessary prerequisite to enable AI in industrial contexts. In this book, we disseminate the insights from our AI and digital journey and the experiences from the development of AI factory.

Materialising the concept of smart machines and enhanced analytics empowered by AI requires know-how. Therefore, in this book, we offer concepts, theories, and best practices packaged in our concept of AI factory, hoping this will accelerate the AI journey of others.

We hope the knowledge, insights, and experiences imparted on these pages will help others in their successful digitalisation and AI journey.

1.2 ARTIFICIAL INTELLIGENCE-EMPOWERED ANALYTICS

Advanced analytics empowered by AI contributes to the achievement of global sustainability and business goals. It also contributes to the global competitiveness of enterprises by enabling fact-based decision-making and improved insight.

The ongoing digitalisation and implementation of AI technologies in industry are highly dependent on the availability and accessibility of data for a geographically distributed system. The digitalisation process in industry and the corresponding implementation of AI technologies require the availability and accessibility of both data and models.

Data and models are considered digital assets (ISO, 2014) that impact a system's dependability during its whole lifecycle.

Digitalisation and implementation of AI in complex technical systems, such as those found in railway, mining, and aerospace industries, are challenging. From a digital asset management perspective, the main challenges can be related to source integration, content processing, and cybersecurity. However, to effectively and efficiently retain the required performance of a complex technical system during its lifecycle, we need appropriate concepts, methodologies, and technologies. Industry is facing challenges in developing and implementing AI to increase the level of autonomy in maintenance. In other words, the digital transformation of industry and the implementation of AI require research and innovation.

Industrial transformation is a matter of scaling innovations derived from research. Hence, the AI factory initiative is designed to bridge research findings with innovative solutions that are scalable for the transformation of industry (Karim et al., 2021).

1.3 AI REVOLUTION IN INDUSTRY

AI refers to the implementation of human intelligence in computer software. Intelligence can be described as the ability to learn from experiences, perceive abstract contexts, cognise, adapt to situations, and act (Karim et al., 2016).

Hence, AI refers to a set of computer science techniques that allow computer software to learn, perceive, cognise, and act.

An important subfield of AI is ML, which enables computers to perform tasks for which they have not been programmed explicitly. Among the numerous ML methods, DL, based on multi-layer neural networks, stands out as particularly promising. With DL, interlinked nodes loosely modelled after the human brain can be trained to perform tasks such as detecting leukaemia earlier than human experts, driving a car, helping a restaurant better predict its food demand or optimising the logistics processes for a global retail company (Modin & Andrén, 2021).

AI is not really new. Yet new things in AI are happening much more rapidly today thanks to emerging computing technologies. More data are available because of Internet of Things (IoT) and sensors; data processing power has exploded (e.g., through cloud/edge computing); and new learning techniques, such as DL, are becoming ubiquitous (Karim et al., 2021).

1.3.1   THE AI REVOLUTION IS HAPPENING NOW

The World Economic Forum attributes the Fourth Industrial Revolution (i.e. Industry 4.0) to the growth and consolidation of technologies such as AI, ML, DL, IoT, and more. Even though we can confidently claim that AI has impacted every facet of most industries, this claim is still an understatement.

The following sections discuss the far-reaching impact of AI across different industries (Cheishvili, 2021).

1.3.1.1   Healthcare

AI experienced a major boom in the healthcare sector with the COVID-19 pandemic. However, it was not the result of overnight changes, as the industry was already becoming increasingly tech-focused.

AI has widespread applications in telemedicine, ranging from making a preliminary diagnosis to formulating a treatment plan. AI platforms can utilise a range of technologies, such as data mining, image processing, and predictive modelling, to make a diagnosis (Cheishvili, 2021).

1.3.1.2   Education

As education becomes more democratised through the power of Internet technologies, AI is serving as both an enabler and an accessory, especially in self-paced learning environments. This too was boosted by the global pandemic when online learning replaced traditional school settings.

AI individualises learning based on the learner's existing competencies. It then establishes a collaborative platform for learners and teachers and changes the difficulty levels based on the knowledge transfer rates. At the back end, automation takes care of routine administrative tasks such as managing attendance or grading, thereby freeing instructors to focus on the teaching aspects (Cheishvili, 2021).

1.3.1.3   Banking, Financial Services and Insurance (BFSI)

In the last few years, the BFSI sector has made slow but highly impactful headway through the power of technologies like AI. Businesses can deploy AI solutions to empower themselves to make smarter and more balanced decisions. Here are a few examples:

- AI helps policy underwriters draft custom insurance policies that account for the risk and customer lifetime value of an individual.
- AI-powered bots can perform high-security authentication while offering access to banking facilities.
- Robo-advisories can make personalised recommendations for investment opportunities for wealth creation (Cheishvili, 2021).

1.3.1.4   Retail and e-Commerce

Most people have already come face to face with AI technologies in the retail and e-commerce space. AI acts as a powerful differentiator in a market segment that is highly competitive. For example, AI, ML, and DL technologies identify customer purchase patterns to yield insight into how businesses can strengthen their marketing capabilities. The value of AI ranges from making personalised recommendations based on customer interactions and preferences to streamlining customer support dialogues (Cheishvili, 2021).

1.3.1.5 Gaming and Entertainment

At one end of the spectrum, AI makes intelligent recommendations to audiences on consumable content depending on their tastes. At the other end of the spectrum, it analyses viewer behaviour and can shed light on the kind of content such platforms must create or acquire.

The gaming industry was one of the first adopters of AI and ML. The result was a highly engaging and interactive game (Cheishvili, 2021).

1.3.2 THE ROAD TO SUPERINTELLIGENCE

Human progress accelerates over time, according to futurist Ray Kurzweil, in what he calls human history's law of accelerating returns. This happens because more advanced societies have the ability to progress at a faster rate than less advanced societies – because they're more advanced.

The average rate of advancement between 1985 and 2015 was higher than the rate between 1955 and 1985 because the former was a more advanced world, so much more change happened in the most recent 30 years than in the prior 30.

So advances are getting bigger and bigger and happening more and more quickly.

In his book *The Age of Spiritual Machines*, Kurzweil suggests that the progress of the entire 20th century would have been achieved in only 20 years at the rate of advancement in the year 2000; in other words, by 2000, the rate of progress was five times faster than the average rate of progress during the 20th century. Because of the law of accelerating returns, the 21st century will achieve 1,000 times the progress of the 20th century. This is because exponential growth isn't totally smooth and uniform. Rather, progress happens in "S-curves", as depicted in Figure 1.1 (Goodell, 2016).

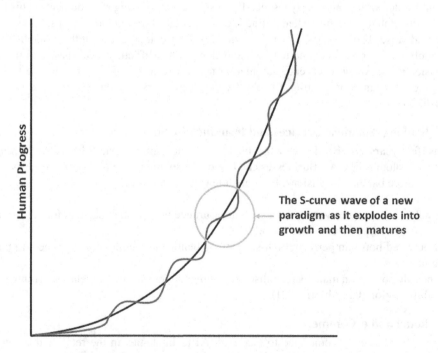

The S-curve wave of a new paradigm as it explodes into growth and then matures

FIGURE 1.1 "S-curves" of progress explained by Kurzweil (Goodell, 2016).

An "S" is created by the wave of progress when a new paradigm sweeps the world. The curve goes through three phases:

- Slow growth (the early phase of exponential growth).
- Rapid growth (the late, explosive phase of exponential growth).
- Levelling off (the particular paradigm matures) (Goodell, 2016).

1.4 AI WINTER, AI SPRING

AI has experienced cycles of "winters" and "springs".

AI winter is a period when interest in and funding for AI research falls significantly. One major AI winter occurred during 1974–1980 and another during 1987–1993. In both cases, disappointing research results led to decreased research funding.

AI spring is a period of significant research activity and progress. The first spring occurred during 1956–1974. This period essentially marked the beginning of AI, with the invention of the perceptron, as well as computers that could solve algebraic word problems, prove theorems in geometry, and speak English. The second AI spring occurred during 1980–1987 and featured the development of the first expert systems.

We are in the midst of a third AI spring. It started in 1993, with the development of the intelligent agent – an autonomous entity that perceives its environment and acts accordingly. A good example is a self-driving car. The AI spring continued to develop momentum in the early 2000s with advances in ML and statistical AI, increased availability of Big Data, and improved processing power (Rose, 2021).

Historically, AI winters have occurred because AI initiatives have been more complicated to carry out than promised. When AI products fail to deliver a robust return on investment (ROI), buyers become disappointed and direct their attention elsewhere. In the past few years, AI has been on an upswing, but after several years of hype, advances, and implementations, some analysts are predicting another AI winter. To forestall another AI winter, some vendors are choosing to label software features "predictive" instead of "artificially intelligent" (TechTarget, 2019).

Figure 1.2 shows a proposed timeline of AI winters and springs (Schuchmann, 2019). The following sections explain these in more detail.

1.4.1 THE FIRST AI SPRING

The first spring started in the 1940s and lasted until the mid-1970s.

Many early ideas about thinking machines appeared in the late 1940–1950s. In 1942, Isaac Asimov published *Runaround*, a short story about a robot developed by two engineers (Haenlein & Kaplan, 2019). In this short story, Asimov formulated what he called the Three Laws of Robotics:

1. A robot may not injure a human being or, through inaction, allow a human being to come to harm;
2. A robot must obey the orders given to it by human beings except where such orders would conflict with the First Law; and

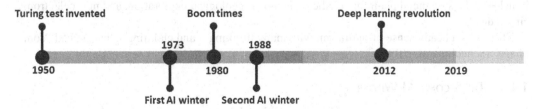

FIGURE 1.2   Timeline of AI winters and springs (Schuchmann, 2019).

3. A robot must protect its own existence as long as such protection does not conflict with the First or Second Laws.

Asimov's work inspired generations of scientists in the field of robotics, AI, and computer science.

Around the same time, English mathematician Alan Turing tried to frame the question "Can machines think?" differently (Schuchmann, 2019). In 1950, he published an article titled "Computing Machinery and Intelligence" in which he described how to create intelligent machines and, in particular, how to test their intelligence. This so-called Turing Test is still considered a benchmark to identify the intelligence of an artificial system: if a human is interacting with another human and a machine and is unable to distinguish the machine from the human, then the machine is said to be intelligent.

The term "artificial intelligence" was officially coined about six years later; in 1956, Marvin Minsky and John McCarthy (a computer scientist at Stanford) hosted the eight-week-long Dartmouth Summer Research Project on Artificial Intelligence (DSRPAI) at Dartmouth College in New Hampshire. The objective of DSRPAI was to unite researchers from various fields to create a new research area aimed at building machines able to simulate human intelligence (Haenlein & Kaplan, 2019).

The perceptron was invented by Frank Rosenblatt in 1958. AI continued to advance: throughout the 1960s, computers were able to solve algebraic word problems, prove theorems in geometry, and speak English.

1.4.2 THE FIRST AI WINTER

Several circumstances combined to create the first AI winter, starting in the mid-1970s. These included:

- Disappointments in machine translation
- Obstacles impeding the progress of perceptrons
- Lighthill's report (Lighthill, 1973)

Arguably the most important of these, James Lighthill's report, "Artificial Intelligence: A General Survey" (Lighthill, 1973), was highly critical of the state of AI research and had a chilling effect on funding. Consequently, research on AI became difficult. DARPA (Defence Advanced Research Projects Agency) started funding more applied AI projects and less fundamental work.

The AI winter lasted for a few years, but another spring was just around the corner (Schuchmann, 2019).

1.4.3 THE SECOND AI SPRING

A new era of AI started in the early 1980s, with more effort focused on creating commercial products. Large conferences, for example, Association for the Advancement of Artificial Intelligence (AAAI), started in the early 1980s and were very popular. There was renewed interest in AI technology across academia, industry, and government.

Expert systems comprised the core of the commercialisation of AI. These systems rest on "if-then" rules. This method is called the "top-down" approach to AI. Expert systems were implemented in fields such as financial planning, medical diagnosis, geological exploration, and microelectronic circuit design.

There was a heady sense of optimism, with many thinking – and claiming – that AI had "come of age" (Schuchmann, 2019).

1.4.4 THE SECOND AI WINTER

Yet these claims were soon tested and found wanting. Expert systems had a number of problems, and expectations could not be met. In 1984, a research report criticised expert systems because they lacked common sense and knowledge of their own limitations. In addition, many tasks were too complicated for engineers to design rules around them manually. For example, systems for vision and speech had too many edge cases.

The general interest in AI declined as people discovered its expected value could not be met. This led to a decrease in funding for AI research, many AI companies closed down, and the AAAI conference attracted over 6,000 visitors in 1986 but dropped to 2,000 by 1991 (Schuchmann, 2019).

1.4.5 ANOTHER SPRING: THE DL REVOLUTION

But like the cycle of the seasons, the cycle of AI winter-spring once again turned into a spring. Things changed in the mid-1990s, with the development of an autonomous entity that could perceive its environment and act accordingly. This was followed in the early 2000s with advances in ML and statistical AI, the advent of Big Data, and improved processing power.

Around 2012, the ML field had breakthroughs in neural networks and other domains, such as speech recognition. ML using DL was key in this more recent part of the current spring cycle. DL refers to the use of neural networks with two or more layers.

The amount of data (Big Data) created every day by the Internet, smartphones, and IoT devices enables DL to flourish. In 2002, the amount of data created per year was estimated to be about 5 exabytes; in 2019, it was about 33 zettabytes, and it is estimated to be about 175 zettabytes by 2025 (Schuchmann, 2019).

At the same time, graphics processing units (GPUs), which can process data in parallel, are becoming widely available, and techniques to train on them are being developed. Not least, computer power has increased astronomically.

Together, the increased computing capabilities and virtually unlimited data access have allowed deep neural networks to outperform classical approaches in many fields, including computer vision, speech recognition, and game-playing, among many others (Schuchmann, 2019).

To put it simply, the first Industrial Revolution was about machines enhancing human muscle power. The AI revolution is about machines enhancing human brain power (Bughin & Hazan, 2017).

1.4.6 PREDICTIONS OF ANOTHER AI WINTER

The jury is out on whether we will see another AI winter. History suggests we will. But some researchers say otherwise.

Some doubters base their scepticism on the following argumentation (Rose, 2021):

- AI research is driving the development of a number of commercially viable technologies, such as self-driving cars, targeted product recommendations, and fraud detection and prevention. As long as new commercial applications continue to appear and continue to be viable, money will continue to be directed towards AI research and development – even if true AI (the thinking and feeling machine) is never achieved.
- Data will continue to grow in volume, variety, and velocity. This will drive innovation, as new uses for all these Big Data are discovered.
- Processors and computer systems will continue to innovate and improve, with increasing processing power, complexity, and speed. This too will drive AI developments.
- Algorithms will continue to be developed, representing the final driver of the ongoing AI spring (Rose, 2021).

The three reasons why spring will not go away, proposed by (Bughin & Hazan, 2017):

1. Clever investors from venture capital and private equity have tripled their AI investments over the past three years and are now investing billions in AI. The investment is growing very quickly, even faster than biotech.

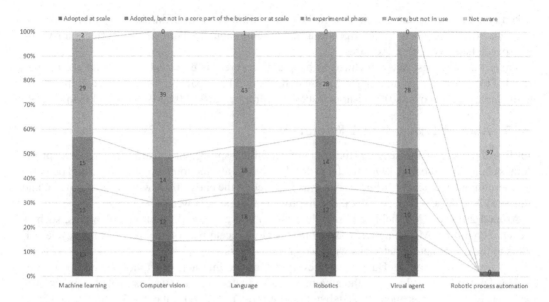

FIGURE 1.3 Degree of AI awareness by technology (Bughin & Hazan, 2017).

2. Corporate investment in AI is three times that of private equity and venture capital firms. Among the corporations betting on AI, the most bullish are high-tech companies such as Intel and Samsung, along with Alphabet, Facebook, and Amazon. Automotive companies are active, too. In addition, AI investments are paying off.

3. AI technologies are actually being deployed (Figure 1.3). In a survey of more than 3,000 businesses, Bughin and Hazan (2017) found that two-thirds were AI-aware. About 20% were serious adopters, mostly deploying ML or computer vision technologies, mirroring the investments made by venture capital, private equity, and high-tech firms. About 40% had started to experiment or were partial adopters. The others were neither experimenting nor implementing. Some said they did not believe in AI; others thought they lacked the technical capabilities to implement AI. Nevertheless, a majority of businesses were trying to deploy AI.

At the moment, investment in the AI sector has reached historical highs, and the preceding discussion suggests a strong sense of optimism among many in the field. Even so, winter is likely to come sooner or later. Knowing when this will happen could be useful in guiding policy decisions and predicting the pace of progress.

Previous AI winters have been triggered by inflated expectations in academic results, and sudden backlashes when those expectations were not met. In other words, the boom (spring) and bust (winter) cycles in AI research have been related to social dynamics amongst academics and related institutions. Yes, some researchers say, we may have another winter, but the next one may be different. These researchers point to the following:

1. Research in AI is no longer dominated by government-funded research institutes. Rather, large private companies play a much larger role relative to government funding than they did in previous AI springs.

2. AI is now prevalent in many consumer products, from search engines to smart speakers and drive-assist software. These applications work well enough to sustain public and private interest even if funding for basic research were cut.

3. Research in AI technology is not concentrated in a few research groups at elite universities, but is widely dispersed.

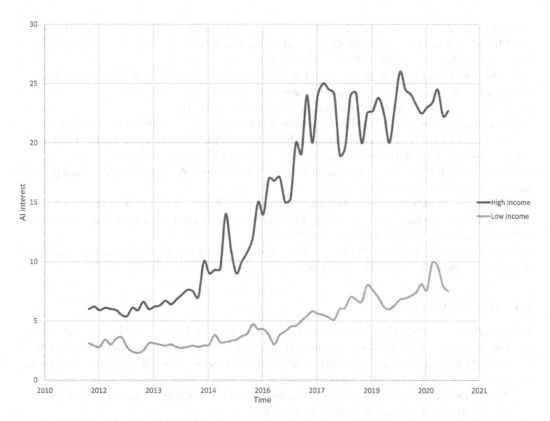

FIGURE 1.4   AI interest (Jebari et al., 2021).

The current development of AI technology relies on massive investments from the private sector, which often (with some notable exceptions) expects a ROI. Whether this return materialises depends on a variety of factors, including consumer interest in AI products, as well as a competent workforce that can create products ready for the market. Both depend on public interest being high. Thus, we can expect public opinion to play a more substantial role in causing or being a relevant proxy for the next AI winter relative to previous winters.

Public interest in AI, as measured by the number of Google searches for AI-related search terms, has increased rapidly in the last ten years (see Figure 1.4). This is true globally, although the interest in high-income countries (with GDP per capita above US$40,000) has increased more and faster than in low-income countries. However, in stark contrast with the exponential increase in funding for AI companies and research, the increase in interest has slowed down considerably in the last few years. In high-income countries, the interest even seems to have plateaued during the last two years (Jebari et al., 2021).

This indicator might not be enough to predict with certainty whether an AI winter is coming but compared to other indicators it is certainly suggestive (Jebari et al., 2021).

1.4.7   Surviving the Next AI Winter: From Myths to Realities

The risk of every AI winter is that the backlash is too great, the disappointment too negative, and potentially valuable solutions are thrown out.

Managing the world is an increasingly complex task: megacities and their "smartification" offer a good example. We have problems of global warming, social injustice, and migration, all of which require ever higher degrees of coordination to be solved. We need good technology to cope with these challenges, and we must put this technology in the service of a better future.

AI can play an important role because we need increasingly smarter ways of processing immense quantities of data sustainably and efficiently. But AI must be treated as a normal technology, and as simply one of the many solutions that human ingenuity has devised.

If a new AI winter is coming, we should be prepared. We should try to avoid a yo-yo effect of unreasonable illusions and exaggerated disillusionment. The winter of AI should not be the end of AI opportunities. It certainly will not be the end of its risks or challenges.

We need to ask ourselves whether AI solutions are going to replace previous solutions (as the automobile did for the horse-drawn carriage), diversify them (as the motorcycle did for the bicycle), or complement and expand them (as the digital smartwatch did for the analogue watch).

We need to determine the social acceptability of AI solutions. Will people really want to wear special glasses to live in a virtual world?

We need to look for feasible AI solutions in everyday life. Before getting excited about an innovation, we should ask whether the necessary skills, datasets, infrastructure, and business models are in place to make an AI application successful.

Ultimately, we need to resist both overstatement and oversimplification. We need to think more deeply and extensively about what we are doing and planning with AI (Floridi, 2020).

1.5   THE VALUE OF AI

AI is everywhere; we use AI on a daily basis for everyday tasks. When we use Siri on our phones or ask Amazon's Alexa a question, we are using AI to complete tasks and answer questions. Facebook Feed uses AI to predict what content is the most relevant to us as users. Netflix uses AI to create suggestions according to our viewing preferences.

AI will undoubtedly transform our lives in multiple ways. The key is to capture the full value of what AI has to offer while avoiding the possible risks.

As the previous section has shown, the idea of AI has been around for quite some time, and we have seen several previous periods of excitement (AI springs) followed by stretches of disappointment (AI winters) when the technology didn't quite live up to the hype. But recent progress in AI algorithms and techniques, more computing power, and massive amounts of available data have engendered significant and tangible advances, thus promising to generate value for individuals, businesses, and society as a whole.

Companies are applying AI techniques in sales and marketing to make personalised product recommendations to individual customers. In manufacturing, AI is being used in predictive maintenance; DL techniques are being applied to high volumes of data from sensors. By deploying algorithms to detect anomalies, organisations can reduce the downtime of machinery and equipment. ML can be used to help enhance human intelligence in many ways. For example, salespeople can review AI-augmented lists of potential deals. Using historic patterns, algorithms automatically prioritise sales calls based on how likely prospects are to buy, which products they are most likely to purchase, and how long the deal is likely to take. Because the data are based on past sales success, the overall effect is to help every salesperson be as good as the best salespeople in the organisation.

AI-augmented analytics can help business people spot outliers and unusual situations faster, and automatically uncover the drivers of key performance measures such as revenue and profit so that business people can spend more time on the decisions that really matter.

AI promises to contribute to economic growth as well by augmenting and substituting labour and capital inputs, driving innovation, and enhancing wealth creation and reinvestment. Some jobs will be lost, but many will be created. Moreover, AI will help us to be more advanced, productive, and engaged. Many jobs are quite routine, and AI can do them for us. If we look at it this way, all this could lead to a happier work environment and more fulfilling professional lives (Mitrovic, 2019).

As a result of overall economic growth, social welfare is likely to improve. In fact, AI could help to improve many aspects of human well-being, from job security and living standards to education and environmental sustainability. Its biggest positive contribution to welfare may be in health and longevity. In one example, AI-driven drug discovery is several times faster than that based on conventional research. In another example, AI-based traffic management significantly reduces the negative impact of air pollution on human health. And an AI disease-detection system can identify skin cancer as well as or even better than dermatologists. AI applications that are currently being field-tested include helping blind people navigate their surroundings (Manyika & Bughin, 2019).

AI's biggest impact may come from democratising the capabilities that we have now. Tech companies have made powerful software tools and data sets open source, so they can be downloaded by anyone, and the computing power used to train AI algorithms is getting cheaper and easier to access. In other words, anybody will be able to do anything (Barber, 2019).

1.5.1 CHALLENGES OF AI

Many challenges remain to be addressed:

- Stage of technology: Most of the technology is still being developed and is not yet widely applicable.
- Data availability: Even though this is an era of Big Data, there are problems with data availability, and AI models need data.
- Impact on work: The nature of jobs will change, as people interact more closely with smart machines in the workplace. This requires new skills; the workforce must be trained and retrained. As demand for high-skill jobs grows, low-skill workers could be left behind, resulting in wage and income imbalances.
- Policy: Policymakers will need to create new policies as AI is adopted at national, regional, and local levels.
- Ethical issues: The wider diffusion of AI will raise difficult ethical questions in areas ranging from surveillance and military applications to social media and politics. Algorithms and social platforms can be used for unethical reasons if left under-regulated (Mitrovic, 2019).
- Biases: Algorithms and the data used to train them may introduce new biases, or institutionalise existing ones.
- Privacy: Data privacy and the use of personal information, cybersecurity, and "deep fakes" to manipulate election results or perpetrate large-scale fraud are other pressing concerns. Deepfakes, AI-generated videos meant to look like real footage, are now accessible to anyone with a laptop. Automated bias and privacy compromises could become normalised swiftly.

Despite these challenges, AI can generate tremendous value, if policymakers and businesses work to capture its full benefits and mitigate the inevitable risks (Manyika & Bughin, 2019).

1.6   POWER OF AI VS. HUMAN INTELLIGENCE

AI will be a huge boost to organisations around the world, but the real opportunity of AI is to unleash the full power of human intelligence. We can use AI to leverage our uniquely human skills such as leadership, adaptability, and creativity. Only humans can understand the full context of what's not working well in business processes and functions and make relevant suggestions on how they could be improved.

But there's one area where the power of human intelligence really shines: innovation. It's a fundamentally human-oriented process that requires coming up with hypotheses, creating experiments, evaluating complex results, and scaling up new ways of working.

Today, business people are often treated as passive "users" of technology. In fact, they are the most important "technology" in the enterprise, and this technology is not being fully leveraged.

Every time people interact with processes and information processes, they add valuable insights. Those insights are often wasted because human-generated information is hard to gather, aggregate, manipulate, and analyse.

Organisations have paid close attention to things like customer and employee feedback for a long time, but people's emotions, expectations, and innovation insights are very different from the structured information that today's information systems are optimised for. This means that gathering experience information has generally been manual, limited, and episodic. But now, new experience management platforms can harness these human insights at scale, gathering the right information, from the right people, at the right time. When combined with traditional data sources and using AI to surface the most important trends, this has the possibility of improving and accelerating innovation at every level and in every business process.

Ultimately, the rise of AI frees workers from drudgery and allows them to spend time on more strategic and valuable business activities. Instead of forcing people to spend time and effort on tasks that we find hard but computers find easy, we will be rewarded for doing what humans do best – and AI will help make us all more human (Elliott, 2020).

1.7   TECHNOLOGIES POWERING AI: ML AND DL

ML is a major factor in digital transformation in industry (Louridas & Ebert, 2016) and can be simply defined as a "machine's ability to keep improving its performance without humans having to explain exactly how to accomplish all the tasks it's given" (Bergdahl, 2018). It does so using algorithms and drawing on either sample data or historical data.

DL is an advancement of ML using superior algorithms. It uses neural networks and can handle much larger data sets.

While data are essential to ML, and the performance of ML systems improves with more data, organisations can still capitalise on the technology and improve performance with smaller amounts of data.

ML creates new approaches to business processes and business models, but it complements human activity – it doesn't replace it. For instance, workflows can be rethought and reformulated to improve efficiency (Bergdahl, 2018).

Although AI is already in use in organisations around the world, the effects of AI will be magnified as industries across the globe transform their business models to take advantage of ML. To give only a couple of examples, some organisations are using ML to determine their trading on Wall Street, and Amazon uses ML to improve product recommendations to customers (Brynjolfsson & Mcafee, 2017).

1.8   PERCEPTION AND COGNITION

Arguably the biggest advancements in the field of AI have been in the fields of perception and cognition:

- Perception: Advances in the category of perception have been in speech recognition and image recognition. Speech recognition is now incredibly fast. The accuracy of image recognition is steadily increasing as well. Five years ago, machines were able to correctly recognise images 70% of the time, while humans succeeded 95% of the time. Better data, improved algorithms, and faster computers have raised machines' accuracy rate to 96%. As humans, we remain stuck at 95% (Bughin & Hazan, 2017). Facebook can recognise the faces of the user's friends in the pictures they upload and will automatically tag them. We are no longer even remotely surprised by this – it is simply an everyday fact.
- Cognition: Cognition has taken great leaps as well. In 2011, IBM's computer system "Watson" played on the game show Jeopardy – and won, beating two previous (human)

winners. Machines have beaten the best human players in games of poker, cybersecurity companies use AI to detect malware, and Paypal uses cognition to prevent money laundering.

The next step in perception and cognition? Some researchers think AI will soon become a digital spokesperson for organisations. When AI-powered conversations are enabled, AI will become the "face" of an organisation (Brynjolfsson & Mcafee, 2017).

REFERENCES

Barber, G. (2019). *The Power, and Limits, of Artificial Intelligence, WIRED.* https://www.wired.com/story/power-limits-artificial-intelligence/

Bergdahl, J. (2018). *The AI Revolution: A Study on the Present and Future Application and Value of AI in the Context of ERP Systems.* http://www.diva-portal.org/smash/record.jsf?pid=diva2%3A1220408&dswid=-5443

Brynjolfsson, E., & Mcafee, A. (2017). How AI fits into your science team. What it can and cannot--do for your organization. *Harvard Business Review*, July 18. https://hbr.org/2017/07/the-business-of-artificial-intelligence

Bughin, J., & Hazan, E. (2017). *The New Spring of Artificial Intelligence, VOX, CEPR Policy Portal.* https://voxeu.org/article/new-spring-artificial-intelligence-few-early-economics

Cheishvili, A. (2021). *The AI Revolution Is Happening Now.* https://www.forbes.com/sites/forbestechcouncil/2021/08/25/the-ai-revolution-is-happening-now/?sh=5604fc5228c8

Elliott, T. (2020). *The Power of Artificial Intelligence Vs. The Power Of Human Intelligence.* https://www.forbes.com/sites/sap/2020/03/09/the-power-of-artificial-intelligence-vs-the-power-of-human-intelligence/?sh=579d823b346c

Floridi, L. (2020). AI and its new winter: from myths to realities. *Philosophy & Technology*, *33*(1), 1–3.

Goodell, J. (2016). Inside the artificial intelligence revolution: a special report (Pt 1). Rolling Stone, February 19. https://www.rollingstone.com/culture/culture-news/inside-the-artificial-intelligence-revolution-a-special-report-pt-1-118333/

Haenlein, M., & Kaplan, A. (2019). A brief history of artificial intelligence: on the past, present, and future of artificial intelligence. *California Management Review*, *61*(4), 5–14. https://doi.org/10.1177/0008125619864925

ISO. (2014). Asset management: management systems, guidelines for the application of ISO 55001, ISO 55002:2014(E). 2014, 38. https://doi.org/10.1007/978-94-007-2724-3

Jebari, K., Strimling, P., & Vartanova, I. (2021). *AI Winter is Coming? AI Futures.* https://www.aifutures.org/2021/ai-winter-is-coming/

Karim, R., Dersin, P., Galar, D., Kumar, U., & Jarl, H. (2021). AI factory: a framework for digital asset management. *Proceedings of the 31st European Safety and Reliability Conference*, 1160–1167.

Karim, R., Westerberg, J., Galar, D., & Kumar, U. (2016). Maintenance analytics: the new know in maintenance. *IFAC-PapersOnLine*, *49*(28), 214–219. https://doi.org/10.1016/j.ifacol.2016.11.037

Lighthill, J. (1973). *Artificial Intelligence: A General Survey.* http://www.chilton-computing.org.uk/inf/literature/reports/lighthill_report/p001.htm

Louridas, P., & Ebert, C. (2016). Machine learning. *IEEE Software*, *33*(5), 110–115. https://doi.org/10.1109/MS.2016.114

Manyika, J., & Bughin, J. (2019). *The Coming of AI Spring, McKinsey.* https://www.mckinsey.com/mgi/overview/in-the-news/the-coming-of-ai-spring

Mitrovic, B. (2019). *The Power of Artificial Intelligence, Bojana Mitrovic, DataDrivenInvestor.* https://medium.datadriveninvestor.com/the-power-of-artificial-intelligence-5cf7d7152b77

Modin, A., & Andrén, J. (2021). *The Essential AI Handbook for Leaders.* Peltaroin. https://peltarion.com/peltarions-essential-ai-handbook-for~....

Rose, D. (2021). *AI Winter is Coming?* https://www.linkedin.com/pulse/ai-winter-coming-doug-rose/

Schuchmann, S. (2019). Analyzing the prospect of an approaching ai winter. *Master's Thesis.* https://doi.org/10.13140/RG.2.2.10932.91524.

TechTarget. (2019). *What is AI Winter? Definition from WhatIs.com.* https://www.techtarget.com/searchenterpriseai/definition/AI-winter

2 Digital Twins

2.1 BASIC CONCEPT OF DIGITAL TWIN

A digital twin (DT) is a virtual model designed to accurately reflect a physical object. It is a dynamic digital replica of a living or non-living physical entity, such as a manufacturing process, medical device, piece of medical equipment, and even a person. It uses physical data on how the components of a thing operate and respond to the environment as well as data provided by sensors in the physical world. A DT can be used to analyse and simulate real world conditions; it responds to changes, can improve operations, and adds value (Gartner, 2022).

An essential component of the DT is the connection of the real physical asset and its virtual twin representation through the Internet of Things (IoT) (IMAG, 2019).

A DT works in the following manner: drawing on sensor data, it combines simulation and analytics to gain insight into the operational state of its physical twin in both the present and future. This type of knowledge allows companies to predict future performance, improve operations and productivity, and diminish risks of unplanned downtime due to failure.

The ultimate goal of DTs is to bring intelligence into business, operation, and maintenance to enable a sustainable asset management (Figure 2.1).

2.2 HISTORY OF DT

The idea of DT was introduced by NASA in the early days of space exploration, but the formal concept was introduced later. In the Apollo project, NASA kept an identical space capsule kept on Earth to simulate the behaviour of the capsule in space, which mirrors the notion of having a separate object simulating the effects of another. However, the space capsule on Earth was not a digital representation but a physical one. Thus, this does not describe the connection between a physical object and its digital representation.

In 2005, the formal concept of DT was introduced in the context of Product Lifecycle Management (PLM) (Grieves, 2005). PLM requires a digital representation of the object. The proposed model has three components: real space, virtual space, and a linking mechanism for the flow of data/information between the two; the model was then referred to as Mirrored Spaces Model.

A similar concept in which software models mimic reality from information input from the physical world was imagined by David Gelernter in 1991 and was called Mirror Worlds. An agent-based architecture, where each product item has a corresponding "virtual counterpart" or agent associated with it, was proposed by Främling et al. (2003), as a solution to the inefficiency of transfer of production information.

By 2006, the name of the conceptual model proposed by Grieves (2005) was changed from Mirrored Spaces Model to Information Mirroring Model. The model emphasises the linking mechanism between two spaces being bidirectional and having multiple virtual spaces for a single real space where alternate ideas or designs can be explored (Figure 2.2). Given the limitations of the technologies, including low computing power, low or no connectivity of devices with the Internet, data storage and management, underdeveloped machine algorithms, etc., DT had no practical applications at the time (Singh et al., 2021).

Within the last decade, the concept of DT has been mostly used for product design and simulation using a data-driven 3D digital companion. Most recently, data and advanced analytics have enabled DT technology to do more than simply mirror key processes within physical assets. Now,

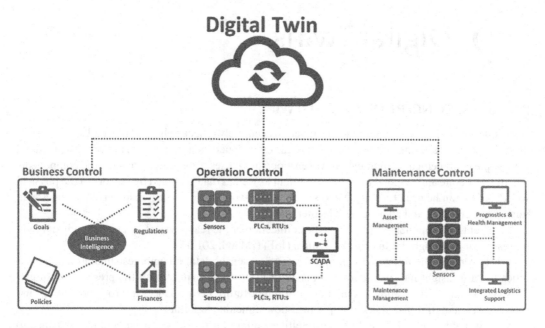

FIGURE 2.1   The concept of DT from an asset management perspective.

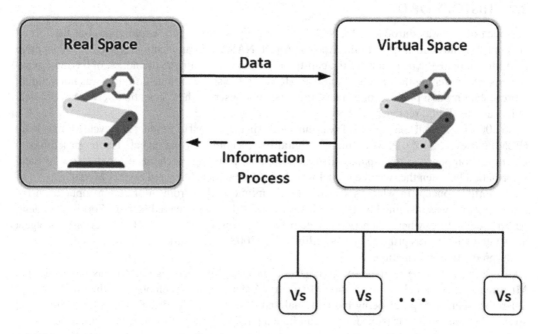

FIGURE 2.2   Mirrored spaces model/information mirroring model (Singh et al., 2021).

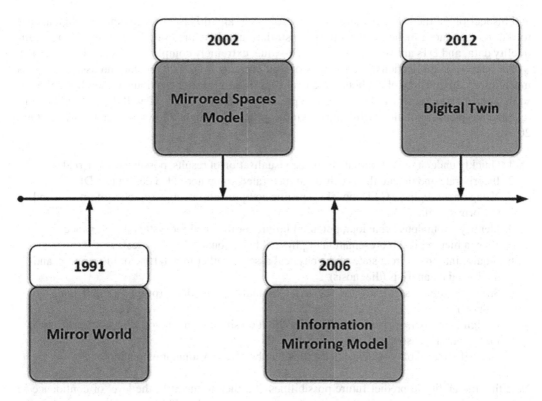

FIGURE 2.3   Timeline of DT (Singh et al., 2021).

a DT strategy can use machine learning (ML) to predict outcomes based on historical data and algorithms specific to parts, systems, sub-assemblies, and assemblies that further consider life-cycle states from as-designed to as-manufactured to as-maintained. Today, predictive analytics and advanced visualisation allow us to explore or identify new opportunities and business models.

The timeline of the evolution of DT is shown in Figure 2.3 (Singh et al., 2021).

2.3   WHAT IS DIGITAL TWIN? ITS INTRINSIC CHARACTERISTICS

A DT is an integrated architecture spanning design, test and evaluation, manufacturing and assembly, sustainment and maintenance, repair, and overhaul. It provides actionable information for making decisions for right now (diagnosis) and for the future (prognosis) (Tuegel, 2013).

A DT has five core characteristics (Erikstad, 2017):

- Identity: the DT is connected to a real physical asset.
- Representation: the DT captures the physical manifestation of the real asset in a digital format.
- State: the DT can determine the asset´s state or condition in close to real time.
- Behaviour: the DT can mimic the physical object's basic responses to external stimuli (e.g. temperature) in the present context.
- Context: the DT can reproduce the external operating context (e.g. wind) of the physical object.

2.3.1   WHY USE DIGITAL TWIN?

There are many inherent opportunities when using a continuously updated digital model, rather than having to assess the real asset directly. For example, it is possible to perform monitoring and inspection on the DT instead of the physical asset, and this is a real advantage when access to the asset is more difficult (e.g. subsea installations). It is also possible to aggregate high-fidelity data, and DTs are very useful for high-value, extremely complex assets (Erikstad, 2017).

For nearly all applications, the primary aim of creating a DT is to enable the user to have as much information as possible about the current status and future behaviour of the physical asset so that optimal decisions can be made. The precise objectives of the DT will depend on the context, but a typical simulation twin for a dynamic application might allow the user to (Wagg et al., 2020):

1. Quickly understand the outputs with fast visualisation of results, possibly even in real time.
2. Incorporate and update the DT through integrated computer-aided design (CAD).
3. Navigate through the CAD model to specific components or sub-assemblies of interest and perform specific tasks.
4. Identify anomalous behaviour, potential failure, or the need for system maintenance.
5. View a hierarchical representation of physical behaviour at different scales.
6. Inquire into the current state of the physical asset, whether in real time or historically, and perform data analysis (diagnosis).
7. Simulate future scenarios for the asset to make predictions (prognosis and decision support).
8. Design controllers, perform hardware-in-the-loop simulation, and/or set control processes for the physical asset.
9. Quantify a level of confidence (trust) that can be given to simulation outputs.

Note that the ability to predict future possibilities and then to quantify the level of confidence in these predictions are particularly important features (Wagg et al., 2020).

To sum up, DTs can do the following (Erikstad, 2017):

- Assess remaining life.
- Detect damage in time for pre-emptive maintenance and thus prevent shutdowns.
- Provide access to aggregated time series for design feedback.
- Offer virtual inspection support.
- Predict the consequences of future operating conditions – especially adverse consequences.
- Provide inspection and monitoring support.
- Visualise and inspect inaccessible/hidden locations.

2.3.2   How Does Digital Twin Work?

The main components of DTs belong to three spaces:

1. A physical asset belonging to the physical space.
2. A virtual asset belonging to the virtual space.
3. Connected data which tie the physical and virtual assets together and belong to the information space (Karim et al., 2016).

The DT is the linked collection of the relevant digital artefacts, including engineering data, operation data, and behaviour descriptions, using simulation models. The simulation models making up the DT are specific for their intended use and apply suitable fidelity for the problem to be solved.

Essentially, DT evolves along with the real system along the whole lifecycle and integrates the currently available knowledge about it. Thus, it can be used to describe behaviour and derive solutions relevant for the real system.

2.3.2.1 Digital Twin and Simulation

DT is a simulation technology. In general, simulation technology offers the chance to integrate data- and physics-based approaches and to reach the next level of merging the real and virtual world in all lifecycle phases.

By using simulation models, it becomes possible to interpret measurements, operational data, and fleet data in a different way – not just detecting deviations. Several modes of failure can be simulated for the current situation trying to reproduce the actual measurement signals. The comparison of the simulated signals with measured ones can help to identify the failure mode.

In essence, simulation is the "imitation of the operation of a real-world process or system" (Banks et al., 1996). In general, the evolution of physical quantities or entities of interest is simulated over time, but other physical domains are also possible. Simulation models express mathematical, logical, and symbolic relationships between the entities of interest for a specific system. As these models are an idealised representation of the physical reality, their design depends on their intended use (Dittrich et al., 2019).

With respect to the asset lifecycle, different stages can be distinguished and many different simulation technologies have emerged for each of these stages. The accuracy and fidelity of the simulation tools continue to increase, thus enabling a deeper understanding of the effects of design decisions on the asset's behaviour in use.

However, the DT is not a single complete model, but a set of linked operation data artefacts and simulation models, which must have suitable granularity for their intended purpose and evolve throughout the asset lifecycle. Consequently, simpler models may be used to make decisions about the concept, while sophisticated simulation models may be better for the actual design.

2.3.2.2 Digital Twin and Cyber-Physical Systems

A Cyber-Physical System (CPS) represents a core-enabling technology for DT. CPS is a key concept of Industry 4.0 architectures and a technical evolution of mechatronic systems. Mechatronic systems combine elements of mechanics, electronics, and computer science.

CPS is equipped with sensors to collect data, actuators to act on their environments and an embedded system. An embedded system is a microcomputer with computing power and an IP address giving the CPS an identity and the ability to store and process data (Figure 2.4).

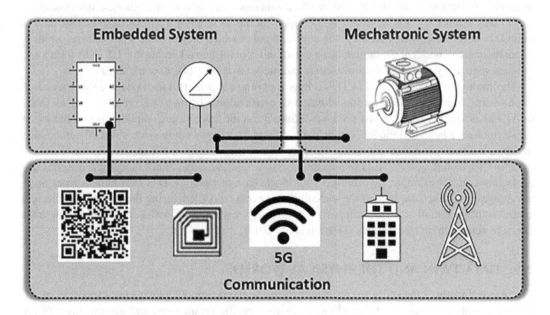

FIGURE 2.4 Components of a CPS (Dittrich et al., 2019).

Several CPS can be connected with each other through a data infrastructure – typically the Internet – to communicate independently and coordinate themselves. Connecting several CPS in a production environment creates what are called cyber-physical production systems (CPPS) (Bauer et al., 2014).

The decentralised data collection and processing offered by CPS is necessary to create a DT, which further processes the data – actually the data of several CPS – centrally.

Key problems are to acquire, transfer, store, protect, and analyse relevant information. This requires a combination of dedicated hardware and software solutions. However, the 5G communication standard is expected to overcome current issues in bandwidth, latency, resilience, and scalability to support multiple devices.

Based on the data provided by CPS, simulations can be run with a DT to test different scenarios. This way, a DT assists in predicting the behaviour of the CPS (Dittrich et al., 2019).

2.4   THE EVOLUTION OF DIGITAL TWIN

The next-generation DT will transport data, information, and executable models of all system elements from development – delivered by the component supplier – to operation. This information can be used for the cost-effective development of assistive systems during operation, e.g. autopilot solutions for production systems and service applications.

Application examples are improved maintenance solutions, which explain anomalies and identify potential failure causes. This networking of information also allows for the increased use of field data in the development of variants and follow-up solutions. The value creation process is closed by a feedback loop (Boschert et al., 2018).

In 2021, the evolution of DT was introduced as a cyber twin (Figure 2.5). In this updated version, a DT is materialised in a digital space, as a set of integrated software, hardware, and liveware. What is new today is the method by which we can facilitate a DT strategy based on advanced technologies such as IoT, cognitive services, and cloud computing to form the basis to develop and deploy dynamic applications and services that cater to enterprise needs.

High-definition maps, examples of a DT built to support self-driving capabilities, are already approaching the precision of 5 cm, mapping reality almost at a 1:1 scale. These maps no longer represent only reality. In fact, they are a meta-reality, adding comprehensive and contextual information, including semantic descriptions of objects, dynamic traffic conditions, and real-time and historical information.

In many realms, we now have a dynamic representational repertoire and sufficient usage data to build DTs of the objects we make and the environment in which they operate. For example, a realistic mathematical model of the human heart exists and is being considered by the US FDA for a more efficient regulatory review of cardiovascular and medical devices (Pigni et al., 2021).

The amount of data generated by DTs is huge and requires powerful methods of data processing. A promising approach is to use a model based on artificial intelligence (AI). While many methods in AI, like neural networks, have been known for quite some time, more computing power has given the technology a boost. AI models can be part of cloud/distributed computing or directly embedded in robots, vehicles, and other physical objects to ensure the security and local processing of private data. In distributed systems, it is important to assure that the data cannot be compromised. Data protection can, for example, be achieved with blockchain technology. DTs may benefit from other advantages of blockchain, such as the traceability of events recorded during the entire lifecycle, and smart contracts (small software snippets) automatically executed to invoke, for instance, maintenance or supply chain transactions (Dittrich et al., 2019).

2.5   DATA TWIN AND THE PHYSICAL WORLD

The physical world of the DT is an intricate, varying, dynamic, manufacturing atmosphere containing users and operators, assets, machinery, goods, specific regulations, and atmosphere (Zheng et al., 2019). All these elements have their own place, but they need to link through IoT systems.

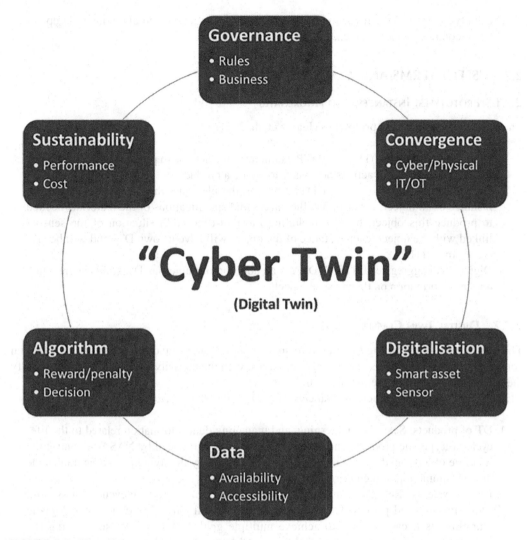

FIGURE 2.5   Essential components of a cyber twin.

For practical purposes, the physical world can be broken down into two main elements (Juarez et al., 2021):

1. Devices: The physical objects from which the DTs are created.
2. Sensors: Elements that are physically connected to the devices and through which data and information are obtained; once the sensor obtains the data, it sends them to be processed. Some widely used sensors are Programmable Logic Controller (PLC), radio frequency identification, and quick response code.

2.6   DATA TWIN AND THE DIGITAL WORLD

The digital world contains two parts (Juarez et al., 2021):

1. Virtual environment platform (VMP): VMPs construct an integrated 3D digital model to execute apps and, at the same time, allow executing actions to prove the functioning of diverse algorithms. There are numerous connections between the VMP and the DTs; VMP offers various models for the development of DTs.

2. Data twin (DT): DTs mirror their physical entity's life course and allow multiple operations (control, prediction, etc.).

2.7 USEFUL TERMS AND CLASSIFICATIONS

2.7.1 PROTOTYPES, INSTANCES, AND AGGREGATES

The following are data twin prototypes (Juarez et al., 2021):

1. Digital twin prototype (DTP): A DTP enumerates the actions to produce a specific object, for example, the list of actions necessary to create a product.
2. Digital twin instance (DTI): A DTI explains the elements that are part of a certain instance of an object, for example, the names and specifications of the materials needed to produce this object, besides including the real-time (RT) situation of the sensors linked with the object; each instance of the object will have its own DTI and will be created using a DTP.
3. Digital twin aggregate (DTA): A DTA is an addition of numerous DTIs; this aggregation obtains information on the physical objects.

2.7.2 DIGITAL TWIN CLASSES

The concept of DT is starting to be used in smart manufacturing, and it has become an essential component to make decisions and manage resources, with the capacity to check the status, modify the behaviour, and realise predictions of the real object.

The following list gives the principal classes of DTs (Juarez et al., 2021):

1. DT of products: Scanning, patterning, and managing data information related to the lifecycle of a specific product. The original concept was introduced by NASA to control the lifecycle of a flying device. The information perceived by the flying device facilitates the distinct simulations which mirror the behaviour of the flying device.
2. DT of systems: Reflecting and predicting conduct during the lifecycle of a system. This class is used primarily in fields such as medical care, fabrication, and logistic planning, as it can be used to achieve multiple goals, for example, supervising the systems to detect failures of the real twin, and from these failures perform predictive maintenance.

2.7.3 DIGITAL TWIN CATEGORIES

The applications of DTs in Industry 4.0 can be divided into the following types (Juarez et al., 2021):

1. Plain models include two main groups of data:
   a. Current value group: Data are obtained by sensors; these data update the DT features.
   b. A set of expectations of values to be obtained.
2. Embedded DTs (EDT): EDTs participate in all operations that include their twins, for example, the simulation models from a specific object or the job scheduling from a system. The interactions between the physical and the digital world occur through a bidirectional connection; the data from the real objects are obtained by the sensors, which allow smart decisions to be made through the DT.
3. Networked twins: Networking allows each integrated EDT to connect with other EDTs, allowing communication amongst each other. This is useful in smart manufacturing environments.

2.8 LEVEL OF INTEGRATION

As we have already established, DTs are digital copies of their physical twins. The expressions digital model (DM), digital shadow (DS), and digital twin (DT) are sometimes used as synonyms. However, these expressions vary in the level of integration of the data from the real object and the DT. Some instances of DTs are simulated and obtain their data from files entered by the operators, while others obtain data directly from their physical twins. The following sections classify DTs based on the level of integration (Kritzinger et al., 2018).

2.8.1 Digital Model

A DM is a virtual portrayal of a simulated or real object that does not utilise any automated information interchange between the real and the virtual objects. The virtual portrayal may contain a rough description of the real object. This means it can contain some models (physical, behaviour, etc.) of the specific object as long as it does not use automated information interchange. Data can be used to create models and simulations as long as they are entered manually.

Changes in the real object may not directly affect the virtual object and vice versa. The flow of data between the twins is shown in Figure 2.6 (Juarez et al., 2021).

2.8.2 Digital Shadow

A DS refers to an automatic unidirectional information interchange between the real object and the virtual object. If there is an alteration in the state of the real object, it will directly lead to an update in the virtual object. However, the reverse is not true. The flow of data between the twins is shown in Figure 2.7 (Juarez et al., 2021).

2.8.3 Digital Twin

In DTs, the information interchange between a real object and a virtual object is bidirectional. Thus, the DT can be an instance of its real twin and used to manage its lifecycle. A change in the real or the virtual object will directly affect the other. The flow of data between the twins is shown in Figure 2.8 (Juarez et al., 2021).

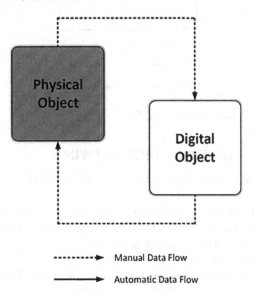

FIGURE 2.6 Flow of data in a digital model (Juarez et al., 2021).

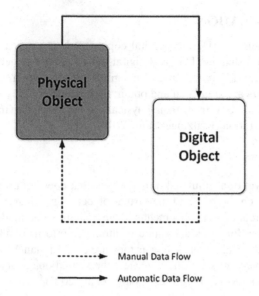

FIGURE 2.7   Flow of data in a digital shadow (Juarez et al., 2021).

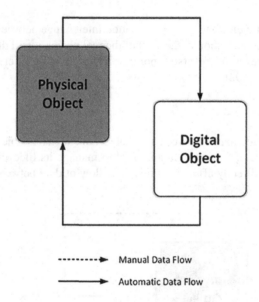

FIGURE 2.8   Flow of data in a DT (Juarez et al., 2021).

2.9   MAIN CHARACTERISTICS OF DIGITAL TWIN

The main characteristics of a DT are the following (Tao et al., 2019):

1. RT mirror reflection: There are two worlds inside a DT, the physical and the digital world. The digital world mirrors the real state of the physical world. Based on the exchange of data between the worlds, the two may be synchronised.
2. Communication and confluence:
   i. Communication and confluence in the physical world: The DT is a complete and unified system which includes the information produced in the entire lifecycle of the real twin. This means the information generated can be fed back.

ii. Communication and confluence between the stored and current information: The information comes from different sources. Thus, the DT is more reliable and complete and can be better used.

iii. Communication and confluence between the physical and the real world: A bidirectional relationship between these worlds allows information exchange between them.

3. Self-evolution: The DT has the capacity to refresh and modify the RT information, thus producing a direct, consecutive, and positive change in the model. It contains change by comparing current information with the information presented in the physical world.

2.10 MODELLING DIGITAL TWINS

There is no generic way to build a DT model. The following sections give some different methods, methodologies, and modelling tools (Tao et al., 2019).

2.10.1 SYSTEMS MODELLING LANGUAGE (SYSML)

SysML is a graphical modelling language that supports the analysis, specification, design, verification, and validation of complex systems. SysML can represent the following aspects of systems, components, and other objects (Makarov et al., 2019):

- Structure, interrelation, and classification;
- Behaviour-based on functions, messages, and states;
- Limitations on physical and operational properties;
- Distribution between behaviour, structure, and limitations;
- Requirements and their relationship with other conditions, design elements, and test cases.

As shown in Figure 2.9, SysML includes nine diagrams: package diagram, requirement diagram, behaviour diagram (activity diagram, sequence diagram, state machine diagram, and use-case diagram), parametric diagram, and structure diagram (block definition diagram and internal block diagram) (Friedenthal et al., 2014).

For example, to present the car specifications, we can use a simplified version of the SysML, with only six diagrams for modelling: package diagram, requirement diagram, activity diagram, and parametric diagram (see block definition diagram in Figures 2.10 and 2.11), (see internal block diagram in Figures 2.12 and 2.13) (Makarov et al., 2019).

The first three diagrams are simple and can be presented in text form.

The package diagram shows all model elements for describing car specifications. This means that they can be diagrammed as a whole. The example contains four folders: requirements, behaviour, structure, and parametric.

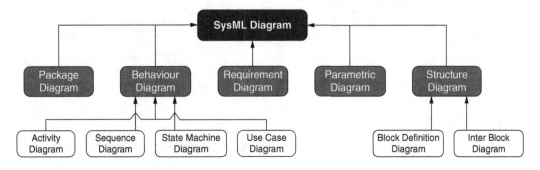

FIGURE 2.9 SysML diagram (Makarov et al., 2019).

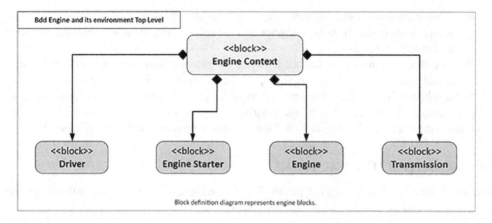

FIGURE 2.10   Block definition diagram – top level (car specification) (Makarov et al., 2019).

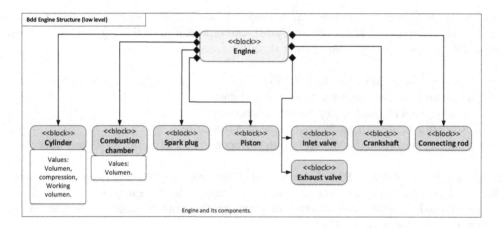

FIGURE 2.11   Block definition diagram – bottom level (car specification) (Makarov et al., 2019).

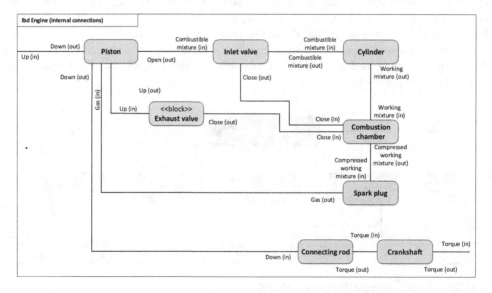

FIGURE 2.12   Internal block diagram (car specification) (Makarov et al., 2019).

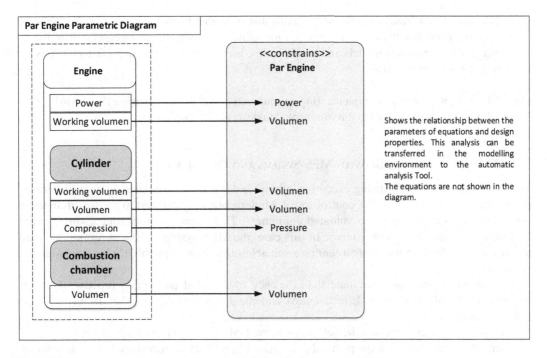

The following text appears within the diagram:

Par Engine Parametric Diagram

Engine
Power
Working volumen

Cylinder
Working volumen
Volumen
Compression

Combustion chamber
Volumen

<<constrains>>
Par Engine

Power
Volumen

Volumen
Volumen
Pressure

Volumen

Shows the relationship between the parameters of equations and design properties. This analysis can be transferred in the modelling environment to the automatic analysis Tool.
The equations are not shown in the diagram.

FIGURE 2.13 Parametric diagram (car specification) (Makarov et al., 2019).

The next diagram, requirements, contains technical and user specifications for car construction and their values (limitations). This diagram includes the following criteria: capacity, vehicle performance, driving comfort, emissions, reliability, and fuel consumption. Insulation and steering gear can limit driving enjoyment.

The behaviour diagram has four integral diagrams, including an activity diagram. Each activity diagram presents one process which describes the driver's activity. In this case, the activity diagram is to set the car in motion. The process starts with the action of inserting the ignition key and ends with ensuring the transmission of torque to the semi-axle of the front wheels. One of the most critical parts (details) of this process is the engine. Therefore, the next three diagrams focus on it. These diagrams are not complete and designed for educational purposes to demonstrate the initial capabilities of the SysML language.

SysML can be used at every level of system specification and helps engineers focus on design, rather than on the traditional hierarchical complexity of documents and drawings. This modelling language facilitates the adoption and use of technology and can be implemented by several teams working on a large project (Makarov et al., 2019).

2.10.2 SIMULATION AS THE BASIS OF DIGITAL TWIN TECHNOLOGY

Simulation is a numerical method for studying complex systems. A heterogeneous mathematical apparatus describes their elements, and a specific connecting model unites them into the informational model.

There is a need to consider several parallel tasks:

- The first is related to the acquisition of data removed from a real object and is necessary for carrying out virtual modelling on real objects.
- The second is to decide on the rationality of using universal software for building simulation models, as in some cases, the most appropriate solution may be the individual development of a simulation model (Makarov et al., 2019).

- The third arises from practical observations that show that the most effective DTs are the main advantage of those areas for which formalised methods are an integral part of the usage of mathematical models and terms, but the main reason for creating DT technology is to use them in all areas.

One of the recognised tools for implementing a simulation model while creating a DT is AnyLogic – a powerful and flexible modelling environment (Makarov et al., 2019).

2.10.3 The Connection Between MES-Systems and Digital Twins

The MES-system (manufacturing execution system) is designed to simulate and control intradepartmental material flows in the control tower. Modern MES is designed to work with modern IoT interfaces and to connect to outdated equipment. This allows it to saturate a vast amount of data with meaning and consistency. In this case, the MES-system works as an intermediate translator layer, turning the data stream into valuable information suitable for making strategic decisions.

Two numerical indicators evaluate the efficiency of a digital production process: the OEE coefficient (Overall Equipment Effectiveness) and the MCE coefficient (Manufacturing Cycle Effectiveness).

The OEE coefficient analyses the behaviour of the DM of the production system; it is the measurement of the proportion of the planned production time, which is necessary for manufacturing the part without taking into account work in progress (Makarov et al., 2019).

The OEE coefficient is calculated as follows (Makarov et al., 2019):

$$OEE = C_t * C_p * C_q = \frac{\sum_j \left[F_{tj} - D_j \right]}{\sum_j \left[F_{tj} \right]} * \frac{\sum_i \left[T_i * O_i \right]}{\sum_j \left[F_{tj} - D_j \right]} * \frac{\sum_i \left[T_i * (O_i - Def_i) \right]}{\sum_i \left[T_i * O_i \right]} \tag{2.1}$$

where C_t is the time coefficient (availability), C_p is the performance coefficient (efficiency), C_q is the quality coefficient (quality level), j is the number of equipment, F_{tj} is the fund of time of work of a unit of equipment (work shift time), D_j is equipment downtime, including planned, i is the number of products produced on this piece of equipment, T_i is the time of the release of the product, O_i is the amount of manufactured product within F_t, Def_i is the reject quantity of a product manufactured within F_t, $\sum_j [F_{tj} - D_j]$ is the time available for the output per unit of equipment, $\sum_i [Ti * Oi]i$ is the amount of time spent on production, and $\sum_i [Ti * (Oi - Def_i]$ is the amount of time spent on the production of a non-defective product.

The second indicator describes the digital production model. It is the coefficient MCE or the ratio of the labour intensity of technological operations performed by the corresponding production units during the processing of products (Makarov et al., 2019).

The MCE coefficient is calculated as follows (Makarov et al., 2019):

$$MCE_{ik} = \frac{T_{ik} * O_{ik}}{\sum_j F_{tj}} \tag{2.2}$$

where O_{ik} is the development of the production site for parts included in the product, T_{ik} is the rhythm of production in area k, and F_{tj} is the operating time of equipment fund.

The *OEE* coefficient characterises the density of equipment loading, which turns into a DM, and the *MCE* coefficient is a characteristic of the dynamics of the material flow in the DT of the production system (Makarov et al., 2019).

2.10.4 APPLICATION TOOLS

A DT's value can be amplified by combining it with other technologies and tools. Data mining techniques, AI, and ML can analyse the model of operations represented by a DT. In a supply chain, for instance, these tools can process and evaluate multiple sources of data to learn about many facets, dimensions, and contexts to accurately forecast operation and performance (Lawton, 2022). DTs play a key role in augmented reality, which involves the RT integration of digital information with users' environments. A DT follows a product's location and movement. Images that are overlaid onto the real world through RT sensor data and analytics can be used to perform product maintenance and services (Kshetri, 2021).

In a blockchain-based supply chain, a DT can function as a reference point to check information in a ledger, which can enhance traceability and the transparency of operations. For example, the blockchain platform for the lifestyle company Lukso utilises DTs of physical goods, such as jackets and shoes, which are stored on a blockchain. Tokenised assets are transferred along with their physical twins to prove ownership. In this way, top fashion designers and luxury merchants can display their collections in Lukso and enhance their reputations in the digital world (Kshetri, 2021).

The DT system consists of four main application tools (Bevilacqua et al., 2020):

1. Control and execution tool: The control and execution tool allows the physical system to communicate with the cyber system at the output through sensors, transducers, etc. and at the input through the control of actuators, switches, etc. This is a computer system dedicated to the management or control of industrial processes. This tool executes a program and elaborates digital and analogue signals coming from sensors and directed to the actuators present in an industrial plant.
2. Simulation tool: The simulation tool allows the company to create virtual modelling of the processes. This is an advanced vision of the DT that includes not only a simulation model, which is coherent with the real plant but also a behavioural and functional model through the creation of mock units.

   The simulation tool can work online or offline, i.e., the inputs can come from the sensors (in the first case) or can be entered manually (in the second case). When working offline, through a virtual representation of the physical assets, the tool allows managers to analyse what-if scenarios without the need to physically realise them, thus avoiding potential situations of risk for operators. In this case, the tool can be used, for example, to commission a new plant in a virtual way to identify the risks for operators before actually activating the plant or to simulate a maintenance activity and identify the risks associated with it.

   In the case where the tool works online, it must be able to receive information from the sensors on the physical asset and it modifies its parameters when the asset changes its conditions. The online application can allow a company to compare the various data provided by the simulation system. The data are actually detected by the sensors in order to activate warning signals if the discrepancy between the two values is beyond defined thresholds (Bevilacqua et al., 2020).
3. Anomaly detection and prediction tool: This tool should predict why faults are occurring, what the causes are (anomaly detection) and how long the system can go on before it breaks down or goes out of the correct plant operating parameters (anomaly prediction and residual life assessment). Figure 2.14 shows the rule of this tool within the reference model. The tool is based on ML algorithms for the analysis of anomaly detection and prediction in the execution of production and maintenance processes within the IoT environment (Bevilacqua et al., 2020).

   Typical anomalies to be predicted through ML in process plants are the following (Bevilacqua et al., 2020):
   • During the operative phase of the plant, the operator erroneously closes a shut-off valve and the plant goes into overpressure, putting at risk the integrity of the piping

and the personnel. Before the safety valve intervenes (which would lead to a partial emptying of the system with consequent stoppage of the system for a long time), the tool detects an increase in pressure at certain points, identifies the problem, and warns the operator about the type of anomaly that is occurring.

- During a pump maintenance operation, the operator does not close the shut-off valve and floods the area.
- The control valve downstream of the tank is blocked and closed due to a fault and the system goes into overpressure.
- A pump vibrates abnormally due to bearing failure.
- A shut-off valve upstream of the pump closes by mistake and the pump goes into cavitation.

4. Cloud server platform: The platform must acquire RT data from the field. Therefore, a normal server architecture is not enough because, in a normal operating environment, the enormous amount of data will not make its operation stable. This is the same with classic relational databases; these are not able to withstand an excessive number of requests for simultaneous access to reading and writing. This implies that the platform must be designed *ad hoc* for data acquisition, sorting, and visualisation through a cloud solution.

The platform provides application programming interfaces (APIs) or external calls with related authentication, to manage:

- Data input from the PLC;
- External engines for input data analysis (sensor readings);
- Elaborations carried out by the data analysis engines, after which they are visualised for comparison;
- Data coming from the sensors to the simulated model of the plant;
- Data coming from the simulated model (what-if scenarios) and the relative comparison of this model with the real one;
- Data coming from the sensors to the 3D model of the plant;
- Data coming from the 3D model and its comparison with the real one.

In addition to the functions listed above, it is necessary to manage the historical data related to both field sensors and analysis. It is also necessary to manage user permissions to avoid inappropriate deletions in non-applicable areas (Bevilacqua et al., 2020).

2.11 SMART MANUFACTURING: AN EXAMPLE OF DIGITAL TWIN DEVELOPMENT AND OPERATION

Smart manufacturing refers to a data-driven paradigm that creates manufacturing intelligence based on the acquired data in order to optimise, monitor, and visualise every aspect of the factory. The smart factory cell (Figure 2.15) serves as an example to demonstrate and evaluate the application of smart manufacturing (Stark et al., 2019).

The smart factory cell is an instantiation of a digital production twin: operational data of the physical smart factory cell is linked to the digital master, i.e., the digital prototype model. The smart factory cell focuses on the following aspects of the information factory (Stark et al., 2019):

- A service for the individualisation of products interacts directly with production;
- The factory operates this service through cloud computing into machine control;
- The factory is linked to its digital master so that its interactions can be processed, controlled, and modified in RT.

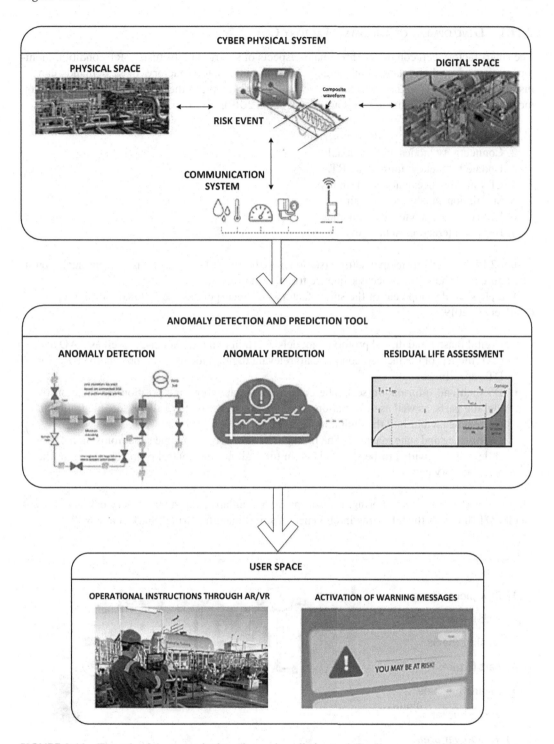

FIGURE 2.14 The rule of the anomaly detection and prediction tool (Bevilacqua et al., 2020).

2.11.1 DEVELOPMENT OF THE SMART FACTORY CELL

The smart factory cell comprises three major aspects of smart manufacturing: RT condition monitoring, control, and simulation. In the context of the information factory, these demands can be instantiated for the DT of the smart factory cell using the example of the digital twin eight-dimension model (Figure 2.16) explained as follows (Stark et al., 2019):

1. Integration breadth: production system.
2. Connectivity modes: bidirectional.
3. Update frequency: immediate RT.
4. CPS intelligence: automated (in ms).
5. Simulation capabilities: dynamic.
6. DM richness: geometry kinematics.
7. Human interaction: smart devices.

Figure 2.15 shows the principal setting (stations) of the smart factory cell, as it is physically built. The figure also shows the process sequence through the various operations.

The physical development of the smart factory cell incorporates the following design elements (Stark et al., 2019):

- Digital master and digital prototype models: Certain numeric models, as well as CAD and CAE models of the factory, comprise all relevant digital models and represent the basis for DT capabilities.
- DS data and information sets: The collection of data about the position information on moving parts, as well as information on the motion of the motors, allows the integration of the real behaviour into the digital models.
- Intelligence and state machine: The linkage richness is based on the synchronisation of the collected data with a to-be status. This, in turn, allows the control of the operation of the smart factory cell.

The central element for monitoring, controlling, and simulating the smart factory cell is the smart factory DT. It covers the following intelligence of smart manufacturing (Stark et al., 2019).

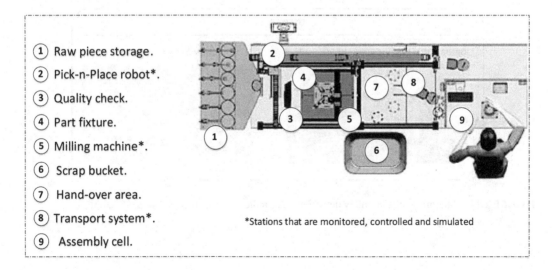

1. Raw piece storage.
2. Pick-n-Place robot*.
3. Quality check.
4. Part fixture.
5. Milling machine*.
6. Scrap bucket.
7. Hand-over area.
8. Transport system*.
9. Assembly cell.

*Stations that are monitored, controlled and simulated

FIGURE 2.15 Principal setting and process of the smart factory cell (Stark et al., 2019).

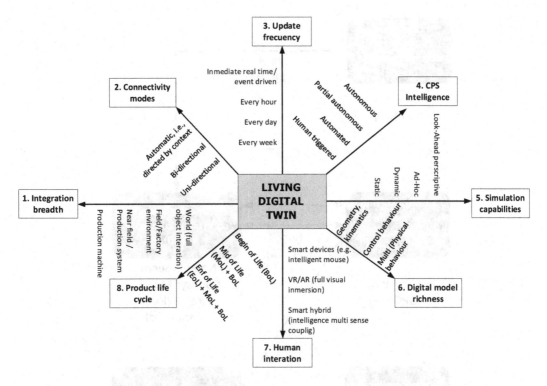

FIGURE 2.16   The digital twin 8-dimension model (Stark et al., 2019).

- Condition monitoring: Monitoring positions of every step such as baselining, order, transport, moving mill, milling, waiting, transport, and end of run.
- Control: Controlling the manufacturing processes with the DT enables an individualised manufacturing process because the whole process is simulated simultaneously. The information collected in the field is used together with the simulation and other information sources to give the control to the DT itself. One example of controlling is monitoring for collisions or intrusions, either of which would lead to the stoppage of the pick-and-place robot.
- RT simulation: Controlling the manufacturing process with the DT needs information on the status of the process and the positions of every object. The positions of moving objects are continuously updated for the RT simulation of the DT. They are directly connected to the mill and the pick-and-place robot.

2.11.2   OPERATION OF THE SMART FACTORY CELL

The DT enables an individual manufacturing process with which virtual and physical interaction takes place. The activity of controlling the manufacturing processes with the DT enables an individualised manufacturing process, due to the simultaneous simulation of the process. The information collected in the field is linked to the simulation and other information sources in order to give the control to the DT itself.

Figure 2.15 shows the principal setting of the smart factory cell, including its stations and process operations. The operations monitored, controlled, and simulated are baselining, order, transport (station 2), moving the mill, milling (station 5), and waiting and transport (station 8). The DT centrally controls the motion of the machines and the condition monitoring with the sensors. Figure 2.17 shows the relevant hardware and software, their interactions, the transport protocols, and the measuring points of the smart factory cell (Stark et al., 2019).

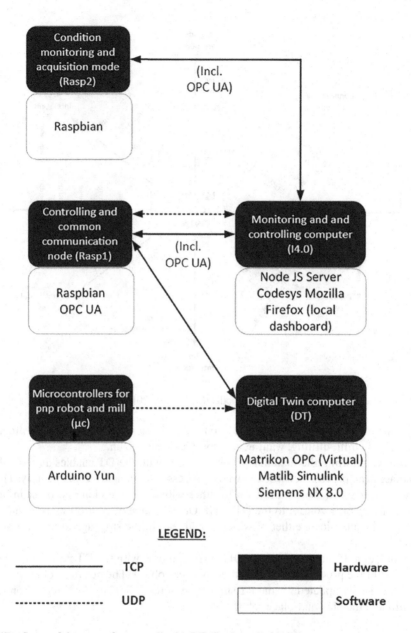

FIGURE 2.17   Setup of the smart factory cell with DT (Stark et al., 2019).

In Figure 2.17, the positions of the controlled machines are continuously updated within the DT simulation, which is run on the DT computer. Intermediate Raspberry Pi's (Rasp 1 and 2) are directly connected to the sensors and actuators, collecting data and synchronising the position information and control. The I4.0 computer interacts with the Rasp 1, which is a PLC shield, and the Rasp 2, a minicomputer with Wi-Fi communication. Two microcontrollers (mc) translate the commands into the motion of the motors of the pick-and-place (pnp) robot and the mill. Each mc serially communicates with the motors of the pnp robot and the mill, respectively. They continuously send the position data to the DT. Rasp1 is used to communicate the monitoring and control commands among the I4.0 and DT computers.

For condition monitoring (temperature, power, and energy consumption), the average package size is around 408 bytes (TCP) and 208 (UDP) with a minimum of 60 bytes and a maximum of

1,296 bytes. The package sizes for motion control for one simple manufacturing process(milling) are on average 187 bytes (DT control) with a minimum of 130 bytes and a maximum of 198 bytes (Stark et al., 2019).

2.12   SOME APPLICATIONS OF DIGITAL TWINS

DTs allow organisations to accurately predict the current state and future of physical assets by ana-lysing their digital counterparts. By implementing DTs, organisations can gain better insights into product performance, improve customer service, and make better operational and strategic deci-sions based on these insights. DTs are currently being applied in the following sectors.

1. Manufacturing: DTs have a significant impact on the way products are designed manu-factured and maintained. DT makes manufacturing more efficient and optimised while reducing throughput times (HappiestMinds, 2022).
2. Automobile: DTs can be used in the automobile sector to create the virtual model of a con-nected vehicle. DT captures the behavioural and operational data of the vehicle and helps analyse the overall vehicle performance, as well as the connected features. It also helps to deliver a truly personalised/customised service for customers.
3. Retail: DT implementation can play a key role in augmenting the retail customer experience by creating virtual twins for customers and modelling fashions for them on it. DT also helps in store planning, security implementation, and energy management in an optimised manner.
4. Healthcare: DTs along with data from IoT can play a key role in the healthcare sector, from cost savings to patient monitoring, preventive maintenance, and personalised health care.
5. Smart cities: Smart city planning and implementation with DT and IoT data enhance eco-nomic development, support efficient management of resources, reduce the ecological footprint, and increase the overall quality of a citizen's life. The DT model can help city planners and policymakers in smart city planning by gaining insights from various sen-sor networks and intelligent systems. The data from the DTs help them arrive at informed decisions regarding the future as well.
6. Industrial IoT: Industrial firms with DT implementation can now monitor, track and control industrial systems digitally. In addition to the operational data, DTs capture environmental data, such as location, configuration, financial models, etc. These data help in predicting future operations and anomalies.

2.13   USES OF DIGITAL TWIN TECHNOLOGY

Creating and using DTs increase intelligence as part of the operational system. Having an up-to-date representation of real operating assets allows organisations to control or optimise assets and the wider system. The representation captures the current state and often incorporates the operating his-tory of the asset. DTs allow organisations to optimise, improve efficiencies, automate, and evaluate future performance. The models can be for other purposes as well, such as virtual commissioning or to influence next-generation designs.

DT models are commonly used in several areas:

1. Operations optimisation: Using variables like weather, fleet size, energy costs, or perfor-mance factors, models run hundreds or thousands of what-if simulations. This enables system operations to be optimised or controlled during operation to mitigate risk, reduce cost, or gain any number of system efficiencies (Figure 2.18) (MathWorks, 2022).
2. Predictive maintenance: In industry 4.0 applications, models can determine the remaining useful life to inform operations on the most opportune time to service or replace equipment (Figure 2.19) (MathWorks, 2022).

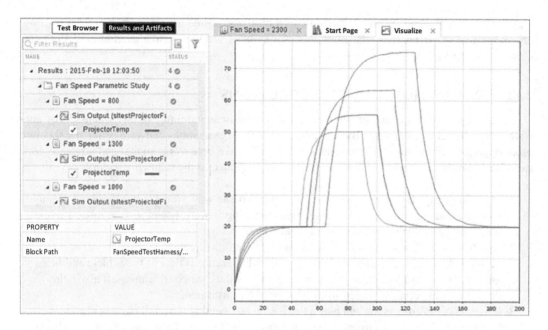

FIGURE 2.18   Monte Carlo simulations to evaluate possible behaviour (MathWorks, 2022).

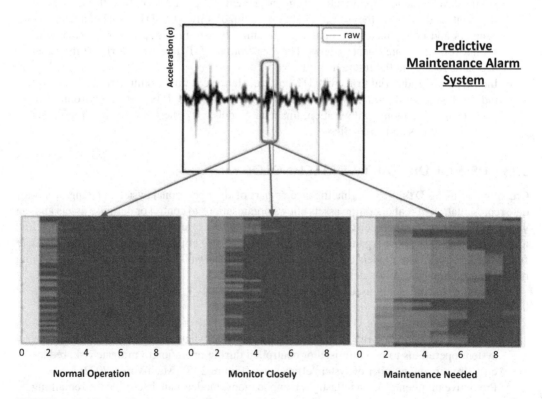

FIGURE 2.19   Baker Hughes' predictive maintenance alarm system, based on MATLAB (MathWorks, 2022).

3. Anomaly detection: The DT runs in parallel to the real assets, and immediately flags operational behaviour that deviates from expected (simulated) behaviour. For example, a petroleum company may stream sensor data from offshore oil rigs that operate continuously. The DT will look for anomalies in the operational behaviour to avoid catastrophic damage (Figure 2.20) (MathWorks, 2022).

4. Fault isolation: Anomalies may trigger a number of simulations to isolate the fault and identify the root cause so engineers or the system can take appropriate action (Figure 2.21).

5. Product design: Today, data from many previous generation product realisations are merged into a common DT of the product to gain more product knowledge in the early stages of new product generation. The application of DTs in the product design stage allows a quantitative design tool for efficient and optimal design decisions by using data from previous product generations. In this context, data from DTs of previous product design can be analysed and used for optimising new designs.

6. Optimisation of tool behaviour: By modelling manufacturing steps and entire machine tools using DTs, the effects of tool behaviour and process parameters can be determined and optimised. Optimum tool geometries and process parameters for surface conditioning, for example, can be determined by using DTs of a cutting tool to achieve advanced products.

7. Additive engineering: In additive manufacturing, DTs are used to evaluate 3D printed metallic components. The goal is to reduce the number of trial and error tests to obtain the desired product attributes and shorten the time between design and production.

8. Complex production systems: Complex systems link manufacturing, quality control and logistics processes. They consist of multiple stochastic and dynamic processes with mostly non-linear dependencies. Analytical methods cannot capture all processes and dependencies so simulation models are used. DTs of production systems can be combined with existing optimisation programs, for selective part assembly to achieve cutting-edge products, scheduling to build robust production schedules or predicting the effect of counter measurements in case of disturbances. In some cases, even human resources systems are considered in the DT.

Human interaction: Human interaction is also modelled in DTs. A developed DT of human-robot collaboration yields important insights and makes it possible to test new operating policies before implementing them in a production setting.

2.13.1 CURRENT STATE OF THE ART

DT modelling methods generally can be grouped into two types: first principles or physics-based methods (e.g. mechanical modelling) and data-driven methods (e.g. deep learning). A DT can also be a composite of various modelled behaviours and modelling methods and is likely to be elaborated on over time as more uses are identified (Figure 2.22) (MathWorks, 2022).

The models must be kept up-to-date and tuned to the assets in operation. This typically involves direct streaming of data from the assets into algorithms that tune the DT. This allows users to consider aspects like asset environment, age, and configuration.

Once the DT is available and up to date, it can be used in myriad ways to predict future behaviour, refine the control, or optimise asset operation. Some examples include simulating sensors that are not present on the real asset, simulating future scenarios to inform current and future operations, or using the DT to extract the current operational state by sending in current real inputs (MathWorks, 2022).

With advancements in technology like cloud computing, IoT, and Big Data, many domains have seen major developments, such as Industry 4.0, Physical Internet, Cyber-manufacturing, Made in China 2025, Cloud Manufacturing, etc. Industry 4.0 rests on digital advancements, IoT, and Big

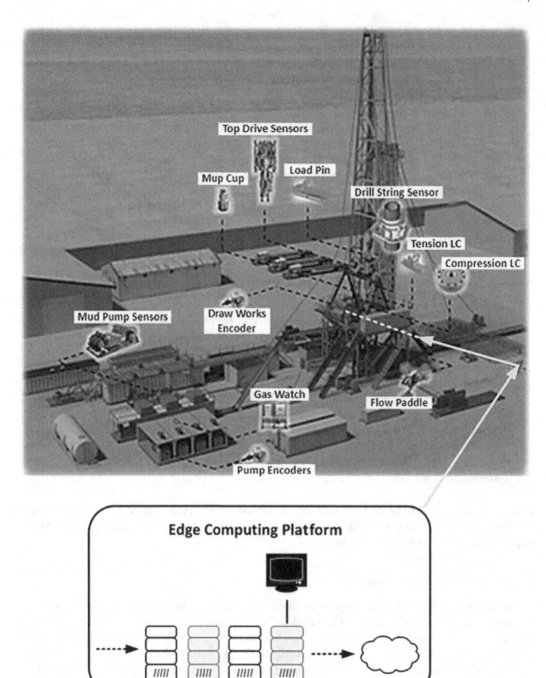

FIGURE 2.20 Prototype of industrial IoT deployment on oil rig using simulink RTe. Image courtesy: National oilwell varco (MathWorks, 2022).

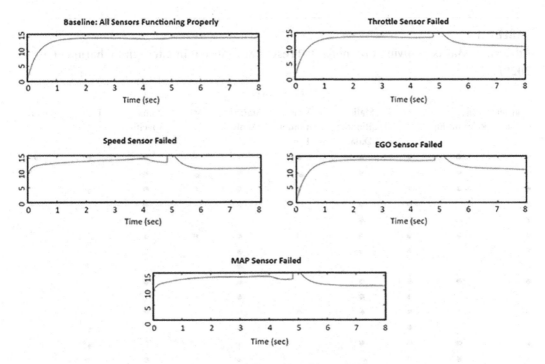

FIGURE 2.21 Fault isolation of a fuel control system (MathWorks, 2022).

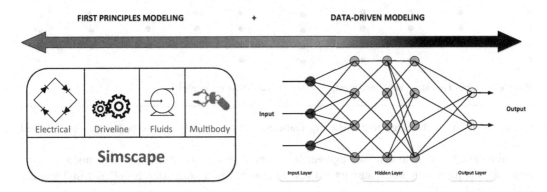

FIGURE 2.22 Modelling methods for DTs: first principles and data-driven (MathWorks, 2022).

Data. With the storage of all data in digital format, and sensors being inbuilt into industrial spaces, Industry 4.0 put DT implementation on the fast track.

Importantly, with the emerging extensive simulation capabilities, it has become feasible to perform realistic tests in a virtual environment (Sharma et al., 2020).

2.13.1.1 Components of DT

DT was introduced by Grieves (see Section 4.2) with three components: the digital component (virtual part), the real physical object, and the connection between them. However, subsequent authors extended this concept to include five components by including data and service as part of DT. They also identified VV&A (verification, validation, and accreditation) as DT components.

When data models entered the picture, the definition extended to include the integration of multiple models of a model-based enterprise; in this understanding, a DT can be formed by creating associations between different models and relations between data stored in different parts. With the

TABLE 2.1

Adjacency Matrix Showing Components Present and Absent in Literature (Sharma et al., 2020)

				Components					
Transfer of Info	Bijective Relationship	IoT	Static Continuous Data	Time-Continuous Data	Statistical Analysis	ML	Domain-Specific Services	Testing	Security
●	●	●	●	●	●	●	●	●*	●
●	●	●	●	●*	●	●*	●	●*	
●	●	●	●	●	●	●	●	●*	
●		●	●		●		●		
●		●*	●				●		
●	●	●	●	●	●	●	●		
●		●	●		●		●		
●					●			●	
●	●	●	●		●		●		
●	●	●	●		●				
●	●	●	●	●	●	●	●		
		●			●			●*	
●	●	●	●	●*	●	●*	●	●*	
●	●	●	●*		●		●	●	●
●	●	●*	*		*		●		
●	●	●	●	●	●	●	●	●*	●
●	●	●	●	●*	●	●	●	●	●*
●	●	●	●	●*	●	●	●	●*	●*
●	●	●	●	●*	●		●*	●*	●
●	●	●	●	●*	●				

Note: '●' Indicates Present; ' ' Indicates Absent; '*' Means Indication but not Explicitly.

advancements in technology (e.g. ML, Big Data, and cybersecurity), these requirements changed again.

Ultimately, there is no common agreement on the components of DT. Components and properties are mentioned by some authors but not by others. The information is collated in Table 2.1 (Sharma et al., 2020).

2.13.1.1.1 Basic Components

The basic components are those without which a DT cannot exist (Sharma et al., 2020):

1. Physical asset (either a product or a product lifecycle).
2. Digital asset (the virtual component).
3. Two-way synchronised relationship establishing information flow between the physical and digital asset.

2.13.1.1.2 Essential Components

The essential components add to the properties of DT. Without any of these, DT would not be unique:

1. IoT devices: The devices collect RT information from various sub-components of the physical asset. It is essential to have high-fidelity connection between all IoT devices, for accurate and timely flow of information.

2. Integrated time continuous data: These data are gathered from different IoT components for ML and analytics and are essential to monitor the system, guarantee correct behaviour, and provide input to the ML system. They require Big Data analysis and storage tools in order to extract useful information.
3. Machine learning: ML is used for predictions and feedback and can propose mitigation strategies, in exceptional circumstances. It requires a joint optimisation feature for all the sub-components of the DT.
4. Security of the data and information flow among the various physical components of the physical asset.
5. DT performance evaluation: This requires evaluation metrics (e.g. accuracy, resilience, robustness, and costs) and evaluation methods and tests (Sharma et al., 2020).

2.13.1.2   Properties of a DT

2.13.1.2.1   Necessary Properties

These are the properties inherent to any DT (Sharma et al., 2020):

1. RT connection with the physical entity.
2. Self-evolution: With this property, DTs can learn and adapt in RT, by providing feedback to both the physical asset (through the human asset) and the DT. This has become relatively straightforward with the development of ML tools: the DT can remodel and redesign itself (e.g. reinforcement learning). This property depends on the update scenarios, such as event-based (supply chain) scenarios, periodic intervals (aircraft), condition-based (logistics) scenarios etc.
3. Continuous ML analysis: This depends on the frequency of the synchronisation and is not just one-time output forecasting.
4. Time-series (or time continuous) data: These data must be available for monitoring and as input to the ML system.
5. Domain dependence (or domain-specific services): Depending on the domain, a DT may provide or prioritise services specific to the industry. These are the domain-specific services which exist in the physical asset (e.g. the optimisation problems for an aircraft and a manufacturing unit will prioritise or add more weight to different parameters).

2.13.1.2.2   Dynamic Properties

Based on these dynamic properties, a DT hierarchy can be created:

- Autonomy: A DT (or any information provider) could make changes to the physical asset itself, or a human in control could make changes to the DT. This applies differently to different hierarchies of components in the DT, such as some parts of the ML system or the decision-making system. Hence, the property of a DT to be autonomous, not autonomous, or partly autonomous is case-dependent. This classification also includes the self-evolution mechanism of DT (what changes it must make to itself, and what changes must be approved by a human).
- Synchronisation: Synchronisation of data could either be continuous or at certain time intervals. This depends on a number of factors, such as technology, resources available, the need for the data, and the type of ML algorithm being used. A DT could have sub-components, which could be partly continuously synchronised and partly event-based synchronised.

Synchronisation can result in different hierarchies based on how often the data are collected and stored, and often the DT is updated.

A reference framework is presented in Figure 2.23 (Sharma et al., 2020).

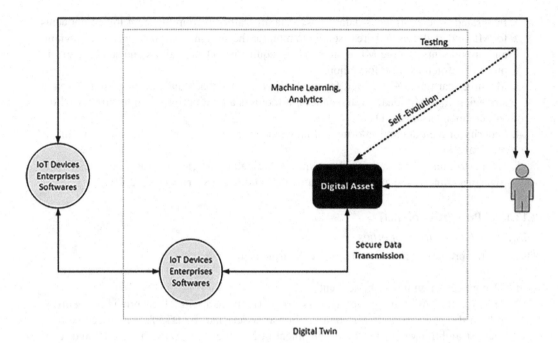

FIGURE 2.23   DT reference framework with components and information flows (Sharma et al., 2020).

TABLE 2.2
DT Compared to Existing Technologies
(Sharma et al., 2020)

Technology	How it Differs from DT
Simulation	No RT twinning
Machine learning	No twinning
Digital prototype	No 10T components necessarily
Optimisation	No simulation and RT tests
Autonomous Systems	No self-evolution necessarily
Agent-based modelling	No RT twinning

2.13.1.3   How DT Differs from Existing Technologies

DT applications include simulation, RT monitoring, testing, analytics, prototyping, and end-to-end visibility. Each can be broadly classified as a subsystem of DT. For example, a DT can be used for testing during prototyping or for RT monitoring and evaluation, or for both. The presence of all the components discussed in the previous section makes a DT different, as described in Table 2.2 (Sharma et al., 2020).

2.13.1.4   A Brief Overview of Similar Concepts That Preceded DT

The concepts of digitising and twinning are not new. Many similar concepts have preceded DT, and the DT technology is built on many of them:

- Digital model: A digital model has only manual exchange of data and, unlike DT, does not showcase the real-time state.
- Digital shadow: A digital shadow is a saved data copy of the physical state, with one-way data flow from physical object to the digital object. The DT has fully integrated data flow; thus, DT reflects the actual state of the physical object.

- Semantic virtual factory data models (VFDMs): VFDMs are virtual representations of factory entities and were used in manufacturing and industrial spaces. DT differs because of its property of RT synchronisation. VF is a data model only, whereas DT is RT and synchronised.
- Product avatar: This is a distributed and decentralised approach to product information management with no concept of feedback. It may represent information on only parts of the asset. In contrast, DT offers feedback and represents a broader perspective.
- Digital product memory: In semantic/digital product memory, a digital product memory senses and captures information related to a specific physical part. In this sense, it can be viewed as an instantiation of DT.
- Intelligent product: New technologies such as IoT, Big Data, and ML have all been built on the concept of Intelligent Product. In other words, DT can be seen as an extension of an Intelligent Product.
- Holons: As an initial computer-integrated manufacturing tool, holons formed the basis for all the technologies described above (Sharma et al., 2020).

2.13.1.5 Added Value of Digital Twins

DT offers the following eight value additions:

1. RT remote monitoring and control: It is almost impossible to gain an in-depth view of a very large system physically in RT. A DT can be accessible anywhere. The performance of the system can not only be monitored but also controlled remotely using feedback mechanisms.
2. Greater efficiency and safety: DTs will enable greater autonomy with humans in the loop as and when required. Dangerous, dull, and dirty jobs will be allocated to robots with humans controlling them remotely.
3. Predictive maintenance and scheduling: A comprehensive DT will ensure that multiple sensors monitoring the physical assets will be generating Big Data in RT. Faults can be detected in advance, enabling better scheduling of maintenance.
4. Scenario and risk assessment: A DT will enable what-if analyses resulting in better risk assessment. It will be possible to synthesise unexpected scenarios and study the response of the system and the corresponding mitigation strategies.
5. Better intra- and inter-team synergy and collaborations: With greater autonomy and all the information at a fingertip, teams can better utilise their time in improving synergies and collaborations leading to greater productivity.
6. More efficient and informed decision support system: Availability of quantitative data and advanced analytics in RT will lead to more informed and faster decision-making.
7. Personalisation of products and services: With detailed historical requirements, preferences of various stakeholders, and evolving market trends and competition, the demand for customised products and services will increase. A DT in the context of factories of the future will enable faster and smoother shifts to account for changing needs.
8. Better documentation and communication: Readily available information in RT combined with automated reporting will keep stakeholders informed, thereby improving transparency.

2.13.2 Specific Applications of Digital Twins in Maintenance

DTs integrate IoT, AI, ML, and software analytics to create living digital simulation models that update and change as their physical counterparts change. A DT continuously learns and updates itself based on multiple sources in order to represent its near RT status, working condition, or position, thus making it ideally suited for maintenance purposes.

2.14   HOW ARE DIGITAL TWINS USED IN MAINTENANCE?

The following are some principal use-cases for DTs in enterprise maintenance (Edge4Industry, 2018):

1. Use #1: Digital simulation

    A DT provides the information needed to execute realistic and accurate simulations about the behaviour of assets and their maintenance. Simulations based on DTs take in information about risk factors, failure modes, operating scenarios, and system configurations in order to produce maintenance-related key performance indicators (KPIs) such as:
    - Maintenance cost
    - System downtime and unavailability
    - Remaining useful life (RUL)
    - End of life (EoL)
    - Mean time between failures (MTBF) and more.

        Such simulations enable the anticipation of future maintenance activities, which is key for developing predictive maintenance systems. At the same time, they can improve the planning of preventive and condition-based maintenance processes as a means of minimising downtimes and unscheduled repairs.

2. Use #2: Support for what-if analysis

    DTs are used for what-if analysis of alternative maintenance scenarios. By simulating different maintenance scenarios, organisations can evaluate and select the most effective asset management strategy. What-if analysis can be exploited both for long-term planning of maintenance strategies (e.g. comparing a predictive maintenance strategy to a preventive one in terms of return on investment) and for short-term on-the-spot decision-making (e.g. whether it's time to replace a tool or not).

3. Use #3: Maintenance system configuration

    In many cases, DTs remain synchronised to the status of the physical assets they represent. Whenever the status of an asset is changed, the DT model updates to reflect the change. Likewise, whenever the status of the DT is changed as part of an information technology (IT) operation, the respective change is reflected in the physical assets based on some IoT or CPS that conveys the status of the digital world to the real world.

    Based on this synchronisation, DTs can be used to configure the operation of assets and related physical systems. For example, if an IoT/CPS application detects a machine's failure or degradation pattern, it could configure the machine to operate at a reduced speed. This can be done through an IT command to the DT of the machine, rather than to the human operator of the machine.

    It's important to note that the use of DTs for the flexible configuration of maintenance systems hinges on the deployment of proper CPS systems on the plant floor; notably, systems that can configure their physical parts based on information and commands from cyber counterparts.

4. Use #4: Open the doors to innovation in enterprise maintenance

    In the medium- and long-term, DTs will drive open innovation in enterprise maintenance based on digital technologies. In particular, they will be used as a vehicle for testing, validating, and evaluating innovative ideas about when and how to maintain or repair an asset, without disrupting plant operations. This will facilitate innovators in their endeavours and will reduce the enterprise's maintenance innovation cycles. In this context, IBM views DTs as a way of transforming engines and other pieces of equipment to digital innovation platforms.

2.15   DIGITAL TWINS AND PREDICTIVE MAINTENANCE

Predictive maintenance evaluates the condition of equipment by performing periodic (offline) or continuous (online) equipment monitoring. The goal of the approach is to perform maintenance at a scheduled point in time when the maintenance activity is most cost-effective and before the equipment loses performance within a given threshold.

Industry 4.0 has been accompanied by a strategic shift from a reactive to a predictive maintenance approach. Analytical solutions for predictive maintenance enable organisations to avoid unwanted, random events, and monitor assets, the entire production line or plant. When combined with the possibility to simulate behaviour, it provides companies with the ability to fully optimise their operations. It also allows for testing variants of production development or planned investments.

The full representation of the system and its dynamics in RT offered by DT allows simulations of the system behaviour. This creates the possibility to test the algorithms of predictive maintenance as a part of various scenarios that may not have occurred thus far. Such simulations of behaviour allow faster and better testing of predictive maintenance solutions (ReliaSol, 2021).

2.16 A DIGITAL TWIN MAINTENANCE USE CASE: POINT MACHINE FOR TRAIN SWITCHES

Railroad switches, also called turnouts or points, are a key element of the rail network infrastructure. They are distributed all over the network, and their maintenance is crucial to guarantee safety and undisturbed operation.

Within a railway network, the turnouts are responsible for a high amount of the operational costs as monitoring and maintenance are mainly manual. Points diagnostics systems like the Sidis W compact from Siemens are used to monitor the current condition of the point machine by analysing the electrical power demand of the drive and point machine operation module. However, a prediction of the future behaviour remains difficult. The interaction of a railway switch and its drive (point machine) is complex. On both subsystems, many different parameters act in a way that make it difficult to predict behaviour (Boschert et al., 2018).

2.17 PLANNING THE DIGITAL TWIN

The DT can become part of a product itself enhancing the original functionality of the product. The additional functionalities covered by the DT can be designed in the same way as normal product features or when the concept of DT is already broadly realised, the functionalities can be assembled based on existing (simulation) modules provided by the DT.

In our example of the railway point machine, physics-based simulation models, as well as live data from the points diagnostics system, are used to identify a possible malfunction of the turnout. Therefore, a "template" of this DT feature is specified during the conceptual design phase. This template describes how the different components are linked together and interact. During the ongoing design and construction process, it will be filled with (sub-)models as soon as they are created and finally result in a complete system model that fulfils the specified product functionalities.

Defining the template during the early planning helps to ensure that the simulation models are created at the time when the lowest effort is needed: during the component development. It is also possible to create the models afterwards, but at a higher cost, as implicit knowledge may have been lost (Boschert et al., 2018).

2.18 DIGITAL TWIN DURING OPERATION PHASE

The system model allows simulating the operation of the point machine for a customer/site-specific configuration. Depending on the complexity of the underlying system, the implementation can be done at different locations, ranging from embedded logic in the control unit of the drive-over included as an assistance module for the switch operator to cloud-based implementation as service on demand (e.g. for maintenance workers).

In the suggested setup (assistance system), the failure identification module compares the measurement data from the live system with results from the physics-based simulation. This direct comparison is possible, as by design, the results of the two input sources (simulation model and points diagnostics system) are comparable.

As soon as the failure identification module detects a significant deviation of the two models, it raises a notification in the dashboard and analyses possible root causes of the failure, also displayed to the operator.

As usual, every turnout has an individual configuration, the failure identification module has to be configured individually. However, in several situations, different turnouts show similar behaviour as they are somehow connected. For example, turnouts that are locally close to each other are subject to similar environmental conditions like temperature or rainfall. Including this kind of information in the analysis using DTs is discussed in the following section (Boschert et al., 2018).

2.19 HYBRID ANALYSIS AND FLEET DATA

The connection between the DT and operational data offers a wide range of new services, from failure detection to diagnosis.

The connection between the DT and a physical instance is established through sensors. Ideally, sensor data are received and processed in RT. But if data are submitted to a cloud and processed there, synchronisation and proper delay management become important due to different time constants. Depending on the application, such sensors measure physical quantities like accelerations, displacements, strains, temperatures, or current signature and power in the case of point machines. In this situation, it is relevant not only to monitor data but also to detect and diagnose failure states, as well as give recommendations for future operation or maintenance.

A second approach is to rely on data and use AI algorithms on those data. However, without a large and old fleet, there can be a lack of data. In this situation, simulation models help to test the system virtually in different environments or failure modes. Fleet data are generated using simulation models and variants of these models. This approach even applies to unique items. Once products are in operation, these data can be gradually enriched by data from the field (Boschert et al., 2018).

2.20 STEPS TO ENSURE WIDESPREAD IMPLEMENTATION OF DIGITAL TWIN

The following steps will advance DT and lead to its widespread useful implementation (Sharma et al., 2020):

1. A formal definition of DT: A lack of consensus exists for the definition of DT; having a formal definition will help to clarify the concept and reach a universally accepted concept.
2. IoT standards for DT: Since DT relies heavily on IoT devices for capturing and sharing data, RT synchronisation and monitoring, knowing what IoT standards are best suited for these operations will enhance the acceptance of DT and make it easier for widespread adoption. A data communication standard is also required.
3. Regulations at enterprise and global levels: As many companies collaborate across industries, having proper legal-binding regulations on the data used in DT is crucial for smooth operation. This also applies to sites spread across the globe which need to adhere to laws applicable of the particular country.

4. Liaison with domain experts to spread DT across sectors: Communicating with domain experts will facilitate the implementation and acceptance of DT in new domains. As domain experts know all there is to know about domain-specific requirements, they can be very useful in designing the DT. Once a design is ready, the implementation of the DT framework can be managed by programmers and developers.

2.21 DIGITAL TWIN AND ITS IMPACT ON INDUSTRY 4.0

As this chapter has made clear, DT is at the core of the fourth industrial revolution or Industry 4.0, which embraces automation, data exchange, and manufacturing technologies. DT is a combined adaptation of the physical and the virtual world. It incorporates technologies like AI, ML, and software analytics with information to make living digital simulation models that update and change with any change in their physical counterparts.

By providing the exact digital replica of machines, the technology helps operators to understand unique features, performance, and potential issues on the virtual simulated model (Figure 2.24). Since the technology supports RT monitoring of a physical plant, with the help of sensors, operators receive an alert on possible machine failures and/or threats of downtime and/or accidents. With RT operation updates, industry workers can optimise the performance of machines in RT, monitor the coordination between all the devices, perform diagnosis on a virtual plant, and repair the faults, if any, with minimal loss to productivity (VizExperts, 2022).

In conclusion, DTs are digital replicas of objects, places, physical systems, or processes. Everything can be artificially represented. The DT is responsible for truthfully showing the operation, response, and behaviour of its "real" counterpart through the combination of physical and virtual data (Figure 2.25) (Blanco, 2022).

With the further evolution of ML and AI, machines will take autonomy to the next level. In such an autonomous world of industrial machines, the role of DT will evolve with increasing self-awareness in the machines. Such machines will be capable of optimising their performance, coordinating with other machines, doing self-diagnosis, and self-repairing the faults, if any, with minimal intervention from a manual operator (HappiestMinds, 2022).

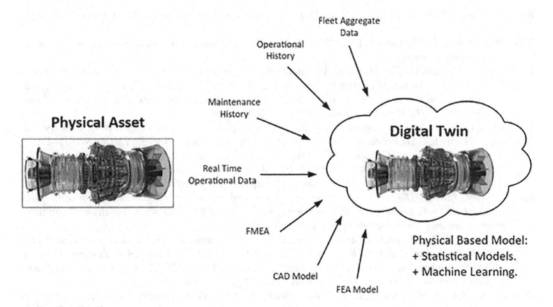

FIGURE 2.24 Technologies incorporated by DT (VizExperts, 2022).

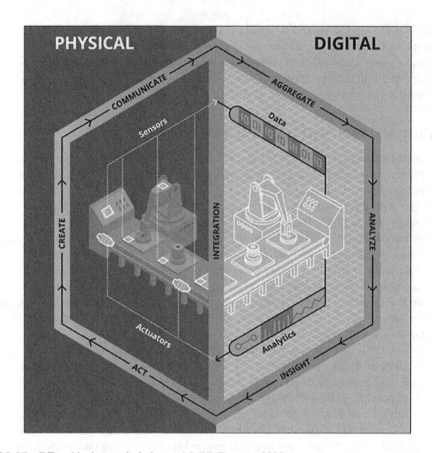

FIGURE 2.25   DT and its impact in industry 4.0 (VizExperts, 2022).

REFERENCES

Banks, J., Carson, J., Nelson, B. L., & Nicol, D. (1996). *Discrete-event system simulation* (4th ed.). Prentice Hall.

Bauer, W., Schlund, S., Marrenbach, D., & Ganschar, O. (2014). *Industrie 4.0: volkswirtschaftliches potenzial für deutschland*. Stuttgart.

Bevilacqua, M., Bottani, E., Ciarapica, F. E., Costantino, F., Donato, D. L., Ferraro, A., Mazzuto, G., Monteriù, A., Nardini, G., Ortenzi, M., Paroncini, M., Pirozzi, M., Prist, M., Quatrini, E., Tronci, M., & Vignali, G. (2020). Digital twin reference model development to prevent operators' risk in process plants. *Sustainability, 12*(3), 1088. https://doi.org/10.3390/SU12031088

Blanco, J. M. (2022). *Digital Twins and Industry 4.0*. https://www.plainconcepts.com/digital-twins-industry-4-0/

Boschert, S., Heinrich, C., & Rosen, R. (2018). Next generation digital twin. *Procedia TMCE, 2018*, 7–11.

Dittrich, M. A., Schleich, B., Clausmeyer, T., Damgrave, R., Erkoyuncu, J. A., Haefner, B., de Lange, J., Plakhotnik, D., Scheidel, W., & Wuest, T. (2019). Shifting value stream patterns along the product life-cycle with digital twins. *Procedia CIRP, 86*, 3–11. https://doi.org/10.1016/J.PROCIR.2020.01.049

Edge4Industry. (2018). *Digital Twins: What are They and How are They Shaking Up Enterprise Maintenance? – Edge4Industry*. https://www.edge4industry.eu/2018/06/19/digital-twins-what-are-they-and-how-are-they-shaking-up-enterprise-maintenance/

Erikstad, S. O. (2017). Merging physics, big data analytics and simulation for the next-generation digital twins. Paper presented at *HIPER (High-Performance)Marine Vehicles Conference*, Zevenwach, South Africa, September. https://www.researchgate.net/publication/320196420_Merging_Physics_Big_Data_Analytics_and_Simulation_for_the_Next-Generation_Digital_Twins

Främling, K., Holmström, J., Ala-Risku, T., & Kärkkäinen, M. (2003). Product agents for handling information about physical objects. *Report of Laboratory of Information Processing Science Series B, TKO-B, 153*, 3.

Friedenthal, S., Moore, A., & Steiner, R. (2014). *A Practical Guide to SysML: The Systems Modeling Language.* *Morgan Kaufmann.*

Gartner. (2022). *Top Strategic Technology Trends for 2022 Gartner.* https://www.gartner.com/en/information-technology/insights/top-technology-trends

Grieves, M. W. (2005). Product lifecycle management: the new paradigm for enterprises. *International Journal of Product Development, 2*(1–2), 71–84. https://doi.org/10.1504/ijpd.2005.006669

HappiestMinds. (2022). *What is Digital Twin Concept Applications.* https://www.happiestminds.com/insights/digital-twins/

IMAG. (2019). *Digital Twin Overview Interagency Modeling and Analysis Group.* https://www.imagwiki.nibib.nih.gov/content/digital-twin-overview

Juarez, M. G., Botti, V. J., & Giret, A. S. (2021). Digital twins: review and challenges. *Journal of Computing and Information Science in Engineering, 21*(3), 030802. https://doi.org/10.1115/1.4050244/1100428

Karim, R., Westerberg, J., Galar, D., & Kumar, U. (2016). Maintenance analytics – the new know in maintenance. *IFAC-PapersOnLine, 49*(28), 214–219. https://doi.org/10.1016/j.ifacol.2016.11.037

Kritzinger, W., Karner, M., Traar, G., Henjes, J., & Sihn, W. (2018). Digital twin in manufacturing: a categorical literature review and classification. *IFAC-PapersOnLine, 51*(11), 1016–1022. https://doi.org/10.1016/J.IFACOL.2018.08.474

Kshetri, N. K. (2021). The economics of digital twins. *IEEE Computer, 54*(4), 86–90. https://doi.org/10.1109/MC.2021.3055683

Lawton, G. (2022). *What is Descriptive Analytics? Definition from WhatIs.com.* https://www.techtarget.com/whatis/definition/descriptive-analytics

Makarov, V. V., Frolov, Y. B., Parshina, I. S., & Ushakova, M. V. (2019). The design concept of digital twin. *Proceedings of 2019 12th International Conference & Management of Large-Scale System Development & MLSD 2019.* https://doi.org/10.1109/MLSD.2019.8911091

MathWorks. (2022). *What Is a Digital Twin? 3 Things You Need to Know.* https://www.mathworks.com/discovery/digital-twin.html

Pigni, F., Watson, R. T., & Piccoli, G. (2021). Digital twins: Representing the future. *SSRN Electronic Journal.* https://doi.org/10.2139/ssrn.3855535

ReliaSol. (2021). *Digital twins and predictive maintenance. What should you know? ReliaSol predictive models and platform for prescription analytics.* https://reliasol.ai/digital-twin-predictive-maintenance-technologies-that-change-the-industry/

Sharma, A., Kosasih, E., Zhang, J., Brintrup, A., & Calinescu, A. (2020). Digital twins: State of the art theory and practice, challenges, and open research questions. arXiv. https://doi.org/10.48550/arXiv.2011.02833

Singh, M., Fuenmayor, E., Hinchy, E. P., Qiao, Y., Murray, N., & Devine, D. (2021). Digital twin: Origin to future. *Applied System Innovation 2021, 4*(2), 36. https://doi.org/10.3390/ASI4020036

Stark, R., Fresemann, C., & Lindow, K. (2019). Development and operation of digital twins for technical systems and services. *CIRP Annals, 68*(1), 129–132. https://doi.org/10.1016/J.CIRP.2019.04.024

Tao, F., Zhang, H., Liu, A., & Nee, A. Y. C. (2019). Digital twin in industry: state-of-the-art. *IEEE Transactions on Industrial Informatics, 15*(4), 2405–2415. https://doi.org/10.1109/TII.2018.2873186

Tuegel, E. (2013). *ADT 101: Introduction to the Airframe Digital Twin Concept.* https://view.office apps.live.com/op/view.aspx?src=https%3A%2F%2Fadt.larc.nasa.gov%2Fwp-content%2Fuploads%2Fsites%2F14%2F2013%2F05%2FADT_Feb2013_101.pptx&wdOrigin=BROWSELINK

VizExperts. (2022). *Digital Transformation Virtual Reality Augmented Reality VizExperts.* https://vizexperts.com/

Wagg, D. J., Worden, K., Barthorpe, R. J., & Gardner, P. (2020). Digital twins: state-of-the-art and future directions for modeling and simulation in engineering dynamics applications. *Journal of Risk and Uncertainty in Engineering Systems, 6*(3), 030901. https://doi.org/10.1115/1.4046739/1081999

Zheng, Y., Yang, S., & Cheng, H. (2019). An application framework of digital twin and its case study. *Journal of Ambient Intelligence and Humanized Computing, 10*(3), 1141–1153. https://doi.org/10.1007/S12652-018-0911-3/FIGURES/10

3 Hypes and Trends in Industry

3.1 ASSET MANAGEMENT

Managing industrial assets efficiently and effectively is necessary for a sustainable society.

An asset is an item, thing or entity that has potential or actual value to an organisation. The value will vary between different organisations and their stakeholders, and can be tangible or intangible, financial or non-financial (ISO55000, 2014).

Asset management is also an enabler of a circular economy, which aims at reduction of material consumption and waste, extension of life lengths (increased life), and optimisation of power consumption. Asset management involves the balancing of costs, opportunities, and risks against the desired performance of assets to achieve organisational objectives. The balancing might need to be considered over different timeframes. Asset management enables an organisation to examine the need for, and performance of, assets and asset systems at different levels. Additionally, it enables the application of analytical approaches towards managing an asset over the different stages of its lifecycle (ISO55000, 2014). The ongoing industrial evolution expressed through the concept of Industry 4.0 is expected to contribute to the achievement of Sustainable Development Goals (SDG). Industry 4.0 featured asset management is highly dependent on underlying technologies such as digitalisation technologies and artificial intelligence to provide advanced analytics for decision support in operation and maintenance.

So how is asset management related to the Reliability, Availability, Maintainability, and Safety (RAMS) concept? Asset management is a management system that focuses on maximising the value of asset by optimising the value creation process in industry. RAMS, on the other hand, focuses on measuring and optimising the performance of the asset.

Is asset management similar to managing asset? Not really! In industrial contexts, managing assets and asset management focus on different aspects:

- Managing assets (things you do to assets) can be done with or without a structured organisational strategy and context. An organisation gains more value from managing assets within a context of organisational purpose and strategy that steers this activity (and becomes asset management) (ISO55000/TC251, 2017).
- Asset management has a broader focus than managing assets, encompassing many organisational levels and applying to all functions or departments. The terms and concepts are explained in ISO 55000 "Asset Management", which shows how the application of broader asset management approaches can help you extract the most value for stakeholders (ISO55000/TC251, 2017).

The differences in focus between asset management and managing assets are explained in Table 3.1.

3.1.1 CHALLENGES TO ASSET MANAGEMENT

There are a number of challenges to optimal asset management:

1. Composition: One challenge is the composition of the asset's technical system (see Figure 3.1), as it often consists of a network of systems or system-of-systems (SoS).
2. Lifecycle: Another challenge is the lifecycle of the asset, as many industrial systems have a long lifetime, for example, 30–50 years.

TABLE 3.1
Managing Assets vs. Asset Management (ISO55000/TC251, 2017)

Asset Management	Managing Assets
Individual perspective: • Information supported decisions • Strategies to select and exploit assets over their lifecycles to support business goals • Collaboration across departments optimise allocated resources and tasks	Individual perspective: • Asset data, location, condition, and health assessment • Current KPl :s • Department budget
Stakeholder perspective: • Triple bottom line and value • Clarity of purpose of the organisation • Focus on impact of the tasks on organisation's objectives	Stakeholder perspective: • Costs • Current performance • Response to maintenance and failures
Top management perspective: • long-term value for the organisation • Developing competence and capability across workforces • Business risks understood, mitigated, and managed	Top management perspective: • short-term gain/loss • Departmental/individual performance • OPEX, savings
Supplier perspective: • long-term contracts/partnering relationship to create value for customer • Understanding customer's strategy and needs	Supplier perspective: • short-term contracts and performance • Service level agreements are focused on contract specifications

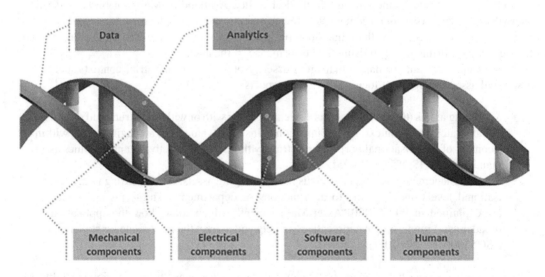

FIGURE 3.1   The DNA of a system-of-systems analytics.

3. Complexity: An additional challenge is the complexity, as the asset often consists of a vast number of items with multiple interfaces.
4. Heterogeneity: A further challenge is heterogeneity of the items in the system, as many components are quite different. For example, the asset can include hardware, software, or liveware.
5. Coexistence: A final challenge is related to the coexistence of new and legacy items of the SoS (Candell et al., 2009; Karim, 2008; Karim et al., 2008, 2016).

3.1.2 INTELLIGENT ASSET MANAGEMENT

An appropriate asset management regime powered by digitalisation and AI is expected to contribute to the achievement of goals related to sustainability, energy efficiency, transportation security, quality of life, and economic growth (Kumari et al., 2022). Asset management empowered by AI capabilities and digitisation technologies, i.e., intelligent asset management (IAM), will enable an industry to achieve operational excellence.

Going toward IAM in complex industrial contexts such as asset management requires a roadmap. When developing a roadmap for an industrial domain, having a holistic understanding of associated challenges is essential. An augmented asset management (AAM) taxonomy developed by Kumari et al. (2022) provides a structured set of challenges to be addressed.

3.1.3 TAXONOMY OF AAM

The challenges listed in this section were identified through an iterative process which began with the identification of challenges in the FM of rolling stock. The AAM concept with SoS thinking was then applied to address these challenges. The application of this approach led to deeper reflection by related organisations within railways, to identify more specific challenges that need to be addressed. The taxonomy of challenges, shown in Figure 3.2, is categorised into three levels.

1. Organisational: Challenges that are related to the organisational complexity
2. Technological: Challenges that are directly related to the management and analysis of asset data
3. Economical: Challenges that can have a direct impact on cost

The specific problems shown within the general taxonomy in Figure 3.2 are explained below.

Cross-organisational operation and maintenance: Railway rolling stock in Sweden is cross-organisational with multiple stakeholders. It is challenging to compose a unified picture of the fleet from several heterogenous sources of data. For instance, maintenance service providers own the data generated on vehicles; the Swedish transport administration owns the data on punctuality and regularity of vehicles; the weather data are extracted from an open source, and so on. Organisations need a common and distributed platform where the complete information regarding operation, maintenance, and asset condition can be integrated.

Rotating components: HVKs are used in different vehicles in their lifetime based on requirement and availability. To predict failures in the fleet, it is important to predict failure in HVKs. It is of value to study the lifecycle of these components and the variation in their behaviour in specific vehicle configurations. It is currently challenging to maintain and access the complete record of operation and maintenance on HVKs because of their varying configurations at different times.

Configuration management: The rolling stock fleet is an SoS of heterogeneous components and sub-components with varying functions and lifecycle processes. The behaviour of any component within this SoS influences the entire structure due to interactions between interfaces. Moreover, the continuous sharing and exchange of components and sub-components between the vehicles in a fleet need a structured condition monitoring system to be able to understand and predict these interactions.

Asset data management: Two types of asset data were identified in this case:

1. Offline data, consisting of maintenance records, failure and damage history, operational condition records, time of train arrival, etc. The challenges observed in the management of such data are heterogeneity in data, data quality issues, data cleaning, data storage, and data retrieval.
2. Live streaming data consist of large volumes of condition monitoring data from on-board systems and wayside detectors. The challenge with this type of data is related to velocity, volume, variety, cybersecurity, meaningfulness of data, data storage, data filtering, and the need for an automated system to continuously process live data.

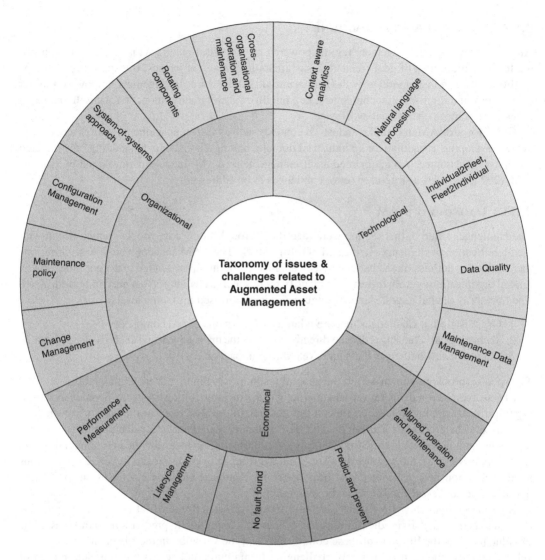

FIGURE 3.2 A taxonomy of issues and challenges in AAM for railways, categorised as organisational, economical, and technological (Kumari et al., 2022).

Data quality: Data quality is assessed on aspects like availability, accessibility, credibility, metadata, integrity, consistency, relevance, readability, and structure based on business requirements. However, even different methods within the same application may require different data quality; therefore, quality cannot be determined as a priori. Some specific data quality issues identified for this case were: missing data, missing parameters needed for analytics, fewer data points leading to uncertainties in prediction, inconsistencies in data formats and language, differentiating anomalies from incorrect data, and redundant data.

Context-aware analytics: Context-aware analytics normally consider the context of the end user to provide relevant information required for decision support. In the scope of this case study, the need to define the context for the analytic services was identified on two more levels.

1. Context adaptation of the analytics to the user based on factors such as the role description, interaction with the interface, and the level of decision support.

2. Context adaptation of the analytics based on the consideration of varying operating conditions for the railway vehicle such as temperature, humidity, operating route, positioning of brakes, speed limit, and so on. Such parameters are numerous and often correlated.
3. Context adaptation of the analytics to maintenance needs. This refers to factors such as lifecycle stage of the asset, safety thresholds, maintenance policy of the organisation, and so on.

Individual2Fleet, Fleet2Individual: AAM for FM involves generalisations based on fleet behaviour and identification of individual outlier behaviour. The industry faces challenges identifying bottlenecks in fleet operation and tracking the party responsible. Top-down and bottom-up approaches (fleet2individual and individual2fleet, respectively) are needed to identify these bottlenecks and their impact on fleet key performance indicators (KPIs).

System-of-systems approach: The vehicles in a fleet are acquired over time and grouped based on routing and operational needs. This creates a heterogenous fleet with varying operation and maintenance history. Developing a common maintenance plan for such a fleet is not insightful, because there are very few common characteristics within the fleet. Defining the fleet as an SoS based on technical, operational, or contextual characteristics such as system design, period of operation, route of operation, maintenance policy, etc. can contribute to better analytics. Suggested specifications to define an SoS for railway vehicles from a maintenance perspective considering some maintenance-related specifications are listed in Table 3.2.

Natural language processing: A substantial amount of maintenance logs consists of manually entered free text by experienced personnel. These logs contain important information related to events, failures, and maintenance of the vehicles and their components. The free text logs cannot be easily classified into specific categories for analysis. In addition, the use of technical terms, acronyms, multilingual entries, incomplete records, and use of organisational language make it challenging to apply out-of-the-box NLP tools to the maintenance context.

Lifecycle management: AM needs to consider interactions between components of an asset that are at different stages of the lifecycle. The maintenance safety thresholds and speed restrictions at an early stage might be different from the advanced stages of degradation with time and mileage. Managing maintenance at each stage of the asset life cycle as shown in Figure 3.3 (adapted from 3), can help in maximising the asset performance. Such a perspective is essential to consider varying expectations related to operation, maintenance, and business at different stages.

TABLE 3.2

Suggested Specifications to Define a SoS for Railway Rolling Stock from a Maintenance Perspective (Kumari et al., 2021)

Maintenance Specifications	Description
Maintenance strategy/policy	Defining the SoS based on the applied maintenance policy such as corrective maintenance, predictive maintenance s
Maintenance indenture levels	Defining SoS based on the number of maintenance indenture levels specified such as SoS, system, equipment, and component. The maintenance tasks are prescribed against each indenture level.
Maintenance echelons	Defining SoS based on the organisational units such as overhaul facilities and repair shops, that are required to carry out maintenance
Maintenance action	Defining SoS based on the suggested maintenance action such as repair, replace, overhaul or "do nothing".
Maintenance support	Defining the SoS based on required maintenance support such as inventory, trained personnel, line replaceable units (LUR) and shop replaceable units (SRU), availability of maintenance window and so on.

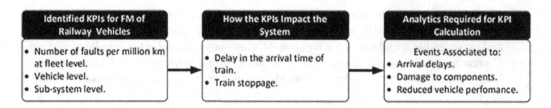

FIGURE 3.3 KPIs for the fleet of rolling stock in railways, with their associated impact and the required analytics for the calculation of the KPIs (Kumari et al., 2021).

No fault found: No fault found (NFF) is a known phenomenon where the reason for interruptions in operation cannot be explained. The system complexity in the fleet of railway vehicles makes it challenging to link faults to specific parties or events in the chain. The reasons for NFF include the lack of understanding about mechanical systems, lack of understanding about the defect logging software, multiple and non-standard ways of fault reporting, variations in interpretations of the maintenance manuals, design of the training and troubleshooting tests, the expertise of engineers, the inability to establish relationships and identify patterns in data, and the organisation's maintenance culture.

Change management: Change management within an organisation includes updating the legacy hardware and software systems, infrastructure, processes, and training the workforce towards adopting new skills. The application of AAM for the rolling stock fleet requires transformation within organisation on all these levels. It is additionally challenging from technical, legal, operational, and organisational aspects due to the larger impact of the change realised at the fleet level.

Performance measurement: For organisations such as railways, availability is an operational success factor for performance measurement. The KPIs that affect the availability of railways have a major impact on business performance and costs. The measurement of these KPIs is challenging, as it needs the integration of several data sources from multiple organisations. Some identified KPIs, their impact on system performance and the analytics needed to extract the KPIs are shown in Figure 3.3.

Maintenance policy: Maintenance policy is based on the approach of an organisation towards maintenance which can be preventive and/or corrective. The optimisation of preventive and corrective maintenance activities is needed to reduce maintenance cost and increase the availability of railway vehicles. Such an optimisation is complex as it depends on several factors like classification of maintenance activities as preventive or corrective and analysing the direct (resources, inventory, man-hours) and indirect (outsourcing, training) associated maintenance cost.

Predict and prevent: The preventive maintenance windows for railway vehicles are normally scheduled based on time or mileage of operation. This is a one-size-fits-all approach that does not consider the asset condition. Predictive maintenance based on advanced analytics of asset condition data and operation and maintenance history can help identify failures before they occur. This transformation from time/mileage-based maintenance to condition-based maintenance is needed to reduce operational failures and unnecessary routine maintenance.

Aligned operation and maintenance: Due to the increased traffic of passengers and goods, the railway traffic in Sweden has steadily increased over the past few years. Performing maintenance action by interrupting operation can increase maintenance cost. The demanding operational needs in combination with complexity in predicting the need for maintenance make it challenging to create and implement a schedule that optimises both operation and maintenance windows.

3.2 TRACKING AND TRACING IN ASSET MANAGEMENT

Tracking is the process of following something or someone's *current position*, as depicted on the left side of Figure 3.4.

FIGURE 3.4 The process of tracking vs. tracing.

In any industry, keeping track of assets is one of the major tasks for overall asset management. Asset tracking is essential for many industrial processes such as logistics, spare part planning, operation, maintenance, and also business. Proper tracking of asset facilitates cost optimisation, diagnostics, prognostics, calculation of the remaining useful life of an asset, quality assurance etc. Tracking asset is also fundamental to the achievement of sustainability goals in the industrial context as it is one of the enablers of circularity in business, production, and consumption.

In industry, insight into the current position in real time can facilitate planning in many processes such as operation, maintenance, procurement, and logistics. It also enables the implementation and optimisation of the Just-In-Time (JIT) approach in the management strategy. Through an appropriate JIT implementation, an organisation will be able to optimise spare part planning, reduce costs, and increase the system availability through effective and efficient supportability.

Tracing is the process of following something's or someone's path to the current position, as depicted on the right side of Figure 3.4.

Tracing brings insight into history of a movement or a process. This history may include spatial data such as a point of interest, ambient data such as temperature, humidity, load, pressure, and processing data such as quality-of-data, quality-of-service, latency, wait time in synchronisation etc. These historical data can be used in data-driven analytics to improve the efficiency of a process and enhance its effectiveness.

3.2.1 What can be Tracked and Traced?

In industry, asset management refers to managing any item, tangible or intangible, that has a value during its whole lifecycle. This means not only physical goods but also digital items are subject to asset management. When we think of assets, it is common to think of physical things, but in a digitalised industrial environment, digital items such as data, models, and algorithms should be considered assets. Some examples of items of interest for tracking and tracing are shown in Figure 3.5.

We have described the relevance of tracking and tracing in asset management and explained why it is important for industry.

But *what challenges need to be addressed to enable tracking and tracing?* As in any digitalisation process, we need a framework that helps us select the appropriate technologies, methodologies, and tools for developing solutions for the system-of-interest and its enabling systems. This framework should be designed based on the needs and requirements from different aspects, as illustrated in Figure 3.6, such as (a) business models; (b) digital and physical governance policies; (c) management strategies; (d) logistics of physical and digital assets; (e) expected level of trust; (f) lifecycle management of physical and digital asset; (g) configuration management of the whole system, including digital and physical assets; (h) needs and requirements on taxonomies and ontologies; and (i) adoption of standards.

3.2.2 Challenges of Tracking and Tracing

As in any digitalisation process, we need a framework to help select the appropriate technologies, methodologies, and tools for developing solutions for the system-of-interest and its enabling-systems.

FIGURE 3.5 Examples of items to track or trace.

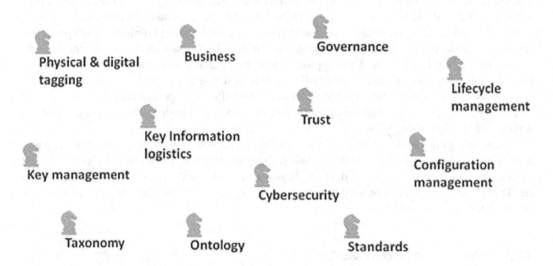

FIGURE 3.6 Key challenges in digital tracking and tracing.

This framework should be designed based on the needs and requirements of different aspects as illustrated in Figure 3.6 and listed below:

- business models;
- digital and physical governance policies;
- management strategies;
- logistics of physical and digital assets;
- expected level of trust;
- lifecycle management of physical and digital asset;
- configuration management of the whole system, including digital and physical assets;
- needs and requirements of taxonomies and ontologies;
- adoption of standards.

3.2.3 Benefits of Tracking and Tracing

There are many benefits of an appropriate mechanism for tracking and tracing:

- Improved capability in planning processes.
- Increased level of customer satisfaction: achieved through real-time online communication on the state of goods and service delivery.

- Quality assurance of delivered goods and services: by analysing ambient data during the internal and external logistic processes.
- Reduced costs: tracking and tracing empowered by digital technology and AI reduces costs by enabling JIT material supply.
- Sustainability: tracking and tracing of used and processed natural resources is essential for circularity, recycling, and upcycling in industry and society.

Benefits can be seen from two perspectives: an internal view and an external view:

- Internal benefits of tracking and tracing are related to effective asset management, improved dependability (including availability, reliability, maintainability, and support-ability), internal logistics, improved cost efficiency, enablement of process mining, and improved optimisation of business, operation, and maintenance.
- External benefits of tracking and tracing are related to improved quality-of-service, increased customer satisfaction, improved lifecycle management, enablement of circular economy, and achievement of sustainability goals.

3.3 GREEN INDUSTRY (SUSTAINABLE)

Simply defined, Green Industry is industrial production and development that does not come at the expense of the health of natural systems or lead to adverse human health outcomes. Green Industry is aimed at mainstreaming environmental, climate, and social considerations into the operations of enterprises. It provides a platform for addressing global interrelated challenges through a set of immediately actionable cross-cutting approaches and strategies that take advantage of emerging industry and market forces.

Green Industry is therefore an important pathway to achieving sustainable industrial development.

It involves a two-pronged strategy to create an industrial system that does not require the ever-growing use of natural resources and pollution for growth and expansion. As shown in Figure 3.7, these two components are the greening of existing industry and the creation of new green industries (UNIDO, 2011).

The first element of Green Industry is fundamentally about the greening of all industries (see Figure 3.8), with a long-term focus on continuously improving environmental performance regardless of sector, size or location. It includes a commitment to and action on reducing the environmental impact of processes and products by (UNIDO, 2011):

- Improving production efficiency: using resources more efficiently and optimising the productive use of natural resources;
- Enhancing environmental performance: minimising environmental impact by reducing the generation of waste, emissions and environmentally sound management of residual wastes; and
- Minimising health risks: minimising health risks to humans caused by environmental emissions, along with the provision of goods and services that support the occurrence of these environmental emissions.

FIGURE 3.7 Components of green industries (UNIDO, 2011).

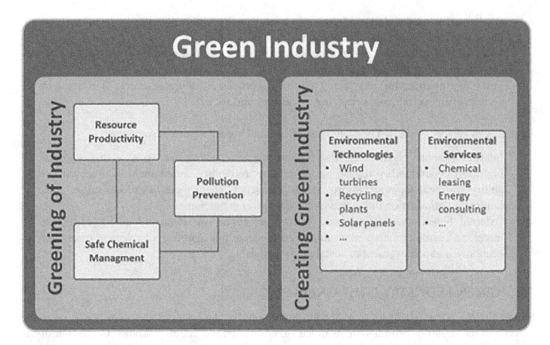

FIGURE 3.8   Green Industry – A two-pronged strategy (UNIDO, 2011).

The second element entails the systematic encouragement and creation of key green industries constituting a diverse sector of the economy that covers all types of services and technologies (see Figure 3.8). Supplying domestic needs with green technologies as well as servicing international markets is a major Green Industry goal. This would include companies that manufacture and install renewable energy equipment, as well as a wide range of companies developing clean technologies for the industrial, transport, building, and automotive sectors. Service industries, including material recovery companies, recycling companies, waste management and treatment companies, as well as companies that transport waste, are also included. Other examples include engineering companies that specialise in wastewater treatment, air pollution control, and waste treatment equipment, as well as companies that provide monitoring, measuring, and analysis services. Green industries also encompass environmental and energy consultants, in addition to the providers of integrated solutions. An example is Energy Service Companies (ESCOS) that offer design and implementation of energy-saving projects, energy conservation, energy infrastructure outsourcing, power generation, energy supply, and risk management. This highly heterogeneous sector of the economy is an essential part of the story in the greening of industry.

This two-pronged strategy aims to bring about an age of Green Industry, in which the production of goods ceases to negatively affect the natural environment and in which it will be possible to upgrade the living standards of the developing world without hurting the climate and environment.

Green Industry approaches are about promoting the transfer and implementation of the best available environmentally sound technologies and environmental practices. While this includes transfers of all types and in all directions, this chapter will focus on the context of the developing world and the potential for Green Industry development there. A Green Industry technology is one which is incorporated or woven into the economic, social, and environmental structures and best serves the interests of the community, country, or region that employs it. For instance, technologies to improve water productivity in industry and prevent the discharge of industrial effluents would thereby protect water resources and reduce the harmful impacts of water pollution. Improvements in, for instance, energy efficiency can often be implemented fairly quickly and have a meaningful impact on climate change mitigation while reducing costs, increasing revenues, and providing competitive advantage. Green Industry stimulates technological advances and innovation, as well as the development of new industries. It not only reduces environmental impacts but also spurs innovation, thereby creating business opportunities and new jobs while helping to alleviate poverty.

Another important aspect of Green Industry approaches is that they encourage companies to take extended responsibility for their operations and products, which can spur the design of more durable, reusable, and recyclable products, often referred to as Design-for Environment (DfE). In many cases, businesses involved in Green Industry approaches have taken the lead in spreading awareness about sustainable production techniques and practices by providing guidance and assistance to other businesses in the sectors, value chains, or communities where they are based. The benefits from DfE also extend to consumers, through improved access to sustainable products and services.

Making a significant impact on reducing pollution, including GHG emissions, will require comprehensive changes in resource usage and waste treatment, and the development of a robust Green Industry sector will be absolutely vital to achieve this transformation. Green Industry also fundamentally improves the health of the environment and its citizens through the development of safer chemical substitutes and non-chemical-based alternative processes (UNIDO, 2011).

3.3.1 SUSTAINABILITY GREEN INDUSTRY 4.0

The Sustainability Green Industry (SGI) 4.0 framework captures the relationships between Industry 4.0, green processes, and sustainability in manufacturing. The purpose of the framework is to explain how Industry 4.0 technologies create sustainability outcomes through green processes (Pech & Vrchota, 2021).

The framework, shown in Figure 3.9, has three vertical levels: technological, process, and development. These are integrated through the circular economy. The horizontal axis consists of three main processes: green design and product development, green manufacturing, and green supply chain and logistics. These are integrated through the lifecycle and the value chain. Industry 4.0 technologies and green technologies ensure their integration at a high level. The development level has various sub-goals of sustainability: organisational and technical sustainability, sustainable manufacturing, sustainable supply chain, and logistics.

Finally, the triple bottom line comprises the three main sustainability outcomes: environmental, economic, and social sustainability (Vrchota et al., 2020).

The SGI 4.0 framework can explain how Industry 4.0 technologies create sustainability outcomes through green processes. Green processes are an important part of the relationship between Industry 4.0 and sustainability outcomes. The core of green processes is based on green technologies. Industry 4.0 technologies enable the full use of green processes to achieve sustainability objectives. The importance of green processes lies in the functions they can perform to create sustainability outcomes (Vrchota et al., 2020):

- The supporting function of green processes connects organisational and technical sustainability with technologies. Green processes use current technologies to create an environment for innovations, working, social and technical conditions at the workplace. This includes processes of eco-design, innovation, maintenance and desirable recovery.
- The facilitating function of green processes refers to technologies and systems that ensure a continuous and uninterrupted material and information flow from suppliers to end customers. These processes also include reverse flow based on reverse logistics of packaging, recycling, reuse, and dismantling of products.
- The activation function of green processes means the creation of sustainable production system via green value creation, appropriate lean practices, monitoring, and the possibility of reprocessing products.

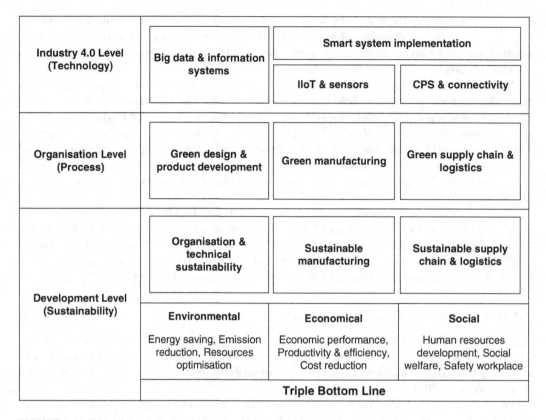

FIGURE 3.9   SGI 4.0 framework (Vrchota et al., 2020).

Products manufactured following these guidelines minimise negative environmental impacts by conserving energy and natural resources (Vrchota et al., 2020).

3.3.1.1   Sustainable Green Industry Model

The model for SGI 4.0 can be divided into technological, organisational, and developmental levels (see Figure 3.9). These are discussed in the following sections.

3.3.1.1.1   *Technological Level*

The technological level of the SGI 4.0 model comprises: Big Data and information systems; Industrial Internet of Things (IIoT) and sensors; cyber-physical systems (CPS) and connection; and smart systems implementation.

- Big data and information systems: Information systems are used to process large amounts of real-time data (Big Data) stored on servers and the Internet in the Cloud. In fact, information systems and Big Data are essential to smart factories; they are integrated into enterprise resource planning (ERP) and visualised via business intelligence technologies. Importantly, users can access data from almost anywhere using a web browser and an appropriate software.
- IIoT and sensors: This part of the technological level includes the technologies (e.g., sensors and switches) that find the information required by a control system (e.g., computers and human brains). It also includes technical devices (e.g., robots and machines) measuring physical and technical quantities of interest (e.g., temperature, pressure, speed, humidity, movement, position, sound, power, and time). These are converted into a signal that is

transmitted and then processed remotely. IIoT devices are useful because they are able to communicate with each other and can send and receive information.

- CPS and connection: Independent control (computer) units make autonomous decisions, manage the technological unit, and become independent and full members of complex production units. Thus, they work together but also work independently. In effect, the intelligent connection of various devices connects the virtual world with people. The goal is to connect the real and digital world via manufacturing execution system (MES) and digital twin (DT) technologies, computer-aided design (CAD) tools, augmented reality (AR), virtual reality (VR), and to support logistics in customer relationship management (CRM) and supply chain management (SCM) applications.

- Smart system implementation: Implementation includes the integration of the various technologies into a fully functional system. It is associated with digitisation, robotics and processes based on automation, and AI. Simply stated, smart systems are based on technologies that allow sensors, databases, and wireless technologies to work together, adapt, and modify their behaviour to adapt to a changing environment and their users' needs. They can learn, draw on their previous experience, anticipate future behaviour, and demonstrate both self-management and self-regulation. Another Industry 4.0 technology associated with smart system implementation is 3D printing used in additive manufacturing (Vrchota et al., 2020).

3.3.1.1.2   Organisational (Process) Level

The organisational or process level of the SGI 4.0 model includes green design and product development, green manufacturing, and green supply chain and logistics.

- Green design and product development: Green design or eco-design includes the use of recyclable and/or recycled materials, parts recovery, reduced use of chemicals, energy saving, further use or reuse of products, a long product lifecycle (LCA), product sharing, durability, the disclosure of environmental information, a low carbon footprint, careful adherence to environmental standards, and a focus on renewable resources.

- Green manufacturing: Simply stated, green manufacturing refers to the use of less energy-intensive equipment and a shift to products with minimal environmental impact. This method of production reduces harmful emissions and leads to less waste of natural resources by using renewable resources and cleaner technologies.

- Green supply chain and logistics: This refers to an organisation's systematic use of measures of green activities and its implementation of logistics focused on recycling, reusing waste, and reducing emissions. It also involves the use of renewable and recyclable packaging, as well as environmentally friendly fuels and means of transport (Vrchota et al., 2020).

3.3.1.1.3   Development (Sustainability) Level

The development level of the SGI 4.0 model includes organisational and technical sustainability, sustainable manufacturing, sustainable supply chain and logistics, the triple bottom line (also see Figure 3.9), and the circular economy.

- Organisational and technical sustainability: This sustainability is focused on the inner workings of the organisation and deals with the optimal use of resources. Issues of concern at this level include the use of human labour, the maintenance of technical equipment and machinery, and the capability of the information technology (IT) infrastructure.

- Sustainable manufacturing: This refers to the sustainability of production processes in the production of environmentally friendly products following environmental protection standards while optimising production costs.

- Sustainable supply chain and logistics: This aspect of sustainability is based on the need to ensure a continuous supply while keeping a careful eye on waste management. The key to optimised management of supplier networks is cooperation between enterprises in various logistics functions, such as distribution, warehousing, transport, and implementation. Logistics also considers the possible negative impact of transport on the environment.
- Triple bottom line: This refers to the outcomes of sustainability and includes economic, environmental, and social aspects. Otherwise stated, the triple bottom line reflects the concept of 3P (people, planet, and profit). Sustainable outcomes mean meeting human needs (people/social outcomes) while allocating resources efficiently (profit/economic outcomes) and conserving natural resources (planet/environment outcomes).
- Circular economy: The circular economy features the transition to renewable energy and materials. It decouples economic activity from the consumption of finite resources and is defined by Wikipedia as: "a model of production and consumption, which involves sharing, leasing, reusing, repairing, refurbishing and recycling existing materials and products as long as possible". In the Green Industry model, it consolidates the use of technologies and resources through the green processes enabling long-term sustainability (Vrchota et al., 2020).

3.4 INDUSTRY 4.0

At this point, it is commonly understood that the rapid development of information technologies has led to the emergence of a new paradigm: Industry 4.0. It was first used by the German government in 2011 as a strategy for this country's manufacturing industry, as part of the High-Tech Strategy 2020 Action Plan. Since then, countries around the world have accepted this paradigm.

All industrial revolutions have focused on the manufacturing sector, and technology has been the enabler of each revolution (Osman & Ghiran, 2019). Industry 4.0 is part of the 4th Industrial Revolution and has introduced a new industrial model. The convergence of new technologies is transforming sectors and markets, and digitisation represents a radical change in the way of doing business. Organisations are thinking and acting differently, becoming agile and collaborative and using interactivity to design products and digitisation to work with their clients (Telukdarie & Sishi, 2018).

Although there are slight differences in how practitioners and researchers comprehend it, Industry 4.0 includes but is not limited to the following:

- 3D printing,
- 3D simulations
- additive manufacturing,
- augmented reality (AR),
- artificial intelligence (AI),
- big data,
- cloud computing,
- cloud technologies,
- cyber-physical production systems (CPPS),
- cybersecurity,
- industrial internet of things Things (IIoT),
- information systems,
- Internet of things (IoT),
- sensors,
- systems integration (horizontal–vertical) (Furstenau et al., 2020; López-Robles et al., 2018; José Ricardo López-Robles et al., 2019).

Through management and transfer processes, these technologies become competitive factors that give organisations a greater probability of permanence in the market.

3.4.1 WHAT IS INDUSTRY 4.0?

Industry 4.0 refers to the intelligent networking of machines and processes for industry with the help of information and communication technology. To put it more simply, people, machines, and products are directly connected with each other (Plattform-i40, 2022).

There are many ways for organisations to capitalise on this type of intelligent networking. The possibilities include, for example:

- Flexible production: In manufacturing a product, many companies are involved in a step-by-step process to develop a product. By being digitally networked, these steps can be better coordinated and the machine load better planned.
- Convertible factory: Future production lines can be built-in modules and be quickly assembled for tasks. Productivity and efficiency would be improved; individualised products can be produced in small quantities at affordable prices.
- Customer-oriented solutions: Consumers and producers will move closer together. The customers themselves could design products according to their wishes; for example, sneakers can be designed and tailored to the customer's unique foot shape. At the same time, smart products that are already being delivered and in use can send data to the manufacturer. With this usage data, the manufacturer can improve his or her products and offer the customer novel services.
- Optimised logistics: Algorithms can calculate ideal delivery routes; machines independently report when they need new material; smart networking enables an optimal flow of goods.
- Use of data: Data on the production process and the condition of a product will be combined and analysed. Data analysis provides guidance on how to make a product more efficiently. More importantly, it is the foundation for completely new business models and services. For example, lift manufacturers can offer their customers "predictive maintenance": elevators equipped with sensors that continuously send data about their condition. Product wear would be detected and corrected before it leads to an elevator system failure.
- Resource-efficient circular economy: The entire life cycle of a product can be considered with the support of data. The design phase would already be able to determine which materials can be recycled (Plattform-i40, 2022).

3.4.2 TALKING ABOUT A REVOLUTION: WHAT IS NEW IN INDUSTRY 4.0?

Since the 1970s, IT has been incorporated into business. Desktop PCs, the use of office IT, and the first computer-aided automation revolutionised the industry. For Industry 4.0, it is not the computer that is the core technology, but rather the Internet. Digitalising production is gaining a new level of quality with global networking across corporate and national borders: The IoT, machine-to-machine communication, and manufacturing facilities that are becoming ever more intelligent are heralding a new era: the fourth industrial revolution, Industry 4.0 (Plattform-i40, 2022).

3.4.3 ON THE PATH TO INDUSTRY 4.0: WHAT NEEDS TO BE DONE?

Implementing Industry 4.0 is a complex project: the more processes companies digitalise and network, the more interfaces are created between different actors. Uniform norms and standards for different industrial sectors, IT security, and data protection play an equally central role as the legal framework, changes in education and jobs, the development of new business models and corresponding research (Plattform-i40, 2022).

3.4.4   Key Paradigms of Industry 4.0

Industry 4.0 is built on three paradigms: the smart product, the smart machine, and the augmented operator:

- Smart products: Simply stated, smart products extend the role of the work piece so that it becomes an active part of the larger system. Smart products have a memory in which operational data and requirements are stored. The smart product requests resources and drives the production process leading to its own completion (Loskyll et al., 2012). The goal is to achieve self-configuring processes in highly modular production systems (Weyer et al., 2015).
- Smart machines: In this paradigm, machines become CPPS. The traditional production hierarchy (i.e., requiring human input) is replaced by a decentralised self-organisation enabled by CPS (Zamfirescu et al., 2014). Smart machines can communicate with other devices, production modules, and products through open networks and semantic descriptions. This allows smart machines to self-organise within the production network. Once this is fully operational, production lines will become so flexible and modular that even the smallest lot size will be produced under conditions of highly flexible mass production. Not least, a CPS-based modular production line will accommodate plug-and-play integrations, replacements, and reconfigurations (Weyer et al., 2015).
- Augmented operators: This paradigm targets the technological support of the worker in the context of modular production systems. Industry 4.0 is not about removing the worker. Instead, human operators are expected to become flexible parts of production systems by adapting to challenging work environments (Schmitt et al., 2013). To meet the challenge of flexibility, workers will be asked to tackle a variety of jobs, ranging from monitoring to intervention in the autonomously organised production system, if required. At the same time, they will be given optimum support through mobile, context-sensitive user interfaces and user-focused assistance systems (Gorecky et al., 2014). Interaction technologies from the consumer goods market (tablets, smart glasses, smart watches, etc.) can be adapted to industrial conditions, allowing workers to handle the steadily rising technical details (Weyer et al., 2015).

3.4.5   Four Components of Networked Production

The four main elements of networked production are the following: smart workpieces; intelligent machines; virtual network connections; and horizontal network connections:

1. Smart workpiece: The product to be manufactured senses the production environment with internal sensors and controls and monitors its own production process to meet the production standards. It is able to communicate with the equipment as well as the components already incorporated and the components to be incorporated.
2. Intelligent machines: Intelligent machines communicate simultaneously with the production control system and the workpiece being processed, so that the machine coordinates, controls, and optimises itself.
3. Vertical network connections: When processing the unique specifications given by the customer for the product to be manufactured, the production control system forwards the digital workpiece created by automated rules to the equipment. The products control their own manufacturing process, as they communicate with the equipment, devices and other workpieces about the conditions of the production.
4. Horizontal network connections: Communication goes beyond an organisation to include the whole supply chain: suppliers, manufacturers, and service providers. The main purpose is to enhance the efficiency of production and to utilise the resources in a more economical way.

3.4.6 CONNECTED TECHNOLOGIES

The importance of production arranged in global networks is that the manufacturing process can flexibly adapt to the unique costumer demands, to the activity of the other parties of the supply chain, and to the rapidly changing economic environment.

Industry 4.0 is not a far-distant technology. In July 2015, Changing Precision Technology (Dongguan, China) became the first factory where only robots work. Each labour process is executed by machines: the production is done by computer-operated robots; transport is implemented by self-driven vehicles; even the storage process is automatic (Gubán & Kovács, 2017).

In 2016, PricewaterhouseCoopers (PWC) identified three main areas where Industry 4.0 affects the corporate world:

1. Integration and digitalisation of horizontal and vertical value chains;
2. Digitalisation of products and services;
3. Formation of digital business models and customer relations.

The connected technologies are shown in Figure 3.10.

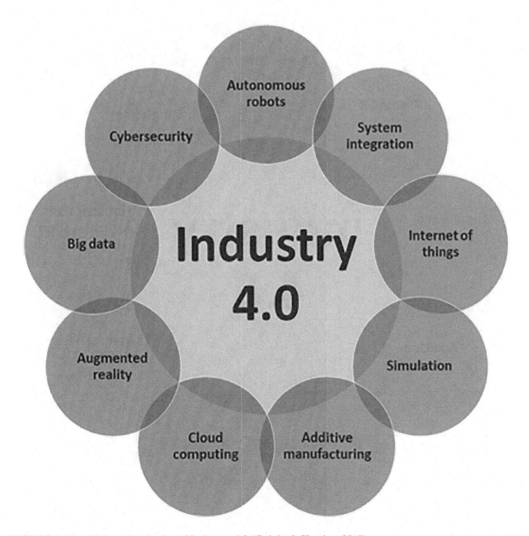

FIGURE 3.10 Main technologies of Industry 4.0 (Gubán & Kovács, 2017).

3.4.7 NINE PILLARS OF TECHNOLOGICAL ADVANCEMENT

Technological advances have always driven dramatic increases in industrial productivity in a series of industrial revolutions. The steam engine changed things in the 19th century; the widespread use of electricity led to mass production in the early 20th century, and in the 1970s, industry became automated. With the rise of digital industrial technology, we are well into the fourth industrial revolution. Industry 4.0 will increase manufacturing productivity, alter the profile of the workplace and the workforce, ultimately changing the competitiveness of not just companies but entire regions (Rüßmann et al., 2015).

In all industrial revolutions, technological advancement has been the key. Now, sensors, machines, and systems are connected along the value chain within and beyond a single enterprise. These connected systems speak to each other and interact via the Internet (e.g., IIoT). They analyse data, predict failure, configure themselves, and adapt to changes.

We have already discussed the technologies driving Industry 4.0 (see Section 3.4), but as defined by Rüßmann et al. (2015) the nine most essential ones are the following: autonomous robots; simulation; horizontal and vertical simulation; IIoT; cybersecurity; the cloud; additive manufacturing; AR; and Big Data and analytics (see Figure 3.11).

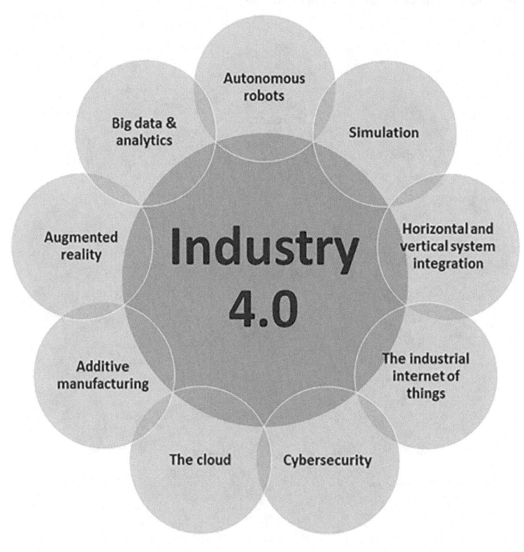

FIGURE 3.11 Industry 4.0 (Rüßmann et al., 2015).

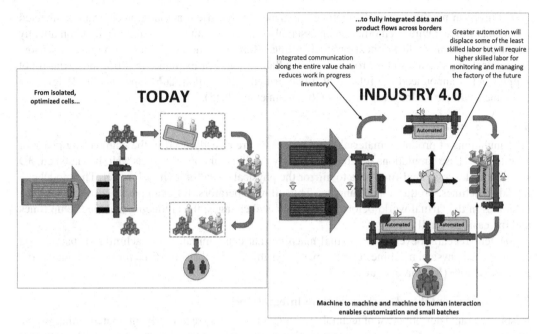

FIGURE 3.12   New manufacturing relationships (Rüßmann et al., 2015).

Many of these nine advances are already used in manufacturing, but as time goes on, they will be used more, transforming production: isolated workpieces will unite as a fully integrated, automated, and optimised production flow. The number one result will be increased efficiency. At the same time, new relationships will form among suppliers, producers, and customers – and between humans and machines (see Figure 3.12). In other words, the workplace will look very different (Rüßmann et al., 2015).

In the following sections, we discuss each of the nine pillars in more detail.

3.4.7.1   Big Data and Analytics

Big Data analytics is a recent innovation in industry, but this analytics will be crucial as we move forward. Simply stated Big Data analytics can optimise production, conserve energy, and improve equipment service. In an Industry 4.0 context, data from many different sources (Big Data=production equipment data+production system data+enterprise management system data+customer-management system data … and so on) can be collected and systematically and comprehensively evaluated. This will become *de rigeur* in real-time decision-making.

One company has decreased product failures by correlating single-chip data captured in the testing phase at the end of the production process with process data collected earlier in the process. The enterprise can identify patterns early in the production process and improve production quality (Rüßmann et al., 2015).

3.4.7.2   Autonomous Robots

Manufacturers in many industries already use robots for some tasks, but these tasks may be relatively restricted in scope. Robots are evolving and becoming even more useful. They are becoming more autonomous, flexible, and cooperative. Before long (perhaps by the time this book appears), they will interact with one another and humans. Humans and robots will work safely together, and robots will learn from their human mentors. These robots will cost less and have a greater range of capabilities than those used in manufacturing today.

A European manufacturer of robotic equipment already offers autonomous but interconnected robots that interact with each other on an assembly line. Importantly, they are able to automatically adjust their actions to fit the next product in line. Moreover, the availability of high-end sensors and control units enables close robot-human collaboration. For example, in 2015, industrial-robot supplier ABB announced the release of a two-armed robot called YuMi specifically designed to assemble small parts alongside humans (Rüßmann et al., 2015).

3.4.7.3   Simulation

3D simulations of products, materials, and processes are already used in the engineering phase of production. These simulations will be increasingly used in plant operations as well. In a nutshell, 3D simulations leverage real-time data to mirror the physical world in a virtual model. The model can include machines, products, and humans. This allows operators, for example, to test and optimise machines in the virtual world before making physical changes, thus reducing machine setup times and increasing overall quality.

Siemens recently developed a virtual machine that can simulate the machining of parts using data from the physical machine. The company says this lowers the setup time for the real machining process by 80% (Rüßmann et al., 2015).

3.4.7.4   Horizontal and Vertical System Integration

Despite the rapid development of technology, many IT systems are not fully integrated, either within an enterprise (vertical integration) or across the supply chain (horizontal integration). Departments such as engineering, production, and service are seldom linked, while links between companies, suppliers, and customers are even rarer. As Industry 4.0 progresses, cross-company, universal data integration networks will evolve and enable automated value chains.

To give one example, in 2014, BoostAeroSpace and Dassault Systèmes launched AirDesign, a collaborative platform for the European aerospace and defence industry. The platform is a common workspace for design and manufacturing collaboration and is available as a service on a private cloud. More specifically, AirDesign tackles the complex task of exchanging product and production data among multiple partners (Rüßmann et al., 2015).

3.4.7.5   Industrial Internet of Things (IIoT)

With IIoT, devices can be networked and enriched with embedded computing and connected using standard technologies. They can communicate and interact with one another and, if necessary, with more centralised controllers. Analytics are decentralised, as is decision-making, so responses are real-time.

In an example of how IIoT networking can be effective, in one company's use of a semi-automated, decentralised production process, products are identified by radio frequency identification (RFID) codes; automated workstations know which manufacturing steps must be performed for each product and can adapt accordingly (Rüßmann et al., 2015).

3.4.7.6   Cybersecurity

The downside of the increased connectivity and use of standard communications protocols that accompany Industry 4.0 is the heightened threat of cybersecurity threats. To protect critical industrial systems, it is essential to have secure, reliable communications, along with sophisticated identity and access to both machines and users (Rüßmann et al., 2015).

3.4.7.7   The Cloud

Cloud-based software is already a reality for enterprise and analytics applications, but as time goes on, more production-related tasks will necessitate increased data sharing across sites and even across company boundaries. Concomitantly, the performance of cloud technologies will improve. Data will increasingly be sent to the cloud, enabling more data-driven services for production systems. Even systems that monitor and control processes may become cloud-based (Rüßmann et al., 2015).

3.4.7.8 Additive Manufacturing

Additive manufacturing includes 3D printing and is used to prototype and produce individual components. In the next stage of development, additive methods will be widely used to produce small batches of customised products. Advantages include complex, lightweight designs. In addition, high-performance, decentralised additive manufacturing systems will reduce transport distances and the amount of stock on hand.

In one use-case, aerospace companies are using additive manufacturing to apply new designs to reduce aircraft weight, thus lowering the costs of raw materials (Rüßmann et al., 2015).

3.4.7.9 Augmented Reality

AR-based systems support a variety of services. They are not yet widely used, but as the technology evolves, organisations will use them to provide workers with real-time information to improve decision-making and work procedures.

In one example, workers may receive instructions on how to replace or repair a particular part as they are actually looking at it. This information may be displayed directly in their field of sight via AR glasses. Virtual training is another use-case scenario (Rüßmann et al., 2015).

3.4.8 OTHER INDUSTRY 4.0 COMPONENTS

3.4.8.1 Cyber-Physical Systems (CPS)

An important component of Industry 4.0 is the fusion of the physical and the virtual world (Kagermann et al., 2013). This fusion is made possible by CPS. CPS integrates computation and physical processes. Embedded computers and networks monitor and control the physical processes, usually with feedback loops where physical processes affect computations and vice versa (Lee, 2008).

The development of CPS can be divided into three phases:

- The first-generation CPS includes identification technologies like RFID tags, which allow unique identification. Storage and analytics must be provided as a centralised service.
- The second generation is equipped with sensors and actuators with a limited range of functions.
- The third generation can store and analyse data, is equipped with multiple sensors and actuators, and is network compatible (Bauernhansl et al., 2014).

One example of a CPS is the intelligent bin (iBin) by Würth. It contains a built-in infrared camera module for C-parts management, which determines the amount of C-parts within the iBin. If the quantity falls below the safety stock, the iBin automatically orders new parts via RFID. This allows consumption-based C-parts management in real time (Günthner et al., 2017).

3.4.8.2 Internet of Things (IoT)

We have already discussed IIoT but we really should have started with the IoT. The IoT allows things and objects, such as RFID, sensors, actuators, and mobile phones, to interact with each other and cooperate with their neighbouring "smart" components to reach common goals (Giusto et al., 2010).

Based on the definition of CPS above, "things" and "objects" can be understood as CPS. Therefore, IoT can be defined as a network in which CPS cooperate with each other through unique addressing schemas. And IIoT can be defined as the application of IoT in an industrial context.

Application examples of the IoT are Smart Factories, Smart Homes, and Smart Grids (Bauernhansl et al., 2014).

3.4.8.3 Internet of Services

The Internet of Services (IoS) enables service vendors to offer their services via the Internet. The IoS consists of participants, an infrastructure for services, business models, and the services themselves. Services are offered and combined into value-added services by various suppliers; they are communicated to users and consumers and are accessed by them via various channels (Buxmann et al., 2009).

It is conceivable that this concept will be transferred from single factories to entire value-added networks. Factories may go one step further and offer special production technologies instead of just production types. These production technologies will be offered over the IoS and can be used to manufacture products or compensate production capacities (Scheer, 2013).

The idea of the IoS has been implemented in Germany in a project named SMART FACE under the "Autonomics for Industry 4.0" program initiated by the Federal Ministry for Economic Affairs and Energy. It proposes a new distributed production control for the automotive industry based on a service-oriented architecture. This allows the use of modular assembly stations that can be flexibly modified or expanded. The transportation between the assembly stations is ensured by automated guided vehicles. Assembly stations and automated guided vehicles both offer their services through the IoS. The vehicle bodies know their customer's specific configuration and can decide autonomously which working steps are needed. Therefore, they can individually compose the required processes through the IoS and autonomously navigate through the production (Mertens, 2016).

3.4.8.4 Smart Factory

Smart factories constitute a key feature of Industry 4.0 (Kagermann et al., 2013). A smart factory is context-aware and assists humans and machines execute their tasks.

These systems accomplish their tasks based on information coming from both the physical and the virtual world. Information from the physical world is, for example, the position or condition of a tool. Information from the virtual world includes electronic documents, drawings, and simulation models (Lucke et al., 2008).

Based on the definitions above for CPS and IoT, the smart factory can be defined as a factory where CPS communicate over IoT and assist people and machines in the execution of their tasks (Schlick et al., 2014).

3.4.9 THE IMPACT OF INDUSTRY 4.0

Companies around the world are adopting elements of Industry 4.0 (Rüßmann et al., 2015).

3.4.9.1 Quantifying the Impact

Industry 4.0 will yield benefits in four areas: productivity, revenue, employment, and investment.

Productivity: As Industry 4.0 is embraced by more companies, productivity will rise across all manufacturing sectors. While all stand to gain, some will gain more than others. For example, automotive companies may see increases in the realm of 10–20%. Figure 3.13 shows what gains will look like in Germany, but other Western countries should be similar.

Revenue: Industry 4.0 will drive growth in revenue in the manufacturing industry, especially as organisations look to buy enhanced equipment and new data applications, while consumers can expect to see a wider variety of increasingly customised products.

Employment: Despite digitisation and automation, Industry 4.0 is expected to increase employment. In fact, the impact of Industry 4.0 is projected to lead to a 6% increase in employment during the next ten years (see Figure 3.14), with a greater demand in some sectors. For example, the demand for workers in the mechanical-engineering sector may rise by as much as 10%. Yet different skills will be needed in the workplace. Initially, the trend toward greater automation is likely to displace low-skilled labourers who perform simple, repetitive tasks (e.g., assembly line work). We should think in terms of competency transformation, not loss, however, because the more general use of software, connectivity, and analytics will increase the demand for employees who understand software development and IT technologies. A good example of a burgeoning field is mechatronics,

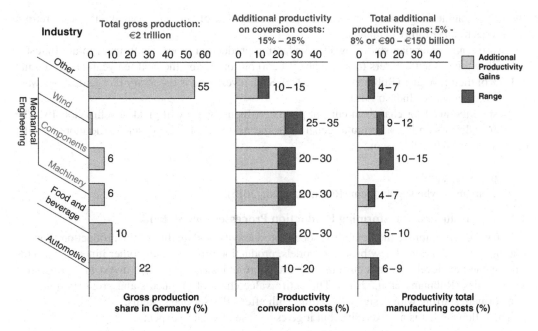

FIGURE 3.13 Productivity gains in Germany (Rüßmann et al., 2015).

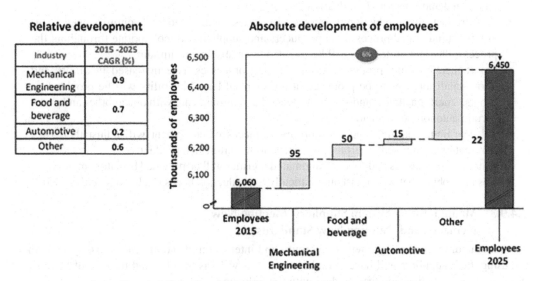

FIGURE 3.14 Increased manufacturing employment (Rüßmann et al., 2015).

an area of engineering comprising several engineering disciplines. The goal should be to retrain employees to meet future demands.

Investment: A German study suggested adapting production processes to incorporate Industry 4.0 will require manufacturers to invest about €250 billion during the next ten years, representing 1–1.5% of their revenues (Rüßmann et al., 2015). Such investment is necessary if organisations want to reap the benefits of Industry 4.0.

Despite the need for change in current practices, Industry 4.0 will yield benefits globally. The preceding discussion has been quite general. In the next sections, we describe the more specific effect Industry 4.0 will have on:

- producers, and
- companies who supply them (Rüßmann et al., 2015).

3.4.9.2 Producers: Transforming Production Processes and Systems

Industry 4.0 will improve the flexibility, speed, productivity, and quality of the production process, leading to the adoption of new business models, production processes, and other innovations. This will enable new levels of mass customisation as more industrial producers invest in cutting-edge technologies (Rüßmann et al., 2015). The entire value chain of producers and production will be transformed, starting with design and ending with after-sales service systems.

The following list is not exclusive, but it gives a sense of what to expect:

- Integrated IT systems: Along the entire value chain, production processes will be optimised via integrated IT systems. Insular manufacturing cells will be replaced by fully automated and integrated production.
- VR: Products and production processes will be designed, tested, and commissioned virtually in an integrated process, and producers and suppliers will collaborate throughout the process. Physical prototypes will be reduced to an absolute minimum.
- Smart machines and products: Manufacturing processes have increased flexibility and allow small lot sizes to be produced at no financial loss. Flexibility will be provided by robots, smart machines, and smart products that communicate with one another and make certain autonomous decisions.
- Self-learning: Learning and self-optimising pieces of equipment will adjust their own parameters as they sense certain properties of the unfinished product.
- Autonomous vehicles and robots: Automated logistics will be provided by autonomous vehicles and robots that will adjust automatically to production needs (Rüßmann et al., 2015).

3.4.9.3 Manufacturing-System Suppliers: Meeting New
Demands and Defining New Standards

As manufacturers demand greater connectivity and interaction of the machines and systems they are using, their suppliers will have to make changes as well, as they expand the role of IT in their products. They will have to face and deal with the following:

- Functionality: Changes are likely to include a greater modularisation of functionality, including in the cloud and on embedded devices.
- Flexibility: Flexibility is a key concern. Online portals for downloading software and collaborative partner relationships may be required to offer more flexible and adaptable equipment configurations. Suppliers themselves must be flexible, as automation architectures will evolve differently for different use-cases. They will have to prepare for a plethora of scenarios and support shifts and changes.
- Competition: IT players are taking a share of the growing market for production-related applications and data-driven services. Suppliers will have to work to retain their share of the market.

- Standards: The interconnectivity of machines, products, and humans will require new international standards defining their interaction in the digital factory. Efforts to develop these standards are being driven by traditional standardisation bodies and emerging consortia. Manufacturing-system suppliers would be well advised to participate and help shape the standardisation agenda (Rüßmann et al., 2015).

3.4.10 How Will Industry 4.0 Impact Equipment?

Investing in intelligent equipment is likely to reduce risk, increase output, and improve profits.

Equipment monitoring devices give users a good sense of how equipment is running, what optimal operation looks like, and how they can improve the way the equipment is being used. Reports from the equipment yield precise and accurate data, allowing operations managers to make real-time decisions that affect the entire facility.

Industry 4.0 has exciting implications, but converting to smart equipment will take both time and money. Accordingly, for many organisations, the shift will be slow (GeneralKinematics, 2020).

3.5 DIGITALISATION AND DIGITISATION

Digitisation represents the replacement of analogue data with digital data and is the first stage of digitalisation.

Digitalisation involves an in-depth transformation of processes whereby physical operations on hardware are, as much as possible, replaced with virtual operations relying on software, and processes are optimised end-to-end. Digitalisation encompasses the provision of digital services that create value to its user.

Achieving digitalisation requires appropriate digitisation technologies. Hence, digitisation can be considered as a digital infrastructure that is necessary for digitalisation.

Examples of digitalisation include virtual prototypes, virtual validation and testing, simulations, and ultimately the DT, which is a virtual replica of the system in its operational context.

Digitalisation includes a vertical dimension, i.e., end-to-end process integration throughout life cycle, from design all the way to operation and maintenance. It also involves a horizontal dimension, i.e., reaching across the entire supply chain to suppliers and sub-suppliers.

Benefits include substantially increased process efficiency, seamless operation, and opportunities for creating new high-value-added data-centric services, such as AI-based decision support for maintenance and operations policies. In addition, a more thorough knowledge of systems' and products' behaviour in operation entails significant benefits to the Original Equipment Manufacturers (OEM), through continuous design improvements.

An indispensable and essential condition for digitalisation is trust in data, so-called digital trust. Digital trust is necessary to be able to provide proof of the integrity and origin of data and models. The AI factory is built with those goals and constraints in mind (Karim et al., 2021).

Examples of digitisation technologies are sensors:

- Stationary sensors: to measure wheel geometry, light beam, noise, loads, angel-of-attack, current etc.
- Mobile sensors: to measure cracks, speed, noise, light beam, thermal, position, fluid, weather, navigation etc.

Data from these sensors are necessary to enable a data-driven approach. A data-driven approach requires also techniques and technologies for data integration, data filtering, data processing, and data visualisation (Karim et al., 2016).

3.6   DATA, MODELS, AND ALGORITHM

Understanding the relationship between data, algorithms, and models is essential to enable digitalisation in any industry:

- Data can be seen as the fuel required to run an engine.
- Algorithms can be described as engines that transform one type of energy to another.
- Models are the description of the context in which the engine is to be run.

Otherwise stated, data are collected by sensors (human and machine) and used to run AI-algorithms which, in turn, are aimed to enable fact-based decision-making and accelerate autonomy (Karim et al., 2021).

3.7   TRANSFORMATIVE TECHNOLOGIES

Technological change is a significant megatrend, constantly reshaping economies and societies, often in radical ways. The scope of technology – in terms of its form, knowledge bases, and application areas – is broad and varied, and the ways it interacts with economies and societies are complex and co-evolutionary. These characteristics create significant uncertainty about the future directions and impacts of technological change. Indeed, predictions about technological timelines – when key developments will arise – are typically inaccurate. In addition, overestimation of the short-run impacts of new technologies is common. Nanotechnology, for instance, considered revolutionary in the 1980s, is only now starting to meet early expectations. But the digital basis and diversity of recent developments offer opportunities for firms, industries, governments, and citizens to shape technology and its adoption.

Technological development can cause multiple forms of disruption:

- shifts in the demand for workforce skills,
- changes in market structure,
- the need for new business models,
- new patterns of trade and investment,
- novel threats to the (digital) security of business, and
- broader challenges to societal and even political processes.

Some potential disruptions could be entirely positive. For instance, recent breakthroughs in materials science – allowing nano-sieves from graphene – might help to address the global challenge of access to clean drinking water.

The list of transformative and potentially transformative technologies is long, from quantum computing and advanced energy storage to new forms of 3D printing, Big Data analytics and neurotechnology. In what follows, we highlight three with the potential to be particularly far-reaching: AI, IoT, and Blockchain (OECD, 2018).

3.7.1   Artificial Intelligence (AI)

AI is the ability of machines and systems to acquire and apply knowledge and carry out intelligent behaviour. Early efforts to develop AI centred on defining rules that software could use to perform a task. Such systems worked on narrowly defined problems but failed when confronted with more complex tasks such as speech recognition.

Increases in computational power, new statistical methods, and advances in Big Data have brought major breakthroughs to the field of AI, especially in "vertical" AI-like automated vehicles as opposed to "general" AI. With machine learning (ML) algorithms that identify complex patterns in large data sets, software applications can perform tasks and simultaneously learn how to improve performance.

AI is not constrained to the digital world. Combined with advances in mechanical and electrical engineering, it has increased the capacity for robots to perform cognitive tasks in the physical world. AI will enable robots to adapt to new working environments with no reprogramming. AI-enabled robots will become increasingly central to logistics and manufacturing, complementing and sometimes displacing human labour in many productive processes.

Sectors likely to experience AI-based transformations in production include agriculture, chemicals, oil and coal, rubber and plastics, shoe and textile, transport, construction, defence, and surveillance and security (OECD, 2018).

3.7.2 The Internet of Things (IoT)

The IoT comprises devices and objects whose state can be altered via the Internet (or in local networks), with or without the active involvement of individuals. The networked sensors and actuators in the IoT can serve to monitor the health, location, and activities of people and animals and the state of production processes and the natural environment, among many other applications.

Development of the IoT is closely related to Big Data analysis and cloud computing. While the IoT collects and distributes data, cloud computing allows the data to be stored and Big Data analysis amplifies the power of data processing and data-based decision-making (OECD, 2018).

3.7.3 Blockchain

Blockchain is a distributed database that acts as an open, shared, and trusted public ledger that nobody can tamper with and everyone can inspect. Protocols built on blockchain (e.g., Bitcoin) specify how participants in a network can maintain and update the ledger. Blockchain technology was originally conceived for Bitcoin, but the expected impacts of blockchain technology go beyond digital money and may significantly affect any activity based on authenticating a transaction (OECD, 2018).

Potential applications can be clustered into three categories:

- Financial transactions: A blockchain may be "unpermissioned", as in Bitcoin, i.e., open to everyone to contribute data and collectively own the ledger. It may also be "permissioned", so that only some users in the network can add records and verify the contents of the ledger. Permissioned ledgers offer many applications in the private sector.
- Record and verification systems: Blockchain technology can be used to create and maintain trustworthy registries. Possible uses include the registration and proof of ownership of land titles and pensions and verification of the authenticity and origin of items ranging from works of art to drugs. Blockchain ledgers could also improve resource allocation in the public sector by consolidating accounting, increasing transparency, and facilitating auditing.
- Smart contracts: Blockchain technology offers the opportunity to append additional data to value transactions. These data could specify that certain rules must be met before the transfer can take place. In this way, a transaction works as an invoice that will be cleared automatically upon fulfilment of certain conditions. Such contracts are also referred to as "programmable money".

The pseudo-anonymity of blockchain-based transactions raises several concerns. While blockchain-mediated transfers are permanently recorded and immutable, they contain information only relative to an agent's Internet identity, which may not be authentic. More effective methods of identification could eventually lead to more effective law enforcement in digital currencies, compared to cash.

However, smart contract applications could also allow the creation and operation of illegal markets that function beyond regulatory oversight (OECD, 2018).

3.7.4 SOME IMPLICATIONS

The transformative technologies are wide-ranging in their origins and potential applications, but they exhibit some common features relevant to policy. One is their dependence on large data sets and Information and Communications Technology (ICT). Technology convergence – with a growing role played by digital technologies in all the sciences – can be aided by cross-disciplinary institutional spaces (e.g., for interdisciplinary R&D and training). Even though G7 governments increasingly support such efforts, more needs to be done to overcome long-established monodisciplinary institutional and organisational arrangements for funding and performing research and development (R&D) (OECD, 2018).

3.8 ARTIFICIAL INTELLIGENCE VS INDUSTRIAL ARTIFICIAL INTELLIGENCE

AI refers to the implementation of human intelligence in computer software. Intelligence can be described as the ability to learn from experience, perceive abstract contexts, cognise, adapt to situations, and act (Karim et al., 2016). Thus, AI refers to a set of computer science techniques that allow computer software to learn, perceive, cognise, and act.

ML is one area of AI used by industry. Machines need data to learn, either large quantities of data for one-time analytical purposes, or streams of data from which learning is continuously taking place. Based on acquired data, either online or offline, ML can reduce complexity and detect events or patterns, make predictions, or enable actions to be taken without explicit programming in the form of the usual "if-then" routines or without classic automation and control engineering.

Deep learning (DL) is another example of how AI can be put to use. In DL, interlinked nodes loosely modelled after the human brain can be trained to do things like detect leukaemia earlier than human experts, drive a car, help a restaurant better predict its food demand, or optimise the logistics processes for a global retail company (Modin & Andrén, 2021).

AI augments human intelligence, facilitates the process of problem-solving, and, as such, has many uses. Yet it also requires deep domain understanding. For example, the performance of ML algorithms is highly dependent on a developer's experience and preferences.

At this point, AI applications tend to be found in the areas of robotics, knowledge management, quality control, and maintenance analytics shifting from traditional approaches to predictive ones.

Industrial AI is a systematic discipline that focuses on developing, testing, validating, and then deploying ML algorithms for industrial applications. It could, in fact, be seen as a bridge connecting academic research on AI to industry practice.

A good field for AI in maintenance in industrial environments is the analysis and interpretation of sensor data, distributed throughout equipment and facilities. The IoT, i.e., distributed data suppliers and data users capable of communicating with each other, is the basis for this use of AI. The IoT acquires the data after pre-processing, records the status of all different aspects of the machines, and performs actions in process workflows on the basis of its analysis. Its central purpose is to identify correlations that are not obvious to humans to enable predictive maintenance, for example, when complex interrelated mechanical setting parameters have to be adjusted in response to fluctuating conditions in the environment to avoid compromising the asset's health (Karim et al., 2021).

Industrial AI distinguishes itself within the field of AI in the following five dimensions:

- Infrastructures: In the areas of hardware and software, there is an emphasis on real-time processing capabilities, ensuring industrial-grade reliability with high-security requirements and interconnectivity.

- Data: Industrial AI requires data characterised by large volume and high-velocity variety, originating from various units, products, and regimes.
- Algorithms: Industrial AI requires the integration of physical, digital, and heuristic knowledge. Algorithms are required to handle this complexity.
- Decision-making: Given the industrial setting, tolerance for error is generally very low, with uncertainty handling being extremely important. Efficiency is especially important for large-scale optimisation problems.
- Objectives: Industrial AI addresses concrete value creation through a combination of factors such as scrap reduction, improved quality, augmented operator performance, or accelerated ramp-up times (Peres et al., 2020).

A useful taxonomy of system autonomy based on AI and applied to industrial scenarios is shown in Figure 3.15. It defines a six-level model of automated decision-making on the basis of industrial processes (Peres et al., 2020).

Level	Industrial Scenario	
Level 0 - No autonomy: Human operators have full control without any assistance from the AI system		A robot performing pick and place operations in pre-defined, fixed positions within fixed system boundaries. The robot is programmed with a pre-set behaviour by humans, who select and prioritise its rules
Level 1 - Assistance with respect to select functions: Human operators have full responsibility and make all decisions		The robot functions similarly to Level 0. However, at autonomy level 1, a robot assistance system programmed using AI can suggest goal-oriented improvements, such as process optimizations concerning cost, energy of time. These suggestion require the approval of a human supervisor to take effect.
Level 2 - Partial autonomy: in clearly defined areas, human operators have full responsibility and define (some) goals		At level 2 the robot is still predominantly programmed in pre-set manner by humans. However, the self-improvements go beyond level 1, with the AI programming allowing the robot to improve its behaviour within specified system boundaries and goals. An example of this behaviour would be the robot being capable of recognising and picking parts which are not in the exact pre-set position. Humans retain decision-making power and intervene when/if necessary.
Level 3 - Delimited autonomy: In larger sub-areas, the AI system warns if problems occur, human beings validate the solutions recommended by the system		The robot is only partially programmed in a pre-set manner by humans. On top of being capable of adjusting its own behavior, the robot can make and implement plans within the specified system boundaries, including for instance autonomous path control. This can be done in collaboratively with other entities in its environment. For this purpose the robotic system should is equipped with sensors necessary to perceive the environment, its context and to learn skills. Humans oversee the system 's decisions, assist in resolving unforeseen disturbances and intervene in case of emergency.
Level 4 - System is adaptable and functions autonomously: Within defined system boundaries, human operators can supervise or intervene in emergency situations		At this level the system behaves as an adaptive, autonomous system in larger sub-areas within known system boundaries, Self optimization within these boundaries is enabled through continuous learning phases and defined (partial) goals, leading to improved predictions and problem-solving capability. Humans relinquish control of a specific part of the system, shifting to a monitoring role and intervening only in emergency cases. If the human fails to intervene, the robotic system is capable of handling some situations according to its own perception of adequate corrective action.
Level 5 - Full autonomy: The AI system operates autonomously in all areas, including in cooperation and in fluctuating system boundaries. Human operators do not need to be present		At level 5 the robotic system acts with full autonomy and in collaboration with other autonomous systems within system boundaries specified by humans. In case of disturbances or fluctuating working parameters, the system is capable of dynamically adapting the plan and communicate it to other autonomous entities. In emergency cases, the system independently puts itself in secure mode.

FIGURE 3.15 Taxonomy of system autonomy based on AI, defining a six-level model of automated decision-making for industrial processes (Silva Peres, 2020).

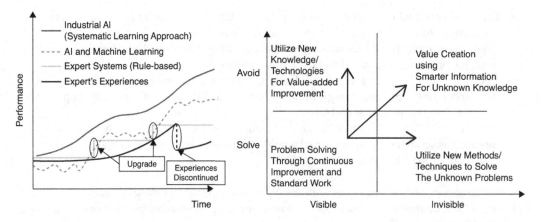

FIGURE 3.16 (A) Comparison of Industrial AI with other learning systems; (B) Impact of Industrial AI from solving visible problems to avoiding invisible problems (Lee et al., 2018).

As Figure 3.15 suggests, industrial AI can be seen as a core technology driving the pursuit of higher degrees of autonomy in industrial systems. Nevertheless, it is important to note that industrial AI is mainly leveraged to augment human performance, not to fully replace humans, and this is likely to remain the case even in more autonomous scenarios in the future (Peres et al., 2020).

Despite its obvious promise, however, industrial AI is still in its very early stages. Its structure, methodologies, and benefits vs. challenges as a framework for industry must be better understood for full adoption. Figure 3.16A compares industrial AI with other learning systems. Figure 3.16B gives guidelines for understanding and implementing industrial AI. It shows how it can be used to solve problems even before they become visible (Lee et al., 2018).

3.8.1 KEY ELEMENTS IN INDUSTRIAL AI: ABCDE

The key elements in industrial AI can be characterised by a simple ABCDE list:

- analytics (A),
- big data (B),
- cloud or cyber technology (C),
- domain know-how (D), and
- evidence (E).

Analytics is the core of AI, including industrial AI, but analytics obviously requires the other four elements to be present as well. Information is essential (Big Data), as is a place to store those data (the cloud). Domain know-how is equally crucial. Domain knowledge includes:

1. understanding a problem and using industrial AI to solve it;
2. understanding the system so the correct data of the right quality can be collected;
3. understanding the physical meanings of the parameters and their association with the physical characteristics of a system or process; and
4. understanding how parameters vary between equipment.

Evidence is the final element. Gathering evidence (e.g., data patterns) on how the AI is actually working can suggest ways to improve the AI model to become more accurate, comprehensive, and robust over time (Lee et al., 2018).

3.8.2 INDUSTRIAL AI ECOSYSTEM

The industrial AI system can be understood as an ecosystem, given the myriad interconnected parts all working together. Each aspect depends on the others for the whole thing to work. Figure 3.17 illustrates this understanding.

Four characteristics of an industrial AI ecosystem, as illustrated in the figure, are:

- self-awareness,
- self-comparison,
- self-prediction,
- self-optimisation.

An industrial AI ecosystem is also resilient.

Figure 3.17 also indicates the four main enabling and interconnected technologies involved in an industrial AI ecosystem:

- data technology (DT),
- analytics technology (AT),
- platform technology (PT),
- operations technology (OT).

These four technologies require a fifth enabler: CPS.

As depicted in Figure 3.17, DT, AT, PT, and OT are the enablers for achieving success in what can be called the 5Cs:

- connection,
- conversion,

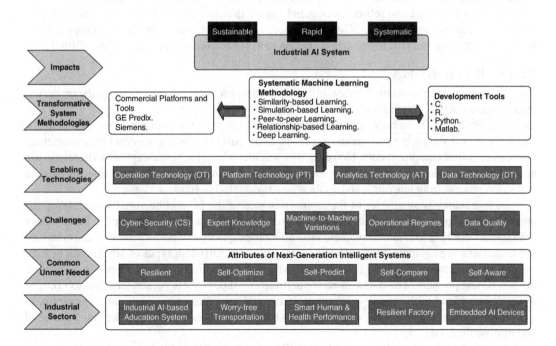

FIGURE 3.17 Industrial AI ecosystem (Lee et al., 2018).

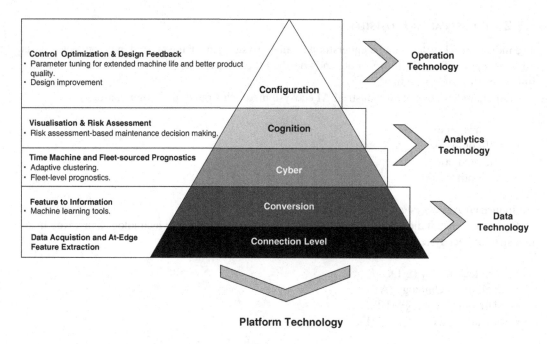

FIGURE 3.18   Industrial AI enabling technologies (Lee et al., 2019).

- cyber,
- cognition, and
- configuration (Lee et al., 2018).

The employment of industrial AI can create smart and resilient industrial systems and enable them to be fault-tolerant, on-demand, and self-organising. In Figure 3.18 industrial AI's four enabling technologies are explained in the context of the 5C-CPS architecture. This architecture provides a comprehensive step-by-step strategy from the initial data collection to the final value creation (Lee et al., 2019).

3.8.2.1   Data Technology

Data technology refers to technology enabling the acquisition of useful data with significant performance metrics across dimensions.

The smart factory must have actionable data that lead to information, knowledge, and insights. The more data analysed, the smarter the decisions. In the past, there was a heavy reliance on manual methods to collect equipment data. However, this was inefficient, highly susceptible to human error, and unable to provide real-time visibility into operations. Technology is crucial: automating the data collection process from machines and applications is essential to future success.

Data technology is an enabler of the *connection* step in the 5C architecture by identifying the appropriate equipment and mechanism for acquiring useful data. Instrumenting the factory floor with sensors can help to create a complete view about the capacity and performance of assets including manufacturing equipment, inventory, people, and so on. Different types of signals can be captured from equipment, including cutting force, vibration, acoustic emission, temperature, current, oil debris, and pressure. The data can be static (machine IDs, process parameters, and job IDs) or dynamic (machine health condition, inventory levels, and asset utilisation). Data can be generated at a component level, machine level, or the shop-floor level and can be broadly divided into structured and unstructured data.

A second key aspect of data technology falling under the 5C architecture is *communication*. Communication extends beyond the relatively straightforward transfer of data from the data source to the point of analysis. It also involves:

1. Interactions in the physical space;
2. Transfer of data from equipment to the cloud;
3. Communication from the physical space to the cyberspace;
4. Communication from the cyberspace to the physical space;
5. Solutions for 3B issues of data systems, i.e., broken data, bad data, and background of data (Lee et al., 2018).

The communication technology should have features such as high data transfer rate, low latency, high reliability, high security, accurate traceability, and scalability.

To sum up: the role of data technologies is to efficiently track, control, and document the voluminous and varied manufacturing data streaming at high speed in real time (Lee et al., 2019).

3.8.2.2 Analytics Technology

Analytics technology converts sensory data into useful information. For example, data-driven modelling can reveal hidden patterns, point to previously unseen correlations, and provide other potentially useful information. This information can be used to predict asset health or remaining useful life, extremely important aspects of machine prognostics and health management (Lee et al., 2018).

Many companies today have made significant investment in data acquisition hardware and sensors, thus capturing and storing massive amounts of process data. But they typically use them only for tracking purposes, not as a basis for improving operations. It is important to know what to do with the collected information. Analytics refers to the application of statistics and other mathematical tools to these data to assess and improve practices. Analytics can enable manufacturers to investigate even the most minute variabilities in production processes and go beyond lean manufacturing programs such as Six Sigma. It can enable them to segment the production process to the most specific task or activity to identify specific processes/components that are underperforming or causing bottlenecks.

Data visualisation tools are another essential element of analytic technologies. Easy-to-interpret and user-friendly graphs, charts, and reports enable manufacturers to more readily comprehend the analysed data, track important metrics, and assess how far or close they are to a target (Lee et al., 2019).

3.8.2.3 Platform Technology

Platform technologies include the hardware for data storage, analysis, and feedback. Platform technology also refers to software that fills a role in application enablement in an industrial environment, such as connecting devices or handling data (collection/extraction, storage, analyses, visualisation).

The use of the right platform architecture to analyse data will realise smart and agile manufacturing. In fact, platforms take centre stage in the concept of industrial AI, providing the tools and flexibility required to develop application-centric functions unique to each industry. Platform technologies help in coordinating, integrating, deploying, and supporting technologies, such as DTs, data storage, connectivity across the shop floor, edge intelligence, and robotics integration.

Platform configurations can be stand-alone, embedded, or cloud. The differentiating factor is the location where the analytics is deployed. Cloud computing is a significant advancement in ICT in the context of computational, storage, and servitisation capabilities. The cloud platform offers rapid service deployment, a high level of customisation, useful knowledge integration, and effective, highly scalable visualisation (Lee et al., 2018, 2019).

3.8.2.4 Operations Technology

In a very general sense, operations technology (OR) refers to decisions made, and actions taken based on the information extracted from data.

While delivering machine and process health information to human operators is valuable, in Industry 4.0, machines can communicate and make decisions. This machine-to-machine collaboration can be between two machines on a shop floor or between machines in two different factories far apart. They can share their experience and adjust their production.

OT is the last step leading to the four capabilities mentioned at the beginning of this section on the industrial AI ecosystem:

1. self-aware,
2. self-predict,
3. self-configure, and
4. self-compare (Lee et al., 2018).

Based on the information derived from the analytics, OT, in conjunction with the other technologies, aims to achieve enterprise control and optimisation via systems such as product lifecycle management, ERP, manufacturing execution systems, CRM, and SCM.

The outcomes of the analytics performed on the collected data can be fed back to the equipment designer for closed-loop lifecycle redesign. In addition, supervisory control and feedback to the physical space are managed through the operations technology level. The advanced OT incorporated in the manufacturing system is used to form a closed-loop management system wherein tasks are generated and executed via intelligent agents running in a distributed and autonomous fashion.

Ultimately, OT enables flexibility and resilience throughout the whole production system and leads to higher efficiency and reduced negative economic impact (Lee et al., 2019).

3.9 AUTONOMY AND AUTOMATION

Autonomy means to be independent or to be able to control and govern oneself by learning and adapting to the environment.

Automation encompasses a series of highly structured and preprogramed tasks that require human supervision and intervention, for example, during abnormal plant operating and equipment conditions (see Figure 3.19) (Fiske & Chen, 2021).

Industrial autonomy maturity is defined by six levels. Level zero represents completely manual operations. In the semi-automated stage (level one), there are many manual operations with mostly paper-based instructions, tracking, and recording results.

The automated stage (level two) is the state of the industry today. Automated systems conduct most production processes and aid in workflows and maintenance tasks. The limited connectivity between disciplines (silos), such as engineering, design, supply chain, manufacturing, and maintenance, severely limits collaboration and real-time decision-making.

Semi-autonomous (level three) is characterised by a mixture of autonomous components and automated assets with human orchestration.

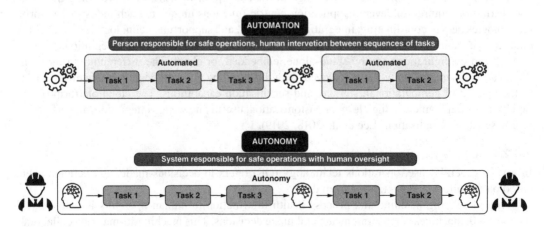

FIGURE 3.19 Automation vs. autonomy (Fiske & Chen, 2021).

In autonomous orchestration (level four), most assets operate autonomously and are synchronised to optimise production, safety, maintenance, and other functions. In this stage, autonomous components perform as a system. However, not all disciplines are integrated, and humans still perform many functions.

Autonomous operation (level five) is a highly idealised state that is difficult to attain and may not be realised in the short- to mid-term. It represents a state in which facilities operate autonomously and are integrated with multiple disciplines that also operate autonomously. This stage extends to supply chain partners and brings together multiple systems to operate as a whole (Fiske & Chen, 2021).

3.9.1 Autonomy and Asset Management

Most organisations have a diverse mixture of old and new assets to operate and maintain. AI allows them to identify anomalous asset conditions that lead to downtime and accidents. Knowing when an asset is predicted to fail permits them to schedule maintenance or repairs before failure.

Autonomous systems will transcend traditional predictive maintenance. For example, control valves with embedded sensors for temperature, pressure, and sound will be able to operate autonomously, determine their maintenance needs, and coordinate service requirements to minimise production disruptions.

Taking an example of a pump, we can explain the shift from industrial automation to industrial autonomy (IA2IA) as follows:

- Manual: Everything, including instructions and paper-based record keeping on pump maintenance, is performed manually.
- Automated: This might include some automated functions, condition monitoring, and predictive analytics. Even in this scenario, many tasks such as opening and closing valves, reading gauges, and making visual inspection rounds are performed manually.
- Semi-autonomous: There is a mixture of manual, automation, and autonomous components. Advanced technologies and analytics are used for predictive and prescriptive condition monitoring and asset management. Some self-aware instruments and equipment are capable of determining optimal outcomes. For example, an autonomous pump might have a leaky seal; however, the pump will know the context in which it operates. If the fluid is hazardous, the process must shut down immediately. If the fluid is water, it might be able to continue until it can be repaired. Perhaps the flow could be diverted or slowed down to allow the process to continue.
- Autonomous orchestration: In this stage, the autonomous pump may determine what to do and when it needs to be fixed. It could shut down the process if the material is hazardous. It could divert the flow if there is auxiliary equipment. If the pump is connected to the asset management system, it could schedule a time for maintenance to fix it. It would select a time that minimises disruption to the process. It will be able to select a technician with the appropriate qualifications to perform the maintenance task.
- Autonomous operations: In autonomous operations, the pump is self-aware and will proceed through the same process as it would in autonomous orchestration. However, this time, the facility will 3D print a part, and a robot will perform the maintenance task (Fiske & Chen, 2021).

3.9.2 Drones and Robots

Many types of drones and robots are becoming popular in the process industries. Remotely operated aerial drones are used in many inspection operations. Robots come in a variety of forms and optimised for specific applications.

Process plant owners are adopting robots and drones to achieve more efficient, reliable, and safer operations. In general, robots and drones better perform mundane or repetitive tasks that humans

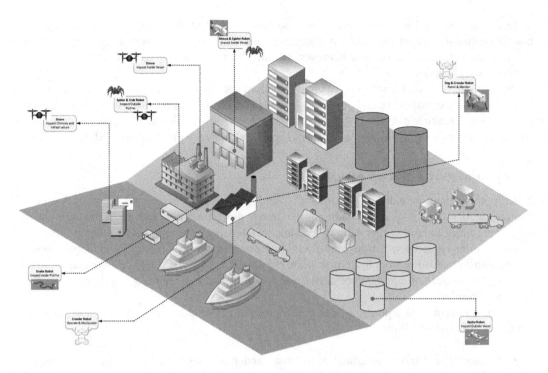

FIGURE 3.20   Drones and mobile robots perform a variety of tasks in process plants (Fiske & Chen, 2021).

find boring and in which they are likely to make mistakes by skipping safety procedures or ignoring important warnings. Robots will not forget or skip steps and can perform tasks in remote areas that are hazardous to humans. Thus, humans can turn their attention to higher value-added activities.

As more intelligence is embedded in drones and robots, they will be able to perform more tasks without human intervention. The data they collect and the tasks they perform must be integrated with IT and OT data.

In the process industries, asset inspection and maintenance are the primary, early targeted applications for robotics. To achieve the optimal benefit, it is necessary to deploy, maintain, integrate, and coordinate the activities of various robots (see Figure 3.20) (Fiske & Chen, 2021).

For example, a snake robot is ideal for inspection inside a pipe. Drones perform numerous upstream oil and gas inspection tasks, such as detecting leaks and fugitive gas emissions, as well as inspecting large, confined spaces. Crawler robots can move around plants and facilities to perform operator tasks. Robots with "arms" can perform simple maintenance tasks, such as turning valves, pushing buttons, painting, and replacing circuit boards in cabinets.

Depending on the task, a robot could be equipped with gas sensors to detect leaks, high-definition cameras to read gauges, infrared cameras to measure temperature, microphones to detect abnormal noises, and accelerometers to detect excess vibration. Drones use cameras to record video from elevated inspection points and to perform Ultrasonic Testing (UT) measurements (Fiske & Chen, 2021).

3.9.2.1 Deploying Robots

Deploying robots in an industrial setting requires a mobile robot management system to coordinate the numerous types of robots and applications. Information integration becomes very important in creating a common graphical interface that allows operators to view the actions and alerts from each robot and drone. Adding to the complexity of the integration task is the fact that some of this information must be sent to automation platforms and some to the asset management systems. The facility requires a platform to integrate and manage all this information effectively (Fiske & Chen, 2021).

3.9.3 Strong Automation Base Layer

There are many benefits to achieving some level of autonomy in the process industries. More integration of automation and domain applications will provide higher levels of productivity, flexibility, efficiency, reliability, and profitability. It will reduce or eliminate human error, provide uninterrupted operations, and remove people from remote or hazardous environments.

High levels of industrial autonomy require a strong automation base layer: the use of more intelligent sensors; remote surveillance and inspection through traditional approaches and with robotics and drones; DT; AI; other analytics to monitor, predict, and mitigate process and equipment failures. Robots and drones will communicate with automation and asset management systems about their missions and perform routine operator rounds, inspections, and routine maintenance tasks (Fiske & Chen, 2021).

3.9.4 Autonomy in Industry Today

Different levels and varying degrees of autonomy can be found across most industries. Some examples include the following:

- Automotive: Swarming robots have been developed for safety in self-driving cars.
- Medicine: AI screening systems have been developed for the early detection of paediatric diabetic retinopathy (DR), a leading cause of vision loss.
- Robots in manufacturing: Autonomous mobile robots (AMRs) handle materials in a manufacturing plant; LiDAR (light detection and ranging) sensors provide accurate range data and larger field views to detect objects and humans and react appropriately to improve material flow, product safety, increase productivity, and optimise floor space.
- Unmanned aerial vehicles (UAVs): These vehicles can do 3D mapping and many other functions, including simultaneous localisation and mapping (SLAM) while dodging objects in their path.
- Delivery services: A food delivery company is already using a fleet of six-wheeled autonomous tiny robots (droids) to deliver groceries and takeout food.
- Unmanned underwater vehicles (UUVs): These can even communicate and collaborate with each other.
- Sports: The Indy Autonomous Challenge is a high-speed autonomous car race (McClean, 2021).

3.9.4.1 Challenges of Autonomy

The challenges of autonomy include eliminating bias, addressing trust, safety, and security concerns, ensuring data privacy is achieved, and meeting ethical standards, including issues of legal liability.

Researchers are making efforts to address the challenges, given the great promise of autonomy. For example, DARPA's Explainable AI program is aiming to build human trust with ML models. More specifically, it draws on ML techniques to allow humans to understand, trust, and manage ML models. As we mentioned earlier, ML models can learn, make decisions, and act without human intervention. DARPA's Explainable AI models will go a step further. They will have the ability to explain their actions and decisions to humans, thus revealing their strengths and weaknesses and suggesting how they will perform in the future.

As we go forward, we will be able to meet and overcome the various challenges as autonomous systems become ubiquitous (McClean, 2021).

3.10 DIGITAL TRANSFORMATION

Addressing continuous change and disruption and creating a more agile organisation requires more than an investment in digital technology or products. It also requires a change in the way the whole organisation works and thinks. Digital transformation is only partly about technology. Ultimately this change succeeds, or not, because of the people on board and the culture created, and the embedded innovation and agility at every level of an organisation. Moreover, technology isn't simply an add-on to the digital transformation process. Now, every organisation has to think like a digital company.

Microsoft (2021) describes "tech intensity" as a blueprint for companies to jump-start their growth. The MSF blueprint has three parts:

1. Every organisation will need to be a fast adopter of best-in-class technology.
2. Every organisation will need to build its own unique digital capabilities, starting with workers who are deeply knowledgeable about the latest technology.
3. Every organisation must invest in human capital and create a workplace culture that encourages capability-building and collaboration to spawn breakthrough concepts.

3.10.1 DEFINING DIGITAL TRANSFORMATION

Digital transformation refers to processes where digital technology is used to change market-facing elements of an organisation. It also refers to changes within organisations that result from, or are carried out to enable, new digital forms of value creation and capture.

Since the primary scope of change is directed at the products, services, and business models of organisations, digital transformation entails alterations to the path-dependent core that defines what an organisation does and how it does it, thus affecting its purpose, boundaries, and activities.

Digital transformation does not occur in isolation, but is influenced by challenges, opportunities, and resources. It unfolds through successive processes of digital innovation and organisational capability-building (Skog, 2019).

There is currently no single, commonly accepted definition for the term digital transformation. Some definitions are shown in Table 3.3 (Schallmo & Daniel, 2018).

3.10.2 DIGITAL TRANSFORMATION – THE FUTURE OF PREDICTIVE MAINTENANCE

Digital transformation is no longer just a concept. It is found in every facet of business and companies that want to build a futuristic business model. The advent of these disruptive technologies is a game-changer and driving a digital revolution in the industrial and manufacturing space. Conventional manufacturing industries are rapidly transforming into digitally connected enterprises by adding OT and IT to their production processes, manufacturing capabilities, and maintenance programs.

The data and insights generated by applying these technologies are helping industrial setups control cost, improve speed to market, drive critical decisions, add customer-centricity, and create competitive advantages (InfiniteUptime, 2021).

3.10.2.1 Applying Digital Transformation in Maintenance

Predictive maintenance (PdM) and condition monitoring (CM) are commonly used strategies in industry largely because of their return-on-investment. Both approaches can benefit from digital transformation.

In this case, digital transformation in both refers to the application of advanced computing technologies to enhance the overall machine efficiency, reliability, outcome, and sustainability in manufacturing operations. It combines a collaborative approach to a man-machine-technology ecosystem along with all its service components (InfiniteUptime, 2021).

Digital transformation provides reliability-engineering teams with a plethora of new tools and approaches to effective machine maintenance and opportunities to accelerate transformation and revenue growth for the top stakeholders. Direct benefits include the following:

TABLE 3.3

Selected Definitions of Digital Transformation (Schallmo & Daniel, 2018)

(Wirtschaft, 2015)	"Digitization stands for the complete networking of all sectors of the economy and society, as well as the ability to collect relevant information, and to analyse and translate this information into actions. The changes bring advantages and opportunities, but they create completely new challenges".
(Bowersox et al., 2005)	Digital business transformation (DBT) is a "process of reinventing a business to digitize operations and formulate extended supply chain relationships. The DBT leadership challenge is about reenergising businesses that may already be successful to capture the full potential of information technology across the total supply chain".
(Westerman et al., 2011)	"Digital transformation (DT) – the use of technology to radically improve the performance or reach of enterprises – is becoming a hot topic for companies across the globe. Executives in all industries are using digital advances such as analytics, mobility, social media, and smart embedded devices – and improving their use of traditional technologies such as ERP – to change customer relationships, internal processes, and value propositions".
(Mazzone, 2014)	"Digital transformation is the deliberate and ongoing digital evolution of a company, business model, idea process, or methodology, both strategically and tactically".
(PricewaterhousewCoopers, 2013)	"Digital transformation describes the fundamental transformation of the entire business world through the establishment of new technologies based on the Internet with a fundamental impact on society as a whole".
(Bouee & Schaible, 2016)	"We understand digital transformation as a consistent networking of all sectors of the economy and adjustment of the players to the new realities of the digital economy. Decisions in networked systems include data exchange and analysis, calculation and evaluation of options, as well as initiation of actions and introduction of consequences".

- Save 30–50% or more on maintenance cost.
- Increase machine uptime significantly.
- Improve visibility in maintenance programs and manufacturing processes with accurate machine data.
- Build a connected enterprise with a man-machine-technology ecosystem.
- Create a digital drive in the enterprise to achieve Industry 4.0 objectives (InfiniteUptime, 2021).

REFERENCES

Bauernhansl, T., Hompel, M. T., & Vogel-Heuser, B. (2014). *Industrie 4.0 in Produktion, Automatisierung und Logistik: Anwendung·Technologien·Migration*. https://link.springer.com/978-3-658-04682-8

Bouée, H.-E., & Schaible, S. (2016). Die digitale transformation vorantreiben. *A European study commissioned by the Federation of German Industries (BDI) and conducted by Roland Berger Strategy Consultants*.

Bowersox, D. J., Closs, D. J., & Drayer, R. W. (2005). The digital transformation: technology and beyond. *Supply Chain Management Review*, *9*(1), 22–29.

Buxmann, P., Hess, T., & Ruggaber, R. (2009). Internet of services. *Business & Information Systems Engineering 2009*, *1*(5), 341–342. https://doi.org/10.1007/S12599-009-0066-Z

Candell, O., Karim, R., Söderholm, P. (2009). eMaintenance-information logistics for maintenance support. *Robotics and Computer-Integrated Manufacturing*, *25*(6), 937–944. https://doi.org/10.1016/j.rcim.2009.04.005

Fiske, T., & Chen, P. (2021). *Industrial Autonomy: How Machines will Perform Their Own Maintenance.* https://www.plantservices.com/articles/2021/automation-zone-industrial-autonomy/

Furstenau, L. B., Sott, M. K., Homrich, A. J. O., Kipper, L. M., Al Abri, A. A., Cardoso, T. F., López-Robles, J. R., & Cobo, M. J. (2020). 20 Years of scientific evolution of cyber security: a science mapping. In *Proceedings of the International Conference on Industrial Engineering and Operations Management (IEOM)* (pp. 314–325). IEOM. http://www.ieomsociety.org/ieom2020/papers/376.pdf

GeneralKinematics. (2020). *Industry 4.0 and What It Means for Mining & Foundry General Kinematics.* https://www.generalkinematics.com/blog/industry-40-and-what-means-for-mining-and-foundry/

Giusto, D., Iera, A., Morabito, G., & Atzori, L. (2010). *The Internet of Things: 20th Tyrrhenian Workshop on Digital Communications.* Springer Science & Business Media.

Gorecky, D., Schmitt, M., Loskyll, M., & Zühlke, D. (2014). Human-machine-interaction in the industry 4.0 era. *Proceedings – 2014 12th IEEE International Conference on Industrial Informatics, INDIN 2014*, 289–294. https://doi.org/10.1109/INDIN.2014.6945523

Gubán, M., & Kovács, G. (2017). Industry 4.0 conception. *Acta Technica Corviniensis - Bulletin of Engineering*, *10*(1). https://www.researchgate.net/publication/317012611_INDUSTRY_40_CONCEPTION

Günthner, W., Klenk, E., & Tenerowicz-Wirth, P. (2017). Adaptive logistiksysteme als wegbereiter der Industrie 4.0. *Handbuch Industrie 4.0 Bd*, *4*, 99–125. https://doi.org/10.1007/978-3-662-53254-6_6

InfiniteUptime. (2021). *Digital Transformation – The Future of Predictive Maintenance.* https://infinite-uptime.com/blog/digital-transformation-the-future-of-predictive-maintenance/

ISO55000. (2014). *International Standard Asset Management – Management Systems – Guidelines for the Application of ISO 55001. 2014.* https://doi.org/10.1007/978–94–007–2724–3

ISO55000/TC251. (2017). *Asset Management – Managing Assets in the Context of Asset Management.* May. https://committee.iso.org/sites/tc251/social-links/resources/guidance.html

Kagermann, H., Wahlster, W., Helbig, J., & others. (2013). Recommendations for implementing the strategic initiative industrie 4.0. *Final Report of the Industrie 4.0 Working Group*, *4*, 82.

Karim, R. (2008). *A Service-Oriented Approach to E-maintenance of Complex Technical Systems.* http://epubl.ltu.se/1402-1544/2008/58/LTU-DT-0858-SE.pdf

Karim, R., Dersin, P., Galar, D., Kumar, U., & Jarl, H. (2021). AI factory – a framework for digital asset management. *Proceedings of the 31st European Safety and Reliability Conference*, 1160–1167.

Karim, R., Kajko-mattsson, M., Söderholm, P., Candell, O., Tyrberg, T., Öhlund, H., Johansson, J. (2008). Positioning embedded software maintenance within industrial maintenance. *IEEE International Conference on Software Maintenance, ICSM*, *1*, 440–443. https://doi.org/10.1109/ICSM.2008.4658099

Karim, R., Westerberg, J., Galar, D., & Kumar, U. (2016). Maintenance analytics – the new know in maintenance. *IFAC-PapersOnLine*, *49*(28), 214–219. https://doi.org/10.1016/j.ifacol.2016.11.037

Kumari, J., Karim, R., Karim, K., & Arenbro, M. (2022). Metaanalyser – a concept and toolkit for enablement of digital twin. *IFAC-PapersOnLine*, *55*(2), 199–204.

Kumari, J., Karim, R., Thaduri, A., & Castano, M. (2021). Augmented asset management in railways – issues and challenges in rolling stock. *Journal of Rail and Rapid Transit*, *236*(7). https://doi.org/10.1177/09544097211045782

Lee, E. A. (2008). Cyber physical systems: design challenges. Invited paper, *International symposium: Object/component/service-oriented real-time distributed computing (ISORC)*, Orlando, May. https://doi.org/10.1109/ISORC.2008.25

Lee, J., Davari, H., Singh, J., & Pandhare, V. (2018). Industrial artificial intelligence for industry 4.0-based manufacturing systems. *Manufacturing Letters*, *18*, 20–23. https://doi.org/10.1016/J.MFGLET.2018.09.002

Lee, J., Singh, J., & Azamfar, M. (2019). *Industrial Artificial Intelligence.* https://doi.org/10.48550/arxiv.1908.02150

López-Robles, J. R., Otegi-Olaso, J. R., Gamboa-Rosales, N. K., Gamboa-Rosales, H., & Cobo, M. J. (2018). 60 Years of business intelligence: a bibliometric review from 1958 to 2017. *Frontiers in Artificial Intelligence and Applications*, *303*, 395–408. https://doi.org/10.3233/978–1–61499–900–3–395

López-Robles, J. R., Rodríguez-Salvador, M., Gamboa-Rosales, N. K., Ramirez-Rosales, S., & Cobo, M. J. (2019). The last five years of big data research in economics, econometrics and finance: identification and conceptual analysis. *Procedia Computer Science*, *162*, 729–736. https://doi.org/10.1016/J. PROCS.2019.12.044

Loskyll, M., Heck, I., Schlick, J., & Schwarz, M. (2012). Context-based orchestration for control of resource-efficient manufacturing processes. *Future Internet 2012, 4*(3), 737–761. https://doi. org/10.3390/FI4030737

Lucke, D., Constantinescu, C., & Westkämper, E. (2008). Smart factory – A step towards the next generation of manufacturing. In M. Mitsuishi, K. Ueda, & F. Kimura (Eds.) *Manufacturing systems and technologies for the new frontier* (pp. 115–118). London: Springer. https://doi.org/10.1007/978-1-84800-267-8_23

Mazzone, D. M. (2014). *Digital or Death: Digital Transformation: The Only Choice for Business to Survive Smash and Conquer*. Smashbox Consulting Inc.

McClean, T. (2021). *The Path From Automation To Autonomy Is Swarming With Activity*. https://www.forbes. com/sites/forbestechcouncil/2021/04/01/the-path-from-automation-to-autonomy-is-swarming-with-activity/?sh=5de60cc43716

Mertens, C. (2016). *Smart Face-Smart Micro Factory für Elektrofahrzeuge Mit Schlanker Produktionsplanung*. https://www.iml.fraunhofer.de/content/dam/iml/de/documents/OE220/Referenzen/ jahresbericht2016/Smart Face_Smart Micro Factory.pdf

Microsoft. (2021). *Roadmap to Digital Infinity*. Microsoft.

Modin, A., & Andrén, J. (2021). *The Essential AI Handbook for Leaders*. Peltaroin. https://peltarion. com/peltarions-essential-ai-handbook-for-leaders

OECD. (2018). *Transformative technologies and jobs of the future*. Background Report for the G7 Innovation Ministers' Meeting, Montreal, March 27–28. https://www.oecd.org/innovation/transformative-technologies-and-jobs-of-the-future.pdf

Osman, C.-C., & Ghiran, A.-M. (2019). When industry 4.0 meets process mining. *Procedia Computer Science*, *159*, 2130–2136.

Pech, M., & Vrchota, J. (2020). Classification of small- and medium-sized enterprises based on the level of Industry 4.0 implementation. *Applied Science, 10*(15), 5150. https://doi.org/10.3390/app10155150

Peres, R. S., Jia, X., Lee, J., Sun, K., Colombo, A. W., & Barata, J. (2020). Industrial artificial intelligence in industry 4.0: Systematic review, challenges and outlook. *IEEE Access*, *8*, 220121–220139. https://doi. org/10.1109/ACCESS.2020.3042874

Plattform-i40. (2022). *Plattform Industrie 4.0 – What is Industrie 4.0?* https://www.plattform-i40.de/ IP/Navigation/EN/Industrie40/WhatIsIndustrie40/what-is-industrie40.html

PricewaterhouseCoopers. (2013). *Digitale Transformation: der größte Wandel seit der industriellen Revolution; wie gelingt der Sprung in die digitale Ära? Wir weisen Ihnen den weg – Deutsche Digitale Bibliothek*. https:// www.deutsche-digitale-bibliothek.de/item/IV2YEHPEKWYJZMLD2WEAKUWMYBU3YVZH

Rüßmann, M., Lorenz, M., Gerbert, P., Waldner, M., Justus, J., Engel, P., & Harnisch, M. (2015). *Industry 4.0: The future of productivity and growth in manufacturing industries*. Boston, MA: Boston Consulting Group (BCG). https://www.bcg.com/publications/2015/engineered_products_project_business_industry_4_future_productivity_growth_manufacturing_industries

Schallmo, A., & Daniel, R. (2018). *Digital transformation now! Guiding the successful digitalization of your business model*. Springer International. https://link.springer.com/content/pdf/10.1007/978-3-319-72844-5.pdf

Scheer, A.-W. (2013). *Industrie 4.0 – Wie sehen Produktionsprozesse im Jahr 2020 aus?* https://www.research-gate.net/publication/277717764

Schlick, J., Stephan, P., Loskyll, M., & Lappe, D. (2014). Industrie 4.0 in der praktischen anwendung. In T. Bauernhansl, M. ten Hompel, & B. Vogel-Heuser (Eds.), *Industrie 4.0 in produktion, automatisierung und logistik* (pp. 57–84). Springer. https://doi.org/10.1007/978-3-658-04682-8_3

Schmitt, M., Meixner, G., Gorecky, D., Seissler, M., & Loskyll, M. (2013). Mobile interaction technologies in the factory of the future. *IFAC Proceedings Volumes*, *46*(15), 536–542. https://doi.org/10.3182/ 20130811-5-US-2037.00001

Skog, D. A. (2019). *The Dynamics of Digital Transformation: The Role of Digital Innovation, Ecosystems and Logics in Fundamental Organizational Change*. UmeåUniversitet.

Telukdarie, A., & Sishi, M. N. (2018). Enterprise definition for Industry 4.0. *2018 IEEE International Conference on Industrial Engineering and Engineering Management,* Bangkok (pp. 849–853). IEEE Xplore. https://ieeexplore.ieee.org/document/8607642

UNIDO. (2011). *Green Industry Initiative for Sustainable Industrial Development*. United Nations Industrial Development Organisation (UNIDO). https://www.unido.org

Vrchota, J., Pech, M., Rolínek, L., & Bednář, J. (2020). Sustainability outcomes of green processes in rela-
    tion to industry 4.0 in manufacturing: systematic review. *Sustainability*, *12*(15), 5968. https://doi.
    org/10.3390/SU12155968
Westerman, G., Calméjane, C., Bonnet, D., Ferraris, P., McAfee, A., & others. (2011). Digital transformation:
    a roadmap for billion-dollar organizations. *MIT Center for Digital Business and Capgemini Consulting*,
    1, 1–68.
Weyer, S., Schmitt, M., Ohmer, M., & Gorecky, D. (2015). Towards Industry 4.0 – standardization as the crucial
    challenge for highly modular, multi-vendor production systems. *IFAC-PapersOnLine*, *48*(3), 579–584.
    https://doi.org/10.1016/J.IFACOL.2015.06.143
Wirtschaft, D. (2015). *Impulse für Wachstum, Beschäftigung und Innovation*. Prpetuum GmbH.
Zamfirescu, C. B., Pirvu, B. C., Loskyll, M., & Zuehlke, D. (2014). Do not cancel my race with cyber-physical
    systems. *IFAC Proceedingss*, *47*(3), 4346–4351. https://doi.org/10.3182/20140824-6-ZA-1003.01600

4 Data Analytics

4.1 DATA-DRIVEN AND MODEL-DRIVEN APPROACHES

Enhanced analytics, based on a combination of data-driven and model-driven approaches, aims to bring insight into asset management by enabling the capability of nowcasting and forecasting (Figure 4.1).

- Nowcasting aims to provide understanding of the current situation and the asset's current condition by providing insight into (Karim et al., 2016):
  1. What happened in the past?
  2. Why did something happen?
- Forecasting aims to provide understanding of the future situation and the asset's estimated condition by providing insight into (Karim et al., 2016):
  1. What will happen in the future?
  2. What needs to be done next?

Today's assets are complex systems whose components may fail over time. Optimal maintenance decisions for such assets require the quick determination of the cause of failure before human intervention is required. A great deal of information needs to be captured to assess the overall condition of a complex asset. Then, the information must be integrated to get an accurate health assessment of the system and determine the likelihood of a stoppage in production. Problematically, the data collected are huge (Big Data) and frequently dispersed across independent systems whose disparate nature and granularity make them difficult to access, fuse, and mine.

Data are gathered and processed on different levels by different Information Technology (IT) systems (Galar & Kans, 2017; Karim et al., 2016; Zhang & Karim, 2014). These include enterprise resource planning (ERP) for business functions and supervisory control and data acquisition (SCADA) for monitoring processes.

The challenge is to have access to intelligent tools to monitor and manage extremely complex assets (machines, plants, products, etc.) proactively through Information and Communications Technology (ICT), with the onus on health degradation monitoring and prognosis rather than fault detection and diagnostics (we discuss this in greater detail later in this chapter).

Maintenance effectiveness depends on the quality, timeliness, accuracy, and completeness of information related to the degradation state of the asset. This translates into the following key requirements: preventing data overload; being able to differentiate and prioritise data (during and after collection); determining which assets have satisfactory performance; and employing efficient analysis and planning tools.

A performance killer is an input element that performs poorly or hinders performance. In this context, a cost driver is an input element to a process that causally affects or drives costs. A cost driver can be interpreted as an element that affects the cost or an element that increases costs considerably. Examples include assets with high failure frequency and long downtime.

The key performance measures or indicators for Reliability Availability Maintainability and Supportability (RAMS) and Lifecycle Costing (LCC) are continuously being developed to facilitate asset maintenance. Effective maintenance and business decision-making in the context of complex assets and multiple stakeholders require the use of maintenance failure data, RAMS analysis, and LCC data analysis to estimate the remaining useful life (RUL). An effective maintenance

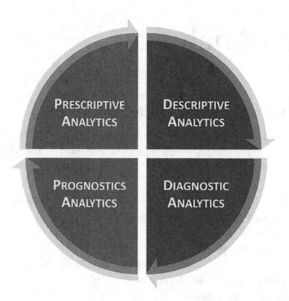

FIGURE 4.1   AI factory's concept of enhanced analytics.

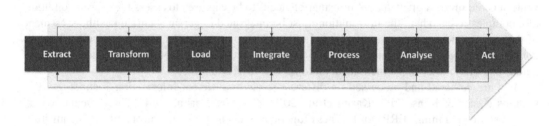

FIGURE 4.2   AI factory's concept of information logistics.

decision-making process also needs a reliable decision support system (DSS) to facilitate knowledge discovery. The steps involved in knowledge discovery are the following: obtaining relevant data and managing their content (data acquisition); communicating the collected data (data transition); compiling data and information from various sources (data fusion); analysing data to extract information and knowledge (data mining); and using the information to support maintenance decisions (data visualisation). The process is shown in Figure 4.2.

Data fusion refers to the integration of data from a multiple-sensor system with information from other sources. Data fusion is required when handling data from various heterogeneous sources or from multiple sensors. The goal is to be able to make inferences from those fused data (Hall & Llinas, 2001).

A recent development in the context of knowledge discovery to facilitate maintenance decisions is eMaintenance. The concept has not been fully accepted for industrial application because it faces organisational, architectural, infrastructural, content and contextual, and integration challenges.

Organisational challenges: Organisations must be restructured to capitalise on eMaintenance. Organisational challenges include aspects related to resource management, and resource planning, for example, for materials or spare parts. Information management and knowledge management change as well, given the need to manage heterogeneity.

Architectural challenges: The architecture of eMaintenance solutions is challenging as well. A framework must be developed for the eMaintenance solution, including models for decentralised data processing and analysis, model-based prognostic tools, models for data and information visualisation to support the human–machine interaction, and models for distributed data storage capability.

Infrastructural challenges: These are essentially related to the technologies and tools that are needed to meet the needs and requirements of eMaintenance. There must be a network infrastructure, either wired or wireless. There must be a way to authenticate and authorise services and users. Safety and security mechanisms are essential, as is the maintainability of eMaintenance services. Mechanisms are required for availability performance management, for tracing and tracking, and for documentation and archiving.

Content and contextual challenges: These types of challenges are data- and information-related. There must be an appropriate ontology allowing data from various data sources to be integrated. This includes process data, product data, condition monitoring data, and business data. A quality assurance mechanism must ensure data are of sufficient quality to improve the quality of decision-making. Another mechanism must be available to assess the user's current situation and thus adapt the information to that user's context. The remaining three challenges are the need to provide a mechanism to describe various contexts, a mechanism to manage uncertainty, and a mechanism for pattern recognition.

4.1.1 DATA MINING AND KNOWLEDGE DISCOVERY

Data produced in asset management can be described in terms of the Big Data 3V architectural paradigm proposed by Zikopoulos and Eaton (2011): variety, volume, and volume (we discuss the 3Vs later in this chapter; see also Lomotey & Deters, 2014). Big Data are a reality, with data from numerous sensors, such as accelerometers or acoustic sensors, acquired at an astounding speed – a rate of tens of 1,000 of samples per second per measuring point. This constitutes the velocity component of Big Data. Moreover, these data can be structured or unstructured. Examples of the latter include textual comments on maintenance actions or failure reports. In addition, data format will likely vary across systems. These aspects comprise the variety of components of Big Data. All these data can have value in asset management, but the data's veracity (data uncertainty) has to be assessed and managed. The value of data also has to be assessed with respect to the data's ability to improve maintenance management and facilitate cost-effective solutions. This constitutes the third V.

Data mining is an important part of the process. Mining Big Data can reveal useful new knowledge in terms of new patterns and relations not visible at a glance. One particularly relevant example in the context of maintenance is the discovery of root causes of failure. This can yield input into design improvement and lead to more accurate maintenance planning.

The term "knowledge discovery and data mining" (KDD) is frequently used in research into pattern recognition (Dhar & Tuzhilin, 1992), machine learning (ML), and techniques in the context of enormous organisational databases. Conceptually, KDD refers to a multiple-step process that can be highly interactive and iterative. The steps include:

1. Selecting, cleaning, transforming, and projecting data;
2. Mining those data to extract patterns;
3. Evaluating and interpreting the extracted patterns to decide what constitutes "knowledge";
4. Consolidating the knowledge and resolving conflicts with previously extracted knowledge;
5. Disseminating the knowledge to stakeholders within the system.

AI techniques have affected all areas of knowledge management: knowledge acquisition, discovery, and distribution, as well as knowledge repositories. Knowledge acquisition includes the acquisition of both tacit and explicit knowledge from domain experts. Knowledge repositories formalise the outcomes of knowledge acquisition and integrate knowledge in distributed corporate environments. Knowledge discovery through data mining explores relationships and trends to create new knowledge (Liu & Ke, 2007).

In decision-making, the processes of dealing with a fault, i.e. the inability to perform as required due to an internal state (IEC-IEV, 2022), and failure, i.e. the termination of the ability of an item to perform a required function state (IEC-IEV, 2022), are essential. Essentially, a fault is the result (state) of an associated failure (event). To deal with both event and state, the MA phases (described in the following sections) can be set in a time-related order.

4.2 TYPES OF ANALYTICS

There are four types of analytics: descriptive, diagnostic, predictive, and prescriptive (Figure 4.3). The more complex an analysis is, the more value it brings (Bekker, 2018; Karim et al., 2016).

The four types of analytics answer different questions (Karim et al., 2016):

1. Descriptive analytics asks what happened.
2. Diagnostic analytics asks why it happened.
3. Predictive analytics asks what could happen in the future.
4. Prescriptive analytics asks how we should respond to those predicted future events.

Descriptive analytics provides information about what happened, for example, an asset's failure. Diagnostic analytics takes a deeper look at data to understand the causes of the event. Precisely why did this asset fail?

Predictive analytics identifies future probabilities and trends based on past behaviour. For example, once the root cause of the asset failure is identified, predictive analytics could help calculate the likelihood of it happening again or to other similar assets.

Prescriptive analytics makes recommendations for action or automates decisions based on a given prediction. It is the most complex of all types.

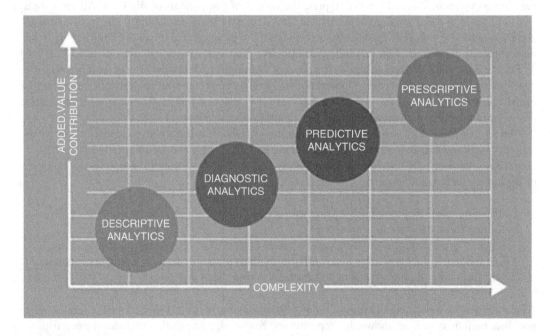

FIGURE 4.3 Types of data analytics (Bekker, 2018).

4.2.1   Descriptive Analytics

Descriptive analytics answers the question of what happened. This type of analytics looks at raw data from multiple data sources and is thus able to give valuable insights into the past. However, these findings simply indicate that something is wrong or right, without explaining why. For this reason, highly data-driven companies should combine descriptive analytics with other types of data analytics (Bekker, 2018; Karim et al., 2016).

4.2.1.1   What is Descriptive Analytics?

Descriptive analytics looks at data statistically to tell us what happened in the past. Descriptive analytics provides context to help stakeholders interpret information. This can be in the form of data visualisations, including graphs, charts, reports, and dashboards (Galar et al., 2012; InsightSoftware, 2021; Zhang et al., 2017).

In this phase, it is very important to have access to data related to system operation, system condition, and expected condition. To understand the relationship between events and states during the phase of descriptive analytics, it is necessary to know the time and time frame associated with each specific log. In addition, events and states need to be associated with the system configuration for the time (T_n). Hence, time synchronisation is an important part of MA.

Descriptive analytics can be used by itself or treated as a preliminary stage of data processing to create a summary or abstraction that, in turn, supports further investigation, analysis or actions performed by other types of analytics (Karim et al., 2016; Lawton, 2022).

How can descriptive analytics help in the real world? In a healthcare setting, for instance, say that an unusually high number of people are admitted to the emergency room in a short period of time. Descriptive analytics tells you that this is happening and provides real-time data with all the corresponding statistics (date, volume, patient details etc.) (Galar et al., 2012; InsightSoftware, 2021; Zhang et al., 2017).

4.2.1.2   How Does Descriptive Analytics Work?

Descriptive analytics uses various statistical analysis techniques to turn raw data into a form that allows people to see patterns, identify anomalies, improve planning, and compare things. Enterprises realise the most value from descriptive analytics when using it to compare items over time or against each other.

Descriptive analytics can work with numerical data, qualitative data, or a combination thereof. Numerical data might quantify things like revenue, profit, or a physical change. Qualitative data might characterise elements such as gender, ethnicity, profession, or political party. To improve understanding, raw numerical data are often binned into ranges or categories such as age ranges, income brackets, or zip codes.

Descriptive analysis techniques perform various mathematical calculations that make recognising or communicating a pattern of interest easier. For example, "central tendency" describes what is normal for a given data set by considering characteristics such as the average, mean, and median. Other elements include frequency, variation, ranking, range, and deviation (Karim et al., 2016; Lawton, 2022).

Descriptive analytics uses two key methods, data aggregation and data mining (also known as data discovery), to discover historical data. Data aggregation is the process of collecting and organising data to create manageable data sets. These data sets are then used in the data mining phase where patterns, trends, and meanings are identified and presented in an understandable way (UNSW, 2020).

Descriptive analytics can be broken down into five steps (UNSW, 2020):

- Create the measurement metrics.
- Identify relevant data sources, including reports and databases.

- Collect and prepare data for analysis.
- Analyse the data, looking for patterns in the data.
- Present the derived information.

4.2.1.3   How is Descriptive Analytics Used?

Descriptive analysis supports a broad range of users in interpreting data. Descriptive analytics is commonly used for the following (Lawton, 2022):

- Financial reports.
- Planning a new program.
- Measuring the effectiveness of a new program.
- Motivating behaviour with KPIs.
- Recognising anomalous behaviour.

Various types of algorithms can be used for descriptive analytics. Common pieces of equipment such as pumps, compressors, and valves are well understood, so engineered analytics based on first principles (1P) and fault trees based on Failure Mode and Effect Analysis (FMEA) data are suited to their analysis, i.e. offering "known solutions to known problems" (Berge, 2020).

4.2.1.4   What Can Descriptive Analytics Tell Us?

Businesses use descriptive analytics to assess, compare, spot anomalies, and identify relative strengths and weaknesses (Lawton, 2022):

- Assess: Important metrics include equipment performance (uptime, repair time, and maintenance cost).
- Compare: Baseline metrics for a characteristic can be compared across time, categories, or interventions. How has this equipment performed over time? How does its performance compare to that of similar equipment?
- Spot anomalies: Taking a close look at descriptive statistics can sometimes reveal outliers worthy of further investigation. These anomalies may prompt additional research using diagnostic analytics to understand their root causes.
- Identify strengths and weaknesses (Lawton, 2022).

4.2.1.5   Steps in Descriptive Analytics

- Quantify goals: The process starts by translating some broad goals, such as better performance, into specific, measurable outcomes, such as longer time to failure.
- Identify relevant data: Teams need to identify any types of data that may help improve the understanding of the critical metric. The data might be buried across one or more internal systems or even in third-party data sources.
- Organise data: Data from different sources, applications, or teams need to be cleaned and fused to improve analytics accuracy.
- Analysis: Various statistical and mathematical techniques combine, summarise, and compare the raw data in different ways to generate data features, revealing hitherto unnoticed patterns.
- Presentation: As a result of analysis, information has been produced. That information can be presented to decision-makers who will determine a course of action. Data features may be numerically presented in a report, dashboard, or visualisation. Common visualisation techniques include bar charts, pie charts, line charts, bubble charts, and histograms (Lawton, 2022).

4.2.1.6 Benefits and Drawbacks of Descriptive Analytics

Descriptive analytics provides the following benefits (Lawton, 2022):

- Numerical data can be more easily and simply disseminated.
- Complex situations are easier to understand.
- Companies can compare performance among and across assets and locations.
- The results can be used to motivate teams to reach new goals.

Some drawbacks of descriptive analytics include the following (Lawton, 2022):

- Results can direct a company's focus to metrics that are not helpful.
- Poorly chosen metrics can lead to a false sense of security.

4.2.2 DIAGNOSTIC ANALYTICS

The diagnostic phase aims to answer "Why has something happened?" The outcome from maintenance descriptive analytics is used to frame the analytics. At this stage, historical data can be measured against other data to answer the question of why something happened and to determine the relationships between the related factors in that event.

Diagnostic analytics involves using data to determine the causes of trends and correlations between variables. It can be viewed as a logical next step after using descriptive analytics to identify trends. This phase requires the availability of reliability data in addition to the data used in the descriptive phase.

Diagnostic analytics is an important step in the maturity model that unfortunately tends to get skipped or obscured (Analytics8, 2021). It can be done manually using an algorithm or using statistical software (such as Microsoft Excel).

Diagnostic analysis is frequently referred to as root cause analysis. It uses processes such as data discovery, data mining, and drill down and drill through. In other words, this analytics is performed on the internal data to understand the "why" behind what happened. It yields an in-depth insight into a given problem provided there are enough data (ProjectPro, 2022).

Diagnostic analytics helps to:

- Identify anomalies: Based on the results of descriptive analysis, analysts can now identify areas that require further research. For example, an asset failed, but it was not close to its end of life.
- Make discoveries: Before explaining the anomalies, analysts must identify the data sources that will help explain them. This may include looking for patterns outside the existing data sets or looking at data from external sources to identify correlations and determine if any are causal in nature.
- Determine causal relationships. Hidden relationships are uncovered by looking at events that might have resulted in the identified anomalies (Yafaa, 2018).

Diagnostic analytics tends to be more accessible and fit a wider range of use cases than predictive analytics (Analytics8, 2021).

Diagnostic analytics gives in-depth insights into a particular problem. At the same time, a company should have detailed information at its disposal; otherwise, data collection may turn out to be individual for every issue and thus time-consuming (Bekker, 2018).

There are several concepts to understand before diving into diagnostic analytics: hypothesis testing, the difference between correlation and causation, and diagnostic regression analysis (Cote, 2021). We explain each of these in the following sections.

4.2.2.1 Hypothesis Testing

Hypothesis testing is the statistical process of proving or disproving an assumption. Having a hypothesis to test can guide and focus diagnostic analysis.

Hypotheses are generally historically oriented (e.g. a decline in production seen last month was caused by a specific failure) and direct the analysis (Cote, 2021).

4.2.2.2 Correlation vs. Causation

When exploring relationships between variables, it's important to be aware of the distinction between correlation and causation.

Causation is simple: it means that event x caused event y to happen.

Correlation is different: If two or more variables are correlated, their directional movements are related. Correlations can be positive or negative. If variables are positively correlated, this means that as one goes up or down, so does the other. If they are negatively correlated, one variable goes up while the other goes down.

Findings of correlations do not necessarily lead to conclusions of causation. Just because two variables are correlated, it doesn't necessarily mean one caused the other to occur (Cote, 2021).

4.2.2.3 Diagnostic Regression Analysis

Some relationships between variables are easily spotted, but others require in-depth analysis. An example is regression analysis. This type of analysis can be used to determine the relationship between two variables (single linear regression) or three or more variables (multiple regression). The relationship is expressed by a mathematical equation that translates to the slope of a line that best fits the variables' relationship.

The insights derived from regression analysis can be extremely valuable for analysing historical trends and developing forecasts. When regression analysis is used to explain the relationships between variables in a historical context, it can be considered diagnostic analytics. The regression can then be used to develop forecasts for the future, an example of predictive analytics (Cote, 2021).

4.2.2.4 How Do You Get Started with Diagnostic Analytics?

A company employing a diagnostic analytics phase has likely adopted a modern analytics tool. Most such tools contain a variety of search-based or lightweight AI capabilities. These features allow detailed insights into a layer deeper (e.g., key drivers visualisation in Power BI, or Qlik's search-based insight functionality) (Analytics8, 2021).

4.2.3 MAINTENANCE PREDICTIVE ANALYTICS

The predictive phase aims to answer "What will happen in the future?" This phase uses the outcome of descriptive analytics.

Predictive analytics is a form of advanced analytics that uses current and historical data to forecast activity, behaviour, and trends. In the maintenance context, both reliability data and maintainability data are needed, as are business data such as planned operations and planned maintenance.

Predictive analytics involves applying statistical analysis techniques, data queries, deep learning (DL) and ML algorithms to data sets to create predictive models that place a numerical value on the likelihood of a particular action or event happening – such as future faults and failures.

Predictive analytics can leverage huge data sets, recognise patterns in Big Data, predict outcomes, and weight probabilities among various outcomes. It draws on contextual data and real-time data from multiple sources and fills in missing data based on observations.

4.2.3.1 What is Predictive Analytics?

Predictive analytics is a key discipline in the field of data analytics, an umbrella term for the use of quantitative methods and expert knowledge to derive meaning from data and answer fundamental questions about many different areas of inquiry (Tucci, 2022). In the context of maintenance, the process is often referred to as MA.

While descriptive analytics focuses on historical data, predictive analytics, as its name implies, is focused on predicting and understanding what could happen in the future. Analysing past data patterns and trends by looking at historical data and expert insights can predict what might happen, allowing companies to set realistic goals, perform more effective planning, manage performance expectations, and avoid risks (UNSW, 2020).

Predictive analytics helps predict the likelihood of a future outcome by using various statistical and ML algorithms but the accuracy of predictions is not 100%, as it is based on probabilities. To make predictions, algorithms take data and fill in the missing data with the best possible guesses. These data are pooled with historical data to look for data patterns and identify relationships among various variables in the data set (ProjectPro, 2022).

Predictive analytics includes a number of sub-sectors and can be further categorised as (ProjectPro, 2022):

- Predictive modelling: Models (i.e., tests) possible scenarios.
- Root cause analysis: Determines the true cause of events.
- Data mining: Identifies correlated data
- Forecasting: Determines what will happen if existing trends continue.
- Monte-Carlo simulation: Determines what could happen.
- Pattern identification and alerts: Suggests when action should be taken to correct a process.

4.2.3.2   How Does Predictive Analytics Work?

Predictive analytics software applications use variables that can be measured and analysed to predict the likely behaviour of individuals, equipment, or other entities. Multiple variables are combined into a predictive model capable of assessing future probabilities with an acceptable level of reliability. The software relies heavily on advanced algorithms and methodologies, such as logistic regression models, time series analysis, and decision trees.

Predictive analytics is based on probabilities. Using a variety of techniques – such as data mining, statistical modelling (mathematical relationships between variables to predict outcomes), and ML algorithms (classification, regression, and clustering techniques) – predictive analytics attempts to forecast possible future outcomes and the likelihood of those events. For example, to make predictions, ML algorithms take existing data and attempt to fill in the missing data with the best possible guesses.

A branch of ML is DL, which mimics how human neural networks work. DL examples include credit scoring using social and environmental analysis and sorting digital medical images such as X-rays to automate predictions for doctors to use when diagnosing patients (UNSW, 2020).

4.2.3.3   What Can Predictive Analytics Tell Us?

Since predictive analytics can tell a business what could happen in the future, this methodology empowers managers to take a more proactive, data-driven approach to strategy and decision-making. They can use predictive analytics for anything from forecasting equipment behaviour to identifying failure trends. Predictions can also help forecast such things as supply chain, operations, and inventory demands (UNSW, 2020).

4.2.3.4   What Are the Advantages and Disadvantages of Predictive Analysis?

Since predictive analysis is based on probabilities, it can never be completely accurate, but it can act as a vital tool to forecast possible future events and inform effective business strategies for the future. Managers can employ predictive analytics to make predictions about what will happen next and use those predictions to plan for the future, set goals, handle performance expectations, and mitigate risk. Importantly, predictive analytics enables fast decision-making.

It requires training to understand the outcomes of predictive analytics and interpret data visualisations. Descriptive analytics is much more accessible. Before a company can effectively apply predictive analytics, it must prepare the data and create and train models – this takes both time and skill. In addition, it may go without saying, but predictive MA is only effective if there are enough data (Peleg, 2021).

4.2.3.5 Predictive Analytics Techniques

Predictive analytics requires a high level of expertise with statistical methods and the ability to build predictive analytics models. It is typically the domain of data scientists, statisticians, and other data analysts, supported by data engineers who gather relevant data and prepare them for analysis, and by business analysts, who help with data visualisation, dashboards, and reports.

Data scientists use predictive models to look for correlations between different data elements in many different types of data sets. Once the data collection has occurred, a statistical model is formulated, trained, and modified as needed to produce accurate results. The model is then run against the selected data to generate predictions. Full data sets are analysed in some applications, but in others, analytics teams use data sampling to streamline the process. The predictive modelling is validated or revised on an ongoing basis as additional data become available.

Once predictive modelling produces actionable results, the analytics team can share them with business executives, usually with the aid of dashboards and reports that present the information and highlight future business opportunities based on the findings. Functional models can also be built into operational applications to provide real-time analytics capabilities (Tucci, 2022).

Beyond predictive modelling, other techniques used in predictive analytics include the following (Tucci, 2022):

- Data mining to sort through large data sets for patterns and relationships that can help solve problems through data analysis;
- Text analytics to mine text-based content, such as Microsoft Word documents, work orders, emails, or social media posts;
- ML, including the use of classification, clustering and regression algorithms that help identify data patterns and relationships;
- More advanced DL based on neural networks emulate the human brain and can further automate predictive analytics.

4.2.3.6 How Can a Predictive Analytics Process be Developed?

The predictive analytics process varies by industry, domain, and organisational maturity. Some organisations have already built robust frameworks for developing, releasing, deploying, and iterating predictive models customised to their particular organisation (Tucci, 2022).

The predictive analytics process isn't always linear, and correlations often present themselves where data scientists aren't looking. Having an open mind about data exploration is a main attribute for effective predictive analytics.

The key steps in deploying predictive analytics are the following (Tucci, 2022):

- Defining requirements: It is necessary to understand the problem at hand. For example, generate questions about the problem and list them in order of importance. Importantly, establish the metrics for measuring success or failure.
- Exploring the data: Identify those data that inform both the problem and the goal. Data must be suitable, available, of good quality, and clean.
- Developing the model: The model must strike a balance between performance, accuracy, and other requirements, such as explainability.
- Deploying the model: Deploy the model at scale in a way that makes a meaningful difference, such as integrating a new algorithm into data on workflow.

- Validating the results: Performance of the model can change over time. Thresholds for updating models vary.

The use and effectiveness of predictive analytics have grown alongside the emergence of Big Data. As enterprises have amassed larger and broader pools of data in Hadoop clusters, cloud data lakes, and other Big Data platforms, they have created more data mining opportunities to gain predictive insights. Heightened development and commercialisation of ML tools by IT vendors have also expanded predictive analytics capabilities (Tucci, 2022).

In manufacturing industries, predictive analytics is employed in predictive maintenance and predictive monitoring. Predictive maintenance provides a timely warning about anomalies, indicating, for example, that a component may be about to fail. Armed with this warning, maintenance teams can schedule repairs before failure. Predictive monitoring applies the same principles to the entire plant, identifying signs of inefficiency or weakness in plant processes.

Various businesses apply predictive analytics to gain visibility into supply chains, especially complex supply chains that cross continents and suppliers (Peleg, 2021).

4.2.3.7 Predictive Maintenance Embraces Analytics

What is the state of the art in asset reliability? Consider a typical production plant. The Human Machine Interface (HMI) graphics flash like a stoplight: red, yellow, and green. Performance values consistently fluctuate up and down. The data are real-time (RT) and they are highly dynamic – professionals equate the data to a plant's vital signs. All the while, operators monitor the HMI waiting for indications of an excursion, and maintenance staff tend to their calendar-based maintenance schedules in an effort to ward off failure. Condition-based tools monitor the few attributes that are readily correlated. With uptime synonymous with profit, this inefficient and risky approach belies the technological advances and industry's investments in improving asset reliability.

Run-to-fail is not a strategy embraced either by plant management or by production staff, and changes in the plant environment present new challenges in maintaining uptime. On the one hand, an ever-increasing supply of operational data is now available, which can provide insights into the health of production assets. On the other hand, dwindling domain experience places a new form of strain on production staff, who must analyse the data in a time frame needed for improving uptime and reducing operations and maintenance (O&M) costs. Data are becoming more abundant as their cost decreases. Although the shift to predictive maintenance provides a meaningful improvement in the manner in which plants maintain normal operation, there remains a strong element of reactive behaviour that manufacturers are looking to overcome. Existing predictive maintenance tools do not fully equip a downsized staff to take advantage of the volume of data now being generated.

Recent innovations in asset reliability and condition-based monitoring are evolving the state of the art. New technologies address both the need for higher-order diagnostics and the challenge of a growing experience gap. These advances possess the ability to process abundant, complex data. Equally important, they are uniquely capable of interpolation – they draw inferences from the data much like a seasoned professional. They have been termed "predictive analytics" as much to distinguish their ability to process and correlate abundant data sources as to reflect their faculty for understanding how changes in asset behaviour lead to failure.

By definition, predictive analytics encompasses a variety of techniques, from statistics to modelling, ML, and data mining, that analyse current and historical data to predict future events. The nature of predictive analytics pushes the pursuit of asset reliability from its residual reactive orientation to one that is fully forward-looking and better aligned with the goals and realities of today's manufacturing environment (Rice & Bontatibus, 2021).

4.2.3.7.1 A Sea Change is Underway

The changing needs of manufacturers have not been lost on suppliers. A Big Data frenzy has captured the attention of thought leaders across industry. They accurately see the deluge of data – both raw and processed – as less an advantage and more a hindrance to effective plant management unless analytics improve.

Moore's law for increases in computer processing power is complemented by equally impressive reductions in the cost of the data. Consider the global market for sensors. For example, forecasts suggest that the average unit cost of a pressure sensor will fall by 30% as unit sales nearly double over the next four years. As the cost to capture data continues to fall, it is conceivable that many manufacturers will drown in their data due to an inability to transform it into actionable information. Although existing asset maintenance and reliability technologies, such as Computerized Maintenance Management Systems (CMMS), Enterprise Asset Management Systems (EAMS), and others, offer the start of a solution, their data-processing limitations underscore the need for more powerful predictive analytic capabilities (Rice & Bontatibus, 2021).

4.2.3.7.2   *Dynamic Data Clustering*
There is a significant gap between existing model-based approaches and predictive analytics in assessing asset health. The former applies a mathematical approach based on equations, whereas the latter utilises statistics and ML in a purely data-driven approach. Modelling tools produce static thresholds based on design or expected levels, and predictive analytics produces a data model that dynamically changes in response to evolving asset conditions. Due to these differences, they can be highly complementary tools for maintaining asset reliability.

Most modelling tools evaluate changes in the condition of a given production asset by comparing the values of various attributes to their respective design levels. Information is usually presented in a trend format. As conditions degrade over time, alerts are raised indicating that attention is required. Negative trends indicative of fouling or other performance-related problems are common health and reliability issues that develop over time. More difficult, however, is identifying imminent asset failure that can result in an unplanned outage. Asset failures are usually due to a combination of factors, which cannot be predicted a priori or detected simply by viewing trend data. Over time, the underlying models lose their efficacy, as the asset has changed with age while the models remain static.

Predictive analytics technologies apply ML algorithms to produce data-driven models of an asset. One technique is to dynamically form and evolve data clusters in sync with each asset's life cycle (Figure 4.4). Clusters are based on numerous data inputs that respond to the changing conditions of an individual asset, and they correspond with the various modes, operating ranges, and products to which the asset is applied. Once catalogued in a knowledge or experience database,

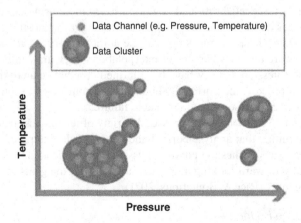

FIGURE 4.4   Dynamic data clustering: shown are clusters associated with just who variables (i.e., data channels). The clusters form from data that describe the true physics of the asset (Rice & Bontatibus, 2021).

clusters associated with asset degradation or other negative attribute trigger alerts. Similarly, the formation of new clusters prompts alerts as the predictive analytics technology identifies new conditions that have yet to be classified. Unlike static and limited input models, the clusters fully account for the asset's condition and recognise both subtle and significant changes in behaviour (Rice & Bontatibus, 2021).

The benefits of predictive analytics are significant, especially when used as a complement to existing maintenance and reliability tools (Rice & Bontatibus, 2021).

4.2.3.7.3   The Benefit of Time

Predictive analytics provides a much-needed supplement to predictive maintenance technologies. It applies ML to cluster large volumes of multi-variable data. Through the cataloguing of data clusters, predictive analytics establishes a comprehensive profile for each asset – unique fingerprints left behind during all phases of operation. Those fingerprints provide detailed knowledge of the asset's performance at varying operating rates, with differing products, and under other changing conditions within the production environment.

A facility that experienced the catastrophic failure of a fan system provides an example where predictive analytics' benefits were made clear. The unit had been equipped with a vibration analysis tool (Figure 4.5). In spite of monitoring standard vibration attributes, the facility's production staff received their first alert only minutes before the failure. By the time vibration levels had triggered an alarm, the damage to the fan system had already occurred, and staff were unable to address the situation with an appropriate corrective action. The ensuing shutdown was costly due to lost production and premiums paid for both replacement equipment and employee overtime. Fortunately, no injuries were sustained (Rice & Bontatibus, 2021).

PlantESP from Control Station, Inc. was subsequently applied to the same unit. Like other predictive analytics tools, it catalogues historical data and compares the associated clusters with

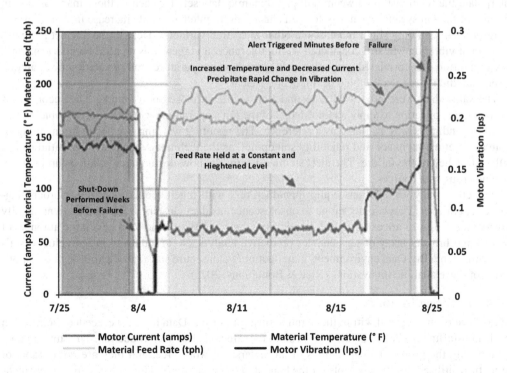

FIGURE 4.5   Vibration analysis: data processed by the company's vibration analysis tool and leading up to the fan's catastrophic failure provide an ambiguous indication of the asset's degrading condition (Rice & Bontatibus, 2021).

current data. Its analytics module is operated in one of two modes: closed book (i.e. operating) and open book (i.e. learning). The two modes allow the application to remember past conditions and to single out new ones, thereby avoiding catastrophic failures.

Predictive maintenance technologies like vibration analysis tools see only part of the picture. In the case of the fan failure, the existing vibration analysis tool utilised a subset of the available asset tags. Although vibration, current, and temperature were constantly monitored, collectively they failed to characterise the true physics of the fan system. With partial information, the plant's predictive maintenance solution provided only part of the answer to what was a complex asset reliability problem.

Adjusting alarms is not a solution to this type of multi-variable problem. Tightening alarm limits on vibration would have resulted in too many nuisance alarms – another problem widely faced by manufacturers. Measurements of vibration and other available data are insufficient to assess an asset's health by viewing them in isolation or relative to a fixed limit. Multi-variable problems require the use of multidimensional solutions.

Hindsight is 20/20, and yet in the case of the fan failure, the forward-looking value of predictive analytics was clearly highlighted. Using historical data from a broader sampling of asset tags, the application was initially run in an open-book mode. With no previous knowledge of the fan's behaviour, several data clusters were generated and quickly attributed to various normal operating conditions – distinctive correlations involving numerous data tags. Another highly distinguishable cluster formed approximately ten hours prior to the failure, signalling a dynamic change in the relationship among and between the asset's measured attributes. Even with that amount of lead time, staff would have been equipped to conduct an investigation and prescribe an appropriate remediation plan.

It is difficult for plant staff to discern subtle changes in the state of seemingly innumerable production assets. The challenge becomes increasingly difficult when the same staff are required to interpolate the relationship between multiple, dynamic data sets for each of those many assets. In the case of the fan system, the newly formed cluster highlighted a notable increase in vibration that corresponded with only slight increases in other measured variables. Despite the distinct increase, the level of vibration was still considered within tolerance, and there was no need for concern. Only when vibration was correlated with other values, such as temperature, and production flow, among other data, did the asset's troubled health become clear.

The same data were processed a second time while in closed-book mode. The second pass allowed the application to apply its knowledge of the fan's operational conditions. A complete catalogue of conditions was available as a reference. The resulting warning was far more meaningful from an asset maintenance and reliability standpoint, as the technology generated an initial alert a full 15 days before the failure. The alert stemmed from the now-documented relationship between the numerous data sources.

Predictive analytics solutions equip manufacturers with much-needed and higher-order diagnostic capabilities. They are not prone to obsolescence, as data clusters are generated dynamically when new conditions are experienced. In addition, their ability to rapidly process large amounts of data from a broader array of tags enables predictive analytics to account for an individual asset's true nature. In a Big Data environment, manufacturers can secure substantial gains from the application of these analytic innovations (Rice & Bontatibus, 2021).

4.2.3.7.4   Facing Forward

Alerts have been triggered within the manufacturing industry. Data have far exceeded their design level, and staffing has fallen below its threshold for safe and effective production. The surge in data is outpacing the processing capabilities of an undersized workforce, and they are not capable of being fully utilised by existing tools for the benefit of manufacturers. The costs are high. New technologies are needed to restore plant operation – a big analytics solution to the Big Data challenge.

The industry continues to embrace technology as an enabler of safe and profitable production. The widespread adoption of predictive maintenance tools signalled a meaningful advancement in the use of technology, and it has reduced the probability of unplanned downtime due to asset failures. Due to their limitations, these tools fall short of the goal and perpetuate aspects of run-to-fail behaviour.

Suppliers across the industry – large and small – have responded to the growing need for higher-order diagnostics. Predictive analytic technologies have been applied successfully to solve complex asset reliability challenges. They are capable of processing the swelling influx of plant data, and they provide a solution to the industry's losses of human capital. Aligned with today's production environment, predictive analytics enables manufacturers to stop looking over their shoulders and face forward (Rice & Bontatibus, 2021).

4.2.3.8   Metrics for Predictive Maintenance Analytics

Broadly, predictive maintenance metrics are categorised into two parts – the first part signals future events (leading indicators) and the second part considers past events (lagging indicators). Using both metrics helps to convert raw data into actionable information (Table 4.1) (DataAnalyticsWiki, 2022).

4.2.3.9   Technologies Used for Predictive Maintenance Analytics

The success of predictive MA depends on the technologies being used. Technologies used throughout global industries are shown in Table 4.2 (DataAnalyticsWiki, 2022).

4.2.3.10   Predictive Maintenance and Data Analytics

Maintenance activities in an organisation are generally driven by preventive measures and these, in turn, are a result of predictive data analytics. Such activities include maintaining the machines, their components, and other infrastructure elements, which, when not working properly, negatively affect the production process. Predictive maintenance can reduce labour and equipment costs, lead to higher overall equipment efficiency (OEE), improve employee productivity and safety, and result in decreased downtime (DataAnalyticsWiki, 2022).

TABLE 4.1
Metrics for Predictive Maintenance Analytics (DataAnalyticsWiki, 2022)

Metric	Description
Overall equipment maintenance (OEE)	The OEE indicates the productivity of equipment and provides information on how proficiently the maintenance process is being carried out. The success of the OEE depends on several factors such as equipment quality, availability, and performance. It is calculated as the product of these three key factors. Thus, the higher the OEE, the lesser the chances of a defect.
Mean time to repair (MTTR)	It focuses on the maintenance of repairable items. As a result, it begins with the start of repair process and continues until operations are restored. It considers repair time, testing period, and return to normal operating state. It is calculated as the sum of downtime periods divided by the total number of repairs.
Planned maintenance percentage (PPC)	The powerful metric provides a percentage representation of time spent on planned maintenance activities in contrast to unplanned ones. In an ideal system, 90% of the maintenance should be attributed to planning with the objective of avoiding unexpected break downs. Thus, it is calculated by dividing scheduled maintenance time by total maintenance hours (multiply by 100 to get the percentage).
Mean time between failure (MTBF)	It is the estimated time from one breakdown to the next in the course of normal operations. Thus, it represents the expected healthy life of equipment before it experiences complete failure. It is calculated by dividing the sum of operational time by the total number of failures.

TABLE 4.2

Technologies Used for Predictive Maintenance Analytics (DataAnalyticsWiki, 2022)

Technology	Application in Predictive Analytics
Vibration analysis	In this method, software identifies significant changes in the machine's standard vibration. Analysis is performed by continuously recording the vibrations with the use of a machine learning algorithm.
Infrared technology	The technology checks the temperature of equipment and tracks its operational conditions. It also plays a prominent role in identifying the hotspots in electronic equipment and the faulty terminations in the circuits.
Oil analysis	Predictive maintenance analytics is gaining importance in the fuel and oil industry where viscosity, wearable particles, and the presence of water are tested in the oil. Its use extends to the transportation industry for the same reasons.
Acoustic monitoring	This imitates the hearing abilities of experienced workers who can diagnose malfunctions based on loud sounds. This monitoring detects certain inappropriate sounds beyond the background noise in industrial contexts.
Motor circuit analysis	This analysis is used across a variety of industries. It measures a motor's starter and rotor and detects contamination and basic faults. It is also used to test new motors prior to installation. Finally, it is used to improve the overall system health.

4.2.3.11 Predictive Asset Maintenance Analytics

Predictive maintenance centres on the idea that service shutdown should be at precisely the right time, not when it's too late and not too soon. The ability of predictive maintenance to meet this goal is helped considerably by recent technological advancements and the Internet of Things (IoT). Advanced MA can reduce the time spent on maintenance planning by 20–50% and increase asset efficiency by 10–20%.

Predictive maintenance algorithms comprise four stages (DataAnalyticsWiki, 2022). The first stage is generating and collecting data. The second stage is finding patterns and relations in the data and modelling the data. The third stage is applying data to the production processes, and the fourth stage is getting feedback data based on model updates.

The use of predictive MA can boost companies in a number of ways:

- Companies will optimise maintenance service time.
- Spare parts will be available in a timely fashion.
- Equipment will be more effective and efficient.
- Maintainers will receive early warning signals about faults and possible failure.

4.2.4 PRESCRIPTIVE ANALYTICS

The prescriptive analytics phase aims to answer the question "What needs to be done?" This phase uses the outcome from both diagnostic analytics and predictive analytics. In the maintenance field, the prediction of upcoming faults and failures requires resource planning data and business data in addition to the data used in the diagnostic and predictive analytics.

Big Data can highlight problems and help a company understand why those problems happened. The company's decision-makers can use the data-backed and data-found factors to create prescriptions for problems.

Prescriptive analytics is the next step of predictive analytics in that it manipulates the future. It uses simulation and optimisation to ask what a business should do to maximise key business metrics (ProjectPro, 2022) and to come up with advice concerning actions and possible outcomes.

It uses diverse rules, including business rules, ML techniques, and algorithms, to predict multiple outcomes and move towards a solution (Logibility, 2019).

4.2.4.1   What is Prescriptive Analytics?

Descriptive analytics tells us what has happened and predictive analytics tells us what could happen. In contrast, prescriptive analytics tells us what should be done. This methodology is the most advanced stage in the analysis process. It calls companies to take action, helping executives, managers, and operational employees make the best possible decisions based on the data available to them (UNSW, 2020).

It suggests various courses of action and outlines what the potential implications would be for each (InsightSoftware, 2021).

Simulating the future, under various sets of assumptions, allows scenario analysis, which, when combined with different optimisation techniques, allows prescriptive analysis to be performed. The prescriptive analysis explores several possible actions and suggests actions depending on the results of descriptive and predictive analytics of a given data set.

Prescriptive analytics is a combination of data and various business rules. The data for prescriptive analytics can be both internal (within the organisation) and external (like social media data). Business rules are preferences, best practices, boundaries, and other constraints. Mathematical models include natural language processing, ML, statistics, operations research, etc.

Prescriptive analytics is comparatively complex in nature, and many companies are not yet using them in day-to-day business activities, as it becomes difficult to manage. Prescriptive analytics if implemented properly can have a major impact on business growth. Large-scale organisations use prescriptive analytics for scheduling the inventory in the supply chain, optimising production etc. to optimise the customer experience (ProjectPro, 2022).

4.2.4.2   How Does Prescriptive Analytics Work?

Prescriptive analytics takes what has been learned through descriptive and predictive analysis and goes a step further by recommending the best possible courses of action. This is the most complex stage of the analytics process, requiring much more specialised analytics knowledge, and thus is rarely used in day-to-day operations (UNSW, 2020).

Prescriptive analytics uses advanced tools and technologies, like ML, business rules, and algorithms, which makes it sophisticated to implement and manage. This type of data analytics requires not only historical internal data but also external information because of the nature of algorithms (Bekker, 2018).

4.2.4.3   What Can Prescriptive Analytics Tell Us?

Prescriptive analytics anticipates what, when, and why something might happen. Decision-makers weigh the possible implications of each decision option, before deciding on a course of action to take advantage of future opportunities or mitigate future risks (UNSW, 2020).

4.2.4.4   What Are the Advantages and Disadvantages of Prescriptive Analytics?

Prescriptive analytics, when used effectively, provides invaluable insights to make the best possible, data-based decisions to optimise performance. However, like predictive analytics, this analytics requires large amounts of data, and those data may not be available. In addition, ML algorithms, on which this analysis often relies, cannot always account for all external variables.

However, there are many advantages.

- Reduction of human error: The use of ML dramatically reduces the possibility of human error (UNSW, 2020).
- Improved operations: It is possible to optimise planning, reduce inefficiencies, and make better operational decisions.

- Efficient resource management: It is possible to use capital, personnel, equipment, vehicles, facilities, capital, personnel, equipment, vehicles, and facilities more efficiently.
- Mitigation of risks: Companies can gain insight into how decisions can have company-wide impacts and hedge against data uncertainty (Yafaa, 2018).

4.2.4.5 Getting Started in Prescriptive Analysis

Prescriptive analytics is comparatively complex, and many companies are not yet using it in day-to-day business activities. If implemented properly, prescriptive analytics can have a major impact on business growth. Large-scale organisations can use prescriptive analytics for scheduling the inventory in the supply chain, optimising production etc. to optimise the customer experience (ProjectPro, 2022).

4.2.4.6 Maintenance Prescriptive Analytics: A Cure for Downtime

Prescriptive maintenance is a combination of prescriptive analytics and predictive maintenance, neither of which is new. Prescriptive maintenance is about scheduling and carrying out predictive maintenance based on predictive analytics and then recommending actions (Figure 4.6) (Berge & Rais, 2021).

Prescriptive maintenance means predictive maintenance based on prescriptive analytics. It considers two separate dimensions (Berge & Rais, 2021) (illustrated in Figure 4.7):

- The time when maintenance is performed.
- The level of actionable analytics.

The first dimension is the time when maintenance is performed according to traditional maintenance approaches: reactive, corrective, preventive, predictive, condition-based, and proactive (Table 4.3) (Berge & Rais, 2021).

The second dimension is understanding how actionable the analytics is using anomaly detection and descriptive and prescriptive techniques (Table 4.4) (Berge & Rais, 2021).

You could say that prescriptive analytics builds on descriptive analytics. After the descriptive analytics has diagnosed the condition of the asset, a corresponding recommended action (i.e. the prescription) is provided (Berge & Rais, 2021).

4.2.4.7 Prescription

The recommended action (prescription) can be provided by the analytics software. This is the easiest solution (Figure 4.8). In a more complex solution, the analytics app presenting the diagnostics to the user may be able to display the recommended action text together with the description. In addition, more than one recommended action may be provided (Berge & Rais, 2021).

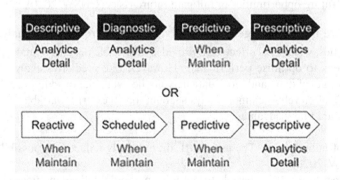

FIGURE 4.6 Prescriptive maintenance (Berge & Rais, 2021).

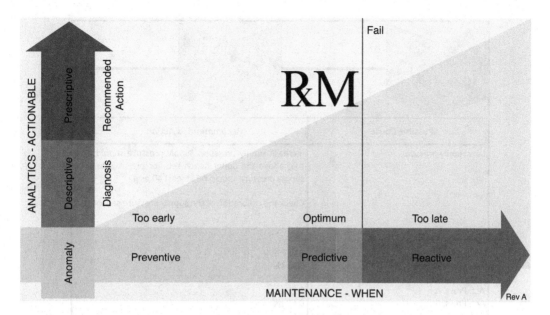

FIGURE 4.7 When "maintenance" is performed and how "actionable" the diagnostics is are two separate dimensions (Berge & Rais, 2021).

TABLE 4.3
The First Dimension (Berge & Rais, 2021)

Time of Maintenance	When
Reactive/corrective	After failure
Preventive (calendar-based schedule)	Before failure, often too early, but may occasionally be too late if the P-F interval is shorter than expected
Predictive, condition-based, and proactive	Before failure, but not too early, just-right, timed based on leading indicators of wear and tear

TABLE 4.4
The Second Dimension (Berge & Rais, 2021)

Analytics Detail	Actionable
Anomaly detection	Unusual, does not say what is wrong
Descriptive	Diagnosis
Prescriptive	Recommended action

4.2.4.8 Scale Out

As we have explained above, prescriptive maintenance involves scheduling and carrying out predictive maintenance when predictive analytics provides recommended actions (Table 4.5). Prescriptive maintenance has already been used in some cases. For example, some plants are applying prescriptive analytics to some instrumentation and control valves. They use the information to schedule and

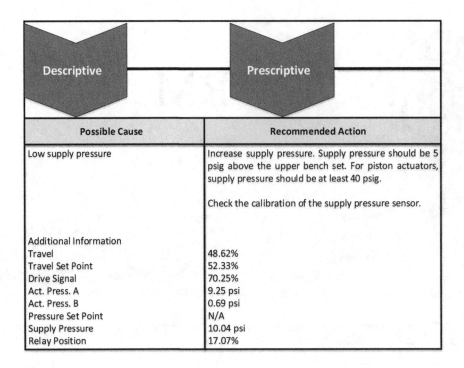

FIGURE 4.8   Descriptive and prescriptive valve diagnostics (Berge & Rais, 2021).

TABLE 4.5

Prescriptive Analytics is Descriptive Analytics with Recommended Action (Berge & Rais, 2021)

Symptom (Pump Example)	Diagnostics (descriptive analytics)	Recommended Action (prescriptive analytics)
Increasing bearing vibration and temperature	Bearing wear	Lubricate bearing Align pump and motor Replace bearing
Discharge pressure instability	Cavitation	Check for upstream or downstream blockage such as closed valve
Strainer pressure drop	Strainer plugging	Clear strainer
Motor temperature high	Motor winding insulation breakdown	Rewind motor
Flush fluid reservoir level drop or reservoir pressure increase	Mechanical seal leak	Replace mechanical seal

carry out maintenance on these assets. Other plants are applying prescriptive maintenance to larger pieces of equipment like pumps and heat exchangers. When the company's instrumentation and control (I&C) engineers instrument these assets and deploy purpose-built predictive analytics for these equipment types, the plant can scale out prescriptive maintenance practices across multiple asset classes in the plant (Berge & Rais, 2021).

4.2.4.9   The Need for Prescriptive Analytics In Maintenance: A Case Study

To sum up the previous discussion, there are four types of analytics. Descriptive analytics (hindsight) looks at what has happened to an asset after it has failed. Diagnostic analytics can look a little deeper and figure out why it failed (the root cause). Predictive analytics can predict the future behaviour of the asset by analysing its RUL. Prescriptive analytics assesses the recommendations provided by predictive analytics and recommends corrective or preventive maintenance actions. This has the capability of designing O&M to adapt continually in the context of Industry 4.0 systems.

Figure 4.9 summarises three potential maintenance scenarios (Galar & Kans, 2017).

In Figure 4.9, the health of the asset is represented by a traffic light. Its health can be good (green light), acceptable (orange light), or bad (red light). Each of these states is related to a different maintenance scenario. The diagnosis phase ("what is happening") may be able to distinguish between the three states, based on two predefined thresholds: maintenance threshold and service threshold. The maintenance threshold is essentially a warning limit telling maintenance personnel to start considering a maintenance action. The service threshold is equivalent to RUL when the asset fails and service is interrupted (Galar & Kans, 2017).

In the first scenario (green light), when neither the maintenance threshold nor the service threshold has been crossed, two computations are of interest to operators and maintainers (see Figure 4.10) (Galar & Kans, 2017):

- Remaining time to get to the maintenance threshold.
- Remaining time to get to the service threshold.

In this first green-light phase of the life span, the system does not suggest any maintenance actions. The component is in an early safety stage and the RUL estimation shows the risk of failure is remote.

Once the maintenance threshold has been crossed, however, the asset enters a risky orange-light stage wherein a relevant maintenance action should be performed in the near future to avoid failure.

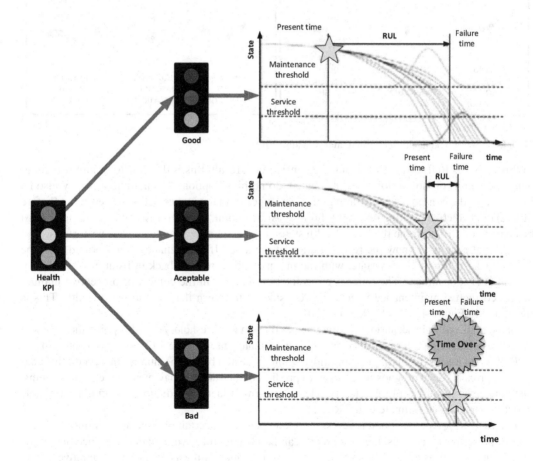

FIGURE 4.9   Maintenance scenarios (Galar & Kans, 2017).

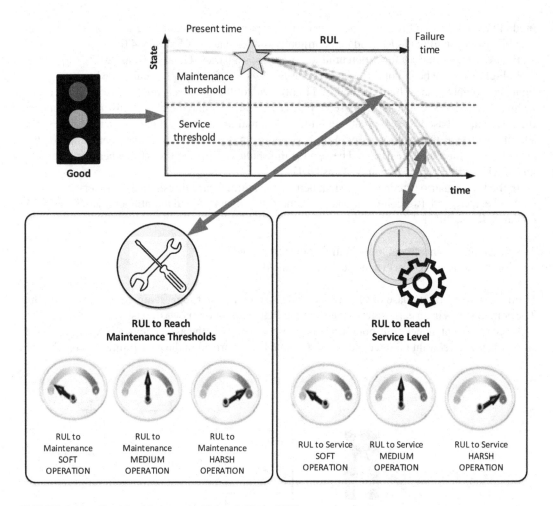

FIGURE 4.10   Good health scenario (Galar & Kans, 2017).

In this case, the RUL estimation should be considered a result: this is the time to failure if mainte-nance personnel do not perform maintenance ("do nothing" option). Yet maintainers may also be interested in the consequences of taking different types of maintenance action – preventive (before failure) or corrective (waiting until after failure). At this point, the RUL restoration parameter must be considered to determine the likely health state of the asset after maintenance is performed.

The challenge is to know the real condition of the asset. If maintenance is performed, will the asset be returned to a healthy state, with the maintenance threshold back in front of it? Or will it remain at risk of failure? The latter is more likely to happen in the context of preventive mainte-nance; corrective maintenance is generally considered to return the asset to good health. This is illustrated in Figure 4.11 (Galar & Kans, 2017).

In the final, red-light scenario, the asset reaches the service threshold. After this point, the only way to restore health is to perform corrective or reactive maintenance (Figure 4.12) (Galar & Kans, 2017).

RUL is no longer the main piece of information requested by the maintainer in a predictive ana-lytics approach. Since prognostics deals with predicting the future behaviour of assets and systems, there are several sources of uncertainty. These, in turn, influence predictions, making it infeasible to obtain an accurate estimate of the RUL.

Before making a prediction, it is necessary to compute the uncertainty associated with RUL. In the case of prescriptive analytics, the uncertainty can be meaningful for the maintainer since one of the uncertainty sources is a lack of knowledge about the operation of the asset. The most intuitive way to show degradation is to determine the evolution over time of a predetermined performance/health index.

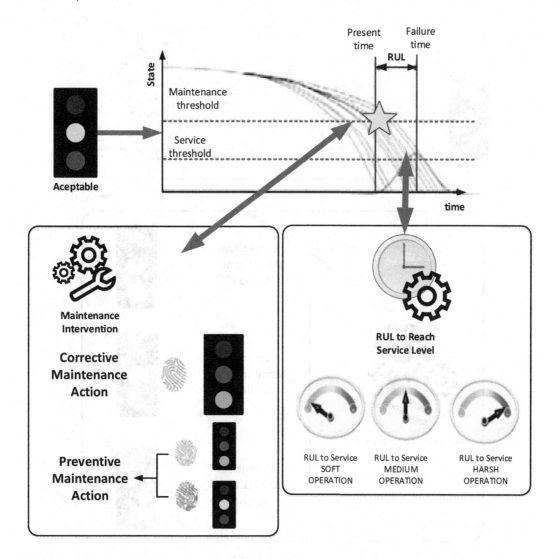

FIGURE 4.11   Risky health scenario (Galar & Kans, 2017).

In Figure 4.13, the blue horizontal line represents the threshold indicating entry into a faulty condition; this will determine the asset's RUL. The black stars show the evolution of the real data points over time. The red lines are uncertainty measures with respect to the operation of the asset. This estimation provides the information required to schedule maintenance (Galar & Kans, 2017).

In addition, the different RUL estimates give decision-makers some options. They can choose different operational sequences to schedule maintenance when it is more convenient. These alternatives are far different from static RUL predictions and represent the type of analytics requested by O&M departments and asset managers in Industry 4.0 (Galar & Kans, 2017).

4.3   BIG DATA ANALYTICS METHODS

Big Data analytics is a strategy or method to process a huge structured, semi-structured, or unstructured data set. This data set could be, for example, data from sensors, data from IoT systems, logging data devices, or data management systems in general, text messages, images, and videos.

The descriptive tasks of Big Data analytics identify the common characteristics of data to derive patterns and relationships that exist in the data. The descriptive functions of Big Data mining

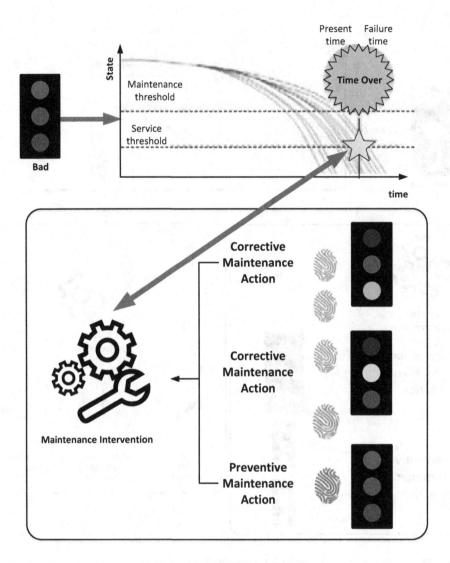

FIGURE 4.12 Faulty health scenario (Galar & Kans, 2017).

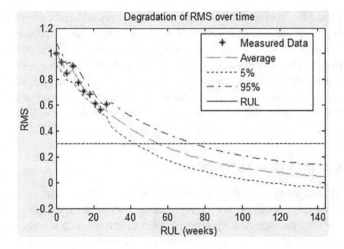

FIGURE 4.13 Degradation over time (Galar & Kans, 2017).

include classification analysis, clustering analysis, association analysis, and logistic regression (Lee et al., 2017):

- Classification analysis: Classification is a typical learning model used in Big Data analytics, which aims to build a model to make predictions on data features from the predefined set of classes according to certain criteria. A rule base classification is used to extract "if-then" rules to classify categories. Examples include neural networks, decision trees, and support vector machines.
- Clustering analysis: Clustering analysis is defined as the process of grouping data into separate clusters of similar objects, thus helping to segment and acquire the data features. Data can be divided into subgroups according to their characteristics. Practitioners may formulate appropriate strategies for different clusters. The common examples of clustering technique are the K-means algorithm, self-organising map, hill climbing algorithm, and density-based spatial clustering.
- Association analysis: The association model helps practitioners recognise groups of items that occur synchronously. The association algorithm is developed to search frequent sets of items with a minimum specified confidence level. The criteria support and confidence level help to identify the most important relationships among the related items.
- Regression analysis: Regression represents the logical relationship of the historical data. Regression analysis focuses on measuring the dependent variable, given one or several independent variables that support the conditional estimation of the expected outcome using the regression function. Linear regression, nonlinear regression, and exponential regression are common statistical methods to measure the best fit for a set of data (Lee et al., 2017).

4.3.1 Defining Big Data Analytics

In Big Data analytics, advanced analytic techniques operate on Big Data. The definition is easy to understand, but do users actually use the term? Figure 4.14 gives some of the interesting responses to a survey on familiarity with Big Data (Russom, 2011).

Most of the survey respondents understood the concept of Big Data analytics, whether they actually knew the term or not (Russom, 2011). Only 7% were totally unfamiliar with the concept. However, many didn't have a name for Big Data analytics; some made up their own name. Terms included large-volume or large-data-set analytics (7%), advanced analytics (12%), analytics (12%), data warehousing (4%), data mining (2%), and predictive analytics (2%) (Figure 4.15). Finally, a few survey respondents entered humorous but revealing terms such as honking big data, my day job, pain in the neck, and we-need-to-buy-more-hardware analytics. Only 28% understood the concept and named it (Russom, 2011).

Figure 4.16 shows three characteristics of a data set which are essential for Big Data analytics platforms. Generally called the 3Vs, these characteristics are variety, velocity, and volume (see Section 4.10; also see Section 4.5.1 for the 5Vs).. These characteristics have a direct impact on the decision about which method to use when analysing a specific data set.

Which of the following best characterizes your familiarity with big data analytics and how you name it?

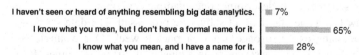

I haven't seen or heard of anything resembling big data analytics.   7%

I know what you mean, but I don't have a formal name for it.   65%

I know what you mean, and I have a name for it.   28%

FIGURE 4.14   Based on 325 respondents (Russom, 2011).

Enter the term you use for big data analytics.

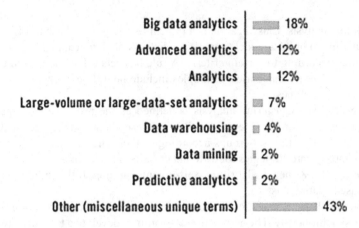

Big data analytics	18%
Advanced analytics	12%
Analytics	12%
Large-volume or large-data-set analytics	7%
Data warehousing	4%
Data mining	2%
Predictive analytics	2%
Other (miscellaneous unique terms)	43%

FIGURE 4.15 Based on 92 respondents who report having a name for Big Data analytics (Russom, 2011).

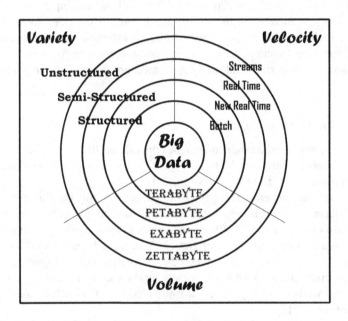

FIGURE 4.16 The three vs of Big Data (Redrawn from Sagiroglu & Sinanc, 2013).

- Variety: A data set can be structured, for example, an Extensible Markup Language (XML) file that follows a specific schema. Another example could be a railML file, which follows a specific data model that can be validated. A semi-structured data set, also known as a self-described structure, is a data set which does not follow specific schemas but is self-described, for example, by tags in the data structure. The unstructured data set does not follow a data schema and is also not self-describing; one example is plain text.
- Velocity: This defines how fast a specific data set should be processed. The data set processing can be batch processing executed once a day or once a week. One example is the analysis and aggregation of warning messages from a cluster of virtual machines. RT processing is the processing of a data set where time plays a role in the veracity of the

information. Streaming is a continuous data flow that is received by the data analysis platform and is processed immediately. One example is the stream of Twitter messages posted by users and sent to the Big Data analytics platform.
• Volume: Volume is related to the size of the data set.

Depending on the combination of the three Vs, certain specific methods or combinations of methods could be more suitable for a specific task (Sagiroglu & Sinanc, 2013).

4.3.2 DEFINING BIG DATA VIA THE THREE VS

Big Data are about more than size. Variety and velocity also matter, and together, the 3Vs constitute a more comprehensive definition. In addition, each of the three Vs has its own ramifications for analytics (Figure 4.17) (Russom, 2011).

4.3.2.1 Data Volume as a Defining Attribute of Big Data

Despite the importance of variety and velocity, data volume is still the primary attribute of Big Data. While most people define Big Data in terms of terabytes – sometimes petabytes – Big Data can also be quantified in terms of numbers of records, transactions, tables, or files. Some organisations find it useful to quantify Big Data in terms of time. For example, given the seven-year statute of limitations in the USA, many companies keep seven years of data available for risk, compliance, and legal analysis.

The scope of Big Data, i.e. what it's intended to do, affects quantification as well. For example, the data collected for general data warehousing may differ from data collected specifically for analytics. In addition, different forms of analytics may have different data sets. Some analysts may create an analytic data set for each analytic project. And of course, Big Data just keep growing. All this makes Big Data tough to quantify (Russom, 2011).

4.3.2.2 Data Type Variety as a Defining Attribute of Big Data

Big Data come from a plethora of sources, including the Web, with sources like clickstreams and social media. Some data are hard to categorise, as they come from audio, video, and other devices.

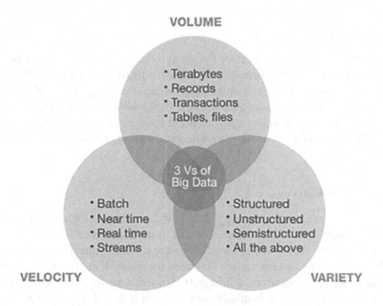

FIGURE 4.17 The three vs of Big Data (Russom, 2011).

In addition, multidimensional data can be drawn from a data warehouse to add historic context to Big Data.

Not all Big Data get used and companies tend to hoard data without using it. Untapped Big Data include RFID data from supply chain applications, text data from call centre applications, semi-structured data from various business-to-business processes, and geospatial data in logistics.

There is a greater recognition now of what Big Data can do, and more organisations are analysing these data at a complex and sophisticated level. The leveraging of these sources for analytics means structured data are being merged with unstructured data (text and human language) and semi-structured data (XML, RSS feeds). In other words, variety is important (Russom, 2011).

4.3.2.3   Data Feed Velocity as a Defining Attribute of Big Data

Big Data can be described by their velocity or speed, i.e. the frequency of data generation or the frequency of data delivery. The collection of Big Data in real time isn't new; many companies have been collecting clickstream data from websites for years, using those streaming data to make purchase recommendations to web visitors.

With sensor and Web data constantly available in real time, the volume builds quickly. Problematically, the analytics that accompanies streaming data has to make sense of the data and take action – also in real time (Russom, 2011).

4.3.3   Text Analytics

Text analytics is used to extract information from textual data such as message chats, emails, forums, and documents in general. Text analytics methods include extracting information (IE), summing up text, answering questions (QA), and analysing sentiment (opinion mining) (Gandomi & Haider, 2015).

4.3.4   Audio Analytics

Audio analytics, also called speech analytics, extracts information from audio data. Audio analytics takes either a transcript-based approach, also known as large vocabulary conversational speech recognition (LVCSR), or a phonetics-based approach (Gandomi & Haider, 2015).

4.3.5   Video Analytics

Video analytics or video content analytics (VCA) involves a variety of techniques to monitor, analyse, and extract meaningful information from video streams (Gandomi & Haider, 2015). For example, railway drones equipped with video cameras are used to monitor railway infrastructure (Flammini et al., 2017) or VCA can be used to count the number of people waiting for a train on a platform. A critical challenge of video analytics is the large amount of data generated. These data can be processed using either a server-based architecture or an edge-based architecture (Gandomi & Haider, 2015).

4.3.6   Social Media Analytics

Social media analytics refers to processing data from social media platforms such as Twitter, LinkedIn, and Facebook. In this case, structured and unstructured data sets are processed to gain information about the data. The user-generated content (e.g., sentiments, images, videos, and bookmarks) and the relationships and interactions between the network entities (e.g., people, organisations, and products) are the two sources of information in social media. Based on this categorisation, social media analytics can be either content-based or structure-based (Gandomi & Haider, 2015).

Information can be extracted in the following ways (Gandomi & Haider, 2015):

- Community detection
- Social influence analysis
- Link prediction-

4.4 MAINTENANCE STRATEGIES WITH BIG DATA ANALYTICS

The Big Data platform has the ability to handle huge amounts of data in manufacturing or production logistics databases, along with the development of CMMS, which assists in decision-making on maintenance strategies.

Under the corrective maintenance strategy, maintenance takes place when a machine failure has occurred. Companies using this strategy keep component inventories for Maintenance, Repair and Operations (MRO) to prevent disruption of the overall production when machine parts or equipment fail.

Preventive maintenance follows a fixed time, interval-based, or condition-based schedule to avoid fatal machine failure. Preventive maintenance is a protective, process-oriented approach in which machine failure and downtime cost could be reduced through proper prevention. Decisions on maintenance schedules are based on a machine's physical properties or asset condition. The assumption of preventive maintenance is that equipment failure follows the bathtub curve shown in Figure 4.18. Scheduled maintenance happens in the wear-out phase to reduce the failure rate. However, a problem with preventive maintenance is the possibility of random failure within the useful life period. The impact of failure in a critical machine is a tremendous risk of downtime costs and becomes a bottleneck in production logistics operations (Lee et al., 2017).

Predictive maintenance helps prevent random machine failure. It involves observing the machine degradation process and monitoring the machine condition from normal to flawed states. Predictive maintenance is a sensor-based content-awareness philosophy based on the IoT. The intelligent maintenance prediction support system monitors the machine status by utilising real-time sensory data. Predictive maintenance is able to provide insights for maintenance scheduling in advance to eliminate unanticipated machine breakdowns and minimise maintenance costs, as well as downtime, before the occurrence of random machine failure.

The important factors associated with predictive maintenance in Maintenance Policy Management (MPM) emphasise criticality, availability of sensory data, reliability, timeliness, relevance, and knowledge-oriented strategy.

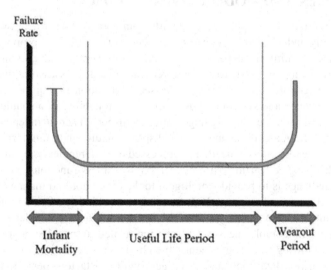

FIGURE 4.18 Classical bathtub curve (Lee et al., 2017).

- Criticality in failures: Predictive maintenance concentrates on RT machine condition monitoring through diagnostics and prognostics to prevent foreseeable machine downtime cost. The critical assets have a higher ranking in priority, as they will have the greatest impact on production. This changes the maintenance objective from avoiding breakdown to accepting downtime and taking maintenance action ahead of schedule (Lee et al., 2017).
- Availability of sensory data: Predictive maintenance is highly dependent on Extract Transform-Load (ETL) operational data in condition-based monitoring. The current operational status and abnormal performance can be assessed by equipping sensors to identify failure modules or machines. Lack of sensory data may result in poor maintenance prediction.
- Reliability: Maintaining critical machine performance and leveraging the overall cost to sustain production are the major targets of predictive maintenance. The system must provide the correct measures and reliable prediction to address feasible and foreseeable machine failure and build confidence in operation.
- Timeliness: The prediction must come before the undesired event occurs, so maintenance can be conducted in a timely manner. The time series of the maintenance schedule and delivery of MRO should be taken into consideration in order to facilitate production, with zero tolerance of equipment failure.
- Relevance: The MPM system needs to be developed based on the opinions of experts. The collected sensory information must be recorded and analysed on an RT basis. To improve data quality, the extraction of relevant data for maintenance decision-making is crucial. Inappropriate integration of a sensor and machine may cause poor estimation and inaccurate predictions of machine performance.

Knowledge-objective oriented strategy: The concept of predictive maintenance involves a belief that the implicit knowledge from the collaboration of sensory information contributes to maintenance in advance of failure. The knowledge transfer system facilitates the disclosure of implicit information to maximise production efficiency and minimises the adverse impact of idling time under maintenance and unawareness of potential failure. Predictive maintenance could be boosted by the involvement of Big Data mining techniques to detect and defeat anomalies at an early stage (Lee et al., 2017).

4.5 DATA-DRIVEN AND MODEL-DRIVEN APPROACHES

Assets are complex mixes of complex systems built from components which, over time, may fail. The ability to quickly and efficiently determine the cause of failures and propose optimum maintenance decisions, while minimising the need for human intervention, is necessary. Thus, for complex assets, much information needs to be captured and mined to assess the overall condition of the whole system. Therefore, the integration of asset information is required to get an accurate health assessment of the whole system and determine the probability of a shutdown or slowdown. Moreover, the data collected are not only huge but often dispersed across independent systems that are difficult to access, fuse, and mine due to their disparate nature and granularity. Data relevant to asset management are gathered, produced, and processed on different levels by different IT systems (Galar et al., 2012; Zhang & Karim, 2014) e.g. ERP for business functions; SCADA for monitoring process. The challenge is to provide intelligent tools to monitor and manage assets (machines, plants, products etc.) proactively through ICT, focusing on health degradation monitoring and prognosis instead of fault detection and diagnostics. Maintenance effectiveness depends on the quality, timeliness, accuracy, and completeness of information related to machine degradation state. This translates into the following key requirements: the ability to prevent data overload; the ability to differentiate and prioritise data; tools and machinery with satisfactory performance; and efficient analysis tools and planning tools. A performance killer is an input element that performs poorly or hinders performance. In this context, a cost driver is an input element to a process that causally affects or drives costs which is tangible. A cost driver can be interpreted as an element that affects cost, or an element that increases costs considerably. Examples include assets with high failure frequency and long downtime.

Some of the key parameters in the form of performance measures or indicators for RAMS and LCC etc. are continuously developed and applied for tracking maintenance activities.

Maintenance decision-making with multiple stakeholders largely depends on the maintenance failure data, RAMS, and LCC data analysis to estimate the RUL and thereby ensure effective business and maintenance decision-making. Thus, an effective maintenance decision-making process needs a trusted DSS based on knowledge discovery. The process of knowledge discovery will essentially consist of: data acquisition to obtain relevant data and manage its content; data transition to communicate the collected data; data fusion to compile data and information from different sources; data mining to analyse data to extract information and knowledge; and information extraction and visualisation to support maintenance decision, as shown in Figure 4.4.

The integration of data, recorded from a multiple-sensor system, together with information from other sources to achieve inferences, is known as data fusion (Hall & Llinas, 2001). Data fusion is a prerequisite when handling data from heterogeneous sources or from multiple sensors. Knowledge discovery when applied for maintenance decision support uses the eMaintenance concept to integrate the data mining and knowledge discovery. However, the development of eMaintenance for industrial applications faces a number of challenges, which can be categorised into: (1) organisational; (2) architectural; (3) infrastructural; (4) content and contextual; and (5) integration.

Organisational challenges mainly focus on aspects related to enterprise resource management. Examples of these challenges are (1) restructuring of the organisations involved in eMaintenance; (2) planning of resources (e.g. materials, spare parts); (3) information management; (4) management of knowledge; and (5) management of heterogeneous organisations.

Architectural challenges deal with issues related to the overall architecture of eMaintenance solutions. Some of these challenges are: (1) development of a framework for the development of eMaintenance; (2) development of models for decentralised data processing and analysis; (3) development of a service model for decentralised data analysis; (4) development of model-based prognostic tools; (5) development of a model aimed for data and information visualisation to support human–machine interaction; and (6) development of a model aimed for distributed data storage capability.

Infrastructural challenges address issues related to the provision of necessary technologies and tools that are required to meet needs and requirements when services, according to SOA, are developed, implemented, and managed in an enterprise. Examples of these are: (1) network infrastructure (e.g. wired and wireless); (2) authentication of services and users; (3) authorisation of services and users; (4) a safety and security mechanism; (5) maintainability of eMaintenance services; (6) availability performance management and tracing and tracking mechanism; and (7) provision of a mechanism aimed for documentation and archiving

Content and contextual challenges are mainly related to data and information provided through the eMaintenance services. Some of these challenges are (1) provision of appropriate ontology through which data from data sources (e.g. process data, product data, condition monitoring data, and business data) can be smoothly and seamlessly integrated; (2) provision of a quality assurance mechanism that ensures that the required data quality is fulfilled and visualised to increase the quality of decision-making; (3) a mechanism for sensing the user's current situation in order to adapt the information to the user's context; (4) provision of a mechanism for describing various context; (5) a mechanism to manage uncertainty in data sets; and (6) provision of a mechanism for pattern recognition.

4.5.1 Data Mining and Knowledge Discovery

Data produced in asset management can be described in terms of the 5Vs (see Lomotey & Deters, 2014; Zikopoulos & Eaton, 2011). These are velocity, volume, variety, veracity, and value.

Data from sensors like accelerometers or acoustic sensors can be acquired at a *velocity* of tens of thousands of samples per second per measuring point. With hundreds or thousands of those points, a big *volume* of data is produced. Some maintenance-related data are structured while others are not, such as free text comments for performed maintenance actions or failure reports. Moreover, data from different systems are in different formats. This is the source of *variety* of data in asset management. Those data have potential *value* when properly employed in asset management, but to achieve this, there is a need to assess and manage the *veracity* of the data, i.e. the data uncertainty. Finally, it is important to understand the *value* of data, i.e. how data can enable efficiency and effectiveness in maintenance management, for instance, for improved decision-making, and to choose the most cost-effective means to process the data.

Data mining in big asset data can discover knowledge in terms of new patterns and relations not visible at a glance. The Big Data approach enables the incorporation of contextual information in Maintenance Decision Support Systems (Galar et al., 2016). One example of useful knowledge that could be discovered is root causes of failure. This can provide an input for design improvement as well as for more accurate maintenance planning. Indeed, more and more authors are using the term KDD synonymously today. They refer to the area of research that draws upon data mining methods from pattern recognition (Dhar & Tuzhilin, 1992), ML, and database techniques in the context of vast organisational databases. Conceptually, KDD refers to a multiple-step process that can be highly interactive and iterative in the following (Fayyad et al., 1996; Strong et al., 1997):

- selecting, cleaning, transforming, and projecting the data;
- mining the data to extract patterns and appropriate models;
- evaluating and interpreting the extracted patterns to decide what constitutes "knowledge";
- consolidating the knowledge and resolving conflicts with previously extracted knowledge;
- making the knowledge available for use by the interested elements within the system.

AI techniques have advanced knowledge management, including knowledge acquisition, knowledge repositories, knowledge discovery, and knowledge distribution. Knowledge acquisition captures tacit and explicit knowledge from domain experts, while knowledge repositories formalise the outcomes of knowledge acquisition and integrate knowledge in distributed corporate environments. Knowledge discovery and mining approaches explore relationships and trends in the knowledge repositories to create new knowledge (Liu & Ke, 2007).

In decision-making, it is essential to deal with with faults, i.e. inability to perform as required due to an internal state (IEC-IEV, 2022), and failures, i.e. the termination of the ability of an item to perform a required function (IEC-IEV, 2022). The relationship between faults and failures can be described as the following: "a fault is result (state) of an associated failure (event)". To deal with both the event and the state, the MA phases can be set in a time-related order, as shown in the following sections.

4.6 MAINTENANCE DESCRIPTIVE ANALYTICS

The descriptive analytics phase of MA aims to answer "What has happened?" In this phase, it is very important to have access to data related to system operation, system condition, and expected condition. Another important aspect to understand the relationship of events and states during the descriptive analytics is time and time frame associated with each specific log. Furthermore, events and states need to be associated with the system configuration for the time (T_n). This means that time synchronisation becomes an important part to support MA.

4.7 MAINTENANCE DIAGNOSTIC ANALYTICS

The diagnostic analytics phase of MA aims to answer, "Why something has happened?" In this phase, the outcome from "maintenance descriptive analytics" is used to frame the analytics. This phase requires the availability of reliability data, in addition to the data used in the descriptive phase.

4.8 MAINTENANCE PREDICTIVE ANALYTICS

The predictive analytics phase of MA aims to answer, "What will happen in the future?" The outcome from "maintenance descriptive analytics" is used in this phase. Reliability data and maintainability data are necessary, in addition to the data used in the descriptive phase. In addition, business data such as planned operation and planned maintenance data are required to predict upcoming failures and faults.

4.9 MAINTENANCE PRESCRIPTIVE ANALYTICS

The maintenance prescriptive analytics phase of MA aims to answer, "What needs to be done?"

This phase uses the outcome from "maintenance diagnostic analytics" and "maintenance predictive analytics". In addition, resource planning data and business data are required to predict upcoming failures and faults.

4.10 BIG DATA ANALYTICS METHODS

Big Data analytics is a strategy or method to process a huge structured, semi-structured or unstructured data set. This data set could contain, for example, data from sensors, data from IoT systems, logging data devices or data management systems in general, text messages, images, and videos.

As shown in Figure 4.19, three characteristics of a data set are essential for Big Data analytics. We discussed the 3Vs earlier (also see Section 4.5.1 a slightly different interpretation, i.e. the 5Vs). These characteristics have a direct impact on the decision about which methods will be used to analyse a specific Big Data set.

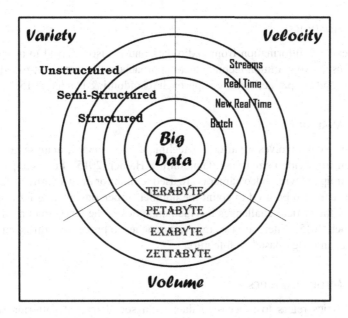

FIGURE 4.19   The three vs of Big Data (Redrawn from Sagiroglu & Sinanc, 2013).

The 3Vs are described below:

- Variety: A data set can be structured, for example, an Extensible Markup Language (XML) file that follows a specific schema. Another example could be a railML file, which follows a specific data model that can be validated. A semi-structured data set, also known as a self-described structure, is a data set which does not follow specific schemas but is self-described, for example, by tags in the data structure. The unstructured data set does not follow a data schema and is also not self-describing (e.g. plain text).
- Velocity: This indicates how fast a specific data set should be processed. It can be a batch processing executed once a day or a week. One example could be the analysis and aggregation of warning messages of a cluster of virtual machines. RT processing is the processing of a data set where time plays a role in the veracity of the information. Streaming is a continuous data flow that is received by the data analysis platform and is processed immediately. One example is the stream of Twitter messages, which are posted by users and sent to the Big Data analytics platform.
- Volume: Volume refers to the size of the data set.

As mentioned above, depending on the combination of the 3Vs, specific methods or a combination of methods could be best-suited for a specific task.

4.10.1 Text Analytics

Text analytics is a method used to extract information from textual data such as message chats, emails, forums, and documents, in general. A brief review of text analytics methods described by Gandomi and Haider (2015) is listed below:

- Information extraction (IE)
- Text summarisation
- Question answering (QA)
- Sentiment analysis (opinion mining)

4.10.2 Audio Analytics

Audio analytics extracts information from audio data and is also referred to as speech analytics. Speech analytics uses two common technological approaches: the transcript-based approach (also known as LVCSR) and the phonetics-based approach (Gandomi & Haider, 2015).

4.10.3 Video Analytics

Video analytics or VCA involves a variety of techniques to monitor, analyse, and extract meaningful information from video streaming (Gandomi & Haider, 2015). For example, in the railway industry, drones equipped with video cameras are used to monitor railway infrastructure (Flammini et al., 2017). VCA can also be used to count the number of persons waiting for a specific train on a platform. One of the critical challenges in video analytics is the large amount of data generated (Gandomi & Haider, 2015). There are two main approaches to processing this kind of data: server-based architecture, and edge-based architecture.

4.10.4 Social Media Analytics

Social media analytics refers to processing data from social media platforms such as Twitter, LinkedIn, Facebook, and Wikipedia. In this case, structured and unstructured data sets are processed to gain information. The user-generated content (e.g. sentiments, images, videos, and bookmarks) and the relationships and interactions between the network entities (e.g. people, organisations, and products) are the two sources of information in social media (Gandomi & Haider, 2015). Based on this categorisation, social media analytics can be classified into two groups: content-based analytics and structure-based analytics.

There are diverse techniques to extract information:

- Community detection
- Social influence analysis
- Link prediction

4.11 BIG DATA MANAGEMENT AND GOVERNANCE

Big Data management refers to the possibility of storing any kind of data, both structured and unstructured, in the storage system of the Big Data Appliance (BDA). Several technologies are available for this task; these are known as Distributed File Systems (DFS). Some examples are Hadoop Distributed File System (HDFS), Ceph, and GlusterFS.

This kind of file system makes it possible to store large amounts of data in a distributed fashion by taking advantage of the capacity included in a cluster of computers, showing them as a single entity, i.e. grouping the single capacity of each node of the cluster into a unique storage system. The computer cluster can contain specialised hardware for data storage, as well as commodity hardware: all the storage will behave in the same way, looking like a unique huge disk, where the complexities of the cluster architecture have been transparently hidden.

Since the file system is distributed, a DFS usually needs to provide some fault-tolerance mechanisms to avoid data losses and to ensure data availability. This issue is addressed with data replication techniques, such as data striping, data sharing, etc. These kinds of mechanisms ensure data are not kept by only one node of the cluster; instead, they are replicated in multiple copies over the cluster, either automatically or by setting some replication rules manually, so that many nodes store the same data. Some DFS divide data into blocks so that every node stores pieces of the same data.

The implementation of data replication mechanisms affects both the way the cluster has to be managed and the performance of the DFS (usually in a positive manner). Therefore, to implement data replication successfully, the DFS has to include a metadata system that records the position of all the pieces of data and all the replicas among the cluster (i.e. which node has stored a particular data shard). The architecture of the file system has to be designed carefully to cope with metadata. The existing technologies feature two different approaches: master-slave and masterless. The former design is based on the implementation of a central metadata repository, which acts as a master database recording the position of all the data distributed over the cluster. The latter design distributes not only data but also metadata over the cluster. There are pros and cons for each design, and the choice depends on the type of data to be stored.

From the performance point of view, data replication allows higher throughputs, as the read-and-write performances of several disks installed in the computers of the cluster are combined. Some DFS perform better than others, but the performance increment is usually a general feature that is common to any DFS. Moreover, some DFS include automatic data replication functionalities that are able to replicate data elastically together with the number of requests for those particular data.

Another performance key point for DFS is the possibility to scale to cluster of thousands of nodes. For instance, modern DFS technologies not only cope with machine and disk failures providing seamless access to data but also allow nodes to be elastically added and removed from a particular cluster with no downtimes. If the capacity of a DFS must be expanded, it is sufficient to add new storage devices or nodes to the cluster.

DFS are usually developed for the specific computing framework they are expected to support. For instance, some DFS have been developed for Hadoop distributed computing platforms and others for High Performance Computing (HPC) and supercomputers.

Finally, DFS are differentiated by the additional functionalities they can provide. For instance, a DFS can be accessed in different ways, by exposing RESTful APIs, by implementing sharing-over-network protocols (e.g. Network File System (NFS) or Microsoft Network File Sharing), and so on. Some DFS include Hadoop access APIs so that they can be connected to a Hadoop computing platform. Finally, DFS usually include tools that make it possible to track data and to present where the data are stored over the cluster in a visual way, using web graphical user interfaces (GUI).

Data governance refers to tools that allow the application of policies to data stored in the DFS. These tools usually implement the concept of "data flow", seeing the data as a flow of information coming into and going out of the BDA. In other words, they manage data processing pipelines, taking responsibility for cleaning data, preparing them for analysis, and removing them from the cluster when they outlive their useful life. Moreover, they are designed to enrich data with metadata and to exchange metadata with other tools and processes within and outside the Hadoop stack. Metadata also enable effective data searching and proscriptive lineage, metadata-driven data access control, flexible modelling of both business and operational data, data classification based on external and internal sources, and metadata interchange with other metadata tools.

4.12 BIG DATA ACCESS AND ANALYSIS

Big Data access and analysis refer to all the tools developed to manipulate data, to implement efficient data storage and retrieval through database management systems (DBMS), to analyse data and generally to perform any kind of computation involving data inside the BDA.

Concerning Big Data access, we usually refer to two different categories of tools: tool for data manipulation, implementing one or more processing modes, and distributed DBMS, which support different storage needs and consequently allow different data access patterns.

Processing modes make possible to deal with different problems at the same time by exploiting a single, powerful architecture: the BDA. We can divide processing modes into the following:

Batch processing: this is the first processing mode that was implemented in BDAs. The MapReduce computing framework allows implementing batch jobs on the cluster, i.e. jobs that extensively use data stored in the BDA and continuously perform the same operations on data as soon as new data are available. Traditionally, these kinds of jobs have been related to MapReduce jobs using data on HDFS. They have been recently put aside in favour of in-memory jobs because the latter have higher performance.

Stream processing: This kind of processing mode involves the management and analysis of data streams, which represent fast sequential data incoming into the BDA. The tools used to deal with streaming data allow data to be efficiently analysed at incredible speeds and in a distributed fashion to cope with the high velocity of data.

In-memory processing: This is currently the fastest processing mode. In-memory processing, for which Apache Spark has become famous, is a processing mode that involves the usage of volatile random access memory in a distributed manner to store and process data. This kind of processing mode has become popular with the drop in the memory prices. Moreover, in-memory processing definitely overtook disk storage solutions that provided poor performance compared to that achievable with memories.

Interactive processing: This particular processing mode became available after the advent of in-memory processing solutions. Interactive processing with Big Data implies the availability of RT processing systems able to deal with large amounts of data, and this was not achievable with past solutions. Interactive processing tools make it possible to perform explorative data analysis by exploiting all the computational power of a BDA.

Appendix 1.3 contains a list of some of the well-known distributed DBMS and general architectural descriptions, as well as some highlights on their most interesting features.

As already mentioned, distributed DBMS support different data storage models, which can be categorised using the following classes.

Relational databases: These are also called "NewSQL" databases; they implement the classical relational model, capable of storing structured data and providing ACID (atomicity, consistency, isolation, durability) semantics, but in a distributed fashion and with superior capabilities than in the past. VoltDB represents an example of database built on this model.

NoSQL databases: Databases of this type support nested, semi-structured, and unstructured data and are particularly suitable for Big Data applications. They can be categorised as follows:

- Key-value stores: This is the simplest of the models, implemented as what is essentially a large hash table. Each data item has a unique key pointing to it. The model is fast and highly scalable. Examples of databases built on this model are Voldemort and Redis.
- Document stores: These can be thought of as nested key-value stores, where a key points to a collection of key-value stores rather than simply a value. Examples are CouchDB and MongoDB.
- Column-oriented stores: Data are stored in columns rather than in the typical row/column structure. Columns are grouped into column families. HBase and Cassandra are examples of column-oriented data stores.
- Graph-based stores: These are designed for data that can be represented as a graph and can be used for tasks such as network analysis. They are more flexible than the other models, with no tables or rows. Examples include Neo4J and OrientDB.

Cassandra file system (CFS) is the DFS residing under the Apache Cassandra distributed DBMS. For this reason, distributed DBMS share most of the considerations mentioned in the previous section about DFS, especially with respect to underlying storage hardware, fault-tolerance, data replication, high availability and high performance, scalability, and reliability. Furthermore, some distributed DBMS implement in-memory data storage to achieve higher performance.

A singular element for some distributed DBMS is the concept of "eventual consistency". A system is considered eventually consistent if it informally guarantees that, if no new updates are made to a given data item, eventually all accesses to that item will return the last updated value. These kinds of systems trade write availability for data consistency by letting distributed data be updated asynchronously with other data replicas stored in the cluster. This eventually results in data conflicts, which are resolved either manually or automatically by implementing various MultiVersion Concurrency Control (MVCC) mechanisms. An example of eventually consistent distributed DBMS is Riak.

At its root, the key requirements of Big Data storage are to be able to handle very large amounts of data and to keep scaling to keep up with growth; it must also provide the Input/Output Operations per Second (IOPS) necessary to deliver data to analytics tools. The choice of the right database depends on the data to be stored, as well as on the demands of the project for which they are being used. Another important factor is the ease of use, as many distributed DBMS use their own query languages instead of SQL-like languages to explore stored data.

Regarding Big Data analysis, it is possible to find many tools, and their development is strictly connected to the particular task they are designed to solve. Some of these tools have been adapted for Big Data scenarios, while others deal with Big Data analysis problems. A list of tools and libraries for Big Data analysis is included in Appendix 1.5.

Big Data analysis solutions can be divided into the following categories:

- Analysis types: alongside processing modes, a BDA includes tools able to perform different types of analysis.

- Search: this kind of analysis is particularly interesting for processing document-oriented data. Big Data search engines enable fast full-text search, near RT indexing, and fast exploration.
- Graph analysis: this kind of analysis is particularly useful it the data to be analysed include large numbers of relationships between records, such as in a graph. For example, social media data usually benefit from graph analysis.
- Data mining: a BDA includes several tools for data mining and ML, providing extensive sets of algorithms able to cope with large amounts of data. The algorithms provided by these tools usually exploit the distributed architecture to solve clustering, predictive modelling, classification, and all other classical ML problems.

4.13 BIG DATA VISUALISATION

Data visualisation is the presentation of data in a pictorial or graphical format. It enables decision-makers to see analytics presented visually, so they can grasp difficult concepts or identify new patterns. Visualisation has proven effective for not only presenting essential information in vast amounts of data but also driving complex analyses. For these reasons, Big Data visualisation tools are considered extremely important.

Big Data visualisation tools can be categorised in different ways. Harger and Crossno (2012) split visualization algorithms into four categories: graphs, trees, n-dimensional data (both continuous and discrete), and geospatial (spatiotemporal) visualisations. A comprehensive set of all the possible visualisations is shown in Figure 4.20.

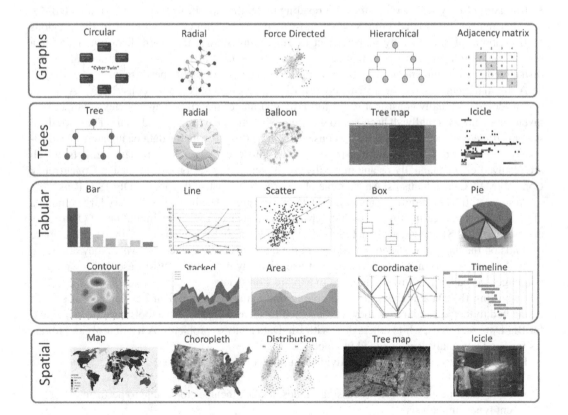

FIGURE 4.20   Data visualisations (Harger & Crossno, 2012).

Graphs are any data that contain information that can be represented as nodes or vertices and edges connecting these nodes. Trees are a special class of graphs that have an explicit hierarchical structure that allows them to be laid out in more ways than graphs in general. Dimensional data are part of a very general class that includes all the information that can be represented in a tabular form (i.e. columns and rows of a table). Finally, the last class is spatial information.

4.14 BIG DATA INGESTION

Big Data ingestion represents the set of interfaces of the BDA with the external world, both inward and outward. To allow the BDA to "ingest" data from any possible data source, the data ingestion tools have to deal with four main categories of data sources:

- Relational database management systems (RDBMS) through standard interfaces such as JDBC and ODBC;
- Data streams, such as log streams of data;
- Messages from messaging interfaces (e.g. STOMP); and
- Unstructured data from NoSQL databases and other sources

Therefore, the data ingestion layer of a BDA has to include tools for bulk data downloaded from and uploaded to traditional relational databases, which are then responsible for inserting data into the distributed DBMS included in the BDA.

The BDA also has to include software tools for dealing with incoming streams of data, which eventually have to be transformed and loaded into internal data storage systems. The same considerations are valid for messaging tools, although they have to deal with a large number of multiple clients at the same time.

Finally, the BDA has to deal with unstructured data by providing tools able to receive them and store them in NoSQL distributed DBMS included into the BDA.

Data ingestion tools can only be successfully developed if they are tightly coupled with the proposed BDA, which not only means that every "connector" needs to have a proper counterpart internally to the BDA, but also that they have to be able to exploit the distributed nature of this kind of system. Indeed, great improvements can result if the ingestion tools are able to work simultaneously from different working nodes in the cluster, virtually eliminating any bottleneck with the external world.

4.15 BIG DATA CLUSTER MANAGEMENT

Big Data cluster managers are fundamental operational tools of a BDA that make it possible to look at the computer cluster as a single computing entity sharing the computing resources of all the nodes.

These systems are responsible for resource management and job scheduling, monitoring, and recovery (in case of failures). The former functionality takes responsibility for managing any computing component (CPU, memory, disk, and network) of every node of the cluster, which is considered a sort of resource container. The usage of every component has to be recorded and reported.

The job scheduling, monitoring, and recovery functionalities are achieved by negotiating resources with the resource monitoring system. Depending on the policies implemented by two distinct systems, jobs will be submitted to certain nodes of the cluster. The job monitoring system tracks which nodes are currently working on the data. If there is a failure or any other problem that prevents a node from completing its part of the job and returning the results, the job recovery system has to deal with the issue, for example, by submitting the same part of the job to another node.

Although resource and job management functionalities are implemented by every cluster manager, the architectural designs can vary with respect to the specific application scenario in which cluster managers are used. For instance, a cluster manager for the Hadoop computing platform, such as YARN, is fundamentally similar to but completely different from SCMS.pro, a cluster manager specifically designed for HPC systems.

4.16 BIG DATA DISTRIBUTIONS

Big Data distributions are pre-built collections of software considered essential for any BDA implementation, usually belonging to the Apache Hadoop ecosystems. They contain tools that cover more than one functional area of a BDA.

Hadoop is an open-source project, and several vendors have developed their own distributions on top of the Hadoop framework to make it enterprise-ready. The beauty of Hadoop distributions lies in the fact that they can be personalised with different feature sets to meet the requirements of different classes of users. Hadoop distributions put together all the enhancement projects included in the Apache repository and present them as a unified product so that organisations do not have to spend time assembling these elements into a single functional component. Among all the options, the most recognised Hadoop distributions available in the market are Cloudera, MapR, and Hortonworks. All these Hadoop distributions are compatible with Apache Hadoop, but they add new functionalities by improving the code base and bundling it with easy-to-use and user-friendly management tools, technical support, and continuous updates.

All three aforementioned distributions use the core Hadoop framework and bundle it for enterprise use. The features offered as part of the core distribution include support service and subscription service models. Commercial vendor MapR offers a robust distribution package that includes real-time data streaming, built-in connectors to existing systems, data protection, and enterprise quality engineering. Cloudera and MapR offer additional management software as part of the commercial distribution so that Hadoop administrators can configure, monitor, and tune their Hadoop clusters.

Cloudera is the best-known player and market leader in the Hadoop space, releasing the first commercial Hadoop distribution. With more than 350 customers and with the active contribution of code to the Hadoop ecosystem, it tops the list when it comes to building innovative tools. The management console Cloudera Manager is easy to use and implement with rich user interface displaying all the information in an organised and clean way. The proprietary Cloudera Management suite automates the installation process and supplies various other enhanced services to users displaying the count of real-time nodes, reducing the deployment time etc. Cloudera offers consulting services to bridge the gap between what the community provides and what organisations need to integrate Hadoop technology in their data management strategy.

The unique features supported by Cloudera are:

- The ability to add new services to a running Hadoop cluster.
- Support for multi-cluster management.
- Node templates; i.e. Cloudera allows the creation of groups of nodes in a Hadoop cluster with varying configurations so that the users do not have to use the same configuration throughout the Hadoop cluster.
- HDFS and the DataNode and NameNode architecture to split up the data and metadata locations.

MapR: Hadoop distribution works on the concept that a market-driven entity is meant to support market needs faster. Leading companies such as Cisco, Ancestry.com, Boeing, Google Cloud Platform, and Amazon EMR use MapR Hadoop distribution for their Hadoop services. Unlike Cloudera and Hortonworks, MapR Hadoop distribution has a more distributed approach for storing metadata on the processing nodes because it depends on a file system known as MapR File System (MapRFS; see Appendix 1.1.10).

The following list includes the unique features supported by MapR:

- MapR is the only Hadoop distribution that includes Pig, Hive, and Sqoop without any Java dependencies because it relies on MapRFS.
- MapR is the most production-ready Hadoop distribution with enhancements that make it more user friendly, faster, and dependable.
- MapR provides multi-node direct access through NFS, so that users of the distribution can mount MapR file system over NFS, allowing applications to access Hadoop data in a traditional way.
- MapR provides complete data protection, ease of use and no single points of failure.
- MapR is considered one of the fastest Hadoop distributions.

Hortonworks: Founded by Yahoo engineers, Hortonworks provides a "service only" distribution model for Hadoop. Hortonworks is different from the other Hadoop distributions, as it is an open enterprise data platform available free for use. Hortonworks' Hadoop distribution can easily be downloaded and integrated for use in various applications. Ebay, Samsung Electronics, Bloomberg, and Spotify use Hortonworks. It was the first vendor to provide a production-ready Hadoop distribution based on Hadoop 2.0. Moreover, only Hortonworks supports Microsoft Windows platforms, so that a Hadoop cluster can be deployed on Microsoft Azure through the HDInsight service.

The following list includes the unique features supported by Hortonworks:

- Hortonworks makes Hive faster through its new Stinger project.
- Hortonworks avoids vendor lock-in by pledging to a forked version of Hadoop.
- Hortonworks is focused on enhancing the usability of the Hadoop platform.

4.17   DATA GOVERNANCE

The two main data governance tools are Apache Falcon and Apache Atlas.

Falcon allows an enterprise to process a single massive data set stored in HDFS in multiple ways – for batch, interactive and streaming applications. Apache Falcon's data governance capabilities play a critical role in cleaning data, preparing them for business intelligence tools, and removing them from the cluster when they outlive their useful life. Falcon simplifies the development and management of data processing pipelines with a higher layer of abstraction, taking the complex coding out of data processing applications by providing out-of-the-box data management services. This simplifies the configuration and orchestration of data motion, disaster recovery, and data retention workflows. Falcon provides a platform for centralised definition and management of pipelines for data ingest, process, and export, it ensures disaster readiness and business continuity, and it includes policies for data replication and retention and performs end-to-end monitoring of data pipelines. Moreover, it is able to visualise data pipeline lineage, to track data pipeline audit logs, and to tag data with business metadata. Finally, it is responsible for replication across on-premise and cloud-based storage targets, for data lineage with supporting documentation and examples, for heterogeneous storage tying in HDFS, and for the definition of hot and cold storage tiers within a cluster.

Atlas provides governance capabilities for Hadoop that use both prescriptive and forensic models enriched by business taxonomical metadata. Atlas, at its core, is designed to exchange metadata with other tools and processes within and outside of the Hadoop stack, thereby enabling platform-agnostic governance controls that effectively address compliance requirements. Apache Atlas empowers enterprises to address effectively and efficiently their compliance requirements through a scalable set of core governance services. These services include search and proscriptive lineage, metadata-driven data access control, flexible modelling of both business and operational data, data classification based on external and internal sources, and metadata interchange with other metadata tools. Apache Atlas is developed around two guiding principles: open development and metadata truth in Hadoop. The former is related to the development of Atlas itself in the context of an open-source community. The latter refers to providing visibility in Hadoop by using both a prescriptive and a forensic model. Atlas provides technical and operational audit, as well as lineage enriched by business taxonomical metadata. Finally, Atlas facilitates the easy exchange of metadata by enabling any metadata consumer to share a common metadata store that facilitates interoperability across many metadata producers.

4.18   DATA ACCESS

Hadoop includes tools implementing different processing modes and several types of distributed DBMS into one single architecture. Hadoop includes Apache Pig, Apache Tez for implementing MapReduce batch processing, Apache Storm for stream processing, and Apache Spark for in-memory data processing. It also includes Apache Hive, Apache HBase, and Apache Accumulo as relational and non-relational (NoSQL) distributed DBMS.

Apache Pig is a scripting language designed to use the traditional MapReduce computing engine, enhanced by the inclusion of YARN in the BDA as cluster manager.

Apache Tez provides a developer API and framework to write native YARN applications that bridge the spectrum of interactive and batch workloads. It allows those data access applications to work with petabytes of data over thousands of nodes. The Apache Tez component library allows developers to create Hadoop applications that integrate natively with Apache Hadoop YARN and perform well within mixed workload clusters. Since Tez is extensible and embeddable, it provides the fit-to-purpose freedom to express highly optimised data processing applications, giving them an advantage over end-user-facing engines such as MapReduce and Apache Spark. Tez also offers a customisable execution architecture that allows users to express complex computations as dataflow graphs, permitting dynamic performance optimisations based on real information about the data and the resources required to process it.

Apache Storm is a distributed real-time computation system for processing large volumes of high-velocity data. Storm is extremely fast, with the ability to process over a million records per second per node on a cluster of modest size. Enterprises harness this speed and combine it with other data access applications in Hadoop to prevent undesirable events or to optimise positive outcomes.

Apache Spark is a fast, in-memory data processing engine with elegant and expressive development APIs to allow data workers to execute efficient streaming, ML, or SQL workloads that require fast iterative access to data sets. With Spark running on Apache Hadoop YARN, developers everywhere can create applications to exploit Spark's power, derive insights, and enrich their data science workloads within a single, shared data set in Hadoop. The Hadoop YARN-based architecture provides the foundation that enables Spark and other applications to share a common cluster and data set while ensuring consistent levels of service and response. Spark is now one of many data access engines that work with YARN in Hadoop. Apache Spark consists of Spark Core and a set of libraries. The core is the distributed execution engine, and the Java, Scala, and Python APIs offer a platform for distributed ETL application development. Additional libraries, built atop the core, allow diverse workloads for streaming, SQL, and ML.

The tables in Hive are similar to tables in a relational database, and data units are organised in a taxonomy from larger to more granular units. Databases are composed of tables, which are made up of partitions. Data can be accessed through a simple query language, and Hive supports overwriting or appending data. Within a particular database, data in the tables are serialised and each table has a corresponding HDFS directory. Each table can be subdivided into partitions that determine how data are distributed within sub-directories of the table directory. Data within partitions can be further broken down into buckets. Hive supports all the common primitive data formats such as BIGINT, BINARY, BOOLEAN, CHAR, DECIMAL, DOUBLE, FLOAT, INT, SMALLINT, STRING, TIMESTAMP, and TINYINT. In addition, analysts can combine primitive data types to form complex data types such as structs, maps, and arrays.

Apache HBase provides random, RT access to data in Hadoop. It was created for hosting very large tables, making it a great choice to store multi-structured or sparse data. Users can query HBase for a particular point in time, making "flashback" queries possible. The following characteristics make HBase a great choice for storing semi-structured data like log data and then providing that data very quickly to users or applications integrated with HBase.

Apache Accumulo was originally developed at the National Security Agency before it was contributed to the Apache Software Foundation as an open-source incubation project. Because of its origins in the intelligence community, Accumulo provides extremely fast access to data in massive tables, while also controlling access to its billions of rows and millions of columns down to the individual cell. This is known as fine-grained data access control. Cell-level access control is important for organisations with complex policies governing who is allowed to see data. It enables the intermingling of different data sets with access control policies for fine-grained access to data sets that have some sensitive elements. Those with permission to see sensitive data can work alongside co-workers without those privileges. Both users can access data in accordance with their permissions. Without Accumulo, those policies are difficult to enforce systematically, but Accumulo encodes those rules for each individual data cell and controls fine-grained access.

4.19   DATA ANALYSIS

Hadoop offers two main tools for data manipulation, MapReduce and Spark. They have been extended with data analysis libraries (i.e. Mahout and MlLib respectively) to perform complex analysis tasks. Moreover, R (one of the most popular open source data analysis tools) can be easily integrated in Hadoop, including sophisticated extension like SparkR (see Appendix 1.5 for more details). H2O is a powerful ML library which can be connected to Hadoop or used alongside it. Finally, search capabilities are achieved by using Apache Solr.

Mahout is one of the more well-known tools for ML. It is known for having a wide selection of robust algorithms, but with inefficient runtimes due to the slow MapReduce engine. In April 2015, Mahout 0.9 was updated to 0.10.0, marking of a shift in the project's goals. With this release, the focus is now on a math environment called Samsara, which includes linear algebra, statistical operations, and data structures. The goal of the Mahout-Samsara project is to help users build their own distributed algorithms, rather than simply a library of Data/Information Management System architecture designs with already-written implementations. They still offer a comprehensive suite of algorithms for MapReduce. One problem with using Mahout in production is that development has moved very slowly; version 0.10.0 was released nearly seven and a half years after the project was initially introduced. The number of active committers is very low, with only a handful of developers making regular commits. The algorithms included in Mahout focus primarily on classification, clustering, and collaborative filtering and have been shown to scale well as the size of the data increases. Additional tools include topic modelling, dimensionality reduction, text vectorisation, similarity measures, a math library, and more. One of Mahout's most commonly cited assets is its extensibility, and many have achieved good results by building from the baseline algorithms. However, to take advantage of this flexibility, strong proficiency in Java programming is required. Some researchers have cited difficulty with configuration or with integration into an existing environment. Nonetheless, several companies have reported success using Mahout in production. Notable examples include Mendeley, LinkedIn, and Overstock.com, which all use its recommendation tools as part of their big data ecosystems. Overstock even replaced a commercial system with it, saving a significant amount of money in the process.

MLlib covers the same range of learning categories as Mahout and adds regression models, which Mahout lacks. It also has algorithms for topic modelling and frequent pattern mining. Additional tools include dimensionality reduction, feature extraction and transformation, optimisation, and basic statistics. In general, MLlib's reliance on Spark's iterative batch and streaming approaches, as well as its use of in-memory computation, enables jobs to run significantly faster than those using

Mahout However, the fact that it is tied to Spark may present a problem for those who perform ML on multiple platforms. MLlib is still relatively young compared to Mahout. As such, there is not yet an abundance of published case studies that have used this library, and there is very little research providing meaningful evaluation. The existing research indicates it is considered a relatively easy library to set up and run, helped in large part by the fact that it ships as part of its processing engine, thus avoiding some of the configuration issues people have reported with Mahout. There have been questions raised about the performance and reliability of its algorithms, and more research needs to be done in this area. Efficiency issues have also been noted due to slow convergence requiring a large number of iterations, as well as high communication costs. Some studies have discussed problems in how the implemented tools handle less-than-ideal data such as very low or very high dimensional vectors. The documentation is thorough, but the user community is not nearly as active as the community developing for it. This issue is expected to improve, as more people are migrating from MapReduce to Spark. The large and active group of developers means that many complaints are fixed before they are even published. Notable examples of companies that use MLlib in production are OpenTable and Spotify, both for their recommendation engines.

H2O is the only one that can be considered a product, rather than a project. While it offers an enterprise edition with two tiers of support, nearly all of offerings are available open source as well and can be used without the purchase of a license. The most notable features of this product are that it provides a GUI, and numerous tools for deep neural networks. DL has shown enormous promise for many areas of ML, making it an important feature of H2O. There is another company offering open-source implementations for DL, Deeplearning4j, but it is targeted towards business instead of research, whereas H2O targets both. In addition, Deeplearning4j's singular focus is on DL, so it does not offer any of the other types of ML tools that are in H2O's library. There are also other options for tools with a GUI, such as Weka, KNIME, or RapidMiner, but none of them offers a comprehensive open-source ML toolkit that is suitable for Big Data. Programming in H2O is possible with Java, Python, R and Scala. Users without programming expertise can still utilise this tool through the web-based UI. Because H2O comes as a package with many of the configurations already tuned, setup is easy, requiring less of a learning curve than most other free options. While H2O maintains its own processing engine, it also offers integrations that allow the use of its models on Spark and Storm. As of May 2015, the ML tools offered cover a range of tasks, including classification, clustering, generalised linear models, statistical analysis, ensembles, optimisation tools, data pre-processing options, and deep neural networks. On its roadmap for future implementation are additional algorithms and tools from these categories, as well as recommendation and time-series. In addition, it offers seamless integration with R and R Studio, as well as Sparkling Water for integration with Spark and MLlib. An integration with Mahout is currently in the works as well. It offers thorough documentation, and staff are very communicative, quickly answering questions in their user group and around the web. More independent research is needed to properly evaluate the speed, performance, and reliability of this tool. One notable example of a company using H2O in production is Share, which uses predictive modelling to maximise advertising return on investment (ROI).

Apache Solr: Hadoop operators put documents in Apache Solr by "indexing" through XML, JSON, CSV, or binary over HTTP. Then users can query those petabytes of data through HTTP GET. They can receive XML, JSON, CSV or binary results. Apache Solr is optimised for high-volume web traffic. Top features include advanced full-text search, near real-time indexing, standards-based open interfaces like XML, JSON and HTTP, comprehensive HTML administration interfaces, server statistics exposed over JMX for monitoring, kinearly scalable, auto index replication, auto failover and recovery, flexible and adaptable, with XML configuration. Solr is highly reliable, scalable, and fault-tolerant. Both data analysts and developers in the open-source community trust Solr's distributed indexing, replication and load-balanced querying capabilities.

4.20   BID DATA FILE SYSTEM

4.20.1   QUANTCAST FILE SYSTEM

Quantcast File System has been developed by Quantcast, and it represents an alternative to the HDFS for large-scale batch data processing. It is a production-hardened, open-source distributed file system, fully integrated with Hadoop and delivering significantly improved performance while consuming 50% less disk space. A key feature of this distributed file system is Reed-Solomon (RS) error correction to deal with data replication and fault tolerance, which are extremely important functionalities on large clusters where unreachable machines and dead disk drives are the rule rather than the exception.

HDFS expands data three times to implement, while QFS uses only half the disk space by leveraging the same error correction technique CDs and DVDs do, providing better recovery power with only a 1.5 times expansion. Moreover, QFS provides higher write throughput thanks to leaner data encoding, which not only saves disk space but also means less data to write. In other words, every job on QFS writes only half as much physical data, so that jobs can complete faster, and more can run at the same time. Furthermore, QFS reads data from (or writes data to) drives in large, sequential bursts. In contrast, normal file I/O APIs permit the operating system to buffer data and swap disk time between different processes, which breaks up big, efficient bursts into small, inefficient ones. QFS uses low-level APIs that give it more control to ensure that disk access stays optimal. In addition, QFS is implemented in C++ so it can carefully manage its own memory within a fixed footprint, leading to fast operations with no interrupts for garbage collection. QFS's memory management helps keep performance high and administration simple. Finally, QFS provides high reliability tested in a suitably demanding environment by Quantcast, which operates daily over about 20 petabytes of data.

Ceph is an open-source distributed object store and file system designed to provide excellent performance, reliability and scalability. Red Hat provides its own non-free version of this file system, rebranded as Red Hat Ceph Storage. Ceph includes interfaces for object-, block- and file-level storage. Ceph delivers extraordinary scalability allowing thousands of clients accessing petabytes to exabytes of data. A Ceph node leverages commodity hardware and intelligent daemons, and a Ceph storage cluster accommodates large numbers of nodes, which communicate with each other to replicate and redistribute data dynamically. Ceph implements data replication and fault tolerance following a self-healing and self-managing design, to minimise administration time and other costs. Ceph does not include some important repair tools (e.g. disaster recovery tools), so it is not recommended for storing mission-critical data. Ceph stripes individual files across multiple nodes to achieve higher throughput. Adaptive load balancing is supported whereby frequently accessed objects are replicated over more nodes. Ceph implements distributed object storage. Its software libraries provide client applications with direct access to the Reliable Autonomic Distributed Object Store (RADOS) object-based storage system and provide a foundation for some of Ceph's features, including RADOS Block Device (RBD), RADOS Gateway, and the Ceph File System. Moreover, software libraries provide interfaces for several programming languages, such as C, C++, Java, PHP, and Python. The RADOS Gateway also exposes the object store as a RESTful interface, exploited by famous cloud computing services such as Amazon S3 and OpenStack Swift. Ceph's RBD integrates with Kernel-based Virtual Machines (KVMs). Ceph's file system (CephFS) runs on top of the same object storage system that provides object storage and block device interfaces. The Ceph metadata server cluster provides a service that maps the directories and file names of the file system to objects stored within RADOS clusters. The metadata server cluster can expand or contract, and it can rebalance the file system dynamically to distribute data evenly among cluster hosts. This ensures high performance and prevents heavy loads on specific hosts within the cluster.

4.20.2 HADOOP DISTRIBUTED FILE SYSTEM

The HDFS is one of many different components and projects contained within the community Hadoop ecosystem. The Apache Hadoop project defines HDFS as the primary storage system used by Hadoop applications. It is an open-source distributed file system designed to run on commodity hardware. Although it has many similarities with existing DFS, the differences are significant. HDFS is highly fault-tolerant and is designed to be deployed on low-cost hardware, provides high throughput access to application data, and is suitable for applications that have large data sets. HDFS relaxes a few POSIX requirements to enable streaming access to file system data. It is designed to address hardware failures by providing data duplication and fault-tolerance mechanisms. Since it is designed more for batch processing than for interactive use, it allows for streaming data access, emphasising high throughput of data access rather than low latency of data access.

HDFS is tuned to support large files from gigabytes to terabytes in size. It provides high aggregate data bandwidth, scales to hundreds of nodes in a single cluster, and supports tens of millions of files in a single instance. HDFS implements a write-once-read-many access model for files, which means that a file once created, written, and closed cannot be changed. This assumption simplifies data coherency issues and enables high throughput data access. Moreover, HDFS is built on the assumption that it is often better to migrate the computation closer to where the data are located than to move the data to where the application is running; this is especially true when the data set is huge. Consequently, HDFS provides interfaces for applications to move themselves closer to where the data are located, minimising network congestion and increasing the overall throughput of the system.

Hadoop and HDFS utilise a master-slave architecture. HDFS is written in Java, with an HDFS cluster consisting of a primary NameNode – a master server that manages the file system namespace and regulates access to data by clients (an optional secondary NameNode for failover purposes also may be configured). In addition, a number of DataNodes manage the storage attached to the boxes that they run on. File blocks are divided up across a set of DataNodes. The NameNode is responsible for tasks such as opening, renaming, and closing files and data directories. It also tackles the job of mapping blocks to DataNodes, which are then responsible for managing incoming I/O requests from clients. The DataNode handles block replication, creation, and removal of data when instructed to do so by the NameNode.

4.20.3 CASSANDRA FILE SYSTEM (CFS)

The Cassandra File System (CFS) was designed by DataStax Corporation to run analytics on Cassandra easily. Cassandra is a massively scalable, no single point of failure, real-time high-performance NoSQL database. CFS provides the storage foundation that makes running Hadoop-styled analytics on Cassandra data hassle-free. In contrast to a master-slave architecture like HDFS, CFS is based on a peer-to-peer distributed "ring" architecture that is elegant, easy to set up, and easy to maintain. All nodes are the same: there is no concept of a master node, with all nodes communicating with each other through a gossip protocol. A user is able to create a cluster that seamlessly stores real-time data in Cassandra, performs analytic operations on that same data, and handles enterprise search operations. Cassandra's built-in replication transparently takes care of replicating the data among all real-time, analytic, and search nodes. CFS stores metadata information regarding analytics data in a Cassandra keyspace, which is analogous to a database in the RDBMS world. Two Cassandra column families (like tables in an RDBMS) in the keyspace contain the actual data, namely inode and sblocks column families. The data contained in these column families are replicated across the cluster to ensure data protection and fault tolerance. CFS implements the Hadoop File System API so it is compatible with the Hadoop stack and third-party tools. CFS is distributed together with Cassandra-distributed DBMS, consequently sharing its open-source nature.

4.20.4 GLUSTERFS

GlusterFS is an open, software-defined scale-out storage platform to easily manage unstructured data for physical, virtual, and cloud environments. GlusterFS combines both file storage and object storage with a scale-out architecture, designed to cost-effectively store and manage petabyte-scale data growth. Red Hat provides its own non-free version of this file system, rebranded as Red Hat Gluster Storage.

GlusterFS is used for storing various kinds of unstructured data including multimedia files (images, videos, and audio files), backup and virtual machine images, Nearline archives, and text files (log files, RFID data, and other machine-generated data). It is optimised for storage-intensive workloads such as archiving and backup, rich media content delivery, enterprise drop-box, cloud and business applications, and virtual and cloud infrastructure storage, as well as emerging workloads such as co-resident applications and Big Data Hadoop workloads. Gluster file system supports different types of volumes based on the requirements (storage size, performance etc.), consequently supporting data distribution, replication, and striping.

GlusterFS architecture does not include a centralised metadata server. It incorporates automatic failover as a primary feature, and it is designed to work seamlessly with industry standard x86 commodity servers. GlusterFS eliminates storage silos by enabling global access to data through multiple file and object protocols. Indeed, Gluster data can be accessed with a range of technologies such as traditional NFS, SMB/CIFS for Windows clients, or the native GlusterFS client. GlusterFS aggregates various storage servers over Ethernet or Infiniband RDMA interconnect into one large parallel NFS. Finally, Gluster allows rapid provisioning of additional storage based on storage consumption needs. Its storage capacity can be easily expanded by adding data nodes to the distributed system.

4.20.5 LUSTRE

Lustre is an open source, parallel file system that supports many requirements of leadership class HPC simulation environments. It provides high performance and is designed for larger network and high-availability environments. Lustre provides a POSIX compliant interface and scales to thousands of clients and petabytes of storage and has demonstrated over a terabyte per second of sustained I/O bandwidth. Many of the largest and most powerful supercomputers on Earth today are powered by the Lustre file system. Traditionally, Lustre is configured to manage remote data storage disk devices within a Storage Area Network (SAN), which is two or more remotely attached disk devices communicating through a Small Computer System Interface (SCSI) protocol. This includes Fibre Channel, Fibre Channel over Ethernet (FCoE), Serial Attached SCSI (SAS) and even iSCSI.

Lustre provides a unique scale-out architecture where metadata services and storage are segregated from data services and storage, with three major functional units. First, a single Metadata Server (MDS) contains a single Metadata Target (MDT) for each Lustre file system. This stores namespace metadata, which includes filenames, directories, access permissions, and file layout. The MDT data are stored in a single disk file system mapped locally to the serving node. Second, Object Storage Servers (OSSes) store file data on Object Storage Targets (OST). An OST is a dedicated object-based file system exported for read/write operations. The capacity of a Lustre file system is determined by the sum of the total capacities of the OSTs. Third, the architecture comprehends clients that access the file data. In a typical Lustre installation on a Linux client, a Lustre file system driver module is loaded into the kernel, and the file system is mounted like any other local or network file system. Client applications see a single, unified file system even though it may be composed of tens to thousands of individual servers and MDT/OST file systems.

The Lustre file system uses inodes on MDTs to store basic information about each file, pointing to one or more OST objects associated with the file rather than to data blocks. These objects are implemented as files on the OSTs. When a client opens a file, the file open operation transfers a set of object pointers and their layout from the MDS to the client, so that the client can directly interact with the OSS node where the object is stored. This allows the client to perform I/O in parallel across all of the OST objects in the file without further communication with the MDS. When more than one object is associated with a file, data in the file is "striped" across the objects. Striping a file over multiple OST objects provides significant performance benefits if there is a need for high bandwidth access to a single large file. Capacity and aggregate I/O bandwidth scale with the number of OSTs over which a file is striped. Each file in the file system can have a different striping layout, so that performance and capacity can be tuned optimally for each file. Finally, the Lustre distributed lock manager (LDLM) protects the integrity of each file's data and metadata. Access and modification of a Lustre file is completely cache coherent among all of the clients.

4.20.6 PARALLEL VIRTUAL FILE SYSTEM

The Parallel Virtual File System (PVFS) is an open-source parallel file system. It distributes file data across multiple servers and provides for concurrent access by multiple tasks of a parallel application. PVFS was designed for use in large-scale cluster computing, so that it focuses on high performance access to large data sets. It consists of a server process and a client library, both of which are written entirely of user-level code. A Linux kernel module and pvfs-client process allow the file system to be mounted and used with standard utilities. The client library provides for high-performance access through the Message Passing Interface (MPI). PVFS is being jointly developed between The Parallel Architecture Research Laboratory at Clemson University and the Mathematics and Computer Science Division at Argonne National Laboratory, and the Ohio Supercomputer Center. PVFS includes several features, such as performance, reliability, optimised MPI-IO support, hardware independence, easy deployment, object-based design, separation between data and metadata, stateless (lockless) servers, user-level implementation and system-level interface.

4.20.7 ORANGE FILE SYSTEM (ORANGEFS)

Orange File System (OrangeFS) is a branch of PVFS. It is an open-source parallel file system designed for use in High-End Computing (HEC) that provides very high-performance access to disk storage for parallel applications. OrangeFS differs from PVFS in some features developed by following inputs from users with specific needs. While PVFS development tends to focus on specific very large systems, Orange considers a number of areas that have not been well supported by PVFS in the past, especially related to metadata operations, small and unaligned accesses, cross-server redundancy, and secure access control.

4.20.8 BEEGFS

BeeGFS was developed at the Fraunhofer Institute for industrial mathematics (ITWM). It was originally released as FhGFS but was newly labelled as BeeGFS in 2014. BeeGFS is an open-source easy-to-use NFS that allows clients to communicate with storage servers through network (Ethernet, InfiniBand, etc.). BeeGFS is also a parallel file system, which means that by adding more servers, the capacity and performance of them are aggregated in a single namespace. In this way, the file system performance and capacity can be scaled to the level that is required for the specific application. BeeGFS is targeted at everyone, who has a need for large and/or fast storage. Traditional fields are High-Performance and HPC/HTC) as well as for storage of (large and growing) research data. First, BeeGFS separates metadata from object data, which means that the moment a client obtains the metadata for a specific file or directory, it can talk directly to the ObjectDataServers to retrieve the information, so that there is no further involvement of the MetaDataServer (unless metadata has to be changed). It is important to underline that the number of ObjectStorageServers as well as the number of MetaDataServers can be both scaled. Moreover, BeeGFS is a Linux-based file system, which means that all parts (clients, servers) run under Linux operating systems. It supports a wide range of Linux distributions (such as RHEL/Fedora, SLES/OpenSuse or Debian/Ubuntu) as well as a wide range of Linux kernels. The storage servers run on top of an existing local file system using the normal POSIX interface, while clients and servers can be added to an existing system without downtime. Furthermore, BeeGFS supports multiple networks and dynamic failover in case one of the network connections is down. Furthermore, it provides best-in-class client throughput (3.5 GB/s write and 4.0 GB/s read with a single I/O stream on FDR InfiniBand), metadata performance (linear scalability through dynamic metadata namespace partitioning) and storage throughput (flexibility over underlying file system to perfectly fit the given storage hardware). Finally, it supports distributed file contents with flexible striping across the storage servers on a by file or by directory base as well as distributed metadata.

4.20.9   MapR-FS

MapR-FS is a random read-write distributed file system that represents a unified data solution for structured data (tables) and unstructured data (files). It allows applications to concurrently read and write directly to disk, while HDFS has append-only writes and can only read from closed files. In other words, an application can write, append, or update more than once in MapR-FS, and can read a file as it is being written. With HDFS, an application can only write once, and the application cannot read a file as it is written. Since HDFS is layered over the existing Linux file system, a greater number of input/output (I/O) operations decrease the cluster's performance. MapR-FS also eliminates the Namenode associated with cluster failure in other Hadoop distributions and enables special features for data management and high availability. The storage system architecture used by MapR-FS is written in C/C++ and prevents locking contention, eliminating performance impact from Java garbage collection. In MapRFS, files are divided into chunks, chunks are assigned to containers and containers are written to storage pools. Indeed, MapR-FS storage architecture consists of multiple storage pools made up of several disks grouped together. The containers that hold MapR-FS data are stored in and replicated among the storage pools in the cluster, so RAID configurations are unnecessary. Moreover, write operations within a storage pool are striped with configurable width and depth across disks to improve write performance. Containers are abstract entities that contain data with the average size of 10–30 GB (the default is 32 GB). Each storage pool can store many containers. Moreover, MapR-FS implements a peer-to-peer architecture in order to manage file system metadata rather that a master-slave one with Namenodes like HDFS. In this way, MapR-FS can store an unlimited number of files at a much lower cost because of less hardware in the cluster compared to HDFS where you require multiple NameNodes to deal with the file limit at scale. Finally, MapR-FS includes a direct access feature that enables RT read/write data flows using the NFS protocol, which also enables direct file modification and multiple concurrent reads and writes with POSIX semantics.

4.20.9.1   Kudu

Kudu is an open-source storage engine for structured data that supports low-latency random access together with efficient analytical access patterns. It distributes data using horizontal partitioning and replicates each partition using Raft consensus, providing low mean-time-torecovery and low tail latencies. Kudu is designed within the Apache Hadoop ecosystem aiming at filling gaps in Hadoop's storage layer that have given rise to stitched-together, hybrid architectures, and contemporarily supporting many integrations with other data analytics projects both inside and outside of the ASF. The project has been recently incubated by the ASF, and currently it is featuring only a beta release. From the architectural point of view, Kudu internally organises its data by column rather than row, allowing for efficient encoding and compression. To scale out to large data sets and large clusters, Kudu splits tables into smaller units called tablets. This splitting can be configured on a per-table basis to be based on hashing, range partitioning, or a combination thereof. Moreover, Kudu uses the Raft consensus algorithm to replicate all operations for a given tablet, ensuring high availability and fault tolerance. Kudu's storage is designed to take advantage of the IO characteristics of solid-state drives, and it includes an experimental cache implementation based on the libpmem library, which can store data in persistent memory. Finally, Kudu is implemented in C++, so it can scale easily to large amounts of memory per node. In addition, because key storage data structures are designed to be highly concurrent, it can scale easily to tens of cores.

REFERENCES

Analytics8. (2021). *Four Types of Analytics and Their Differences, Analytics8*. https://www.analytics8. com/blog/what-are-the-four-types-of-analytics-and-how-do-you-use-them/

Bekker, A. (2018). 4 types of data analytics to improve decision-making. *Harvard Business School Online*, July 10. https://online.hbs.edu/blog/post/types-of-data-analysis

Berge, J. (2020). *(10) Prescriptive Maintenance (RxM) or Predictive Maintenance (PdM)?*. https://www.linkedin. com/pulse/prescriptive-maintenance-rxm-predictive-pdm-jonas-berge/

Berge, J., & Rais, A. (2021). *Prescriptive Maintenance: A Cure for Downtime*. https://www.process-worldwide. com/prescriptive-maintenance-a-cure-for-downtime-a-1021275/

Cote, C. (2021). *What Is Diagnostic Analytics? 4 Examples, HBS Online*. https://online.hbs.edu/blog/post/ diagnostic-analytics

DataAnalyticsWiki. (2022). *Predictive Maintenance Analytics – Data Analytics Website*. https:// dataanalyticswiki.com/predictive-analytics/predictive-maintenance-analytics/

Dhar, V., & Tuzhilin, A. (1992). Abstract-driven pattern discovery in databases. Center for Research on Information Systems. https://archive.nyu.edu/bitstream/2451/14327/1/IS-92-11.pdf

Fayyad, U., Piatetsky-Shapiro, G., & Smyth, P. (1996). From data mining to knowledge discovery in databases. *AI Magazine*, *17*(3), 37–54. http://www.aaai.org/ojs/index.php/aimagazine/article/viewArticle/1230

Flammini, F., Pragliola, C., & Smarra, G. (2017). Railway infrastructure monitoring by drones. *2016 International Conference on Electrical Systems for Aircraft, Railway, Ship Propulsion and Road Vehicles and International Transportation Electrification Conference, ESARS-ITEC 2016*, 1–6. https://doi.org/10.1109/ ESARS-ITEC.2016.7841398

Galar, D., & Kans, M. (2017). The impact of maintenance 4.0 and big data analytics within strategic asset management. In D. Galar & D. Seneviratne (Eds.), *Maintenance Performance and Measurement and Management conference proceedings,* (pp. 96–104). Lulea University of Technology. http://www.diva-portal.org/smash/get/diva2:1083352/FULLTEXT01.pdf

Galar, D., Thaduri, A., Kumar, U., & Pascual, R. (2016). SMART maintenance and prescriptive asset management for mining. Paper presented at *Mine Planning and Equipment Selection: 08/11/2015-13/11/2015*. http://urn.kb.se/resolve?urn=urn:nbn:se:ltu:diva-39497

Galar, D., Wandt, K., Karim, R., & Berges, L. (2012). The evolution from e(lectronic) maintenance to i(ntelligent) maintenance. *Non-Destructive Testing and Condition Monitoring*, *54*(8), 446-455. https:// doi.org/10.1784/insi.2012.54.8.446

Gandomi, A., & Haider, M. (2015). Beyond the hype: Big data concepts, methods, and analytics. *International Journal of Information Management*, *35*, 137–144. https://doi.org/10.1016/j.ijinfomgt.2014.10.007

Hall, D., & Llinas, J. (2001). *Multisensor data fusion*. CRC Press.

Harger, J., & Crossno, P. J. (2012). Comparison of open-source visual analytics toolkits. *Society of Photo-Optical Instrumentation Engineers (SPIE) Proceedings*, *8294*(24), 133–142. https://doi.org/10.1117/12.911901

IEC-IEV. (2022). *IEC 60050- International Electrotechnical Vocabulary – Welcome*. https://www.electropedia. org/

InsightSoftware. (2021). *Comparing Descriptive, Predictive, Prescriptive, and Diagnostic Analytics – Insightsoftware*. https://insightsoftware.com/blog/comparing-descriptive-predictive-prescriptive-and-diagnostic-analytics/

Karim, R., Westerberg, J., Galar, D., & Kumar, U. (2016). Maintenance analytics: The new know in maintenance. *IFAC-PapersOnLine*, *49*(28), 214–219. https://doi.org/10.1016/j.ifacol.2016.11.037

Lawton, G. (2022). *What is Descriptive Analytics? Definition from WhatIs.com*. https://www.techtarget.com/ whatis/definition/descriptive-analytics

Lee, C. K. M., Cao, Y., & Ng, K. H. (2017). Big data analytics for predictive maintenance strategies. In *Supply Chain Management in the Big Data Era* (pp. 50–74). IGI Global.

Liu, D. R., & Ke, C. K. (2007). Knowledge support for problem-solving in a production process: A hybrid of knowledge discovery and case-based reasoning. *Expert Systems with Applications*, *33*(1), 147–161. https://doi.org/10.1016/j.eswa.2006.04.026

Logibility. (2019). Descriptive, predictive, and prescriptive analytics explained. Blog. https://www.logility.com/blog/descriptive-predictive-and-prescriptive-analytics-explained/

Lomotey, R. K., & Deters, R. (2014). Towards knowledge discovery in big data. *Proceedings - IEEE 8th International Symposium on Service Oriented System Engineering, SOSE 2014*, 181–191. https://doi.org/10.1109/SOSE.2014.25

Peleg, L. A. (2021). *Advanced Analytics vs. Predictive Analytics vs. Descriptive Analytics - Precognize*. https://www.precog.co/blog/advanced-vs-predictive-vs-descriptive-analytics/

ProjectPro. (2022). *Types of Analytics:Descriptive, Predictive, Prescriptive Analytics*. https://www.projectpro.io/article/types-of-analytics-descriptive-predictive-prescriptive-analytics/209

Rice, R., & Bontatibus, R. (2021). *Predictive Maintenance Embraces Analytics*. https://blog.isa.org/predictive-maintenance-embraces-analytics

Russom, P. (2011). TDWI best practices report. *Fourth Quarter*, *19*(4), 1–34.

Sagiroglu, S., & Sinanc, D. (2013). Big data: a review. *2013 International Conference on Collaboration Technologies and Systems (CTS)*, 42–47. https://doi.org/10.1109/CTS.2013.6567202

Strong, D. M., Lee, Y. W., & Wang, R. Y. (1997). Data quality in context. *Communications of the ACM*, *40*(5), 103–110.

Tucci, L. (2022). *What is Predictive Analytics? An Enterprise Guide*. https://www.techtarget.com/searchbusinessanalytics/definition/predictive-analytics?_gl=1*1c1mmdo*_ga*NzU5NTg3MjU2LjE2ND I5MzcwMDQ.*_ga_TQKE4GS5P9*MTY0Mjk0NzYyMi4yLjEuMTY0Mjk0ODk0MS4w

UNSW. (2020). *Descriptive, Predictive, Prescriptive Analytics UNSW Online*. https://studyonline.unsw.edu.au/blog/descriptive-predictive-prescriptive-analytics

Yafaa, a. (2018). *(10) 4 TYpes of Data Analytics to Improve Decision-Making: A Three-Minute Guide*. https://www.linkedin.com/pulse/4-types-data-analytics-improve-decision-making-guide-yafaa-ahres/

Zhang, L., & Karim, R. (2014). Big data mining in eMaintenance: An overview. *International Workshop and Congress on EMaintenance: 17/06/2014–18/06/2014*, 159–170. https://www.diva-portal.org/smash/get/diva2:1009104/FULLTEXT01.pdf

Zhang, L., Lin, J., & Karim, R. (2017). Sliding window-based fault detection from high-dimensional data streams. *IEEE Transactions on Systems, Man, and Cybernetics: Systems*, *47*(2), 289–303. https://doi.org/10.1109/TSMC.2016.2585566

Zikopoulos, P., & Eaton, C. (2011). *Understanding Big Data: Analytics for Enterprise Class Hadoop and Streaming Data*. McGraw-Hill Osborne Media.

5 Data-Driven Decision-Making

5.1 DATA FOR DECISION-MAKING

Data are the source for generating the information and knowledge needed to make proper operational and strategic maintenance management decisions. Maintenance data comprise:

1. Data collected during the execution of preventive maintenance (PM) and condition monitoring (CM).
2. Various kinds of supplementary data (e.g. age of machines, spare parts, waiting time, and travel time for repair and service).

Data analysis is the process of extracting information from the data collected for this purpose and can be either qualitative or quantitative.

Data represent a collection of realisations of a measurable quantity such as component failure times, component material property, load on the component etc. Information is extracted from data through analysis to understand possible relationships (such as cause and effect) between pieces of data.

Often data and information are used either interchangeably as synonyms or with only slight differences. Data are raw facts that have not been organised or cannot possibly be interpreted. Information is data that are understood. Knowledge is the ability of humans to understand the information and how it can be used in a specific context (such as prediction). It includes theories, models, tools and techniques, technical standards, and so forth (ITF, 2021).

When data are analysed using artificial intelligence (AI) technology, the data maturity level of the organisation has a significant impact on the reliability of the analytics services and achievement of overall business goals. Data maturity often refers to the capabilities of a data consumer, for example, an organisation, to utilise data produced by a data provider.

Four levels of data maturity are the following (Onis, 2016):

1. Data aware: manual compilation of non-standardised analysis.
2. Data proficient: data islands are available.
3. Data confident: data are used in critical decision-making processes.
4. Data-driven: no decision is made without data.

These phases of data maturity in an organisation reflect not only the technology maturity but also the business maturity in utilising data as an asset in the organisation's value-creating process (Karim et al., 2021).

5.1.1 DATA-DRIVEN DECISION-MAKING

Once gathered, data should be used wisely. Data-driven decision-making (DDDM) is defined as using data to facilitate strategic decisions that align with pre-set goals and objectives.

When organisations realise the full value of their data, better decisions will inevitably be the result. This requires the following:

- choosing the appropriate analytics technology;
- creating a culture that encourages critical thinking and curiosity;

DOI: 10.1201/9781003208686-5

- developing data skills through practice and application;
- making data accessible;
- maintaining proper security; and
- developing proficiency by creating training and development opportunities for employees to learn data skills.

Establishing these core capabilities will help encourage DDDM across all job levels (Tableau, 2022).

5.1.2   THE PROCESS OF DATA-DRIVEN DECISION-MAKING

Through the process of DDDM, data are used to assess, test, and improve a program, activity, or strategy. These activities occur in four iterative stages, as summarised in Figure 5.1 (Keating et al., 2018) and explained below.

1. Formulating key questions: The process begins with identifying and clarifying the key questions to be answered. These questions may address the need to solve a specific problem, learn more about a target population, or improve a program or organisational process.
2. Collecting and analysing data: Guided by the key questions, available data are identified and new data are collected as needed. Access to high-quality data is critical.
3. Communicating results to decision-makers: Results are shared with key decision-makers within and between levels of the organisation or broader service system. Dissemination may take place through various communication channels and formats depending on the information needs of stakeholders.
4. Refining processes, organisations, or systems: Decision-makers use information gathered during the previous stage to assess gaps in services, strengthen the performance of programs, organisations, or systems, and assess the impact of services on outcomes of interest. As more information is collected, the process continues in an iterative manner, with additional evidence producing new insights and subsequent questions for further data collection and analysis.

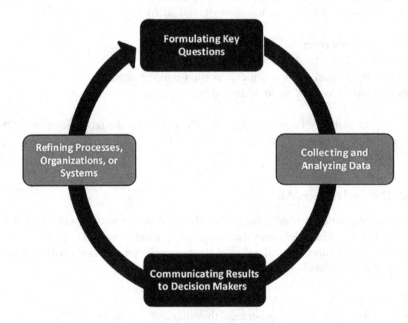

FIGURE 5.1   Stages of the data-driven decision-making process (Keating et al., 2018).

5.1.3 THE CONTEXT OF DATA-DRIVEN DECISION-MAKING

DDDM works at the program, organisation, or system level. It can be used to improve a single program activity or process, or it can be used to improve the functioning of an entire organisation or system (Keating et al., 2018).

1. Program: The least complex use of DDDM involves a single program activity or process. For example, data could be used to evaluate knowledge gains from staff.
2. Organisation: The next level of DDDM addresses the overall functioning of an organisation.
3. System: The highest level of DDDM supports coordinated decisions across organisations and systems. It requires integrated data systems that include information from multiple organisations, often in the interests of effecting collective impact on a common problem or need.

5.1.4 THE IMPORTANCE OF DATA-DRIVEN DECISION-MAKING

We are in an era of Big Data. Not only are there enormous volumes of data – the data are also very complex, making it difficult for organisations to manage and analyse their data.

While many organisations would like to capitalise on DDDM, it can be difficult to do so. For example, the emphasis may be wrong: an organisation may prioritise the acquisition of cutting-edge technology but then can't use it appropriately.

Becoming data-driven requires three core capabilities:

- data proficiency,
- analytics agility, and
- data community or culture.

Incorporating data and analytics into decision-making cycles while continuing to improve and refine analytics will ultimately have a transformative impact (Tableau, 2022).

5.1.5 COMMON CHALLENGES OF DATA-DRIVEN DECISION-MAKING

Although DDDM has great promise, there are a number of challenges for organisations to overcome before they reap the benefits (ParadoxMarketing, 2022).

5.1.5.1 A Lack of Infrastructure and Tools

Gathering data can be a challenge without the right infrastructure and tools. Organisations must develop a system to collect, gather, and organise their data in one centralised location. A good example in the maintenance context is a computerised maintenance management system (CMMS). The next requirements are tools to analyse and visualise data so they will be useful (ParadoxMarketing, 2022).

5.1.5.2 Poor Quality Data

Data are frequently of poor quality, making them difficult to analyse. Issues include duplications, inaccuracies, lack of consistency, and incompleteness. These all affect the quality of data. Out-of-date and obsolete data are problematic, as are inaccurate or irrelevant data (ParadoxMarketing, 2022).

5.1.5.3 Siloed Data

A silo generally refers to a certain unit working on its own with no knowledge of other units. Siloed data happen when different data sources aren't properly integrated. For example, the maintenance department may need access to data from another department. To avoid silos, everyone in an organisation should have access to the same data (Paradox Marketing, 2022).

5.1.5.4   A Lack of Buy-In

Not everyone likes change. Some people, for example, may prefer to make decisions based on experience. When people don't buy-in to DDDM, they may not enter the data required to analyse the full scenario, or they may not use the available data. Convincing everyone of the value of change is the key to effectiveness (ParadoxMarketing, 2022).

5.1.5.5   Not Knowing How to Use Data

An organisation may have accurate and plentiful data – but not know what to do with it. Thus, the data cannot be leveraged to make key decisions. Not knowing what to do with the data or what actions to take based on the analytics defeats the whole purpose of DDDM (ParadoxMarketing, 2022).

5.1.5.6   Being Unable to Identify Actionable Data

It is essential to determine which data will be useful. The data must match the key decisions to be made (ParadoxMarketing, 2022).

5.1.5.7   Too Much Focus on Data

In some cases, a human decision is needed, and focusing only on data can be counterproductive. A balance between data and creativity is needed for optimal results (ParadoxMarketing, 2022).

5.1.6   Data-Driven Decision-Making for Industry 4.0 Maintenance Applications

This section discusses how the nine pillars of Industry 4.0, shown in Figure 5.2, affect and converge with DDDM for maintenance. The nine pillars are augmented reality (AR), Internet of Things (IoT), system integration, cloud computing, Big Data analytics, cyber security, additive manufacturing, autonomous robots, and simulation (Bousdekis et al., 2021).

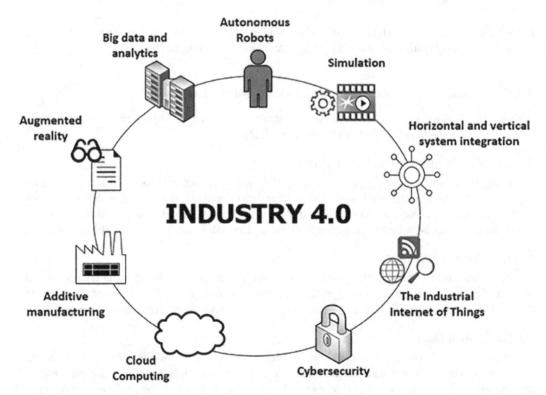

FIGURE 5.2   The nine pillars of Industry 4.0 (Bousdekis et al., 2021).

TABLE 5.1

Research Agenda of Data-Driven Decision-Making for Industry 4.0 Maintenance Applications (Bousdekis et al., 2021)

Industry 4.0 Pillars		Future Research Directions
Augmented Reality (AR)	1. 2.	Interfaces with decision-making algorithms for maintenance applications. Can be applied to shop floor during actual manufacturing operations.
Internet of Things (IOT)	1. 2. 3.	Supporting the autonomy of networked manufacturing systems and machines. Eliminating uncertainty to avoid implementing inappropriate autonomous maintenance actions. Fast learning from the shop floor, exploiting the large availability of data sources.
System integration	1. 2. 3. 4.	Horizontal and vertical integration according to Industry 4.0 principles. Effective interoperability taking into account RAMI 4.0, CPS architectures, and communication protocols. Decision-making algorithms take into account the whole context of the manufacturing enterprise. Humans are an integral part of system integration.
Cloud computing	1. 2. 3. 4.	Aligned with the concept of cloud manufacturing. Seamless and modular communication through cloud-based platforms. Communication protocols and standards for guiding the development of future algorithms. Addresses the challenges of reliability, availability, adaptability, and safety.
Big Data analytics	1. 2. 3. 4.	Maintenance decision-making can benefit from prescriptive analytics for Big Data. Automated data-driven model building to represent the decision-making process instead of the physical process. Efficient algorithms for processing streams of failure predictions and providing meaningful insights. Human feedback mechanisms for improving the decision-making algorithms.
Cyber security	1. 2.	Encryption techniques, risk assessment methodologies, and cyber-attack detection and response methods. Modular integration of decision-making software services in a secure and reliable way.
Additive manufacturing	1.	Decision-making algorithms for manufacturing processes in the context of additive manufacturing.
Autonomous robots	1. 2. 3. 4.	Consider robots as production resources in decision-making algorithms. Assign appropriate maintenance tasks to robots Decide which tasks will be assigned to robots and which ones to humans. Uncertainty of decision-making is a significant challenge in automatic action implementation through autonomous robots.
Simulation	1. 2. 3.	Approaches for digital twins (DTs) in predictive maintenance. Decision-making algorithms for enhancing the capabilities of DTs, eg. by evaluating different scenarios. Information fusion methods incorporated in decision-making algorithms for fully exploiting the available data and knowledge.

Table 5.1 shows where research is being done to advance DDDM in maintenance, looking at each of the nine pillars of Industry 4.0 in turn (Bousdekis et al., 2021).

The following sections discuss the Industry 4.0 pillars in the context of maintenance.

5.1.6.1 Augmented Reality

AR provides a seamless interface combining the real and virtual world aiming at enhancing the collaboration between humans and smart environments. With the advancement of portable devices' processing and visualisation capabilities, AR is evolving into an intuitive user interface for displaying information and interacting with machines and services in smart factories.

Although the potential of AR in maintenance operations has been outlined in the literature, its use as an advanced user interface with decision-making algorithms (e.g. recommending mitigating actions to implement and guiding maintenance personnel in how to implement them, eliminating the impact of a predicted failure) has not been investigated. AR has mostly been used for training purposes, and its application on the shop-floor during the actual manufacturing and maintenance operations remains a challenge (Bousdekis et al., 2021).

5.1.6.2   Internet of Things

IoT provides a dynamic global network infrastructure with self-configuring capabilities based on standard and interoperable communication protocols where physical and virtual "things" are interconnected and integrated into the information network.

In the manufacturing context, the value chain should be intelligent, agile, and networked by integrating physical objects, human factors, intelligent machines, smart sensors, the production process, and production lines. Since increasingly more physical objects are connected to the manufacturing network, and high-speed transactional data and information are generated, scalability is a major challenge in Industry 4.0.

The evolutionary process will lead to networked manufacturing systems with a high degree of autonomy, as well as self-optimisation capabilities. They will be organised in a decentralised manner, increasing robustness and adaptability. Therefore, the increasing availability of sensors and actuators will result in the need for decision-making algorithms capable of supporting the autonomy of networked manufacturing systems. However, the uncertainty in decision-making algorithms for maintenance increases the risk of implementing inappropriate autonomous maintenance actions. To this end, methods and techniques for eliminating uncertainty and ensuring fast learning from the shop-floor are extremely important (Bousdekis et al., 2021).

5.1.6.3   System Integration

System integration increases the value of a system by creating new functionalities through the combination of sub-systems and software applications. The paradigm of Industry 4.0 comprises three dimensions of integration:

1. horizontal integration across the entire value creation network,
2. vertical integration and networked manufacturing systems, and
3. end-to-end engineering across the entire product life cycle.

The full digital integration and automation of manufacturing processes in the vertical and horizontal dimensions also imply automation of communication and cooperation, especially along standardised processes.

Some research has considered joint scheduling and planning, thus attempting to integrate operational with maintenance decision-making in manufacturing processes. System integration aspects of decision-making algorithms in terms of interoperability, service communication, modularity, scalability, and flexibility are less studied.

Architectures that include decision-making functionalities for maintenance have started to emerge. Following the trend of diagnostic and prognostic algorithms, these decision-making algorithms need to be integrated horizontally and vertically according to Industry 4.0 principles. In this way, the algorithms will be able to consider the whole context of the environment (e.g. production plan, supply chain, and inventory) by communicating effectively and interchanging data and information with other manufacturing operations. RAMI 4.0 and Cyber Physical Systems (CPS) architectures are significant enablers towards this direction.

Finally, integration deals also with the human as an integral part of the manufacturing environment in the sense that there is a cognitive interaction between the human and the system. To this end, the Human Cyber Physical System (H-CPS) concept paves the way for the use of emerging technologies implementing human–machine symbiosis (Bousdekis et al., 2021).

5.1.6.4 Cloud Computing

The use of cloud-based architectures and technologies is strongly related to effective systems' integration, e.g. with the use of RESTful Application Programming Interfaces (APIs) for accessing services provided by cloud computing vendors. Cloud consumers use APIs as software interfaces to connect and consume resources in various ways, although the optimal or contemporary route is to use a RESTful protocol-based API. To this end, the services implementing DDDM functionalities should allow seamless and modular communication through cloud-based platforms. This direction must be developed in alignment with the concept of cloud manufacturing.

Cloud manufacturing is a smart networked manufacturing model that incorporates cloud computing. It aims at meeting the growing demands for broader global cooperation, knowledge-intensive innovation, and increased market-response agility. Apart from the technological perspective, this will lead to decision-making algorithms facilitating implementation in a cloud-based computational environment and to domain-specific communication protocols and standards for guiding the development of future algorithms requiring higher computational power.

This requires addressing the challenges of reliability, availability, adaptability, and safety on machines and processes across spatial boundaries and disparate data sources. In addition, privacy and security aspects of the cloud must be tackled. This calls for robust algorithms that can accurately support decision-making in the presence of uncertainty and methods to quantify their confidence in a real-time (RT) and computationally demanding environment (Bousdekis et al., 2021).

5.1.6.5 Big Data Analytics

The collection and processing of data from many different sources have significantly enabled the information that is available to engineers and operators in manufacturing facilities. Data management and distribution in the big data environment are critical for achieving self-aware and self-learning machines and for supporting manufacturing decisions.

Data analytics can be categorised into three main stages characterised by different levels of difficulty, value, and intelligence:

1. Descriptive analytics answers the questions: "What has happened?" and "Why did it happen?", along with "What is happening now?"
2. Predictive analytics answers the questions: "What will happen?" and "Why will it happen?"
3. Prescriptive analytics answers the questions: "What should I do?" and "Why should I do it?"

Although Big Data analytics has been extensively used for real-time diagnosis and prognosis in the context of predictive maintenance, its use in decision-making algorithms remains in the early stages. There has been more interest in descriptive and predictive analytics, so prescriptive analytics has not developed as far as it might. This has inevitably affected the predictive maintenance decision-making algorithms. The vast majority of the existing predictive maintenance decision-making algorithms rely on traditional mathematical programming methods. Prescriptive analytics has been realised mainly for domain-specific expert systems or optimisation models.

There is a need for data-driven generic decision-making algorithms representing the decision-making process instead of the physical process. Building physical models of industrial assets and processes is a complex and laborious task that does not necessary exploit the knowledge that can be discovered from data, such as failure patterns or patterns of causes and effects. Moreover, knowledge-based decision-making methods tend to be static, not capable of self-adaptation on the basis of emerging data. However, dynamic shop-floor conditions require RT decision-making, which requires both advanced data infrastructures, for example, distributed cloud computing for processing and storing data, and new functionalities, for example, computationally efficient, probabilistic algorithms tailored for streaming data and capable of handling uncertainty.

Finally, feedback mechanisms should be employed to adapt decision-making on the basis of changing conditions such as new operating constraints. Although feedback mechanisms for diagnostic and prognostic algorithms have been well received, there are a few mechanisms for tracking the recommended actions (Bousdekis et al., 2021).

5.1.6.6   Cyber Security

With the increased connectivity and use of standard communications protocols that come with Industry 4.0, the need to protect critical industrial systems and manufacturing lines from cyber security threats increases significantly. As a result, secure, reliable communications, as well as sophisticated identity and access management of machines and users on the basis of a cloud infrastructure, are essential.

Existing technologies may not be sufficient for industrial applications that have their own safety and security rules and requirements. With respect to decision-making algorithms for maintenance, these cybersecurity techniques and algorithms will enable the efficient and modular integration of decision-making software services with existing diagnostic and prognostic information systems in a secure and reliable way (Bousdekis et al., 2021).

5.1.6.7   Additive Manufacturing

Companies have just begun to adopt additive manufacturing such as 3D printing, mostly using it to prototype and produce individual components. As time goes on, additive manufacturing methods will be more widely used to produce faster and in a more cost-effective way small batches of customised products that offer construction advantages, such as complex, lightweight designs.

A maintenance solution should deal with the specific requirements of such products and their respective manufacturing processes. Decision-making algorithms in this context will deal with laser repairing processes, taking into account the contextual background of additive manufacturing (Bousdekis et al., 2021).

5.1.6.8   Autonomous Robots

Autonomous robots are beneficial for manufacturing processes, as they can facilitate production tasks that are difficult for humans to perform (e.g. lifting heavy tools), need high accuracy and flexibility, constitute boring routines, or even involve the need to access dangerous areas. However, the high automation of production processes poses new challenges in the execution of production tasks.

Autonomous robots constitute additional resources that need to be managed along with the manufacturing equipment and the personnel. Therefore, maintenance decision-making algorithms need to take into account the fact that certain maintenance actions may be implemented by autonomous robots, and this affects the scheduling of the maintenance tasks to be performed. These algorithms will assign the appropriate maintenance tasks to humans or robots according to the nature of the task, the knowledge of humans and robots, the trade-off between the efficiency of humans and the efficiency of robots for this particular task, the trade-off between the cost of executing the task by a robot or a human etc.

Another important factor is the uncertainty of the prognostic information and thus the suitability of the recommended predictive maintenance actions. Recommendations about maintenance actions with high uncertainty of suitability may be difficult to address automatically by robots that do not have the intelligence to understand the whole context and potential consequences of applying an inappropriate action. In contrast, humans can ignore the recommendations or react during their execution if they realise the actions are not suitable (Bousdekis et al., 2021).

5.1.6.9   Simulation

Simulation is a well-established approach in manufacturing environments for avoiding high costs and issues of reliability and safety when implementing new approaches on the shop floor. For example, decision-making algorithms for maintenance have utilised such methods for evaluating different scenarios of potential failures and mitigating or corrective actions.

This has changed with the arrival of Industry 4.0, characterised by the strong connection between the physical and the digital world in which natural and human-made systems (physical space) are tightly integrated with computation, communication, and control systems (cyberspace). This concept is termed cyber-physical systems (CPS).

In the context of Industry 4.0, simulation has reached the next frontier: digital twin (DT). A DT is a virtual representation of a physical object generated with digital data. It can be used to run simulations throughout the design, build, and operation life cycle. However, its aim is not just to digitally represent a physical counterpart.

DTs that address maintenance operations will need decision-making algorithms capable of generating various scenarios, along with their expected impact. To do this, they will need to incorporate information fusion methods to automatically or semi-automatically transform information from different sources and different points in time into a representation that provides effective support for human or automated decision-making. Such sources can be sensors, legacy systems, physical models, and expert knowledge. In this way, they will be able to exploit all the available information sources to construct scenarios and select the most appropriate ones according to the business objectives and constraints.

Generic approaches for incorporating decision-making algorithms in DTs addressing predictive maintenance aspects are a new area of research (Bousdekis et al., 2021).

5.1.7 Data-Driven Decision-Making Versus Intuition

Smart cities integrate and monitor critical infrastructure using smart computing to deliver core services to the public. The idea of smart cities is technological, but it also includes aspects such as governance and economy, among others. Each decision made by the different services or infrastructure in a city should be based on definitions of situations of normality. With these definitions, it is possible to detect non-normal situations. This is a key aspect for monitoring infrastructure and services. The goal is to prevent risk situations, or in the worst case scenario, detect them in real time.

Measurement and evaluation processes are critical for knowing the current state of each service or infrastructure in the city. That is to say, if we do not measure, we will not know the state of each element. This is critical for DDDM because each decision should be based on the current situation of different elements in the city.

Without data, decisions are often based on intuition, and intuition is subjective. Decision-making based on intuition could have a catastrophic social impact. For example, the city of Santa Rosa in Argentina uses pluviometry to measure the level of rainfall. This allows data to be gathered. However, it cannot monitor in RT the situations associated with rainfall across the city, for example, the volume of water circulating in the sewers. In March 2017, within a week, the city received a volume of water equivalent to one year's worth of rainfall. The consequences of the flooding are still being felt. Natural disasters cannot be prevented, but it is possible to monitor the infrastructure and services in the city and anticipate future scenarios. The monitoring of the infrastructures and services could improve the quality of life, anticipate disasters, and even save the lives of citizens (Divan, 2018).

5.2 DATA QUALITY

The quality of the data influences decision-making in maintenance and has an impact on the quality of the decisions in a data-driven approach. Poor data quality is characterised by incomplete data, missing data, and noisy data.

To improve data quality and support the decision-making process, the current status of data needs to be measured and evaluated before making any decisions based on the collected data.

Although data quality has been studied in different operational areas, few studies address the data quality assessment process (Aljumaili, 2016).

High-quality data are crucial to DDDM. The data must be accurate, complete, timely, and actionable:

1. Accurate: Tools for data collection should be grounded in the research literature with proven validity and reliability.
2. Complete: Data should be complete, well defined, and easily identified.
3. Timely: Data should be accessible and compatible across data systems so multiple users can readily view and use them.
4. Actionable: Data should be actionable so the desired outcomes can be achieved. Establish fidelity metrics to ensure that strategies are implemented as intended and to help identify the need for course corrections to improve implementation (Keating et al., 2018).

Quality is the degree to which a set of inherent characteristics fulfils requirements. Hence, data quality can be described as the degree to which a set of permanent characteristics in the data or dataset meet a data consumer's requirements or stated expectations. Furthermore, information can be described as meaningful data. Simultaneously, information quality can be described as the degree to which a set of permanent characteristics in the information fulfils a certain consumer's requirements or stated expectations.

For most contemporary organisations, quality management is well known and integrated into everyday work for improving the quality of a product or service. However, when it comes to the quality of the information that is produced and consumed, the focus is not that extensive. High-quality information depends on the quality of the raw data and the process through which they are processed. Without control of the data quality, there will be no control of the output (Aljumaili, 2016).

In general, there are two types of information sources: subjective and objective:

- Subjective sources include human observers, experts, and decision-makers. Information is normally based on subjective beliefs, hypotheses, and opinions about what they see or learn. Therefore, the quality of data differs from one person to another.
- Objective information sources include sensors, models, and automated processes. Information is free from biases inherent to human judgement but depends on how well the sensors are calibrated and how adequate the models are.

A study found that about 80% of the identified data quality problems in maintenance are related to subjective sources (Aljumaili, 2016).

Maintaining data at a high-quality level involves significant costs. These costs are associated with efforts to:

- detect and correct defects,
- set governance policies,
- redesign processes, and
- invest in monitoring tools

These are four intrinsic (system-oriented) data quality dimensions to specify whether data are complete, unambiguous, meaningful, and correct. Other approaches classify data into levels: form, meaning, and application according to the use of data and quality needed. Techniques to improve data quality include data profiling, data standardisation, data linking, and data cleaning.

In maintenance decision-making, data quality is crucial, since without controlling it, there is no control of the accuracy of the output. In a CMMS, three important parties may affect the quality of data; data producers, data custodians, and data consumers. Data producers are people or systems that generate data. Data custodians are people who provide and manage computing resources for storing and processing data. Finally, data consumers are people or systems that use data, i.e. data users (Aljumaili, 2016).

5.2.1 eMAINTENANCE AND DATA QUALITY

eMaintenance is a multidisciplinary domain based on maintenance and Information and Communication Technology (ICT), ensuring maintenance services are aligned with the needs and business objectives of both customers and suppliers during the whole product life cycle. More simply stated, eMaintenance uses new technologies for maintenance support. From a generic perspective, eMaintenance is maintenance managed and performed through computing.

eMaintenance provides information resources and information services which enable the development and establishment of a proactive decision-making process through enhanced use of ICT.

eMaintenance solutions may include different services such as:

- eMonitoring,
- eDiagnosis, and
- ePrognosis.

Data quality is extremely important when designing an eMaintenance solution and during its operational phase. High-quality content (i.e. accurate, complete, and relevant) leads to better product cost control and increased organisational efficiency (i.e. increased decision-making efficiency). When developing eMaintenance solutions as support to maintenance decision-making, an integration architecture for data exchange between different data sources is important. Therefore, eMaintenance ontologies may contribute to enhancing the quality of data in maintenance (Aljumaili, 2016).

5.2.1.1 Problems in Data Quality

A number of problems in eMaintenance can be related to different aspects of data quality. A non-exhaustive list includes problems of data multiplicity, manual input and transfer of data, usability of systems, performance indicators missing or difficult to obtain, poor information logistics between teams, and knowledge recycling:

- Data multiplicity: This problem concerns the duplication of information and its existence in different systems or parts of a system. For example, certain information on technical documentation and drawings may be stored both in the maintenance system and in other media (e.g. computer hard drives, paper). Moreover, information related to certain equipment may be stored in different subparts of the system. In many cases, there is no technical information, whether drawings or work instructions, in the maintenance system. Or the stored information is not regularly updated or maintained, thus making it difficult to know if it can be trusted. At times, the information sources may contain conflicting information, making it difficult to know which one to trust. The issue with data duplication is worsened when the responsibility for updating the different data sources is not clear and therefore seldom done.
- Manual input and transfer of data: Manually entering data can lead to the data being of varying quality. Moreover, each time data are manually transferred between systems, there is a risk of data being lost or corrupted. This makes it hard to trust the data, and valuable time is lost finding additional information.
- Usability of systems: This problem points to the interface and functionality of the systems used in the maintenance processes. Simply stated, users must know how to use the systems and have relevant information available.

- Performance indicators missing or difficult to obtain: To continuously follow up and improve maintenance, it is important to have indicators of its status and efficiency. This includes such things as salaries for the maintenance staff and costs for subcontractors, as well as the costs of materials. The latter costs must be available on an equipment level. The efficiency of the maintenance organisation can also be determined by work time execution and the status of work orders. If any or all of these are missing, it is impossible to assess maintenance performance.
- Poor information logistics between teams: This problem relates to the transfer of information between different maintenance teams, such as mechanical and electrical. A problem may require a shared solution, but if the teams do not communicate, this can be difficult. The organisational structure should promote and facilitate communication.
- Knowledge recycling: This problem concerns the issue of not making use of previous knowledge in the maintenance work. Analyses of past failures may be difficult to access or rarely consulted or followed up on to find systematic or recurring problems (Aljumaili, 2016).

5.2.1.2   Data Quality in The Maintenance Phases

The above problems are all rooted in different aspects of data quality. This section provides a classification of these problems based on the four categories of data quality: intrinsic, contextual, representational, and accessibility (Table 5.2).

- Intrinsic data quality denotes that data have quality in their own right. For example, mismatches among sources of the same data are a common cause of intrinsic data quality problems.
- Contextual data quality highlights the requirement that data quality must be considered within the context of the task at hand. This could refer to issues concerning missing (incomplete) data, inadequately defined or measured data, and data that could not be appropriately aggregated.
- Representational data quality emphasises that high-quality data should be clearly represented. Examples of issues related to this are interpretability, ease of understanding, concise representation, and consistent representation.
- Accessibility data quality refers to the fact that data must be accessible to the data consumer (i.e., user) in a secure way. Accessibility data quality problems are, for example, characterised by underlying concerns about technical accessibility, data-representation issues interpreted by data consumers as accessibility problems, and data-volume issues interpreted as accessibility problems.

The problem of data multiplicity is classified as an intrinsic problem, as the accuracy of the data may be affected because of the problem of proving the correctness of the data.

The issue of manual input and transfer of data is an intrinsic problem, as the accuracy also may be affected by the manual processes. But it can also constitute a contextual problem, as the completeness of the data may be affected as well.

The problem related to the usability of systems is a representational problem, as the data may be accurate but difficult to utilise due to poor usability of the system.

The problem of performance indicators missing is classified as a contextual problem because data are missing and incomplete.

Finally, poor information logistics between teams and difficult-to-access analyses both reflect accessibility problems, as data are difficult to access.

Effective and efficient maintenance requires proper information logistics, which can be delivered through eMaintenance solutions. The development of eMaintenance solutions faces extensive challenges, however. There is a need for quality assurance mechanisms. These mechanisms should

TABLE 5.2

Data Quality Issues and Their Linkage to Maintenance (Aljumaili, 2016)

Data quality problem	Maintenance Management phase	Maintenance Support Planning phase	Maintenance Preparation phase	Maintenance Execution phase	Maintenance Assessment phase	Maintenance Improvement phase	Type of data quality problem
Multiple information sources in spare parts			v				Intrinsic
Lacking progress information for spare part orders		v	v				Contextual Accessibility
Manually inputted work orders varies in quality			v	v	v		Intrinsic Contextual
Information needed is not connected to work orders				v			Contextual Accessibility
Lack of information needed to follow up work					v	v	Intrinsic Contextual
Multiple failure notices			v	v	v		Intrinsic
Usability of systems	v	v	v	v	v	v	Representational
Information duplication and poor maintenance of information		v	v	v	v	v	Intrinsic
Performance indicators missing or difficult to obtain	v				v	v	Contextual
Bad information logistics between teams			v	v			Accessibility
Poor support for work planning by system		v	v				Representational Accessibility
Route cause analysis poorly utilized					v	v	Accessibility

encompass all phases of the maintenance process. They should be able to manage data quality from different data sources and at various aggregation levels, be able to visualise data quality for the user, be able to adapt to the user's context and the decision-making process, and be able to tackle criticality management. In addition, it is important to have an overarching plan for information management that covers a system's life cycle (Aljumaili, 2016).

5.2.2 DATA QUALITY PROBLEMS

A few final problems related to data quality include the following:

1. Subjective judgement can be introduced into data, thus biasing the information
2. Big Data, i.e. the sheer volume of data, may make it difficult to access information as and when needed
3. Data may come from heterogeneous systems with different definitions, formats, and values
4. Nonnumeric information is difficult to index (Aljumaili, 2016).

5.3   DATA AUGMENTATION

Data augmentation refers to techniques to generate new synthetic datasets based on original datasets, for example, by copying and slightly modifying or enriching the features in a dataset. Otherwise stated, data augmentation involves creating new and representative data (Takimoglu, 2022).

Data augmentation includes geometric manipulation. It also includes adding noise, changing colour settings, and other effects such as blur and sharpening filters to repurpose existing training examples as new data. For example, a coloured photo can be augmented by generating a grey-scaled-version of the same photo, and both photos can be fed to the AI-engine to increase its recognition capability. These techniques are commonly used in the learning phase of AI (Karim & Kumar, OECD). Data augmentation can be applied to other types of data as well. For text datasets, nouns and verbs can be replaced with their synonyms. In audio data, training examples can be modified by adding noise or changing the playback speed (Dickson, 2021).

Data augmentation is especially useful for supervised learning because the labels are already available, and the new examples do not need to be annotated. Data augmentation is also useful for other classes of machine learning (ML) algorithms such as unsupervised learning, contrastive learning, and generative models.

5.3.1   IMPORTANCE OF DATA AUGMENTATION IN MACHINE LEARNING

Data augmentation has become a standard practice for training ML models for computer vision applications. Popular ML and deep learning (DL) programming libraries have easy-to-use functions to integrate data augmentation into the ML training pipeline.

Data augmentation techniques may be a good tool in the face of new challenges in the AI world. More specifically, ML applications, especially in the DL domain, continue to diversify and are rapidly increasing. Data augmentation can help organisations handle this challenge in the following ways:

- Data augmentation can enhance the performance and outcomes of ML models by forming new and different examples to train datasets. Rich datasets result in better model performance.
- Data augmentation techniques lead to more robust ML model results because they create real-world scenarios.
- Collecting and labelling data for ML models can be time-consuming and expensive. The application of data augmentation techniques can transform datasets and lead to reduced operational costs (Takimoglu, 2022).

Interest in data augmentation techniques has been growing, partly because of the increasing interest in DL models (Takimoglu, 2022). Figure 5.3 shows the pattern over the past five years.

5.3.2   ADVANCED MODELS FOR DATA AUGMENTATION

Some advanced models for data augmentation are the following:

1. Adversarial training/adversarial ML: Adversarial examples are generated and injected into the dataset for training purposes.
2. Generative adversarial networks (GANs): GAN algorithms can learn patterns from input datasets and automatically create new examples which are injected into the training data.
3. Neural style transfer: These models can blend content image and style image and separate style from content.
4. Reinforcement learning: Reinforcement learning models use a virtual environment to train software agents to reach their goals and make decisions (Takimoglu, 2022).

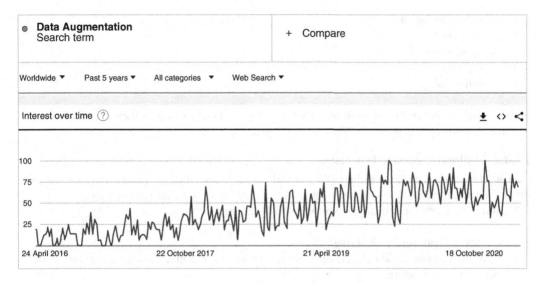

FIGURE 5.3   Data augmentation growth over the last five years (Takimoglu, 2022).

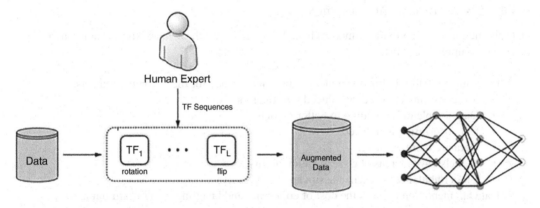

FIGURE 5.4   Techniques in data augmentation for image recognition and NLP (Takimoglu, 2021).

5.3.3   IMAGE RECOGNITION AND NATURAL LANGUAGE PROCESSING

Classic and advanced techniques used in data augmentation for image recognition and natural language processing (NLP) are shown in Figure 5.4 (Takimoglu, 2022).

5.3.3.1   Image Classification and Segmentation

As mentioned above, data augmentation includes making simple alterations to visual data. Some classic image-processing activities for data augmentation are the following (Takimoglu, 2022):

- re-scaling
- padding
- random rotating
- cropping
- flipping vertically or horizontally
- moving image along x, y direction (translating)
- zooming
- darkening & brightening

- colour modification
- grayscaling
- changing contrast
- adding noise
- random erasing

Note that all of the above are commonly used today by many people – they are not linked to advanced knowledge. Anyone can "Photoshop" something.

5.3.3.2   Natural Language Processing

Data augmentation is not as popular in the natural language domain as in computer vision domain, simply because the complexity of language makes it difficult to augment textual data.

Common methods for data augmentation in NLP are the following:

- Contextualised word embedding.
- Easy data augmentation (EDA) operations: synonym replacement, word insertion, word swap, and word deletion.
- Back translation (Takimoglu, 2022).

5.3.4   Benefits of Data Augmentation

Data augmentation can provide numerous benefits, some of which we have already mentioned. Here is a more comprehensive list:

1. Data augmentation improves model prediction accuracy for the following reasons:
   - More training data are introduced into the models.
   - Data are plentiful, leading to better models.
   - Data overfitting is reduced.
   - Data are more variable.
   - Models have increased generalisation ability.
   - Class imbalance issues in classification are resolved.
2. Data augmentation reduces the cost of collecting and labelling data (Takimoglu, 2022).

5.3.5   Challenges of Data Augmentation

Despite the many advantages, there are still some challenges to be overcome.

1. Organisations need systems to evaluate the quality of their augmented datasets. As the use of data augmentation methods increases, organisations will also need to assess the quality of their output.
2. The domain of data augmentation needs to develop new ways to create new/synthetic data with advanced applications.
3. If a dataset contains biases, the data augmented from it will have biases (Takimoglu, 2022). The data augmentation process also needs to be adjusted to address other potential problems, such as class imbalance (Dickson, 2021).
4. Data augmentation still requires data. Based on the target application, a fairly large training dataset with enough examples is still required.
5. In some applications, training data might be too limited for data augmentation to help. It may be possible to use transfer learning, where an ML model is trained on a general dataset (e.g., ImageNet) and then repurposed by fine-tuning its higher layers on the limited data that are available.

Used wisely, data management can be a powerful tool (Dickson, 2021), but it is important to identify an optimal data augmentation strategy.

5.3.6 DATA AUGMENTATION METHODS

Existing image augmentation methods can be put into one of two very general categories: traditional, white-box methods or black-box methods based on deep neural networks. In this section, we briefly introduce groups of methods that have made the biggest impact in the field of image synthesis and augmentation (Mikołajczyk & Grochowski, 2018).

5.3.6.1 Traditional Transformations

A common practice of data augmentation is a combination of affine image transformation and colour modification. Figure 5.5 shows the affine techniques of rotation, refection, scaling (zoom in/out) and shearing (Mikołajczyk & Grochowski, 2018).

Geometric distortions or deformations are commonly used to increase the number of samples for training deep neural models. They are also widely used as affine transformations for data augmentation. The most popular methods are histogram equalisation, enhancing contrast or brightness, white balancing, sharpening, and blurring (Figure 5.6).

Those easy-to-understand methods are fast and reproducible. Their implementation code is relatively easy and is available to download for most DL frameworks, making them even more popular (Mikołajczyk & Grochowski, 2018).

5.3.6.2 Generative Adversarial Networks

GAN is a relatively new and powerful tool to perform the unsupervised generation of new images using the min-max strategy.

GANs are extremely useful in many different image generation and manipulation problems like text-to-image synthesis, super resolution (generating high-resolution images out of low-resolution ones), image-to-image translation (e.g. converting sketches to images), image blending (mixing

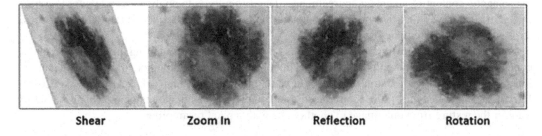

Shear	**Zoom In**	**Reflection**	**Rotation**

FIGURE 5.5 Same image after different types of affine transformations (Mikołajczyk & Grochowski, 2018).

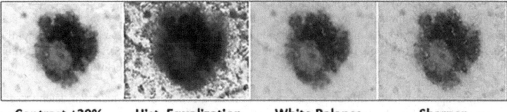

Contrast +20%	**Hist. Equalization**	**White Balance**	**Sharpen**

FIGURE 5.6 Same image after different types of colour transformations (Mikołajczyk & Grochowski, 2018).

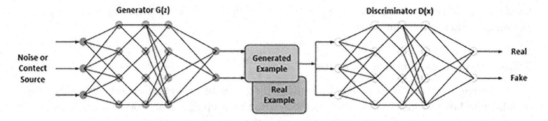

FIGURE 5.7   Simplified idea of GAN (Mikołajczyk & Grochowski, 2018).

selected parts of two images to get a new one), and images in painting (restoring missing pieces of an image).

The overall idea of GANs is to use two adversarial networks (G(z) and D(x)), where one generates a photorealistic image to fool the other (generator G(z)). The goal is to distinguish fake images from real ones (discriminator D(z)). In other words, the generator's task is to minimise a cost (value) function V(D, G) (e.g. maximum likelihood), while the discriminator needs to maximise it (Figure 5.7) (Mikołajczyk & Grochowski, 2018).

Although this technique can yield satisfactory outcomes, it is still unclear how to quantitatively evaluate generative models. Models that generate good samples can have poor maximum likelihood (the probability that the model is similar to the training data), and models that obtain good likelihood can generate bad samples. Other limitations include problems of compliance with reality (e.g. generating e animals with the wrong number of body parts), lack of a three-dimensional perspective (e.g. generating the images of objects that are too flat or too highly axis-aligned), and difficulty coordinating a global structure (e.g. a structure seen both from the front and from the side) (Mikołajczyk & Grochowski, 2018).

5.3.6.3   Texture Transfer

The goal of texture transfer is to synthetise a texture from a texture-source image while constraining the semantic content of a content-source image. The difficulty is to apply a given texture to a new image in such a way that the visual attributes of the original image, like contour, shading, lines, strokes, and regions, remain visible.

Most of the classical texture transfer methods rely on the idea of resampling the texture to a given content image. For example, image quilting, a famous technique, is a method of synthesising a new image by stitching together small patches of existing images (Mikołajczyk & Grochowski, 2018). Hertzman and colleagues (2001) introduced a technique called image analogies which is able to transfer the texture from one image to another one with a pixel resampling.

5.3.6.4   Convolutional Neural Networks

Another image augmentation methods rely on the use of a convolutional neural network (CNN). In DL, a CNN is a class of artificial neural network.

One interesting approach is a random erasing technique. It is fast and relatively easy to implement yet gives good results in the generalisation ability of CNNs. In the method, one randomly paints a noise-filled rectangle in an image, resulting in changing original pixels values. Expanding the dataset with images of various levels of occlusion reduces the risk of overfitting and makes the model more robust.

Another approach was initiated by the need to create a robust CNN which can defend itself against adversarial attacks. A data set of images is augmented by adding a stochastic additive noise to the images, making them more robust against the noise adversarial attacks (Mikołajczyk & Grochowski, 2018).

5.3.7   Data Augmentation for Data Management

This section focuses on two main problems, data preparation and data integration, and describes how existing ML-based solutions benefit from the data augmentation process (Li et al., 2021).

5.3.7.1   Data Augmentation for Data Preparation

Data preparation plays an essential role in many data analytic applications. Two significant tasks in data preparation are information extraction and data cleaning. ML-based solutions, especially those enhanced by data augmentation, have recently become important parts of these tasks.

1. Information extraction: Information extraction focuses on extracting structured information from unstructured or semi-structured data sources. It is an area of interest for both data management and NLP (NLP). The core tasks of information extraction are:
   - Named entity recognition: The named entity recognition task is often formulated as a sequence tagging problem. Some researchers adapt basic data augmentation operators, commonly used for sequence classification tasks, to perform the sequence tagging task; others use conditional generation to produce synthetic training examples.
   - Relation extraction: Relation extraction focuses on assigning a relation label for two entities in a given context. To augment examples in the training set, some researchers use dependency path between entities to classify the relation and augment the paths via entity directions. Others leverage external ontology knowledge to augment training examples (Li et al., 2021).
   - Co-reference extraction: Many recent solutions to these core information extraction tasks rely on training examples and ML approaches. Thus, data augmentation can be beneficial: it can diversify and enrich the training dataset, simultaneously reducing the cost of collecting high-quality labelled data and improving the model accuracy.
2. Data cleaning: Error detection is an essential step in data cleaning. Error detection seeks to determine whether the values of a certain cell in a database are correct (i.e., clean). ML can thus be used for error detection as it can classify whether the given cell is clean.
   One suggestion is to use a data augmentation-based approach to error detection. This approach essentially enriches and balances the labels of small training data through the learned-data transformations and data augmentation policies.

5.3.7.2   Data Augmentation for Data Integration

The research on data integration has expanded in several core directions. Two of these are schema matching/mapping and entity matching. These core tasks have benefited from advances in ML and human-annotated datasets (Li et al., 2021).

- Schema matching: Schema matching purports to find the correspondence among schema elements in two semantically correlated schemas. To use ML in this case, the problem can be formulated as a classification problem: for each schema element from the source schema, the task is to assign labels corresponding to schema elements in the target schema.
  Augmenting training examples has been used in schema-matching solutions for quite some time. One possibility is to use mapping between schemas in the same corpus to augment training examples. Another is to adapt a similar augmentation method to enrich training examples for an ML model that predicts the similarity between two schema elements. A final possibility is to augment the training data of similarity matrices to improve the schema-matching results.
- Entity matching: Entity matching is also called record linkage and entity resolution. It is the problem of identifying all records that refer to a real-world entity, thus making it an

important task in data integration. A basic step in entity matching is to classify entity pairs as either matching or non-matching.

One possible technique to enrich training examples for entity matching is to apply different basic data augmentation operations on different levels to transform existing data examples into new (synthetic) ones. It may also be possible to use data augmentation to create new training examples from the unlabelled dataset by assigning both positive and negative labels to a transformed data point in the set, to enforce a strong co-regularisation on the classifier.

5.3.8 ADVANCED DATA AUGMENTATION

Advanced data augmentation techniques can be used in data management. The ones we discuss here are interpolation-based data augmentation, generation-based data augmentation, and learned-data augmentation. These advanced techniques draw on recent ML techniques, such as representation learning, neural sequence generation, and natural language programming/computer vision (Li et al., 2021).

5.3.8.1 Interpolation-Based Data Augmentation

New techniques in interpolation-based data augmentation include MixUp, an advanced data augmentation method for image classification. It produces virtual training examples by combining two randomly sampled training examples into their linear interpolations. Variants of this method have shown significant improvements in tagging and sequence classification. Some data management methods have adapted the MixUp technique to sequential data by performing interpolations between two sequences in their embedding space (Li et al., 2021).

5.3.8.2 Generation-Based Data Augmentation

By leveraging the most recent advancements in generative pre-trained language modelling, this type of advanced data augmentation attempts to overcome the lack of diversity in simple data augmentation. These kinds of techniques filter out low-quality generations using the target model or apply conditional generation on the given labels with the aim of reducing the label corruptions and to further diversify the augmented examples.

InvDA is a recent method trained on the task-specific corpus in a self-supervised manner; it learns how to augment existing examples by "inverting" the effect of multiple simple data augmentation operators and is effective for entity matching and data cleaning.

Another line of generation-based data augmentation methods uses GANs (see Section 6.3.6.2). For relational data, GANs can be used to synthesise tables, and these can be used for data augmentation (Li et al., 2021).

5.3.8.3 Learned-Data Augmentation

This category of advanced data augmentation methods aims at automatically finding the best data augmentation policies (i.e. a combination of data augmentation operators) by solving an additional learning task. The first step is to introduce different optimisation goals for the data augmentation learning task, along with the various searching techniques to solve the task, such as Bayesian optimisation, reinforcement learning, and meta-learning searching techniques. Of these three approaches, meta-learning-based searching techniques show better efficiency as they enable the use of gradient descent by differentiating the search space.

Rotom is a meta-learning-based framework (Miao et al., 2021) that adapts the most popular optimisation objective (i.e. minimising the validation loss) to select and combine augmented examples (Li et al., 2021).

5.3.9 DATA AUGMENTATION WITH OTHER LEARNING PARADIGMS

The possibility of combining data augmentation with learning paradigms other than supervised learning for data preparation and integration has promise, but certain challenges remain salient (Li et al., 2021). We discuss some of these other learning paradigms: semi-supervised and active learning, weak supervision, and pre-training for relational data.

5.3.9.1 Semi-Supervised and Active Learning

Data augmentation can be applied to unlabelled data in either a semi-supervised or active-learning manner.

- Semi-supervised: Data augmentation can be applied in a semi-supervised manner to exploit a large number of unlabelled examples to regularise consistency.
- Active learning: Active learning can be used in data integration tasks. It selects the most informative unlabelled examples for humans to assign labels and update the model.

Both the initial model training and the iterative labelling process of active learning can benefit from data augmentation to further reduce the label requirement, but a challenge remains, in that it is non-trivial to make the data augmentation process and the fine-tuning of deep learning models interactive enough to support user inputs (Li et al., 2021).

5.3.9.2 Weak Supervision

Weak supervision mainly applies in the data programming field. In this context, data augmentation refers to the use of noisy sources such as crowd-sourcing and user-defined heuristics to provide supervision signals from unlabelled examples. This works in the following way: data programming enables developers to provide data programs (i.e. labelling functions) that label a subset of the unlabelled examples. Similarly, user-defined data augmentation operators (i.e. transformation functions) can be used as input and applied in sequence; this can accompany data augmentation methods.

An ongoing challenge in data programming is the difficulty involved in generating functions by enumerating heuristics rules. This is now being addressed by data transformation techniques that have been extensively studied in the database community (Li et al., 2021).

5.3.9.3 Pre-Training for Relational Data

Pre-trained language models can be used to construct distributed representations of relational data entries and thus yield significant performance gains. Yet language models do not characterise the structure information and factual knowledge inherent to relational data. A recent suggestion points to the promise of structure-aware representation learning for relational data in different data integration tasks; however, it is challenging to have pre-trained models for different domains and tasks.

We expect pre-trained models for relational data will provide effective data augmentation for data integration tasks, for example, language models for text data augmentation. Given the success of pre-trained language models in the NLP community, we think having publicly available pre-trained models for relational data would boost future research on data integration and improve understanding.

5.4 INFORMATION LOGISTICS

The context of the information on the maintenance of complex technical systems with long life-cycles is both dynamic and comprehensive, making appropriate information logistics a necessity (Blanchard & Blanchard, 2004; Muller et al., 2008; Tsang, 2002).

Simply stated, information logistics provides just-in-time information to targeted users. It makes the right information available at the right time and in the right place.

Solutions for information logistics need to deal with the following four concerns:

1. Time management: When information should be delivered. In the information society, the just-in-time delivery of information is of utmost importance. Information is only useful if provided at the required time and if it is not outdated. Information logistics enables a timely supply of information that fulfils these requirements.
2. Content management: What information should be delivered. Each individual has information demands that differ from those of other persons. Information logistics ensures that each person is supplied only with the content he or she needs.
3. Communication management: How information should be delivered. An information logistics information supply involves various methods of providing individuals with information via several communication channels. The supplied information is adjusted to the technical environment of the recipient.
4. Context management: Where information should be delivered and why. The goal is to ensure people receive information where they need it and are not given information that is of no value at their current location (Haseloff, 2005).

The main objective of information logistics is an optimised information provision and information flow. The scope can be a single person, a target group, a machine/facility, or any networked organisation (Sandkuhl, 2007).

Information logistics focuses on information supply to individuals and aims to optimise this process using a purpose-oriented provision of information adjusted to people's demands. It ensures that only the right information is made available to individuals at the right time and in the right context. This includes the transformation of information in accordance with people's preferences and the available communication media to ensure that the supplied information can be processed by the recipient (Haseloff, 2005).

Managing information in the proper way is vital to an organisation's long-term competitive success. If companies want to add value to customers by helping them make substantial and lasting improvements in performance, managing information is a critical tool. Almost every company has exploitable information assets, but few companies systematically explore the opportunities they create. However, the rewards can certainly justify the effort (Jagersma, 2011).

Information logistics offers a number of benefits, including the following:

- Better overall business and customer understanding by linking a mass of customer data to a mass of sales and product data at a single point in time and over time.
- Cost reduction opportunities through more efficient and effective use of the information such as seamless sharing of different kinds of information.
- Improved quality of decision-making by ensuring the decision-makers are receiving the key information they need on time and nothing more.
- Innovation and creativity by using the information for cross-fertilised thinking to develop new customer propositions and underpin new forms of commercial activity.
- Speed of management decisions by improving processes and customer relations (Jagersma, 2011).

5.4.1 Information Logistics and eMaintenance

Manufacturing and process industries, as well as maintenance and in-service support providers, are experiencing ever-increasing customer requirements to increase dependability and decrease Life Support Cost (LSC). To achieve this, a central problem for these industries is to manage the rapidly increasing information flow that follows the development of more complex and technologically advanced systems. Customers are also demanding improved system availability, safety, sustainability, cost-effectiveness, operational flexibility, and tailored worldwide support 24 hours a day, seven days a week (24/7). This changing business environment requires new and innovative solutions as support products and services to satisfy the needs of customers and end-users.

Maintenance and support concepts for modern complex technical systems, such as civil airliners and military combat aircraft, can be described as focusing on optimising two fundamental and interdependent elements. In the aviation example, the first element is the aircraft (i.e. the system-of-interest), which should be designed to maximise the inherent availability through proper reliability and maintainability design within available Lifecycle Cost (LCC) constraints. This design should be balanced with the support system, which is the second element. The support system should be designed to provide necessary support during the utilisation and support phases of the system-of-interest's lifecycle, which is measured through the support system's maintenance support performance. The support system is an enabling system, i.e. a system that complements a system-of-interest during its lifecycle stages, but does not necessarily contribute directly to its function during operation. An enabling system provides functions and services to users and other stakeholders to ensure a proper and efficient function of the system-of-interest. eMaintenance has the potential to improve the management and performance of activities related to the whole maintenance process and thereby improve the dependability, safety and LCC of critical systems. This can be realised through a coordinated application of ICT throughout the maintenance and support processes, thus integrating Built-in Test (BIT) systems, external tests at different maintenance echelons, technical information, diagnostics, prognostics, and other sources of support information.

On an operational level, end-users and managers utilising the support system of a modern aircraft are confronted with a multitude of computerised functions and ICT solutions. However, today there is little or no integration of functions and services related to the support system, such as technical information (publications), maintenance programs, maintenance plans, job cards, fault diagnosis support, amendment services, health and usage monitoring, and operational feedback.

At the same time, producers and suppliers of maintenance products and customer support services are facing escalating challenges trying to sustain high quality and increase service levels for increasingly complex technical systems in an environment characterised by multiple products, suppliers, and customers with increasingly stringent requirements. This environment is also to a great extent becoming purely digital; an increasing amount of software and hardware products, design data, and other information exchange is provided and communicated solely in digital form. Hence, both customers and suppliers are facing increased complexity levels in information related to configuration control and change management for both the system-of-interest (e.g. the aircraft) and its support system. This high complexity level of information logistics will hamper the operational effectiveness and drive up the LCC.

One way to increase aircraft availability and improve maintenance and support efficiency is to speed up the turnaround time for scheduled and unscheduled maintenance. The ultimate goal is risk-based utilisation and support, where true condition-based maintenance (CBM) is integrated with current operational requirements and available resources in RT. This aims at the elimination of all preventive scheduled maintenance based on fixed time intervals and execution of only corrective maintenance that has been predicted and turned into scheduled maintenance facilitated by proper support. To address the challenge of information logistics of digital product data and information within maintenance in-service support, providers need to adapt new methodologies and tools that enable full utilisation of the advantages of digital product data and information in processes and business models, e.g. Service-Oriented Architecture (SOA). To implement such improved support solutions in a global-support environment, eMaintenance is seen as one important building block. eMaintenance includes monitoring, collection, recording and distribution of real-time system health data, maintenance-generated data, and other decision and performance-support information to different stakeholders independent of organisation or geographical location, 24 hours a day, seven days a week (24/7).

Therefore, suppliers need to change methodologies, tools, and processes for information logistics to be both more customer-focused and more efficient for internal development and sustainability. New concepts for the application of ICT need to address information quality, lead time, accessibility 24/7, usability, and an overall reduction of cost for information logistics related to maintenance and support. Simultaneously, since much of the managed data and information related may be sensitive and confidential (especially in our example of aircraft), the aspect of information security is of outmost importance and needs to be considered, e.g. through content classification, authentication and authorisation. In fact, information security is so fundamental that it can override the functionality of any solution.

Information logistics in the case of aircraft needs to integrate and exploit the use of maintenance data and consider fleet status, flight operations, and maintenance sources. This would provide maintenance planners, operations and others with tailored information for decision support, derived from common data sources.

Examples of these trends are manufacturers' airline in-flight information systems. These can include multifunction e-applications for flight operations, passenger, cabin crew, and maintenance features. Capabilities in flight operations include performance calculations, electronic manuals, technical logbook, crew e-mail, graphical weather, and charts and maps. For maintenance, capabilities include technical logbooks, manuals, maintenance tools, and performance monitoring.

Capability also needs to be developed to enable more agile and efficient use of new maintenance and support functions integrated with the aircraft, exploitation of operational feedback, and rapid supplier adaptation to continuously changing customer-specific requirements on hardware and software products, as well as services.

An example of such solutions is again manufacturers' innovative support strategies, where customers pay for a significant portion of purchased services with data collected during operations. Maintenance, Repair, and Overhaul (MRO) providers are also required to provide data such as man hours, downtime, and reliability data. In return, the manufacturer commits to include promotion of services from the MRO providers, provide information exchange in terms of access to specific information (e.g. draft service bulletins, information on market requirements, advance information on major retrofit programs), and offer management reviews (Candell et al., 2009; Karim et al., 2009).

5.4.2 INFORMATION LOGISTICS AND INFORMATION FLOW IN AN ERA OF INDUSTRY 4.0

Under Industry 4.0, the manufacturing industry is creating and employing increasingly intelligent, autonomous, and decentralised sub-systems that will, in turn, lead to more competitive production and logistics processes. This renders the effective and economical integration of information and decision-making bodies, especially salient. If this integration is efficiently performed on all system and corporate levels, it can be the key to organisational success.

Despite the increased use of newer technologies such as radio frequency identification (RFID) or semi-autonomous control of production and logistics facilities, the immediate intra- and intercompany transfer of information along the supply chain is often very limited. However, in times of growing competitiveness and shorter times-to-market, an efficient and cost-optimised material flow can arise only through the sophisticated integration of production and information processes. Thus, the collection and use of information are becoming increasingly important.

Due to recent developments such Big Data, information is omnipresent. This apparent advantage can be quickly turned into a drawback: there is an oversupply of data that do not provide beneficial information to their environment. This offers more disadvantages than potential opportunities for a company. The flood of data means the truly relevant information may not be located at the time it is needed. While this aspect is often underestimated, it is a strategic necessity for companies to bring information flows and material flows into harmony. ICT can work to embed the information flows with the production processes (Altendorfer-Kaiser, 2015).

It is not the quantity of data that is important. It is more about the quality of the resulting information, and of course it is equally important to have information in the right place at the right time.

TABLE 5.3
6Rs of Logistics Applied to Information Flow (Altendorfer-Kaiser, 2015)

IR's	Information context
Right information	Necessary for the user
Right time	Decision-supportive
Right quantity	As much as necessary
Right place	Accessible for the user
Right quality	Detailed enough and usable
Right costs	Reasonable price

The so-called "6Rs" of logistics matter for proper information flow management in an era of Big Data:

- **R**ight information
- **R**ight time
- **R**ight quantity
- **R**ight place
- **R**ight quality
- **R**ight costs.

Table 5.3 shows the 6Rs of logistics applied to information flow (Altendorfer-Kaiser, 2015).

To realise an adequate information flow management, a change in information systems may be necessary. However, information system aspects have often been left out of consideration, and organisations often lag behind in their IT. Software systems are often outdated and poorly structured. The need for agile software architecture becomes evident when the need for more flexibility and reduced costs in the daily business urges companies to restructure.

Today's companies can be considered open socio-technical systems with the goal to supply their customers while making profit (Martin, 2013). As open systems, they have a lot of interfaces to the outside world, as shown in Figure 5.8 (Altendorfer-Kaiser, 2015).

Highlighted in this figure is the information flow, which runs in parallel to the material flow. This indicates the importance of a well-defined information flow and a well-established information flow management. The latter is not only necessary for intra-company flows; it is also necessary for the whole supply chain (Altendorfer-Kaiser, 2015).

5.4.3 INFORMATION LIFE CYCLE

Information logistics has many parallels to production logistics. Thus, the information lifecycle has similarities with the product lifecycle. The lifecycle model for information shown in Figure 5.9 identifies the phases information passes through (Altendorfer-Kaiser, 2015).

In a further step, corresponding tasks can be defined and assigned to appropriate technologies to realise the individual phases.

An interesting possibility is the ability to handle the flood of information by controlling the information lifecycle and thus categorising value-added vs non-value-added information.

Modern hardware and software solutions promise greater transparency and increased efficiency through the collection and analysis of numerous data. However, because of the high density of information (i.e. Big Data), it is often difficult to assess data according to their percentage of completion. The tendency to hoard all the relevant data may result in losing sight of what is essential.

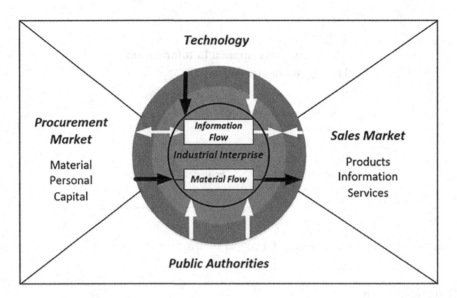

FIGURE 5.8   Interfaces of a company (Altendorfer-Kaiser, 2015).

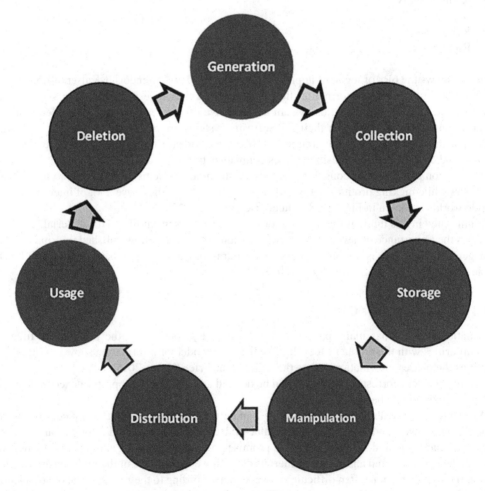

FIGURE 5.9   Information life cycle (Altendorfer-Kaiser, 2015).

TABLE 5.4

Muda of Information Compared to Muda of Production (Altendorfer-Kaiser, 2015)

Muda of production	Muda of information
Over production	Production of wrong information
Idle times	Delay in information retrieval
Transport	Too many interfaces
Production	No clear definition of what kind of information is needed
Movements	High effort of transformation
Stock	Inefficient storage
Maintenance	Missing or wrong information

Internet technologies allow an enterprise-wide manipulation. On the one hand, this is a significant advantage of modern technology, but on the other hand, it enhances the potential for information-related waste. A strict editing and plausibility check of information is required. To this end, the organisation must establish standards for cross-company practices. This, in turn, will enable the identification of information-related waste (Altendorfer-Kaiser, 2015).

The left side of Table 5.4 shows how Toyota identified waste in its production processes (termed "muda"). The right side shows a comparable identification of waste in information.

The creation of common structures and standards represents a proven form to reduce and prevent information-related wastes (Altendorfer-Kaiser, 2015).

5.4.4 eMaintenance – Information Logistics for Maintenance Support

Frameworks, concepts, methodologies, and platforms for information logistics related to maintenance are often collapsed under the heading of eMaintenance (Bangemann et al., 2004, 2006; Karim, 2008).

eMaintenance is the application of ICT to achieve effective information logistics within the maintenance area. eMaintenance includes monitoring, collecting, recording, and distributing RT system health data, maintenance-generated data, and other decision and performance-support information to stakeholders no matter who or where they are, 24/7.

One of the main objectives of eMaintenance is to enhance and support the maintenance process by establishing a content-sharing process based on ICT that provides the right information at the right time and in the right format to the right actor (i.e. information logistics). Content sharing includes various processes: data collection, data filtering, data aggregation, data analysis, data distribution, and data visualisation.

The process of information sharing is especially complex when the underlying data that need to be shared are produced by different processes within the organisation, for example, the business, operations, and maintenance processes. Each process may utilise several different technologies implemented in a complex ICT environment. These heterogeneous ICT environments put new burdens on the process of content sharing.

When establishing an eMaintenance program, organisations need to tackle two main issues:

- Content format: One of the major requirements is content format. Simply stated, sharable content must be packaged in a format that is not proprietary (i.e. not limited to one part of the organisation, e.g. maintenance) and can be managed by every part of the process.
- Content structure: Another requirement is the structure of the content. In essence, sharable content must be structured in accordance with a known and accepted content model that incorporates the structure, semantics, and validity of the content.

In other words, content format and content structure are significant issues for organisations to consider when they are establishing an eMaintenance solution (Karim et al., 2009).

Other significant issues to consider are the following:

- Ever-increasing customer requirements to increase dependability and decrease LSC.
- Increasing customer demands for improved system availability, safety, sustainability, cost-effectiveness, operational flexibility, and tailored support.
- Rapidly increasing information flows accompanying the development and use of complex and technologically advanced systems.

This changing business and work environment requires new and innovative solutions to satisfy the needs of customers and end-users.

Maintenance and support concepts for modern complex technical systems focus on optimising two fundamental and interdependent elements:

1. System-of-interest: The first element is the system-of-interest. It should be designed to maximise availability through proper reliability and maintainability within the given LCC constraints.
2. Support system: The support system should be designed to provide support during the utilisation and support phases of the system-of-interest's lifecycle, measured as the support system's maintenance support performance. The support system is an enabling system, in that it complements a system-of-interest during its lifecycle but does not necessarily contribute directly to its function during operation. Simply stated, an enabling system provides functions and services to users and other stakeholders to ensure the system-of-interest functions correctly and efficiently throughout the lifecycle.

eMaintenance has the potential to improve the management and performance of activities related to the whole maintenance process and thus improve the dependability, safety and LCC of critical systems. This requires a coordinated application of ICT throughout the maintenance and support processes, thus integrating technical information, diagnostics, prognostics, and so on.

To address the challenge of information logistics of digital product data and information within maintenance in-service support, providers need to adapt new methodologies and tools that allow them to capitalise on the advantages of digital product data and information in processes and business models. One example is SOA. eMaintenance is seen as an important building block in the implementation of such improved support solutions in a global-support environment. To reach this type of solution, the following steps are required:

- Information logistics need to integrate and exploit the use of maintenance data to provide maintenance planners, operations, and others with tailored information for decision support derived from common data sources.
- Users must demonstrate agile and efficient use of new maintenance and support functions integrated with the system-of-interest.
- Operational feedback must be exploited.
- Suppliers must rapidly adapt to continuously changing customer requirements.

Some manufacturers have already inaugurated innovative support strategies, where customers pay for a significant portion of purchased services with data collected during operations. MRO providers are required to provide data such as work hours, downtime, and reliability data. In return, the manufacturer promotes the MRO provider's services, gives access to specific information, and offers management reviews (Candell et al., 2011; Candell & Karim, 2008; Szymanowski et al., 2010).

TABLE 5.5
List of Challenges

Governance	eGovernance	Governance of a digital infrastructure for enabling a data-driven approach refers to the regulation of the collaboration and cooperation of the digital community in a digitalised environment including aspects of organisation, processes, policies etc.	
	Regulation	Regulation refers to establishment of a regime for management of a system by a set of rules.	
	Democratisation	In a digitalised environment, the democratisation refers to availability and accessibility of data and models for the "digital citizens", i.e. individuals and organisations committed to the defined digital governance model.	
	Standardisation	Standardisation refers to the conventions, patterns, guidelines, etc. agreed upon by the partners committed to the governance model.	
Business	Incentive model	This refers to models and incentives that stimulate digital transactions between involved parties in the community. These models support the agreed-upon governance model and facilitate the implementation of the data-driven approach.	
	Ownership	In the context of the data-driven approach, this refers to the aspects of ownership, e.g. right-to-use and freedom-to-operate, related to data and models.	
	Freedom-to-operate	This refers to freedom-to-operate and right-to-use related to data and models.	
	Business model	For digital assets, the selection of a service-based or product-based approach has an impact on the governance model and the selection of the technology.	
Technology	Autonomy	Autonomy in the data-driven approach refers to the level of intelligence and perception implemented in a digital asset.	
	Information logistics	Data are obviously required in a data-driven approach. Information logistics in this context refers to the digital logistics regime for managing the flow of data, information, and models between the digital community governed by the agreed-upon governance model.	
	Distribution	Supporting a distributed system such as railway requires a supporting distributed digital infrastructure. Distribution in the data-driven approach refers to models that enable the distribution of data, models, storage, networking, and computing.	
	Integration	Distributed digital assets must be supported by smart integration. Integration in the data-driven approach refers to mechanisms for the orchestration, fusion, and integration of digital assets, e.g. datasets and models.	
	Quality	Quality in the data-driven approach refers to the measurement of aspects related to quality-of-services, quality-of-data, and quality-of-model. Measuring and explaining the precision of data-driven components are very important for acceptance and fidelity models.	
	Cybersecurity	Cybersecurity is a critical aspect to be addressed in a data-driven approach.	

5.5 DATA-DRIVEN CHALLENGES

The data-driven approach has evolved significantly. With the emergence of AI technologies and digitalisation, it has become a tool for industry in general. The data-driven approach offers fact-based decision-making, the ability to predict the remaining useful life (RUL) of assets, improved capacity, cost efficiency, and improved sustainability with respect to environment, technology, and economy. At the same time, new challenges must be addressed and overcome. Some of these are shown in Table 5.5.

REFERENCES

Aljumaili, M. (2016). *Data Quality Assessment: Applied in Maintenance Operation and Maintenance Engineering*. LTU.

Altendorfer-Kaiser, S. (2015). Information logistics means to support a flexible production? *IFIP Advances in Information and Communication Technology, 459*, 414–421. https://doi.org/10.1007/978-3-319-22756-6_51/TABLES/2

Bangemann, T., Rebeuf, X., Reboul, D., Schulze, A., Szymanski, J., Thomesse, J.-P., Thron, M., & Zerhouni, N. (2006). Proteus-creating distributed maintenance systems through an integration platform. *Computers in Industry, 57*(6), 539–551. https://doi.org/10.1016/j.compind.2006.02.018

Bangemann, T., Reboul, D., Szymanski, J., Thomesse, J.-P., & Zerhouni, N. (2004). Proteus – an integration platform for distributed maintenance systems. *Proceedings of the Intelligent Maintenance Systems (IMS) 2004 International Conference*. https://hal.science/hal-00327189/

Blanchard, B. S., & Blanchard, B. S. (2004). *Logistics Engineering and Management*. Pearson Prentice Hall.

Bousdekis, A., Lepenioti, K., Apostolou, D., & Mentzas, G. (2021). A review of data-driven decision-making methods for industry 4.0 maintenance applications. *Electronics 2021, 10*(7), 828. https://doi.org/10.3390/ELECTRONICS10070828

Candell, O, Karim, R., & Parida, A. (2011). Development of information system for e-maintenance solutions within the aerospace industry. *International Journal of Performability Engineering, 7*(6), 583-592. http://www.scopus.com/inward/record.url?eid=2-s2.0-84861360207&partnerID=MN8TOARS

Candell, O., & Karim, R. (2008). e-Maintenance: Information driven maintenance and support. In L. J. de Vin (Ed.), *Proceedings of the 18th International Conference on Flexible Automation and Intelligent Manufacturing: June 30-July 2, Skövde, Sweden* (pp. 365–372). Högskolan i Skövde. http://www.diva-portal.org/smash/get/diva2:1001726/FULLTEXT01.pdf

Candell, Olov, Karim, R., & Söderholm, P. (2009). eMaintenance-information logistics for maintenance support. *Robotics and Computer-Integrated Manufacturing, 25*(6), 937–944. https://doi.org/10.1016/j.rcim.2009.04.005

Dickson, B. (2021). What is data augmentation? *TechTalks*. https://bdtechtalks.com/2021/11/27/what-is-data-augmentation/

Divan, M. J. (2018). Data-driven decision making. *2017 International Conference on Infocom Technologies and Unmanned Systems: Trends and Future Directions, ICTUS 2017*, January, 50–56. https://doi.org/10.1109/ICTUS.2017.8285973

Haseloff, S. (2005). *Context awareness in information logistics*. Dissertation, Berlin Technical University. https://core.ac.uk/download/pdf/57701839.pdf

Hertzman, A., Jacobs, C., Oliver, N., Cureless, B., & Salesin, D. (2001). Image anomalies. *Proceedings of the 28th annual conference on Computer graphics and interactive techniques*. DOI:10.1145/383259.383295

ITF. (2021). Data-driven transport infrastructure maintenance. International Transport Forum Policy Papers, No. 95. OECD Publishing.

Jagersma, P. K. (2011). Competitive information logistics. *Business Strategy Series, 12*(3), 136–145. https://doi.org/10.1108/17515631111130103

Karim, R. (2008). A service-oriented approach to e-maintenance of complex technical systems. http://epubl.ltu.se/1402-1544/2008/58/LTU-DT-0858-SE.pdf

Karim, R., Candell, O., & Söderholm, P. (2009). E-maintenance and information logistics: aspects of content format. *Journal of Quality in Maintenance Engineering, 15*(3), 308–324. https://doi.org/10.1108/13552510910983242

Karim, R, Dersin, P., Galar, D., Kumar, U., & Jarl, H. (2021). AI factory – A framework for digital asset management. In B. Castanier, M. Cepin, D. Bigaud, & C. Berenguer (Eds.), *Proceedings of the 31st European Safety and Reliability Conference (ESREL 2021)* (pp. 1160–1167). Research Publishing Services. http://www.diva-portal.org/smash/record.jsf?pid=diva2%3A1626359&dswid=5463

Keating, K., Coleman, C., Melz, H., Graham, E., & Thomson, A. (2018). *Guide to data-driven decision-making: Using data to inform practice and policy decisions*. James Bell Associates (JBA). https://www.jbassoc.com/resource/guide-data-driven-decision-making-using-data-inform-practice-policy-decisions-child-welfare-organizations/

Li, Y., Wang, X., Miao, Z., & Tan, W. C. (2021). Data augmentation for ML-driven data preparation and integration. *Proceedings of the VLDB Endowment, 14*(12), 3182–3185. https://doi.org/10.14778/3476311.3476403

Martin, H. (2013). *Transport-und lagerlogistik: planung, aufbau und steuerung von transport-und lagersystemen*. Springer-Verlag.

Miao, Z., Li, Y., & Wang, X. (2021). Rotom: A meta-learned data augmentation framework for entity matching, data cleaning, text classification, and beyond. *Proceedings of the 2021 International Conference on Management of Data*, 1303–1316. https://doi.org/10.1145/3448016.3457258

Mikołajczyk, A., & Grochowski, M. (2018). Data augmentation for improving deep learning in image classification problem. *2018 International Interdisciplinary PhD Workshop, IIPhDW 2018*, 117–122. https://doi.org/10.1109/IIPHDW.2018.8388338

Muller, A., Crespo Marquez, A., & Iung, B. (2008). On the concept of e-maintenance: Review and current research. *Reliability Engineering and System Safety*, *93*(8), 1165–1187. https://doi.org/10.1016/j.ress.2007.08.006

Onis, T. (2016). The four stages of the data maturity model. *CIO Online*. https://www.cio.com/article/238210/the-four-stages-of-the-data-maturity-model.html

ParadoxMarketing. (2022). Data driven decision making . *Knowledge Management*. https://paradoxmarketing.io/capabilities/knowledge-management/data-driven-decision-making

Sandkuhl, K. (2007). Information logistics in networked organizations: Selected concepts and applications. *International Conference on Enterprise Information Systems*, *12*, 43–54.

Szymanowski, M., Candell, O., & Karim, R. (2010). Challenges for interactive electronic technical publications in military aviation. *The 1st International Workshop* …. http://pure.ltu.se/portal/files/4922774/Article.pdf

Tableau. (2022). A guide to data-driven decision making. https://www.tableau.com/learn/articles/data-driven-decision-making

Takimoglu, A. (2022). What is data augmentation? Techniques & examples in 2022. *AI Multiple*. https://research.aimultiple.com/data-augmentation/

Tsang, A. H. C. (2002). Strategic dimensions of maintenance management. *Journal of Quality in Maintenance Engineering*, *8*(1), 7–39. https://doi.org/10.1108/13552510210420577

6 Fundamental in Artificial Intelligence

6.1 WHAT IS DECISION-MAKING?

Artificial intelligence (AI) is considered a powerful tool that can support and facilitate or even generate decisions normally made by humans, but *what is making decisions*? Making decisions can be described as the individual activity of selecting one option among several options. However, the step of selecting one among several options is normally associated with other pre-activities and post-activities. In industry, this set of interconnected activities is often recognised as the decision-making process.

In the context of the workplace, management is nothing but a continuous process of decision-making. It is the responsibility of business managers to make operational decisions and ensure that their teams execute the tasks. Decisions are needed both to tackle the problems and to take maximum advantage of the opportunities available. Correct decisions reduce complexities, uncertainties, and diversities of the organisational environments. In fact, the success of every manager depends largely on his or her decision-making skills.

The process of business planning depends on the art of decision-making. During the planning stage, managers need to make various decisions such as setting organisational goals. The care and research put in before making a decision shape the impact it will have. Managers decide individual targets, team goals, and various rules and regulations related to the team's functioning and conflict resolution, wherever needed (Harapan et al., 2020). They decide on key products, marketing strategies, role assignments, and timelines for every task.

In situations where plans don't deliver the desired outcome or are derailed for some reason, such as external issues or lack of performance, it is the managers who need to bring things back on track by making contingency decisions (Harapan et al., 2020).

Decision-making in the context of work management has three different but inter-related aspects (Sharma, 2022a):

1. When making a decision, managers exercise choice. They decide what to do based on conscious and deliberate logic or judgement.
2. When making a decision, managers are faced with alternatives. An organisation does not need a wise manager to reach a decision when there are no other possible choices. It does require wisdom and experience to evaluate several alternatives and select the best one.
3. When making a decision, managers have a purpose. They propose and analyse the alternative courses of action and finally make a choice that is likely to move the organisation in the direction of its goals.

6.1.1 IMPORTANCE OF DECISION-MAKING

It doesn't matter whether you are working in a small company with fewer than ten employees or in a large enterprise that has thousands of employees – things and situations always change. Over time, old practices, rules, and personnel make space for new processes, especially in uncertain situations, whether economic or political. Changes in conditions are the usual rule, but these situations call for actions that involve decision-making. Thus, managers are constantly called upon to reassess old decisions and make new ones.

Many decisions are critical to the ongoing success of the organisation, such as pricing a product, deciding which products to market, controlling production and maintenance costs, advertising, capital investments, creating a policy for dividends, and taking care of employee issues, among others.

Critical decisions also need to be made by managers in government or social service enterprises where profit is not the criterion of success (Harapan et al., 2020). Decision-making is the number one job of managers, regardless of their workplace. All managers must plan and assess the efficacy of their plans as they unfold.

When managers plan, they decide on many matters, such as what goals their organisation will pursue, what resources they will use, and who will perform each required task. When plans go wrong or off track, managers have to decide what to do to correct the deviation.

In fact, the whole planning process involves the managers constantly in a series of critical decision-making situations. The quality of managerial decisions largely affects the effectiveness of the plans they make (Sharma, 2022a). In sum, then, the decision-making process is both omnipresent and universal in the workplace.

6.1.2 Features or Characteristics of Decision-Making

The following are some important features of managerial decisions:

1. Rational thinking: Decision-making is based on rational thinking wherein the decision-maker tries to envision various possible effects of a decision before selecting one. It is invariably based on rational thinking. The human brain makes the rationality possible with its ability to learn, remember, and relate many complex factors.
2. Process: Decision-making is not a single moment in time but a process that includes both deliberations and reasoning (i.e. rational thinking).
3. Selective: Decision-making is selective, in that it represents the choice of the best alternative among several possibilities.
4. Purposive: Decision-making has a purpose. There is an expected end result wherein a specific goal will be met.
5. Positive: Decision-making is positive in that something will be done, and some action will be taken. That said, it is possible to decide not to decide – to put something off, say. However, even here, an end product has been created.
6. Commitment: Every decision is based on the concept of commitment. Decision-makers must be committed to their decisions. This promotes the stability of the organisation. Managers can't change their minds every few weeks and expect their employees to respect their decisions. Every decision should become a part of the expectations of the people involved in the organisation. Decisions are usually so inter-related with the entire organisational life of an enterprise that any change in one area of activity may change the other areas too. Thus, the decision-maker's commitment should extend to the decisions' successful implementation.
7. Evaluation: Decision-making involves evaluation in two ways. The first is in initial planning when the decision-maker evaluates the alternative choices. The second is a later step when the decision-maker evaluates the results of the previous decisions and selects among various possible responses. In either case, the best alternative will be chosen only after all pros and cons have been carefully considered.
8. Decision-making as art and as science: As the preceding analysis suggests, decision-making is both an art and a science. It rests on facts, but it requires human analysis (sometimes subjective) of those facts (Chand, 2022; Sharma, 2022a, 2022b).

6.1.3 Principles of Decision-Making

Effective decision-making involves two important aspects: the purpose for which it is intended and the environmental context. If either of these aspects is not considered, a decision that seems good in the beginning may turn out to be the wrong one.

In a helpful approach to this dilemma, Sharma (2022a) has delineated the main principles of decision-making. These are shown in Figure 6.1 and discussed in more detail below.

1. Subject of decision-making: Decision-making can be a routine and repetitive process that occurs in a cyclical and/or ongoing fashion. Or it can be non-repetitive, non-routine, and novel. The latter type may require individual attention and analysis, but it is also wise to take care of the former type, not to make assumptions.
2. Organisational structure: This refers to who actually makes the decision. Is it made from the top of the organisational structure? Is the decision-making rigid and highly centralised? Or are those at lower levels included in the process? Decision-making is very different between the two possibilities. If power is overly concentrated at the top, those at the bottom may feel alienated. But if the organisational structure provides scope for delegation and decentralisation of authority, the decision-making process may be more flexible and closer to the actual operating centres.
3. Analysis of objectives and policies: Decision-makers should have a clear understanding of the objectives of the decision-making. An organisation's objectives and policies should underlie and guide decision-making. Otherwise, decision-making may lack purpose and ultimately be unproductive – or even counterproductive.
4. Analytical study of the alternatives: Decision-makers need to weigh all possible alternatives, looking at possible upsides and downsides. This refers back to the concept of "rational" decision-making.
5. Proper communication systems: A decision cannot be a good one if those affected don't know about it, or if they know about it, they don't understand it. Effective decision-making requires a machinery for proper communication of information to all relevant parts of the organisation.
6. Sufficient time: On the one hand, decision-makers need enough time to think about various ideas and properly evaluate alternatives. On the other hand, delay is never good. They should have a clear deadline in mind.
7. Study of the impact of a decision: Decision-makers need to think globally within the organisation. How will a maintenance decision affect production and the goals of production? A decision in one particular area may have an adverse effect on other areas of the organisation. The impact of any decision should be analysed before it is made.

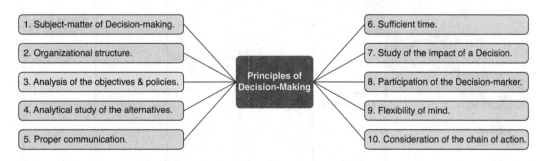

FIGURE 6.1 Principles of decision-making (Sharma, 2022a).

8. Participation of the decision-maker: Obviously, the decision-maker participates in the decision-making. However, he or she should also participate in completing the work for which the decision was made. This experience will help in future decision-making. Was the decision a practical one?

9. Mental flexibility: Unfortunately, few decisions satisfy everybody. A decision-maker must be ready to face criticism and must be flexible enough to change the decision if it turns out to be widely critiqued. Flexibility will lead to more co-operation across the board.

10. Consideration of the chain of action: This is related to point number 7. Any decision to change a particular task brings a change in other tasks. Decision-makers need to take a close look at the chain of action among activities (see Sharma, 2022a).

6.2 GENERAL DECISION-MAKING PROCESS

Decision-making is a process. Being able to identify the steps required may help generate better decisions by organising relevant information and defining alternatives. Figure 6.2 shows seven steps in an effective decision-making process, as identified by UMass (2022). We discuss these seven steps in more detail below.

1. Step 1: Identify the decision

   If there is a lack of clarity about exactly what must be decided, it will be virtually impossible to make a good decision. So the first step is to clearly define the nature of the decision to be made.

2. Step 2: Gather relevant information

   Even if the decision is a recurring one, it is essential to gather any new and relevant information before making a decision. If it refers to an ongoing situation, has anything changed? It is a new decision, what information is needed? Where can the information be

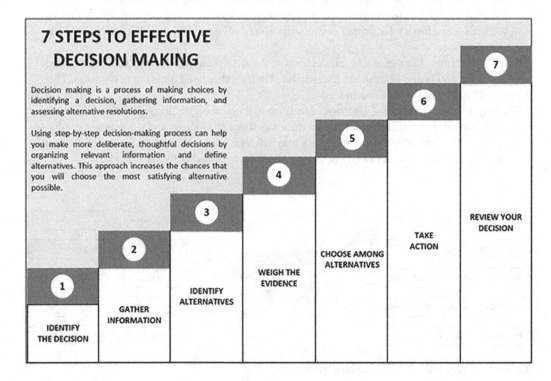

FIGURE 6.2   Steps in effective decision-making process (UMass, 2022).

found? Is it outside the organisation, for example, online or in books? Can other organisations be helpful?

3. Step 3: Identify the alternatives

There may be only one possible choice, but this seldom happens. In real life, there are likely to be several possible paths of action or alternatives. In this step, decision-makers should list all possible alternatives.

4. Step 4: Weigh the evidence

This step is arguably the most difficult because it requires decision-makers to imagine what would happen for each of the alternatives and to have a clear understanding of Step 1. Some alternatives may clearly be bad ones, but others may seem to have similar potential to reach a particular goal. Ultimately, the alternatives should be placed in a priority order, based on the decision-maker's value system.

5. Step 5: Choose among alternatives

The final choice is mostly likely to be the choice that made it to the top of the list in Step 4. However, it is also possible to opt for a combination of alternatives.

6. Step 6: Take action

This step is self-explanatory. The decision is made and the selected alternative is implemented.

7. Step 7: Review the decision and its consequences

This is a vital step in the decision-making process. Does the decision satisfy the need identified in Step 1? If not, it may be necessary to repeat all or part of the decision-making process to make a new decision. Perhaps more information is required, for example (UMass, 2022).

6.3 PROBLEM-SOLVING PROCESS IN INDUSTRIAL CONTEXTS

Decision-making may involve solving problems, but the two processes are not one and the same. In this section, we discuss the problem-solving process in the industrial domain. Note that many of the points we make will repeat those in the previous section on general decision-making.

The problem-solving process often emphasises certain generic actions (Figure 6.3).

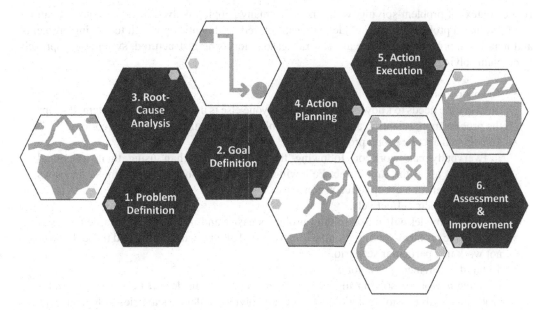

FIGURE 6.3 A generic problem-solving process.

1. Problem definition: The aim is to define which problem needs to be solved and to understand the characteristics of the problem situation, such as when and how the problem can be observed, recognised, and isolated. The main objective is to define what is called the *As-Is* state of the system-of-interest.
2. Goal definition: The aim is to envision a desired state of the system, called the *To-Be* state. The To-Be state often represents a future expected context to which the system-of-interest needs to be adapted. Transforming a problem situation from its As-Is state to its To-Be state requires a set of actions to be formulated and then taken.
3. Root cause, effect, and consequence identification: The aim is to provide a better understanding of the underlying mechanisms causing a specific problem and the consequences of the problem on, for example, the performance and/or the lifecycle of the system-of-interest.
4. Action plan development: The aim is to develop a roadmap, consisting of interconnected prioritised actions that, when conducted, result in the transformation of the context state of the system-of-interest, from As-Is to To-Be. Action plan development encompasses many aspects, including business, regulation, technology, and governance.
5. Action execution: The aim is to materialise the developed action plan in the addressed context. Executing actions is highly dependent on the selection of appropriate strategies and efficient support planning.
6. Continuous assessment and improvement: As in any other processes, retaining the effectiveness and efficiency of the problem-solving process requires an appropriate learning loop. The continuous assessment of the problem-solving process provides insight into how the various actions of the process can improve to improve overall performance.

A systematic approach to problem-solving allows:

- Making decisions based on data, rather than hunches.
- Determining root causes of problems, rather than reacting to superficial symptoms.
- Devising permanent solutions, rather than relying on quick fixes (Qureshi, 2008).

6.3.1 Six-Step Problem-Solving Model

In the context of problem-solving, when there are many people involved in the decision, it can be helpful to use a problem-solving model, i.e. a structured, systematic approach to solving problems and making improvements. There are several reasons for using a structured, systematic approach to problem solving:

- To ensure consistency.
    Everyone needs to know what method everyone else is using to solve a problem. It keeps the process more scientific and less susceptible to individual biases and perceptions.
- To help manage the group process.
    Everybody can work on following the model rather than using their individual approaches all at the same time. Following a method and using data to make decisions make it easier for a group to reach consensus.
- To solve problems effectively.
    Using a model will make solving problems easier and ultimately yield a better result because the problem-solving group will have tested all ideas and eliminated those that will not work in a particular scenario.
- To build a convincing case for change.
    Using a problem-solving model enables a group to consider all possible causes of a problem and all possible solutions. A problem-solving model uses a series of logical steps to help a group identify the most important causes and the best solution. Following the

model not only helps the group arrive at a solution, but also helps the group arrive at a justifiable solution.
- To present a clear and convincing rationale for action.
  A process improvement model is also useful as a methodology for presenting the conclusions of process improvement activities. The diagrams and charts used in the process improvement cycle help make the proposal for change more convincing (Qureshi, 2008).

Problem-solving models can be highly sophisticated and technical. The model shown in Figure 6.4 has only six steps (also see Section 6.2, steps in decision-making). Despite its simplicity, this model is comprehensive enough to address all but the most technical problems (Qureshi, 2008).

The steps in the sequence are arranged in a circle to emphasise the cyclical, continuous nature of the problem-solving process. All six steps must be followed in the order shown in Figure 6.4, beginning with Step 1, Identify the Problem. Each step must be completed before the group proceeds clockwise to the next step (Qureshi, 2008).

There are several important characteristics of this model:

- The steps are repeatable.
  At any step in the process, a group may decide to go back and repeat an earlier step. For example, diagnosing a problem can often lead back to redefining the problem.
- The process is continuous.
  Simply implementing a solution does not end the problem-solving process. Evaluation of that solution may identify new aspects of the problem or new problems that need to be addressed, leading the group back to step one, where the new problem is identified.

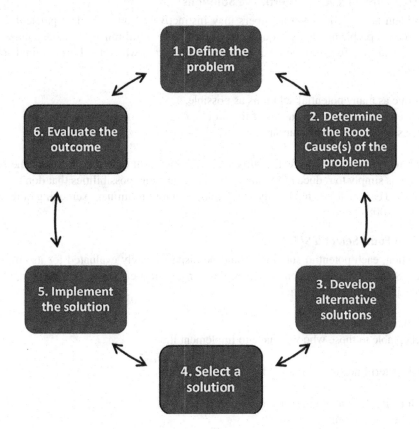

FIGURE 6.4   A problem-solving model (Qureshi, 2008).

Although the steps all have distinct names, there is no clear demarcation between them. For example, "identifying" a problem and "diagnosing" a problem frequently overlap (Qureshi, 2008).

6.3.1.1   Step One: Identify the Problem

The first step, identifying the problem, is a broad review of the current situation – a fitting together of information, like pieces of a puzzle. In this first stage, a group identifies and discusses the symptoms and scope of the problem. That is, it determines what "hurts", the degree to which the symptoms are shared, and the urgency of relieving the symptoms. Groups use tools such as brainstorming, interviewing, and completing questionnaires to gather this information.

As groups go through this step, they will find themselves raising, reviewing, and discarding statements of the problem as they sort out what are merely symptoms of the problem and then look behind those symptoms to make a tentative definition of the underlying problem (Qureshi, 2008).

6.3.1.2   Step Two: Determine the Root Cause(s) of the Problem

Once the group has recognised the symptoms and tentatively defined the problem, it can begin to collect information about the nature of the problem. At this step, tools such as the Fishbone diagram or Pareto analysis may help organise this information and zero in on the underlying causes of the problem. In this way, the group determines the root causes of the problem. When the problem is restated, the definition will reflect the causes. Efforts over the next two steps can thus be directed to finding solutions that address the roots of a documented problem, not merely its random symptoms (Qureshi, 2008).

6.3.1.3   Step Three: Develop Alternative Solutions

Once a problem is defined, group members may instinctively lean towards a particular solution. However, creative problem-solving requires them to explore a full range of viable solutions before reaching a conclusion. To assemble a variety of solutions from which to choose a final solution, it is necessary to:

- Generate as many potential solutions as possible.
- Relate each solution to the causes of the problem.
- Merge similar or related solutions.

No matter how confident people feel, at this stage, they are still not ready to select the best solution. The goal is simply to reduce redundancy and eliminate any possibilities that don't address the causes identified earlier. Force field analysis is a good tool for preliminary screening of this solution field (Qureshi, 2008).

6.3.1.4   Step Four: Select a Solution

Before selection, each potential solution should be dispassionately evaluated for its strengths and weaknesses. Selecting a solution entails searching for the most effective solution by applying two general criteria. An effective solution:

- Is technically feasible.
- Is acceptable to those who will have to implement it.

Feasibility is determined by asking the following questions:

- Can it be implemented in a reasonable time?
- Can it be done within cost limits?
- Will it work reliably?

- Will it use staff and equipment efficiently?
- Is it flexible enough to adapt to changing conditions?

Ask these questions when evaluating a solution's acceptability:

- Do the implementers support the solution, perceiving it as worth their time and energy?
- Are the risks manageable?
- Will the solution benefit the persons affected by the problem?
- Will it benefit the organisation?

Simply stated, selecting a solution requires selecting the one that will be effective – one that has sufficient technical quality to resolve the problem and is acceptable to those who will implement it (Qureshi, 2008).

6.3.1.5   Step Five: Implement the Solution

Choosing a solution does not immediately solve a problem. Putting a solution into action may prove as difficult as deciding on one. The implementation stage requires action planning:

- What must be done?
- Who will do it?
- When will it be started?
- When will key milestones be completed?
- How will the necessary actions be carried out?
- Why are these actions a solution?

Once the group has answered these questions, the proposed solution can be implemented (Qureshi, 2008).

6.3.1.6   Step Six: Evaluate the Outcome

In simple terms, evaluation is the monitoring that any project needs to ensure its milestones are met, costs are contained, and work is completed. Unfortunately, most groups neglect or short-change the evaluation step and therefore do not get the continued results or performance they were hoping to achieve.

- Establishing feedback mechanisms will detect the need for midcourse corrections and ensure the problem is solved without creating new problems.
- Collecting data and reporting on what has been accomplished keeps a group credible with its constituents.
- Reflecting on its own processes and results keeps a group effective. It also brings the problem-solving process full circle, as reflecting on results helps a group identify its next step (Qureshi, 2008).

6.4   SYSTEM THINKING AND COMPUTER SCIENCE

When empowering highly complex industrial technical systems with digital technologies and AI, it is essential to take a holistic approach to these systems. At the same time, however, there is a need to understand a system's various inherent items and their interactions. This is commonly referred to as the system structure.

Defining, identifying, and understanding the system structure is extremely important when selecting approaches, methodologies, technologies, models, algorithms, and tools in the digital transformation of the system. Two essential aspects to consider are system decomposition and system abstraction.

1. System decomposition: System decomposition aims to identify and understand a system's inherent items, by breaking a more complex item down into several simpler items. This means that we reduce the complexity of the system to facilitate our understanding of it.

When decomposing a system, the number of items in the system structure description increases. Think of an aircraft, for example: it is considered a complex technical system. During the decomposition of aircraft, we may identify: engine left, engine right, landing gear left, landing gear right, left wing, right wing, main avionic computer, secondary avionic computer etc. The landing gear may further be decomposed into axel, down lock, side strut, actuator etc. Today's complex systems can all be similarly decomposed.

Even though the main purpose of decomposition is to simplify things, the increased number of items brings new complexity into the picture.

2. System abstraction: System abstraction deals with the challenge of decomposition, whereby the sheer number of items determined by decomposition works to increase the complexity. The purpose of system abstraction is to reduce complexity when describing an item's characteristics, through classification. A class created by abstraction represents common characteristics of similar items. It is important to note that we cannot always describe all the characteristics of an item through its abstract representation, i.e. its class. This means we need to differentiate between the description of an individual item and its type description.

Returning to the aircraft example, let's assume the aircraft has four engines of the same type. At first glance, we might think these four engines can be described by single abstract class. However, we also know that an engine is subject to maintenance, repair, and overhaul. Moreover, an engine can be replaced during maintenance to retain the required availability of the aircraft. This means the replaced engine in the aircraft might have individual characteristics that need to be managed, even though it is of the same class as the original engine.

Abstraction may facilitate the understanding and management of items' common characteristics and behaviour, but it many cases, we still need to manage and understand an item's individual characteristics and behaviour, as illustrated in Figure 6.5.

Why do system decomposition and item abstraction matter in digital transformation and implementation of AI?

1. First, decomposition helps us understand the characteristics of the system and the structure of its inherent items which we plan to empower with AI and digitalisation. It also helps us understand the interactions between the items, i.e. the interfaces. This insight can be used to identify relevant data sources and features that are essential in data processing. Understanding the characteristics of an item is a must when developing AI-based algorithms. Without knowing the physics of a system, digital transformation is very difficult.

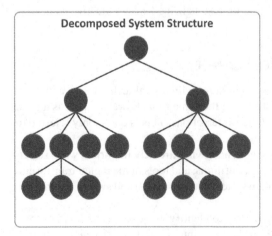 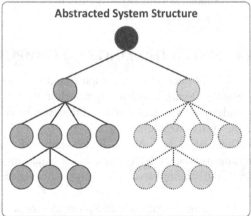

Decomposed System Structure   **Abstracted System Structure**

FIGURE 6.5   System structure decomposed and abstracted.

2. Second, abstraction helps to simplify context sensing, context adaptation, and data processing via pattern recognition. It provides the necessary input to increase the efficiency of the execution and initiation of the AI algorithms. Finally, abstraction can be used to implement an appropriate architecture for distributed computing and distributed cybersecurity. Without an appropriate system abstraction, the lifecycle management of the digital transformation and AI will be costly.

6.5 DECISION SUPPORT SYSTEMS

Making decisions effectively and efficiently requires an appropriate support system. The decision support system (DSS) is illustrated in Figure 6.6.

A decision-making process can be aided with analytic services at different levels of autonomy. A simple DSS passively provides information which has been complied, without considering the context in which the information will be used. A simple DSS doesn't provide the capability to evaluate the options and give them a weighting relative to their consequences.

An enhanced DSS provides built-in capability to evaluate options, estimate the consequences, and manage the risks. Based on the risk assessment, it also takes action.

In other words, a simple DSS has a low level of autonomy and requires the involvement of liveware (i.e. humans) for additional post-processing before a decision is made. An enhanced DSS can be considered an autonomous mechanism that can perceive its context, adapt to the context, solve complex problems, act, and learn from its previous actions.

As illustrated in Figure 6.6, a DSS is often characterised by the following set of services:

1. Collecting data from various data sources;
2. Transforming collected data for data processing;
3. Loading data to storage (e.g. the cloud);
4. Integrating collected datasets;
5. Processing data;
6. Analysing the processed data;
7. Delivering input for acting.

When the maturity of a DSS increases and it has the capability to mimic human cognition and perceptions for problem-solving, it is often called an expert system or knowledge-based system.

6.6 DATA IN A DECISION-MAKING PROCESS

Data are the essential raw materials that are processed by the DSS to facilitate the decision-making process.

Data can be collected, harvested, and generated using a number of different approaches. The process can be knowledge-driven, data-driven, model-driven, or a hybrid.

- Knowledge-driven: The knowledge-driven approach is mainly based on the transferring of known facts (from experts, for example) to the decision-making process, using, for example, communication channels or documentation. To validate the reliability and quality of

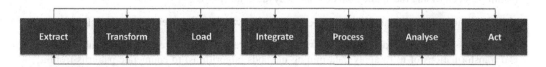

FIGURE 6.6 Decision support services.

the data provided by a knowledge-driven approach, we need to establish indicators and documentation on how the original knowledge was gained. Establishing a proper quality assessment is one of the main challenges in the knowledge-driven approach, however, as it is strongly based on the perceptions and cognition of humans.

- Data-driven: The data-driven approach is mainly based on the utilisation of artefacts, such as soft and hard sensors, for data collection. These sensors measure the parameters from the operation of a system in its real-world environment. The data-driven approach fills the gap between assumptions of expected behaviour and actual behaviour. However, in a data-driven approach, a human might be considered a specific type of sensor and source of data generation. In the data-driven approach, assessing the reliability and quality of data requires an appropriate strategy to establish a security and calibration program.
- Model-driven: The model-driven approach is mainly based on the description of expected system behaviour in its assumed environment through a model. A model can be considered a simplified description of a real-world phenomenon. Simplification in modelling is a common approach to reduce the model complexity to make the model more manageable. As in any simplification process, there is trade-off between losing system properties, quality or quantity, and level of complexity.
- Hybrid: The hybrid approach is simply any combination of the approaches mentioned above. The main reason for combining data collection approaches is to improve the quality and reliability of data sets used in the analytics and enhance the accuracy of the decision-making process.

In industrial contexts, selecting the appropriate data collection and data generation approach is important and needs to be considered based on the context and the required outcome for that context – in other words, an outcome-driven approach.

An outcome-driven approach is a mindset that is result-centric. This approach puts the focus on the overall business objective (the outcome), rather than the means (the output) to achieve the objectives.

6.7 KNOWLEDGE DISCOVERY

Knowledge discovery (KD) can be described as the process of extracting useful information for data. Over time, many approaches, technologies, and methodologies have been developed to facilitate KD. Today, KD is tightly connected with cognitive technologies such as machine learning (ML), deep learning (DL), and natural language processing (NLP) for enabling analytics-driven business (see data-driven decision-making in Chapter 5). Besides the cognitive technologies, visualisation technologies are important to enhance the overall usefulness and experience of KD.

KD can be used to bring intelligence to many industrial contexts, such as marketing, operation, maintenance, and business (El Sheikh & Alnoukari, 2012). .
Knowledge discovery in data (KDD) has been defined as:

> ...the entire knowledge extraction process, including how data are stored and accessed, how to use efficient and scalable algorithms to analyse massive datasets, how to interpret and visualise the results, and how to model and support the interaction between human and machine. It also concerns support for learning and analysing the application domain. (Fayyad et al., 1996)

As this definition makes clear, KD is a process. The knowledge discovery process (KDP) is:

> ...the process of using the database along with any required selection, pre-processing, subsampling, and transformations of it; to apply data mining methods (algorithms) to enumerate patterns from it; and to evaluate the products of data mining to identify the subset of the enumerated patterns deemed knowledge. (Fayyad et al., 1996)

6.7.1 Approaches to KDP Modelling

The following are the main KDP modelling approaches:

1. Traditional KDP approach: This approach is widely used by most KDP modelling innovators. Starting with KDD process modelling, many KDP models use the same process flow, including most of the following steps: business understanding, data understanding, data processing, data mining/modelling, model evaluation, and deployment/visualization.
2. Ontology-based KDP approach: This approach is the integration of ontology engineering and traditional KDP steps. The approach includes ontology for KDP, KDP for ontology, and the integration of the two.
3. Web-based KDP approach: This approach mainly deals with web log analysis. It is similar to the traditional KDP approach, but it has some unique steps to deal with log web data.
4. Agile-based KDP approach: This approach integrates agile methodologies and KDP traditional methodologies (Fayyad et al., 1996).

6.7.2 The Leading KDP Models

The following leading KDP models based on their innovation and their applications in both academia and industry are the following:

1. KDD process model.
2. Information flow in a data mining lifecycle model.
3. SEMMA, steps for the practical implementation of Fayyad et al.'s (1996) model.
4. Refined KDD paradigm model.
5. Knowledge discovery lifecycle (KDLC) model.
6. Cross-industry-standard process for data mining (CRISP-DM) model.
7. Generic data mining lifecycle (DMLC) model.
8. Ontology-driven knowledge discovery (ODKD) process model.
9. Adaptive software development-data mining (ASD-DM) process model (El Sheikh & Alnoukari, 2012).

The main measures used when evaluating the models are the following:

1. Data: Define the exact data sources (where data originated) such as online transaction processing (OLTP) databases, data warehouse, data marts etc. Also define the data destination (where data are stored) such as data repository, knowledge repository etc. This measure is crucial in any KDP modelling as it defines the main inputs and outputs.
2. Process: Define all process steps or phases involved in the KDP model extended by the process flows throughout the model's lifecycle. The following process steps have been identified as critical and are necessary to build a comprehensive KDP model: business understanding, data understanding, objectives/hypotheses, data preparation/ ETL, modelling/data mining, evaluation, and deployment.
3. People: Define the human resources involved throughout the KDP model. The model should address different kinds of skills, including business analyst, data engineer, data miner, domain expert, knowledge engineer, and strategic manager.
4. Adaptive: Define how the KDP model could be adaptive to environment changes. This measure is crucial for applications where requirements are uncertain or volatile (such as data mining and BI).
5. Knowledge: Define how the KDP model could enhance knowledge capture and sharing. Knowledge is the core outcome of any KDP model. Models are evaluated by how they gain new knowledge, and how they store and maintain the discovered knowledge for future use.

6. Strategy: Define how the KDP model could help formulate the organisation's mission and long-term objectives and help it implement and achieve its strategies (El Sheikh & Alnoukari, 2012).

6.8 BUSINESS INTELLIGENCE

Business intelligence (BI) is a term that is often used to describe tools and technologies to facilitate KD in an organisation. BI tools are often associated with features such as the capability to process a large amount of data from data sources, data filtering, data processing, and data visualisation. The main goal of these tools is to enable an analytics-driven approach in an organisation by increasing efficiency in analytics and facilitating the decision-making process.

Demand for BI applications continues to grow even when demand for most information technology (IT) products is soft. Yet information systems (IS) research in this field is notably lacking.

Although the term "business intelligence" is relatively new, computer-based business intelligence systems appeared close to 41 years ago. BI as a term replaced decision support, executive IS, and management IS. With each new iteration, capabilities increased as enterprises grew ever-more sophisticated in their computational and analytical needs and as computer hardware and software matured.

Simply stated, BI systems combine data gathering, data storage, and knowledge management with analytical tools to present complex internal and competitive information to planners and decision-makers. In other words, BI systems provide actionable information delivered at the right time, in the right place, and in the right form to assist decision-makers. The objective is to improve the timeliness and quality of inputs to the decision process, hence facilitating decision-making.

Sometimes business intelligence refers to online decision-making, requiring an instant response. Most of the time, it refers to shrinking the time frame so that the intelligence is still useful to the decision-maker when the decision time comes. In all cases, the use of business intelligence is viewed as being proactive (Negash, 2004).

Essential components of proactive BI are:

- real-time data warehousing,
- data mining,
- automated anomaly and exception detection,
- proactive alerting with automatic recipient determination,
- seamless follow-through workflow,
- automatic learning and refinement,
- geographic IS,
- data visualisation.

Figure 6.7 shows the variety of information inputs available to provide the intelligence needed in decision-making (Negash, 2004).

6.8.1 BUSINESS INTELLIGENCE ON A PRACTICAL LEVEL

BI is simply a technology that collects, stores, accesses, and analyses data to help decision-makers make good well-informed decisions. Otherwise stated, BI converts raw data into meaningful information, producing, for example, reports and dashboards, thus permitting decision-makers, whether individuals or organisations, to make informed data-driven decisions by optimising and capitalising on historical data.

To arrive at that meaningful information and produce those reports, BI employs statistical methods to analyse the data. To that end, it draws on cutting-edge tools, such as data mining and data warehousing, along with others (GlobalData365, 2022).

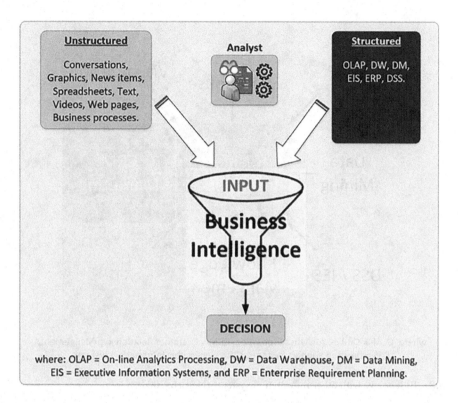

FIGURE 6.7   Inputs into business intelligence systems (Negash, 2004).

6.8.2   What Does Business Intelligence Do?

BI assists in strategic and operational decision-making. In fact, BI is a natural outgrowth of a series of previous systems designed to support decision-making. The emergence of the data warehouse as a repository, the advances in data cleaning that lead ideally to a single truth, the greater capabilities of hardware and software, and the boom of Internet technologies that provide a user interface all combine to create a richer BI environment than was available previously.

BI pulls information from many other systems. Figure 6.8 depicts some of the IS used by BI (Negash, 2004).

BI converts all these data from all these systems into useful information. At the end of the process, the human analysis turns the information into knowledge.

Some of the tasks performed by BI are:

- Creating forecasts based on historical data, past and current performance, and estimating the future direction.
- Performing "What if" analysis of the impacts of changes and alternative scenarios.
- Providing ad hoc access to data to answer specific, non-routine questions.
- Offering strategic insight (Negash, 2004).

The three key performance indicators of BI are security, simplicity, and speed (GlobalData365, 2022).

6.8.3   Differences Between Artificial Intelligence and Business Intelligence

BI and AI are frequently confused. Both assist organisations in making crucial decisions, but there are significant differences between them.

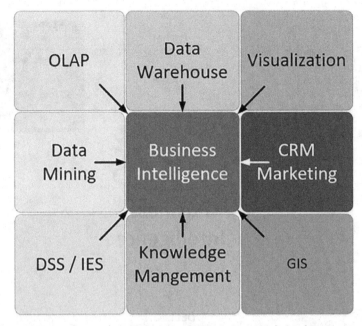

where: OLAP = On-line Analytics Processing, CRM = Customer Relationship Mangement,
DSS = Decision Support Systems, GIS = Geographic Information Systems.

FIGURE 6.8   BI relations with other information systems (Negash, 2004).

In a nutshell, AI refers to computer intelligence that is similar to human intelligence, while BI refers to intelligent decision-making. Table 6.1 shows their most salient differences (GlobalData365, 2022).

On the one hand, AI wants to create machines replicating human thought. On the other hand, BI hopes to assist organisations to evaluate and understand the past and thus predict the future. BI enables organisations to gain access to the data they need to make fast, better-informed decisions – a crucial element of survival in today's rapidly evolving business environment.

Despite their differences (or because of them), BI may be a driver of AI integration. BI-savvy organisations can better plan for thinking machines and lay the foundations for machine-augmented decision-making by investing in BI now (GlobalData365, 2022).

6.9   DATABASE AND KNOWLEDGE BASE IN DECISION SUPPORT SYSTEMS

In a DSS, data have to be managed properly. If the DSS also aims to provide cognitive and perception capabilities, knowledge management becomes equally important. In other words, both a database and a knowledge base must be managed. The terms can be defined as follows:

- Database: A database is a collection of data representing facts in their basic form. In simple terms, it stores and manages facts, i.e. elements of data, for example, temperature, load, thickness, and so on. Automation software typically helps to transform and load data into a database. It takes a database management system (DBMS) to then access, manipulate, and use these data (ThinkAutomation, 2022).
- Knowledge base: A knowledge base stores information as answers to questions or solutions to problems. Otherwise stated, it is used to manage the knowledge expressed by the facts and the relations between them. We can make inquiries against a knowledge base; information in a knowledge base is typically fully developed and ready to be applied.

TABLE 6.1

Key Differences Between Artificial Intelligence and Business Intelligence (GlobalData365, 2022)

Factors	Artificial Intelligence	Business Intelligence
Concept	Artificial intelligence refers to human-like computer intelligence.	Business intelligence refers to intelligent decision-making.
Emphasis	It requires the use of statistical methods to analyse data.	It involves machine learning and DL algorithms.
Application	It is primarily used in robotics, virtual reality, image recognition, and ML.	It is primarily used in data warehouse, data modelling. data visualisation and dashboards, analytics, and reporting.
Usage	Its usage is linked to future events.	Its usage is linked to available historical data.
Inputs	It benefits subjects such as biology and computer.	It benefits enterprise management data reporting and data analysis, as well as online analytical processing.
Algorithm	It utilises the breadth-first algorithm (BFS) and follows the first-in-first-out (FIFO) principle.	It uses a linear aggression module to organise data.
Limitations	It poses security and privacy risks.	It can lead to the misuse of data by using improving technology.
Objective	The main aim of AI is to produce machines that have the potential to work like the human brain.	The main aim of BI is to analyse present conditions and make future predictions by using historical data.
Tools	It makes use of complex algorithms to make logic.	It makes use of spreadsheets. query software, dashboards, and tools of data mining analysis.

As such, it permits rapid search, retrieval, and reuse (GetGuru, 2022). Whereas a database stores simple structures (i.e. facts), a knowledge base is designed to manage complex nested structures and context-based rules (or predicates). There are many approaches and techniques for knowledge representation and reasoning (KRR), some of which are in the area of ontology engineering, such as the semantic web. In the area of AI, several programming languages aimed at rule-based logical reasoning have been developed, for example, Prolog and Lisp. A knowledge base can take the form of an FAQ section, a web portal, PDFs, spreadsheets, Wikis, and so on (ThinkAutomation, 2022).

When managing data and knowledge, some common issues that need to be addressed are the *redundancy* of data and knowledge (often solved using a break-down-approach) and the *consistency* of data and knowledge during an update.

6.9.1 Differences Between a Database and a Knowledge Base

Table 6.2 shows some of the differences between a database and a knowledge base (Webeduclick, 2022). Two very basic differences include the form of data and the purposes.

1. Form of data: Knowledge bases and databases store and provide access to different types of information. Databases store data in their basic form. These need to be further processed and analysed to be of any use. Data are not answers. They simply represent the information needed to find the answers. Knowledge bases contain information that is ready to apply, such as, for example, formulated answers, how-to guides, or troubleshooting instructions (ThinkAutomation, 2022).

2. Purpose: Just as databases and knowledge bases contain different data, they also have different purposes. The purpose of a database is to take raw data and store them safely, making

TABLE 6.2
Differences Between Database and Knowledge Base (Webeduclick, 2022)

Database	Knowledge Base
1. Database doesn't consist of fuzzy facts	1. Knowledge base may consist of fuzzy facts.
2. Database doesn't contain the more sophisticated relationship between facts.	2. Knowledge base contains more sophisticated relationships between facts
3. Database doesn't contain factual and heuristic knowledge.	3. Knowledge base contains both factual and heuristic knowledge.
4. It doesn't emulate the decision-making processes of humans.	4. It emulates the decision-making processes of humans.
5. It doesn't capture and distribute knowledge.	5. It captures and distributes knowledge.
6. Databases are sometimes inconsistent.	6. Knowledge bases are accurate and consistent.
7. Databases aren't dependable.	7. Knowledge bases are dependable.
8. A database expert is needed to update databases.	8. Expert knowledge of the domain is needed to update a knowledge base.
9. Databases are sometimes not profitable.	9. Knowledge bases are profitable.

them easily accessible and readily usable. The required data should be easy to find, manipulate, and filter. The purpose of a knowledge base is to make it easy to find answers to questions. Thus, ease of use is a common purpose for both databases and knowledge bases. However, a knowledge base is basically a self-service tool (ThinkAutomation, 2022).

6.10 INFERENCE MECHANISMS IN ARTIFICIAL INTELLIGENCE

Reasoning can be seen as the process of building a theory. It is fundamental in building theories, making conclusions, and supporting decision-making. In science, there are mainly three reasoning mechanisms:

1. deduction
2. induction
3. abduction (Patel & Davidson, 2003).

These are illustrated in Figure 6.9. These reasoning mechanisms are also applicable, implemented, and used in reasoning in AI. Besides these fundamental mechanisms, there are additional complementary reasoning mechanisms developed by the AI community.

6.10.1 DEDUCTIVE REASONING

Deductive reasoning uses general rules and theories to explain a specific case. For example, we might start with the theory: "All birds can fly". We can then test this theory by observing a selected population of birds. The population we observe will have a direct impact on whether we conclude that the test shows our theory is true or false. For example, if we look at penguins, the result will be different from looking at seagulls.

Deductive reasoning in AI uses knowledge to make conclusions. In this *model-driven approach* to analytics, the model represents the known knowledge (i.e. the theory).

Deductive reasoning starts with the assertion of a general rule and proceeds to a specific conclusion. In deductive reasoning, if the original assertions are true, the conclusion must also be true. For example, math is deductive, as the following shows:

- If $x=4$,
- and if $y=1$,
- then $2x+y=9$.

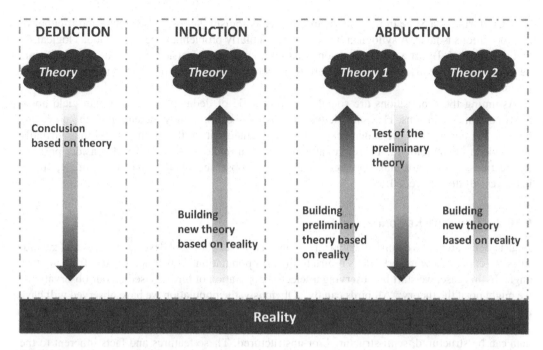

FIGURE 6.9   Some reasoning mechanisms.

In this example, it is a logical necessity that $2x+y$ equals 9. Interestingly, formal symbolic logic uses a language that looks very like this math equality, with its own operators and syntax. Moreover, a math equality expressed in English, i.e. a deductive syllogism, can be expressed in ordinary language:

- If entropy (disorder) in a system will increase unless energy is expended,
- and if my kitchen is a system,
- then disorder will increase in my kitchen unless I clean it.

In this syllogism, the first two statements are propositions or premises; they lead logically to the conclusion, the third statement. Here is another example:

- A medical technology ought to be funded if it has been used successfully to treat patients.
- Adult stem cells are being used to treat patients successfully in more than 65 new therapies.
- Adult stem cell research and technology should be funded.

A conclusion is sound (true) or unsound (false), depending on the truth of the original premise (any premise may be true or false). At the same time, independent of the truth or falsity of the premise, the deductive inference itself (the process linking the premise to the conclusion) is either valid or invalid. Thus, the process of inference can be valid even if the premise is false, as the following example shows:

- There is no such thing as drought in the American West.
- California is in the American West.
- California never needs to make plans to deal with a drought.

In this case, the inferential process is valid, but the conclusion is false because the first proposition is false. There is indeed a problem with drought in the American West. The second proposition is true: California is a State in the American West. A syllogism yields a false conclusion if either of its propositions is false. A syllogism like this is particularly problematic because it looks logical. In fact, it is logical. But if a policy decision is based upon it, and decision-makers decide California never needs to make plans to deal with a drought, there is likely to be a problem in the not-so-distant future.

Assuming the propositions are sound, the rigid logic of deductive reasoning can yield absolutely certain conclusions. That said, deductive reasoning cannot really increase human knowledge because the conclusions are statements that are contained within the premises and thus virtually self-evident, i.e. tautologies. Therefore, although we can make observations and consider possible implications, we cannot make predictions about non-observed phenomena, for example, future instances (ButteCollege, 2019).

6.10.2 INDUCTIVE REASONING

Inductive research uses empirical data from many cases to explain and develop theories and general rules. To explain how it works, let's return to the bird population. This time, we start from another angle. In this case, we start by observing a selected population of birds. Based on our observations, we might posit the theory: "All birds can fly". Obviously, the population we have observed will have a direct impact on whether our new theory is valid.

Inductive reasoning in AI uses facts (i.e. data) to describe features of the observed objects. The data can be structured, semi-structured, or unstructured. These features and facts inherent to the data are then used to build the theory.

In this *data-driven approach* to analytics, the facts (i.e. the data) are used to explain a phenomenon of interest.

Inductive reasoning begins with observations that are specific and limited in scope and proceeds to a generalised conclusion that is likely, but not certain, in light of the accumulated evidence. In a nutshell, inductive reasoning moves from the specific to the general. A great deal of scientific research uses the inductive method: gathering evidence, seeking patterns, and forming a hypothesis or theory to explain what has been seen.

Conclusions reached by the inductive method are not logical necessities; no amount of inductive evidence guarantees the conclusion simply because there is no way of knowing that all the possible evidence has been gathered. Some further bit of hitherto unobserved evidence may invalidate a hypothesis. Thus, the scientific literature tends to use cautious language, the language of inductively reached, probable conclusions, with such words as "suggest", "may", "possibly", and so on.

Because inductive conclusions are not logical necessities, inductive arguments are not simply true. Rather, the evidence seems complete, relevant, and generally convincing, i.e. cogent, so the conclusion is probably true. By the same token, inductive arguments are not simply false; rather, the evidence is incomplete or unconvincing; i.e. the argument is not cogent, and the conclusion is therefore probably false.

While inductive reasoning cannot yield an absolutely certain conclusion, unlike deductive reasoning, it can actually increase human knowledge. Moreover, unlike deductive reasoning, it can make predictions about future events or as-yet unobserved phenomena. Many scientific theories have evolved in this manner (ButteCollege, 2019).

6.10.3 ABDUCTIVE REASONING

Abductive reasoning is a combination of deductive and inductive reasoning approaches. In abduction reasoning, the most likely theory is selected based on observations. The preliminary selected theory is then tested on real-world data, and a new theory is built. Returning to our bird example, we might observe some birds, for example, a flock of seagulls, and using deductive reasoning, we select the theory: "Birds can fly". Then, we test our theory on new observations and include a different bird population, say penguins. Now the new theory might be expressed as: "Birds can typically fly".

Abductive reasoning in AI uses facts (i.e. data) and knowledge (i.e. model) to observe, test, and build theories. In this *hybrid approach* to analytics, the data-driven and model-driven approaches are combined to build new theories and reach conclusions.

Abductive reasoning typically begins with an incomplete set of observations and proceeds to the likeliest possible explanation for the set. It lends itself to the kind of daily decision-making that does the best it can with the information at hand, which often is incomplete.

A medical diagnosis is an application of abductive reasoning: given this set of symptoms, what diagnosis best explains most of them? We might call this a "best guess" type of reasoning.

While cogent inductive reasoning requires the evidence to be fairly complete, abductive reasoning is characterised by a lack of completeness, either in the evidence, or in the explanation, or both. In our medical diagnosis analogy, a patient may fail to report every symptom, resulting in incomplete evidence, or a doctor may arrive at a diagnosis that fails to explain several of the symptoms. Still, she must reach the best diagnosis she can.

The abductive process can be creative and intuitive. Einstein's work, for example, involved a creative leap of imagination and visualisation, so much so, that some of his peers discredited his ideas. Nevertheless, his amazing and unsubstantiated conclusions about space-time continue to be verified by others (ButteCollege, 2019).

6.10.4 CASE-BASED REASONING

Case-based reasoning (CBR) is an approach to provide conclusions based on historical conclusions. This approach relies on similarity analysis and uses a matching mechanism to identify similar cases. It is assumed that historical solutions are applicable to new problems, if the cases in which the problems exist have a high degree of similarity.

CBR is a paradigm of AI and cognitive science that models the reasoning process as primarily memory-based (Whitney et al., 2001). It is based on the paradigm of human thought in cognitive psychology that contends human experts derive their knowledge from solving numerous cases in their problem domain. Although humans may generalise patterns of cases into rules, the principal unit of knowledge is "the case". Thus, the reasoning is by analogy or association with the solutions for previous similar cases.

CBR can be particularly useful in areas where traditional rule-based reasoning is relatively weak, such as knowledge acquisition, ML, and reasoning with incomplete information. At present, prototype computer programs are being tested for their effectiveness in problem-solving tasks using the CBR approach. Manual systems have been successfully used in medicine, law, and design and failure analysis. Such systems have dealt with the conceptual design of office buildings and building failure analysis. A possible application of CBR to concrete problems is the identification of causes of concrete deterioration where the records are incomplete, and traditional methods of analysis are inconclusive (Ramachandran & Beaudoin, 2000).

The CBR process can be described as cyclic, as shown in Figure 6.10. The description of a new problem to be solved is introduced in the problem space. This is followed by three steps: retrieval, adaptation, and learning.

During the first step, retrieval, a new problem is matched against problems of the previous cases by computing similarity function, and the most similar problem and its stored solution are found. If the proposed solution does not meet the necessary requirements of a new problem situation, the next step, adaptation, occurs and a new solution is created. A received solution and a new problem together form a new case that is incorporated into the case base during the learning step. In this way, the CBR system evolves as the capability of the system is improved by extending the stored experience (Grievink & Van Schijndel, 2002).

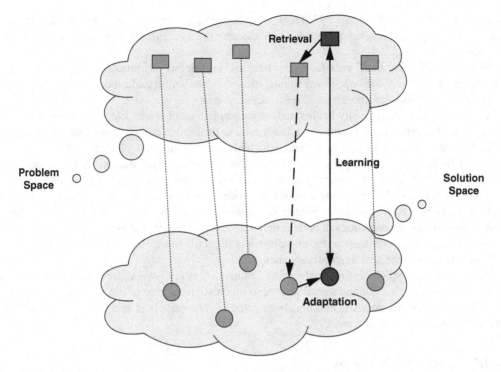

FIGURE 6.10   Illustration of the CBR process (Grievink & Van Schijndel, 2002).

CBR has been used in chemical engineering for equipment selection, process synthesis, and support of preliminary design (Grievink & van Schijndel, 2002).

6.10.5 MONOTONIC REASONING AND NON-MONOTONIC REASONING

In monotonic reasoning, the conclusions are static; when a conclusion is reached, it remains the same, even if we add new information.

In non-monotonic reasoning, the conclusions may be invalid when new facts are added.

6.11 KNOWLEDGE INTERPRETATION: THE ROLE OF INFERENCE

In AI, the software component that is responsible for interpreting the rules is often called the "inference engine". The inference engine applies facts, which are stored in the knowledge base. Inferencing is an iterative process, executed by the inference engine, during which rules are applied to the facts, and new rules are deduced. In other words, the inference engine creates a chain of logic during interpretation, in which each logic is selected based on the previous interpretation. This is called logical reasoning.

In general, the inference engine executes a logical chain based on two implementations: forward chaining and backward chaining.

- Forward chaining is the implementation of deductive reasoning. It starts with the known facts and asserts new facts.
- Backward chaining is the implementation of inductive reasoning. It starts with goals and works backward to determine what facts must be asserted so that the goals can be achieved (Feigenbaum et al., 1981; Sterling & Shapiro, 1986; Van der Gaag & Lucas, 1990).

The inference engine is based on the logical rule of *modus ponens* (in Latin "mode that affirms") for the interpretation of mode, as shown in Equation 6.1. *Modus ponens* is a powerful basic logic for reasoning that can be used for concluding based on an *If-Then* logic. The *If*-part of the logic is called antecedent and the *Then*-part of the logic is called consequent.

According to the *modus ponens* logic, *If* antecedent (*P*) implies consequent (*Q*), *and* antecedent (*P*) is true, *then* consequent (*Q*) is true. The negation reasoning logic, *modus tollens*, is used to express when the consequent (*Q*) does NOT hold. According to the *modus tollens* logic, *If* antecedent (*P*) implies consequent (*Q*), *and* consequent (*Q*) is false, *then* antecedent (*P*) is false.

Equation 6.1. Logic of Modus Ponens

$$\frac{P \to Q, P}{\therefore Q} \tag{6.1}$$

Example of *modus ponens*:

1. *If* you own a Tesla (*P*) *then* you own a car (*Q*)
2. You own a Tesla (*P*)
   - Thus, you own a car (conclusion)

Example of *modus tollens*:

1. *If* you own a Tesla (*P*) *then* you own a car (*Q*)
2. You don't own a car (*Q*)
   - Thus, you don't own a Tesla (conclusion)

Managing uncertain situations in reasoning and deriving conclusions is important. Several techniques in reasoning deal with uncertainty using probability and logic. Examples include Certainty Factory, fuzzy logic, and Bayes theorem (Bayesian statistics).

6.11.1 Inference Engine Architecture

As mentioned above, the logic that an inference engine uses is typically represented as *If-Then* rules. The general format of such rules is IF <logical expression> THEN <logical expression>.

Before the development of expert systems and inference engines, early AI researchers focused on more powerful theorem prover environments that offered much fuller implementations of first-order logic, for example, general statements that included universal quantification (for all X some statement is true) and existential quantification (there exists some X such that some statement is true). The researchers discovered that the power of these theorem-proving environments was also their drawback. It was easy to create logical expressions that could take an indeterminate or even infinite time to terminate. For example, it is common in universal quantification to make statements over an infinite set, such as the set of all natural numbers. Such statements are perfectly reasonable and even required in mathematical proofs but their inclusion in an automated theorem prover executing on a computer may cause the computer to fall into an infinite loop.

Focusing on *If-Then* statements (or *modus ponens*) gave developers a very powerful general mechanism to represent logic, but one that could be used efficiently with computational resources. There is also some psychological research that indicates humans tend to favour *If-Then* representations when storing complex knowledge.

A simple example of *If-Then* often used in introductory logic books is "If you are human then you are mortal". This can be represented in pseudocode as:

Rule1: Human(x) => Mortal(x)

A trivial example of how this rule would be used in an inference engine is as follows.

- In forward chaining, based on the statement "If you are human then you are mortal", the inference engine would find any facts in the knowledge base that matched Human(x) and for each fact it found would add the new information Mortal(x) to the knowledge base. If it found an object called Socrates that was human it would deduce that Socrates was mortal.
- In backward chaining, the system would be given a goal, for example, to answer the question "Is Socrates mortal?" It would search the knowledge base and determine if Socrates was human and, if so, would assert he was also mortal. However, in backward chaining, a common technique was to integrate the inference engine with a user interface. In that way, rather than simply being automated, the system could now be interactive.

In this trivial example, if the system was given the goal to answer the question if Socrates was mortal and it didn't yet know if he was human, it would generate a window to ask the user the question "Is Socrates human?" and would then use that information accordingly.

This innovation of integrating the inference engine with a user interface led to the second early advancement of expert systems: explanation capabilities. The explicit representation of knowledge as rules rather than code made it possible to generate explanations to users: explanations both in real time and after the fact. If the system asked the user "Is Socrates human?", the user might wonder why she was being asked that question, and the system would use the chain of rules to explain why it was currently trying to ascertain that bit of knowledge: that is, it needs to determine if Socrates is mortal and to do that it needs to determine if he is human.

At first, these explanations were not much different than the standard debugging information that developers deal with when debugging any system. However, an active area of research was using natural language technology to ask, understand, and generate questions and explanations using natural languages rather than computer formalisms.

An inference engine cycles through three sequential steps: match rules, select rules, and execute rules. The execution of the rules will often result in new facts or goals being added to the knowledge base which will trigger the cycle to repeat. This cycle continues until no new rules can be matched.

1. In the first step, match rules, the inference engine finds all of the rules that are triggered by the current contents of the knowledge base. In forward chaining, the engine looks for rules where the antecedent (left-hand side) matches some fact in the knowledge base. In backward chaining, the engine looks for antecedents that can satisfy one of the current goals.
2. In the second step, select rules, the inference engine prioritises the various rules that were matched to determine the order to execute them.
3. In the final step, execute rules, the engine executes each matched rule in the order determined in step two and then iterates back to step one again. The cycle continues until no new rules are matched (HandWiki, 2019).

6.11.2 INFERENCE ENGINE IMPLEMENTATIONS

Early inference engines focused primarily on forward chaining. These systems were usually implemented in the Lisp programming language. Lisp was a frequent platform for early AI research because of its strong capability to do symbolic manipulation. Moreover, as an interpreted language, it offered productive development environments appropriate for debugging complex programs. A necessary consequence of these benefits was that Lisp programs tended to be slower and less robust than compiled languages of the time such as C.

A common approach in these early days was to take an expert system application and repackage the inference engine used for that system as a reusable tool other researchers could use for the development of other expert systems. For example, MYCIN was an early expert system for medical diagnosis, and EMYCIN was an inference engine extrapolated from MYCIN and made available for other researchers.

As expert systems moved from research prototypes to deployed systems, there was more focus on issues such as speed and robustness. One of the first and most popular forward chaining engines was OPS5 which used the Rete algorithm to optimise the efficiency of rule firing. Another very popular technology was the Prolog logic programming language. Prolog focused on backward chaining and featured various commercial versions and optimisations for efficiency and robustness.

As expert systems prompted significant interest in the business world, various companies guided by prominent AI researchers created productised versions of inference engines. These inference engine products were also often developed in Lisp at first. However, demands for more affordable and commercially viable platforms eventually made personal computer platforms popular (Sterling & Shapiro, 1986).

6.12   FROM DATA TO WISDOM

When establishing AI-based solutions, such as the AI factory, in industrial contexts, identifying the purpose of the individual micro-services (i.e. a software component) is essential. This will help the solution architecture to select appropriate frameworks, approaches, technologies, and methodologies for design, development, and implementation of the solution.

In addition, understanding the relationship between data, information, knowledge, and wisdom, as illustrated in Figure 6.11, helps data scientists and software engineers select and develop proper models and algorithms for implementation, based on the expected outcome of the individual micro-service.

The relationship between data, information, knowledge, and wisdom has been widely discussed by researchers (e.g. Ackoff, 1989; Dammann, 2019). Most are inspired by Ackoff (1989).

The relationship can be understood as follows:

1. Data: Data are symbols that represent the properties of objects and events.
2. Information: Information consists of processed data. The processing is directed at increasing their usefulness. Like data, information represents the properties of objects and events, but it does so more efficiently and usefully than data. The difference between data and

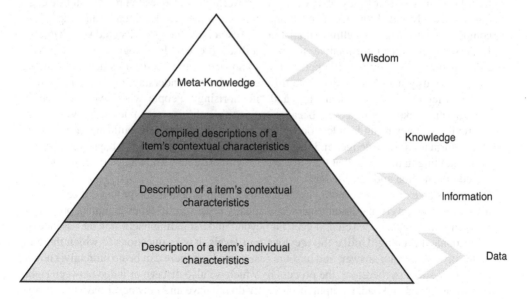

FIGURE 6.11   Data to wisdom ontology (Ackoff, 1989; Dammann, 2019).

information is functional, not structural. Information is contained in descriptions and answers to questions that begin with such words as who, what, when, where, and how many.
3. Knowledge: Knowledge is conveyed by instructions and answers to how-to questions.
4. Understanding: Understanding is conveyed by explanations and answers to why questions.
5. Wisdom: Wisdom can be understood as evaluated understanding.

Together, data information, knowledge, and understanding enable us to increase efficiency, but not effectiveness. Wisdom gives us the ability to increase effectiveness. The difference between efficiency and effectiveness – that which differentiates wisdom from understanding, knowledge, information, and data – is reflected in the difference between development and growth.

The first four categories relate to the past; they deal with what has been or what is known. Only the fifth category, wisdom, deals with the future because it incorporates vision and design. With wisdom, people can create the future rather than just grasp the present and past. But achieving wisdom isn't easy; people must move successively through the other categories (Ackoff, 1989; Bellinger et al., 2003).

6.12.1 DATA, INFORMATION, KNOWLEDGE, AND WISDOM

Ackoff's (1989) definitions can be elaborated as follows:

- Data simply exist and have no significance beyond their existence. They can exist in any form, usable or not. They do not have meaning by themselves. For example, a spreadsheet generally starts out by holding data.
- Information is data that have been given meaning by way of relational connection. This "meaning" can be useful but does not have to be. For example, a relational database makes information from the data stored within it.
- Knowledge is a collection of information intended to be useful. Knowledge is a deterministic process. When someone "memorizes" information, then he or she has amassed knowledge. This knowledge has useful meaning, but it does not provide, in and of itself, an integration that would infer further knowledge. For example, elementary school children memorise, or amass knowledge of, the "times table". They can tell you that "$2\times2=4$" because they have amassed that knowledge. But when asked what is "1267×300", they cannot respond correctly because that entry is not in their times table. Correctly answering such a question requires a true cognitive and analytical ability that is only encompassed in the next level, understanding. Most computer applications (modelling, simulation etc.) exercise some type of stored knowledge.
- Understanding is an interpolative and probabilistic process. It is cognitive and analytical. It is the process by which a person takes knowledge and synthesises new knowledge from previously held knowledge. The difference between understanding and knowledge is the difference between "learning" and "memorising". People who have understanding can undertake useful actions because they can synthesise new knowledge with what is previously known (and understood). That is, understanding can build upon currently held information, knowledge, and understanding itself. For example, AI systems possess understanding in the sense that they are able to synthesise new knowledge from previously stored information and knowledge.
- Wisdom is an extrapolative and non-deterministic, non-probabilistic process. It calls upon all the previous levels of consciousness, specifically upon special types of human programming (moral, ethical codes etc.). It goes far beyond understanding itself. It is the essence of philosophical probing. Unlike the previous four levels, it asks questions to which there is no (easily-achievable) answer, and in some cases, to which there can be no humanly-known answer. Wisdom is, therefore, the process by which we also discern or judge between right and wrong, good and bad. Computers currently do not have and may never have the ability to possess wisdom, as it may be a uniquely human quality (Bellinger et al., 2003).

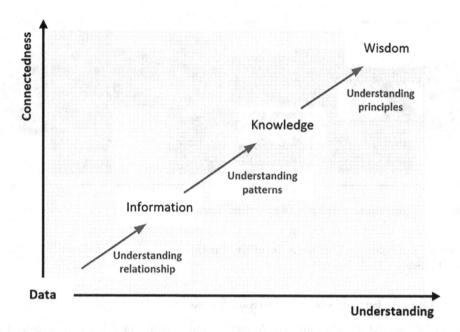

FIGURE 6.12   The transitions from data, to information, to knowledge, and finally to wisdom (Bellinger et al., 2003).

Figure 6.12 represents the transitions from data, to information, to knowledge, and finally to wisdom. In this formulation, understanding supports the transition from one stage to the next. It is not a stage in and of itself (Bellinger et al., 2003).

6.13   AI AND SOFTWARE ENGINEERING

AI in industrial contexts is often discussed from a data science perspective, with an emphasis on exploring, identifying, and understanding the relationships between facts and events related to items described in the data set, and the item's real characteristics described by the item's physical properties.

These relationships are then implemented in set of instructions (called algorithms) aiming to process the data (facts) and provide an output. The algorithms can be used to understand and match the pattern of the data sets to our assumptions or hypotheses. They may also be used to validate the assumptions as such, which give us a measure accuracy of the algorithm (also called model precision). These algorithms might be implemented using a learning paradigm, such as ML and DL, or they might be implemented based on a classic statistical approach.

Producing knowledge using a knowledge management system empowered by AI requires understanding the characteristics of knowledge types. There are two fundamental categories of knowledge which have relevance in industrial contexts: procedural knowledge and declarative knowledge.

1. *Procedural knowledge* is the practical knowledge used to perform a task.
2. *Declarative knowledge* is knowledge that describes an object or event.

In AI-based solutions, the intelligent agents, i.e. the software components, may provide support for procedural and/or declarative knowledge extraction.

Development and deployment of AI solutions require extensive knowledge and skills in software engineering, in addition to knowledge of ML or DL to achieve high levels of availability, reliability, maintainability, and supportability in the performance of the AI solution.

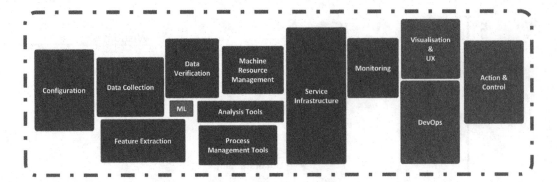

FIGURE 6.13   Components of real-world AI solutions (Sculley et al., 2015).

Some of the components that affect the efficient performance of an AI solution are depicted in Figure 6.13 (Sculley et al., 2015).

6.13.1 ARTIFICIAL INTELLIGENCE AND SOFTWARE ENGINEERING

During the last decades, the disciplines of AI and software engineering (SE) have developed separately without much exchange of research results. Research in AI has looked for techniques for computations that make it possible to perceive, reason, and act. Research in SE has been concerned with supporting human beings to develop better software faster.

Today, several research directions of both disciplines are coming closer together and beginning to build new research areas. Software agents play an important role as research objects in distributed AI (DAI) and in agent-oriented software engineering (AOSE). Knowledge-based systems (KBS) are being investigated for learning software organisations (LSO) and for knowledge engineering. Ambient intelligence (AmI) is a new research area for distributed, non-intrusive, and intelligent software systems from two directions: how to build these systems and how to design the collaboration between ambient systems. Last but not least, computational intelligence (CI) plays an important role in research on software analysis or project management and in KD in databases or ML.

The following sections will examine these various research directions with a focus on how the two disciplines are drawing upon each other (Rech & Althoff, 2004).

6.13.1.1 Aspects of AI

As a field of academic study, many AI researchers reach to understand intelligence by becoming able to produce effects of intelligence: intelligent behaviour. One element in AI's methodology is that progress is sought by building systems that perform: synthesis before analysis (Wachsmuth, 2000). Wachsmuth, (2000) says: "it is not the aim of AI to build intelligent machines having understood natural intelligence, but to understand natural intelligence by building intelligent machines".

AI has two main strands, a scientific strand and an engineering strand, which overlap considerably in their concepts, methods, and tools, though their objectives are very different.

AI also has two different types of goals: one motivated by cognitive science and the other by the engineering sciences (see Figure 6.14) (Rech & Althoff, 2004).

A further subdivision of AI into sub-fields, methods, and techniques is shown in Figure 6.15.

For SE, the scientific strand orienting itself towards cognitive science and humanities in general could be a helpful guide for interdisciplinary research. Of course, there is a strong overlap between SE and the engineering strand of AI. An important part of the latter is KBS.

KBS comprises three layers: the cognitive layer (human-oriented, rational, informal), the representation layer (formal, logical), and the implementation layer (machine-oriented, data structures and programmes). These levels are shown in Figure 6.16.

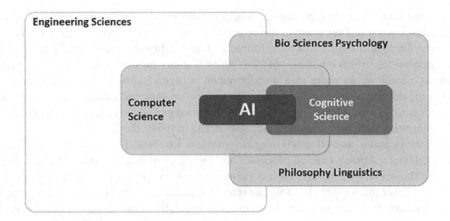

FIGURE 6.14 AI and related research areas (Rech & Althoff, 2004).

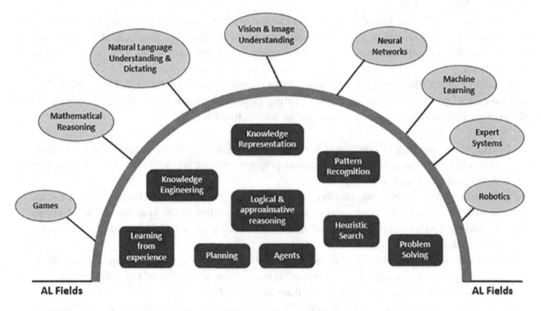

FIGURE 6.15 AI fields, methods, and techniques (Rech & Althoff, 2004).

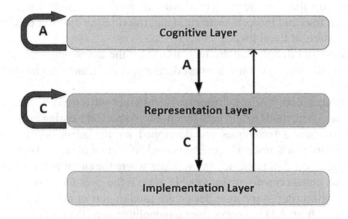

FIGURE 6.16 The three levels of knowledge-based systems (Rech & Althoff, 2004).

Between the knowledge utterance and its machine utilisation several transformations have to be performed (thick arrows). They point to the direction of increased structuring within the layers and proceed from the cognitive form to a more formal and more efficiently processed form. The letter A stands for Acquisition (which is human-oriented) whilst C stands for Compilation (machine-oriented). Each syntactic result in the range of a transformation between layers has to be associated with a meaning in the domain of the transformation. The most interesting and difficult arrow is the inverse transformation back to the cognitive layer; it is usually called explanation (Rech & Althoff, 2004).

AI is interesting for SE researchers because it can provide the initial technology and first (successful) applications, as well as a testing environment for ideas. The inclusion of research supports the enabling of human-enacted processes and increases user acceptance. AI technology can help to base the overall SE method on a concrete technology, providing sufficient detail for the initial method description using the available reference technology clarifying the semantics of the respective method. In addition, other AI techniques naturally substituting/extending the chosen technology can be used for improved versions of the SE method (Rech & Althoff, 2004).

6.13.1.2   Aspects of SE

The discipline of SE was initially mainly concerned with the efficient and effective development of high-qualitative and mostly very large software systems. The goal was (and still is) to support software engineers and managers in order to develop better software faster with (intelligent) tools and methods.

Several research directions have developed and matured in this broad field. Figure 6.17 shows a software development reference model integrating important phases in a software lifecycle. Some of the main research directions in SE can be set within this lifecycle:

1. Project engineering is concerned with the acquisition, definition, management, monitoring, and control of software development projects and the management of risks emerging during project execution.
2. Requirements engineering supports the formal and unambiguous elicitation of software requirements from the customers to improve the usability of the systems and to establish a binding and unambiguous definition of the resulting system during and after software project definition.
3. Software design and architecture advance techniques for the development, management, and analysis of (formal) descriptions of abstract representations of the software system, along with the required tools and notations (e.g., UML).
4. Software programming research looks for techniques to develop highly maintainable, efficient, and effective source code.
5. Verification and validation are concerned with the planning, development, and execution of (automated) tests and inspections (formal and informal) to discover defects or estimate the quality of parts of the software.
6. Implementation and distribution are responsible for the development of methods for the introduction at the customer's site, support during operation, and integration in existing IT infrastructures.
7. Software evolution occurs after delivery to the customer software systems. Thus, the focus of research lies on methods to add new functions and perfect existing ones.
8. Software maintenance techniques are developed for the adaptation to environmental changes, prevention of foreseeable problems, and correction of noticed defects.
9. Reengineering research is interested in situations where the environment changes dramatically or further enhancements are impossible. Here techniques for software understanding and reverse engineering of software design are used to port or migrate a system to a new technology (e.g., from Ada to Java or from a monolithic to a client/server architecture) and obtain a maintainable system (Rech & Althoff, 2004).

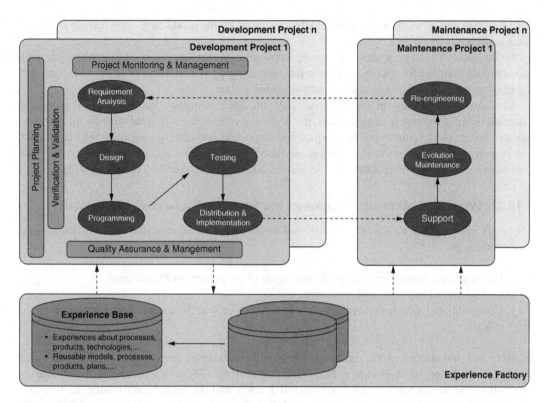

FIGURE 6.17   Software development reference model (Rech & Althoff, 2004).

A related area not shown in Figure 6.17 is experience factory (EF) or, alternatively, LSO. The systematic reuse and management of experiences, knowledge, products, and processes have been researched since the 1980s. This field researches methods and techniques for the management, elicitation, and adaptation of reusable artefacts from SE projects.

SE is of interest to AI researchers because it supports systematic AI application development, as well as the operation of AI applications in real-life environments. More specifically, it allows them to be evaluated, maintained, continuously improved, and systematically compared to alternative approaches (e.g., another modelling method). Finally, SE supports the systematic definition of the respective application domains, for example, through scoping methods (Rech & Althoff, 2004).

6.13.2   THE ROLE OF ARTIFICIAL INTELLIGENCE IN SOFTWARE ENGINEERING

AI is about making machines intelligent, whilst SE is the activity of defining, designing, and deploying some of the most complex and challenging systems mankind has ever sought to engineer. Though SE is one of the most challenging of all engineering disciplines, it is often not recognised as such, because software is so well concealed.

The scale of the engineering challenge posed by software remains entirely invisible. When one of the Eiffel Tower's 2.5 million rivets fails, the tower itself does not fail. Compare this enormous engineering edifice with a typical tiny smartphone, which may contain five to ten million lines of code, the failure of any one of which could lead to total system failure. The space of inputs to even the smallest app on the phone is likely to comfortably exceed 10^{80} (a reasonable current estimate for the number of atoms in the observable universe), yet all but a single one of these inputs may fail to reveal the presence of just such a critical fault.

Faced with the daunting challenge of designing, building, and testing engineering systems at these scales, software engineers have one critical advantage that other engineers do not possess;

their software can be used to attack the challenges posed by the production of systems in this very same material.

At this point, AI can be a useful tool in the software engineer's toolbox: AI algorithms are well suited to such complex SE problems because they are designed to deal with one of the most demanding challenges of all – the replication of intelligent behaviour.

As a result of this natural technological pull, the SE community has adopted, adapted and exploited many of the practical algorithms, methods, and techniques offered to them by the AI community. These AI algorithms and techniques find important and effective applications that impact almost every area of SE activity. Of course, neither SE nor AI is a static field of activity. We will continue to see important breakthroughs in SE and AI, alone and together (Harman, 2012).

6.13.3 When Does Artificial Intelligence for Software Engineering Work Well?

The areas in which AI techniques have proved to be useful in SE research and practice can be characterised as:

1. Fuzzy and probabilistic methods for reasoning in the presence of uncertainty,
2. Classification, learning, and prediction, and
3. Computational search and optimisation techniques or search-based software engineering (SBSE).

In fuzzy and probabilistic work, the aim is to apply AI techniques developed to handle real world problems which are, by their nature, fuzzy and probabilistic. There is a natural fit here because, increasingly, SE needs to cater to fuzzy, ill-defined, noisy, and incomplete information, as its applications reach further into our messy, fuzzy, and ill-defined lives. This is true not only of the software systems we build but also of the processes by which they are built, many of which are based on estimates.

One example of a probabilistic AI technique that has proved to be highly applicable in SE has been the use of Bayesian probabilistic reasoning to model software reliability, one of the earliest examples of the adoption of what might be called, perhaps with hindsight, AI for SE. Another example of the need for probabilistic reasoning comes from the analysis of users, inherently requiring an element of probability because of the stochastic nature of human behaviour.

In classification, learning, and prediction work, there has been great interest in modelling and predicting software costs as part of project planning. For example, a wide variety of traditional ML techniques, such as artificial neural networks, case-based reasoning, and rule induction have been used for software project prediction, ontology learning and defect prediction.

In SBSE work, the goal is to re-formulate SE problems as optimisation problems that can then be attacked with computational search. This has proved to be a widely applicable and successful approach, with applications from requirements and design to maintenance and testing. Computational search has been exploited by all engineering disciplines, not just SE. However, the virtual character of software makes it an engineering material ideally suited to computational search (Harman, 2012).

6.13.4 Relationship Between Approaches to Artificial Intelligence for Software Engineering

The various ways AI techniques have been applied in SE have considerable overlaps. For instance, the distinctions between probabilistic reasoning and prediction for SE are blurred, if not arbitrary. We can easily think of a prediction system as nothing more than a probabilistic reasoner. We can also think of Bayesian models as learners and of classifiers as learners, probabilistic reasoners, and/or optimisers.

Indeed, all the ways AI has been applied to SE can be regarded as ways to optimise either the engineering process or its products and, as such, they are all examples of SBSE. That is, whether we think of our problem as one couched in probability, formulated as a prediction system, or characterised by a need to learn from experience, we are always seeking to optimise the efficiency and effectiveness of our approach and to find cost-benefit trade-offs.

These optimisation goals can usually be formulated as measurable objectives and constraints, the solutions to which are likely to reside in large spaces, making them ripe for computational search.

There is a very close interplay between ML approaches to SE and SBSE approaches. ML is essentially the study of approaches to computation that improve with use. To improve, we need a way to measure improvement and, if we have this, then we can use SBSE to optimise according to it. Fortunately, in SE situations we typically have a large number of candidate measurements against which we might seek to improve.

Previous work on ML and SBSE also overlaps through the use of genetic programming as a technique to learn/optimise. Genetic programming has been one of the most widely used computational search techniques in SBSE work, with exciting recent developments in automatic bug fixing, porting between platforms, languages, and programming paradigms, and trading functional and non-functional properties.

However, genetic programming can also be thought of as an algorithm for learning models of software behaviour, a lens through which it appears to be both an ML approach and an optimisation technique. In other words, there are close connections between ML for SE and SBSE: one way of learning is to optimise, whilst one way to think of the progress that takes place during optimisation is as a learning process.

The first step for the successful application of any AI technique to any SE problem domain is to find a suitable formulation of the SE problem so that AI techniques become applicable. Once this formulation is accomplished, it typically opens a technological window of opportunity through which many AI techniques may profitably pass (Harman, 2012).

6.13.5 Intersections Between Artificial Intelligence and SE

The intersections between AI and SE remain relatively rare but are multiplying and growing. First points of contact emerged from the application of techniques from one discipline to the other. Today, methods and techniques from each discipline support the practice and research of the other. Figure 6.18 depicts some research areas in AI and SE and their intersections (Rech & Althoff, 2004).

Figure 6.18 suggests the following relations:

- Systematic software development, such as requirements engineering, engineering of designs, and source code, as well as project management methods, helps to build intelligent systems while using advanced data analysis techniques.
- Knowledge acquisition techniques help to build the experience factory.
- Intelligent ambient systems like domain modelling techniques support the construction of requirements for software systems and product lines.
- CBR is used to support the retrieval and management of data in the experience factory.
- Information agents are used in SE to simulate development processes or to distribute and explain change requests (Rech & Althoff, 2004).

6.13.5.1 Agent-Oriented Software Engineering

Software agents are typically small intelligent systems that cooperate to reach a common goal. These agents are a relatively new area wherein research from AI and SE intersects. From the AI side, the focus is on even more intelligent and autonomous systems to solve more complex problems using communication languages between agents. In SE, meanwhile, agents are seen as systems that need more or less specialised formal methods for their development, verification, validation, and maintenance.

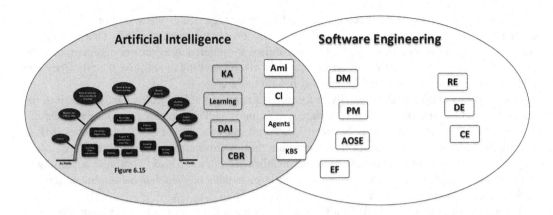

FIGURE 6.18 Research areas in AI and SE and their intersections (Rech & Althoff, 2004).

AOSE (Figure 6.18), otherwise known as agent-based software engineering (ABSE), as related to object-oriented SE (OOSE) is centred on systems where objects in a model of a software system are intelligent, autonomous, and proactive. The systematic development and representation of software agents is the topic of research, with languages being created for their representation during development, such as Agent UML. Methods include MASSIVE, GAIA, MESSAGE, TROPOS, and MAS-CommonKADS.

ABSE and AOSE are currently applied in many areas, including intelligent and agent-based user interfaces to improve system usability, trading agents in eCommerce to maximise profits, or assisting agents in everyday work to automate common tasks (e.g. booking hotel rooms). Furthermore, software agents are increasingly used to simulate real-world domains (e.g. traffic control) or work processes in SE (Rech & Althoff, 2004).

6.13.5.2 Knowledge-Based SE

SE is a dynamic field in terms of research and knowledge, and it depends heavily upon the experience of experts for the development and advancement of its methods, tools, and techniques. The tendency to focus on "best practices" or "lessons learned" is a distinctive aspect of the literature. Thus, the SE field first introduced the concept of the experience factory to explicitly and systematically deal with experience. An experience factory is a logical and/or physical infrastructure for continuous learning from experience and includes an experience base for the storage and reuse of knowledge. It supports organisational learning (Figure 6.18) (Rech & Althoff, 2004).

6.13.5.3 Computational Intelligence and Knowledge Discovery

CI is attracting the interest of both AI and SE researchers. KD techniques like neural networks, evolutionary algorithms, or fuzzy systems are increasingly applied and adapted for specific SE problems. They are used to estimate the progress of projects to support software PM, to discover defective modules to ensure software quality, or to plan software testing and verification activities to minimise the effort of quality assurance.

Many application areas for KDD in SE have been established in fields like quality management, project management, risk management, software reuse, and software maintenance (Rech & Althoff, 2004).

6.13.5.4 Ambient Intelligence

The idea behind ambient intelligence (AmI) is the creation of sensitive, adaptive, and reactive systems that are informed about the user's needs, habits, and emotions to support the user in his or her daily work. Techniques for autonomous, intelligent, robust, and self-learning systems are needed to enable communication between systems (machine-machine interfaces and ontologies) or users and systems (human–machine interfaces).

AmI is based on several research areas, including ubiquitous and pervasive computing, intelligent systems, and context awareness. Research on AmI tries to build an environment similar to the previously mentioned research areas, such as intelligent software agents, KBS, and KD (e.g. to detect and analyse foreign systems and software).

Several AI research areas are developing smart algorithms for AmI applications, such as user profiling, context awareness, scene understanding, and planning and negotiation tasks. Meanwhile, SE research is concerned with model-driven development for mobile computing, the verification of mobile code, the specification of adaptive systems, or the design of embedded systems. In addition, we need intelligent human interfaces from a usability perspective that translate between users and a new configuration of the ambient system. A fusion of these two fields could be established to analyse and evaluate foreign software systems that try to connect with a system to be executed on its hardware (Rech & Althoff, 2004).

REFERENCES

Ackoff, R. (1989). From data to wisdom. *Journal of Applied Systems Analysis, 16*(1), 3–9. https://doi.org/10.5840/du2005155/629

Bellinger, G., Castro, D., & Mills, A. (2003). Data, information, knowledge, and wisdom. *Systems Thinking.* http://outsights.com/systems/dikw/dikw.htm

ButteCollege. (2019). Deductive, inductive and abductive reasoning. TIP Sheet. Butte College. http://www.butte.edu/departments/cas/tipsheets/thinking/reasoning.html

Chand, S. (2022). Decision making: 7 essential nature of decision making – explained! Your Article Library. https://www.yourarticlelibrary.com/decision-making/decision-making-7-essential-nature-of-decision-making-explained/25655

Dammann, O. (2019). Data, information, evidence, and knowledge: A proposal for health informatics and data science. *Online Journal of Public Health Informatics, 10*(3). https://doi.org/10.5210/ojphi.v10i3.9631

El Sheikh, A. A. R., & Alnoukari, M. (2012). *Business intelligence and agile methodologies for knowledge-based organizations: Cross-disciplinary applications.* Business Science Reference. http://projanco.com/Library/Business%20Intelligence%20and%20Agile%20Methodologies%20for%20Knowledge-Based%20Organizations.pdf

Fayyad, U., Piatetsky-Shapiro, G., & Smyth, P. (1996). From data mining to knowledge discovery in databases. *AI Magazine.* http://www.aaai.org/ojs/index.php/aimagazine/article/viewArticle/1230

Feigenbaum, E. A., Barr, A., & Cohen, P. R. (1981). *The handbook of Artificial Intelligence.* HeurisTech Press; William Kaufmann.

GetGuru. (2022). Knowledge base: Definition, examples, & step-by-step guide guru. GetGuru. https://www.getguru.com/reference/types-of-knowledge-bases

GlobalData365. (2022). Artificial intelligence (AI) vs. business intelligence (BI). *Global Data 365.* https://globaldata365.com/artificial-intelligence-ai-vs-business-intelligence-bi/

Grievink, J., & van Schijndel, J. (2002). *European Symposium on Computer Aided Process Engineering-12.* Elsevier.

HandWiki. (2019). Philosophy: Inference engine. HandWiki. https://handwiki.org/wiki/Philosophy:Inference_engine

Harapan, H., Itoh, N., Yufika, A., Winardi, W., Keam, S., Te, H., Megawati, D., Hayati, Z., Wagner, A. L., & Mudatsir, M. (2020). Coronavirus disease 2019 (COVID-19): A literature review. *Journal of Infection and Public Health, 13*(5), 667–673. https://doi.org/10.1016/J.JIPH.2020.03.019

Harman, M. (2012). The role of artificial intelligence in software engineering. *2012 First International Workshop on Realizing AI Synergies in Software Engineering (RAISE)*, 1–6. https://doi.org/10.1109/RAISE.2012.6227961

Negash, S. (2004). Business intelligence. *Communications of the Association for Information Systems, 13*, 177–195. https://doi.org/10.17705/1CAIS.01315

Patel, R., & Davidson, B. (2003). *Forskningsmetodikens grunder Att planera, genomföra och rapportera en undersökning.* Studentlitteratur.

Qureshi, Z. (2008). Six-step problem solving model. https://www.academia.edu/8229711/Problem_Solving_Overview_SIX_STEP_PROBLEM_SOLVING_MODEL

Ramachandran, V. S., & Beaudoin, J. J. (2000). *Handbook of analytical techniques in concrete science and technology: Principles, techniques and applications*. Elsevier.

Rech, J., & Althoff, K.-D. (2004). Artificial intelligence and software engineering: Status and future trends. *Kinetics Information*, *18*(3), 5–11.

Sculley, D., Holt, G., Golovin, D., Davydov, E., Phillips, T., Ebner, D., Chaudhary, V., Young, M., Crespo, J. F., & Dennison, D. (2015). Hidden technical debt in machine learning systems. *Advances in Neural Information Processing Systems*, *2015*, 2503–2511.

Sharma, P. (2022a). Decision-making: Definition, importance and principles management. Your Article Library. https://www.yourarticlelibrary.com/management/decision-making-management/decision-making-definition-importance-and-principles-management/70038

Sharma, P. (2022b). Decision making: Definition, characteristics and importance. Your Article Library. https://www.yourarticlelibrary.com/management/decision-making-management/decision-making-definition-characteristics-and-importance/70292

Sterling, L., & Shapiro, E. Y. (1986). *The art of prolog: Advanced programming techniques*. MIT Press.

ThinkAutomation. (2022). Knowledge base vs database: What's the difference? ThinkAutomation. https://www.thinkautomation.com/eli5/knowledge-base-vs-database-whats-the-difference/

UMass. (2022). 7 Steps to effective decision making. https://www.umassd.edu/media/umassdartmouth/fycm/decision_making_process.pdf

Van der Gaag, L., & Lucas, P. (1990). An overview of expert system principles. In M. Masuch (Ed.), *Organization, management, and expert systems: Models of automated reasoning* (pp. 195–224). Walter De Gruyter. https://www.degruyter.com/document/doi/10.1515/9783110869088-fm/html

Wachsmuth, I. (2000). The concept of intelligence in AI. In H. Cruse (Ed.), *Prerational intelligence: Adaptive behavior and intelligent systems without symbols and logic*, Vol. I (pp. 43–55). Kluwer Academic Publishers. https://doi.org/10.1007/978-94-010-0870-9_5

Webeduclick. (2022). Differentiate between database and knowledge base. Webeduclick. https://webeduclick.com/differentiate-between-database-and-knowledge-base/

Whitney, P., Smelser, N. J., & Baltes, P. B. (2001). *International encyclopedia of social behavioral sciences*. Pergamon.

7 Systems Thinking and Systems Engineering

7.1 DEFINITION OF SYSTEM

Understanding the definition of a system and various types of systems is fundamental in systems thinking and systems engineering. It also helps us select appropriate frameworks, approaches, and tools when developing artificial intelligence (AI)-based solutions manifested through, for example, the concept of digital twin (DT).

A system is two or more components that combine to produce from one or more inputs, one or more results that could not be obtained from the components individually (Grieves, 2012).

Systems can be categorised based on the level of complexity, as depicted in Figure 7.1. Systems can be simple, complicated, or complex.

Simple systems are just that. The outside observer has no problem recognising the operation of the system. The system is completely predictable. The inputs are highly visible. The actions performed on those inputs are transparent. The outputs are easily predictable (Grieves & Vickers, 2017).

Complicated systems are also completely predictable and follow well-defined patterns (Sargut & Gunter McGrath, 2011). The difference between simple systems and complicated systems is the number of inherent components. Complicated systems have many more components. However, the inputs and outputs of complicated systems are well known. The connection between components is linear and straightforward (e.g. a mechanical watch) (Grieves & Vickers, 2017).

Complex systems are a different class of systems entirely. There is little agreement on how to even describe a complex system. In fact, there is little agreement on the term complexity, 2008. Complex systems have been characterised as a large network of components, many-to-many communication channels, and sophisticated information processing that makes prediction of system states difficult (Mitchell, 2009).

There are many different classifications, or taxonomies, of systems. One of the widely accepted classifications is the one by Peter Checkland (1999), as illustrated in Figure 7.2.

Checkland's five types of generic systems are as follows:

- Natural systems: Open systems whose characteristics are beyond the control of humans, such as weather systems, nature, the environment, or time.
- Designed physical systems: Physical artefacts that represent the real-world manifestation of the system, almost any object you can think of, from computer games to cars.
- Designed abstract systems: Systems without a physical artefact but used to understand or explain an idea or concept, such as models, equations, or thought experiments.
- Human activity systems: People-based systems that can be seen or observed in the real world, typically consisting of different sets of people interacting to achieve a common goal or purpose, such as a political system or a social group.
- Transcendental systems: Systems that go beyond our current understanding, such as deities or unknown problems.

7.1.1 CHARACTERISTICS OF A SYSTEM

A common set of characteristics can be associated with all these various types of systems, despite their differences. These characteristics allow the systems to be understood and developed.

DOI: 10.1201/9781003208686-7

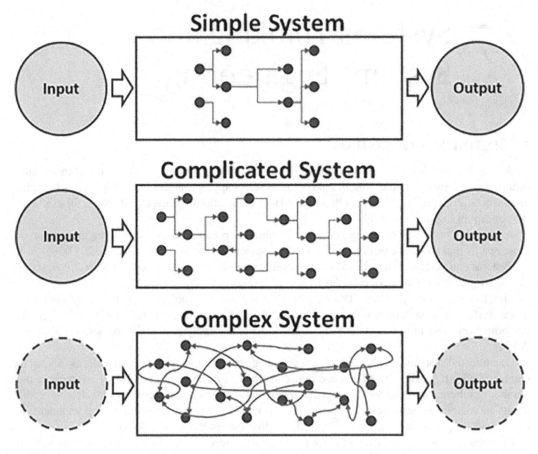

FIGURE 7.1 Types of systems (Grieves & Vickers, 2017).

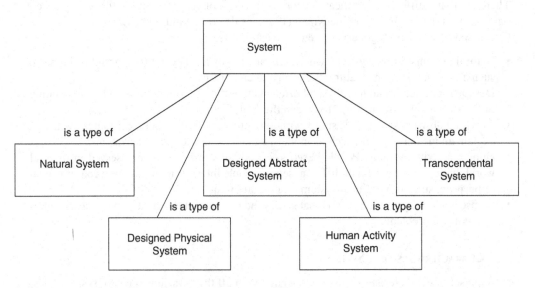

FIGURE 7.2 Checkland's five types of systems (Holt, 2021).

7.1.1.1 System Structure

All systems have a natural structure and comprise a set of interacting system elements, as shown in Figure 7.3.

As the figure shows, a system can be a system of interest or an enabling system. System of interest refers to a system under development, whereas enabling system refers to any system with an interest in, or interacting with, a system of interest.

In fact, the structure of the system is more complex than the figure suggests, as a system element itself may be broken down into lower-level system elements. Ultimately, a system hierarchy of several levels can be identified for a specific system.

System elements interact with other system elements. This is a key concept in system engineering. When considering any system or system element, it is important to understand that it will interact with other system elements. They do not exist in isolation. Understanding the relationships between system elements is just as important as understanding the system elements themselves.

The interactions between system elements also allow interfaces between them to be identified and defined. Understanding interfaces is crucial to be able to define all types of systems. It is also necessary to understand the information or material (anything that is not information) that flows across the interfaces (Holt, 2021).

7.1.1.2 System Stakeholders

A key aspect of a system is the stakeholders associated with it, as shown in Figure 7.4 (Holt, 2021). A stakeholder is any person, organisation, or thing with an interest in the system.

Understanding stakeholders is key to successful system engineering. The following should be kept in mind:

- The *role* of the stakeholder is of interest, not the name of the person, organisation, or thing associated with it. For example, say you own a car – the system of interest. You will likely play a number of stakeholder roles such as owner, driver, and maintainer. At some point,

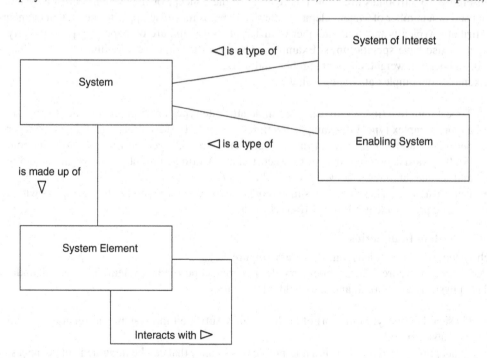

FIGURE 7.3 System elements (Holt, 2021).

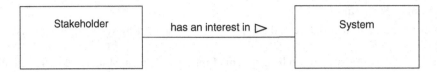

FIGURE 7.4   System stakeholders (Holt, 2021).

you may be a passenger. Each of these stakeholder roles views the system of the car in a different way.
- Stakeholders are not necessarily people. They can be organisations as well. Returning to the example of the car, it may be a company car; in this case, the organisation takes on the stakeholder role.
- There is not a one-to-one correlation between stakeholders and the person, organisation, or thing that takes on the stakeholder role. For example, a single person may take on multiple stakeholder roles, but it is also possible for many people to take on one stakeholder role. Say several friends travel in the car with you. In this situation, several people take on the stakeholder role of passenger.
- Stakeholders lie outside the boundary of the system, as do enabling systems (Figure 7.3). A stakeholder is anything with an interest in the system, so an enabling system is actually just a special type of stakeholder, as the basic definition is the same.

Identifying stakeholders is an essential part of systems engineering, as stakeholders will all look at the same system in different ways, depending on their stakeholder role (Holt, 2021).

7.1.1.3   System Attributes
It is possible to describe high-level properties of any given system by identifying a set of attributes (Holt, 2021).

In Figure 7.5, attributes are shown as relating to the concept of the system, but as a system is composed of a number of system elements; these attributes may also apply to the system elements.

Attributes typically take on a number of different values and are of a specific, predefined type. They may also have specific units. Examples of simple attributes include dimension (e.g. length, width, and height), weight, element number, and name.

Examples of complex attributes include:

- Timestamp: In a timestamp, a set of simple attribute types are brought together to provide a more complex type. For example, the timestamp may be a combination of day (an integer between 1 and 31), month (an integer between 1 and 12), year (an integer ranging from 0000 upwards), hour (an integer between 1 and 24), minute (an integer between 0 and 59), and second (an integer between 0 and 59).
- Data structures: These attributes may represent an audio or video file that complies with a specific protocol (e.g. MP3 or MP4) (Holt, 2021).

7.1.1.4   System Boundaries
Each system will have at least one boundary (Figure 7.6).

As shown in Figure 7.6, the boundary defines the scope of the system. Types of boundaries include physical, conceptual, and stakeholder boundaries:

- Physical boundary: Some sort of enclosure may surround the system and separate it from the outside world.
- Conceptual boundary: This is a non-physical boundary that can be imagined but not necessarily observed.

FIGURE 7.5 System attributes (Holt, 2021).

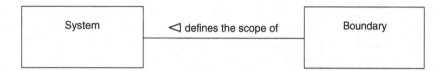

FIGURE 7.6 Defining the scope of a system – boundary (Holt, 2021).

- Stakeholder boundary: Different stakeholders may look at the same system in different ways and, therefore, where they perceive the boundary of the system to be may differ. For example, in the case of a car, a driver, a passenger, and a maintainer may perceive different boundaries (Holt, 2021).

The concept of boundary allows key aspects of the system to be understood:

- What is inside the boundary: Identifying elements that are inside the boundary of the system will help to define the scope of the system.
- What is outside the boundary: Things identified outside the boundary of the system are considered to be either stakeholders or enabling systems or both.
- Where key interfaces exist: When an interaction occurs across the boundary of a system, it identifies an interface to that system. A boundary is therefore important to identify all interfaces between a system and the outside world (Holt, 2021).

7.1.1.5 System Needs

All systems have a purpose, and this purpose is described by a set of needs (Figure 7.7) (Holt, 2021). Figure 7.7 shows three types of needs: goals, requirements, and features:

- Requirement: A requirement represents a statement of something that it is desirable for the system to do, often related to the desired specific functionality of the system. For example, a requirement for a car may be that the driver must be able to stop the car by using the brake.
- Feature: A feature represents a higher-level need of the system that does not necessarily relate to a specific function but may relate to a collection of functions. An example of a feature may be adaptive cruise control in a car.
- Goal: A goal is a very high-level need representing a need of the overall system. A goal could be to transport a driver and three passengers in an electric car over a distance of 300 miles on a single charge (Holt, 2021).

7.1.1.6 System Constraints

All systems will be limited in some way in terms of how they can be realised, and these limitations are called constraints. Their relationship is shown in Figure 7.8 and explained below (Holt, 2021). Constraints that are associated are often grouped into categories:

- Quality constraints: In almost all systems, certain constraints will be related to best practice sources, such as standards. For example, a standard in the automotive industry is ISO 26262.

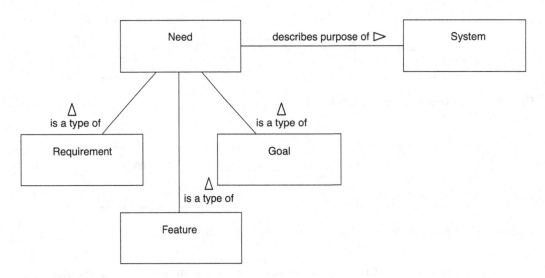

FIGURE 7.7   Defining the purpose of the system – needs (Holt, 2021).

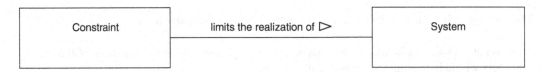

FIGURE 7.8   Defining constraints (Holt, 2021).

- Implementation constraints: These constraints will limit the way in which a system can be built, including the materials used; for example, a car may be limited to being made out of aluminium.
- Environmental constraints: Many systems will be deployed in a natural environment, and certain constraints must be met. For example, a car may be limited in its emissions to minimise the impact on the environment.
- Safety constraints: Almost all systems will have constraints placed on them to ensure the system can operate safely and minimise damage if things go wrong. For example, cars are required to have safety bags installed (Holt, 2021).

7.1.2   SYSTEMS ENGINEERING

Systems engineering is interdisciplinary, combining engineering and engineering management. It includes designing, integrating, and managing complex systems over a system's lifecycle, drawing on the principles of systems thinking to do so. The outcome of systems thinking is an engineered system, defined as a combination of components that work together to perform a useful function.

Issues such as the requirements of engineering, reliability, logistics, coordination of different teams, testing and evaluation, maintainability, and many other factors necessary for successful system design, development, implementation, and ultimate decommission become more difficult when dealing with large or complex projects. Systems engineering deals with work processes, optimisation methods, and risk management tools in such projects. It overlaps technical and human-centred disciplines such as industrial engineering, process systems engineering, mechanical engineering, manufacturing engineering, production engineering, control engineering, software engineering, electrical engineering, cybernetics, aerospace engineering, organisational studies, civil engineering, and project management. Systems engineering ensures all aspects of a project or system are considered and integrated into a whole.

The systems engineering process is a discovery process that is quite unlike a manufacturing process. A manufacturing process is focused on repetitive activities that achieve high-quality outputs with minimum cost and time. The systems engineering process must begin by discovering the real problems that need to be resolved, and identifying the most probable or highest-impact failures that can occur – systems engineering involves finding solutions to these problems.

Systems engineering signifies an approach and, more recently, a discipline in engineering. The aim of education in systems engineering is to formalise various approaches simply and in doing so, identify new methods and research opportunities similar to those in other fields of engineering. As an approach, systems engineering is holistic and interdisciplinary (Wikipedia, 2022).

7.1.2.1   Holistic View

Systems engineering comprises a number of steps. It elicits and analyses customer needs and required functionality during development and then proceeds with design synthesis and system validation, while always bearing in mind the lifecycle of the system. This includes fully understanding all the stakeholders involved. Oliver and colleagues (1997) claimed the systems engineering process can be decomposed into a technical process and a management process.

In their model, the management process aims to organise the technical effort in the lifecycle, while the technical process includes assessing available information, defining effectiveness measures, creating a behaviour model, creating a structure model, performing trade-off analysis, and creating a sequential build and test plan (Oliver et al., 1997).

Depending on their application, although several models are used in industry, they all aim to identify the relations between the various stages and incorporate feedback. Examples of such models include the Waterfall model and the VEE model (also called the V model) (Wikipedia, 2022).

7.1.2.2   Interdisciplinary Field

System development often requires contribution from diverse technical disciplines. By providing a systems (holistic) view of the development effort, systems engineering helps turn all the separate technical contributors into a unified team, creating a structured development process that proceeds from concept to production to operation and, in some cases, to termination and disposal. In an acquisition, the holistic integrative discipline combines contributions and balances trade-offs among cost, schedule, and performance while maintaining an acceptable level of risk covering the entire lifecycle of the item.

This perspective is often replicated in educational programmes, in that systems engineering courses are taught by faculty from other engineering departments, thus creating an interdisciplinary environment (Wikipedia, 2022).

7.1.2.3   Managing Complexity

The need for systems engineering arose with the increased complexity of systems and projects; this exponentially increased the possibility of friction between components and therefore the unreliability of the design. In this context, complexity incorporates not only engineering systems but also the logical human organisation of data. At the same time, a system can become more complex due to an increase in size or an increase in the amount of data, variables, or the number of fields involved in the design. The International Space Station is an example of such a system.

The development of smarter control algorithms, microprocessor design, and analysis of environmental systems also comes within the purview of systems engineering. Systems engineering encourages the use of tools and methods to comprehend and manage complexity in systems. Some examples of these tools are the following (Wikipedia, 2022):

- System architecture;
- System model, modelling, and simulation;

- Optimisation;
- System dynamics;
- Systems analysis;
- Statistical analysis;
- Reliability analysis;
- Decision-making.

7.1.2.4   Systems Engineering Processes

Systems engineering processes encompass all creative, manual, and technical activities necessary to define a product and which need to be carried out to convert a system definition to a sufficiently detailed system design specification for product manufacture and deployment. Design and development of a system can be divided into four stages (Wikipedia, 2022):

- Task definition: informative definition;
- Conceptual stage: cardinal definition;
- Design stage: formative definition;
- Implementation stage: manufacturing definition.

Depending on their application, different tools are used for various stages of the systems engineering process (Wikipedia, 2022):

The four main features of the systems engineering process are the following:

1. Requirements analysis;
2. Functional analysis/allocation;
3. Synthesis;
4. System analysis and control.

These are shown in Figure 7.9 in the context of the military. The process requires a variety of inputs, delineated in the figure as "process input". The outputs are shown under the heading "process output" The more general view of systems engineering and its management is considerably broader, however (Eisner, 2002).

7.2   SYSTEMS-OF-SYSTEMS

As the term implies, a system-of systems (SoS) consists of components that are themselves systems. But the whole must possess two properties for it to be considered an SoS (Maier, 1998):

- Operational independence of components: The component systems fulfil valid purposes in their own right and continue to operate to fulfil those purposes if disassembled from the overall system.
- Managerial independence of components: The component systems are managed (at least in part) for their own purposes rather than the purposes of the whole.

The "independence" aspect implies autonomy is inherent in SoS – not just in the function of the SoS but also in the function of component systems. Autonomy in this context does not necessarily mean human-free operation; the human element may be part of the component system. But this subsystem must be able to function independently on one occasion and be a cog in a larger machine on another occasion. Dynamics in the evolving structure are a peculiarity of SoS (Maier, 1998).

The prospect of developing a large, functionally rich, behaviourally complex SoS is unrealistic, especially given the requirement that component systems be useful entities in their own right. SoS tend to exhibit evolutionary development – intermediate systems are developed that perform useful

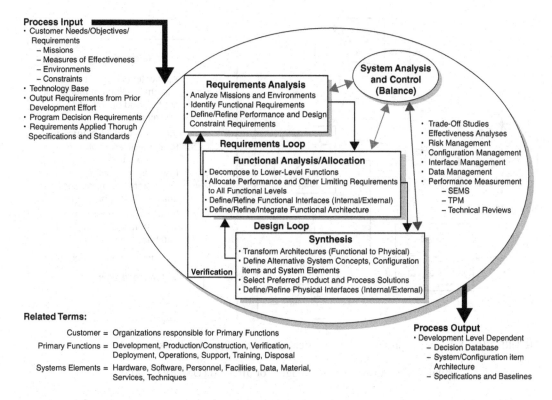

Process Input
- Customer Needs/Objectives/
  Requirements
  – Missions
  – Measures of Effectiveness
  – Environments
  – Constraints
- Technology Base
- Output Requirements from Prior
  Development Effort
- Program Decision Requirements
- Requirements Applied Thorough
  Specifications and Standards

Requirements Analysis
- Analyze Missions and Environments
- Identify Functional Requirements
- Define/Refine Performance and Design
  Constraint Requirements

Requirements Loop

Functional Analysis/Allocation
- Decompose to Lower-Level Functions
- Allocate Performance and Other Limiting Requirements
  to All Functional Levels
- Define/Refine Functional Interfaces (Internal/External)
- Define/Refine/Integrate Functional Architecture

Design Loop

Synthesis
- Transform Architectures (Functional to Physical)
- Define Alternative System Concepts, Configuration
  items and System Elements
- Select Preferred Product and Process Solutions
- Define/Refine Physical Interfaces (Internal/External)

Verification

**System Analysis
and Control
(Balance)**
- Trade-Off Studies
- Effectiveness Analyses
- Risk Management
- Configuration Management
- Interface Management
- Data Management
- Performance Measurement
  – SEMS
  – TPM
  – Technical Reviews

Related Terms:
Customer = Organizations responsible for Primary Functions
Primary Functions = Development, Production/Construction, Verification,
   Deployment, Operations, Support, Training, Disposal
Systems Elements = Hardware, Software, Personnel, Facilities, Data, Material,
   Services, Techniques

Process Output
- Development Level Dependent
  – Decision Database
  – System/Configuration item
    Architecture
  – Specifications and Baselines

FIGURE 7.9   Military standard 499B view of systems engineering process (Eisner, 2002).

functions and are then integrated into larger systems. SoS will typically evolve through stable intermediate forms (Rechtin & Maier, 1997).

Other characteristics of SoS include the following (Maier, 1998):

- SoS will be heterogeneous. From components to subsystems to systems, different technologies and implementation media will be involved.
- SoS will exhibit emergent behaviour. Given their architectural complexity, the interaction of the SoS component elements will inevitably result in behaviours that are not predictable in advance.
- SoS will be a large-scale system. "Scale" should be interpreted in a logical sense, not necessarily a geographical sense, as an SoS can be a local entity with collocated subsystems.

Although these defining properties and characteristics do not explicitly invoke control, the relevance of the technology to SoS is evident, given the dynamics involved in the component systems and compounded by the meta-system. Individual components will require control applications within them, and these control applications will interact explicitly (e.g. through coordination signals) or implicitly (e.g. through physical influences). Information technologies will provide the integration infrastructure, which is an enabler for closing the loop and optimising design and operations (Figure 7.10).

Dynamics and control aspects of SoS are also critical for non-functional properties; SoS requirements cannot be limited solely to their core performance-related functions. SoS must be designed to provide assurances of predictability, dependability, and safety. Verification at several levels of abstraction will be required, given the safety- and mission-criticality of engineered SoS, and such verification will need to be informed by the dynamics of SoS (Samad & Parisini, 2011).

Note that although SoS is a system, not all systems are SoS.

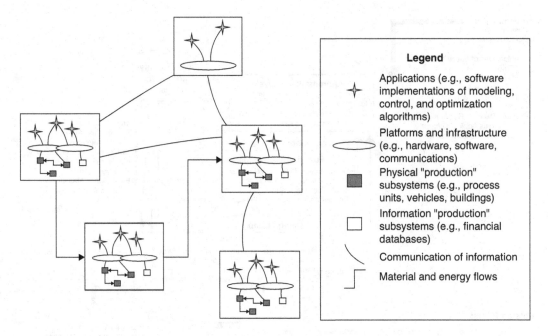

FIGURE 7.10   Schematic representation of a system of systems (Samad & Parisini, 2011).

SoS can be virtual, collaborative, acknowledged, or directed (US DoD, 2008):

- Virtual SoS: These lack a central management authority and a centrally agreed-on purpose. Large-scale behaviour emerges – and may be desirable – but this type of SoS relies
  on relatively invisible mechanisms.
- Collaborative SoS: In this type, the component systems interact more or less voluntarily
  to fulfil agreed-on central purposes. An example of a collaborative system is the Internet.
  The Internet Engineering Task Force sets standards but cannot enforce them. Instead, the
  central players collectively decide how to provide or deny service, thereby enforcing and
  maintaining standards.
- Acknowledged SoS: These types have recognised objectives, a designated manager, and
  resources, but the constituent systems retain their independent ownership, objectives,
  funding, development, and sustainment approaches. Changes are based on collaboration
  between the SoS and the system.
- Directed SoS: In this case, the integrated SoS is built and managed to fulfil specific purposes. It is centrally managed during long-term operation to continue to fulfil those purposes, along with any new ones the system owners might want to add. The component
  systems can operate independently, but their normal operational mode is subordinated to
  the centrally managed purpose.

Examples of SoS, either existing or proposed, are found in all societal sectors: air and road transportation, power grids, healthcare, water management, industrial processes, building complexes,
critical infrastructures, enterprise systems, smart homes and cities, and others. In the following
sections, we discuss a few examples (Samad & Parisini, 2011).

7.2.1   MANUFACTURING SUPPLY CHAINS

A large-scale manufacturing facility is an SoS in itself, and connectivity with upstream and downstream entities is a possibility, especially through IT integration – platforms and communications

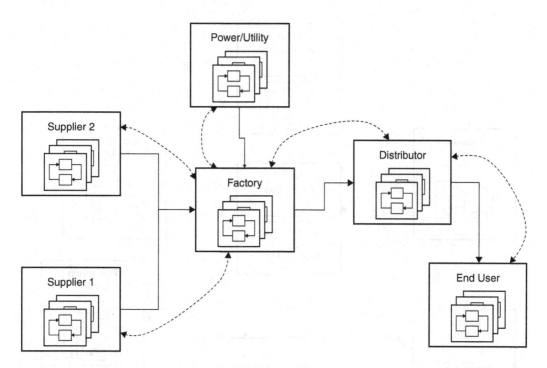

FIGURE 7.11 Control-centric view of an enterprise-level system of systems. Solid arrows show material and energy flows; dashed lines show information flows. Individual systems contain optimisation and control loops, and intersystem interactions realise higher-level control loops (Samad & Parisini, 2011).

that can, for example, automate ordering from suppliers based on inventory and production levels. Although the benefits of such automation are significant, the real value of the infrastructure is as a foundation for the optimisation of the overall supply chain – enabling responsiveness to market conditions, maximising energy efficiency, coordinating inventories with production plans dynamically, and so on.

Control loops exist within the entities in a supply chain; even suppliers and distributors who do not have manufacturing operations have feedback processes operating to service requests, accommodate inputs, and manage inventories; these are typically discrete event processes, with simpler dynamics than a production operation. An interconnected supply chain establishes additional control structures with complicating factors. Different business entities are involved with their own and often competing, priorities. Centralised or global optimisation is not feasible. See Figure 7.11 for an illustrative sketch (Samad & Parisini, 2011).

7.2.2 Embedded Automotive Systems

Today's cars are embedded systems on wheels. Much of the innovation in the automotive industry in the last decade or two has been as a result of on-board computing, control, and communication, and these innovations have dramatically improved safety, fuel economy, emissions, and reliability. A number of separate embedded systems exist in a modern automobile. Those related to safety include collision impact warning, airbag deployment and seatbelt pre-tensioners, antilock and differential braking, intelligent cruise control, and traction and stability control.

Often designed independently, these systems are nevertheless interdependent through the physics of the vehicle and the environment and the actions of the driver. This can lead to failure modes. For example, cars may lock themselves if the driver gets out with the engine running and shuts the

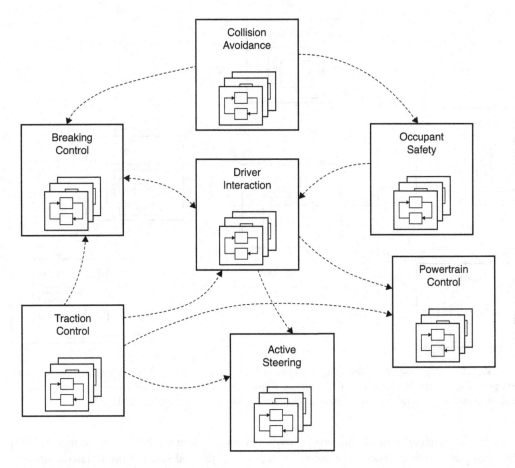

FIGURE 7.12 An "embedded" SoS example (automotive) illustrating control applications and their dependencies. Dependencies can be realised through the physics of the vehicle-driver-environment SoS or through explicit control commands (Samad & Parisini, 2011).

door, or antitheft systems may disengage and doors unlock if cars are rocked side-to-side, triggering rollover detection.

The solution is to adopt an SoS viewpoint when designing automotive systems (Figure 7.12). Standard network protocols and buses have already been adopted in vehicles. Some level of algorithmic integration has also occurred – some systems coordinate traction control and antilock braking, for example. But much remains to be done, and with the continuing rollout of X-by-wire systems (e.g. active steering), more opportunities will arise.

With developments in intelligent road transportation systems, communication and coordination among vehicles and between vehicles and infrastructure elements (road signage, traffic lights, etc.) will further increase the SoS web (Figure 7.12) (Samad & Parisini, 2011).

Intra-automobile systems are especially useful to explain the SoS vision and its strong control connections, but similar systems are found in other embedded electronic domains.

7.2.3 Smart Grids

Smart grids are of tremendous interest worldwide. They represent a revolutionary advance over traditional power grids as they are enabled by a two-way flow of electricity and information. Smart grids incorporate an overlay of communication and control over a modernised power system infrastructure, resulting in a cyber-physical system extending from generation to consumption and facilitating the integration of distributed storage and generation (especially from renewable sources) and electric and plug-in hybrid vehicles.

Today, electricity consumption is mostly independent of the exigencies of supply. Adjustment of consumption may be desired for several reasons – generation shortfalls, desires to ramp down the use of polluting or expensive generation assets, better use of renewable generation, and bottlenecks in the transmission system – but no system-wide infrastructure exists to realise such adjustment. Similarly, opportunities to effect optimised control of transmission and distribution grids, accurately monitor and communicate system state, closely connect power markets with power flows, and achieve other advanced power system capabilities are limited by the existing infrastructure.

A smart grid, as an SoS, will enable such functions. One example is depicted in Figure 7.13. Autonomous control units manage generation (including renewables and combined heat and power [CHP]), storage devices such as fuel cells, electric vehicles, and building loads, and the future may bring as-yet-unknown technologies. Utilities and system operators can interact with these master controllers and also with market entities. Individual control systems must satisfy local objectives, but they also need to cooperate to ensure the reliable and efficient operation of the power system. In Figure 7.13, the coordination is through a central node; this is closer to today's situation. In the future, we can anticipate less hierarchical, more collaborative decision and control architectures (Samad & Parisini, 2011).

7.3 SYSTEM OF INTEREST

In systems thinking and computer science, identifying the system of interest (SoI) is very important. The SoI can be a single specific system or a class of systems which is under consideration in

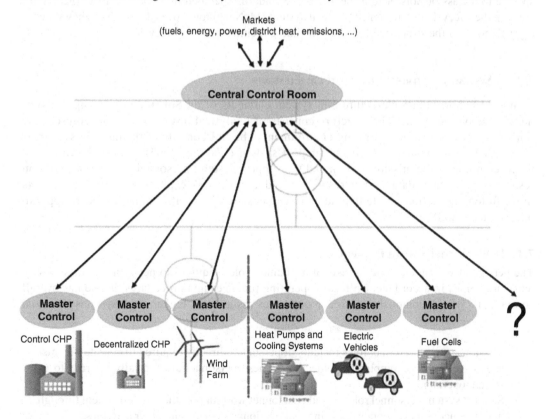

FIGURE 7.13 Smart grid SoS example (Samad & Parisini, 2011).

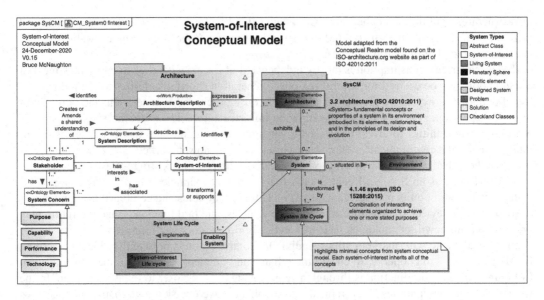

FIGURE 7.14   SoI conceptual mode (McNaughton, 2023).

a given context (ISO/IEC, 2008). The set of stakeholders and the stakeholders' concerns shape the determination of the SoI.

The SoI can be approached through its architecture or its lifecycle. The architecture can be specific to a class of SoIs or to a specific SoI. Standards specified by ISO/IEC/IEEE 15288:2015 concern the lifecycle of a designed physical system (McNaughton, 2023). Figure 7.14 shows a conceptual model of the structure of the SoI, including architecture and lifecycle.

7.3.1   System of Interest Architectural Elements

Figure 7.15 shows the architecture and system elements of an SoI in an operating environment. The system element architecture consists of analytical abstractions that represent the SoI's interactions with its operating environment. The SoI consists of the mission system as an abstraction with interfaces to the support system (Wasson, 2005). Table 7.1 shows elements common to the mission system and the support system: personnel, equipment, mission resources, procedural data, system responses, and facilities. We explain each of these concepts in the following sections. Note that many references are to aircraft, but the concepts apply to other areas as well.

7.3.1.1   Personnel System Element

The personnel system element consists of all human roles required to perform the mission system's operations in accordance with safe operating practices and procedures. It also has overall accountability for accomplishing mission objectives assigned by higher-order systems (Wasson, 2005).

- Mission system personnel roles include all personnel directly required to operate the mission system and accomplish its objectives. These personnel are typically referred to as system operators.
- Support system personnel roles include personnel who support the mission system through maintenance, supply support, training, publications, security, and other activities.

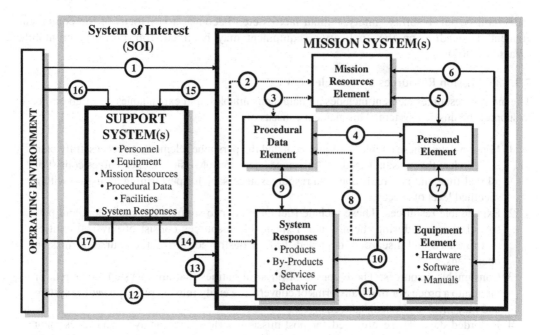

FIGURE 7.15   SoI architecture and its system elements (Wasson, 2005).

TABLE 7.1

System Elements Common to Mission System and Support System (Wasson, 2005)

System Element	Mission System Role	Support System Role
Personnel	●	●
Equipment	●	●
Mission resources	●	●
Procedural data	●	●
System responses	●	●
Facilities		●

7.3.1.2   Equipment System Element

The equipment system element consists of any physical, multi-level, electromechanical optical device that represents an integration of the hardware element and the software element, if applicable. This integration of elements can be:

1. Developed and/or procured to satisfy a system entity's capability and performance requirement.
2. Used to operate and maintain the system.
3. Used to generate or store energy required by the system.
4. Used to dispose of a system.

The success of the mission system requires that the equipment element be operationally available and fully capable of supporting the mission system and the safety of its personnel to ensure a level of success. As a result, specialty engineering (reliability, availability, maintainability, vulnerability, survivability, safety, human factors etc.) becomes a key focus of the equipment element. Depending on the application, equipment may be fixed, transportable, or mobile (Wasson, 2005).

7.3.1.3 Mission Resources System Element

The mission resources element includes all data, consumables, and expendables required on-board to support the mission system. This element consists of:

1. Mission data: These enable the equipment and the personnel elements to successfully plan and conduct the mission based on "informed" decisions. Mission data resources consist of all real-time and non-real-time data resources necessary for performing a mission with a specified level of success.
2. Expendable resources: These include fuel and water to support the equipment and personnel elements during the mission. Expendable resources consist of physical entities that are used and discarded, deployed, lost, or destroyed during the course of mission operations.
3. Consumable resources: These consist of physical entities that are ingested, devoured, or input into a processor that transforms or converts the entity into energy to power the system and may involve physical state changes.
4. Recorded data: These are used for post-mission performance analysis and assessment (Wasson, 2005).

7.3.1.4 Procedural Data System Element

The procedural data element consists of all documentation that specifies how to safely operate, maintain, deploy, and store the equipment element.

In general, the procedural data element is based on operating procedures. Operating procedures document sequences of personnel actions required to ensure the proper and safe operation of the mission system to achieve its intended level of performance under specified operating conditions. The procedural data element includes items such as reference manuals, operator guides, standard operating practices and procedures (SOPPs), and checklists (Wasson, 2005).

7.3.1.5 System Reponse Element

Every natural and human-made system, as a stimulus-response mechanism, responds internally or externally to stimuli in its operating environment. The responses may be explicit (reports, communications, altered behaviour etc.) or implicit (thoughts, strategies, lessons learned, behavioural patterns etc.).

System responses occur in a variety of forms that we characterise as behavioural patterns, products, services, and by-products throughout the system's pre-mission, mission, and post-mission phases of operation.

- System behaviour consists of system responses based on a plan of action or physical stimuli and audio-visual cues, such as threats or opportunities. The stimuli and cues invoke system behavioural patterns or actions that may be categorised as aggressive, benign, defensive, or everywhere in between. Behavioural actions include strategic and tactical tactics and countermeasures.
- System products include any type of physical outputs, characteristics, or behavioural responses to planned and unplanned events, external cues, or stimuli.
- System by-products include any type of physical system output or behaviour that is not deemed to be a system, product, or service.
- System services refer to any type of physical system behaviour, excluding physical products, that assists another entity in the conduct of its mission (Wasson, 2005).

7.3.1.6 Facilities System Element

The facilities element includes all entities required to support and sustain the mission system elements and the support system elements.

System support for pre-mission, mission, and post-mission operations requires facilities to enable operator and support personnel to accomplish their assigned tasks and objectives in a reasonable work environment. Depending on the type of system, these facilities support the following types of tasks:

1. Plan, conduct, and control the mission.
2. Provide decision support.
3. Brief and debrief personnel.
4. Store the physical system or product between missions.
5. Configure, repair, maintain, refurbish, and replenish system capabilities and resources.
6. Analyse post-mission data.

Where practical, the facilities element should provide all the necessary and sufficient capabilities and resources required to support the mission system and human activities during pre-mission, mission, and post-mission operations. Facilities may be owned, leased, rented, or provided on a limited one-time use agreement.

In general, people tend to think of facilities as enclosures that provide shelter, warmth, and protection. This thought process is driven by human concerns for creature comfort rather than the mission system. An aircraft will not know it is sitting in the rain, but members of the support system's personnel element are aware of the conditions.

Perhaps the best way to think of the facilities element is to ask the question: What type of interface is required to support the following mission system elements during all phases of the mission: equipment element, personnel element, mission data element, and resources element?

The facilities element fulfils a portion of the support system role. Depending on the mission system and its application, the facilities element may or may not be used in that context. For example, an aircraft – which is a mission system – does not require a facility to perform its primary mission. However, between primary missions, facilities are required to maintain and prepare the aircraft for its next mission. To understand the various relationships, refer to Figure 7.16 (Wasson, 2005).

7.4 ENABLING SYSTEMS

An enabling system complements and provides support to an SoI during its lifecycle stages but does not necessarily contribute directly to its function during operation. An enabling system has a lifecycle of its own (ISO/IEC, 2008).

Furthermore, enabling systems are not necessarily delivered with the SoI and do not necessarily exist in the operational environment of the SoI (ISO/IEC/IEEE 15288, 2015).

Enabling system elements: These provide the means for putting a capability into service, keeping it in service, or ending its service, for example, processes or products used to enable system development, testing, production, training, deployment, support, and disposal (Gaska et al., 2015).

As Figure 7.17 shows, the systems design for an operational effectiveness model incorporates primary and enabling systems across the lifecycle of the SoI (Gaska et al., 2015).

Complexity is increased once an SoI is deployed. The operational framework shown in Figure 7.18 encompasses the data collection and analytics for the control system to be able to affordably manage operations and sustainment across the lifecycle. This framework can support definition and advanced application of data analytics and Big Data approaches to the digital threads that define the interaction between primary and enabling systems, the enterprise, and the deployed environment, providing the variables which contribute to operational outcomes and effectiveness (Gaska et al., 2015).

To / From System Element	Personnel	Equipment	Procedural Data	Mission Resources	System Responses	Facilities
Personnel	①	②	③	④	⑤	⑥
Equipment	⑦	⑧	⑨	⑩	⑪	⑫
Procedural Data	⑬	⑭	⑮	⑯	⑰	⑱
Mission Resources	⑲	⑳	㉑	㉒	㉓	㉔
System Responses	㉕	㉖	㉗	㉘	㉙	㉚
Facilities	㉛	㉜	㉝	㉞	㉟	㊱

Where: Ⓧ = entity relationships and associated capabilities

FIGURE 7.16 System element entity relationship matrix system analysis, design, and development concepts, principles, and practices (Wasson, 2005).

The analysis of feedback from actual operations compared to planned suitability analysis during the design phase may necessitate system modifications to adapt to changes (Gaska et al., 2015).

7.5 SYSTEM LIFECYCLE

The system lifecycle can be defined as the evolution over time of an SoI from conception through to the retirement of the system (ISO/IEC, 2008).

The system lifecycle in systems engineering is a view of a system or proposed system that addresses all phases of its existence to include system conception, design and development, production and/or construction, distribution, operation, maintenance and support, retirement, phase-out and disposal (Blanchard & Fabrycky, 2006).

The IEEE Standard for application and management of the systems engineering process specifies the following:

The systems engineering process (SEP) shall be applied during each level of system development (system, subsystem, and component) to add value (additional detail) to the products defined in the prior

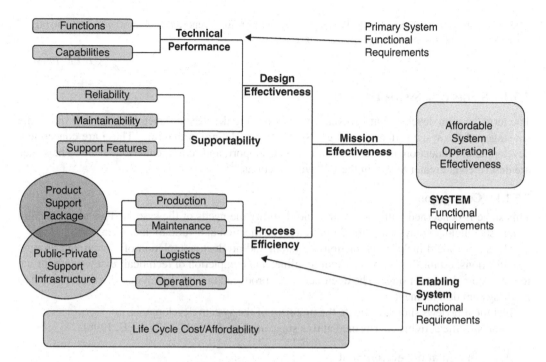

FIGURE 7.17 Systems design for operational effectiveness model incorporating primary and enabling systems across the lifecycle (Gaska et al., 2015).

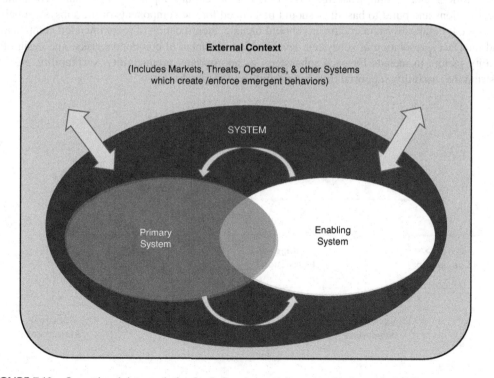

FIGURE 7.18 Operational data analytics for SoS and external context (Gaska et al., 2015).

application of the process. The SEP shall be applied to resolve reported problems, and for evolving products to improve performance or extend service life.

(IEEE, 1998)

7.5.1 STAGES OF A SYSTEM LIFECYCLE

The term "system development lifecycle" may be used to describe a system. Figure 7.19 shows the six stages of the system lifecycle using a SysML block definition diagram. These are conception, development, production, utilisation, maintenance/support, and retirement (Holt, 2021). The stages are described at greater length in the following sections.

7.5.1.1 Conception

This stage is concerned with identifying and defining the needs of the system. This also typically covers stakeholder analysis and the definition of verification and validation criteria.

The stage should include completion of system and product, completion of system and product specifications, establishment of a system baseline, and completion of technical reviews appropriate to the system definition stage. The documentation produced during system definition is required to guide system development.

Technical reviews should evaluate the maturity of the system development.

Some specific activities performed at this stage are listed in Table 7.2 (IEEE, 1998).

7.5.1.2 Design and Development

This stage is concerned with identifying potential candidate solutions for the problems associated with the needs and then finding the preferred solution. This stage may also involve developing a prototype prior to the production stage.

The preliminary design stage is executed to initiate subsystem design and create subsystem-level specifications and design-to baselines to guide component development. Preliminary component specifications and build-to baselines should be defined for the components of the subsystem being developed. Final subsystem documents should include: identification of recommended components and interfaces; resolution of subsystem-level risks; assessment of component risks; and design for quality factors to include for each subsystem, as appropriate, producibility, verifiability, ease of distribution, usability, supportability, trainability, and disposability.

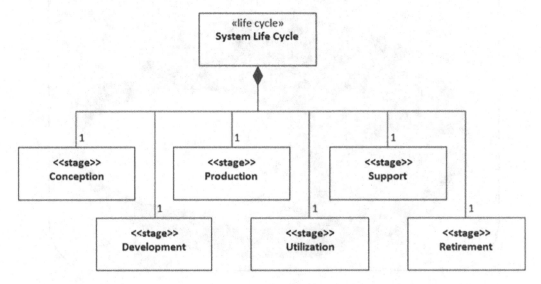

FIGURE 7.19   A lifecycle definition view showing the stages of a system lifecycle (Holt, 2021).

TABLE 7.2

System Definition (IEEE, 1998)

Establish system definition

(a) Select system concept

(b) Establish initial project and technical plans

(c) Mitigate system risks

(d) Assess subsystem risks

(e) Identify subsystems and subsystem interfaces

(f) Identify human/system interface issues

(g) Define life cycle quality factors

   (i) Producibility

   (ii) Verifiability

   (iii) Ease of distribution

   (iv) Usability

   (v) Supportability

   (vi) Trainability

   (vii) Disposability

   (viii) Total ownership costs

(h) Revise engineering and technical plans for preliminary design

Complete specifications

(a) Complete system and product interface specifications

(b) Complete system and product specifications

(c) Complete subsystem interface specifications

(d) Complete preliminary subsystem specifications

(e) Complete preliminary human/system interface

(f) Complete preliminary manpower, personnel, and training

Establish baselines

(a) Establish system baseline

(b) Establish preliminary subsystem "design-to" baselines

Complete technical reviews

(a) Complete alternative concept review

(b) Complete system definition review

The detailed design stage of the system lifecycle is intended to complete system design down to the lowest component level and create a component specification and build-to-component baseline for each component. The outputs of this stage are used to guide the fabrication of preproduction prototypes for development testing.

Identified component functions must be decomposed into lower-level functions, and functional and performance requirements should be allocated throughout the resulting lower-level functional and design architectures.

Each preliminary component specification and build-to baseline generated during the preliminary design of the subsystem should be evolved into a component specification and a build-to baseline, respectively.

Final component documents should include identification of recommended parts and interfaces, resolution of component-level risks, and for each component, down to the lowest subcomponent, the design for quality factors to include, as appropriate, producibility, verifiability, ease of distribution, usability, supportability, trainability, and disposability (IEEE, 1998).

7.5.1.3 Production

This stage takes the preferred solution and creates the actual system. It will also involve various testing activities to ensure the system is built right (verification) and the right system is built (validation). The purpose of this stage is to resolve product deficiencies when system, product, subsystem, assembly, or component specifications are not met, as determined by inspection, analysis, demonstration, or testing.

The main activities of this stage are shown in Table 7.3 (IEEE, 1998).

7.5.1.4 Utilisation

This stage describes what happens when the system is being used by end users and the operator stakeholders. This stage will also include training the appropriate stakeholders to use the system effectively. It takes place in parallel with the support stage (IEEE, 1998).

7.5.1.5 Maintenance and Support

The support stage is concerned with providing all the support services such as reporting errors, maintenance, correcting deficiencies discovered during production, assembly, integration, and acceptance testing of products and/or lifecycle process products, and so on. This will ensure the system is being run effectively. This stage taked place in parallel with the utilisation stage.

The major events of these two stages of a product's lifecycle are shown in Figure 7.20 (IEEE, 1998).

7.5.1.6 Retirement

This stage includes how and when the system is decommissioned and disposed of in a safe and secure manner.

7.5.1.7 Applications of the Six Lifecycle Stages

The six lifecycle stages (conception, design, development utilisation, maintenance/support, and retirement) may also be used as the stages for the following:

TABLE 7.3

Subsystem Definition – Fabrication, Assembly, Integration & Test (FAIT) (IEEE, 1998)

Conduct system integration and testing

- (a) Fabricate hardware components, implement software components
- (b) Assemble, integrate, and test components and assemblies
- (c) Assemble. integrate, and test subsystems and products
- (d) Establish life cycle processes
- (e) Analyse and fix failures/deficiencies and retest
- (f) Update all specifications and baselines
- (g) Revise engineering and technical plans for production

Complete technical reviews

- (a) Complete component test readiness reviews
- (b) Complete subsystem test readiness reviews
- (c) Complete system test readiness review
- (d) Complete component functional configuration audits
- (e) Complete subsystem functional configuration audits
- (f) Complete system functional configuration audits
- (g) Complete component production approval reviews
- (h) Complete subsystem production approval reviews
- (i) Complete system production approval review

Production	Customer support

Produce system products
  a) Perform production inventory and control activities
 	
  b) Produce and assemble consumer products
  c) Correct product- and process-design deficiencies
  d) Dispose of by-products and wastes
 	
Complete technical reviews
  a) Complete component physical configuration audits
 	
  b) Complete subsystem physical configuration audits
  c) Complete system physical configuration audits
	Provide customer support
	  a) Provide customer service
	
	  b) Provide "after market" products
	
	Complete system evolution
	  a) Evolve design to
	    1) Make an incremental change
	    2) Resolve product deficiencies
	    3) Exceed competitive products

FIGURE 7.20 Production and customer support (IEEE, 1998).

- Project lifecycle: The project lifecycle describes the evolution of a specific project. It is possible for several project lifecycles to be contained within a single system lifecycle. Likewise, as a programme comprises a number of projects, there is a strong link between these two.
- Programme lifecycle: The programme lifecycle sits at a level of abstraction above the project lifecycle, as a programme comprises a number of projects. A programme, therefore, relates to a number of projects or a portfolio of programmes.
- Product lifecycle: The product lifecycle refers to the end result of a project or the thing that is sold to the end customer. There is a close relationship between a product and a system as it may be considered that all products are systems, but not all systems are products.

The use of the same set of stages for a number of different lifecycles can lead to confusion, making it important to understand the scope of the lifecycle being considered (IEEE, 1998).

7.5.2 DEFINING LIFECYCLE MODELS

As the preceding analysis indicates, lifecycles are defined by identifying a set of stages that describe the evolution of an entity. A lifecycle is a structural construct. However, a lifecycle model is a behavioural construct that describes the execution of a lifecycle, specifically the order of the execution of the stages. The six stages (conception, design, development utilisation, maintenance/support, and retirement) may be executed in different sequences, depending on the nature of the system.

A SysML sequence diagram is often used to visualise the various lifecycle models, as the emphasis is on the order of the execution of the stages that comprise the lifecycle. This is good for the consistency of the overall model but can lead to diagrams that differ in appearance from some of the traditional visualisations of lifecycle models.

Most lifecycle models are visualised using non-standard, ad hoc notations, and this leads to a set of very different-looking and difficult-to-compare diagrams. This illustrates one of the benefits of using a standard notation, such as SysML: all of the different lifecycle models may be compared and contrasted easily as they are visualised in the same way.

Several well-established lifecycle models that may be used on different types of projects are described in the following sections (Holt, 2021).

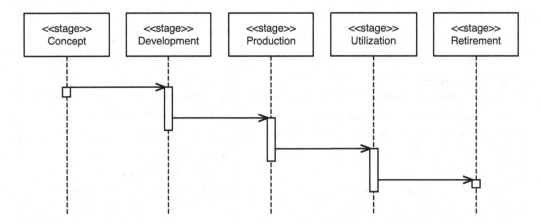

FIGURE 7.21   A lifecycle model view showing a simple linear lifecycle model (Holt, 2021).

7.5.2.1   A Linear Lifecycle Model

In a linear lifecycle model, the stages are executed in a simple linear sequence. The classic example used to illustrate a linear lifecycle model is the waterfall model by Royce (1970). The The The waterfall model is arguably the original lifecycle model and, like many of its comparators, its origins lie in the world of software engineering. An example of a linear lifecycle model, based on the waterfall model, is shown in Figure 7.21 (Holt, 2021).

Figure 7.21 visualises a lifecycle model using a SysML sequence diagram. The execution of each stage of the lifecycle is visualised using a lifeline, and the interactions show the order of the execution of the stages. In a linear lifecycle model, each stage is executed in a specific order, and each stage is executed after the completion of the previous stage.

There is typically no route to go back to a previous stage. The linear lifecycle model is used predominantly for projects where the original needs are well-specified and not likely to change. The product being developed and the technologies used are typically well understood. In terms of the project, the resources are easily managed and readily available, and the timeframe tends to be short.

There tends to be little variation, if any, in the processes that are executed in each stage; often, only a single process is executed in each stage.

The linear lifecycle model is still used extensively in industry, primarily for small, well-understood projects with robust needs. It has the advantage of being simple and easy to understand with a very clear process application and clearly defined gates for each stage.

This model is not suitable for large, complex projects and systems where the needs are prone to change. It does not work well for long-term projects, as the products are delivered in a single release at the end of the project. Bearing in mind that systems engineering is typically applied to complex projects and systems, the linear lifecycle model is not particularly well suited to it (Holt, 2021).

7.5.2.2   An Iterative Lifecycle Model

The iterative lifecycle model differs from the linear lifecycle model in that instead of a single pass through the lifecycle stages, there are several passes through the stages. These are known as iterations. Iterative lifecycle models have been used successfully for decades and have seen a resurgence in the last two decades with the widespread use of Agile techniques.

Figure 7.22 shows how the iterative lifecycle model works (Holt, 2021).

In Figure 7.22, the iterative model is visualised using a SysML sequence diagram. The execution of each stage of the lifecycle is visualised using a lifeline, and the interactions show the order of execution of the stages.

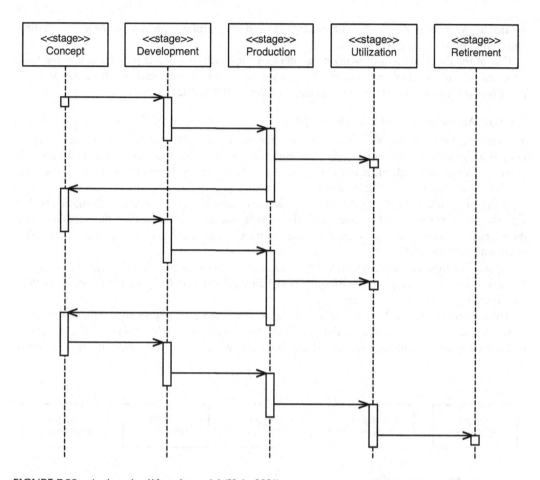

FIGURE 7.22   An iterative lifecycle model (Holt, 2021).

The iterative lifecycle approach assumes that if a linear lifecycle model works well for short, well-defined projects and systems, then it is possible to break a large, complex system into a series of shorter, simpler projects. Each of these mini-lifecycles is known as an iteration.

Each iteration represents a single pass through the stages, starting at the concept stage and progressing until after the production stage and into utilisation. The result of each iteration is a workable version of the final system that can be deployed in the target environment.

This has a number of advantages, as each iterative release of the system is a more complete and typically improved version compared to the previous one. This also means that if a specific release of the system does not work or is a disaster in some way, it is relatively easy to go back to a previous release and restore some level of functionality.

Each iteration will also take a short period of time. In some cases, the first iteration may take longer than the subsequent iterations to get the original working release completed. It is quite usual for these subsequent iterations to be very short, and in many organisations that are employing an Agile approach, new versions of the system may be produced on a weekly or even daily basis.

The classic iterative approach is used heavily in the software world, rather than on large systems projects, due to the perceived ease of creating software releases. This has the disadvantage that the emphasis is often on getting a release out on time rather than waiting for something that works.

There is a common misconception that model-based systems engineering (MBSE) cannot be applied to iterative approaches, but this is simply not the case. A model-based approach can be applied at any point in a lifecycle where there is a need to control complexity, define understanding, and communicate with stakeholders.

One of the disadvantages of applying an iterative approach to systems projects is that the basic needs may be changed quite frequently by stakeholders, so it is important to have a robust needs process in place. Unfortunately, this is often not the case (Holt, 2021).

7.5.2.3   An Incremental Lifecycle Model

The incremental lifecycle model is similar in some ways to the iterative lifecycle model. There is not just a single pass through the stages but multiple passes so that the final system is deployed in a number of releases. Indeed, both iterative and incremental lifecycle models are often known collectively as evolutionary lifecycle models.

In this approach, the concept stage is executed as the first stage but will cover all the needs. The subsequent development and production of the system take different subsets of the needs and produce a partial solution that does not comprise the whole system and can be deployed in the target environment (Holt, 2021).

Figure 7.23 shows an incremental lifecycle model, visualised using a SysML sequence diagram. The execution of each stage of the lifecycle is visualised using a lifeline, and the interactions show the order of execution of the stages.

The incremental lifecycle model results in the system being deployed in an incremental fashion, rather than as a single release, as in the case of the linear lifecycle model. This is a clear advantage as the final system can be seen to be working, and the system is deployed, albeit in a reduced form.

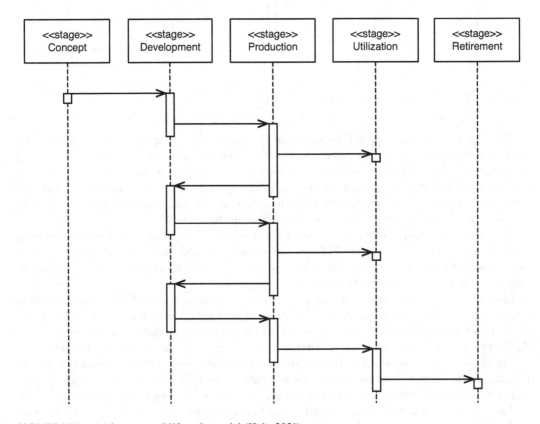

FIGURE 7.23   An incremental lifecycle model (Holt, 2021).

The incremental lifecycle model is, therefore, useful for very long projects where some functionality of the system is required before the end of the project. There is a downside to this, as not all systems can be broken down into subsets of the overall system and, in such cases, the approach is not suitable (Holt, 2021).

7.6 HIERARCHIES

Hierarchies are organisational representations of partitioned relationships. Otherwise stated, the hierarchy represents a partitioning of the entity into smaller more manageable entities. All systems have a natural hierarchy. It is an essential part of the modelling endeavour to capture this hierarchy and to ensure all elements in the model adhere to it.

While there is no universally accepted nomenclature for hierarchy, the following definitions are particularly useful to understand how the system hierarchy actually works:

- System: An integrated set of elements, subsystems, or assemblies that accomplish a defined objective. These elements include products (hardware, software, firmware), processes, people, information, techniques, facilities, services, and other support elements. An example is an air transportation system.
- Element: A major product, service, or facility of the system, for example, the aircraft element of an air transportation system.
- Subsystem: An integrated set of assemblies, components, and parts which performs a cleanly and clearly separated function involving similar technical skills or involving a separate supplier. Examples are an aircraft on-board communications subsystem or an airport control tower as a subsystem of the air transportation system.
- Assembly: An integrated set of components and/or subassemblies comprising a defined portion of a subsystem, for example, the pilot's radar display console or the fuel injection assembly of the aircraft propulsion subsystem.
- Subassembly: An integrated set of components and/or parts that comprise a well-defined portion of an assembly, such as a video display with its related integrated circuitry or a pilot's radio headset.
- Component: A clearly identified item constituting a key constituent part of an object, such as the earpiece of a pilot's radio headset.
- Part: The lowest level of separately identifiable items, for example, a bolt to hold a console in place (INCOSE, 2007).

The system hierarchy should be balanced, with appropriate fan-out and span of control. Appropriate fan-out and span of control refer to the number of elements subordinate to each element in the hierarchy.

System hierarchies are analogous to organisational hierarchies. Both can suffer from improper balance, that is, too great a span of control or excessive layers in the hierarchy. A rule of thumb useful in evaluating this balance is that a system should have no more than 7 ± 2 elements reporting to it. In the same way, an element should have no more than 7 ± 2 subsystems reporting to it, and so on.

A design level with too many entities reporting suffers from too much complexity. The design and corresponding test activities run the risk of running out of control or acquiring an informal partitioning that guides the work without proper control or visibility.

A level of design with too few entities likely does not have distinct design activity, and both design and testing activities contain redundancy.

An example of a common hierarchy is shown in Figure 7.24 (INCOSE, 2007).

The depth of the hierarchy can be adjusted to fit the complexity of the system. For example, in the complex Apollo programme, NASA added a Module Level in the hierarchy to differentiate it from the Command Module, Lunar Module etc. of the Space Vehicle Element. Simple systems may have fewer levels in the hierarchy than complex systems.

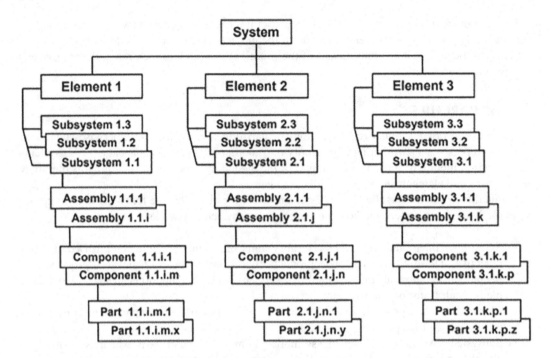

FIGURE 7.24 Hierarchy within a system (INCOSE, 2007).

Some examples of the hierarchy of systems terminology are shown in Figure 7.25 (INCOSE, 2007).

Figure 7.26 (Holt, 2021) shows an expanded ontology defining several new levels of hierarchy, using a SysML block definition diagram. In the figure, each level is represented by stating a higher level and a lower level. The following rules apply:

- Each system comprises a number of owned subsystems (shown by SysML composition) and may be made up of an optional number of non-owned subsystems (shown by SysML aggregation).
- Each subsystem comprises a number of owned assemblies (shown by SysML composition) and may be made up of an optional number of non-owned assemblies (shown by SysML aggregation).
- Each assembly comprises a number of owned components (shown by SysML composition) and may be made up of an optional number of non-owned components (shown by SysML aggregation).

This results in a set of four levels of system hierarchy that may be permitted to exist. The relationships between each of the levels are shown by both compositions and aggregations. Each level can have both owned and non-owned lower-level elements. This will allow greater flexibility, but importantly, the goal is not flexibility; the goal is to represent what is necessary in the hierarchy.

Each of these relationships must be considered carefully before inclusion in, or exclusion from, the ontology.

The presence of these relationships shows the legal relationships that may be visualised. Any relationships that are not present are therefore illegal. For example, it is clear that it is legal for a system to comprise at least one subsystem, as it is in the ontology. The following relationships, however, are not legal:

- A system comprises a number of assemblies.
- A system comprises a number of components.
- A component comprises a number of subsystems.

System	Air Logostics	Information	Electric Car
Elements	Aircraft Package Processing Support Equipment Air & Ground Crews Hub, Base, Facility	Computers Network Printers Data Storage Personnel	
Sub-systems		Data Processor Operating System Software	Power Train Body Chassis
Components		Input Devices Output Devices Processing Memory	Battery Motor(s) Generator Controller

FIGURE 7.25 Examples of system hierarchy (INCOSE, 2007).

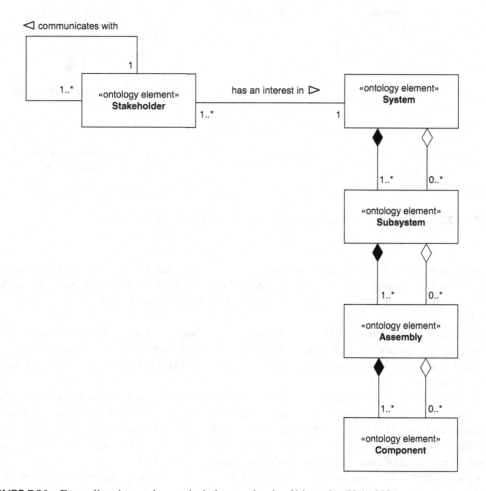

FIGURE 7.26 Expanding the ontology to include more levels of hierarchy (Holt, 2021).

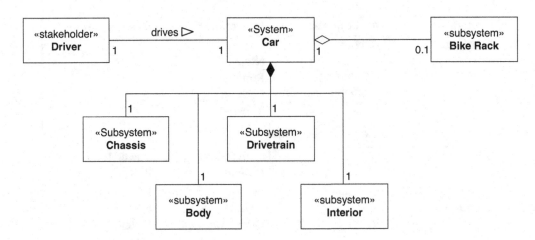

FIGURE 7.27   Structural breakdown view showing compositions and aggregation (Holt, 2021).

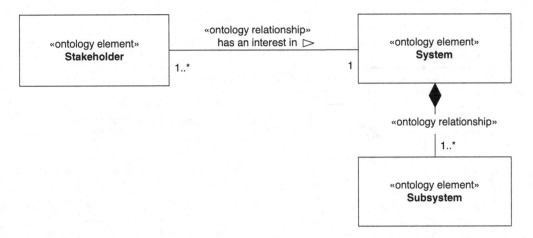

FIGURE 7.28   Simple system hierarchy with a single level (Holt, 2021).

This list shows just a few of the relationships that are illegal as their corresponding relationship does not exist in the ontology. The ontology therefore shows the legal ontology elements and ontology relationships that may be visualised and prohibits the visualisation of anything that is not on the ontology.

The diagram in Figure 7.27 (Holt, 2021) shows an example of legal visualisations of ontology. In other words, it is a valid view forming part of the overall model. The figure shows a very simple system hierarchy with only one lower level of abstraction, that of the subsystem, using a SysML block definition diagram.

In Figure 7.28, the stakeholders with an interest in the system sit at the same level of abstraction as the system. This may be inferred by the fact that the relationship between stakeholder and system is visualised using an association that makes both model elements exist at the same level. The relationship between system and subsystem, however, uses a composition that means that the subsystem sits at a lower level of abstraction than that of the system (Holt, 2021).

By locating the compositions and aggregations, it is possible to quickly identify the various levels of abstraction that exist in the diagram and to easily identify the highest level. This is important as it provides a good starting point for reading the diagram. In the diagram in Figure 7.28, therefore, the natural place to start to read it is at the highest level of abstraction. This means the diagram will be read as:

One or more stakeholders have an interest in the system, and each system comprises a number of subsystems.

(Holt, 2021)

7.7 SYSTEM ITEM STRUCTURE

The basic three elements of a system are:

- Input;
- Processing;
- Output.

For ease of interpretation, these are visualised in Figure 7.29 (MentorWay, 2022).
Additional important elements are:

- Control,
- Feedback,
- Environment,
- Boundaries and interfaces.

Therefore, the key elements of a system can be stated as output, input, processes, control, feedback, environment, and boundaries and interfaces and explained as follows:

- Output: First of all, we must determine what the objectives or goals are and what we intend to achieve. Once we know our aim, we can try to achieve it in the best possible way – that constitutes the planned output.
- Input: Once we know the output, we can determine what the input should be.
- Processes: Processes refer to the details of how the inputs and files are converted into outputs. Processes may modify the input totally or partially depending on the specifications of the output.

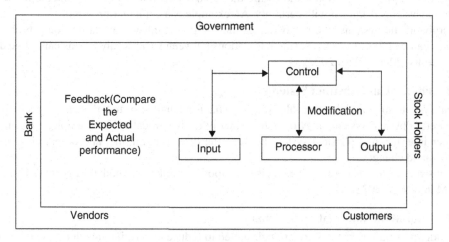

FIGURE 7.29 System items (MentorWay, 2022).

- Control: The decision-maker controls the activities of accepting input processing and producing output. For example, in an organisational context, management as a decision-making body controls the inflow, handling, and outflow of activities that affect the welfare of the business.
- Feedback: The feedback on the output allows the output to be measured against certain established standards and to make adjustments in the processing accordingly.
- Environment: The environment is the source of external elements with an effect on the system. It determines how a system must function.
- Boundaries and interfaces: A system should be defined by its boundaries. These are the limits that identify its components, processes, and interrelationships when it interfaces with another system. For example, a teller system in a commercial bank is restricted to the deposits, withdrawals, and related activities of customers' checking and savings accounts (MentorWay, 2022).

7.7.1 TYPES OF SYSTEMS

Common classifications of systems are the following:

- Open and closed systems;
- Deterministic and probabilistic systems;
- Physical or abstract systems;
- Man-made information systems (MentorWay, 2022).

Each of these is described in more detail in the following sections.

7.7.1.1 Open and Closed Systems

An open system is a system that interacts freely with its environment. This type of system can adapt to changing internal and environmental conditions. Examples are business organisations and human beings.

A closed system is one which is self-contained. It has no interaction with its environment. An example is a computer program which processes predefined input in a predefined way (MentorWay, 2022).

7.7.1.2 Deterministic and Probabilistic Systems

The behaviour of a deterministic system is completely known. There is no uncertainty involved in defining the outputs of the systems knowing the inputs. This implies that the interaction between various subsystems is known with certainty. An example is a computer program.

In probabilistic systems, the behaviour cannot be predicted with certainty; only probabilistic estimates can be given. In this case, the interactions between various subsystems cannot be defined with certainty (MentorWay, 2022).

7.7.1.3 Physical and Abstract Systems

Physical systems are tangible or visible systems. That is a tangible system that can be seen, touched, counted etc. Physical systems may operate statically or dynamically. For example, a programmed computer is a dynamic physical system because the data, programme, and output change as the user's demand changes.

An abstract system is not tangible or visible. Good examples are models, algorithms, and equations (MentorWay, 2022).

7.7.1.4 Man-Made Information Systems

Man-made information systems are often designed to reduce uncertainty about a state or event. For example, information that the weather will be good tomorrow reduces uncertainty about whether a football game will be played. Thus, a good example of a man-made information system is a weather forecast (MentorWay, 2022).

7.7.2 INFORMATION SYSTEMS IN THE ORGANISATIONAL CONTEXT

Information systems used within organisations can be formal, informal, or computer-based (MentorWay, 2022).

7.7.2.1 Formal Information Systems

Formal information systems can be strategic, tactical, or operational. Figure 7.30 sets these within an organisational hierarchy.

7.7.3 INFORMAL INFORMATION SYSTEMS

In the organisational context, an informal information system is an employee-based system designed to meet personnel and vocational needs and to help solve work-related problems. It also directs information upward, through indirect channels. In this way, it is considered to be a useful system because it works within the framework of the business and its stated policies.

7.7.4 COMPUTER-BASED INFORMATION SYSTEMS

Common computer-based information systems are the following:

1. Transaction processing system (TPS): TPS carries out simple but repetitive computations on a large number of records like maintenance of inventory records, payroll preparation etc. Figure 7.31 shows how TPS works (MentorWay, 2022).
2. Management information system (MIS): (MIS) is required to obtain tactical information. These systems assist lower management in problem-solving and decision-making. They use the results of transaction processing, as well as other information. Figure 7.32 shows how this system works (MentorWay, 2022).

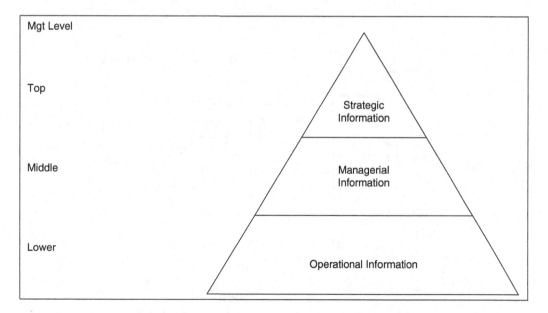

FIGURE 7.30 Types of formal information systems (MentorWay, 2022).

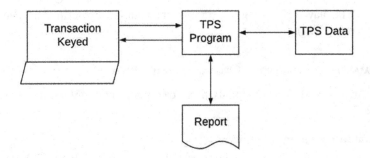

FIGURE 7.31   Transaction processing system (TPS) (MentorWay, 2022).

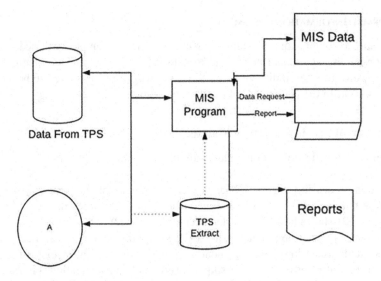

FIGURE 7.32   Management information system (MIS) (MentorWay, 2022).

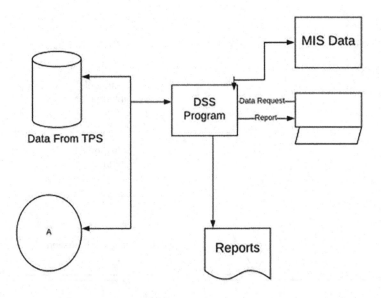

FIGURE 7.33   Decision support system (DSS) (MentorWay, 2022).

3. Decision support system (DSS): DSS is used to obtain strategic information. These systems assist higher management to make long-term decisions. Decisions can be unstructured or semi-structured. DSS is shown in Figure 7.33 (MentorWay, 2022).

REFERENCES

Blanchard, B.S., & Fabrycky, W.J. (2006). *Systems engineering and analysis*. Pearson Prentice Hall.

Checkland, P. (1999). *Systems thinking, systems practice*. Wiley.

Eisner, H. (2002). *Essentials of project and systems engineering management*. Wiley.

Gaska, M.T., Bobinis, J.S., & Galluzzo, V. (2015). Application of system design for operational effectiveness for architectural modelling of the SoS relationship between primary and enabling systems. *Procedia Computer Science*, *61*, 240–245. https://doi.org/10.1016/j.procs.2015.09.204

Grieves, M. (2012). Virtually indistinguishable. In L. Rivest, A. Bouras, & B. Louhichi (Eds.), *Product lifecycle management. Towards knowledge-rich enterprises* (pp. 226–242). PLM 2012. IFIP Advances in Information and Communication Technology, vol 388. Springer. https://doi.org/10.1007/978-3-642-35758-9_20

Grieves, M., & Vickers, J. (2017). Digital twin: Mitigating unpredictable, undesirable emergent behavior in complex systems. In F-J. Kahlen, S. Flumerfelt, & A. Alves (Eds.), *Transdisciplinary perspectives on complex systems: New findings and approaches* (pp. 85–113). Springer. https://link.springer.com/chapter/10.1007/978-3-319-38756-7_4

Holt, J. (2021). *Systems engineering demystified: A practitioner's handbook for developing complex systems using a model-based approach*. Packt Publishing.

IEEE. (1998). IEEE 1220:1998. Standard for application and management of the systems engineering process. https://ieeexplore.ieee.org/document/741941

INCOSE. (2007). *International Council on Systems Engineering (INCOSE) systems engineering handbook: A guide for system life cycle processes and activites, version 3.1*. INCOSE. https://www.amazon.com/International-Council-Systems-Engineering-Handbook/dp/B0088BGAAM

ISO/IEC. (2008). ISO/IEC 15288:2008 (en). Systems and software engineering: System life cycle processes. https://www.iso.org/obp/ui/#iso:std:iso-iec:15288:ed-2:v1:en

ISO/IEC/IEEE. (2015). ISO/IEC/IEEE 15288:215. Systems and software engineering: System life cycle processes. https://www.iso.org/standard/63711.html

MentorWay. (2022). What are the elements of a system? Types of systems. https://www.mentorway.in/what-are-the-elements-of-a-system-types-of-systems/

Maier, M.W. (1998). Architecting principles for systems-of-systems. *Systems Engineering*, *1*(4), 267–284. https://doi.org/10.1002/(SICI)1520-6858(1998)1:4<267::AID-SYS3>3.0.CO;2-D

McNaughton, B. (2023). System of interest conceptual model. https://sysdesc.info/Content/System/CM_System-of-Interest.htm

Mitchell, M. (2009). *Complexity: A guided tour*. Oxford University Press. https://www.academia.edu/40227220/Complexity_A_Guided_Tour_Melanie_Mitchell_2009_

Oliver, D.W., Kelliher, T.P, & Keegan Jr, J.G. (1997). *Engineering complex systems with models and objects*. McGraw-Hill.

Rechtin, E., & Maier, M.W. (1997). *The art of systems architecting*. CRC Press.

Royce, W.W. (1970). Managing the development of large software systems. *Proceedings IEEE Wescon* (pp. 1–9). Institute of Electrical and Electonics Engineers. http://www-scf.usc.edu/~csci201/lectures/Lecture11/royce1970.pdf

Samad, T., & Parisini, T. (2011). System of systems. ePaper, *IEEE Control Systems Society*. https://www.yumpu.com/en/document/view/6064499/systems-of-systems-ieee-control-systems-society

Sargut, G., & Gunter McGrath, R.D. (2011). Learning to live with complexity. *Harvard Business Review*, *89*(9), 68–76. https://www.researchgate.net/publication/51662670_Learning_to_live_with_complexityttps://www.researchgate.net/publication/51662670_Learning_to_live_with_complexity

US Department of Defence (DoD). (2008). *Systems engineering guide for systems of systems*. Washington, DC: Pentagon.

Wasson, C.S. (2005). *System analysis, design, and development: Concepts, principles, and practices*. John Wiley & Sons.

Wikipedia. (2022). Systems engineering. https://en.wikipedia.org/wiki/Systems_engineering

8 Software Engineering

8.1 SOFTWARE ENGINEERING OVERVIEW

Software engineering refers to the development of software products using scientific principles, methods, and procedures. The outcome of software engineering is a reliable software product (TutorialsPoint, 2022).

The term "software engineering" was created in the 1960s when researchers began to address what many saw as a "software crisis", defined by Krueger (1992) as "the problem of building large, reliable software systems in a reliable, cost-effective way". To this point, industry and academia had concentrated on developing capable and competent hardware. As a result, powerful and inexpensive machines were readily available.

The next step was to create software to fully utilise the capability of the available hardware. In other words, researchers needed to create software that could solve real-world problems. The resulting field of endeavour was called software engineering (Tiwari & Kumar, 2020), and the outcomes were software products created with specific requirements in mind (TutorialsPoint, 2022). The process of product creation is shown in Figure 8.1.

The term "software engineering" can be broken down as follows:

1. Software: The first half of the term, "software", refers to more than a programme code. A programme is an executable code serving a certain computational purpose. Software is a collection of executable programmes, associated libraries, operational manuals, data structures, and documentation (Tiwari & Kumar, 2020).
2. Engineering: The second half of the term, "engineering", refers to the use of scientific principles and methods to create the software product (TutorialsPoint, 2022). Engineering is the step-by-step evolution of constructs in an organised, well-defined, and disciplined manner (Tiwari & Kumar, 2020),

Some leading definitions of software engineering produced by eminent researchers and practitioners are as follows:

1. IEEE Standard 610.12-1990 defines software engineering as the application of a systematic, disciplined, and quantifiable approach to the development, operation, and maintenance of software, that is, the application of engineering to software (TutorialsPoint, 2022).
2. Software engineering is the establishment and use of sound engineering principles to obtain economically developed software that is reliable and works efficiently on real machines (Naur & Randell, 1969).
3. Software engineering is the application of science and mathematics by which the capabilities of computer equipment are made useful to man through computer programmes, procedures, and associated documentation (Boehm, 1984).
4. Software engineering is the introduction of formal engineering principles to the creation and production of software. A scientific or logical approach replaces the perhaps more traditional unstructured (or artistic) methods (Partridge, 2013).
5. Software engineering is a discipline whose aim is the production of quality software, software that is delivered on time, within budget, and that satisfies its requirements (Schach, 1990).

DOI: 10.1201/9781003208686-8

FIGURE 8.1 Software product (TutorialsPoint, 2022).

In short, the goal of software engineering is to develop quality software within reasonable time limits, and at an affordable cost (Tiwari & Kumar, 2020).

8.2 FROM PROGRAMMING LANGUAGES TO SOFTWARE ARCHITECTURE

A framework or architecture is defined as a meta-level model (a higher-level abstraction) through which a range of concepts, models, techniques, and methodologies can be clarified and/or integrated (Jayaratna, 1994). Software architecture involves the description of systems' inherent elements, the interactions between the elements, and their composition guided by patterns and constraints on those patterns (Shaw & Garlan, 1996; Sowa & Zachman, 1992).

One characterisation of progress in programming languages and tools has been regular increases in abstraction level or the conceptual size of software designers' building blocks. In the following sections, we discuss the historical development of abstraction techniques in computer science (Garlan & Shaw, 1994).

8.2.1 High-Level Programming Languages

When digital computers emerged in the 1950s, software was written in machine language; programmers placed instructions and data individually and explicitly in the computer's memory. Insertion of a new instruction in a programme might require hand-checking of the entire programme to update references to data and instructions that moved as a result of the insertion.

Eventually, researchers realised that the memory layout and updating of references could be automated, and symbolic names could be used for operation codes and memory addresses. Symbolic assemblers were the result. They were followed by macro processors, which allowed a single symbol to stand for a commonly used sequence of instructions. The substitution of simple symbols for machine operation codes, machine addresses yet to be defined, and sequences of instructions were perhaps the earliest form of abstraction in software.

In the latter part of the 1950s, it became clear that certain patterns of execution were commonly useful. Indeed, they were so well understood that it was possible to create them automatically from a notation more like mathematics than machine language. The earliest patterns were for the evaluation of arithmetic expressions, for procedure invocation, and for loops and conditional statements.

These insights were captured in a series of early high-level languages, of which Fortran was the main survivor.

Higher-level languages allowed more sophisticated programmes to be developed, and patterns in the use of data emerged. Whereas in Fortran, data types served primarily as cues for selecting the proper machine instructions, data types in Algol and its successors served to state the programmer's intentions about how data should be used. The compilers for these languages could build on experience with Fortran and tackle more sophisticated compilation problems. Among other things, they could check adherence to these intentions, thereby providing incentives for the programmers to use this type of mechanism.

Progress in language design continued with the introduction of modules to provide protection for related procedures and data structures, with the separation of a module's specification from its implementation and with the introduction of abstract data types (Garlan & Shaw, 1994).

8.2.2   ABSTRACT DATA TYPES

In the late 1960s, some programmers had an intuition about software development: if you get the data structures right, the effort will make the development of the rest of the programme much easier. The abstract data type work of the 1970s can be viewed as a development effort that converted this intuition into a real theory. The conversion from an intuition to a theory involved understanding the following:

* Software structure, including a representation packaged with its primitive operators;
* Specifications (mathematically expressed as abstract models or algebraic axioms);
* Language issues (modules, scope, user-defined types);
* Integrity of the result (invariants of data structures and protection from other manipulation);
* Rules for combining types (declarations);
* Information hiding (protection of properties not explicitly included in specifications).

The effect was to raise the design level of certain elements of software systems, namely abstract data types, above the level of programming language statements or individual algorithms. This form of abstraction led to an understanding of a good organisation for an entire module that serves one particular purpose. This involved combining representations, algorithms, specifications, and functional interfaces in uniform ways. Certain support was required from the programming language, but the abstract data-type paradigm allowed some parts of systems to be developed from a vocabulary of data types rather than from a vocabulary of programming-language constructs (Garlan & Shaw, 1994).

8.2.3   SOFTWARE ARCHITECTURE

Just as good programmers recognised useful data structures in the late 1960s, good software system designers now recognise useful system organisations. One of these is based on the theory of abstract data types. But this is not the only way to organise a software system.

Many other organisations have developed informally over time and are now part of the vocabulary of software system designers. Thus, a number of architectural patterns, or styles, form the basic repertoire of a software architect (Garlan & Shaw, 1994).

Many software architectures are carefully documented and often widely disseminated. Examples include the International Standard Organization's Open Systems Interconnection Reference Model, the NIST/ECMA Reference Model (a generic software engineering environment architecture based on layered communication substrates), and the X Window System (a distributed windowed user interface architecture based on event triggering and call-backs) (Garlan & Shaw, 1994).

8.3 SYSTEM SOFTWARE

System software is software written to service and support other programmes. Compilers, editors, debuggers, operating systems, and hardware drivers are examples of such software. Most system software deals with computer hardware, multiple users, concurrent operations and process scheduling, resource sharing and virtualisation, complex data structures, and multiple external interfaces (University of Cape Town, 2011).

On a more basic level, system software refers to the files and programmes that make up a computer's operating system. System files include libraries of functions, system services, drivers for printers and other hardware, system preferences, and other configuration files. The programmes that are part of the system software on a computer include assemblers, compilers, file management tools, system utilities, and debuggers. Since system software runs at the most basic level of a computer, it is called "low-level" software. It generates the user interface and allows the operating system to interact with the hardware (Uerikasakura, 2020).

8.3.1 FUNCTIONS OF SYSTEM SOFTWARE

System software includes operating systems such as device drivers, servers, windowing systems, and utilities. System software runs the hardware and computer system. The two main categories of system software are operating systems and utility software.

The three major functions of system software are allocating system resources, monitoring system activities, and managing disks and files(Uerikasakura, 2020).

1. Allocating system resources: The system resources are time, memory, input, and output. The time in the central processing unit (CPU) is divided into time slices. The time slices are measured in milliseconds. Based on the priority of tasks, the time slices are assigned. Memory is also managed by the operating system. Disk space is a part of the main memory. The data flow is controlled by the operating system.
2. Monitoring system activities: System security and system performance are monitored by system software. System performance includes response time and CPU utilisation. System security is a part of the operating system. Multiple users can't gain access without the security code or password.
3. Managing files and disks: The user needs to save, copy, delete, move, and rename files. The system software will handle those functions. Disk and file management is a technical task.

8.3.2 APPLICATION SOFTWARE

Application software is designed to solve a specific business need. Most software programmes operating with business and technical data are application software, as are most real-time (RT) systems (University of Cape Town, 2011).

8.3.3 ENGINEERING/SCIENTIFIC SOFTWARE

This software supports the use and production of scientific and engineering datasets. It is used in almost all engineering and scientific disciplines, from simulating water flow, lighting conditions, and aerodynamics, to examining the large-scale structure of the universe. Engineering software is also used for design purposes, i.e. computer-aided design (CAD) software, and automation of manufacturing of goods, i.e. computer-aided manufacturing (CAM) software (University of Cape Town, 2011).

8.3.4 EMBEDDED SOFTWARE

This software resides directly within some hardware component to provide control over the component or other vital features required for it to function. Embedded software is widespread and can be found in everything from phones and microwave ovens to cars, aeroplanes and medical equipment (University of Cape Town, 2011).

8.3.5 WEB APPLICATIONS

A web application software is an application accessed through a web browser over a network. Web applications offer a variety of functions, and some application software products are now implemented as web applications, such as Google Docs (University of Cape Town, 2011).

8.3.6 ARTIFICIAL INTELLIGENCE SOFTWARE

Artificial intelligence (AI) software has been used in the domains of robotics, expert systems, pattern recognition, theorem proving, and game playing (University of Cape Town, 2011).

8.4 SOFTWARE EVOLUTION

Software evolution refers to the process of developing a software product using software engineering principles and methods. This includes the initial development of software and its maintenance and updates until a software product which satisfies the stated requirements is developed (TutorialsPoint, 2022). The process is shown in Figure 8.2.

Evolution starts when developers ascertain the users' requirements. Based on what they learn, the developers create a prototype of the intended software and show it to the users to get their feedback. The users suggest changes and updates. This iterative process changes the original software and continues until the desired software product is created.

Even after the users have the software, the product will continue to evolve because of changing technology and changing user requirements. Starting over again at the beginning is neither feasible nor economical. Instead, the existing software must be updated (TutorialsPoint, 2022).

8.4.1 SOFTWARE EVOLUTION LAWS

In software engineering, the laws of software evolution refer to a series of laws formulated by Belady and Lehman (1976, 1985). The laws describe a balance between forces that drive new developments on the one hand, and forces that slow down progress on the other hand.

Lehman (1980) divided software into three categories: static-type, practical-type, and embedded-type. Each evolves differently (TutorialsPoint, 2022).

8.4.1.1 Static-Type (S-Type)

The S-type software works strictly according to predefined specifications and solutions. The solution and the method are understood before coding begins. The S-type software is the simplest type

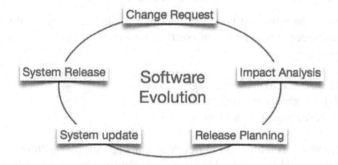

FIGURE 8.2 Software evolution (TutorialsPoint, 2022).

because it is the least subject to changes. An example of S-type software is a calculator programme for mathematical computation (TutorialsPoint, 2022).

8.4.1.2   Practical-Type (P-Type)

The P-type software comprises a collection of procedures and is defined by what those procedures can do. In this software, the specifications can be described, but the solution is not immediately obvious. An example of the P-type is gaming software (TutorialsPoint, 2022).

8.4.1.3   Embedded-Type (E-Type)

The E-type software works closely with the real-world environment. This software is very likely to evolve because real-world situations are subject to change. An example of the E-type is online trading software (TutorialsPoint, 2022).

Lehman's eight laws for E-type software are the following:

1. The software will undergo continuous change;
2. The software will become increasingly complex;
3. For continuity, it is essential to remember how/why the software was developed;
4. The software will continue to grow;
5. The quality of the software will decrease unless it is maintained and adapted;
6. The software is a multi-loop, multi-level feedback system and must be treated as such to be modified;
7. The software is capable of self-regulation;
8. The software has organisational stability (Lehman, 1980).

8.5   PARADIGMS OF SOFTWARE ENGINEERING

Many software development paradigms have evolved over the years. These paradigms act as a guiding tool for the development community, not only making the development process systematic and disciplined but also making the lifecycle of their developed product easy for users to understand.

On the basis of their evolution, development models can be classified into two broad categories:

1. Traditional software engineering paradigms; and
2. Advanced software engineering paradigms (Tiwari & Kumar, 2020).

In the following sections, we discuss and give examples of these paradigms.

8.5.1   Traditional Software Engineering Paradigms

With the evolution of the term "software engineering", a number of software development paradigms came into existence. These traditional software engineering models can be categorised into three broad categories:

- Classical lifecycle development paradigms,
- Incremental development paradigms, and
- Evolutionary development paradigms.

Each of these paradigms has a finite set of development steps starting with requirement-gathering and progressing through to deployment. Traditional software engineering paradigms and their three categories are shown in Figure 8.3 and discussed below (Tiwari & Kumar, 2020).

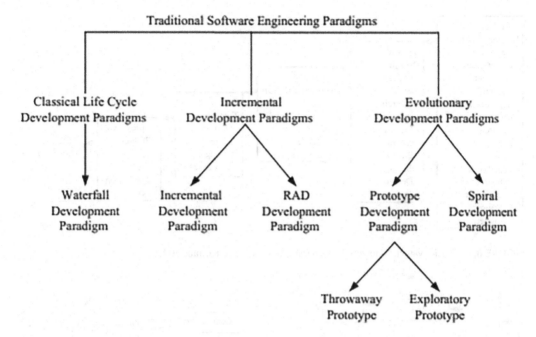

FIGURE 8.3   Traditional software engineering paradigms (Tiwari & Kumar, 2020).

8.5.1.1   Classical Lifecycle Development Paradigms

These very early software development paradigms came into existence in the 1960s. Their development phases are based on the development lifecycle of systems in general (Tiwari & Kumar, 2020). An example of a classical lifecycle paradigm is the basic waterfall paradigm.

8.5.1.1.1   Basic Waterfall Development Paradigm

Basic waterfall was one of the first paradigms showing development as a defined and disciplined process. In this linear development paradigm, the accomplishment of one phase is followed by the start of the next. It is an organised, step-by-step engineering software process, not considering changes in requirements, the possibility of enhancements, or feedback from customers.

Basic waterfall's orderly chronological approach starts with a requirements analysis and then moves through design, implementation, testing, deployment, and finally reaches maintenance. This process is shown in Figure 8.4 (Tiwari & Kumar, 2020).

8.5.1.2   Incremental Development Paradigms

Incremental development paradigms have some attributes of the basic waterfall paradigm in that the development phases are sequential. However, changes can occur throughout development (Tiwari & Kumar, 2020).

Incremental development paradigms can be categorised into two classes:

1. Incremental paradigm, and
2. Rapid application paradigm.

8.5.1.2.1   Incremental Development Paradigm

The incremental paradigm draws on the linear and sequential approach of the basic waterfall paradigm but does so in an iterative manner. Each iteration includes a small set of requirements and produces a working version of the software. The incremental paradigm can start development with the set of requirements that is initially available, but this can change throughout development. The

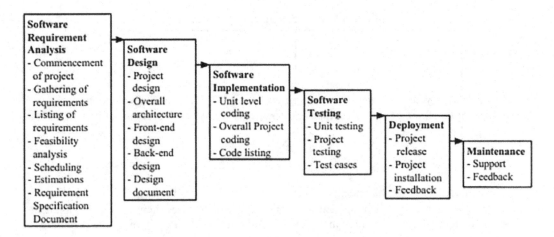

FIGURE 8.4   Basic waterfall development paradigm (Tiwari & Kumar, 2020).

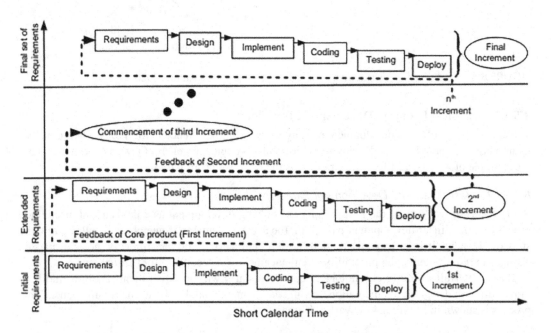

FIGURE 8.5   Incremental development paradigm (Tiwari & Kumar, 2020).

first increment produces what is called the "core product". To this core software product, as a result of user feedback, further requirements can be added. In other words, each increment contains additional features based on the discovery of further requirements. Figure 8.5 shows the incremental process (Tiwari & Kumar, 2020).

8.5.1.2.2   Rapid Application Development Paradigm

Rapid application development (RAD) was one of the first software development paradigms to consider the concepts of both the componentisation of complex software (see Section 9.7.4) and the parallel development of components. In the RAD paradigm, large projects are divided into smaller modules. The software's componentisation or modularisation starts after the initial requirements are formulated. The division of modules is based on the requirements and early-stage planning by

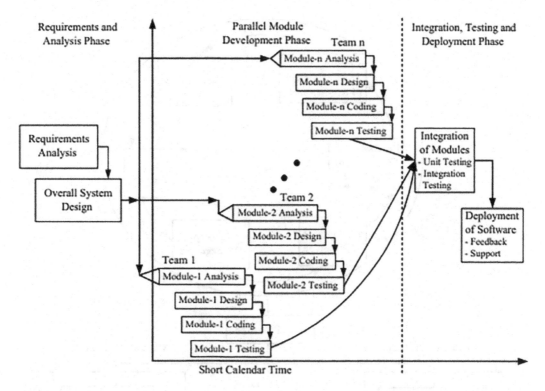

FIGURE 8.6   Rapid application development (RAD) paradigm (Tiwari & Kumar, 2020).

analysts and systems engineers. Different development teams then develop the modules in parallel; in the final step of the process, these modules are integrated and tested.

The RAD paradigm differs from other paradigms because it focuses on more than just development; it also optimises the use of the development team and the available resources.

One goal of RAD is to shorten the overall development time and deliver the software product in the shortest possible time. RAD is shown in Figure 8.6 (Tiwari & Kumar, 2020).

8.5.1.3   Evolutionary Paradigms

The software environment is dynamic. As time passes, customer requirements are likely to change. At the same time, with the evolution of technology and the appearance of new platforms, software will acquire new shapes and dimensions. In dynamic and rapidly changing environments, linear software development is unlikely to meet the needs of customers. Evolutionary paradigms solve this problem. In this approach, large and complex software is developed iteratively, with customers involved in each iteration (Tiwari & Kumar, 2020).

Evolutionary paradigms are classified as the following:

1. Prototyping development paradigm, and
2. Spiral development paradigm.

8.5.1.3.1   Prototyping Development Paradigm

The prototyping paradigm is useful for new and innovative projects where customers are unsure of what their requirements are, and the development team is unsure about the technology needed to meet them. Prototyping is suitable for both small-scale projects and large and complex projects. Moreover, prototyping can be associated with the other development paradigms discussed here. Figure 8.7 shows the basic working of the prototype paradigm.

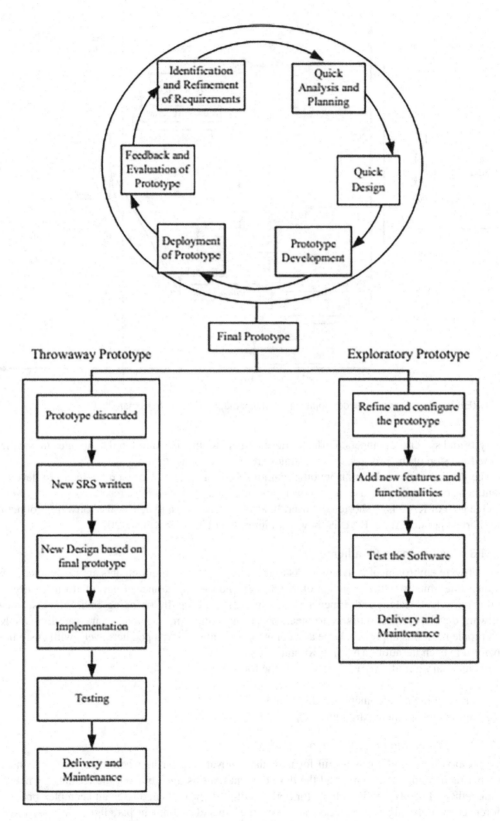

FIGURE 8.7 Prototyping development paradigm (Tiwari & Kumar, 2020).

The prototyping paradigm starts with interactive meetings between customers and development teams. Both parties try to understand the overall behaviour and intentions of the software. They try to define previously undefined problems and identify the platforms and technologies needed to design and develop the software. Based on this, the developers design and make prototype systems; these, in turn, are evaluated by customers. The customers give feedback, and the next iteration begins.

Prototyping is one of two types: throwaway prototyping or exploratory prototyping:

1. Throwaway prototyping: Once the development team and the customer finalise the prototype, the designers set it aside. They do not entirely throw it away, however, as they take it as the basis for the model. They build on it by writing a new software requirements specification (SRS) and creating and building a new design using new tools and technologies. In a sense, the discarded prototype works as a guide to refine the requirements.
2. Exploratory prototyping: Exploratory prototyping is different. In this case, the finalised prototype is treated as a half-finished product. New features and additional functionalities are added, as needed, to make the prototype operational. After customers give feedback and the developers test it, the product is deployed to the customer's site.

8.5.1.3.2 Spiral Development Paradigm

The spiral paradigm is an extremely well-known traditional development paradigm. It was one of the first paradigms to include the assessment of risk factors. It combines the features of prototype and classic sequential development paradigms in an iterative fashion. The spiral model consists of a series of loops, with each 360° loop denoting a cycle. The cycle consists of four quadrants:

- In quadrant 1, developers define objectives, identify alternative solutions, and determine constraints.
- In quadrant 2, developers evaluate alternative solutions, identify possible risks, and mitigate those risks.
- In quadrant 3, developers create, construct, and verify software.
- In quadrant 4, developers plan the next cycle.

After the completion of each spiral cycle, some goals are reached and others are established. Figure 8.8 shows how the spiral works (Tiwari & Kumar, 2020).

8.5.2 ADVANCED SOFTWARE ENGINEERING PARADIGMS

The field of software engineering has been around for a long time, and it has evolved with time and experience. Software has become increasingly complex. In this section, we discuss a few of the most common software engineering paradigms appearing in recent years and explain how each approaches development.

Out of a plethora of advanced development paradigms, we focus on the following four:

1. Agile development paradigm;
2. Component-based development paradigm;
3. Aspect-oriented development paradigm;
4. Cleanroom development paradigm (Tiwari & Kumar, 2020).

These four development paradigms are shown in Figure 8.9.

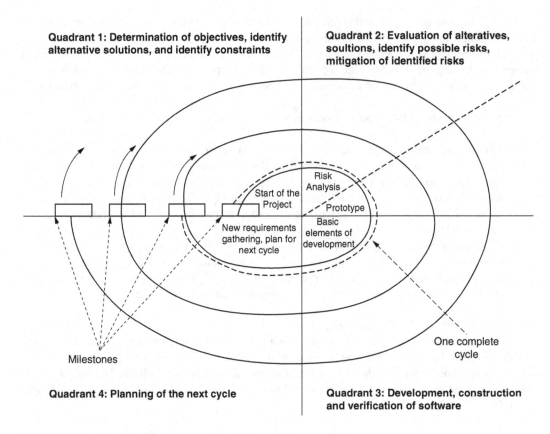

FIGURE 8.8   Spiral development paradigm (Tiwari & Kumar, 2020).

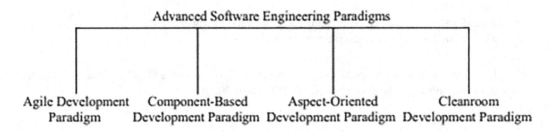

FIGURE 8.9   Advanced software engineering paradigms (Tiwari & Kumar, 2020).

8.5.2.1   Agile Development Paradigm

The agile development paradigm is, in fact, a combined development paradigm. It includes a set of guidelines, self-organising and motivated teams, and collaborations with customers. The sole aim of the agile paradigm is customer satisfaction. It emphasises continuous planning that can adapt to changes, evolutionary and iterative design and development, continual improvements, and rapid and flexible response to change.

In 2001, Kent Beck and 16 other developers and researchers who called themselves "the Agile Alliance" published their "Manifesto for Agile Software Development" (https://agilemanifesto. org/). It has since become the fundamental guide to the agile development paradigm. Agile development, they say, values:

1. Individuals and interactions over processes and tools;
2. Working software over comprehensive documentation;
3. Customer collaboration over contract negotiation; and
4. Responding to change over following a plan (Beck et al., 2001).

In other words, agile development prioritises interactions with customers, not development processes and tools, the provision of working and operational deliverables, not documents, customer involvement in development and developer ownership, not simply delivery, and changes and adaptations at any stage, not waiting for the review phase (Tiwari & Kumar, 2020).

Agility is actually a philosophy of development, not a development paradigm. There is no set plan, and there are no predefined activities and operations. Instead, agile development is a collaborative endeavour across all stakeholders – customers and designers – to achieve a single over-riding goal: customer satisfaction (Tiwari & Kumar, 2020).

Various frameworks are available to implement this methodology, including the following:

- Adaptive software development (ASD)
- Scrum.
- Crystal.
- Extreme programming (XP).
- Lean software development (LSD).
- Feature drive development (FDD).
- Dynamic systems development method (DSDM).

8.5.2.2 Aspect-Oriented Development Paradigm

Cost and complexity increase simultaneously with the size of the software (Tiwari & Kumar, 2020). A problem may arise because certain functions can be repeated throughout the software, in every component or module. Some may even be required in all components of the software. Examples include resource sharing, logging, memory management, RT constraints, exception handling, error handling, business rules, and transaction processing. Problematically, when a function is changed, every module in which it appears must also be changed. If these small function codes are neglected, simply because they are small and overlooked, there will be problems in the software.

In a worst-case scenario, adding or modifying a single functionality/module/component will mean almost all the software modules must be changed.

In the aspect-oriented development paradigm, these elements are called "aspects" or "concerns". Aspect-oriented software seeks to modularise or isolate these complex concerns or aspects. More specifically, the aspect-oriented development paradigm represents a set of processes and techniques to identify, define, design, and construct aspects (Tiwari & Kumar, 2020).

8.5.2.3 Cleanroom Development Paradigm

The term "cleanroom" expresses the property of correctness in the developed software. The cleanroom development paradigm provides correctness through formal specifications, mathematical proofs and foundations, walkthroughs, formal verification, and inspection methods. It does not rely on the code-and-test methods of traditional development paradigms. It provides a certain level of software reliability from the outset, as its goal is to prevent defects, not to detect and then remove them.

To this end, cleanroom avoids dependence on costly defect removal by writing code increments correctly the first time and verifying their correctness before testing. Its process model incorporates the statistical quality certification of code increments as they accumulate in a system.

Cleanroom produces software in small increments rather than developing and delivering the complete software in a single go. Each increment is tested, verified, and certified by the developer. Then, the increments are assembled to construct the complete software. The phases of each increment are shown in Figure 8.10.

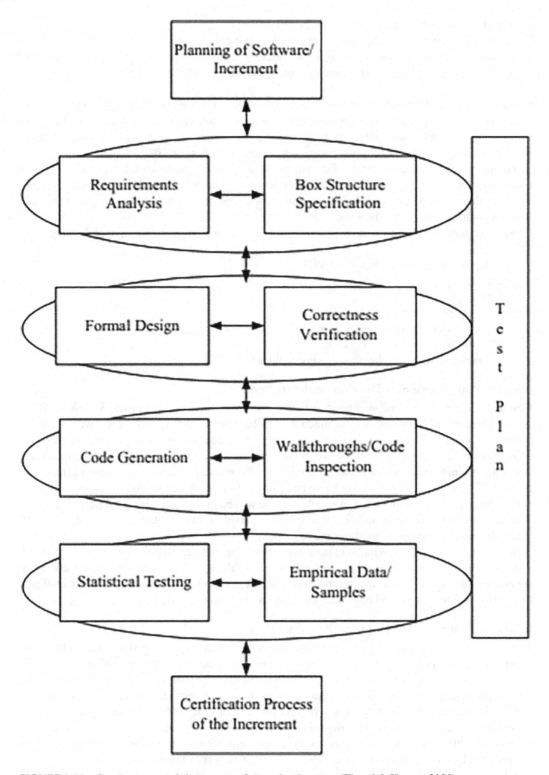

FIGURE 8.10 One increment of cleanroom software development (Tiwari & Kumar, 2020).

Each increment consists of the following: planning; requirement analysis; box-structure specification; formal design and correctness verification; code generation, inspection, and walkthroughs; statistical testing with empirical data; and certification of increments. These are explained, respectively, as follows:

- Planning requires special care, as available increments must be easily adapted and integrated.
- Requirements can be collected using any methods and tools, both traditional and advanced.
- Specifications are defined using box structures. Box structures are useful because they can isolate behaviour, data, and procedures at each level of refinement. Three types of box structures are used in the cleanroom development paradigm:
  1. Black box: specifies system behaviour when a function is applied to a set of inputs.
  2. State box: can be likened to an encapsulated object putting input data and transition operations together; it is used to state the states of the system.
  3. Clear box: transmits the inputs to the outputs.
- Designs use formal specification methods, in addition to traditional design methods, at both architectural and component levels. The cleanroom development paradigm regressively focuses on design verification. Mathematical proofs and logics are used to determine the correctness of the proposed design.
- The cleanroom development paradigm translates the design into an appropriate programming language. Code inspections, technical reviews, and decisional charts are used to check the correctness of the developed code.
- Testing is conducted using statistical data sets and samples. Testing methods are mathematically verified. Exhaustive testing is performed regressively.
- Once all phases are tested and verified, the developer begins the certification of the increment. All the required tests are conducted. Finally, the increment is released and is integrated with other certified increments (Tiwari & Kumar, 2020).

8.5.2.4 Component-Based Development Paradigm

The component-based development paradigm focuses on the reusability of pre-constructed code constructs and other deliverables. It can be used with traditional or advanced development paradigms. Reusability can be at any level and with any deliverable, including documentation, requirements, design construct, test cases, and coding (Tiwari & Kumar, 2020). This is discussed at greater length in Section 9.7.

8.6 SOFTWARE ARCHITECTURE MODELS

8.6.1 Layered Architecture

Components within the layered architecture pattern are organised into horizontal layers, each layer performing a specific role within the application (e.g. presentation logic or business logic). Although the layered architecture pattern does not specify the number and types of layers that must exist in the pattern, most layered architectures consist of four standard layers: presentation, business, persistence, and database (Figure 8.11). In some cases, the business layer and persistence layer are combined into a single business layer, particularly when the persistence logic (e.g. SQL or HSQL) is embedded within the business layer components. Thus, smaller applications may have only three layers, whereas larger and more complex business applications may contain five or more layers. Each layer of the layered architecture pattern has a specific role and responsibility within the application. For example, a presentation layer would be responsible for handling all user interfaces and browser communication logic, whereas a business layer would be responsible for executing specific business rules associated with the request. Each layer in the architecture forms an abstraction around the work that needs to be done to satisfy a particular business request.

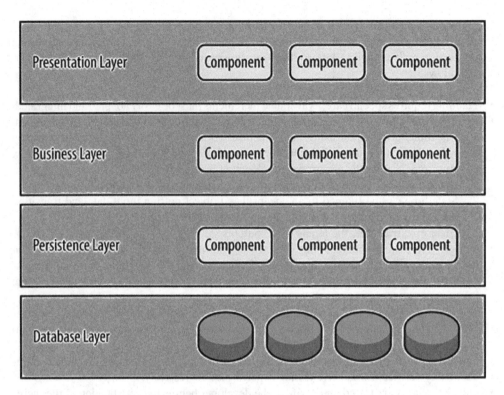

FIGURE 8.11 Layered architecture (Richards, 2022).

One of the powerful features of the layered architecture pattern is the separation of concerns among components. Components within a specific layer deal only with logic that pertains to that layer. For example, components in the presentation layer deal only with presentation logic, whereas components residing in the business layer deal only with business logic. This type of component classification makes it easy to build effective roles and responsibility models into the architecture, and also makes it easy to develop, test, govern, and maintain applications using this architecture pattern due to its well-defined component interfaces and limited component scope. The layered architecture pattern is a solid general-purpose pattern, making it a good starting point for most applications, particularly when users are not sure what architecture pattern is best suited for their application. However, there are a couple of things to consider from an architectural standpoint when choosing this pattern (Richards, 2022).

8.6.2 Event-Driven Architecture

The event-driven architecture pattern is a popular distributed asynchronous architecture pattern used to produce highly scalable applications. It is also highly adaptable and can be used for small applications and as well as large, complex ones. The event-driven architecture is made up of highly decoupled, single-purpose event-processing components that asynchronously receive and process events.

The event-driven architecture pattern consists of two main topologies: the mediator and the broker. The mediator topology is commonly used when it is necessary to orchestrate multiple steps within an event through a central mediator, whereas the broker topology is used when the goal is to chain events together without the use of a central mediator. Because the architecture characteristics and implementation strategies differ between these two topologies, it is important to understand each one to know which is best suited for a particular situation. The mediator topology is useful for events that have multiple steps and require some level of orchestration to process the event. For example, a

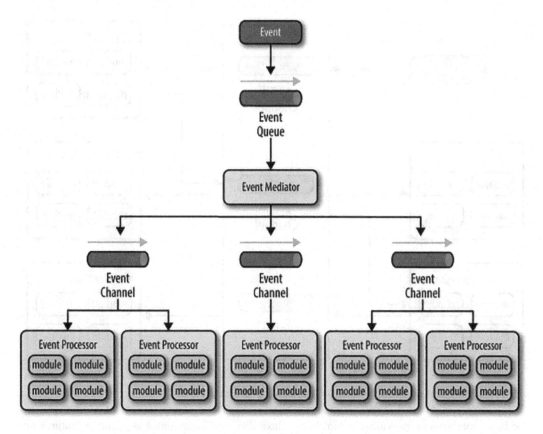

FIGURE 8.12 Event-driven architecture mediator topology (Richards, 2022).

single event to place a stock trade might first require validating the trade, then checking the compliance of that stock trade against various compliance rules, assigning the trade to a broker, calculating the commission, and finally placing the trade with that broker (Figure 8.12) (Richards, 2022).

The broker topology differs from the mediator topology in that there is no central event mediator; rather, the message flow is distributed across the event-processor components in a chain-like fashion through a lightweight message broker (e.g. ActiveMQ, HornetQ, etc.). This topology is useful when the event processing flow is relatively simple, and central event orchestration is neither wanted nor needed.

There are two main types of architecture components within the broker topology: a broker component and an event-processor component. The broker component can be centralised or federated and contains all of the event channels that are used within the event flow. The event channels contained within the broker component can be message queues, message topics, or a combination of both. The event-driven architecture pattern is a relatively complex pattern to implement, primarily due to its asynchronous distributed nature. When implementing this pattern, it is necessary to address various distributed architecture issues, such as remote process availability, lack of responsiveness, and broker reconnection logic in the event of a broker or mediator failure (Figure 8.13) (Richards, 2022).

8.6.3 MICROKERNEL ARCHITECTURE

The microkernel architecture pattern consists of two types of architecture components: a core system and plug-in modules. Application logic is divided between independent plug-in modules and

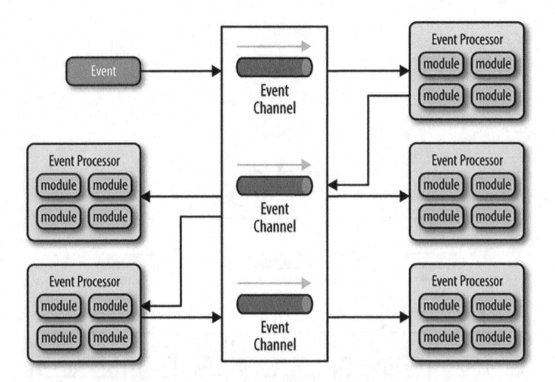

FIGURE 8.13   Event-driven architecture broker topology (Richards, 2022).

the basic core system, providing extensibility, flexibility, and isolation of application features and custom processing logic. Figure 8.4 illustrates the basic microkernel architecture pattern. The core system of the microkernel architecture pattern traditionally contains only the minimal functionality required to make the system operational.

Many operating systems implement the microkernel architecture pattern, hence the origin of this pattern's name. From a business-application perspective, the core system is often defined as the general business logic without a custom code for special cases, special rules, or complex conditional processing. The plug-in modules are stand-alone, independent components that contain specialised processing, additional features, and custom code that are meant to enhance or extend the core system to produce additional business capabilities. Generally, plug-in modules should be independent of other plug-in modules, but it is possible to design plug-ins that require other plug-ins to be present. Either way, it is important to keep the communication between plug-ins to a minimum to avoid dependency issues.

One great thing about the microkernel architecture pattern is that it can be embedded or used as part of another architecture pattern. For example, if this pattern solves a particular problem with a specific volatile area of the application, it may not be possible to implement the entire architecture using this pattern. In this case, the microservices architecture pattern can be embedded in another pattern (e.g. layered architecture). Similarly, the event-processor components described in the previous section on event-driven architecture could be implemented using the microservices architecture pattern (Figure 8.14) (Richards, 2022).

8.6.4 Microservices Architecture

The microservices architecture pattern is quickly gaining ground in industry as a viable alternative to monolithic applications and service-oriented architectures. Because this architecture pattern is still evolving, there's a lot of confusion about what this pattern is all about and how it is implemented. This section explains the key concepts and provides foundational knowledge necessary to understand the benefits (and trade-offs) of this important architecture pattern and whether it is the right pattern for a given application.

Regardless of the topology or implementation style selected, several core concepts apply to the general architecture pattern. The first of these concepts is the notion of separately deployed units. As illustrated in Figure 8.5, each component of the microservices architecture is deployed as a separate unit, allowing easier deployment through an effective and streamlined delivery pipeline, increased scalability, and a high degree of application and component decoupling within the application. The microservices architecture pattern solves many of the common issues found in both monolithic applications and service-oriented architectures. Since major application components are split up into smaller, separately deployed units, applications built using the microservices architecture pattern are generally more robust, provide better scalability, and can more easily support continuous delivery (Figure 8.15) (Richards, 2022).

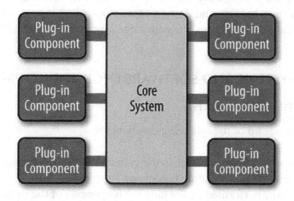

FIGURE 8.14 Microkernel architecture (Richards, 2022).

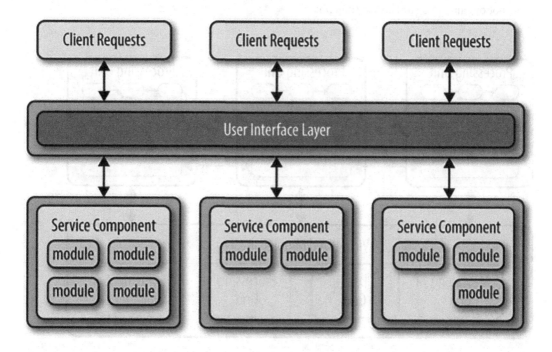

FIGURE 8.15 Basic microservices architecture (Richards, 2022).

8.6.5 SPACE-BASED ARCHITECTURE

The space-based pattern (sometimes called the cloud architecture pattern) minimises the factors that limit application scaling. This pattern gets its name from the concept of tuple space, the idea of distributed shared memory. High scalability is achieved by removing the central database constraint and using replicated in-memory data grids instead. Application data are kept in memory and replicated among all the active processing units. Processing units can be dynamically started up and shut down as user load increases and decreases, thereby addressing variable scalability. Because there is no central data base, the data base bottleneck is removed, providing near-infinite scalability within the application.

There are two primary components within this architecture pattern: a processing unit and virtualised middleware. Figure 8.6 illustrates the basic space-based architecture pattern and its primary architecture components. The space-based architecture pattern is a complex and expensive pattern to implement. It is a good architecture choice for smaller web-based applications with variable load (e.g. social media sites, bidding and auction sites). However, it is not well suited for traditional large-scale relational data base applications with large amounts of operational data (Figure 8.16) (Richards, 2022).

8.7 SOFTWARE SYSTEMS AND SOFTWARE ENGINEERING PROCESSES

8.7.1 SOFTWARE SYSTEM COMPONENTS

Software systems are made up of the following components:

- Users: the people who add information to the system, request information from the system, and perform some of the information processing functions.
- Procedures: the tasks performed by the human components of the information system.
- Information: meaningful data that the system stores and processes.
- Documents: manuals on how to use the system, sometimes even files of data which should not or cannot be stored electronically.

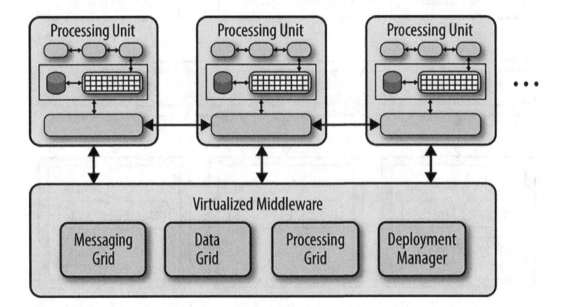

FIGURE 8.16   Space-based architecture pattern (Richards, 2022).

- Hardware: the computers in the system and any networks linking the computers, the input devices, and the output devices.
- Software: computer applications performing some of the system functions to record, process, and regulate access to some of the information that the information system works with.

Software is typically defined as instructions that provide desired features, functions, and performance. It contains data structures that allow the software programme to manipulate the information contained in an information system. Importantly, software also includes documentation describing how the software performs the actions that it does, and how it may be used. Some of the documentation is for the software users, while other portions of the documentation are for its developers and maintainers (University of Cape Town, 2011).

8.7.2 PROPERTIES OF SOFTWARE

Some important properties of software include the following:

- Software is engineered rather than manufactured. Once the software has been developed, no significant "manufacturing" process could possibly lower the software's quality (i.e. introduce software errors, cause the software to deviate from what the customer requested, etc.). The cost of developing software lies almost completely in the engineering of the software, not in the manufacturing of a product that customers can hold in their hands.
- Software does not wear out with use, as hardware might. However, this does not mean that software does not degrade over time. A software programme is continuously changed over its lifetime. If these changes occur too frequently, the bugs introduced by each change may slowly degrade the performance and utility of the software as a whole. Moreover, when software degrades in quality, no "spare parts" can be used as replacements.
- Unlike hardware, most software is custom-built, not using "off-the-shelf" components (University of Cape Town, 2011).

8.7.3 THE IMPORTANCE OF SOFTWARE ENGINEERING

Over the last few decades, software systems and the software that run them have become important to many aspects of our society, from commerce to medicine, engineering, the sciences, and entertainment.

The infrastructures of all developed countries rely heavily on software systems. Therefore, it is important that the software we use is of high quality and meets our requirements. Gaining this high quality does not happen randomly or by accident – rather, we need to engineer that quality into the software.

When software fails, people may be bankrupted and even killed (consider safety critical systems which run planes, medical equipment, etc.). Because so much depends on software, software has become important to business and the economy. This means the software engineer is always part of a larger environment, consisting of customers, other software engineers, managers, and so on. It is important that the engineer be able to interact appropriately with all of these individuals, and this, too, is part of software engineering (University of Cape Town, 2011).

8.7.4 THE SOFTWARE ENGINEERING PROCESS

Software engineers are concerned with issues of complexity, scalability, quality, and cost. In addition, software must be able to adapt to the dynamic nature of the environment (TutorialsPoint, 2022).

An improved process should produce software that is correct, reliable, usable, and maintainable. By understanding the process, it should be possible to plan projects with more accurate predictions of cost and time, to provide ways of monitoring intermediate stages of project progress, and to be able to react and re-plan if a project begins to go off budget or timescale. Software engineering is the discipline of producing such software.

The following is a list of some very basic, commonly agreed-upon aspects of the software development process:

- Some software development activities are common to all successful projects.
- Some activities need to occur before others.
- There is a need to both understand that requirements change and manage this change.
- Any existing systems need to be understood before working on the design of a new one.
- It is wise to delay decisions that will constrain the final system – this can be achieved by initially designing an implementation-independent logical design (see Chapter 9), before committing to a detailed design for a particular physical set of hardware and software (University of Cape Town, 2011).

Understanding this list led to a model of what is called the software process or system lifecycle. The software process is the process of engineering and developing software; a process model, or life-cycle model is a descriptive model giving the best practices for carrying out software development (i.e. for carrying out the software process). However, a process model is often treated as a prescriptive model that needs to be followed precisely, without any deviation. This should not be the case. The specific model of the software process used should be tailored to meet the specific needs of the project and the developers working on the project.

Note: software process, software lifecycle, system development lifecycle, system lifecycle, and development lifecycle are all used to describe the same concept (University of Cape Town, 2011).

8.7.4.1 The Layers of Software Engineering

Software engineering is a discipline that can be pictured as built of layers, as shown in Figure 8.17 (University of Cape Town, 2011).

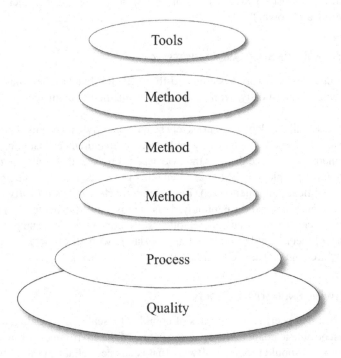

FIGURE 8.17 Layers of software engineering (University of Cape Town, 2011).

Software engineering demands a focus on quality. This is the first layer.

Next comes the foundation of software engineering: the software process. The process is the framework on which the rest of software engineering is built. The process defines the required input and output products, the milestones to be reached, and so on. The process also describes how quality should be ensured.

The various methods are next. These describe how the different portions that make up the software engineering process should be carried out, for instance, how to communicate with clients, how to test the software, how to gather requirements, and so on.

The tools that support the software engineering process comprise the final layer. Such tools are called computer-aided software engineering tools (University of Cape Town, 2011).

8.7.4.2 A Generic Framework of the Software Process

A software process consists of the activities that are carried out during the development of every software system. There are specific activities which are carried out at specific times, as well as activities carried out throughout the project's lifetime. Such life-long activities are called umbrella activities.

A generic framework defining these activities for the software process identifies activities common to most of the models of the software process, although each model adapts the activities to its own ends. The activities are as follows:

- Communication: This activity involves the gathering of software requirements from the customer, and related sub-activities.
- Planning: This is the activity of planning the work required to develop the software. This includes managing risk, listing the associated outputs, and producing a schedule for the work.
- Modelling: This activity is involved with modelling both the requirements and the software design so that both the developers and the customers can better understand the work being carried out.
- Construction: This is the development of the software. This activity also includes sub-activities for testing the software.
- Deployment: The software is delivered, and the customer provides feedback on it (University of Cape Town, 2011).

8.8 COMPONENT-BASED SOFTWARE ENGINEERING

Component-based software engineering (CBSE) is an elite form of software engineering that offers the feature of reusability. It aims at assembling large software systems from previously developed components (these, in turn, may be constructed from other components). Reusing software artefacts and the process of reusability rather than developing software constructs from the beginning make CBSE a specialised paradigm. Figure 8.18 illustrates the CBSE paradigm.

CBSE applications are constructed by assembling reusable, pre-existing, and new components (including classes, functions, methods and operations) which are integrated through error-free interfaces. The basic idea is to develop a component and then reuse it in various applications rather than re-constructing it every time. Reusing pre-developed and pre-tested components shortens the development lifecycle, reduces time to market, and increases the reliability of the overall application (Tiwari & Kumar, 2020). CBSE can develop large complex software systems by integrating previously designed commercial off-the-shelf components (COTS), third-party contractual components, and newly developed components to minimise development time, effort, and cost.

CBSE offers an improved and enhanced reuse of software components, but it also permits the addition of other properties, such as extendibility, flexibility, and better service quality, thus

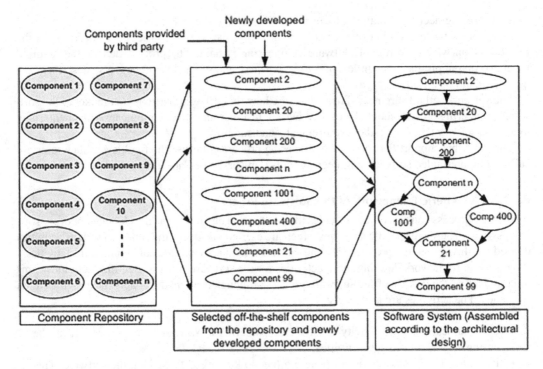

FIGURE 8.18 Component-based software engineering (Tiwari & Kumar, 2020).

better meeting customers' needs. It can be involved in the creation of more than one application concurrently.

8.8.1 Construction-Based Software Engineering Processes

As shown in Figure 8.19, CBSE is used to develop both generalised and specific components in four parallel processes:

1. Development of new components,
2. Selection of pre-existing components,
3. Integration of components, and
4. Control and management.

Each of the first three processes must have a feedback method to address problems, errors, and side effects. Note that the control and management procedure must assess the development process and also manage the analysis of requirements, the selection and integration of components, and the quality of components that are likely to be reused (Tiwari & Kumar, 2020).

Other researchers label the concurrent processes differently:

1. Creation process: Development of new applications by reusing existing software components.
2. Management process: Management of activities of development, including selection of components, cost of components, and schedule for new application development.
3. Support process: Provision of help and maintenance in the development of new applications and the provision of existing components from the repository.
4. Reuse process: Collection and analysis of the requirements to select the appropriate components from the repository. Note that this final process is responsible for ensuring reusability is a part of development (Tiwari & Kumar, 2020).

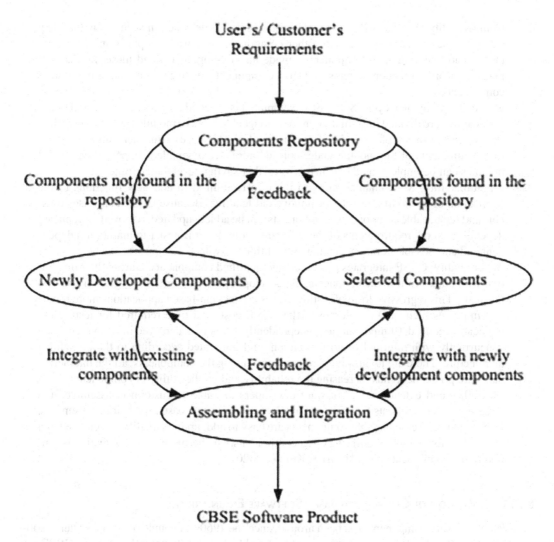

FIGURE 8.19 Concurrent component-based software development processes (Tiwari & Kumar, 2020).

8.8.2 CHARACTERISTICS OF COMPONENT-BASED SOFTWARE ENGINEERING

Heineman and Council (2001) list three fundamental properties of CBSE:

1. First, software systems are developed from existing software entities;
2. Second, these pre-existing entities can be used along with newly developed software entities in other applications;
3. Third, these entities can be preserved, maintained, and fabricated for future implementations.

CBSE possesses a number of properties over and above those of other software engineering paradigms. These include the following:

- Reusability: This is the key property of CBSE – through the principle of reusability, software systems can be created from existing software. Simply stated, software reuse is the process of integrating predefined specifications, design architectures, tested codes, and/or test plans with the proposed software. CBSE reuses these various artefacts; it does not re-develop them. Therefore, components are developed with reusability in mind.

- Composability: The individual reusable components are designed in such a way that they can be reused in composition with other components in various applications with little or even no fabrication. A component is made up of components, and these, in turn, are made up of still other components. In fact, a component can be a part of one or more other components.
- Reduced development cycle: Software development is speeded up. First, complex and bulky applications are divided into smaller, more manageable units or modules. Then, rather than starting to code a complete module from the first line of code, existing elements that satisfy the requirements of the module under consideration are assembled. Importantly, several modules can be implemented concurrently, further saving development time.
- Maintainability: Maintenance refers to the effort required to add new functions to the application or to modify, update, or remove old features. Because CBSE comprises reusable and replaceable components, components can be added, updated, removed, or replaced depending on the requirements of the software. Note that it is easier to maintain independent and composable components than monolithic software.
- Better quality: CBSE integrates pre-tested and qualified components. During their integration with other pre-tested components, the developer performs further integration and system tests. This regressive form of testing makes component-based applications more robust and improves their quality. Moreover, the effort, cost, and time required for testing are noticeably reduced. Components are independently developed, deployed in various contexts concurrently with minimal or no fabrication, and integrated according to the predefined architecture. There are no unwanted interactions among the components; all the interaction paths are predefined, thus increasing the reliability and predictability of components.
- Flexibility and extendibility: Software developers are able to customise, assemble, and integrate the components from a set of available components based on their requirements. Replaceable and compassable components are easy to add, update, modify, or remove from the application without modifying other components. Furthermore, error navigation is limited to the component level (Tiwari & Kumar, 2020).

8.8.3 EVOLUTION OF COMPONENT-BASED SOFTWARE ENGINEERING

The idea of software components has been around since the 1960s. A couple of decades later, a software component was understood to comprise a building block and architectural unit. Now, CBSE is a well-established paradigm for the development of large, complex, and high-quality software systems.

The development of the CBSE paradigm went through four phases: preparation, definition, progression, and expansion (Tiwari & Kumar, 2020).

8.8.3.1 Preparations

In the early stages of CBSE, researchers started from the beginning, defining possible approaches, challenges, and implications. By the end of the preparatory phase, CBSE was a popular software development paradigm, and the literature on CBSE had begun to grow. Importantly, the software component was considered a pre-existing and reusable entity (Tiwari & Kumar, 2020).

8.8.3.2 Definitions

Terms relating to CBSE were defined and classified in the second phase. These included such terms as component specification, component architecture, component adaptation, and component acquisition.

At conferences and workshops, researchers discussed new areas of interest, such as component trust, predictable assembly, automated CBSE, and component specifications. As the topics of discussion increased, so too did the number of research publications (Tiwari & Kumar, 2020).

8.8.3.3 Progression

In the third phase, beyond the interest of research groups, the software industry itself began to take a closer look at the benefits of CBSE. Collaboration sprang up between the component-based paradigm and other areas in software engineering. Among other topics, work proceeded on critical systems, RT systems, embedded systems, hierarchical frameworks for component-based RT systems, performance attributes, component-based system modelling and design, component testing frameworks, estimation of resources at dynamic time in multi-task CBS environments, and component structure for critical dynamically embedded contexts (Tiwari & Kumar, 2020).

8.8.3.4 Expansion

This final phase is ongoing, with parallel approaches being recognised in software engineering and software development. Research into areas like service-oriented development, model-driven engineering, and aspect-oriented programming is being run in parallel with CBSE research.

Research topics of the moment include development, customisation, and deployment of CBSE systems, component-based web services, service-oriented architectures (SOA), components supporting grid computing, prediction and monitoring of distributed and service components, techniques and methods for constructing component-based service systems, and components for networked dynamic and global information systems-linking sensors, among many others (Tiwari & Kumar, 2020).

8.8.4 COMPONENTISATION

Componentisation involves identifying the quantity of components in a specific application. It addresses the need to maintain a balance between the number of components and the system complexity. Simply stated, the level of componentisation equals the level of requirement sufficiency. To determine the requirement sufficiency, developers consider as many components as are needed to fulfil the software application's intention.

If a large number of components provide small functions, this will increase the cost of integration and the number of interactions. The coding complexity and testing effort will increase as well. However, if an application is componentised, fewer components will each provide a number of functions. Thus, both testing and maintenance will cost less. The goal is to achieve a minimum cost region so that cost and effort can be balanced against the number of components. Figure 8.20 sums this up, showing the costs of componentisation versus integration (Tiwari & Kumar, 2020).

8.9 SOFTWARE MAINTENANCE OVERVIEW

Software maintenance is part of the software development lifecycle. Maintenance refers to modifications and updating after the software product is delivered to the consumer. Modifications may be required for the following reasons:

- Market conditions: Policies, such as taxation, change over time, and new constraints, for example, in bookkeeping, may be introduced. These and other market conditions may trigger the need for software modification.
- Client requirements: Over time, customers are likely to need new features or software functions, thus requiring maintenance to be updated.
- Host modifications: The host's hardware and/or platform, for example, the operating system, may change; to maintain adaptability, the software must change as well.
- Organisational changes: Organisations are constantly evolving. Business-level changes may call for modifications in software (TutorialsPoint, 2022).

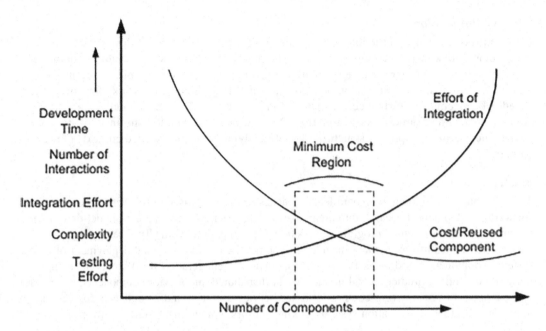

FIGURE 8.20   Componentisation vs integration cost (Tiwari & Kumar, 2020).

8.9.1 Types of Maintenance

Throughout its lifetime, software will undergo various types of maintenance: corrective, adaptive, perfective, and preventive:

- Corrective maintenance includes modifications and updates to fix problems, either discovered by the user or spotted in user error reports.
- Adaptive maintenance includes modifications and updates to keep the software up to date with changes in technology.
- Perfective maintenance includes modifications and updates to keep the software usable over time. Maintainers may add new features based on new user requirements or simply work to improve the software's reliability and performance.
- Preventive maintenance includes modifications and updates to prevent future problems. Problems may be presently insignificant but may cause serious issues in due course (TutorialsPoint, 2022).

8.9.2 Cost of Maintenance

While it is necessary, maintenance can be expensive and is estimated to be as much as two-thirds of the cost of the entire software process cycle. Figure 8.21 shows the cost of maintenance compared to other costs (TutorialsPoint, 2022).

A number of factors explain the high cost of maintenance

Real-world factors: Most maintenance engineers use trial and error methods, and the changes they make may hurt the original structure of the software, making it hard to perform subsequent changes. In addition, changes are often left undocumented, and this could exacerbate problems in the future.

Software factors: Software is expected to last only 10–15 years, and older software cannot compete with new software running on modern hardware. As technology advances, it becomes increasingly expensive to maintain old software. The structure of the software programme and

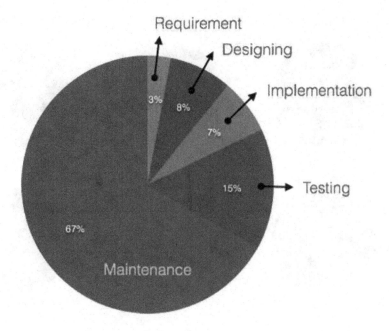

FIGURE 8.21   Associated software costs (TutorialsPoint, 2022).

the programming language it uses can be out of date, making the software costly to maintain (TutorialsPoint, 2022).

8.9.3   MAINTENANCE ACTIVITIES

A framework for sequential maintenance process activities is shown in Figure 8.22 and explained below. It can be used iteratively and extended to include customised items and processes (TutorialsPoint, 2022).

- Identification and tracing: This phase involves identifying the need for modification or maintenance. It is either generated by the user or by the system itself through logs or error messages.
- Analysis: A proposed modification is analysed with respect to its impact on the system, including safety and security implications. If the probable impact is severe, maintainers look for alternative solutions. A set of required modifications is created, and the cost of modification/maintenance is determined.
- Design: New modules are designed according to the requirement specifications determined in the analysis phase. Test cases are created for validation and verification.
- Implementation: In this phase, the new modules are coded.
- System testing: This phase involves integration testing between the newly created modules and between the new modules and the system. Then, the system is tested as a whole using regressive testing techniques. This is an internal testing.
- Acceptance testing: After the system has been tested internally, it is tested for acceptance by users. Any user complaints are addressed at this point or will be addressed in the next iteration.
- Delivery: In this phase, the system is deployed in the organisation and constitutes the final testing. Deployment may represent a small update or the re-installation of the entire system.

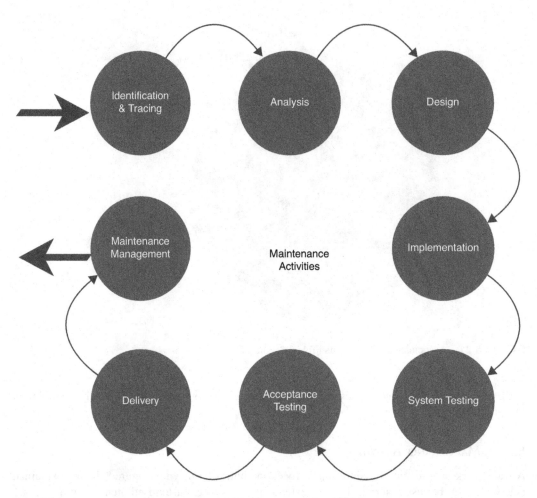

FIGURE 8.22   Diagram of maintenance activities (TutorialsPoint, 2022).

- Maintenance management: Configuration management is an essential part of system maintenance. Maintainers use version control tools.

8.9.4   SOFTWARE RE-ENGINEERING

Updating software to keep it current without impacting its functionality is called software re-engineering. In this process, the design of software can be changed and programmes re-written.

Legacy software cannot keep up with the latest technology, and this calls for re-engineering. For example, Unix was developed in assembly language. When language C came into existence, Unix was re-engineered in C, because working in assembly language was now too difficult.

If maintainers notice that certain parts of software need more maintenance than others, these parts will need re-engineering (TutorialsPoint, 2022).

The process of re-engineering is shown in Figure 8.23. Reverse engineering, restructuring and forward engineering are part of the process and are explained below.

8.9.4.1   Reverse Engineering

An existing system is a previously implemented design. Reverse (or backward) engineering figures out the system specifications by analysing and understanding the existing system. Designers do reverse engineering by looking at the code and trying to understand the design. Once they

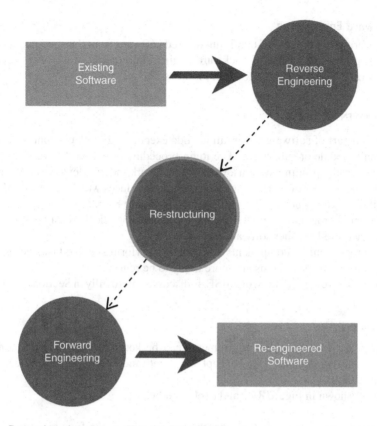

FIGURE 8.23   Re-engineering process (TutorialsPoint, 2022).

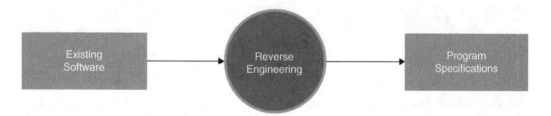

FIGURE 8.24   Reverse engineering (TutorialsPoint, 2022).

understand the design, they can determine the specifications, thus going backwards from the code to the system specification. This process can be seen as a reverse software development lifecycle (SDLC) model and is shown in Figure 8.24 (TutorialsPoint, 2022).

8.9.4.2   Programme Restructuring

Programme restructuring attempts to restructure and reconstruct the existing software. The source code is rearranged, either in the same programming language as the original or in a different language. Restructuring can comprise source code restructuring or data restructuring or both.

Restructuring does not impact the functionality of the software. However, it can improve both reliability and maintainability, as programme components that have caused frequent errors can be changed or updated. Restructuring can also remove the dependence of software on obsolete hardware platforms (TutorialsPoint, 2022).

8.9.4.3 Forward Engineering

Forward engineering is a process of obtaining desired software from the specifications determined by the previous process of reverse or backward engineering. In fact, it is always carried out after reverse engineering. The process is shown in Figure 8.25.

8.9.5 COMPONENT REUSABILITY

A component is a part of software programme code executing an independent task in the system. It can be a small module or subsystem. The login procedures used on the web can be considered components, as can the printing systems. Components work independently and can perform tasks without depending on other modules. They also provide interfaces which can establish communication among different components. This is illustrated in Figure 8.26.

In object-oriented programming (OOP), components are specifically designed for a purpose and are unlikely to be reused in other software.

In modular programming, components are coded to perform specific tasks across a number of other software programmes and thus are more likely to be reused.

The reuse of software components, or CBSE, is discussed more fully in Section 8.8 (TutorialsPoint, 2022).

8.9.5.1 Reuse Process

There are two reuse scenarios: the requirements can be kept the same and the components can be adjusted, or the components can be kept the same and the requirements can be modified (TutorialsPoint, 2022).

The process is shown in Figure 8.27 and explained below.

- Requirement specification: In this step, the functional and non-functional requirements of the software are specified, using information from the existing system, user input, or both.

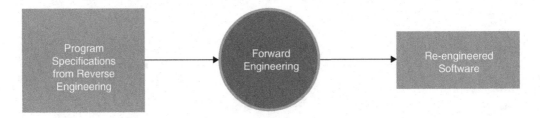

FIGURE 8.25 Forward engineering (Lee et al., 2014).

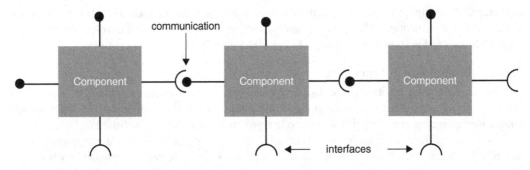

FIGURE 8.26 Example of reusable components (TutorialsPoint, 2022).

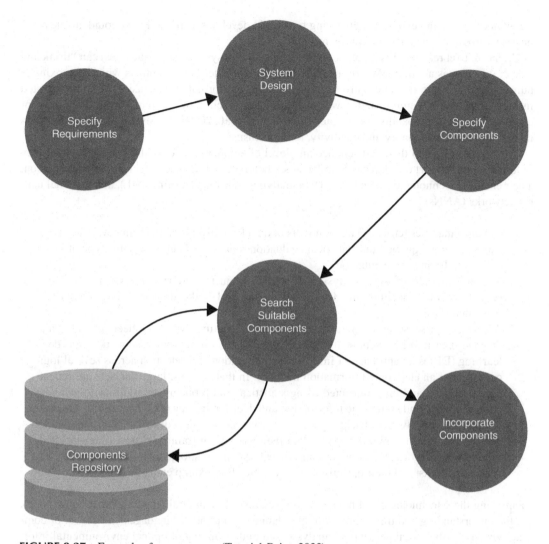

FIGURE 8.27   Example of reuse process (TutorialsPoint, 2022).

- Design: In this standard SDLC process step, the requirements are defined in software terms. The step includes the design of the basic architecture of system as a whole and its sub-systems.
- Specify components: In this step, the designers divide the entire system into smaller components or subsystems. Instead of a single software design, there is a collection of components working together.
- Search for suitable components: Designers look for existing components to reuse on the basis of functionality and requirements, drawing on a software component repository.
- Incorporate components: In this final step, all components are integrated to become a complete software.

8.10   APPLICATIONS OF AI IN CLASSICAL SOFTWARE ENGINEERING

A common understanding of AI is that computers will take over human engineering and development jobs and may even take over human productivity by intelligent automation. In such scenarios, classical software engineers could become obsolete, as machines take over their tasks. Software might not require any external engineering but would develop self-reliantly. AI could enable computers to produce code and solve problems.

AI has not yet reached this stage, but intelligent artificial systems (e.g. machines) can "think and learn". AI today is an umbrella term used for a set of computer-based routines which approximate human intelligence in that alternatives are weighed, new information is considered and integrated into existing data structures, and new conclusions are reached by inference from qualitative or quantitative data or probabilistic estimates (Barenkamp et al., 2020). However, other forms of mental activity, like emotionality and creativity, remain elusive.

AI routines differ in their self-reliance and level of automation, i.e. in the extent to which they require human support or ask for human feedback before they implement decisions or information. Their enabling technologies include Big Data analytics, machine learning (ML), and artificial neural networks (ANNs):

- Big data analytics retrieves large amounts of data from diverse sources and evaluates them using particular queries and statistical evaluation routines. AI automates this type of information gathering and evaluation.
- ML is a method of data analysis directed to identify patterns in unstructured data sets. It enables machines to draw conclusions and make decisions based on these classifications.
- ANNs comprise several layers of mathematical routines which collect, classify, and arrange data into new sets to find parameters or solutions. Neural network-based deep learning (DL) is an approach of information integration and selection across several logical layers of an electronic information network. In that process, large datasets are repeatedly evaluated and interconnected using statistical and probabilistic routines to generate comprehensive and systematic information and decision frameworks. Algorithms are used to train neutral networks (backpropagation, variants of gradient descent). Neural networks can be distinguished by the type of data they use during training or test time (labelled, unlabelled, categorical, and numerical), their loss/error/cost/objective function, their connection patterns, and their optimisation algorithm (Barenkamp et al., 2020).

In applying these technologies AI manages complex tasks like natural language processing (NLP), i.e. the understanding and translation of human language into other languages and codes, or computer vision, i.e. the visual perception, analysis, and understanding of optical environmental information (Barenkamp et al., 2020).

8.10.1 AI in The Software Engineering Lifecycle

AI has relevance to software engineering. The application of AI instruments at every stage of the development process results in an increase in efficiency throughout the whole process flow, as illustrated in Figure 8.28. The potential, limitations, and development requirements of AI applications in software engineering are explained in the following sections (Barenkamp et al., 2020).

8.10.1.1 AI in Software Project Planning

At the stage of software project planning, software developers and clients come together to determine the project objectives and customer requirements Software development scheduling and planning are crucial to ensure the technical effectiveness and economic efficiency of software projects.

Search-based software engineering is involved with the optimisation of project targets, for example, costs, duration, and quality under certain constraints. The concept originated in the late 1990s. While early algorithms were based on conventional linear programming, coefficient interdependencies, non-linearities, several decision layers, dynamic conditions, and uncertainties are increasingly

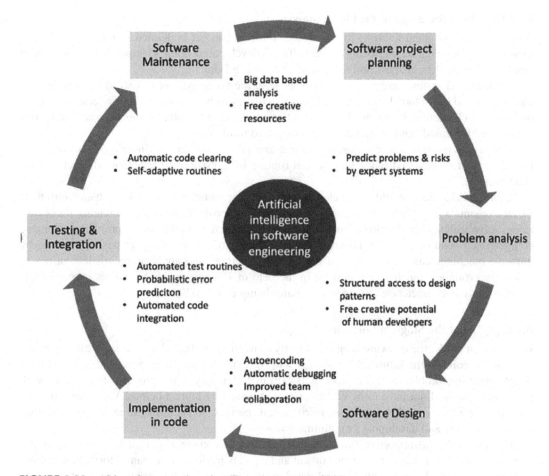

FIGURE 8.28 AI in software engineering (Barenkamp et al., 2020).

included in models. The growing complexity of decision layers and the reference to previous experiences and documentations in external data bases justify the label of AI assigned to innovative scheduling systems.

AI is useful in the following ways:

- Duration and cost of projects are contradictory goals at first glance, and human planners struggle to harmonise them. AI tools are useful to support this process.
- Task assignment in the project planning phase can be a source of conflict for developers and project planners and optimal task, time, and budget allocation regularly exceed human planning capacities. AI is useful to support software project management at the stage of task assignment and human resource allocation.
- Conventional scheduling models face the challenge of a very broad search space, comprising multiple input factors and scenarios, and usually have to make simplifying assumptions to deliver reproducible results. AI algorithms based on non-linear and self-optimising algorithms, like ant colony optimisation, can solve such problems successfully by iteratively reducing decision complexity.

At this point, however, AI still requires human assistance to select an adequate planning algorithm for a problem set. The practical application of AI algorithms for devising and scheduling new projects remains to be done (Barenkamp et al., 2020).

8.10.1.2   AI at the Stage of Problem Analysis

At the stage of problem analysis in the SDLC, the problem set is defined in terms of software tools and development requirements by the software development team. Computers have long been employed for problem analysis and the compilation of Big Data.

Analytical AI systems are more comprehensive in the complexity of statistical approaches and have embedded self-reliant learning algorithms that distinguish patterns based on a series of similar or recurring characteristics to enable new creative solutions. AI analytics uses external data bases to become "informed" and further develop established routines.

AI analytics is applied at the stage of problem analysis in software engineering, for example, to predict project success and risk – an essential routine in assessing and selecting prospective software projects.

In future, AI systems could be developed to decompose complex real-world problems into their fuzzy elements and probabilistic components to structure programme codes managing these routines. Software engineering problems could be reformulated as optimisation problems to enable computerised solutions. So far, however, the structuring of the problem set has to be done by humans; machines can only reproduce predefined structures and apply probabilistic routines to assess uncertainties. Further development in the field of software problem analysis is required to develop analytic competencies in machines (Barenkamp et al., 2020).

8.10.1.3   AI at the Stage of Software Design

In the design phase, the software project is clearly structured, and development tasks are assigned.

At some point in the future, Software 2.0 will develop its own programme codes, based on a simple input (the problem set). The code will gain in complexity in the process of neural network processing and will not have to be understood or reviewed by human beings. Visual recognition, speech recognition, speech synthesis, self-driving car routines, and gaming are early manifestations of self-improving and developing programme codes.

AI search takes a supportive function in the design of computer games, for instance, and is applied to model, generate, or evaluate content and agent behaviour in the game story. AI simulates play and thus contributes to enhance and develop the game, create believable actors, and provide a conclusive computational narrative. AI software is also employed to continuously test new game routines for practicability and has been used to train future developers in a university environment.

When developers are confronted with probabilistic problem sets and have to develop codes for ill-defined, noisy, and incomplete information environments, they rely on the stochastic approximations and iterations AI provides.

Although neural networks are self-enhancing, they still operate on human-defined routines in the phase of software design. There are tools for specifying and structuring particular problem sets, but the work strategy and the actual design of the software still has to be defined by the human engineer. Although computer-aided software engineering, which supports the process of software design by automated activities, is common practice today, AI implementation still requires clearly structured tasks and the support of human developers. Steps that can be automated have to be defined and integrated in an automated development environment package, which can then perform these functions self-reliantly.

In the future, AI could enhance computer-aided software engineering competencies by adding intellectual skills and might substitute human activity in that process to some extent. Future AI systems could, according to some researchers, build causal models that self-reliantly explain real-world phenomena instead of recognising pre-programmed patterns only. They may be self-adjusting and self-learning instead of just optimising predefined routines (Barenkamp et al., 2020).

8.10.1.4   AI at the Stage of Software Implementation

Software implementation comprises the actual coding process of the software application.

Neural networks have been developed to assist software coding. Processing natural language into software code has been researched since the 1980s; with increasing complexity of pattern recognition routines, the technology has advanced to class-model builders in recent years.

Gathered data are transformed into contingent vectors and used for model training to interconnect code levels systematically. AI software generates prototypes of codes from human language, which then are refined and adjusted by human programmers. AI classification strategies are also useful to directly transform human language and real-world phenomena into pieces of code and software models. Some researchers develop an AI for automated semantic code search, i.e. the retrieval of relevant code from a natural language query. The software contains several million functions for automatic queries from natural language, which dissect and systematises human language elements.

Today, AI in software implementation still requires specific and well-defined problem sets, such as equations to fit and probabilistic environments for simulation. Discovering new ideas, new parameters to be optimised, or even new problems remains a field of creative human mental activity.

In future, AI could be developed to produce more coherent codes and possibly even implement the code into existing routines self-reliantly. Some researchers argue that software generated automatically may not be understood by human beings any more and could damage existing routines. AI could ignore risks involved with the automated implementation of auto-generated software codes. Mechanisms to control automatic programming routines will have to be developed to avoid AI-related coding risks (Barenkamp et al., 2020).

8.10.1.5 AI at the Stage of Software Testing and Integration

In the testing phase, the developer and client test the functionality of the software product in practice, identify and analyse errors, and tailor the product to practice requirements. AI uses strategies of pattern recognition and ML to support software testing and integration.

Automated software testing refers to the transference of certain sections of a programme into a script, which is then repeatedly executed by a machine, which then collects, stores, and interprets the test results. AI programme browsers check existing codes for necessary changes automatically and suggest changes to the programme code to make it work. Probabilistic routines support error detection by predicting the likelihood of failure occurrence based on experiences with large data sets.

Software integration refers to the compilation of different codes into a uniform software system. SOA aims at integrating open software standards into firm-specific solutions (Karim, 2008). AI assists developers in integrating different platforms into service-oriented designs and enhances the management of generic quality attributes. AI captures conversation semantics prevalent in different web-based architectures and identifies unifying elements by pattern recognition. AI discovers similar architectures and eliminates redundant code units in the SOA and thus supports developers in clearing up software interfaces so that a contingent SOA tailored to the requirements of specific businesses results.

Fuzzing is an automated software testing technique that is not itself based on AI but is sometimes combined with AI elements. Fuzzing uses invalid, partly incomplete, or random data as input to test programmes systematically and then evaluates the effects. The fuzzing results are summarised in the form of an output protocol. Some researchers use deep neural networks (DNNa) to combine several error routines to identify complex code defects. The DNN adapts to programme reactions in a metamorphic way to identify rare and linked errors and systematically enhance code quality. AI fuzzers are superior to manual or hybrid fuzzing routines.

Although automated AI-based testing and integration functions today are self-improving and use dynamically changing routines, human coders are still required to define the testing process and requirements to the programme, while the test implementation can be done by the machine. A survey of 328 experts found about 35% assumed that a complete substitution of human programmers by machines in the testing phase will never be possible.

AI abbreviates the testing process and saves manpower to perform, document, and evaluate the tests; time to market and development costs are reduced. Yet human control and intervention are still necessary to prevent erroneous testing routines and to critically reflect on the validity and reliability of test results.

8.10.1.6 AI at the Stage of Software Maintenance

In the maintenance phase, the software company assists the customer in product application, provides regular upgrades, and makes further adjustments based on the customer's requirements.

AI instruments support the maintenance and updating of software to meet changing requirements in an Internet environment.

In the maintenance phase, AI can support the classification of user queries; this is useful to classify and direct software users depending on their query pattern.

Using principles of pattern recognition and ML, AI equally supports software modernisation. In ancient codes, structural information is frequently lost because of poor documentation. AI pattern recognition techniques are useful to extract coherent sets of code. ML functions are used to trace and check their functionality. Pattern tracing functions extract redundant elements from codes, automatically generate implementation artefacts, and test software functions.

AI neural networks trained by DL algorithms are useful for software security assessment. AI identifies and simulates attack patterns to discover security gaps, defects, and errors in a targeted way. Neural network error and security gap tracking works by slicing software code into formal routines prone to typical attack patterns in a systematic way and exploring a broad set of viral strategies to each element. Neural security assessment networks can reach an accuracy of more than 90%.

In the future, AI software systems could be useful to manage critical large-scale software infrastructure, like servers, and adapt these to environmental changes or new unexpected conditions. To date, however, there is no single AI system that could manage this task self-reliantly. Lacking human understanding of autonomously regulating AI units could induce self-enforcing cycles which would be beyond human control. Unmanaged AI autonomy could entail unpredictable risks to electronic and even physical infrastructures (Barenkamp et al., 2020).

REFERENCES

Barenkamp, M., Rebstadt, J., & Thomas, O. (2020). Applications of AI in classical software engineering. *AI Perspectives*, 2(1), 1–15.

Beck, K., Beedle, M., Van Bennekum, A., Cockburn, A., Cunningham, W., Fowler, M., Grenning, J., Highsmith, J., Hunt, A., & Jeffries, R. (2001). *Manifesto for agile software development*. https://agilemanifesto.org/

Belady, L. A., & Lehman, M. M. (1976). A model of large program development. *IBM Systems Journal*, 15(3), 225–252.

Boehm, B. W. (1984). Software engineering economics. *IEEE Transactions on Software Engineering*, 1, 4–21.

Garlan, D., & Shaw, M. (1994). An introduction to software architecture. Technical Report. Carnegie Mellon University: Software Engineering Institute. https://resources.sei.cmu.edu/library/asset-view.cfm?assetid=12235

Heineman, G.T., & Council, W.T. (2001). *Component-based software engineering: Putting the pieces together*. Addison-Wesley.

Jayaratna, N. (1994). *Understanding and evaluating methodologies: NIMSAD, a systematic framework*. McGraw-Hill.

Karim, R. (2008). A service-oriented approach to e-maintenance of complex technical systems. http://epubl.ltu.se/1402-1544/2008/58/LTU-DT-0858-SE.pdf

Krueger, C. W. (1992). Software reuse. *ACM Computing Surveys (CSUR)*, 24(2), 131–183. https://doi.org/10.1145/130844.130856

Lee, S., Tewolde, G., & Kwon, J. (2014). Design and implementation of vehicle tracking system using GPS/GSM/GPRS technology and smartphone application. *2014 IEEE World Forum on Internet of Things (WF-IoT)*, 353–358. https://doi.org/10.1109/WF-IoT.2014.6803187

Lehman, M. M. (1980). Programs, life cycles, and laws of software evolution. *Proceedings of the IEEE*, 68(9), 1060–1076.

Lehman, M. M., & Belady, L. A. (1985). *Program evolution: Processes of software change.* Academic Press Professional, Inc.

Naur, P., & Randell, B. (1969). *Software engineering: Report of a conference sponsored by the NATO Science Committee, Garmisch, Germany, 7–11 October 1968.* NATO, Scientific Affairs Division. http://homepages.cs.ncl.ac.uk/brian.randell/NATO/nato1968.PDF

Partridge, D. (2013). *Artificial intelligence and software engineering.* Routledge.

Richards, M. (2022). *Software architecture patterns.* O'Reilly Media.

Schach, S. R. (1990). *Software engineering.* Aksen Associates.

Shaw, M., & Garlan, D. (1996). *Software architecture: Perspectives on an emerging discipline.* Prentice-Hall.

Sowa, J. F., & Zachman, J. A. (1992). Extending and formalizing the framework for information systems architecture. *IBM Systems Journal, 31*(3), 590–616.

Tiwari, U. K., & Kumar, S. (2020). *Component-based software engineering: Methods and metrics.* CRC Press.

TutorialsPoint. (2022). *Software engineering overview.* https://www.tutorialspoint.com/software_engineering/software_engineering_overview

Uerikasakura. (2020). System software. https://uerikasakura.wordpress.com/types-2/system-software/

University of Cape Town. (2011). *Information systems and software.* https://www.cs.uct.ac.za/mit_notes/software/htmls/ch01s03.html

9 Distributed Computing

9.1 CLOUD COMPUTING

Cloud computing enables convenient, ubiquitous, on-demand network access to a shared pool of configurable computing resources, including networks, servers, storage, applications, and services. It can be rapidly provisioned and released with minimal management effort or service provider interaction.

Data and programs can be removed from PCs and organisations' server rooms and installed into the compute cloud. Thus, cloud computing refers to the general geographical shift of computation. This influences all parts of the computational ecosystem starting from the user and ending with the software developer, IT manager, and hardware manufacturer.

Cloud computing integrates network technology and traditional computing technology. It includes such technologies as distributed computing, grid computing, parallel computing, utility computing, network storage, load balancing, and virtualisation (Zou et al., 2013).

9.1.1 ADVANTAGES OF CLOUD COMPUTING

The advantages of cloud computing include the following:

1. Transformation: Cloud computing has the potential to transform the IT industry, making software even more attractive as a service and shaping the way IT hardware is designed and purchased.
2. Speed: Companies with large batch-oriented tasks can get results as quickly as their programmes can scale (Figure 9.1) (Armbrust et al., 2009). Instead of waiting for months and weeks to purchase and configure the hardware, cloud computing services provide a large amount of computing resources within minutes (KnowledgeNile, 2022).
3. On-demand self-service: A consumer can unilaterally provision computing capabilities, such as server time and network storage, as needed automatically without requiring human interaction with each service provider.
4. Broad network access: Capabilities are available over the network and accessed through standard mechanisms that promote use by heterogeneous thin or thick client platforms, for example, cell phones, tablets, laptops, and workstations.
5. Savings: Developers with ideas for new Internet services no longer need to make significant capital outlays for hardware to deploy their service or for the human resources to operate it. Cloud computing eliminates most of the cost and efforts of purchasing the data centres, hardware, and software, the electricity needs to power-up and cool the data centres and hardware, and the installation and maintenance of the infrastructure (KnowledgeNile, 2022).
6. Resource pooling: The computing resources are pooled to serve multiple consumers with different physical and virtual resources dynamically assigned and reassigned according to consumer demand. Examples of resources include storage, processing, memory, and network bandwidth.
7. Measured service/work to scale: Cloud systems automatically control and optimise resource use by leveraging a metering capability at a level of abstraction appropriate to the type of service, for example, bandwidth, processing, storage, and active user accounts. Cloud

DOI: 10.1201/9781003208686-9

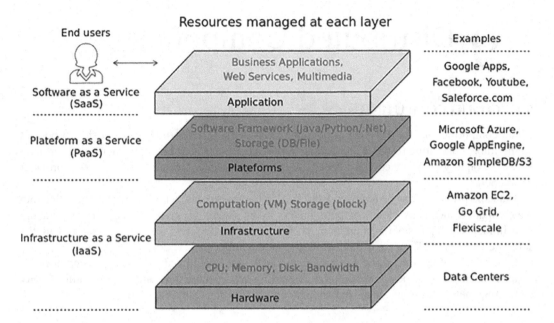

FIGURE 9.1   Cloud computing architecture (Zhang et al., 2010).

computing services deliver the right number of resources. Organisations can scale the capacity as per their needs and avoid purchasing excess capacity (KnowledgeNile, 2022).

8. Rapid elasticity: Capabilities can be elastically provisioned and released, sometimes automatically, to scale rapidly outward or inward based on demand. The capabilities available for provisioning often appear unlimited to consumers, giving them the sense that they can be appropriated at any time and in any quantity (Mell & Grance, 2011).

The following advantages make cloud computing particularly appealing to businesses:

1. No upfront investment: Cloud computing uses a pay-as-you-go pricing model. A service provider does not need to invest in the infrastructure to start gaining benefit from cloud computing. It simply rents resources from the cloud according to its own needs and pays for the usage (Zhang et al., 2010).

2. Reduced operating cost: Resources in a cloud environment can be rapidly allocated and de-allocated on demand. Hence, a service provider no longer needs to provision capacities according to the peak load. This provides huge savings since resources can be released to save on operating costs when service demand is low. Moreover, rather than owning a data centre or a computing infrastructure, companies can rent cloud service providers for applications and storage purposes (KnowledgeNile, 2022).

3. Scalability: Infrastructure provides a large number of resources from data centres and makes them easily accessible. A service provider can easily expand its service to large scales to handle a sudden rapid increase in service demands (e.g. flash-crowd effect). This model is sometimes called surge computing (Armbrust et al., 2009).

4. Easy access: Services hosted in the cloud are generally web-based. Therefore, they are easily accessible through a variety of devices with Internet connections. These devices go beyond desktop and laptop computers to include cell phones.

5. Reduced business risks and maintenance expenses: By outsourcing the service infrastructure to the clouds, a service provider shifts its business risks (e.g. hardware failures) to infrastructure providers, who often have better expertise and are better equipped for managing these risks.

9.1.2 Challenges of Cloud Computing

Despite the many advantages of cloud computing, there are some challenges. A notable one is the ownership of data, and another is the location of data storage (Abadi, 2009):

- Data are stored at an untrusted host: In general, moving data off-premises increases the number of potential security risks, calling for appropriate precautions. Although the name "cloud computing" gives the impression that the computing and storage resources are elsewhere – perhaps somewhere in the sky – the data are physically located in a particular country and are subject to that country's rules and regulations (Thompson, 2008). Since most cloud computing vendors give the customer little control over where data are stored, the customer has to simply hope the data are encrypted using a key not located at the host. Otherwise, a third party may access the data without the customer's knowledge.
- Data are replicated: Data availability and durability are key concerns for cloud storage providers, as data loss or unavailability can be damaging to their ability to meet targets set in service-level agreements (Amazon, 2022) and also to their reputation. Thus, they typically resort to data replication, mostly automatically without customer interference or requests to do so. Cloud computing providers with data centres across the globe can provide high levels of fault tolerance by replicating data across large geographic distances. Customers should question the details of the replication scheme, however, to determine the probability of its failure. The availability of replicated data is not a certainty.
- Transmission rates can be slow: Although cloud computing has many advantages and efficient uses, its centralised nature has proven to be inefficient for latency-sensitive applications in terms of transferring and processing the data. Given the growing amount of data produced every second (i.e. Big Data), slow transmission rates are expected due to heavy traffic in the cloud. Accordingly, since computation powers and the network bandwidth are finite with no major improvement in the latter, cloud computing cannot accommodate the transmission of vast amounts of data and real-time (RT) processing.

9.1.3 Relationship of Cloud Computing with Other Technologies

Cloud computing is not really a new technology. Rather, it represents the evolution and integration of several technologies (Luo et al., 2012), including the following:

- Web service: Using web service, each software or application is packaged as a "service". A service is independent of the context of other services, and various services can interact. A service is self-described and self-contained to provide certain functions. Standardised machine-interpretable interfaces and protocols are formulated to describe a service, publish a service, and transport messages among services. Users can link a number of services together to create complex applications. In the cloud computing platform, complex power system applications can be created by joining services from different service providers.
- Grid computing: Grid computing aggregates geographically distributed computational resources and uses this coordinated grid to accomplish certain tasks. It works in the following manner: users submit tasks to the grid portal. The grid broker chooses suitable resources to execute the job, and when the job is finished, returns the results to users. Thousands of distributed resources comprise the cloud computing platform, and grid computing can aggregate thousands of resources to create a resource pool. Cloud computing takes this technology farther by leveraging virtualisation technologies at multiple levels (i.e. hardware level, application platform) for resource sharing and dynamic resource provisioning.

- Utility computing: In the utility environment, users assign a "utility" value to their job. The utility represents a certain measurable requirement (e.g. execution time, throughput), and the value is the amount of money users are willing to pay the service providers. In other words, this environment constitutes a marketplace, wherein service providers maximise profits while users compete for resources based on the utility value of their jobs.
- Hardware virtualisation: Virtualisation technology allows users to easily access and use distributed heterogeneous resources in a uniform way. Virtualisation actually comprises the foundation of cloud computing, as it provides the capability of pooling computing resources from clusters of servers and dynamically assigning or reassigning virtual resources to applications on-demand. A virtualised server is called a virtual machine (VM).
- Autonomic computing: The goal of autonomic computing is to overcome the management complexity of today's computer systems. To that end, it aims at building computing systems capable of self-management, i.e. able to react to internal and external observations without human intervention. Although cloud computing exhibits certain autonomic features, for example, automatic resource provisioning, its objective is to lower the resource cost, not reduce system complexity (Zhang et al., 2010).

9.1.4 CLOUD COMPUTING SERVICE MODELS

9.1.4.1 Software as a Service

Simply stated, in software as a service (SaaS), the consumer uses the provider's applications running on a cloud infrastructure. The applications are accessible from various client devices through a thin client interface (e.g. a web browser) or a program interface. The consumer does not manage or control the underlying cloud infrastructure, including network, servers, operating systems, storage, or even individual application capabilities, with the possible exception of limited user-specific application configuration settings (Goyal, 2013).

SaaS is emerging as a viable outsourcing option for clients interested in paying for the right to access a standardised set of business software functions through the network. With the SaaS model, software applications are deployed on vendors' premises prior to a client's adoption. Clients do not purchase software or infrastructure upfront but pay for their access to the services over time via the Internet on a pay-as-you-use basis.

Each consumer has two options. The first option is to share access to the software with other consumers (multi-tenancy), thus enabling shared total costs and creating economies of scale. The second option is to be a single tenant, thus providing greater control and security but foregoing the possibility of reduced expenses.

9.1.4.2 Benefits of Software as a Service

SaaS is of interest to many organisations for a number of reasons:

1. The implementation cycle is shortened, as applications are already deployed on SaaS vendor sites.
2. The SaaS model allows extensive cost savings in operating standard business components on a large scale. Firms with high capital costs may find the SaaS model interesting, as it enables them to economise on fixed capital costs by spreading the service cost over time, allowing faster time to value, and potentially yielding significant cost savings.
3. Although the consumer loses some level of control, the SaaS model shifts the burden of getting and keeping an enterprise application up and running from the consumer to the vendor. It permits users to leverage software functionality without the burden of deploying and managing the software themselves. The SaaS model includes systematic support of the software, rather than annual maintenance, and upload of fixes and patches to all

subscribers. It also enables every consumer to benefit from the vendor's latest techno-logical features without the disruptions and costs associated with software updates and upgrades.

4. SaaS applications are accessed through a web-based interface typically run from a web browser. This delivery mechanism allows easy scalability as new users are added.
5. The SaaS model eliminates the added costs and complexities of deploying additional hard-ware and software or dedicating additional staff resources to support an enterprise applica-tion on an ongoing basis.
6. The load on the computer is greatly reduced if all the software applications are built and run on the SaaS platform.
7. Because the SaaS application is part of cloud computing architecture, it represents a highly reliable, more powerful, secure, and redundant hardware infrastructure.
8. SaaS solutions are web-based; deployment is quick, rapid, and quite easy. This gives organisations instant access to all the software applications they may need.
9. The SaaS platform is easily accessible. Data related to the software application can be accessed at any point from anywhere with only an Internet connection.
10. Most SaaS applications are compatible with varied computer systems and telecommunica-tions technology, such as smart phones (Goyal, 2013).

9.1.4.2.1   Challenges in Software as a Service Adoption
Some limitations slow down the acceptance of SaaS and prohibit it from being used in some cases:

1. With data stored on the vendor's servers, data security becomes an issue.
2. SaaS applications are hosted in the cloud, far away from the application users. This intro-duces latency into the environment; for example, the SaaS model is not suitable for applica-tions that demand response times in the milliseconds.
3. Multi-tenant architectures drive cost efficiency for SaaS solution providers but may limit the customisation of applications for large clients, inhibiting such applications from being used in scenarios (applicable mostly to large enterprises) for which such customisation is necessary.
4. Some business applications require access to or integration with the customer's current data. When such data are large in volume or sensitive (e.g. end-users' personal informa-tion), integrating them with remotely hosted software can be costly or risky or may conflict with data governance regulations.
5. Constitutional search/seizure warrant laws do not protect all forms of SaaS dynamically stored data. Thus, a link is added to the chain of security where access to the data, and by extension, misuse of these data, are limited only by the assumed honesty of third parties or government agencies able to access the data on their own recognizance.
6. Switching SaaS vendors may involve the slow and difficult task of transferring very large data files over the Internet.
7. Organisations who adopt SaaS may find they are forced into adopting new versions, which might result in unforeseen training costs or an increase in the probability that a user may make an error.
8. Relying on an Internet connection means data are transferred to and from a SaaS firm at Internet speeds, rather than at the potentially higher speeds of a firm's internal network (Goyal, 2013).

9.1.4.3   Platform as a Service
Platform as a service (PaaS) is a category of cloud computing that provides a platform and envi-ronment to allow developers to build applications and services over the Internet. PaaS services are hosted in the cloud and accessed by users simply via their web browser. The consumer does not

manage or control the underlying cloud infrastructure, including network, servers, operating systems, or storage, but has control over the deployed applications and possibly configuration settings for the application-hosting environment (Mell & Grance, 2011).

Otherwise stated, PaaS allows users to create software applications using tools supplied by the provider. PaaS services can consist of preconfigured features that customers can subscribe to; they can choose to include the features that meet their requirements while discarding those that do not. Consequently, packages can vary from offering simple point-and-click frameworks where no client-side hosting expertise is required to supplying the infrastructure options for advanced development.

The infrastructure and applications are managed for customers, and support is available. Services are constantly updated, with existing features upgraded and additional features added. PaaS providers can assist developers from the conception of their original ideas to the creation of applications, through to testing and deployment. This is all achieved in a managed mechanism.

The services offered by PaaS to users include operating system, server-side scripting environment, database management system, server software, support, storage, network access, hosting, and tools for design and development (Goyal, 2013).

9.1.4.3.1 Benefits of Platform as a Service

PaaS has a number of benefits:

1. PaaS provides the architecture, as well as the overall infrastructure, to support application development. It is therefore ideal for the development of new applications that are intended for the web, mobile devices, and PCs (Goyal, 2013).
2. As with most cloud offerings, PaaS services are generally paid for on a subscription basis with clients paying just for what they use.
3. Clients benefit from the economies of scale that arise from the sharing of the underlying physical infrastructure by users, and this results in lower costs.
4. Capital costs are reduced, as organisations don't have to invest in physical infrastructure or purchase hardware.
5. Organisations do not need to hire experts to run the system, leaving them free to focus on the development of applications.
6. PaaS makes development possible for non-experts. With some PaaS offerings, anyone can develop an application through a web browser using one-click functionality. Salient examples of this are one-click blog software installs, such as WordPress.
7. PaaS provides flexibility. Clients can have control over the tools that are installed within their platforms and can create a platform that suits their specific requirements. They can pick and choose the features they feel are necessary.
8. Adaptability is easy for PaaS users. Features can be changed if circumstances dictate that they should be. Teams in different locations can work together, as an Internet connection and web browser are all that is required. Developers spread across several locations can work together on the same application build.
9. PaaS providers offer data security, backup, and recovery (Goyal, 2013).

9.1.4.3.2 Challenges in PaaS Adoption

Three limitations characterise the PaaS security platform (Goyal, 2013): information processing, information interactivity, and data storage.

- Information processing: Information processing refers to the stage when data are processed to create information that will be disseminated. Sometimes these data are so bulky that the creation process occurs live on a remote server. This increases the document's risk of being intercepted by others. However, PaaS can provide apps that reinforce the security of the document even in the process of open processing on a shared server. It is critical to note that this platform provides great data protection in its stored format. Thus, problems occur only in the processing stage.

- Information interactivity: This is the process of sharing data across the board. Data go through various PCs, seep through networks, and migrate through other devices like phones. They also find their way through nodes that switch them from the access to the core layers. This interaction sometimes connects local networks that have confidential data with the free web where everybody gains access. This is where issues of security come in. PaaS basically enables users to control data through automated apps from their sources. If a client wants to view confidential data over the Internet, he or she may do so in a cloud environment where no one can hack. In a reverse situation, there can be firewalls all over, which restrict how much data outsiders can view. News sites use proxies to deny access to some information to people outside the home country such that they only see what matters to the rest of the world.

- Data storage: This signifies the hosting aspect of cloud computing. Thanks to the mechanisms in PaaS that endorse multiple applications to encrypt data in servers, many documents do not leak. However, this is hard to verify because data are always in shared servers. This has been a prominent issue in the entire cloud community, but the advent of independent clouds even inside dedicated hosting platforms could help to overcome this issue (Goyal, 2013).

9.1.4.4 Infrastructure as a Service

Infrastructure as a service (IaaS) refers to the capability provided to consumers to provision processing, storage, networks, and other fundamental computing resources where they can deploy and run arbitrary software (Goyal, 2013).

As with all cloud computing services, IaaS provides access to computing resources in a virtualised environment. The computing resource provided is specifically that of virtualised hardware, in other words, computing infrastructure. The definition includes such offerings as virtual server space, network connections, bandwidth, IP addresses, and load balancers. Physically, the pool of hardware resources is pulled from a multitude of servers and networks usually distributed across numerous data centres, all of which the cloud provider is responsible for maintaining.

Meanwhile, consumers are given access to the virtualised components so they can build their own IT platforms. Consumers do not manage or control the underlying cloud infrastructure but have control over operating systems, storage, and deployed applications, as well as possibly limited control of select networking components (Mell & Grance, 2011).

9.1.4.4.1 Benefits of Infrastructure as a Service

The benefits of IaaS include the following:

1. Consumer control: Consumers can choose the operating system, database and application development environment, giving them greater control over the hardware than in PaaS. They can configure the servers based on their needs. This results in more maintenance than for PaaS but also more options (Goyal, 2013).
2. Scalability and cost effectiveness: IaaS can be utilised by enterprise consumers to create cost-effective and easily scalable IT solutions where the complexities and expenses of managing the underlying hardware are outsourced to the cloud provider. If the scale of a consumer's operations fluctuates, or it is looking to expand, it can tap into the cloud resource as and when required, rather than purchasing, installing, and integrating hardware itself (Goyal, 2013).
3. Accommodation to growth: Expanding businesses can scale their infrastructure in accordance with their growth while private clouds (accessible only by the business itself) can protect the storage and transfer of the sensitive data that some businesses are required to handle.

4. Pooled resources: Cloud hosting of websites on virtual servers is founded upon pooled resources from underlying physical servers. A website hosted in the cloud, for example, can benefit from the redundancy provided by a vast network of physical servers and on-demand scalability to deal with unexpected demands placed on the website.
5. Virtual data centres (VDCs): These virtualised networks of interconnected virtual servers can be used to offer enhanced cloud hosting capabilities and enterprise IT infrastructure or to integrate all of these operations within either a public or a private cloud implementation.
6. Reduced capital costs: There is no investment in hardware. The underlying physical hardware that supports an IaaS service is set up and maintained by the cloud provider, saving the time and cost of doing so on the consumer side.
7. Utility style costing: The service can be accessed on demand, and consumers only pay for the resources they actually use.
8. Location independence: The service can usually be accessed from any location as long as there is an Internet connection, and the security protocol of the cloud allows it.
9. Physical security of data centre locations: Services available through a public cloud or private clouds hosted externally with the cloud provider benefit from the physical security afforded to the servers, which are hosted within a data centre.
10. No single point of failure: If one server or network switch, for example, were to fail, the broader service would be unaffected because of the remaining multitude of hardware resources and redundancy configurations. For many services, if one entire data centre were to go offline, the IaaS service could still run successfully.

IaaS has the potential to accelerate growth and deliver massive new revenue streams while moving service providers up the value chain. It can provide better return on investment (ROI) through high-margin multi-tenancy services, improved ability to create new competitive offerings, and open market opportunities with enterprise consumers (Goyal, 2013).

9.1.4.4.2 Challenges in Infrastructure as a Service Adoption
Primary factors that limit organisations' interest in using a cloud-based IaaS solution are:

- Concerns about the security and confidentiality of data.
- Lack of time and resources to sufficiently analyse the offerings and the providers.
- Uncertainty about providers living up to their promises.
- Lack of confidence in a shared infrastructure.
- Concern that the provider may not be capable of adding capacity in a dynamic enough fashion.
- The lack of an internal strategy for IaaS.
- The lack of personnel to design and implement solutions.
- The relative immaturity of the technologies that would have to be installed and managed.
- The lack of significant enough cost savings (Goyal, 2013).

9.2 CLOUD COMPUTING TYPES

Clouds can be private, community, public, or hybrid.

- Private cloud: The term private cloud refers to internal data centres of an organisation that are not made available to the public (Armbrust et al., 2009). Rather, the cloud infrastructure is aimed at exclusive use by a single organisation comprising multiple consumers, for example, business units within a company. It may be owned, managed, and operated by the organisation, a third party, or some combination, and it may exist on or off the organisation's premises (Mell & Grance, 2011). In essence, a private network maintains the services offered (KnowledgeNile, 2022).

- Community cloud: This particular cloud infrastructure is provisioned for exclusive use by a specific community of consumers from organisations with shared concerns, for example, mission, security requirements, policy, and compliance considerations. It may be owned, managed, and operated by one or more of the organisations in the community, a third party, or some combination, and like the private cloud, it may exist on or off premises (Mell & Grance, 2011).
- Public cloud: In a public cloud, the cloud infrastructure is provisioned for open use by the public. It may be owned, managed, and operated by a business, by an academic organisation, or by a government organisation, or by some combination of the three. It exists on the premises of the cloud provider (Mell & Grance, 2011). This third-party cloud service provider owns and manages public clouds, delivering the required computing resources over the Internet (KnowledgeNile, 2022). Public cloud services are elastic and readily scalable.
- Hybrid cloud: The hybrid cloud infrastructure is a composition of two or more distinct cloud infrastructures (private, community, or public). Each retains its unique identity. They are bound together by a standardised or proprietary technology that enables data and application portability (Mell & Grance, 2011). A hybrid cloud gives more flexibility by allowing data and application shareability between private and public clouds (KnowledgeNile, 2022).

9.2.1 Advantages of Hybrid Clouds

Both private and public clouds are efficient and sufficient in their fields, but during a large-scale development process and with shared agendas, there is a need for more specific and broadly accessed sharing of information and data.

In the simplest terms, the hybrid model is primarily a private cloud that allows an organisation to tap into a public cloud as and when required to share information. This model provides a more efficient means of keeping data and applications secure. In contrast to a purely public cloud model, the hybrid cloud can provide a higher level of security for sensitive data in instances when companies are affected by industries and financial regulations.

This is the most utility-oriented technique and the most used model in the business-oriented sectors. The cloud model allows companies to adjust the amount of computing power used based on their individual fluctuations in actual usage. Therefore, for companies that have a great deal of variation in their computing needs, a hybrid model speeds things up by using a public cloud at times when more computing capacity is needed.

Generally, adding public space to a company's cloud model is a much easier proposition than growing its private cloud to meet mounting needs. In this way, a hybrid is more cost-efficient in providing world-class computing power that is available anytime, anywhere, without as big a budget commitment as a private cloud.

There are various ways to amend a hybrid cloud. This includes the selection of the required applications and other services to be interconnected with the cloud technology and redistribution and sharing of information (Srinivasan et al., 2015).

9.2.2 Cloud Computing Architecture

The architecture of cloud computing is shown in Figure 9.2 and explained below (Al-Qamash et al., 2018).

- Front-end platform: This is the platform that is visible to the cloud clients. The interface that the client uses to access the cloud can be any software or hardware, depending on the type of cloud computing used to get these services. Some examples are browsers, operating systems, tablets, mobile phones, or other devices.

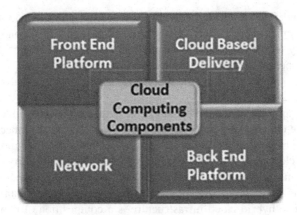

FIGURE 9.2 Architectural components of cloud computing (Al-Qamash et al., 2018).

- Backend platform: This is the platform used by a service provider. It consists of servers and storage resources which are generally defined as the cloud.

9.3 FOG COMPUTING

Fog computing, also known as fog networking or fogging, is a decentralised computing structure located between devices that produce data, such as Internet of Things (IoT) devices, and the cloud (KnowledgeNile, 2022). The main goal is to provide basic analytic services by extending the traditional cloud computing architecture to the edge of the network. Reducing the degree of involvement of the cloud by bringing the processing units closer to the end devices allows fog computing to improve the utilisation of the computation power, task execution time, and processing time.

Fog computing places intelligence in the local area network (LAN). It uses edge devices and gateways, with the LAN providing processing capability (WinSystems, 2022). Data are transmitted from endpoints to a gateway, where they are transmitted to sources for processing and return transmission.

To put it simply, fog computing pushes intelligence down to the LAN level of network architecture, processing data in a fog node (the devices which extend the cloud closer to the source of data are called fog nodes) or IoT gateway. On a very basic level, it comprises moving computers closer to the sensors they are connected with.

9.3.1 BENEFITS OF FOG COMPUTING

Benefits of fog computing include the following:

- Enhanced security.
- Increased business agility.
- Improved reliability.
- Minimised latency.
- Flexible mobility.
- Improved performance: It improves performance and overall network efficiency because there is less distance across the network.
- Time-sensitive: Fog computing analyses data at the network edge, instead of sending the IoT data to the cloud.
- Fast response time: It takes milliseconds to act on the data (KnowledgeNile, 2022).

9.3.2 DISADVANTAGES OF FOG COMPUTING

Fog computing's architecture relies on many links in a communication chain to move data from the physical world of our assets into the digital world of IT. Each of these links is a potential point of failure (SCC, 2022).

Although fog computing is considered to be a huge improvement from cloud computing for RT applications, its performance is still limited in terms of latency and bandwidth, and its dependency on the cloud can be considered a drawback (Al-Qamash et al., 2018).

9.3.3 THE FOG PARADIGM

The fog computing paradigm resembles a layered model that extends the traditional cloud computing model by offering a distributed and decentralised platform. The model can be divided into three major layers: cloud, fog, and terminal as shown in Figure 9.3 (Al-Qamash et al., 2018).

1. The cloud layer, referred to as the cloud stratum, represents the data centres and servers with high storage and computation powers that manage, operate, and process the data received from the fog layer.

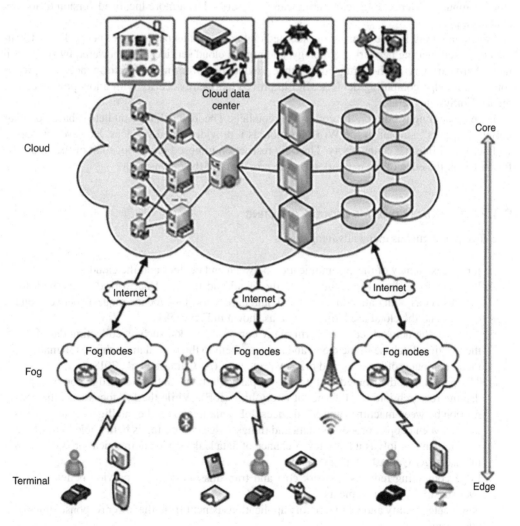

FIGURE 9.3 Fog computing paradigm model (Al-Qamash et al., 2018).

2. The fog layer is composed of multiple fog nodes, also called fog cells. Each includes a set of network devices with sufficient processing and temporary storage capabilities. The fog nodes receive requests from the IoT or end-user devices and are responsible for recognising their processing needs to decide whether the request should be processed locally or sent to the cloud.
3. The terminal layer, also referred to as the device layer, consists of two domains: the IoT devices and the end-user devices. Either is sufficient to complete the fog paradigm. These devices are responsible for sensing and collecting data from the physical world and sending the data to the fog layer.

The layered nature of this paradigm allows each layer to efficiently communicate with the neighbouring layers to process the data in a timely manner.

9.4   EDGE COMPUTING

Edge computing is a novel computing model that places computing resources and storage at the edge of the network closer to the end user. It provides intelligent services by collaborating with cloud computing. Hence, edge computing can be described as a more localised version of fog and cloud computing.

Edge computing is an extension of older technologies such as peer-to-peer networking, distributed data, self-healing network technology, and remote cloud services. It is powered by small form factor hardware with flash-storage arrays that provide highly optimised performance. The processors used in edge computing devices offer improved hardware security with a low power requirement (WinSystems, 2022).

Edge computing is built on the concept of cloudlets. The idea behind cloudlets is based on computing "hotspots", similar to the Wi-Fi hotspot, as it provides cloud services. However, it does so without Wi-Fi Internet connectivity. The only restriction imposed on the location of the cloudlet is for it to be at the edge of the network or in the proximity of the end user.

9.4.1   ADVANTAGES OF EDGE CLOUD COMPUTING

The edge paradigm has many advantages:

1. It reduces latency of the communication between end devices and the cloud.
2. It efficiently utilises the resources of the cloud and the local network devices, because devices act as both data consumers and data producers. This means requests between end devices and the cloud are bidirectional, as shown in Figure 9.4.
3. Nodes at the network edge perform many computing tasks, such as collecting data from the existing database in the cloud and sending them to the user, data caching, IoT management, computer offloading, and privacy protection (Al-Qamash et al., 2018).
4. The paradigm's distributed architecture is particularly advantageous. Edge computing is driving research into the Internet of Everything (IoE). While the IoT focuses on the connection between machines and IoT devices, IoE's main focus is the intelligent communication between people, processes, data and things. Edge computing is better able to meet the requirements of IoE as it has a lower chance of data leaks since communication is closer to the users (Al-Qamash et al., 2018).
5. Edge computing reduces network cost and transmission delay to provide better control over sensitive data movements.
6. Augmented reality and virtual reality applications benefit from the lower response times of edge computing.

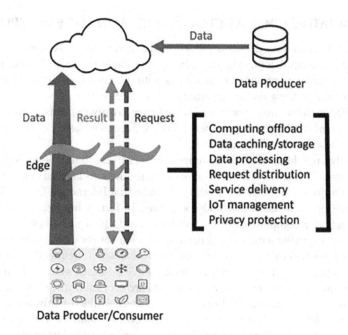

FIGURE 9.4 Edge computing paradigm (Al-Qamash et al., 2018).

7. Edge computing enhances security because the data do not travel over a network. It encrypts data closer to the network core while optimising data farther from the core for performance (WinSystems, 2022). Moreover, data are distributed so the local data remain safe if the data centre is compromised (KnowledgeNile, 2022).
8. It is challenging to transfer many data to the cloud at once. Edge computing stores data locally and can send some of the data to the cloud. It can also wait to send data until adequate bandwidth is available, thus avoiding problems of Internet access (KnowledgeNile, 2022).
9. Edge computing optimises resource usage in a cloud computing system.
10. Performing computations at the edge of the network reduces network traffic, reducing the risk of a data bottleneck (WinSystems, 2022).

9.4.2 How Edge Computing Works

Edge computing processes sensor data away from the centralised nodes and close to the logical edge of the network, in other words, towards the individual sources of the data. Rather than taking data to the cloud for analysis, edge computing moves closer to the data's source. Edge computing triages data locally, reducing traffic to the central repository. Thus, it simplifies the communication chain required in fog computing and reduces possible failure points.

Edge devices can be anything with sufficient computing capacity and capability, including switches, routers, and the sensors collecting the data (SCC, 2022).

9.4.3 Edge Computing and Internet of Things

IoT devices, such as sensors, are a source of data and are connected to the Internet. An edge device collects and processes these data. Edge computing devices stay closer to the source of data, i.e. the IoT devices. Because edge computing moves computing services, including storage and servers, closer to the source of data, data processing becomes much faster with lower latency and saves bandwidth. Without edge computing, the data from IoT devices would be sent back and forth to the cloud, resulting in slower response time and less efficiency (KnowledgeNile, 2022).

9.5 A COMPARATIVE LOOK AT CLOUD, FOG, AND EDGE COMPUTING

The recent development in data-driven applications has given rise to advancements in computational and storage resources. Cloud, fog, and edge computing are used in various applications that rely on data. Such paradigms provide organisations with the ability to use various computing and data storage services depending on the organisational requirements.

These computing architectures appear similar but vary greatly in terms of their characteristics. This allows them to meet different requirements that are needed to satisfy certain real-world applications. Table 9.1 shows some of their differences.

Organisations that rely heavily on data are increasingly likely to use cloud, fog, and edge computing infrastructures. These architectures allow organisations to take advantage of a variety of computing and data storage resources, including the Industrial Internet of Things (IIoT).

Most enterprises are familiar with cloud computing. In fact, it has become standard in many industries. Fog and edge computing are both extensions of cloud networks; these represent collections of servers comprising a distributed network. Such a network can allow an organisation to greatly exceed the resources that would otherwise be available to it, freeing it from the requirement to keep infrastructure on site. The primary advantage of cloud-based systems is they allow data to be collected from multiple sites and devices; these data are accessible anywhere in the world.

However, the other layers immediately come into play. Embedded hardware obtains data from on-site IIoT devices and passes them to the fog layer. Pertinent data are then passed to the cloud layer, which is typically in a different geographical location. The cloud layer is thus able to benefit from IIoT devices by receiving their data through the other layers. Organisations often achieve superior results by integrating a cloud platform with on-site fog networks or edge devices. Most enterprises are now migrating towards a fog or edge infrastructure to increase the utilisation of their end-user and IIoT devices (WinSystems, 2022).

That said, it is important to remember that these are different technologies, and they are non-interchangeable. For example, time-sensitive data are processed on edge computing, whereas cloud computing is used for data that are not time-driven. .

Edge computing for the IIoT allows processing to be performed locally at multiple decision points for the purpose of reducing network traffic (WinSystems, 2022). It performs much of the processing on embedded computing platforms directly interfacing to sensors and controllers. Meanwhile, fog computing uses a centralised system that interacts with industrial gateways and embedded computer systems on a LAN (WinSystems, 2022).

9.6 DATA STORAGE

Data are stored in databases. These can be relational or non-relational databases, file-based or document-based, or even completely unstructured file systems.

TABLE 9.1

Edge, Cloud, and Fog Computing: Key Differences (KnowledgeNile, 2022)

Points of Difference	Cloud Computing	Fog Computing	Edge Computing
Location of data processing	Central cloud server	Within an IoT gateway or fog nodes located in the LAN network	Device itself
Purpose	Long-term in-depth analysis	Quick analysis and real-time response	Quick analysis and real-time response
Latency	High	Low	Very low
Security	Less secure	High security	High security
Geographical distribution	Centralised	Distributed	Distributed

9.6.1 RELATIONAL DATABASES

Relational databases are structures that present information in tables with rows and columns. A table is referred to as a relation in the sense that it is a collection of objects of the same type (rows). Data in a table can be related according to common keys or concepts, and the ability to retrieve related data from a table is the basis for the term relational database.

The systems used to maintain and access these databases are known as relational database management systems (RDBMS). They use the ANSI/ISO standard Structured Query Language (SQL) as an interface between the user and the stored information.

In addition to being relatively easy to create and access, a relational database has the important advantage of being easy to extend. After the original database creation, a new data category can be added without requiring that all existing applications be modified. As drawbacks, relational databases present low performance and high physical storage consumption for large datasets.

Some variations of the relational database model have been implemented. For instance, in the object-oriented database model, information is stored in the form of objects, as used in object-oriented programming. The dimensional model is an adaptation of the relational model used to represent data in data warehouses.

9.6.2 NON-RELATIONAL DATABASES

Not only SQL or non-relational SQL (NoSQL) databases allow the storage and retrieval of data without the restrictions of RDBMS. They have been around since the late 1960s, but were given this label more recently, with the rise of Big Data.

NoSQL databases were introduced to solve the scalability issues and Big Data performance issues that relational databases weren't designed to address. They are especially useful in Big Data and real-time web applications, where there is a need to access and analyse massive amounts of unstructured data or data stored remotely in virtual servers in the cloud.

NoSQL databases are usually harder to configure and create than relational databases, and because they are relatively new, they lack maturity compared to RDBMS.

NoSQL suitability depends on the problem to solve; sometimes one of the data structures in NoSQL is the most efficient while at other times, SQL-based relational databases are the best option.

Many database structures are classified as NoSQL:

- Key-value stores: Also known as Map or Dictionary, these are the simplest of the NoSQL database structures. Every single value is stored together with an attribute name (or "key"). Data are represented as a collection of key-value pairs, such that each possible key appears at most once in the collection.
- Document-based stores: These are collections of structured (XML, railML, PMML, and CSV) and/or unstructured files (doc, pdf, and xls). Document-based stores are an extension of the key-value model; they rely on the internal structure in the document to extract metadata that the database engine uses for further optimisation.
- Column-oriented databases: These databases are optimised for queries over large datasets, with columns of data stored together, instead of rows. These are the most used in Big Data applications. The goal of a columnar database is to efficiently write and read data to and from hard disk storage to speed up the time it takes to return a query.
- Graph-oriented databases: These databases are a collection of nodes and edges. Each node represents an entity, such as a person or business, and each edge represents a connection or relationship between two nodes. Every node is defined by a unique identifier, a set of outgoing edges and/or incoming edges, and a set of properties expressed as key/value pairs. Graph databases are usually faster and are appropriate for analysing data interconnections.

- Multi-model databases: These databases were designed to apply the Polyglot Persistence concept to data modelling. The concept argues that applications should be written in a mix of languages to take advantage of the fact that different languages are suitable for tackling different problems. A multi-model database provides a single back end that supports multiple data models, such as key-value stores, document-based stores, column-oriented databases, and graph-oriented databases.

9.6.3   OTHER DATABASE STRUCTURES

NewSQL is a recent database concept that aims to provide the same performance features as NoSQL databases to standard relational database systems, while still offering robust consistency and transaction capabilities that NoSQL sometimes lacks. The types of applications that benefit from NewSQL have a large number of short transactions accessing small amounts of data. NewSQL systems vary greatly in their internal architectures, but all support relational database models, as well as SQL, as primary interface.

Because of a lack of means or because of a lack of knowledge of how to implement proper database structures, some organisations may simply have a set of unstructured files in a file-system directory.

9.6.4   MESSAGE BROKERS

Data sources may be available via data streams, usually supported by message brokers. A message broker is a middleware program that translates a message from the formal messaging protocol of the sender to the formal messaging protocol of the receiver. Instead of communicating with each other, the sender and the receiver communicate only with the message broker.

In data streams, message brokers usually work under a publish/subscribe model, where the receiver subscribes information. Then, when the publisher sends the information to the message broker, the message will be redirected to all its subscribers.

Message brokers provide increased security because the receiver and the sender never communicate with one another. They also provide increased integrability, as applications that communicate with the message broker do not need to have the same interface.

However, message brokers are not the best option when it comes to performance, as they add an intermediate hop which incurs overhead. They may also cause single-point failure problems, but technology is available to minimise this problem.

9.7   INFORMATION MANAGEMENT

Some common data storage systems are centralised databases, decentralised databases, web-based databases, cloud databases, data lakes, and object storage. In the following sections, we discuss these and their management.

9.7.1   CENTRALISED DATABASES

A database that supports data located at a single site is called a centralised database. Data are accessed from these databases via database management systems (DBMS), as visualised in Figure 9.5. A DBMS is a collection of programmes that manage the database structure and control access to the data stored in the database (Loebbecke & Powell, 1998).

DBMS makes data management more efficient and effective for the following reasons:

- Data sharing: End users have better access to more data and to better-managed data, thus allowing them to respond more quickly to changes.

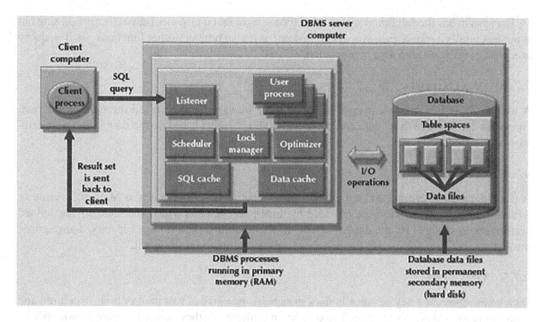

FIGURE 9.5 Standalone DBMS system (Loebbecke & Powell, 1998).

- Data security: A DBMS provides a framework for better enforcement of data privacy and security policies.
- Data integration: A DBMS promotes an integrated view of the organisation's operations and a better understanding of the overall picture. Users can see how actions in one unit of the organisation affect other units.
- Data access: The DBMS provides fast answers to queries. In database terms, a query is a specific request issued to the DBMS to manipulate data.
- Decision-making: Better-managed data and improved data access make it possible to generate better-quality information, thus leading to better decisions – and faster ones.
- Less data inconsistency: At times, similar data are stored in different formats and in different files. A DBMS can reduce data redundancy and inconsistency by minimising isolated files wherein data are repeated. The DBMS may not eliminate data redundancy, but it will certainly help control it.

9.7.2 DECENTRALISED DATABASES

A distributed or decentralised database is a collection of multiple logically interrelated databases distributed over a computer network. A distributed DBMS is a software system that permits the management of the distributed database and makes the distribution transparent to users (Karim et al., 2009).

The distributed database is not simply a collection of files that can be stored individually at each network node. In a distributed database, distributed data should be logically related according to some structural formalism, and access to data should be at a high level via a common interface.

Data are stored at several sites. Each site should have a single processor. Even if some sites have multiprocessors, the distributed DBMS is not concerned with the storage and management of data on them.

The processors at sites are interconnected by a computer network rather than a multiprocessor configuration. Importantly, although they are connected, processors have their own operating systems and operate independently.

The system has the full functionality of a DBMS. Note that it provides transaction processing but is not essentially a transaction-processing system, as it also provides other functions, such as query processing and structured data organisation.

9.7.3   WEB DATABASES

A web database is a database system designed to be managed and accessed through the Internet. Operators can manage these data and present analytical results based on the data in the web database application.

9.7.4   CLOUD DATABASE

A cloud database is created and maintained using cloud data services such as Microsoft Azure or Amazon AWS. These services are provided by third-party vendors. These services provide defined performance measures for the database, including availability, data storage capacity, and required throughput, but may not specify the necessary infrastructure to implement it.

9.7.5   DATA LAKES

Data lakes represent a key advance in data storage. A data lake is vast pool of both structured and unstructured raw data at any scale. The data are not filtered as they would be in a data warehouse. The structure of the data or schema is not defined when data are captured, and the data can be stored from any source.

9.7.6   OBJECT STORAGE

The concept of object storage was introduced in the early 1990s (Factor et al., 2005). Object storage systems allow the retention of massive amounts of unstructured data. Object storage is used for purposes such as storing pictures, files, songs, and videos on Facebook, Spotify, or Dropbox.

9.8   DATA FUSION AND INTEGRATION

Data are processed and integrated through a data fusion process and transformed into an eMaintenance information warehouse system. Data quality needs to be considered throughout the process, from data collection to data fusion and integration (Aljumaili, 2016).

9.8.1   PROBLEMS WITH DATA FUSION

The majority of issues with data fusion derive from information coming from different sensors. The data fusion process should be able to deal with the following multisensory data fusion problems:

- Imprecision and uncertainty: Not all collected data are perfect. To some extent, they are likely to be imprecise, and measurements may have a level of uncertainty.
- Spurious data: Data could be noisy, making them hard to interpret.
- Outliers: Data could contain outliers, possibly due to faulty or imprecise measurement.
- Modality: Data may be heterogeneous containing a combination of visual, auditory, and physical measurements.
- Conflict: Different sensors could report conflicting data. These are difficult to fuse.
- Operational timing: Data may have timing variations. In distributed fusion settings, different parts of the data may traverse different routes before reaching the fusion centre, possibly causing data to arrive out-of-sequence.
- Dynamic vs static: Some data may come from a phenomenon that is time-invariant while other data are time-variant, i.e. changing over time.

- Dimensionality: Data may be collected in different dimensions, thus calling for the pre-processing of the measurement data, either locally at sensor nodes or globally at the fusion centre to be compressed into desired dimensions.
- Correlation: Some sensor nodes are likely to be exposed to the same external noise biasing their measurements; if such data dependencies are not accounted for, the algorithm may yield inconsistent results.
- Alignment/registration: Different sensors will have different local frames. Their data must be set into a standard frame before fusion can occur.

Other important terms in data fusion:

- Data association: As the term suggests, this involves discovering interesting relations between variables, often quite disparate ones, in large databases.
- Processing framework: Data can be fused in a centralised or decentralised manner. The decentralised method is usually preferred in wireless sensor networks, as it decreases the communicational burden required by a centralised approach and allows each sensor node to process its own locally collected data (Khaleghi et al., 2013).

9.9 DATA QUALITY

The list of potential problems in data fusion that we give above suggests the importance of data quality and the need for organisations to understand what data quality means to them. In developing data quality measures, an organisation must determine what is to be measured and what set of data quality dimensions are essential to meet its goals and accommodate its specific operations (Lee et al., 2016).

A list of 20 attributes of data quality (Knight & Burn, 2005) is provided below:

- accurate and error-free,
- consistent format, compatible with previous data,
- secure and appropriately restricted,
- timely and up to date,
- complete and sufficiently deep,
- concise and compactly represented,
- reliable and correct,
- accessible and easily retrievable,
- available and physically accessible,
- objective, unbiased, and impartial,
- relevant, applicable, and helpful,
- usable,
- understandable, unambiguous, and easily comprehended,
- appropriate amount with respect to quantity or volume,
- believable, true, and credible,
- discoverable, easily found, and clearly linked to the task at hand,
- reputable in terms of source and/or content,
- useful, applicable, and helpful for the task at hand,
- efficient and able to quickly meet the information needs for the task at hand,
- added value, wherein the use of information provides extra benefits (Knight & Burn, 2005).

9.10 COMMUNICATION

Communication is a key aspect of AI, as the end goal is to have machines communicate with users and vice versa. Recent developments in AI have introduced new challenges and opportunities for communication. Technologies such as machine translation of human languages, spoken dialogue systems like Siri, algorithms capable of producing publishable journalistic content, and social robots are all designed to communicate with users in a human-like way (Gunkel, 2020).

9.10.1 Machine Learning in Communications

ML algorithms are used in various fields of communications, from smart infrastructure and IoT to image and video communication. Figure 9.6 shows the wide range of their applicability (Samek et al., 2017). We discuss some of these applications in the following sections.

9.10.1.1 Routing in Communication Networks

Routing has a significant impact on the network's performance, and it is a well-studied topic in communications. ML methods have been used to tackle different types of routing problems in the past, including shortest path routing, adaptive routing, and multicasting routing.

An algorithm has been proposed for package routing in dynamically changing networks based on reinforcement learning. This algorithm learns a routing policy which balances the route length with the possibility of congestion along the popular routes. Others have approached the routing problem with genetic algorithms. Here alternative routes are created by crossover and mutation of the existing routes. Genetic algorithms have been also used to tackle the multicasting routing problem which emerges when data are sent to multiple receivers through a communication network. In addition, in mobile ad hoc networks, the construction of multicast trees has been addressed using genetic algorithms. Here, additional objectives are added to the optimisation, such as bounded end-to-end delay and energy efficiency.

It is also possible to use ML techniques for throughput or traffic prediction in communication networks. This is an important topic, as a dynamic throughput control and allocation allows users to fulfil the quality of service (QoS) requirements, while efficiently utilising the network resources. For instance, neural networks can be used to predict variable-bit-rate video traffic to dynamically allocate throughput for RT video applications.

Traffic identification is another important topic for network operators as it helps them to manage their networks, assure the QoS and deploy security measures. Here, machine learning methods

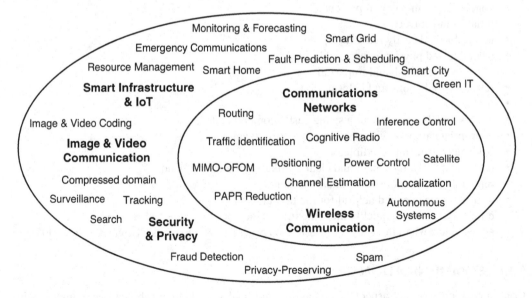

FIGURE 9.6 Applications of machine learning in different areas of communications (Samek et al., 2017).

recognise statistical patterns in the traffic data by analysing packet header and flow-level information (Samek et al., 2017).

9.10.1.2   Wireless Communications

To achieve high efficiency at the desired QoS in wireless systems, it is essential to continuously adapt different parameters of MIMO-OFDM systems, especially the link parameters, to the variations in the communication environment. Various work tackles this parameter selection problem using ML. Due to the dynamic nature of the wireless communication environment, there is a strong need to adapt hardware parameters, for example, to select a suitable set of transmit and receive antennas (Samek et al., 2017).

9.10.1.3   Security, Privacy, and Communications

ML methods play a pivotal role in tackling privacy and security-related problems in communications. For instance, they monitor various network activities and detect anomalies, i.e. events that deviate from the normal network behaviour. Various ML methods have been applied for network anomaly detection in the past.

Other security applications are automatic spam filtering and phishing attack detection. Preserving data privacy is an important security aspect in communications, especially when sensitive data are involved. The design of ML algorithms that respect data privacy has recently gained increased attention. For example, it is possible to build a decision-tree classifier from corrupted data without significant loss in accuracy compared to the classifiers built with the original data, but it is not possible to accurately estimate the original values in the corrupted data records. We can hide private information from the algorithm, but still obtain accurate classification results (Samek et al., 2017).

9.10.1.4   Smart Services, Smart Infrastructure, and Internet of Things

With the recent advances in communication technology, "smart" applications have gained increased currency (e.g. smart homes, smart cities, smart grids, and IoT). ML algorithms are often the core part of such applications. For instance, researchers used a neural network-based prediction algorithm to forecast and manage the power production of a photovoltaic plant. Other researchers applied similar techniques to traffic light control in smart cities or context-aware computing in IoT.

ML can also help detect malicious events before they occur, for example, in smart-grid networks. Tasks such as the prediction of a resource usage, estimation of task response times, data traffic monitoring, and optimal scheduling can also be approached through learning algorithms (Samek et al., 2017).

9.10.1.5   Image and Video Communications

ML methods have been used for various tasks in multimedia communication and processing. Signal compression is one important field of application of these methods, as it is part of almost every multimedia communication system. Tracking is another well-studied topic in ML which is also relevant in multimedia communication.

New methods include a new generation of object tracking methods based on deep neural networks and tracking algorithms which make use of the compressed video representation. In multimedia applications, such as video streaming, the quality of the displayed video is extremely important. Different ML methods have been proposed to estimate the subjective quality of images perceived by a human (Samek et al., 2017).

9.11   COGNITIVE COMPUTING

Cognitive computing is an emerging paradigm of intelligent computing methodologies and systems that implements computational intelligence by autonomous inferences and perceptions mimicking the mechanisms of the brain. On the basis of cognitive computing, next-generation cognitive computers and autonomous intelligent systems that think and feel may be designed and implemented (Ahmed et al., 2017; Wang, 2009).

We generally define cognitive computing in terms of its functions, as it is not easy to define precisely and completely. Thus, we may say cognitive computing is a computational environment comprised of the following:

1. A high-performance computing infrastructure powered by special processors, such as multicore CPUs, GPUs, TPUs, and neuromorphic chips;
2. A software development environment with intrinsic support for parallel and distributed computing, powered by the underlying computing infrastructure;
3. Software libraries and ML algorithms for extracting information and knowledge from unstructured data sources;
4. A data analytics environment whose processes and algorithms mimic human cognitive processes; and
5. Query languages and APIs for accessing the services of the cognitive computing environment.

In cognitive computing, classic symbolic and rule-based approaches to problems such as machine translation and speech-to-speech translation are being superseded by statistical learning approaches. For example, consider the problem of recognising handwritten digits. Rule-based approaches entail developing a number of rules which aim to explicitly capture ways different users may write digits. This results in too many rules. Furthermore, additional rules are needed to accommodate new users who might write a digit differently from the ways that are incorporated in the current rule set.

In contrast, artificial neural network (ANN) approaches use several small pieces of evidence in the form of features and combine them to produce higher-level features. ANN approaches are more robust as they perform better with data which are not seen in the training phase (Gudivada et al., 2016).

9.11.1 Theoretical Foundations for Cognitive Computing

Theories and methodologies of cognitive computing are inspired by the latest advances in cognitive informatics and denotational mathematics. This section elaborates some of these (Wang, 2009).

9.11.1.1 Cognitive Informatics for Cognitive Computing

The fundamental theories and methodologies underpinning cognitive computing can be called cognitive informatics. Cognitive informatics is a cutting-edge and multidisciplinary research field that tackles the fundamental problems shared by modern informatics, computation, software engineering, AI, computational intelligence, cybernetics, cognitive science, neuropsychology, medical science, systems science, philosophy, linguistics, economics, management science, and life sciences. The development of and the cross-fertilisation between these science and engineering disciplines have led to a range of emerging research areas known as cognitive informatics.

The architecture of the theoretical framework of cognitive informatics includes the information-matter-energy (IME) model, the layered reference model of the brain (LRMB), the object-attribute-relation (OAR) model of information representation in the brain, the cognitive informatics model of the brain, natural intelligence (NI), neural informatics (NeI), the mechanisms of human perception processes, and cognitive computing (Wang, 2009).

9.11.1.2 Neural Informatics for Cognitive Computing

NeI is a branch of cognitive informatics, where memory and its neural and logical models are recognised as the foundation and platform of any form of natural or artificial intelligence. The major memory organ that accommodates acquired information and knowledge in the brain is the cerebrum or the cerebral cortex, in particular, the premotor cortex in the frontal lobe, the temporal lobe, sensory cortex in the frontal lobe, visual cortex in the occipital lobe, primary motor cortex in the frontal lobe, supplementary motor area in the frontal lobe, and procedural memory in the cerebellum (Wang, 2009).

9.11.1.3 Denotational Mathematics for Cognitive Computing

Whilst formal logic and Boolean algebra are the mathematical foundations of von Neumann computers, the mathematical foundations of cognitive computing are contemporary denotational mathematics. This is a category of expressive mathematical structures dealing with high-level mathematical entities beyond numbers and simple sets such as abstract objects, complex relations, behavioural information, concepts, knowledge, processes, intelligence, and systems (Wang, 2009).

9.11.2 Models of Cognitive Computing

On the basis of cognitive informatics and denotational mathematics, new computing architectures and technologies known as cognitive computing adopt non-von Neumann architectures and extend traditional computing capabilities from imperative data processing to autonomous knowledge processing. The following subsections describe the abstract intelligence and behavioural models of cognitive computing (Wang, 2009).

9.11.2.1 Abstract Intelligence Model of Cognitive Computing

According to functional reductionism, a logical model of the general form of intelligence known as abstract intelligence is needed to formally explain high-level mechanisms of the brain based on observations at the biological, physiological, functional, and logical levels. Building on the logical model of abstract intelligence, the paradigms of intelligence, such as natural, artificial, machinable, and computational intelligence, may be unified into a coherent framework.

Abstract intelligence, αI, is a human enquiry involving both natural and artificial intelligence at embodied neural, cognitive, functional, and logical levels from the bottom up (Wang, 2009).

9.11.2.2 Computational Intelligence Model of Cognitive Computing

Computational intelligence (CoI) is an embodying form of abstract intelligence (αI) that implements intelligent mechanisms and behaviours using computational methodologies and software systems, such as expert systems, fuzzy systems, autonomous computing, intelligent agent systems, genetic/evolutionary systems, and autonomous learning systems.

The fundamental mechanisms of αI can be described by the Generic Abstract Intelligence Model (GAIM). In the GAIM model, different forms of intelligence are described as driving forces that transfer between a pair of abstract objects in the brain, such as data (D), information (I), knowledge (K), and behaviour (B). It is noteworthy that each abstract object is physically retained in a particular type of memory. This is the neural informatics foundation of NI and the physiological evidence showing why NI can be classified into four forms: instructive intelligence I_i, reflective intelligence I_r, cognitive intelligence I_c, and perceptive intelligence I_p.

Cognitive computing aims to implement all forms of abstract intelligence in the GAIM model through imperative computing C_I, autonomic computing C_A, and cognitive computing C_C from the bottom up (Wang, 2009).

9.11.2.3 Behavioural Model of Cognitive Computing

The abstract intelligence model of cognitive computing can be refined by a behavioural model that evolves computing technologies from the conventional imperative behaviours to autonomic and cognitive behaviours.

The entire behavioural space of cognitive computing, B_{CC}, is a layered hierarchical structure that encompasses the imperative behaviours B_I, autonomic behaviours B_A, and cognitive behaviours B_C

from the bottom up, i.e. where B_I is modelled by the event-, time-, and interrupt-driven behaviours, B_A is modelled by the goal- and decision-driven behaviours, and B_C is modelled by the perception- and inference-driven behaviours (Wang, 2009).

9.11.3 APPLICATIONS OF COGNITIVE COMPUTING

Cognitive computing as a generic intelligence/knowledge processing methodology and technology can be applied to develop next-generation cognitive computers and autonomous systems. Two paradigms of cognitive computing, i.e. autonomous agent systems (AAS) and cognitive search engines, mimic higher-level intelligent capabilities of αI and NI beyond conventional imperative computing (Wang, 2009).

9.11.3.1 Autonomous Agent Systems

An AAS is a composition of distributed agents that possesses autonomous computing and decision-making abilities, as well as interactive communication capability with peers and the environment (Wang, 2009).

9.11.3.2 Cognitive Search Engines

Search is not only a basic computational application; it is also a fundamental cognitive process of human brains. Thus, cognitive search engines represent another application paradigm of cognitive computing. Simply stated, a search engine is a cognitive process to allocate and retrieve a piece of knowledge in the memory and/or cyberspace (Wang, 2009).

9.12 DISTRIBUTED LEDGER

The operations of large technical systems, such as railways, for example, with various layers of horizontal and vertical separation, depend on the availability, integrity, and authenticity of data and, in turn, consensus on the overall state of the system. Building consensus among multiple entities in a distributed system with the possibility of entities giving different answers to the same question at different times is described as the Byzantine generals' problem. This is a game theory problem describing the difficulty decentralised parties have arriving at consensus without relying on a trusted central party (Lamport et al., 1982).

Distributed ledgers are a mechanism to create consensus among participants in an untrusted environment. To investigate the properties of distributed ledger and categorise the issues and challenges in the creation of a secure and distributed digital environment for stakeholders, the first step is to collect data. These data must then be analysed, considering the needs of various stakeholders, such as regulating agencies, manufacturers, operators, and service providers, while also addressing the challenges inherent to the creation of data sharing in an untrusted environment (Patwardhan et al., 2021).

Distributed ledgers can be implemented through various mechanisms like blockchain (Nakamoto, 2008) or directed acyclic graphs (Benčić & Žarko, 2018). In what follows, we go into more detail on blockchain.

9.12.1 DISTRIBUTED LEDGER AND BLOCKCHAIN

Blockchain started in the world of cryptocurrencies, such as Bitcoin (Nakamoto, 2008). However, the technology has now spread to other areas of life – including "smart contracts" or trackable, irreversible transactions carried out directly between buyers and sellers without the involvement of a third party. It is widely seen as a possible solution to some of the biggest challenges today in industry, including in areas such as machine-to-machine communication, secure data transactions, component origin, and location tracking. It is also posited as a gateway to new products and services (Roland Berger, 2018).

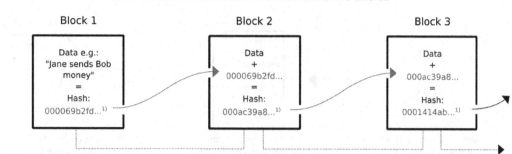

A hash is the unique digital fingerprint of the data which changes
when an element recorded on the blockchain is altered

| Block 1 | Block 2 | Block 3 |

Data e.g.:
"Jane sends Bob money"
=
Hash:
000069b2fd...[1]

Data
+
000069b2fd...
=
Hash:
000ac39a8...[1]

Data
+
000ac39a8...
=
Hash:
0001414ab...[1]

All data used to record a transaction produces a unique hash

The hash is sensitive to the data included in previous blocks...

...making it impossible to change previous blocks

1) Has number is usually 32 digits

FIGURE 9.7   Blockchain digital fingerprint (Roland Berger, 2018).

A blockchain is essentially a decentralised, distributed, shared, and immutable database ledger, or distributed ledger technology (DLT) that stores a registry of assets and transactions across a peer-to-peer network. We go into detail in the next section, but for now, we simply note that it has blocks of data that are chained, timestamped, and validated by data miners (Khan & Salah, 2018). Once transactions are validated and verified by consensus, block data are immutable; in other words, once a piece of information goes in, data cannot be erased or altered.

Blockchains do not actually store the information being transferred; rather, they record the proof of the transaction with what is called the "hash", as shown in Figure 9.7, and explained at greater length in the next section.

This unmatched security makes blockchain relevant for any industrial application that requires an audit trail. The technology grants universal proof of anything that has occurred and been recorded on the blockchain.

9.12.1.1 How Blockchain Works

The design structure is composed mainly of the block header and the block body. The latter contains a list of transactions. The former contains various fields, one of which is a version number to track software on protocol upgrades. The header also includes a timestamp, the block size, and the number of transactions (Khan & Salah, 2018).

Blockchain works by collecting transactions (Antonopoulos, 2014) together in blocks and creates a chain by using the "hash" of the previous block within the newly created block. This connection between the parent and the child has a one-to-one relationship. As more transactions come in, new blocks are created. Since this is an untrusted environment, each participant stores the entire chain of blocks locally and can check the authenticity of any new transaction request. Figure 9.8 (Roland Berger, 2018) gives an overview of the process.

The creation of a new block is called "mining," performed by miners who are the participants competing to find a block with a hash value numerically less than the global set value. The hash calculated for a block uses the hash of all the included transactions, time, and a random value called a nonce (number used only once), where the miner (the entity performing the job of mining) checks through all the possible values for the nonce. This is the work done by the miner; if a legal value is found, the miner shares the crypto-graphically signed block with all the neighbours who check its correctness; if it is found legal, they include it as the latest block.

Finding a legal block requires a large number of calculations repeatedly for different nonce values, and block creation rights are awarded to the miner who first reports the block. This process requires massive amounts of processing power and consumes both time and energy.

Blockchain is a technology that enables transections to be safely and transparently executed

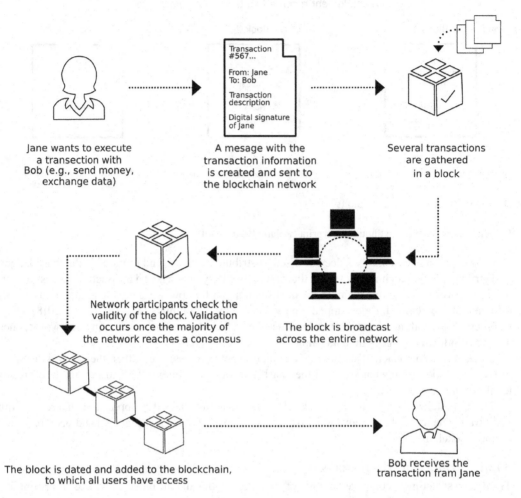

FIGURE 9.8 Blockchain transactions (Roland Berger, 2018).

Blockchain creates a distributed ledger shared by all the participants and any new block consisting of many transactions made by participants can be verified for authenticity by all the other participants before appending it to their copy of the chain. If a malicious agent wants to revert a transaction, it must convince or control more than 50% of the miners to join and generate all the legal blocks after the modified block.

9.12.1.2 Types of Blockchain

Blockchain can be classified as a public (or permissionless), consortium, or private (or permissioned) blockchain:

- Public or permissionless blockchains provide complete anonymity and operate in an untrusted environment with all participants responsible for the authentication of transactions. Anyone can join in.
- Consortium and private or permissioned blockchains are restricted to a particular group of participants who may not be responsible for the authentication of transactions all the time (Monrat et al., 2019).

Permission blockchains provide more privacy and better access control (Khan & Salah, 2018).

Anyone interested in joining a permissionless blockchain may do so without any requirement of authentication or the need to declare their identity. This mechanism of acknowledging the authority of an unknown entity in a permissionless blockchain based on its ability to solve time-consuming mathematical problems and associating the work performed to a unique user through cryptography is called proof-of-work (Nakamoto, 2008).

Consortium and private blockchain based on proof-of-stake and proof-of-authority are capable of significantly higher throughput than proof-of-work (Monrat et al., 2020). Proof-of-stake protocols are a class of consensus mechanisms for blockchains that work by selecting validators in proportion to their quantity of holdings in the associated cryptocurrency; the purpose is to avoid the computational cost of proof-of-work schemes (Wikipedia, 2022c, 2022b). Proof-of-authority is an algorithm used with blockchains; it delivers comparatively fast transactions through a consensus mechanism based on identity as a stake (Wikipedia, 2022a).

Many industries that require data sharing among known partners operating in a closed environment and that attempt to integrate distributed ledgers and smart contracts to ensure secure data transactions do not require the stringent security of public blockchain. In such cases, proof-of-work and the associated computation is not required, simply proof-of-stake (Dinh et al., 2017) or proof-of-authority (De Angelis et al., 2018).

9.12.1.3   Advantages of Blockchain

The main benefits of this technology can be summarised as follows:

- Integrity: Once a piece of information goes in, or a block is written, it cannot be altered.
- Traceability: Problems can be easily located; furthermore, there is no central point of failure.
- Security: Blockchains are extremely hard to break into, thanks to the block encryption; to hack a blockchain we would need a yet unrealistic amount of computational power. Furthermore, each user participating in the network is provided with a unique identity, linked to the user's account.
- Faster transactions: Blockchain-based operations are faster than standard contracts and transactions – the latter are time-consuming and costly.
- No need for a central authority: Blocks are ordered by a decentralised time-stamping algorithm, which allows users to vote on the validity of database updates and eventually agree on the correct order of transactions and a shared system state at any given point. As a result, the users of a blockchain system can interact without the need for a central authority to resolve conflicting views of the correct order of transactions (Hawlitschek et al., 2018).

9.12.1.4   Uses of Blockchain

The use of blockchain has been explored in various domains, including the following:

1. Blockchain has been applied in healthcare data management (Khatoon, 2020; Kuo et al., 2017) to provide patient data protection regulation while opening new opportunities for data management and the convenience of data sharing.
2. Blockchain has been used in IIoT to provide product traceability, smart diagnostics and maintenance, product certification, machine-to-machine transaction, supplier identity, reputation tracking, and registry of assets and inventory (Bahga & Madisetti, 2016; Brody & Pureswaran, 2014).
3. Blockchain has been applied to vehicular networks to provide user privacy, information security, remote track and trace, regulatory compliance, and remote software updates (Astarita et al., 2020; Dorri et al., 2017).

4. Blockchain has been used in supply chain scenarios to connect the chain of provider, producer, processor, distributor, retailer, and consumer while optimising transparency and traceability (Caro et al., 2018; Francisco & Swanson, 2018).

5. Blockchain has been used for land records management, including process redesign, technology readiness, and socio-political requirements (Benbunan-Fich & Castellanos, 2018).

However, there is still a need to move from a technology-driven to a need-driven approach, with accompanying changes in technology and administrative processes to ensure information integrity (Ølnes et al., 2017).

9.12.1.5   Limitations of Blockchain

In spite of the huge advantages of blockchain, some limitations should be acknowledged:

- Privacy protection: The generation of a decentralised consensus requires the public availability of historical data and the pseudonymous disclosure of the various transacting parties. Thus, privacy protection is a particular challenge (Hawlitschek et al., 2018).
- Reliance on predefined rules: As autonomous transactional database systems, blockchains rely on the correctness of predefined rules; thus, it is crucial to make sure they are secure, reliable, and accurate.
- Throughput: As the frequency of transactions in blockchain increases, the blockchain network's throughput will need to be improved (Yli-Huumo et al., 2016).
- Power use: A real-time ledger is one of the reasons for the increased consumption; every time it creates a new node, it communicates with every other node (DataFlair, 2018).
- Uncertain regulatory status: Smart money is created and controlled by central governments around the world. It is difficult for blockchain applications such as Bitcoin to be accepted by established financial institutions (DataFlair, 2018).

9.12.1.6   Blockchain and Smart Contracts

Smart contracts are computer protocols intended to facilitate, verify, or enforce the negotiation or performance of a contract. More simply stated, a smart contract is an agreement or set of rules that govern a business transaction. The smart contract is stored on the blockchain and is executed automatically as part of a transaction. For example, it could encapsulate the terms and conditions of travel insurance; the contract is automatically executed when the terms are not met, for example, if a train is delayed more than a pre-established length of time.

It is important to remember that smart contracts are not "legal contracts": rather, they are simply pieces of code running on top of a blockchain network, able to deploy "if-then-else logic" to enable the execution of "rules" (although these may be derived from legal contractual obligations). When the conditions predefined in the smart contract are fulfilled, the smart contract will auto-execute a transaction according to the defined arbitrary rules (Figure 9.9).

Smart contracts have the following features:

- Fast: Smart contracts represent software code to automate tasks and, as such, can be operated quickly, while standard contracts take time and money.
- Safe: It is difficult, if not impossible, to hack the smart contract. Encryption keeps the documents safe.
- Trustworthy: All the transactions are encrypted and saved on the ledger; data cannot be lost.
- Autonomous: There are no intermediaries; users can make their own contracts, as execution is managed automatically by the network.
- Cost-effective: Smart contracts save money because intermediaries are eliminated (Roland Berger, 2018).

Blockchain enables contracts without the involvement of third party

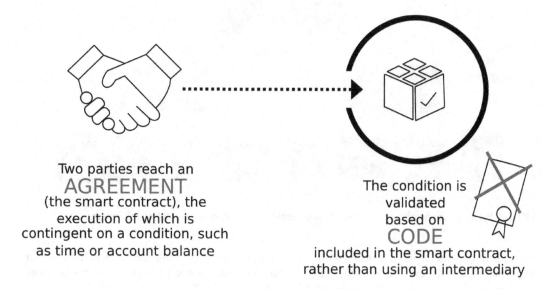

Two parties reach an
AGREEMENT
(the smart contract), the
execution of which is
contingent on a condition, such
as time or account balance

The condition is
validated
based on
CODE
included in the smart contract,
rather than using an intermediary

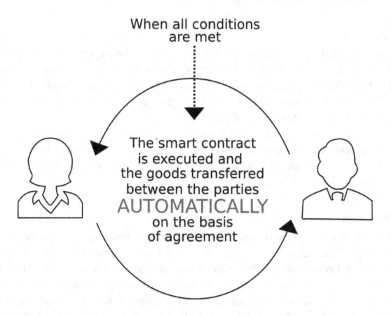

When all conditions
are met

The smart contract
is executed and
the goods transferred
between the parties
AUTOMATICALLY
on the basis
of agreement

FIGURE 9.9   Smart contracts (Roland Berger, 2018).

9.12.1.7   Blockchain Frameworks in Use

Different enterprise blockchain platforms are available and applicable to real business scenarios. Figure 9.10 shows the distinctions between the two families of DLT, i.e. private/permissioned vs. public/permissionless, together with examples of real implementations (In2Dreams, 2018). The examples are explained below.

9.12.1.8   Bitcoin

Bitcoin's blockchain is essentially a distributed ledger system recording transactions taking place in the Bitcoin network. This peer-to-peer payment network operates on a cryptographic protocol. Each

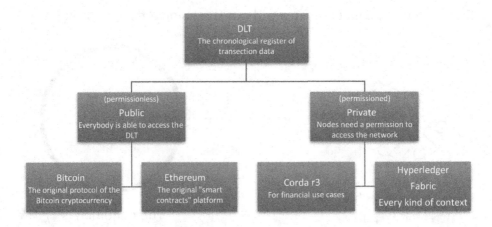

FIGURE 9.10 Classification of distributed ledger technology and some examples (In2Dreams, 2018).

transaction has one or more transaction inputs. These represent previous transactions from which the present user has received Bitcoins. Each transaction also has one or more transaction outputs; these are the users who are going to get the Bitcoins (Fersht, 2018).

9.12.1.9 Ethereum

Ethereum is a decentralised platform running smart contracts. This open software platform is based on blockchain technology, has a built-in cryptocurrency called ether, and is programmed in a language called Solidity. The Ethereum network is a virtual state machine called the Ethereum Virtual Machine (EVM). This distributed global computer gives a platform for developers to build and deploy decentralised transactions and applications.

Ethereum is currently being used in some countries for land title services, drawing on the data trail inherent to blockchain to record property ownership and changes over time. It is also being used to protect e-services, smart devices, and national data, in areas such as national health, legislative, and judicial registries (Fersht, 2018).

9.12.1.10 R3 Corda

Launched in 2015, R3 is a consortium of some prominent financial institutions that have created an open-source distributed ledger platform called Corda (hence the name). Its partners now include more than 60 companies. While Corda was designed with banking in mind, other use cases in the areas of supply chain, healthcare, trade finance, and government are emerging. Corda does not have built-in tokens or cryptocurrency. Furthermore, it is a permissioned blockchain, restricting access to data to those explicitly entitled to them, not to the whole network. It is advantageous for three reasons: its consensus system considers the reality of managing complex financial agreements; it focuses on interoperability; it offers ease of integration with legacy systems (Fersht, 2018).

9.12.1.11 Hyperledger Fabric

Hyperledger is an open-source collaborative effort to advance cross-industry blockchain technologies. Hosted by Linux Foundation, it was launched in 2016. The main goal of Hyperledger is to create enterprise-grade distributed ledger frameworks and codebases. This is a large and growing consortium; by 2018, it already had more than 185 collaborating enterprises across a variety of sectors, including finance, banking, IoT, supply chain, manufacturing, and technology. Hyperledger Fabric is one of eight ongoing Hyperledger projects. Its modular structure offers an attractive blockchain framework for enterprise solutions; notably, it allows plug-and-play components in both consensus and membership services (Fersht, 2018).

9.12.1.12 Comparison of Distributed Ledger Technologies

Table 9.2 comparatively sums up the various DLT technologies (In2Dreams, 2018).

9.13 INFORMATION SECURITY

As the preceding sections of the chapter have made clear, security is a key concern in the development of technology, especially in an era of cloud computing and Big Data. This section provides an overview of information security control requirements when managing a corporate IT project or an existing corporate IT asset and the project or asset's compliance with standards, policies, and the security assurance framework (SAF). Using a railway company as an example, we suggest guidelines to ensure appropriate information security controls are built and operating for corporate IT systems and services throughout their lifecycle (Burrell & Inwood, 2016).

We propose four classification levels, based on the levels of data sensitivity: public, internal, confidential, and secret (Burrell & Inwood, 2016). Table 9.3 indicates how these can be applied. We note, however, that this is taken from the railway industry. Each organisation should obviously set the appropriate classifications for a system or service based on the data it uses.

Table 9.4 (Burrell & Inwood, 2016) shows a checklist to identify the controls applicable to a project based on a certain data classification. This information security control framework project spreadsheet is designed to help project managers and/or information owners understand which controls should be implemented. Although this is taken from the railway industry and the work of Burrell and Inwood (2016), it can be adapted and applied elsewhere.

Controls can be mandatory or non-mandatory:

1. A mandatory control is considered critical to adequately protect information and ensure compliance with the organisation's policies and standards.
2. A non-mandatory control is a discretionary control assigned by project managers and/or information owners.

Table 9.4 can be updated with further controls when personally identifiable information (PII) is contained in the project, as shown in Table 9.5, again taken from the rail industry and the work of Burrell and Inwood (2016).

A given project may be unable to apply a particularly recommended control, generally because the software is inadequate. Two possible ways to deal with this issue are risk acceptance or exception waivers:

Risk acceptance: In this case, the organisation accepts the risk, generally in writing. For example, if a control cannot be implemented for at least 12 months, then rather than turning to a waiver process, the organisation will provide a written agreement saying it accepts the risk. The risk will be documented in a risk register.

Exception waiver: In this case, the recommended control is not applied. The organisation may opt to document a security exception to policy, whereby an exception is defined as authorised non-compliance based on the business requirements exceeding the related risks. An exception can be accepted through a documented security exception waiver process. An exception waiver, i.e. an Exception to Information Security Policy Statement of Authorisation, can be authorised for a maximum of 12 months in certain situations. The exception waiver describes further controls that can be implemented to mitigate risk and includes:

- A summary of requirements,
- A description of non-compliance, and
- The identified risks.

TABLE 9.2
Comparison of Blockchain Platforms and Their Characteristics (In2Dreams, 2018)

	Open source	Currency	Public	Description of platform	Consensus	Governance	Smart contracts
Ethereum	Yes	• Ether • Tokens via smart contracts	• Yes • (Permission less, public or private)	Generic blockchain platform	• Mining based on proof-of-work (PoW) • Ledger level	Ethereum developers	• Yes • Smart contract code(Solidity)
Hyperledger Fabric	Yes	• None • Possibility for currency and tokens via chain code	• No • Private (Permisioned)	Modular blockchain platform	• Freedom of choice between more types of consensus • Transaction level	Linux Foundation	• Yes • Smart contract code (Go, Java)
R3 Corda	Yes	None	• No • Private (Permissioned)	Specialised distributed ledger platform for financial industry (and possible broad use)	• Freedom of choice between more types of consensus • Transaction level	R3	• Yes • Smart contract code (Kotlin, Java) • Smarts ledger contract (legal prose)
Bitcoin	Yes	Bitcoin	Yes	Generic blockchain platform	• Mining based on proof- of-work (PoW) • Ledger level	Bitcoin developers	No
Stellar	Yes	Lumens	Yes	Distributed payment infrastructure, micropayments -	Stellar consensus protocol (SCP)	Stellar developers	Yes

TABLE 9.3
Classification of Data Sensitivity (Burrell & Inwood, 2016)

Classification	Anticipated Audience	Description
Public	Media, railway line neighbours, and the general public	Information authorised for release by the railway company
Internal	All rail staff, contractors, and key business partners	Information freely available within the railway company
Confidential	Defined groups with a need to know	Information with a possibly significant impact if available outside the authorised groups
Secret	Defined individuals with a need to know	Information with a possibly significant impact if available to more than authorised individuals

TABLE 9.4
Checklist to Identify Mandatory Controls Applicable to a Project Containing Information of a Particular Data Classification (Burrell & Inwood, 2016)

	Control		Public	Internal	Confidential
1	**Authentication**				
	1.1	Authentication credentials securely protected in transit and at rest	x	x	x
	1.2	Account ownership and responsibility		x	x
	1.3	Use of strategic user authentication system		x	x
	1.4	Use of multi-factor authentication when connecting from an untrusted device			x
2	**Password management**				
	2.1	Enforcement of password controls		x	x
	2.2	Passwords are not displayed on screen by default		x	x
	2.3	One-time passwords are distributed securely		x	x
	2.4	Users can select their passwords		x	x
3	**Asset management**				
	3.1	Business system owner must take responsibility for information security of the asset	x	x	x
	3.2	Information is clearly labelled to communicate its sensitivity	x	x	x
	3.3	The lifecycle of the asset is mapped and how it is processed is described	x	x	x
	3.4	Access right requests are formally documented and approved	x	x	x
	3.5	Use of approved process for secure disposal of storage media		x	x
	3.6	Segregation of duties			x
	3.7	Asset permissions are reviewed periodically		x	x
4	Account management				
	4.1	Appropriate access rights in place (read/write/edit/delete)	x	x	x

(Continued)

TABLE 9.4 (*Continued*)

Checklist to Identify Mandatory Controls Applicable to a Project Containing Information of a Particular Data Classification (Burrell & Inwood, 2016)

	Control		Public	Internal	Confidential
	4.2	Ability to set expiry dates on accounts		x	x
	4.3	Ability to detect inactive accounts and disable them		x	x
	4.4	Login banner is presented to the user	x	x	x
	4.5	Session termination after defined period		x	x
5	**Data in transit**				
	5.1	Data secured with strong encryption while in transit			x
6	**Data at rest**				
	6.1	Data secured with strong encryption while at rest if indicated in an information security assurance questionnaire (ISAQ)			x
7	**Removable and physical media**				
	7.1	Use of encryption for removable media			x
	7.2	Paper documentation and physical media must be sent using a secure courier service			x
8	**Auditing/logging**				
	8.1	Audit records for authentication events	x	x	x
	8.2	Audit records for authorisation changes	x	x	x
	8.3	Integrity of audit records	x	x	x
	8.4	Reliable time stamps	x	x	x
	8.5	Ability to audit account disabling	x	x	x
	8.6	Ability to audit account termination	x	x	x

TABLE 9.5

Two Further Controls to be Implemented when Personally Identifiable Information (PII) is Contained within the Project (Burrell & Inwood, 2016)

	Control	
9	Personally Identifiable Information (PII)	
	9.1	Registration with organisation's data protection officer
	9.2	Documentation regarding how the DPA principles are met

The waiver will also require the organisation to derive a clear plan of action and create timescales. The two types of waiver exceptions are temporary non-compliance and non-compliance pending change to policy.

- Temporary non-compliance: This waiver exception is applied when immediate compliance with policy would unacceptably disrupt business activities and is not feasible. However, there is a time limit on this: the maximum allowable period for temporary non-compliance is 12 months. Therefore, a plan to work towards compliance should be developed and agreed upon.

- Non-compliance pending change to policy: A better solution is available and, as such, will be written into the official policy. Therefore, an exception is granted until the policy is updated. Again, there is a time limit: the maximum allowable period for non-compliance pending policy change is 12 months (Burrell & Inwood, 2016).

9.14 CYBERSECURITY

Cybersecurity is a serious concern today, and, as such, it merits a separate section in the chapter. Simply defined, cybersecurity is the "ability to protect or defend the use of cyberspace from cyberattacks," and cyberspace is "a global domain within the information environment consisting of the interdependent network of information systems infrastructures including the Internet, telecommunications networks, computer systems, and embedded processors and controllers" (Kissel, 2013).

Types of cyberattacks seem almost limitless: malware, phishing, man-in-the-middle attacks, DDoS, cross-site scripting, SQL injection, botnets, social botnets, espionage-based attacks that steal data and information, drive-by-downloads, last-mile interceptions, transmission bugs/intercepts, critical infrastructure, cyber kidnapping, cyber extortion, and hacktivism.

Cyberattacks have negative consequences, including reputational damage, heavy costs, and service unavailability, and, as such, can affect the sustainability of the system, with subsequent economic, environmental, and social impacts. Thus, cybersecurity is one of the main prerequisites to achieve operational excellence in any industry utilising complex technical system-of-systems empowered by AI and taking a data-driven approach. In this section, we discuss cybersecurity in the context of the railway, but the discussion is equally applicable to any industrial domain operating complex technical systems.

9.14.1 Challenges and Responses

Complex technical systems, such as railways, depend on the collaboration of multiple stakeholders. Consequently, issues of developing and maintaining digital trust in secure data sharing become a core aspect of future growth. The challenges of maintaining data integrity, knowledge of ownership, and security of stored data must be met and resolved to create a trustable platform for data sharing among the stakeholders. These challenges can be addressed by using blockchain and smart contracts.

Although stakeholders mostly perceive digitalisation as an opportunity, they also see it as a challenge - specifically in the context of cybersecurity. Cyberattacks are rapidly growing, threatening complex critical infrastructures and creating concerns about the privacy and security of the data underlying these infrastructures. In the railway industry, digitalisation in operation and maintenance provides such benefits as sustainability, availability, reliability, maintainability, capacity, safety, and security. However, cybersecurity is the weakest link in digitalisation of the transport system.

One problem is that railway asset management is complex; it involves many stakeholders collaborating, cooperating, and also competing. In addition, from a technological perspective, railway asset management is highly heterogeneous with a vast number of technologies deployed at different stakeholder organisations. The railway system (infrastructure, signalling, and rolling stock) is a complex technical system consisting of many items with a long lifecycle. It should therefore be studied in the context of a complex technical system with a vast number of stakeholders. Thus, dealing with cybersecurity requires a holistic approach.

Essentially, cybersecurity in a globalised economy needs to serve the constraints of individual stake-holding organisations while simultaneously facilitating the adaptation to joint multistakeholder constraints. In this context, cybersecurity needs to provide mechanisms to manage not only common interests between stakeholders but also possible conflicts of interest.

It is commonly understood that distributed ledger implemented in blockchain ushered in a new era of digital currency. Yet the underlying technology addresses much deeper issues of trust, integrity, and decentralised consensus in a digital environment. Blockchain implements secure, distributed append-only data storage with global consensus, with strong resistance to cyber threats. Smart contracts are event-driven executable codes capable of accessing, evaluating, and appending data on the blockchain. Together, blockchain and smart contracts provide a robust foundation for the creation of secure and decentralised data and a model exchange platform supporting authentication and consensus. Consensus-based cybersecurity is believed to be an appropriate approach to facilitate issues and challenges related to information assurance in industrial contexts.

The reliability of a sector-wide cybersecurity technology chain is dependent on the maturity of cybersecurity in individual organisations in the chain. Hence, an overarching cybersecurity mechanism must consider the variability of this system-of-systems. This is one of the issues addressed by the AI Factory concept.

9.14.2 A CYBERSECURITY FRAMEWORK

There is a need for researchers to develop a generic cybersecurity framework for the digitalised railway (and digitalised industry more generally) to facilitate proactive cybersecurity and threat intelligence-sharing. Some of the main security concerns are discussed in the following sections. A viable framework should be able to handle these concerns. Researchers recently developed such a framework (i.e. OSA-CBM) by integrating open system architecture (OSA) and condition-based maintenance (CMB) technologies at different stages (Kour, 2020).

9.14.3 ACCESS CONTROL SECURITY

Access control security is the key to safeguarding system safety. Access control security comprises such issues as global identity management, customer identity authentication, and the single login problem. There are several basic approaches to access control security, including the following: access control list (ACL), role-based access control (RBAC) (Edwards, 1996), task-based access control (TBAC), team-based access control (TMAC), spatial access control for collaborative environment (SPACE), and context-aware access control (Tolone et al., 2005).

9.14.4 INFORMATION TRANSMISSION SECURITY

Enterprise service bus (ESB) technology or OPC unified architecture (OPC UA) is used when several systems share data and service in the railway information-sharing platform. Yet information security remains a basic problem in the transmission process. Web and cloud services are other information-sharing platforms.

9.14.5 DATA STORAGE SECURITY

Data storage security is a significant concern in railway information-sharing. Using technology such as cloud data storage and management of decentralised computing technology can improve the safety of important data. At the same time, however, the technology requires a complex system structure and leads to complex management problems. Problems of off-site storage, disaster recovery, data recovery, security technology, and information-sharing platforms must all be resolved to ensure data security.

REFERENCES

Abadi, D. J. (2009). Data management in the cloud: challenges and opportunities. *IEEE Data Engineering Bulletin, 32*(1), 3–12. https://doi.org/10.2200/s00456ed1v01y201211dtm032

Ahmed, S. N., Gagnon, J., Naeem, R., & Wang, J. (2017). New methods and equipment for three-dimensional laser scanning, mapping and profiling underground mine cavities. In M. Hudyma & Y. Potvin (Eds.), *UMT 2017: Proceedings of the First International Conference on Underground Mining Technology* (pp. 467-473). Perth: Australian Centre for Geomechanics. https://doi.org/10.36487/ACG_rep/1710_37_Ahmedhttps://doi.org/10.36487/acg_rep/1710_37_ahmed

Aljumaili, M. (2016). *Data quality Assessment: Applied in Maintenance Operation and Maintenance Engineering.* Doctoral Dissertation, LuleåUniversity of Technology. https://doi.org/10.13140/RG.2.1.3386.6641

Al-Qamash, A., Soliman, I., Abulibdeh, R., & Saleh, M. (2018). Cloud, fog, and edge computing: a software engineering perspective. *2018 International Conference on Computer and Applications (ICCA),* 276–284. https://doi.org/10.1109/COMAPP.2018.8460443

Amazon. (2022). *Amazon S3 Service Level Agreement.* https://aws.amazon.com/s3/sla/

Antonopoulos, A. M. (2014). *Mastering bitcoin: Unlocking digital cryptocurrencies.* O'Reilly Media, Inc.

Armbrust, M., Fox, A., Griffith, R., Joseph, A. D., Katz, R., Konwinski, A., Lee, G., Patterson, D., Rabkin, A., Stoica, I., & Zaharia, M. (2009). Above the clouds: A Berkeley view of cloud computing. *Communications of the ACM, 53*(4), 50–58. https://doi.org/10.1145/1721654.1721672

Astarita, V., Giofrè, V. P., Mirabelli, G., & Solina, V. (2020). A review of blockchain-based systems in transportation. *Information (Switzerland), 11*(1), 21. https://doi.org/10.3390/info11010021

Bahga, A., & Madisetti, V. K. (2016). Blockchain platform for industrial internet of things. *Journal of Software Engineering and Applications, 09*(10), 533–546. https://doi.org/10.4236/jsea.2016.910036

Benbunan-Fich, R., & Castellanos, A. (2018). Digitalization of land records: From paper to blockchain. *International Conference on Information Systems (ICIS): 2018 Proceedings.* https://aisel.aisnet.org/icis2018/ebusiness/Presentations/15

Benčić, F. M., & Žarko, I. P. (2018). Distributed ledger technology: Blockchain compared to directed acyclic graph. *2018 IEEE 38th International Conference on Distributed Computing Systems (ICDCS),* 1569–1570. https://doi.org/10.1109/ICDCS.2018.00171

Brody, P., & Pureswaran, V. (2014). Device democracy: Saving the future of the internet of things. *IBM, September, 1*(1), 15. https://public.dhe.ibm.com/common/ssi/ecm/gb/en/gbe03620usen/GBE03620USEN.PDF

Burrell, M., & Inwood, J. (2016). Information security controls framework: Guidelines for Implementation. Network Rail UK. https://www.networkrail.co.uk/running-the-railway/railway-upgrade-plan/

Caro, M. P., Ali, M. S., Vecchio, M., & Giaffreda, R. (2018). Blockchain-based traceability in agri-food supply chain management: A practical implementation. *2018 IoT Vertical and Topical Summit on Agriculture – Tuscany,* 1–4. https://doi.org/10.1109/IOT-TUSCANY.2018.8373021

DataFlair. (2018). Advantages and disadvantages of blockchain technology. DataFlair Web Services. https://dataflair.training/blogs/advantages-and-disadvantages-of-blockchain/

De Angelis, S., Aniello, L., Baldoni, R., Lombardi, F., Margheri, A., & Sassone, V. (2018). PBFT vs proof-of-authority: Applying the CAP theorem to permissioned blockchain. *CEUR Workshop Proceedings, 2018,* 1–11. https://eprints.soton.ac.uk/415083/

Dinh, T. T. A., Wang, J., Chen, G., Liu, R., Ooi, B. C., & Tan, K. L. (2017). Blockbench: A framework for analyzing private blockchains. *Proceedings of the ACM SIGMOD International Conference on Management of Data,* 1085–1100. https://doi.org/10.1145/3035918.3064033

Dorri, A., Steger, M., Kanhere, S. S., & Jurdak, R. (2017). Blockchain: A distributed solution to automotive security and privacy. *IEEE Communications Magazine, 55*(12), 119–125. https://doi.org/10.1109/MCOM.2017.1700879

Edwards, W. K. (1996). Policies and roles in collaborative applications. *Proceedings of ACM Conference on Computer-Supported Cooperative Work (CSCW'96),* 11–20. https://doi.org/10.1145/240080.240175

Factor, M., Meth, K., Naor, D., Rodeh, O., & Satran, J. (2005). Object storage: The future building block for storage systems a position paper. *Local to Global Data Interoperability – Challenges and Technologies, 2005, 2005,* 119–123. https://doi.org/10.1109/lgdi.2005.1612479

Fersht, P. (2018). The top 5 enterprise blockchain platforms you need to know about. *HFS Online.* https://www.hfsresearch.com/blockchain/top-5-blockchain-platforms_031618/

Francisco, K., & Swanson, D. (2018). The supply chain has no clothes: Technology adoption of blockchain for supply chain transparency. *Logistics, 2*(1), 2. https://doi.org/10.3390/logistics2010002

Goyal, S. (2013). Software as a service, platform as a service, infrastructure as a service – A review. *International Journal of Computer Science \& Network Solutions, 1*(3), 53–67. https://www. semanticscholar.org/paper/Software-as-a-Service%2C-Platform-as-a-Service%2C-as-a-Goyal/7f8b0b5e73d04f6fa0802108085d9648d74170a7

Gudivada, V. N., Irfan, M. T., Fathi, E., & Rao, D. L. (2016). Cognitive analytics: Going beyond big data analytics and machine learning. In V.N. Gudivada, V.V. Raghavan, V. Govindaraju, & C.R. Rao (Eds.), *Handbook of Statistics* (pp. 169–205). Elsevier.

Gunkel, D. J. (2020). *An introduction to communication and artificial intelligence.* John Wiley \& Sons.

Hawlitschek, F., Notheisen, B., & Teubner, T. (2018). Electronic commerce research and applications the limits of trust-free systems: A literature review on blockchain technology and trust in the sharing economy. *Electronic Commerce Research and Applications, 29*, 50–63. https://doi.org/10.1016/j.elerap.2018.03.005

In2Dreams. (2018). The data transactions model in railways ecosystems. *Intelligent solutions 2ward the development of railway energy and asset management systems in Europe.* IN2Dreams.

Karim, R., Candell, O., & Söderholm, P. (2009). E-maintenance and information logistics: Aspects of content format. *Journal of Quality in Maintenance Engineering, 15*(3), 308–324. https://doi.org/10.1108/13552510910983242

Khaleghi, B., Khamis, A., Karray, F. O., & Razavi, S. N. (2013). Multisensor data fusion: A review of the state-of-the-art. *Information Fusion, 14*(1), 28–44. https://doi.org/10.1016/j.inffus.2011.08.001

Khan, M. A., & Salah, K. (2018). IoT security: review, blockchain solutions, and open challenges. *Future Generation Computer Systems, 82*, 395–411. https://doi.org/10.1016/j.future.2017.11.022

Khatoon, A. (2020). A blockchain-based smart contract system for healthcare management. *Electronics (Switzerland), 9*(1), 94. https://doi.org/10.3390/electronics9010094

Kissel, R. (2013). Glossary of key information security terms. *NISTIR 7298 Rev 2.* Computer Security Resource Center. https://doi.org/http://dx.doi.org/10.6028/NIST.IR.7298r2

Knight, S., & Burn, J. (2005). Developing a framework for assessing information quality on the world wide web. *International Journal of an Emerging Transdiscipline, 8*(May), 159. https://doi.org/10.28945/493

KnowledgeNile. (2022). Edge & cloud & fog computing: What is the difference between them? https://www.knowledgenile.com/blogs/edge-cloud-fog-computing-what-is-the-difference-between-them/#CloudComputing

Kour, R. (2020). *Cybersecurity in railway: A framework for improvement of digital asset security.* Doctoral Dissertation, LuleåUniversity of Technology. http://urn.kb.se/resolve?urn=urn:nbn:se:ltu:diva-78488

Kuo, T. T., Kim, H. E., & Ohno-Machado, L. (2017). Blockchain distributed ledger technologies for biomedical and health care applications. *Journal of the American Medical Informatics Association, 24*(6), 1211–1220. https://doi.org/10.1093/jamia/ocx068

Lamport, L., Shostak, R., & Pease, M. (1982). The byzantine generals' problem. *ACM Transactions on Programming Languages and Systems, 4*(3) 382–401.. https://doi.org/10.1145/357172.357176

Lee, Y. W., Pipino, L. L., Funk, J. D., & Wang, R. Y. (2016). *Journey to data quality.* MIT Press.

Loebbecke, C., & Powell, P. (1998). Competitive advantage from it in logistics: The integrated transport tracking system. *International Journal of Information Management, 18*(1), 17–27. https://doi.org/10.1016/S0268-4012(97)00037-6

Luo, F., Member, S., Dong, Z. Y., Member, S., & Chen, Y. (2012). Hybrid cloud computing platform: The next generation IT backbone for smart grid. *2012 IEEE Power and Energy Society General Meeting*, 1–7. https://doi.org/10.1109/PESGM.2012.6345178

Mell, P., & Grance, T. (2011). *The NIST definition of cloud computing.* National Institute of Standard Technology. https://doi.org/10.1136/emj.2010.096966

Monrat, A. A., Schelén, O., & Andersson, K. (2019). A survey of blockchain from the perspectives of applications, challenges, and opportunities. *IEEE Access, 7*, 117134–117151. https://doi.org/10.1109/ACCESS.2019.2936094

Monrat, A. A., Schelén, O., & Andersson, K. (2020). Performance evaluation of permissioned blockchain platforms. *2020 IEEE Asia-Pacific Conference on Computer Science and Data Engineering (CSDE)*, 1–8. https://doi.org/10.1109/CSDE50874.2020.9411380

Nakamoto, S. (2008). Bitcoin: A peer-to-peer electronic cash system. *SSRN Electronic Journal.* https://doi.org/10.2139/ssrn.3440802

Ølnes, S., Ubacht, J., & Janssen, M. (2017). Blockchain in government: Benefits and implications of distributed ledger technology for information sharing. *Government Information Quarterly, 34*(3), 355–364. https://doi.org/10.1016/j.giq.2017.09.007

Patwardhan, A., Thaduri, A., & Karim, R. (2021). Distributed ledger for cybersecurity: Issues and challenges in railways. *Sustainability*, *13*(18), 10176. https://doi.org/10.3390/su131810176

Roland Berger. (2018). The blockchain bandwagon – Is it time for automotive companies to start investing seriously in blockchain? *Focus*.

Samek, W., Stanczak, S., & Wiegand, T. (2017). The convergence of machine learning and communications. *ICT Discoveries*, *Special Issue* (1), 49–58. https://www.itu.int/dms_pub/itu-s/opb/journal/S-JOURNAL-ICTF.VOL1-2018-1-P06-PDF-E.pdf

SCC. (2022). The three layers of computing – Cloud, fog and edge https://www.scc.com/insights/it-solutions/data-centre-modernisation/the-three-layers-of-computing-cloud-fog-and-edge

Srinivasan, A., Quadir, A., & Vijayakumar, V. (2015). Era of cloud computing: A new insight to hybrid cloud. *Procedia – Procedia Computer Science*, *50*, 42–51. https://doi.org/10.1016/j.procs.2015.04.059

Thompson, B. (2008). Storm warning for cloud computing. BBC News. http://news.bbc.co.uk/2/hi/technology/7421099.stm

Tolone, W., Ahn, G.-J., Pai, T., & Hong, S.-P. (2005). Access control in collaborative systems. *ACM Computing Surveys*, *37*(1), 29–41. https://doi.org/10.1145/1057977.1057979

Wang, Y. (2009). On cognitive computing. *International Journal of Software Science and Computational Intelligence*, *1*(3), 1–15. https://doi.org/10.4018/JSSCI.2009070101

Wikipedia. (2022a). Proof of authority. https://en.wikipedia.org/wiki/Proof_of_authority

Wikipedia. (2022b). Proof of stake. https://en.wikipedia.org/wiki/Proof_of_stake

Wikipedia. (2022c). Proof of work. https://en.wikipedia.org/wiki/Proof_of_work

WinSystems. (2022). Cloud computing – Fog computing & edge computing. https://www.winsystems.com/cloud-fog-and-edge-computing-whats-the-difference/

Yli-Huumo, J., Deokyoon, K., Choi, S., Park, S., & Smolander, K. (2016). Where is current research on blockchain technology? A systematic review. *Plos One*, *11*(10), e0163477. https://doi.org/10.1371/journal.pone.0163477

Zhang, Q., Cheng, L., & Boutaba, R. (2010). Cloud computing: State-of-the-art and research challenges. *Journal of Internet Service Applications, 2010*, 7–18. https://doi.org/10.1007/s13174-010-0007–6

Zou, C., Deng, H., & Qiu, Q. (2013). Design and implementation of hybrid cloud computing architecture based on cloud bus. *Proceedings – IEEE 9th International Conference on Mobile Ad-Hoc and Sensor Networks, MSN 2013*, 289–293. https://doi.org/10.1109/MSN.2013.72

10 Case Studies

10.1 CASE STUDY 1 – AI FACTORY FOR RAILWAY

Various technologies are used to monitor the condition of railway vehicles. These include acoustic-bearing detectors, hot box detectors (HBDs), temperature trending, hot and cold wheel detectors, track performance detectors, hunting detectors, cracked axle detectors, cracked wheel detectors, machine vision, and wheel impact load detectors (WILDs).

In most cases, defective wheels generate high-impact load on the track. This is detected by WILD, as it weighs each wheel several times when the wheel passes a detector at a certain distance. Strain-gauge-based technologies are used by WILD to measure the performance of a railcar in a dynamic mode by quantifying the force applied to the rail. Once a train is detected, WILD generates different levels of data, including train data, equipment data, track data, and wheel data.

In addition to vehicle deterioration, the conditions of the railway track can degrade over time, either gradually or abruptly. This can occur due to cumulative tonnage, defective wheels, and the impulsive force on tracks. Defects can worsen if no recovery action is undertaken. They may finally result in complete rail breakage, a major cause of train derailment. Railway tracks have two types of spot defects: track structural defects and track geometry defects. Track structural defects occur when the structure and support system of railway tracks fail. This could happen on the rail, ballast, ties, subgrade, or drainage systems. Track geometry defects arise due to irregularities in various track geometry measurements, such as profile, alignment, and gauge. The presence of structural defects, such as cracks and track misalignment, is a major threat to the safe operation of a railway system.

Railway companies collect massive amounts of inspection data, including service failure data, signal data, ballast history, grinding history, remedial action history, traffic data, inspection data, and curve and grade data. These data are collected in different ways (ITF, 2021):

- Track inspection cars are used to detect defects before they deteriorate. Two common types of monitoring cars are ordinary measurement cars, which measure the rail geometry and surface deterioration, and ultrasonic inspection (USI) cars, which measure rail breakage and internal cracks.
- Drones have recently gained popularity for track inspections. Images are usually processed from the front camera of the drones. Fast image processing and analysis will be used in the near future in drone-based track inspection.
- Track degradation models are used to better predict defects. They can be based either on the physical laws describing the behaviour of the asset using mechanistic models or on data-driven models, which rely mainly on ML algorithms.

Preventive maintenance on tracks is expensive. Costs include inspection, different types of maintenance, track downtime, labour, and material, among others. Preventive maintenance becomes worthwhile when the cost incurred by device failure is larger than that of preventive maintenance. Preventive maintenance is expensive when performed too early or too late.

Researchers have attempted to identify the most cost-effective maintenance policy for the railway. In an assessment of the track inspection and maintenance policy deployed for railroads in North America, some researchers found savings can be made by replacing repetitive minor maintenance actions with slightly more major maintenance actions. They termed this the optimal policy. The cost of major maintenance increases as the number of major maintenance actions increases.

DOI: 10.1201/9781003208686-10

However, repeated minor maintenance on the same section of the track decreases, and the costs decrease in kind. The optimal policy is able to remove unnecessary minor maintenance (ITF, 2021).

10.1.1 AI FACTORY FOR RAILWAY

The ongoing digitalisation and implementation of AI technologies in the railway are highly dependent on the availability and accessibility of data for a geographically distributed system. AI Factory for Railway (AIF/R) will facilitate this by providing a platform for data sharing.

AIF/R is a set of smart cloud/edge-based data services aimed to accelerate digitalisation in railway. AIF/R services will provide capabilities such as acquisition, integration, transformation, and processing of railway-related data across endpoints, such as authorities, industries, academia, and small- and medium-sized enterprises (SMEs). AIF/R's integrated services can be invoked on-premises or in multiple cloud-based environments. Its architecture is built on loosely coupled storage and computing services, as shown in Figure 10.1.

AIF/R will provide digital pipelines between data providers and data consumers, as illustrated in Figure 10.1. Each pipeline represents a set of orchestrated activities aimed to extract, transfer, load, and process datasets between the provider and the consumer. AIF/R's pipelines are configurable entities, which can utilise a palette of technologies for communication, storage, and processing to enable context-adaptability and meet users' requirements. Selection of appropriate technologies for each pipeline will be based on context-specific requirements, such as requirements of scalability, authentication, and authorisation.

We believe a generic data factory for railway should be hosted as a neutral open platform governed by a body with a focus on research and innovation (Table 10.1).

AIF/R will provide railway stakeholders, nationally and internally, with cloud/edge-based services and supporting governance processes that can be used to access various types of datasets.

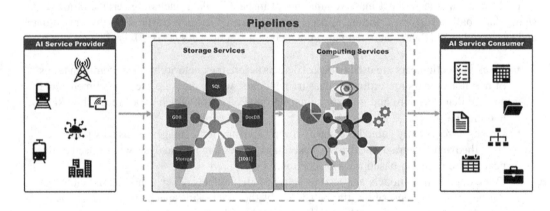

FIGURE 10.1   AIF/R conceptual model.

TABLE 10.1
AIF/R Platform

Vision	AIF/R's vision is to be the most internationally recognised and leading node for data and analytics services for railway data.
Goal	AIF/R's goal is to create value for its stakeholders by establishing a reliable and resilient platform for data sharing and analytics. The platform consists of a set of services and governing structures enabling railway stakeholders, nationally and internationally, to provide and consume data and services securely.

AIF/R will also offer a cyber security platform including authentication mechanisms at various levels. The cyber security platform will manage access to data based on data openness characteristics, such as:

1. Fully open data (require no authentication),
2. Semi-open data (require weak authentication), and
3. No-open data (strong authentication).

The data services will include various application programming interfaces (APIs) to facilitate dynamic and context-based integration between back-end and front-end services. Examples include Logic Apps, Services Bus, Event Grid, REST, etc.

AIF/R will also provide computing capabilities for AI, besides capabilities for storage, networking, and communication. These capabilities will be materialised in a set of interconnected and loosely coupled services, orchestrated dynamically to adapt to various contexts. The overarching architecture of AIF/R is illustrated in Figure 10.2. AIF/R's services will fulfil stakeholders' requirements on data access and knowledge discovery. Finally, AIF/R will enable integration with other AI environments and initiatives.

AIF/R relies on four main pillars:

- A technology platform (AI Factory): AIF/R's technology platform is a service-oriented scalable environment for enabling capabilities for information logistics, including services data acquisition, data filtering, data quality, data transformation, cyber security, data processing, and visualisation.
- A digital governance platform (eGovernance): AIF/R's eGovernance platform deals with all activities necessary to enable governance of digital assets in a heterogeneous technology environment with a large number of stakeholders.
- A communication platform: AIF/R's communication platform will support and facilitate the achievement of the overall goals. Communications will be built on scientific results, which will be reviewed and published in peer-reviewed journals.
- A coordinating platform: AIF/R's coordinating platform is built upon an agile mindset with related tools to facilitate collaboration between stakeholders and to increase the efficiency of AIF/R's DevOps (development and operations) processes (Figure 10.3).

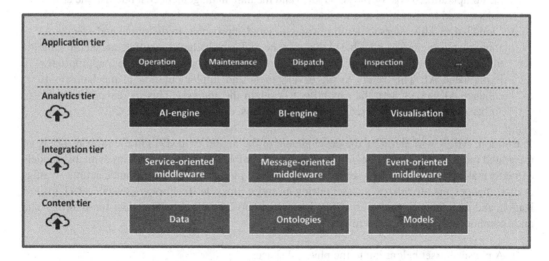

FIGURE 10.2 AIF/R overarching architecture.

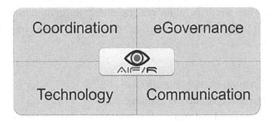

FIGURE 10.3 AIF/R main pillars.

10.1.1.1 Technology Platform (AI Factory)

AIF/R's technology platform is a service-oriented scalable environment for enabling capabilities for information logistics, including services data acquisition, data filtering, data quality, data transformation, cyber security, data processing, and visualisation. These services can be utilised to support, for example, diagnostics, prognostics and health management, condition monitoring and assessment, risk management, asset management, etc.

Furthermore, the platform will enhance the reliability, availability, and sustainability of the railway systems, including rolling stock and infrastructure, through the enablement of Industrial AI (IAI). Industrial AI is applied research within AI which focuses on the deployment of ML, Industrial Internet of Things (IIoT), Big Data, and context information in industrial contexts. IAI is explorative to bring insight into and understanding of industrial phenomena. It can generate problem-solving findings that are practically useful in various industrial contexts, such as prescriptive analysis of asset health, diagnostics, and prognostics.

AIF/R will focus on:

1. Data accuracy and usefulness: This refers to the characteristics, such as quality, completeness, and consistency of the datasets fed to the ML models. In industrial contexts, data accuracy and data availability are issues, not because of the lack of data with respect to volume, but because of the insufficient quality in acquired data due to insufficiency in the data acquisition process, the complexity of the asset structure, and the co-existence of obsolete and new technologies.
2. Analysis fidelity: This refers to the identification and definition of cost functions to assess the fidelity of models such as the predictors. The cost functions have to consider not only the computational cost of the AI models and the data management cost but also the cost of risks related to operation and maintenance.
3. Cloud2edge: This refers to defining strategies and approaches to distribute and execute AI components as close as possible to the asset, i.e. industrial edge computing, and at the same time harmonise edge solutions with the power of cloud computing whenever appropriate.
4. Explainable AI: This refers to the development and implementation of mechanisms to enhance AI models with the capability to explain the analysis. This increases the creditability of and trust in the predictions, prescriptions, diagnosis etc.

In addition, AIF/R will facilitate the development of the digital twin (DT) in the railway. DT is an integrated multi-physics, multi-scale simulation of a complex product which uses available models and information updates (such as sensor measurements, procurement, maintenance actions, configuration changes, etc.) to mirror an asset during its entire lifecycle. Technologies such as IAI, visualization, and maintenance analytics will be integrated into DT for augmented decision-making. The main components of DTs are the following:

1. A physical asset belonging to the physical space,
2. A virtual asset belonging to the virtual space,

3. Connected data tying together the physical and virtual assets and belonging to the information space.

The success of DT is dependent on the convergence of Information Technology (IT) and Operation Technology (OT). For this purpose, AIF/R will focus on:

1. Interaction and convergence between the physical space and the digital space: The connection between physical and virtual spaces must be smooth, easy, and seamless, while ensuring the continuity of the DT during the asset's lifecycle.
2. Synchronisation of digital assets and physical asset configuration: The configuration changes in the physical system structure and the digital system structure must be synchronised to maintain accuracy in the system indenture.
3. Behaviour replication between physical and digital systems: The requested (pull) and required (push) behaviour, including models, properties, and data, must be replicated.

10.1.1.2 Digital Governance Platform (eGovernance)

A railway system involves an extensive number of stakeholders with heterogeneous interests and needs. To fulfil stakeholders' needs effectively and efficiently, the rail system needs to provide flexible and adaptive services and functions. Need identification is one of the key success factors in design and development of flexible and adaptive services. The need-identification process is highly dependent on input from involved stakeholders. Hence, AIF/R will:

1. Create an environment for cooperation and collaboration;
2. Identify key areas for joint innovative governance activities;
3. Design and test neutral and holistic governance models;
4. Identify key processes for cooperation and collaboration; and
5. Coordinate heterogeneous needs related to gender, equality, disability, age, etc.

Risk management is an important aspect of AIF/R. Risk management in relation to the railway system is the set of processes through which all stakeholders together identify, analyse, and, where necessary, respond appropriately to risks that might adversely affect the realisation of the transport policy goals. Hence, AIF/R will focus on:

1. Assessing and defining risk management value and risk ownership;
2. Defining risk assessment metrics; and
3. Conducting simulations and stress tests.

10.1.1.3 Communication Platform

One of the main purposes of AIF/R is to increase the utilisation of the developed platform for data sharing. For this purpose, a proper communication and dissemination platform is extremely important. The communication platform will support and facilitate the achievement of the overall goals.

Communications will be built on scientific results, which will be reviewed and presented. A major outlet for communication is the research community, and articles in peer-reviewed journals will be of high importance. These results will also be presented at selected scientific conferences.

10.1.1.4 Coordinating Platform

To achieve overall project goals and ensure the quality of the outcomes, AIF/R will have the following organisation. The *steering board* is responsible for the achievement of the project's overall goals and for the selection of appropriate strategies for execution. The *project manager* is responsible for the execution of the project activities and quality assurance of the outcomes. The *technology team* is responsible for the technology development and implementation of AIF/R. The *communication team* is responsible for internal and external communication, and the dissemination of results and findings to railway stakeholders. The *collaboration team* is responsible for facilitating the collaboration and cooperation between primary and secondary stakeholders. The *support team* is responsible for the provision of support resources as described in service level agreements (SLAs) between AIF/R and data providers or data consumers.

The focus of AIF/R is to secure sustainability, including social aspects of sustainability. One aspect of social sustainability is equality, not only between genders but also between people with different ethnic and social backgrounds. More precisely, the development of mobility systems influences people's everyday lives and therefore needs to consider how that development can support the integration and inclusion of all members of society. Therefore, gender and equality play a central role in AIF/R.

10.2   CASE STUDY 2 – AI FACTORY FOR MINING

The sustainability and circularity of natural resources have amplified the need for seamless integration of information-driven decision-making in the mining sector to achieve operational excellence. Emerging digital technologies empowered by AI are expected to facilitate decision-making processes in mining industries and to provide necessary societal value. Mining assets empowered by AI and digital technologies will generate environmental, societal, and economic benefits, such as safety, sustainability, resilience, robustness, reliability, effectiveness, and efficiency.

The mining sector needs to become data-, model-, and information-driven. However, to implement information-driven decision-making in the mining sector, insight into the decision-making processes, understanding of the domain knowledge, and perception of characteristics of the system-of-interest are critical to exploit the power of AI and digitalisation for enhanced safety, sustainability, and resilience.

Hence, the objective of AI Factory for Mining (AIF/M) is to provide a platform and toolkit empowered by AI and digital technologies. This platform and toolkit aim to contribute to the achievement of sustainable and resilient operational excellence in the mining industry. AIF/M will have a special focus on:

1. Sharing of data and models;
2. Toolkit for augmentation of context-aware needs-based information-driven analytics;
3. Cybersecurity;
4. Innovative business models; and
5. AI-based toolkit based on energy-efficient distributed computing.

AIF/M will enable data-driven and model-driven decision-making tools, technology, and roadmaps to implement AI-empowered business solutions in mining processes.

From a collaboration perspective, the AIF/M's consortium consists of organisations representing end-users (LKAB and Boliden), mining equipment system integrator (Epiroc), the digital solution providers to mining industries (IBM), and academia (LTU). The consortium is also supported by an industrial connectivity solution provider (Ericsson), as an associate partner. This unique constitution of partners brings extensive domain knowledge, deep insight into mining processes, and associated challenges in IAI.

From a technology perspective, the project will be built upon some of the universal concepts and components developed within the AI Factory platform.

10.2.1   AIF/M Concept

Information-driven decision-making in the mining sector contributes to the achievement of global sustainability goals and system resilience. It also contributes to augmented asset management and operational excellence through improved effectiveness and efficiency of processes, including business, asset management, operation, and maintenance.

However, information is considered as interpreted data, adapted to a given mining context. To be able to interpret data appropriately, we need a good understanding of the specific industrial domain. We also need knowledge and insight to process the relevant and related data for the given context. This data processing is often done using algorithms. AI represents a package of algorithms with some common characteristics and capabilities aimed to extract information out of data. In AI, ML and deep learning (DL) refer to subsets of these algorithms.

In the mining industry, achieving operational excellence is highly dependent on the availability and accessibility of information. Information can be used to augment the decision-making processes and to take action. Industrial automation expects to provide profit to the business and contribute to improved sustainability in natural resource consumption. Automation is not limited to the production process; it can be of benefit to other processes as well, such as business, operation, and maintenance. The increased level of automation in industry requires appropriate information-driven governance, management, and execution strategies. An information-driven industrial process, in turn, requires a data-driven approach that facilitates knowledge discovery through information extraction.

The ongoing digitalisation and implementation of AI technologies in the mining industry depend on the availability and accessibility of data for a geographically distributed system. Going from data to decisions or from data to action is a necessary evolution for any sustainable and competitive industry, and it can be accelerated by means such as digital technologies and AI.

The vision of AIF/M is to contribute to the achievement of sustainable and resilient operational excellence in the mining industry through the utilisation of digital technologies and AI. AIF/M will have a special focus on:

1. Enabling mechanisms for sharing data and models between mining stakeholders;
2. Developing a toolkit for enhanced context-aware needs-based information-driven analytics aimed at asset management, operation, and maintenance;
3. Developing mechanisms to achieve the necessary cybersecurity in sharing and processing data and models;
4. Developing new innovative business models to facilitate long-term business-driven implementation;
5. Enabling a digital platform including an AI-based toolkit based on an energy-efficient distributed computing architecture that contributes to sustainability and circularity in the context of digital and physical, i.e. cyber-physical asset management, in the mining sector.

AIF/M is conceptually based on a factory metaphor. It consists of a set of lines-of-production (LoPs), as shown in Figure 10.4. The LoPs are configurable digital units consisting of specialised data processing steps. The LoP data processing steps will be designed developed and implemented based on the architectural design approach of micro-services. AIF/M's micro-services will be built and deployed independently to enable required scalability and flexibility in orchestration as required in industrial contexts. AIF/M's micro-services will be implemented based on a distributed computing approach and deployed on cloud, fog, and edge to serve the requirements of the individual LoP.

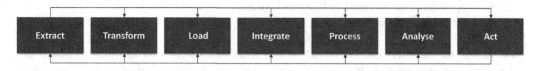

FIGURE 10.4   AI Factory's concept of line-of-production.

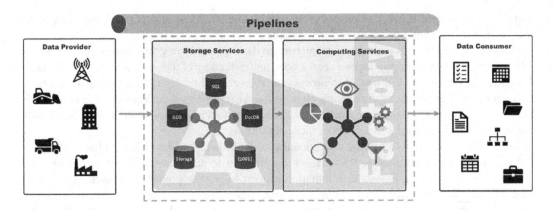

FIGURE 10.5 AIF/M conceptual model.

Simply stated, AIF/M is a set of smart cloud/edge-based data services aimed to accelerate digitalisation in the mining industry. It will provide a platform for data and model sharing. AIF/M
will provide capabilities such as acquisition, integration, transformation, and processing of mining-
related data across endpoints, such as authorities, industries, academia, and SMEs. Data analytics
within AIF/M will help to ensure the safety, sustainability and profitability of mines. AIF/M analytical engines and AI-based algorithms will facilitate the processing of real-time (RT) data streams
and complex events to support prescriptive analysis of asset health, diagnostics, and prognostics.
AIF/M's integrated services can be invoked on-premises or in multiple cloud-based environments.
The AIF/M architecture is built on loosely coupled storage and computing services (Figure 10.5).

AIF/M provides digital pipelines between data providers and data consumers, as illustrated in
Figure 10.5. Each pipeline represents a set of orchestrated activities aimed to extract, transfer, load, and
process datasets between the provider and the consumer. AIF/M's pipelines are configurable entities,
which can utilise a palette of technologies for communication, storage, and processing to enable context-
adaptability and meet users' requirements. Selection of appropriate technologies for each pipeline will
be based on context-specific requirements, such as scalability, authentication, and authorisation.

We believe a generic data factory for mining should be hosted as a neutral open platform governed by a body with a focus on research and innovation.

AIF/M will undertake a feasibility study for digital transformation of the mining industry
through utilisation of digitalisation and AI technologies. To create value for mining industry value
chains and achieve operational excellence, AIF/M will address issues and challenges in a number
of areas related to mining maintenance. These are depicted in Figure 10.6. It will also create a roadmap for the enablement of automated AI services and an appropriate architecture that can be used
for distributed computing, data integration, information logistics, and cybersecurity.

When implemented, AIF/M will provide mining stakeholders, nationally and internally, with
cloud/edge-based services and supporting governance processes that can be used to access various types of datasets. AIF/M will also provide a digital security platform, including authentication
mechanisms at various levels. The digital security platform will manage access to data based on the
following data openness characteristics:

1. Fully open data (require no authentication),
2. Semi-open data (require weak authentication), and
3. Bo-open data (strong authentication).

Furthermore, the data services in AIF/M will provide various APIs to facilitate dynamic and
context-based integration between back-end and front-end services. Examples are Logic Apps,
Services Bus, Event Grid, REST, etc.

FIGURE 10.6 AIF/M focus areas.

TABLE 10.2

AIF/M Project

 AIF/M's vision is to contribute to the achievement of sustainable and resilient operational excellence in the mining industry by providing a platform and a toolkit empowered by digital technologies and AI.

 AIF/M's goal is to create value for its stakeholders by developing a trustworthy, reliable, and resilient concept, platform, and toolkit for data and model sharing, and enhanced analytics for the mining sector using AI and digitalisation.

 AIF/M's objective is to provide a platform and toolkit empowered by AI and digital technologies. The concept, platform, and toolkit will be validated though a system demonstrator in the mining sector that includes aspects of framework, technologies, methodologies, security, business, and governance.

 AIF/M's strategy is to combine relevant and necessary digitalisation technologies for data sharing and service provisioning for AI, with appropriate processes and regulations for effective and efficient digital collaboration and governance. AIF/M will be built on existing technology platforms (e.g. LTU) and existing collaborative platforms for mining stakeholders (i.e. CMIS).

Providing a platform which enables the management and sharing of Big Data among many stakeholders with diversified requirements is an essential prerequisite but is not sufficient. It is believed the main benefit will be gained through analytics. Hence, AIF/M is designed to consider characteristics of advanced analytic technologies such as AI, ML, and DL. Accordingly, AIF/M will provide computing capabilities for AI, in addition to capabilities for storage, networking, and communication. These capabilities will be materialised in a set of interconnected and loosely coupled services, orchestrated dynamically to adapt to various contexts. The overarching architecture of AIF/M is the same as that for AIF/R shown in Figure 10.2. AIF/M services will meet stakeholders' requirements for data access and knowledge discovery.

The main purpose is to enable and conduct research and innovation that contribute to improved efficiency and effectiveness of operation and maintenance in the mining industry with a particular focus on increased utilisation of digital technology and AI. Table 10.2 specifies the vision, goal, objective, and strategy.

10.2.2 EXPECTED RESULTS AND EFFECTS

Current decision-making processes in the mining sector are not fully integrated and are operated and managed in silos. AIF/M will facilitate the integration of decision-making processes and provide innovative business solutions leading to improved overall equipment efficiency, achieved through augmented asset management using AI and digitalisation. AIF/M will bring step changes into the economic performance and enhance the competitiveness of the mining sector.

AIF/M is a holistic, innovative approach to asset management as it is built upon a unique integrated collaborative and technology platform – the AI Factory. AI Factory's innovative technology platform and toolkit facilitate provision of the necessary technology capabilities for AIF/M. The use cases focus on the innovation of products and services, which can be further deployed in the context of interested stakeholders. The development of these products and services can address issues related to data integration, analytics, visualisation, business models, cybersecurity, and digital governance.

Many of the use case examples are a continuation of work started in AIF/M Phase I. All use cases contribute to improved asset knowledge. This has the potential to offer new products and services. AI and digital technologies merge historical data with other data sources (e.g. asset data, condition data, operation data, maintenance data, and business data) to enhance the quality of the input information for better decision-making at the operational level. This information can enable fact-based decision-making through data-driven and model-based approaches. These products and services, in combination with expert knowledge in the industrial domain, will lead to long-term, innovative, and sustainable asset management, operation, and maintenance.

The evolutionary process of AIF/M and the relationship between the first two steps are depicted in Figures 10.7 and 10.8. The proof-of-concepts from Phase I will help to develop system demonstrators within AIF/M that include ML and DL models for prescriptive analysis of asset functional health, diagnostics, and prognostics and measure cost-benefit analyses in the mining industry.

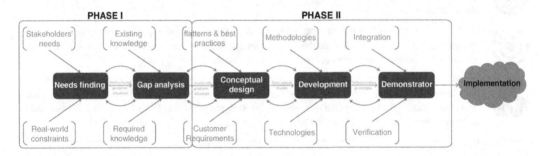

FIGURE 10.7 AIF/M phase I & phase II.

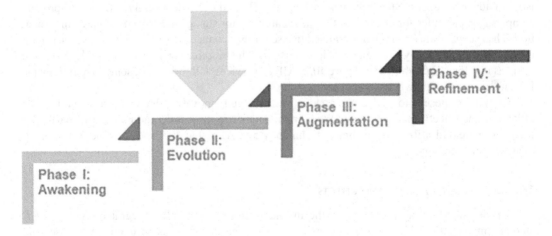

FIGURE 10.8 AIF/M evolutionary process.

The concept of AI Factory can generate great benefits in mining through the transformation of knowledge (i.e. transferred learning). The following are the expected results for AIF/M Phase II:

1. AIF/M analytical engines and AI-based algorithms will process RT data streams and complex events to enable prescriptive analysis of asset health, function performance monitoring, diagnostics, and prognostics.
2. AIF/M will provide mining stakeholders, nationally and internationally, with cloud/edge-based services and supporting governance processes to access various types of datasets.
3. The data services in AIF/M will provide various APIs to facilitate dynamic and context-based integration between back-end and front-end services. Examples include Logic Apps, Services Bus, Event Grid, and REST.
4. AIF/M will provide a cybersecurity platform including authentication mechanisms at various levels. The platform will manage access to data based on the data openness characteristics specified previously.
5. AIF/M will improve the overall effectiveness and efficiency of operation and maintenance in the mining industry.

The final system demonstrator will provide proof-of-concept by integrating data and models coming from geographically distributed systems in a standardised and secured manner. This will show the results of analytics applied to different mining assets in a unique human-system interaction. The demonstrator can be extended as a DT for the system-of-interest.

10.2.3   Four Pillars of AIF/M

Like AIF/R, AIF/M relies on four main pillars:

- A technology platform (AI Factory),
- A digital governance platform (eGovernance),
- A communication platform, and
- A coordinating platform.

10.2.3.1   Technology Platform (AI Factory)

AIF/M's technology platform is a service-oriented scalable environment to enable capabilities for information logistics, including service data acquisition, data filtering, data quality, data transformation, cyber security, data processing, and visualisation. These services can be utilised to support diagnostics, prognostics and health management, condition monitoring and assessment, risk management, asset management, and so on.

The platform will enhance the reliability, availability, and sustainability of the mining process industry through the enablement of IAI. IAI focuses on the deployment of ML, IIoT, Big Data, and context information in industrial contexts. IAI is explorative and brings insight into and understanding of industrial contexts. It can also generate problem-solving findings that are practically useful in various industrial contexts, such as prescriptive analysis of asset health, diagnostics, and prognostics.

AIF/M will focus on:

1. Data accuracy and usefulness,
2. Analysis fidelity,
3. Cloud2edge,
4. Explainable AI.

AIF/M will facilitate the development of DT in the mining process industry. DT is an integrated multi-physics, multi-scale simulation of a complex product which uses available models and information updates (e.g. sensor measurements, procurement, maintenance actions, and configuration changes) to mirror an asset during its entire lifecycle. Technologies such as IAI, visualisation, and maintenance analytics will be integrated into DT for augmented decision-making. DTs comprise the following:

1. A physical asset belonging to the physical space,
2. A virtual asset belonging to the virtual space, and
3. Connected data which tie together the physical and virtual assets in the information space.

The success of DT is dependent on the convergence of IT and OT. For this purpose, AIF/M will focus on:

1. Interaction and convergence between the physical space and the digital space;
2. Synchronisation of digital assets and physical asset configuration;
3. Behaviour replication between physical and digital system, i.e. CPS.

10.2.3.2   Digital Governance Platform (eGovernance)

A mining process industry involves an extensive number of stakeholders with heterogeneous interests and needs. To fulfil their needs effectively and efficiently, the mining process needs to provide flexible and adaptive services and functions. Need identification is one of the key success factors in the design and development of flexible and adaptive services. The need-identification process depends on input from involved stakeholders. Hence, this platform will:

1. Create an environment for cooperation and collaboration.
2. Identify key areas for joint innovative governance activities.
3. Design and test neutral and holistic governance models.
4. Identify key processes for cooperation and collaboration.
5. Coordinate heterogeneous needs related to gender, equality, disability, age, etc.

Risk management is an important aspect of AIF/M. Risk management in relation to the mining process is the set of processes through which all the stakeholders together identify, analyse, and, where necessary, respond appropriately to risks that might adversely affect the realisation of the mining policy goals. Hence, AIF/M will focus on:

1. Assessing and defining risk management value and risk ownership;
2. Defining risk assessment metrics; and
3. Conducting simulations and stress tests.

10.2.3.3   Communication Platform

One of the main purposes of AIF/M is to increase the utilisation of the developed platform for data sharing. For this purpose, a proper communication and dissemination platform is important. The communication platform will support and facilitate the achievement of the overall goals.

Communications will be built on scientific results, which will be reviewed, published in peer-reviewed journals, and presented at selected scientific conferences.

10.2.3.4   Coordinating Platform

To achieve overall project goals and ensure the quality of the outcomes, AIF/M will have the following organisation. The steering board is responsible for the achievement of the project's overall goals, and for the selection of appropriate strategies for execution. The project manager is responsible for the execution of the project activities and the quality assurance of the outcomes. The technology team is responsible for the technology development and the implementation of AIF/M. The communication team is responsible not only for internal and external communication but also for dissemination of results and findings to mining stakeholders. The collaboration team is responsible for facilitating the collaboration and cooperation between primary and secondary stakeholders. The support team is responsible for the provision of support resources as described in SLAs between AIF/M and data providers or data consumers.

10.3 CASE STUDY 3 – AI FACTORY – AUGMENTED REALTIY AND VIRTUAL REALITY SERVICES IN THE RAILWAY

The ongoing digital transformation is changing asset management across industry, including in the railway. Emerging digital technologies and AI are expected to facilitate decision-making in the management, operation, and maintenance of the railway by providing integrated data-driven and model-driven solutions.

An important aspect when developing decision-support solutions based on AI and digital technology is user experience. The user experience design process aims to create relevance, context awareness, and meaningfulness for end-users. In railway contexts, applying a human-centric design model in the development of AI-based artefacts will enhance the usability of the solution, with a positive impact on decision-making processes. In this section, we propose a human-centric design model for the enhancement of railway asset management using AI, VR, and mixed reality (MR) technologies. Their use could lead to increased efficiency and effectiveness of the operation and maintenance processes.

The railway is complex because of its inherently distributed and networked nature with long lifetimes of its subsystems and components. It is one of the major contributors to the economy of a country. Railway infrastructure consists of tracks, catenary/carrier wires, wayside monitoring systems, switches and crossings, bridges and tunnels, and railway platforms. In addition, the railway is a time-critical system with strict timetables for maintenance activities.

Maintenance is a process that comprises a combination of the various technical, administrative, and managerial actions taken during an item's lifetime intended to keep it in, or restore it to, a state in which it can perform the required function. Otherwise stated, the purpose of the maintenance process is to sustain the capability of a system to provide a service. The maintenance process consists of a number of activities, including planning, preparing, executing, assessing, and improving maintenance (Figure 10.9).

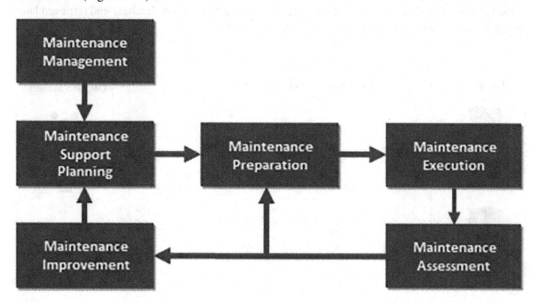

FIGURE 10.9 A generic maintenance process (IEC, 2004).

It can be difficult to inspect the physical railway assets (e.g. tracks, switches, mast, catenaries, etc.) in remote areas, under harsh weather conditions, and during pandemic situations like Covid-19. Under such situations, the use of advanced technologies like VR integrated with AI has the potential to accelerate the procedure of maintenance activities to save time, cost, and energy. With these technologies, railway personnel can visualise the asset's condition or inspection information remotely on a screen using VR devices. Visual inspection is an important part of the maintenance process, which makes the management of assets easier and results in improved railway efficiency. This will further improve the overall efficiency of data management platforms (DMPs) within the maintenance process.

We propose a holistic human-centred design (HCD) model that will enhance the railway asset management by using AI and extended reality (XR). This will help railway stakeholders to augment the DMP within all the stages of maintenance process. This model for railway asset management has been adapted from the conceptual model of E365 Analytics® and the eMaintenance solution for maintenance analytics. In this model, 3D analytics and immersive experience provide services for the whole DMP, including data fusion and integration, data modelling and analysis, and context sensing and adaptation. It provides a set of interconnected, loosely coupled services, which can be orchestrated to fulfil users' demands with respect to decision support. These services are built upon technologies such as Big Data, data analytics, computer vision (CV), speech recognition, DL, context awareness, cloud computing, and edge computing. When users interact with such end solutions, their experience is very important to consider; therefore, this model considers the human perspective on the navigability, visibility, satisfaction, motivating, and usability of the solution.

The AI-integrated human-centric design model is depicted in Figure 10.10.

The three main parts of the model are data fusion and integration, data modelling and analysis, and context sensing and adaptation.

10.3.1   DATA FUSION AND INTEGRATION

The purpose of this step is to integrate data from various sources, such as condition monitoring data (Optram), light detection and ranging (LiDAR) data, 3D images of railway infrastructure, and maintenance data into the eMaintenance cloud to construct 3D models and access asset information in the later stages of the proposed XR model. LiDAR data are transferred to the eMaintenance cloud in the form of point cloud. Most of the data are stored in an SQL server database and retrieved later during the data modelling and analysis and data visualisation steps.

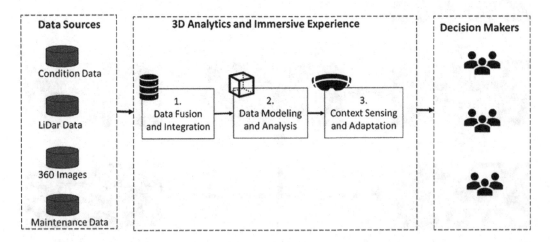

FIGURE 10.10   AI-integrated human-centric design model for railway AM (Karim et al., 2016).

10.3.2 Data Modelling and Analysis

The purpose of this step is to generate 3D models of railway assets using AI technology.

LiDAR is one of the main data sources. LiDAR generates point cloud data with (X Y Z) coordinates, by scanning a laser beam over the area. The reflected beams are used to compute the distance through time-of-flight calculations. The scan results are stored in standard formats; each point has its absolute GPS coordinates or other coordinates, along with its altitude, intensity, colour information, classification codes, etc. In contrast to standard image formats where the stored data of pixels' location are relative to a real-world view, the point cloud data generated by LiDAR do not have any such relationship. A single LiDAR scan may contain millions of points; generally, 10% fall in the region of interest, in this case, railway assets. The following sections discuss the various steps involved in the generation of 3D models from point cloud. Figure 10.11a shows a view of a point cloud containing 8.5 million points.

10.3.2.1 Point Cloud Pre-Processing

Pre-processing of point cloud involves the decimation of points; a random selection of 25–50% of points reduces the time and space impact while computations are performed. The final extraction of features for the creation of models is taken from the original point cloud.

The LiDAR scan in the example data has a range of about 100 m forward but much less in other dimensions. (X Y Z) coordinates in the point cloud can be stored in different formats and may have large values if absolute values are used for representation. During computation, such large values can cause integer overflow and generate computing error, so data must be transformed. Preservation of relative information is required to maintain the aspect ratio along the (X Y Z) axis.

The Random Sample Consensus (RANSAC) method has been applied for plane and line detection. RANSAC is an iterative method to estimate the parameters of a mathematical model from a set of data containing outliers.

10.3.2.2 Classification

One option for clustering and segmentation is the density-based spatial clustering of applications with noise (DBSCAN) algorithm. DBSCAN can find arbitrarily shaped clusters and, therefore, is very suitable for LiDAR point cloud data. Point cloud clustering performed by applying the DBSCAN algorithm is presented in Equation 10.1.

$$DBSCAN(DB, distFunc, eps, minPts) \tag{10.1}$$

where DB is the database consisting of the dataset to be scanned, eps is the epsilon that defines the radius of the neighbourhood around a point x (the ϵ-neighbourhood of x), minPts is the minimum number of neighbours within "eps" radius, and distFunc computes distance and checks epsilon.

This algorithm groups points based on how closely packed they are while rejecting the points away farther from the cluster (Figure 10.11b). However, the algorithm is sensitive to the parameter values and needs to be set based on the application and dataset. After the classification is performed, the height of clusters and position relative to the scan are used to classify the clusters. Figure 10.11c and d show segmentation for the overhead catenary system and track respectively.

10.3.2.3 Labelling

Once the segmentation is completed through clustering, assets are labelled based on their features. Clusters of point clouds like masts, catenary/cables, beams, etc. are extracted; information about their centroid bounding box as coordinates is extracted and stored in the database for further processing. The mast locations are used to form a convex hull for the next stage of processing.

10.3.2.4 Object Extraction

This stage involves extracting objects of interest such as railway masts (Figure 10.11e). One possibility is to use voxelisation for the extraction of these assets. Extraction of individual objects

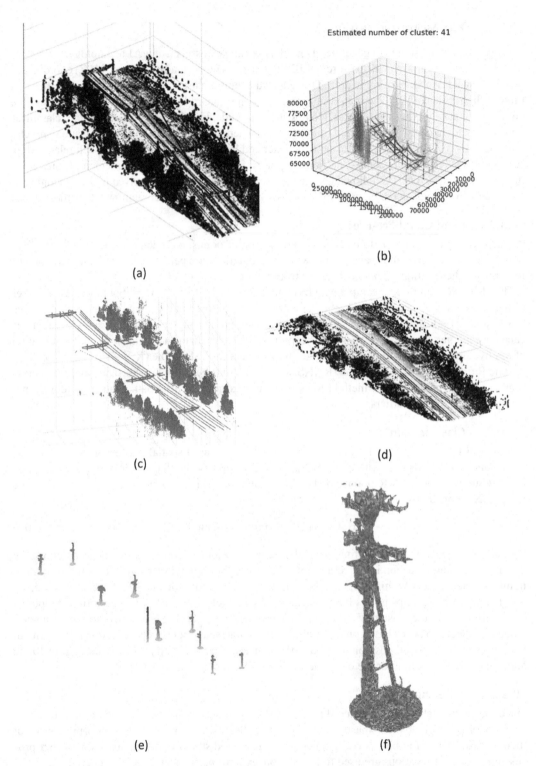

FIGURE 10.11   (a) View of the point cloud: 8.5M points for a short track section; (b) point cloud cluster-ing; (c) point cloud segmentation for the overhead catenary system; (d) point cloud segmentation for track; (e) extracted tower shapes from point cloud after labelling; (f) 3D model of individual mast; (g) 3D model of catenary; (h) 3D model of beam bridge.

involves filtering all the points from the point cloud fitting inside a cylinder or a cuboid at the location of the object within known asset dimensions; its geometry is defined by length (l), width (w), and height (h). The index (i, j, k) of each point in the point cloud is calculated using Equations 10.2–10.4:

$$i = \frac{\text{floor}(X - X\min)}{l} \tag{10.2}$$

$$j = \frac{\text{floor}(Y - Y\min)}{w} \tag{10.3}$$

$$k = \frac{\text{floor}(Z - Z\min)}{h} \tag{10.4}$$

where (Xmin, Ymin, Zmin) are the minimum coordinates.

The extracted set of points corresponding to individual railway assets are stored as separate files for further processing.

10.3.2.5 Model Creation

The generation of a 3D model (Figure 10.11f–h) involves the generation of a surface mesh of triangles from the point cloud, discarding points not required for surface formation. One option for model creation is to use the ball-pivoting algorithm.

10.3.3 Context Sensing and Adaptation

The purpose of this final step is to create and adapt visualisation models based on user experience.

To explain the application of XR technology in the railway, especially in asset management, we created three prototypes for an XR proof-of-concept application for railway asset management. These three XR prototypes for asset management contain a railway track section (approximately 200 metres) as one complete game scene. Once all the 3D models are ready (extracted from point cloud), they are imported into the Unity environment for interaction. The C# script is used to create dynamic objects inside a simulation. All associated assets, in this case, mast, catenaries, and beam bridge, are included and offer a salient level of detail. It also contains a relevant code that executes the interactions of the objects mentioned. Thus, users have all the desirable components for an experiment in one consistent package.

These three prototypes were developed as a guided user interface (GUI) to visualise and interact with railway assets using XR technologies. The prototypes are shown in Figure 10.12.

Prototype 1 (Figure 10.12a) uses 3D models extracted from point cloud data (Figure 10.11f–h) during the second step of the proposed model using AI algorithms. These models consist of railway mast, catenaries and beam bridge. The prototype has two views to visualise and interact with railway assets, i.e. front view and top view. Within prototype 1 for railway asset management, each individual asset is intractable. By using a VR laser pointer of a hand-held controller, information can be displayed related to the inspection/condition monitoring of particular assets (mast, catenary, and beam bridge) within the VR environment. A person wearing VR glasses can move forward, backward, left, or right in this VR environment. Thus, instead of going out in the field, the 3D models of railway assets are constructed from the point cloud within the eMaintenance lab to overlay asset inspection information as presented in Figure 10.12a. This information will help the railway stakeholder visualise health information of the assets and determine the next time for inspection.

Prototype 2 uses 360° images (Figure 10.12b). By using gaming technology, this 360° VR environment is user interactive. With a VR laser pointer, the condition of the railway asset of interest can be displayed within the VR environment using hand-held controllers. In this prototype, three traffic light buttons are used to show the condition of railway assets (Figure 10.12b). To visualise 360°

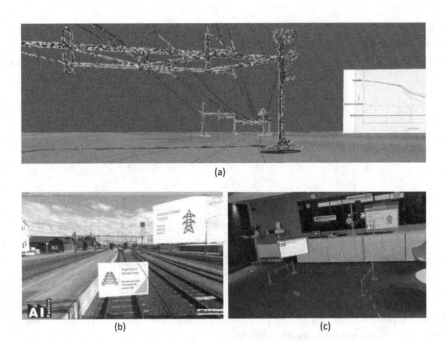

FIGURE 10.12   (a–b) Virtual reality prototypes and (c) mixed reality prototype.

images within a Unity environment, these images are imported from the eMaintenance cloud data source. To see these 360° images with VR glasses, the following steps within Unity are required:

1. In the inspector window, set Texture Shape of 360° image to Cube and apply the changes; this will create a cubemap of the 360° image.
2. Next, create a material. In the inspector window of the created material, set Shader to Skybox/Cubemap.
3. Next, drag and drop the created cubemap of the 360° image in the material window.
4. In the last step, drag this created cubemap material to the scene window.

To interact within this 360° image environment, various interactive buttons are created. When the buttons are clicked, visual inspection/condition monitoring information is displayed in the VR environment. The initial idea is to understand what the MR environment will look like when used in the real railway environment.

Prototype 3 also uses 3D models extracted from point cloud data (Figure 10.11f–h) using AI. However, in MR, these digital objects are merged within the real world as shown in Figure 12c. The person wearing HoloLens 2 (Figure 10.12c) can interact with these 3D models in the real world to see the overlaid inspection or condition monitoring information of the railway asset. The 3D models used for HoloLens 2 are optimised using AI technology.

All three prototypes have been tested by a group of experts from industry and academia. The evaluation results from interviews, workshops, seminars, and questionnaires show that the proposed model will help railway stakeholders augment their DMP within operation and maintenance.

10.4   CASE STUDY 5 – AI FACTORY – CYBERSECURITY SERVICES IN THE RAILWAY

Railway is a critical infrastructure for any country. The operations of freight and passenger services require reliability, availability, maintainability, and safety. Consistency of railway transport in terms of schedule and availability is affected by various factors of operation and maintenance of overall infrastructure and the support of various railway stakeholders.

Previously run by the state, the deregulation of railways started in Europe in the 1980s to ensure the best use of public funds and to create a sustainable environment within economic and legal requirements. Reducing the state monopoly allowed private actors to come into the domain and improve efficiency by combining competition, investment through entrepreneurship, and lack of government constraints with innovative practices to provide a better quality of service at a lower cost to society. Over time, deregulation led to a common European market for services, materials, equipment, and standardisation in railways, setting railways as the preferred mode of transport.

Railway systems' functionality depends on various factors, including people, policies, processes, software applications, information, infrastructure, etc. The vertical segregation of overall operations and services resulting from deregulation has created an array of stakeholders who are responsible for different aspects of the system while working within the regulations to fulfil the requirements. Stakeholders support different parts of the system.

Stakeholders in railways include regulators, infrastructure managers, manufacturers of high-value equipment, manufacturers of rolling stock, rail-set owners, rail-set operators, maintenance service providers, etc. Operators compete through a tendering process to gain the rights to operate in a certain region or route; however, to reduce the cost of operations, the operators do not own the rail sets. Rather, they acquire them on lease from rail-set owners. In the Swedish context, rail-set (locomotive with passenger coaches and freight wagons) owners and operators are separate entities. This creates a condition where different operators may use the same equipment at different points in time. Segregation of stakeholders and the necessity of equipment being shared in space and time increases the complexity of data sharing and requires the resolution of various governance, business, and technology-related issues.

Regular use and exposure to elements lead to deterioration and eventually failure of components, equipment, and infrastructure. Failure of equipment in a connected and dependent railway infrastructure affects multiple stakeholders and disturbs overall operations. Smooth and secure railway operations require constant maintenance of infrastructure and rolling stock. The steps of inspection, detection and prediction, maintenance planning, scheduling, and process are indispensable to maintain high availability. The development of tools and techniques in condition-based maintenance has led to improvement in the overall utilisation of equipment. These maintenance methods are, in turn, dependent on the fusion of a large amount of sensor data, inspection reports, maintenance processes, and eventually domain knowledge. The collection, storage, communication, processing, and management of data, processing models, and results are imperative to deliver the expected results to end-users in the context of data-driven decision-making.

Increasing requirements of railways in terms of data collection, transmission, storage, processing, and overall data management have increased the need for digitalisation. The Internet, the digital expressway connecting the edge devices, and the cloud infrastructure simplify the creation and maintenance of scalable communication and computing infrastructures to support requirements in the digital domain. However, the digital domain is plagued by issues of cybersecurity and cyber threats. Railways have an ever-increasing need for communication and computation resources, and, in turn, their dependence on digitalisation exposed them to cyber threats.

Data storage and sharing have traditionally used a centralised architecture. However, cyber threats engender the single point of failure. In addition, data integrity is questionable, as a malicious agency can not only access the data but also modify the stored contents to represent false conditions. Complexity, lack of resources, and issues pertaining to cybersecurity cause reluctance to share data, and large amounts of collected data are not used within the organisation or shared among the stakeholders.

In a multi-stakeholder environment, such as the railway, confidence in security is difficult due to secrecy about the cybersecurity practices. During a data transfer, the source and destination require authentication for each transaction, while the communication and sharing of credentials themselves can be insecure. The data or the models exchanged do not provide any assurance of integrity and lack metadata, ownership, and lineage. A low level of the expected level of trust (ELoT) requires a higher level of cybersecurity. The lowest level of ELoT, zero trust, is the most challenging scenario.

Enabling cybersecurity for the zero-trust scenario in railway can be achieved using different approaches. One is a decentralised consensus-based governance model, implemented through the concept of distributed ledgers. Distributed ledgers provide data security through open algorithms with well-evaluated resilient security practices and usage guidelines. All participants apply the practices following the same set of guidelines, setting the same and known level of security, and decreasing the level of ELoT (for more on distributed ledgers, see Chapter 11).

Distributed data storage for a multi-stakeholder environment like the railways requires support for maintaining data integrity and data security. Maintaining integrity, authenticity, and consensus for the stored data has limitations when implemented through centralised data storage. In recent years, developments in distributed consensus algorithms have provided the base for distributed ledgers. Distributed ledgers provide a robust data storage layer with strong resistance to cyber threats. Distributed ledgers have been applied in the railway context to solve technical issues involving ticketing, customs clearance, data collection, and so on.

Technological issues represent only one aspect in the application of technology. A unified environment for sharing data among the railway stakeholders in a security-conscious manner is also needed. Dynamic ownership transfer based on time, location, and equipment is a domain requirement for railways. A mechanism to share data, models, information, and introduction of partners with data processing expertise is required to advance the data-driven decision-making process.

As an example, think of a route with a train shuttling between two towns. By considering the maintenance point of view, we can explore the requirements and interdependency of various stakeholders. The data collected by on-board sensors about the train operations will be of interest to several stakeholders, such as the locomotive manufacturer, railcar manufacturer, rail-set owner, operator, infrastructure owner, and maintenance provider. Similarly, the data collected by the wayside detectors or LiDAR equipment is under the ownership of the infrastructure owner but useful to the locomotive manufacturer, railcar manufacturer, rail-set owner, operator, and maintenance provider, in addition to the infrastructure owner. The locomotive and the railcars may be exchanged between operators for reasons of replacement or maintenance requirements. Further, it is of interest to share the data with data processing experts to facilitate improved data analytics and the generated information with correct stakeholders.

10.4.1 RAILWAY SYSTEM STAKEHOLDERS

The data collected over a period even from a single route may have different ownership and many interested parties. A holistic perspective is necessary to create a secure data-sharing environment to address the challenges for governance, business operations, and technical requirements. In the following sections, we discuss the various railway stakeholders in the context of security.

10.4.1.1 Infrastructure Manager

Railway infrastructure is the physical support of the whole railway system. Infrastructure managers are responsible for the management of infrastructure, exploitation, development, and organisation and supervision of predictive and corrective maintenance, including maintenance work to replace old assets or complete installations.

With predictive maintenance, failures are avoided with programmed actions based on statistics or experience, performing adequate maintenance actions or replacing the corresponding assets before the foreseen failure.

For corrective maintenance, infrastructure managers are responsible for tracking these activities, supervising the repairs, and reviewing and updating statistics for the occurred failure, studying the case and proposing (if needed) changes in the predictive maintenance schedule and/or procedures.

They are main agents of the railway system and, as such, are responsible for making it available to the rest of the stakeholders, to allow them to operate according to the technical specifications and safety rules.

10.4.1.2 Maintainer

Maintainers are responsible for performing the scheduled maintenance activities following the established procedures and producing maintenance reports for the infrastructure managers. For corrective maintenance, maintainers perform the activities to re-establish the correct railway operation, preparing the respective reports for the infrastructure manager.

10.4.1.3 Passenger Operator

Passenger services are managed by passenger operators in coordination with traffic management to organise passenger trains' schedules with responsibility for the readiness of trains and passenger services on-board. Passenger services may include Internet connection on board, and this service can be provided by the infrastructure manager.

10.4.1.4 Interaction with Other Operators

Operators, both freight and passenger operators, obtain their slots for traffic from the traffic manager. International traffic (both passengers and freight) needs additional exchange of information to coordinate services (ticket selling, freight tracking, etc.) usually through dedicated virtual private networks (VPNs) and receive information on the traffic situation from the traffic manager.

10.4.1.5 Dependencies with External Stakeholders

Several external stakeholders also have information interchange with traffic and maintenance managers, such as ticket sellers, last mile transporters, and external maintenance companies. For them, information exchange with the railway manager is critical for performing their work, so safe and reliable communication between their systems must be assured.

10.4.1.6 Interaction in Public Areas

Stations are growing not only as passenger boarding places but also as commercial areas and places of leisure. Station managers are responsible for providing passenger information services, providing ticket sales services, and even, in some cases, providing telecommunication services to stores and restaurants.

10.4.1.7 Interactions in Operational Environments

The operational environment often includes intermodal stations and ports, where passengers and freight switch the transport method. This implies coordination for all the transport methods for better efficiency by exchanging information in RT about the actors involved (trains, trucks, boats, buses, etc.). This information interchange requires the information from the different stakeholders to be linked (Shift2Rail, 2017).

REFERENCES

IEC. (2004). *Dependability management - Part 3-14: Application guide - Maintenance and maintenance support*. IEC 60300-3-14:2004. International Electrotechnical Commission. https://webstore.iec.ch/publication/1298

ITF. (2021). Data-driven transport infrastructure maintenance. International Transport Forum (ITF) Policy Papers, No. 95. OECD Publishing. https://www.itf-oecd.org/sites/default/files/docs/data-driven-transport-infrastructure-maintenance.pdf

Luleå tekniska universitet. (LTU). *AI Factory Mining*. https://www.ltu.se/research/subjects/Drift-och-underhall/Forskningsprojekt/AI-Factory/AI-Factory-Mining?l=en

Luleå tekniska universitet. (LTU). *AI Factory Railway*. https://www.ltu.se/research/subjects/Drift-och-underhall/Forskningsprojekt/AI-Factory/aifr

Karim, R. Westerberg, J., Galar, D., & Kumar, U. (2016). Maintenance analytics: The new know in maintenance. *IFAC-PapersOnLine*, *49*(28), 214–219. https://doi.org/10.1016/j.ifacol.2016.11.037.

Shift2Rail. (2017). D2.1 – Safety and security requirements of rail transport system in multi-stakeholder environments. *CYbersecurity in the RAILway sector*, EU Project 730843. Shift2Rail.

11 AI Factory
A Roadmap for AI Transformation

11.1 WHAT IS THE AI FACTORY?

A key AI technology that is used in business today is machine learning (ML). These algorithms are essentially statistical engines with the capacity to reveal patterns in past observations and predict new outcomes. Along with other key components such as data sources, experiments, and software, ML algorithms can create what we have labelled the AI Factory.

The AI Factory is a set of interconnected components and processes nurturing learning and growth. Quality data obtained from internal and/or external sources train ML algorithms to make predictions on specific tasks. In some cases, such as in the healthcare field with the diagnosis and treatment of diseases, these predictions can help human experts make decisions. In others, ML algorithms can automate tasks with little or no human intervention.

The algorithm- and data-driven model of the AI Factory allows organisations to test new hypotheses and make changes that improve their systems, including new features added to existing products/methods or entirely new products/methods. The process is ongoing, as these changes yield new data, allowing organisations to improve their AI algorithms, and find new ways to increase performance, create new products/methods, grow, and move across markets and perhaps into new ones.

It has been stated that AI factory creates a virtuous cycle between user engagement, data collection, algorithm design, prediction, and improvement (Iansiti & Lakhani, 2020).

The cycle itself is not a new concept. But AI factory takes the cycle to a new level by including such innovations as natural language processing and computer vision. The result is that organisations can offer more services to more people at less cost (Dickson, 2020).

11.1.1 INFRASTRUCTURE OF THE AI FACTORY

ML algorithms require huge amount of data. But the simple provision of Big Data cannot ensure good AI algorithms. In fact, many organisations have vast amounts of data, but their data and software exist in separate organisational sections (e.g. maintenance and operations), inconsistently stored in incompatible models and frameworks.

Data cannot be aggregated if internal systems and data are fragmented across organisational units and functions. Without aggregation, the power of analytics and AI cannot be leveraged.

Furthermore, before being fed to AI algorithms, data must be pre-processed. For instance, we might want to use the history of past correspondence with customers to develop an AI-powered chatbot that automates parts of our customer support. In this case, the text data must be consolidated, tokenised, stripped of excessive words and punctuations, and go through other transformations before they can be used to train the ML model.

Even when dealing with structured data such as sales records, there might be gaps, missing information, and other inaccuracies that need to be resolved. And if the data come from various sources, they need to be aggregated in a way that doesn't cause inaccuracies. Without pre-processing, we will be training our ML models on low-quality data, resulting in AI systems that perform poorly.

Finally, internal data sources might not be enough to develop the AI pipeline – by which we mean a set of components and processes that consolidate data from various internal and external sources, clean the data, integrate them, process them, and store them for use in different AI systems. At times, we may need to complement our existing information with data from external sources, such

DOI: 10.1201/9781003208686-11

as data obtained from social media, stock market, news sources, and more. An example is BlueDot, a company that uses ML to predict the spread of infectious diseases. To train and run its AI system, BlueDot automatically gathers information from hundreds of sources, including statements from health organisations, commercial flights, livestock health reports, climate data from satellites, and news reports. Much of the company's efforts and software are designed to gather and unify the data.

The data pipeline should work in a systematic, sustainable, and scalable way, with little manual effort involved to avoid causing a bottleneck in the AI (Iansiti & Lakhani, 2020).

Other challenges in the AI Factory include establishing the right metrics and features for supervised ML algorithms, finding the right split between human expert insight and AI predictions, and tackling the challenges of running experiments and validating the results (Dickson, 2020).

11.1.2 BECOMING AN AI COMPANY

In many ways, building a successful AI company is as much a product management challenge as an engineering one. Many successful organisations have figured out how to build the right culture and processes on long-existing AI technology instead of trying to fit the latest developments in deep learning (DL) into an infrastructure that doesn't work.

This applies to both startups and long-standing firms. To not just survive but also thrive, organisations must continuously transform their operating and business models (Iansiti & Lakhani, 2020).

Startups building AI factories from the ground up, such as Peleton, are able to disrupt the traditional market. At the same time, established companies can evolve; for example, Walmart leveraged digitisation and AI to avoid the fate of Sears, the retail giant that filed for bankruptcy in 2018.

The rise of AI has also brought new meaning to "network effects", a phenomenon studied by tech companies since the first search engines and social networks. AI algorithms integrated into networks can boost growth, learning, and product improvement.

Advances in AI will have implications for everyone running an organisation, not just the people developing the technology. For example, managers will have to learn the foundational knowledge behind AI and the ways that technology can be effectively deployed in their organisation's business and operation models (Iansiti & Lakhani, 2020). They do not need to become data scientists, statisticians, programmers, or AI engineers, but they have to understand the reasons to use AI and appreciate both its challenges and its advantages (Dickson, 2020).

11.2 MASTERING AI IN MANUFACTURING: THE THREE LEVELS OF COMPETENCY

Manufacturers have been facing continual pressure to improve their technology base, reduce costs, and improve quality since the first Industrial Revolution. Organisations are used to change, but not everyone can or will embrace it at the same rate, and no organisation is an immediate expert in the new playing field. This certainly applies to AI (Locke, 2020).

AI in manufacturing can be split into two core areas: robotics and processes.

1. Robotics: Robotics works to make machines more readily adapt to tasks humans do with ease like picking up different objects with different strengths. For all but the biggest manufacturers, the development of bespoke robotics solutions might be infeasible. Buying new machinery like robots is a big investment and can't happen frequently.
2. Processes: The other area of AI, processes, can often be done using the existing data from the shop floor or with making a more limited investment to retrofit some sensors into the environment. Processes include optimising flow through the manufacturing process, identifying quality issues, and minimising downtime for machinery. These are areas where existing data consolidation options can be used to support off-the-shelf AI solutions or specialist development of bespoke solutions. A single data scientist or AI engineer is going

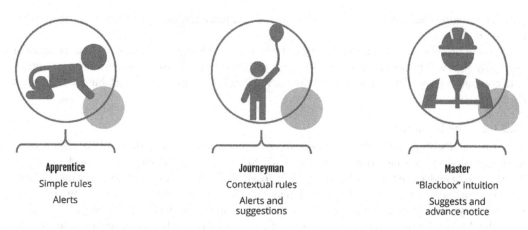

FIGURE 11.1 AI competency (Locke, 2020).

to be less costly than most investments a manufacturer has to make. Manufacturers can use sensor data consolidated by devices like historians to start improving processes with a growing AI competency (Locke, 2020).

11.2.1 AI COMPETENCY

AI competency comprises three levels: apprentice, journeyman, and master (Figure 11.1).

AI competency for a manufacturer starts at the apprentice level, where the basics are learned and people learn exactly how much they don't yet know. It's a formative stage where the foundations of important knowledge and the establishment of trust occur.

The next level is journeyman status. At this point, people are fairly competent and can be trusted to make suggestions.

The final level is the master level, based on an intimate knowledge of what's happening and why, coupled with ongoing learning. Master-level engineers are trusted to make decisions with limited oversight, and errors are few and far between.

These levels of competency add more responsibility, trust, and scope as time goes on (Locke, 2020).

11.2.1.1 The Apprentice

Like all apprenticeships, knowledge acquired at this stage often feels like a struggle and can be initially painful. Apprentices are tasked with simpler tasks and are not expected to be proactive. They are closely monitored and are not tasked with anything too critical.

In the manufacturing world, the apprentice might be expected to monitor a few critical systems and flag any unusual changes in the system to the supervisor. This type of task is also a perfect start for the organisation's first AI solutions.

Anomaly detection can be used to monitor some key systems, with alerts sent if something appears off. At its simplest (the apprenticeship stage), this could be generating alerts whenever a value exceeds a threshold. In the long run, however, this can become a relatively sophisticated process that takes into account patterns of work over recent weeks, so that any issues are contextualised by what is expected at a given point in time.

These types of systems, like human apprentices, can be too nervous (generating more alerts than they needed to) or too relaxed (generating an insufficient number of alerts), but it is a learning process where the right level of attention and signals is the goal.

As the anomaly detection process usually works on a single sensor, many "apprentices" (anomaly detection routines) may work on the shop floor, each potentially generating lots of alerts. It may be difficult to improve each one; thus, it may be better to use just a few and spend more time improving each individually.

Working on anomaly detection processes allows the organisation to develop its data processing capability so it will be able to raise alerts in near real time (RT). It also starts establishing comfort with computers prompting action – something that might be new and uncomfortable for employees (Locke, 2020).

11.2.1.2   The Journeyman

Over time and with practice, the apprentice evolves into a journeyman. Having established some trust, the journeyman is tasked with more difficult things. At the journeyman level, workers should be expected to understand at a high level what factors drive issues, so that they can start understanding when things might go wrong. This is a transition period from being reactive to being proactive, but a journeyman still lacks the responsibility and trust required to make big decisions.

In the AI world, this is equivalent to building and using ML methods that involve known variables and will be used for explaining the drivers of behaviours of interest. Regression and decision trees are common techniques in this area. Experts determine the most important machines and sensors that are most relevant for determining things like imminent breakdowns, quality reduction, or processing speed. These sensor values are matched against the outcome under study.

The next step is the construction of a model that describes how the sensor readings impact the outcome. This model can be used to understand the situation, enabling manual controls or rule-based processes to be put into place. It could be deployed to actively monitor for a high chance of a breakdown, for instance, and generate an alert.

These types of models are typically harder to build and deploy than anomaly detection processes because they require historic data from multiple sensors and whatever it is the organisation is trying to predict/understand. It is also hard if many things are simultaneously happening because the models are intended to be given to a human to think about and reflect upon.

Developing these models validates the organisation's ability to work with historic data and uncover insights. It starts establishing the next level of trust in employees that AI is able to arrive at sensible conclusions. Significant return on investment (ROI) can be generated by being able to prevent issues or optimise processes using the insight generated (Locke, 2020).

11.2.1.3   The Master

The final level in the competency path is master status. Masters are trusted to understand the breadth of the field and have deep knowledge; thus, they are likely to have intuitions about issues before they arise. They are trusted to make decisions mostly autonomously with limited oversight. They still learn on the job, but at this point, they refine and hone their knowledge.

In the context of AI, this is the use of DL and reinforcement learning to construct models that integrate into the manufacturing environment. These models might actually be used to automatically generate tasks, work orders, or control the machines.

With DL, we are able to take a huge amount of data from myriad sensors and build a model that doesn't just use a few rules that someone else says is important, but actually integrates information from the whole suite of sensors to make predictions. The model's predictions are optimised using RT signals about how good it is at predicting things.

These techniques are much more complicated to build, but they can provide stronger coverage of a situation and be more accurate. Ideally, there should always be a human in the loop to monitor what decisions are being made, as models, like humans, are fallible and can make mistakes.

Attaining master status involves the curation of trusted data, trusted models, and strong RT processing capabilities. Employees have worked around the increasingly sophisticated models and have seen benefits to them and to the organisation from their use. They trust the solutions to not just give them insight, but to also start assisting them in the execution of their daily tasks (Locke, 2020).

11.3   IS AI READY TO RUN A FACTORY?

The concept of machine-to-machine (M2M) communication isn't new. In the early 1970s, Theodore Paraskevakos patented the transmission of information from a calling telephone to a called telephone. By the late 1990s, M2M communication included devices sharing data over networks. Over the following decades, more and more data were shared over global Internet. Today, the IoT encompasses some 50 billion data-sharing devices worldwide. It's estimated by 2025 the number of IoT devices will reach 75 billion.

Data are being produced on an unprecedented scale. For example, in 2016, the world generated 2,500,000,000 GB of data each day. Nearly 90% of all data that ever existed prior to 2016 came into existence during 2016. As impressive as the ability to generate data has become, it pales in comparison to the ability to store it. Worldwide data storage capacity (i.e. Global Storage Sphere) doubles every four years. Today, the Global Storage Sphere stands at 6,200,000,000,000 GB. Roughly 60% of this space is currently being used.

11.3.1   CYBER-PHYSICAL SYSTEMS

The ability to generate and store continuous streams of data has allowed engineers to construct "virtual factories". In this digital world, discrete event modelling is used to describe the flow of products through production steps. "Agent-based modelling" allows programmers to place production elements (i.e. people, facilities, products, and orders) inside simulated environments to observe system behaviours.

Virtual factories are routinely used by Volvo Group Global to validate proposed production changes before they are introduced into actual plants (Jain et al., 2017). However, simulating factories has a number of limitations. A factory is an open system. Any number of outside variables (e.g. absenteeism, training, product mix, on-time delivery, inventory levels, machine breakdowns, and scrap) impact what is happening inside the system. Factories, like all open systems, never settle into a steady state. This presents serious problems for modelling. Cyber-physical systems (CPS) address this weakness by continuously feeding information back into models. Consequently, computations monitor and control physical processes while feedback loops allow physical processes to update computations.

The ability for machines to collect, share, analyse, and act upon vast amounts of data requires extremely fast and flexible computer processors (CPUs). Multicore CPUs are capable of executing billions of calculations per second (GHz). CPS, however, requires more: clusters of multicore processors working in parallel. One such cluster, the IBM AC922, is made up of 4,608 computer servers. In one second, this supercomputer can perform 200 quadrillion (i.e. 200 with 15 zeros) calculations. Fast processor speeds and memory transfers are at the heart of smart manufacturing (Seidelson, 2021).

11.3.1.1   Manufacturing and Cyber-Physical Systems

From a manufacturing industry perspective, a CPS is an Internet-enabled physical entity, such as a pump or compressor, embedded with computers and control components consisting of sensors and actuators. Such an entity is IP address-assigned and is capable of self-monitoring, generating information about its own functioning, and communicating with other associated entities or even outside. It is a self-regulating and autonomous operation.

In the years to come, industrial firms will begin to leverage the tenets of CPS more and more to help achieve operational excellence through productivity improvements, efficient deployment of all resources (including material and human), customer fulfilment, and the enhancement of shareholder value. The term "Fourth Industrial Revolution" (Industry 4.0) has been coined to describe the trend.

The foundation for Industry 4.0 was laid during the Third Industrial Revolution in the latter part of the 20th century, characterised by the extensive application of electronics and computers to automate industrial production processes. The expanding use of electronics and computers contributed to their declining prices, the miniaturisation and robustness of computers, and a massive increase in computing and processing power. Digital and communication technologies began to converge. We witnessed the first stages of development of edge/cloud computing, the Industrial Internet of Things (IIoT), AI, autonomous robots, and more. The integration of digital technologies with industrial technologies is set to transform manufacturing and help realise the vision of Industry 4.0.

The tenet of Industry 4.0 is that a manufacturing company will be able to achieve higher efficiency, productivity, and the autonomous operation of production processes by ensuring that machines/plant equipment, logistics systems, work-in-progress components, and other elements (including people) directly communicate with each other to achieve collaboration. A manufacturing company that wants to align its vision with that of Industry 4.0 must take steps to convert existing physical entities into CPS.

Based on its own assessment, each company has to identify machinery, equipment, or other physical systems with the potential to deliver maximum value. The company must integrate them with cyber systems and evolve this into a network of CPS. A refinery complex, for example, may have on-site and off-site tank farms with pipelines, control valves, and pumping stations connecting them to the main plant. In tank farm upkeep, the present practice is manual inspection and periodic maintenance, which is expensive and inefficient. By converting these assets into CPS and supporting them with suitable analytics software, the refinery will be able to switch to remote monitoring, and predictive maintenance can benefit (Arcot, 2021).

11.3.2 ARTIFICIAL INTELLIGENCE

As we have discussed throughout the book, AI refers to a set of technologies in which computer systems are programmed to model complex behaviour in challenging environments. A major goal is to mimic human intelligence in computer software. Human intelligence, broadly speaking, encompasses the ability to learn from experience, perceive abstract contexts, cognise, adapt to situations, and act (Karim, 2008; Karim et al., 2016, 2021; Kour et al., 2020; Kumari et al., 2022; Patwardhan et al., 2021). Accordingly, AI constitutes a set of computer science techniques permitting computer software to learn, perceive, cognise, and act (ITF, 2021).

11.3.2.1 Industrial AI

From an industrial point of view, AI technologies are methods and procedures that enable technical systems to perceive their environments through context and situation awareness, process what they have monitored and modelled, solve problems, find new solutions, make decisions, and learn from experience to improve the processes and performance of tasks under AI supervision.

There are myriad reasons to turn to AI in industry. AI is expected to increase both the efficiency and effectiveness of industrial processes. It should save time, reduce costs, improve quality, and amp up the robustness of industrial processes.

As we mentioned in earlier chapters, AI is not well integrated into industry, largely because of the certainty about enormous changes and high costs. Organisations are quite rightly approaching the technology with caution. At this point, AI applications are mainly found in knowledge management, robotics, and quality control. Another key area is maintenance analytics, as organisations are switching from traditional approaches to maintenance to predictive maintenance.

One area of interest for maintenance in industrial environments is the collection, analysis, and interpretation of sensor data, driven by the capabilities of IoT. IoT acquires the data after preprocessing, records the status of various aspects of interest in the equipment, and performs actions on the basis of its analysis. Its central purpose is to enable predictive maintenance. For example, complex interrelated parameters may need to be adjusted in response to fluctuating conditions in the environment to avoid compromising asset health – and this state would most likely be invisible to the human eye.

AI is also frequently used for data augmentation, whereby new synthetic datasets are generated based on original datasets, for example, by copying and slightly modifying or enriching the features in a dataset (ITF, 2021).

11.3.2.2 Machine Learning

A factory's enterprise resource planning (ERP) systems transfer all of the accounting, production, supply chain, sales, marketing and human resources data using in-memory, relational databases. ERP provider SAP requires a minimum 60 GB of storage capacity. The amount of data storage needed to run a business might seem like a lot – but it isn't when you consider that sensors, solenoids, and actuators on a single IoT-enabled device will typically generate 5 GB of data per week. Even with clustered processors, it can take the order of hours to extract structured (and unstructured) data in multiple disparate formats, transform those data into a format that can be analysed, and then load it into a data warehouse. Collectively, delays in data extraction, transformation, and loading are referred to as exact, transform, and load (ETL) lag.

Machine learning in near real time at factories must compensate for ETL lag. This is commonly done using a lambda (λ) architecture, which gives quick answers based on some of the data and accurate answers based on all of the data.

The continuous flow of high variety data at high volume into λ architecture is accomplished by breaking data into manageable chunks using a queuing system like Kafka and a streaming system like Storm, Spark, or Flink. Algorithms on each coding layer become inputs to other algorithms on other coding layers. In this way, batches of data transfer between layers once an hour or once a day. As more data pass through more computations on more layers, DL model parameters are self-adjusted (i.e. trained) to make better predictions about future data. To the extent existing labelled data matches predict data, the model is validated. To the extent new data matches predict data, the model is tested for use. New and old data continuously retrain batch layer programmes in the hope of improving how well algorithms can monitor and control physical processes. Periodically, model-predicted data are uploaded to serving layers for factory managers to view using NoSQL (not only structured query language (SQL)) key value queries.

Because the batching and serving layers operate on the full dataset, these ML algorithms are the most accurate. Accuracy, however, comes at a high price. Batch layers need to store an immutable, constantly growing master dataset and compute arbitrary functions on that dataset. Even with open-sourced Hadoop batch clustering systems parallelising data storage and computations, ETL lag time to propagate new data through batch layers can take hours. Near RT monitoring and control of physical processes in a factory require a speed layer.

ML algorithms on a λ speed layer perform computations on the most recent data before uploading those data to batch layers. Fast reads and writes are possible because speed layer programs, unlike those on batch layers, aren't continuously re-computing batch views from scratch. Creating a DL model from scratch can take days or weeks to train, because of the large amount of data and extended rate of learning. Databases on the speed layer, such as Cassandra or HBase, are capable of near RT monitoring and control of physical processes because they incrementally update views (i.e. transfer learning) created by analytics programs, such as MapReduce, Hive, or Spark, on batch layers.

Incremental programming logic makes the speed layer fast. For example, with clusters of processors operating in parallel, speed layer training times decrease from weeks to minutes. Unfortunately, transfer learning and the random database reads and writes mean the speed layer is also by far the most complex. The beauty of λ ML architecture is that system complexity is isolated to computing layers where data only exist temporarily. Once data are uploaded to batch layers, they are purged from the speed layer, making room for more incoming data and calculations.

Given the data storage, transfer, and computations needed to support ML, smart manufacturing is primarily done on server-less, pay-for-use network clusters known as clouds. Indeed, spending

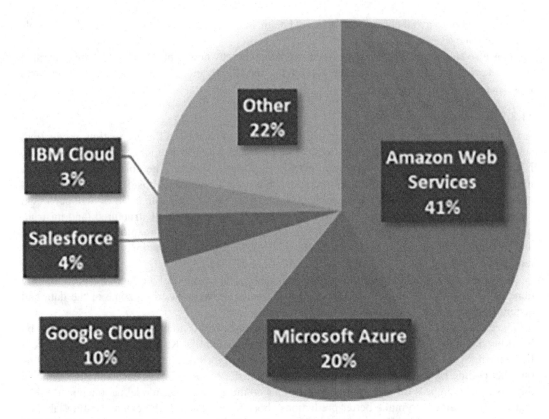

FIGURE 11.2   The public cloud is controlled by a few providers (Seidelson, 2021).

on cloud infrastructure as a service (IaaS) and software as a service (SaaS) reached $20 billion in 2019. By 2025, it's estimated that almost half of the world's data will be stored in clouds. As shown in Figure 11.2, five companies account for nearly 80% of the public cloud (Seidelson, 2021).

Today, the leading public cloud providers offer their own automated ML packages. Microsoft has the Machine Learning Studio. Google offers Cloud AutoML, and AWS uses Sage Maker. Widespread availability of cloud and coding architecture means more organisations can begin AI initiatives.

Even with automatically scalable cloud resources and 20× faster 5G downlink speeds capable of supporting 10× more connected devices per unit of floor space, there are latency concerns when sending data across networks and devices. Near RT ML on a speed layer requires bringing data storage and processing off centralised clouds closer to the edge where computation outputs are needed. This is particularly true in factories when ML data may only be of interest to those applications generating data. By leveraging a wide range of local devices and nearby data centres, edge computing is key to supporting near RT CPS (Seidelson, 2021).

11.3.2.2.1   AI Managed Facilities

The real manufacturing world is on the verge of converging with the digital manufacturing world, thus enabling organisations to digitally plan and project the entire lifecycle of products and production facilities. Smart factories represent an attempt to undertake production without human involvement. Reaching this end involves a pyramid of four levels:

1. Device level,
2. Supervisory control and data acquisition (SCADA) level,
3. Manufacturing operations management (MOM) level, and
4. Enterprise level.

A factory is "smart" to the extent that its answers to the following ten statements are "yes".

1. Algorithms decide inventory and production levels.
2. Machines provide customers and associates with RT answers to their questions.
3. Machines detect, sort, and make corrections for nonconforming products.
4. Algorithms predict quality issues.
5. Algorithms predict maintenance needs.
6. Image recognition locates parts in storage and production.
7. Material handling equipment is self-directed.
8. Algorithms create and validate designs.
9. Production machines are self-operating.
10. Production machines are self-programmed.

Smart manufacturing is expected to grow at an exponential rate. In spite of optimistic projections, a 2018 US Census Bureau survey of 583,000 US businesses found only 2.8% had actually adopted ML. A Capgemini Research Institute survey of 1,000 manufacturers with smart factory initiatives underway found only 14% described their deployments as successful.

At this point, a key issue holding back AI is conductivity between devices and analytics (Seidelson, 2021).

Scaling AI implementations beyond a proof-of-concept (POC) level remains another challenge in manufacturing, as well as other industries, including but not limited to logistics, healthcare, insurance, finance, and audit industries.

Taking advantage of the technology isn't enough – there is also a wider aspect of people and cultural change that needs to be addressed. Stakeholders and end-users must be convinced of the reliability of the data generated with AI and their ability to yield insights. For instance, even when people are aware that the inventory recommendations for raw materials or deliverables are accurate, they feel more comfortable holding a little extra stock or being somewhat protective in the supply chain. Therefore, incorporating human heuristics becomes a challenge (Pressley, 2021).

11.3.2.3 Why is the Adoption of AI Accelerating?

A few key advantages make the adoption of AI particularly suitable as a launching pad for manufacturers to embark on their cognitive computing journey – intelligent maintenance, intelligent demand planning and forecasting, and product quality control.

The deployment of AI is a complex process, as with many facets of digitisation, but it has not stopped companies from moving forward. The ability to grow and sustain the AI initiative over time, in a manner that generates increasing value for the enterprise, is likely to be crucial to achieving early success milestones on an AI adoption journey.

Manufacturing companies are adopting AI and ML with such speed because by using these cognitive computing technologies, they can optimise their analytics capabilities, make better forecasts, and decrease inventory costs. Improved analytics capabilities enable companies to switch to predictive maintenance, thus reducing maintenance costs and reducing downtime.

The use of AI allows organisations to predict when or if functional equipment will fail so that maintenance and repairs can be scheduled in advance. It is important because equipment can operate more efficiently – and cost-efficiently – when AI-powered predictive maintenance is used. The ability to predict breakdowns and optimise scheduling before the equipment fails makes AI excellent for maintaining reliable equipment and maintaining smooth production (Pressley, 2021).

11.3.2.4 Digital Twins in Industry

Digital twins (DTs) are increasingly being used to improve quality control, supply chain management, predictive maintenance, and customer experiences. As IoT implementations enable greater access to Big Data and vast digital ecosystems, creating and maintaining high-fidelity DT gets easier and easier (Pressley, 2021).

DTs work by evolving profiles of past and current behaviours of physical objects or processes that can be analysed to optimise business performance. These can be used in a variety of ways to improve operations and help engineering, production, sales, and marketing to work together using the same data, making better decisions.

DT also helps transform the manufacturing process as it shows variances in equipment or manufacturing processes that indicate a need for maintenance before something major happens. The ease of access to operational data through DT facilitates collaboration, improves communication, and leads to faster decision-making (Pressley, 2021).

11.4   THE DATA-DRIVEN APPROACH AND AI

As discussed in previous chapters, the main objective of implementing a data-driven approach is to augment human capabilities. Improved capabilities include:

- better fact-based decision-making;
- increased cost-efficiency;
- lower latency in planning;
- improved logistics;
- enhanced analytics;
- better ability to predict and prevent; and
- improved sustainability.

However, augmenting human intelligence is not just a matter of data provisioning. The augmentation needs intelligence techniques – such as deep learning (DL) – to perceive and understand data, adapt to situations, and act accordingly.

This, in turn, leads to two dilemmas. The first dilemma is related to data acquisition. In the data-driven approach, data are necessary to solve a problem, but how can we know which datasets are useful? The second dilemma is related to the algorithms that process the data. Selecting an appropriate or the best-fit algorithm is a major optimisation challenge. At the same time, measuring the precision of the algorithm can be an indicator of its accuracy, but measuring model precision requires known knowledge for validation. What if the knowledge that describes a real-world phenomenon is not yet known? Can we use explainability in algorithms to improve their trustworthiness?

As both dilemmas suggest, the data-driven approach depends on what is commonly called domain knowledge. Domain knowledge refers to the in-depth understanding of an industrial sector. It can be used, for instance, to describe the physics-of-failure, which refers to the relationship between physical, thermal, chemical, and electrical mechanisms over time within a given context. In short, domain knowledge helps us select the relevant datasets and the best-fit algorithms. In practice, it isn't easy to apply a data-driven approach due to the lack of efficient procedures to obtain training data and specific domain knowledge. Domain knowledge is key, but can be a complex issue.

Assuming that we have found our data and algorithms, data-driven approaches are very useful. One key strength is their ability to transform high-dimensional noisy data into lower-dimensional information for diagnostic/prognostic decisions identifying remaining useful life (RUL) and facilitating maintenance decision-making (Dragomir et al., 2009). Data-driven approach techniques and ML have been increasingly applied in industry to estimate RUL and have shown improved performance over conventional approaches (Karim et al., 2021).

11.4.1   Pros of AI and a Data-Driven Approach

Opting for a data-driven approach yields the following advantages (Figure 11.3):

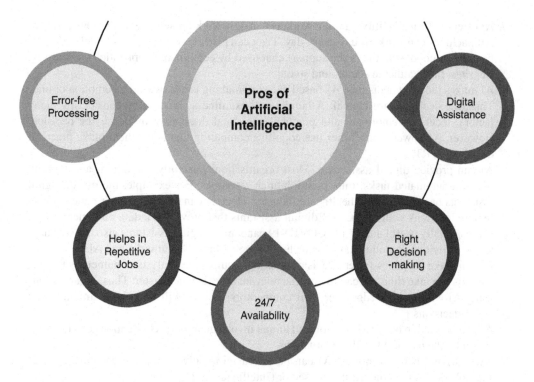

FIGURE 11.3 Pros of artificial intelligence (Intellipaat, 2022).

1. AI enables fact-based decision-making: Embracing a data-driven approach changes the decision-making process. The use of digital technologies powered by AI enables enhanced reasoning using advanced high-performance computing. Organisations can process the ever-increasing datasets and understand the patterns and relations in the data. Consequently, they are better able to recognise and predict both visible and hidden real-world phenomena.
2. AI improves transparency: Increased availability and accessibility of data and models in a unified manner promotes transparency in decision-making. Moreover, organisations can share data and models.
3. AI permits enhanced collaboration: A data-driven approach promotes a culture that endorses communication and collaboration. Improved collaboration, in turn, increases effectiveness and efficiency within an organisation and between collaborating organisations.
4. Reduced bias: Decision-making based on intuition is likely to be biased and may lead to errors and disruptions in operation and maintenance. Opting for a data-driven approach will reduce this type of bias.
5. AI can perform error-free processing: Humans are likely to make mistakes when doing a specific task, but AI-based machines programmed to accomplish that specific task will not make errors. Thus, the use of AI helps reduce unnecessary errors. Algorithms used to build AI-based models implement complicated mathematical constructs, resulting in greater efficiency and fewer errors. Thus, AI helps solve complex real-world problems.
6. AI is useful for repetitive jobs: Unlike humans, machines do not require breaks. Many day-to-day tasks performed by a human are repetitive. Our efficiency drops when we continuously perform the same job. AI-based machines perform repetitive tasks for a long time with no slowdown and no loss of productivity. Thus, AI is useful to manufacturers who want to continuously produce goods to meet market demand and make a profit.

7. AI offers 24/7 availability: Human workers can only work for seven or eight hours per day. AI machines can work all day every day. They can provide services without delay or inefficiency. A good example is the support chat used by ecommerce applications, e-learning websites, the healthcare sector, and so on.
8. AI makes the right decisions: AI-based decision-making is not swayed by emotion or bias. Thus, the decisions are logical. A human will examine a situation by considering many factors, including emotional and practical ones, and these may influence the decision. However, AI-powered machines use cognitive computing that helps them make practical decisions in RT.
9. AI can provide digital assistance: Most organisations currently use digital assistants to perform automated tasks, thus saving human resources. For example, the use of digital assistants has changed the healthcare industry. Doctors can look after their patients from remote locations with the help of digital assistants that provide RT data on patients. This was especially useful during the COVID-19 pandemic. Digital assistants also assist in day-to-day activities. Popular examples include Google Maps, Grammarly, and Alexa.
10. AI can make decisions faster: Decision-making requires the analysis of numerous factors, and this can take time. AI can review the relevant aspects much faster. Thus, organisations using AI will have an edge over their competitors, as they will have more time to make better decisions.
11. AI can be used in high-risk situations: Human involvement in risky situations can be minimised by the use of AI in those situations.
12. AI is driving new inventions: AI can be leveraged to solve complex problems. A good example of this is in the healthcare sector (Intellipaat, 2022).

11.4.2 Cons of AI and a Data-Driven Approach

Despite the numerous advantages of AI given above, there is a downside. In this section, we list the various challenges to the full implementation of AI and the data-driven approach (Figure 11.4).

1. AI needs good-quality data: The data-driven approach requires the analysis of massive amounts of data collected from many data sources to bring insight to decision-making. Insights depend on the quality of the data. Poor data quality can lead to less-reliable decisions.
2. AI requires context knowledge: The data-driven approach for analytics is built on assumptions, simplifications, and descriptions of usage contexts. These assumptions and simplifications

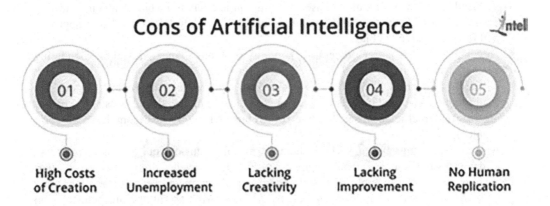

FIGURE 11.4 Cons of artificial intelligence (Intellipaat, 2022).

need to be measured, quantified, and explained for decision-makers. Not knowing the assumptions and the full context might lead to inaccurate decision-making not based on facts.

3. AI requires knowledge transformation: AI and the data-driven approach implement know-how and experience in a set of algorithms. One of the main challenges for organisations implementing a data-driven approach is to retain the level of knowledge in the organisation over the long term. In practice, maintenance decisions are not purely data-driven, because they need to be adapted to national and international contexts and conditions (Karim et al., 2021).

4. AI is expensive to create: The creation of AI machines is very costly, in the millions for large-scale projects. This means smaller organisations will not be able to implement AI. Even larger companies may feel the cost of developing an AI project is too high. The cost of development depends on the hardware and software selected, and both should be regularly updated – another expense. In the future, the cost of developing machines using AI should drop.

5. AI will change employment patterns: AI will create jobs for some, but at the same time, it is likely to leave others unemployed. It will create jobs for people skilled in technologies, but low-skilled jobs will be taken over by AI machines. As AI-based machines can work non-stop, organisations will invest in AI rather than employ humans.

6. AI machines lack creativity: At this point, machines cannot be as creative as humans. AI can provide functionality to learn from data but cannot mimic the human brain and human skills. AI cannot invent anything. It can simply perform the task it is programmed for and improve itself by experience. Although AI can collaborate with other technologies such as Big Data, IoT, and advanced sensors to give the best automation, the smartness and creativity of AI-based machines depend on how intelligent and creative the algorithms are – and these are created by humans.

7. AI can suffer learning failure: AI algorithms allow machines to learn by themselves and improve by exploring data. But problems in the data may cause failures in learning, and improvement may be inconsistent. The algorithms may need to be readjusted for new data.

8. AI lacks humanity: AI machines are based on algorithms, mathematical computing, and cognitive technologies. They may be highly advanced but still cannot act or think like a human. For example, they lack judgemental power as they are not aware of ethics, morals, and right and wrong. They will break down or yield unpredictable results if they are not programmed to make a particular decision (Intellipaat, 2022).

11.4.3 IMPLEMENTING THE DATA-DRIVEN APPROACH

Organisations wishing to implement a data-driven approach should address the challenges associated with it. They should develop a regulatory framework and governance model, considering barriers and potential solutions, addressing the aspects of both business and technology and analysing the various stakeholders, preferences of all parties, and existing technological and business solutions.

In other words, a data-driven approach requires the integration of all the influencing factors. These include issues of governance, business, and technology. A summary of the policy recommendations for the successful implementation of a data-driven approach is given in Table 11.1.

11.4.3.1 Governance

A CPS, for example, a transport system consisting of a combination of physical and digital assets, requires a holistic approach. The digital governance model needs to consider the particularity of digital assets to stimulate collaboration and cooperation between stakeholders, and at the same time provide consistent control and regulatory mechanisms.

TABLE 11.1

Enablers of the Data-Driven Approach

Enabler	Description	Expected Benefits
eGovernance	Digital world needs digital models for governance with supporting regulations and policies.	Improved transparency and democratisation.
Business	Data-driven approach requires new business models and investment scenario.	Enables new line-of-business
Collaboration	Regulatory framework and governance model should facilitate collaboration.	Attractive for investment and innovation in business and technology.
Asset management of digital assets	It is important to establish a management philosophy that considers and values digital assets, such as data and models	Improves innovation and creates a new line of business analysis.
Change management	Promoting AI and digitalisation changes the culture of an organisation.	Facilitates adaptation to new business models.
Data-driven and model-driven	Combining data-driven and model-driven approach increases analytics capabilities.	Improved analytics by utilising the best of two worlds.
Data democratisation	Availability and accessibility of data and models are essential for fact-based decision-making.	Increased accuracy in decision-making and reduced bias.
Cybersecurity	Achieving openness in digital environment requires good understanding and supporting security mechanisms,	Improved democratisation.
Data and model sharing	Sharing data and models requires not only technology, but also what sharing is meant to achieve.	Improved identification of key performance indicators for sharing. Regulatory framework for information logistics.
System-of-system	Understanding the concept of system-of-systems is essential to identify the system-of-interest and enabling-systems.	Enables organisation to focus on the right challenge to address.
Knowledge management	AI is about outsourcing know-how to machines. Strategies for retaining the level of knowledge in an organisation when implementing AI need to be adopted to new changes.	Better knowledge management

Such a governance model can be established by developing a roadmap based on the following questions:

- What are the advantages and disadvantages of the existing organisational forms, structures, and processes if we want to implement a data-driven approach to maintenance?
- How can we encourage coordination?
- Is there an effective incentive structure?
- How should we measure performance?

11.4.3.2 Business

Enabling business models for CPS requires an understanding of the characteristics of the various digital assets. Digital assets are not subject to the same type of degradation by usage as physical assets, and they are not as limited as physical assets to space and time. This means they may be used in more contexts. Thus, business models must adapt to new contexts to bring value to the digital asset's owner.

A roadmap for digital business models may be developed by asking the following questions:

- What are the future financing possibilities?
- What are the incentives and barriers to efficiency improvements?

- How can we ensure that adequate resources are available?
- What are the effects of different forms of ownership in a data-driven approach?

11.4.3.3   Technology

It is essential to select the appropriate technologies based on the governance models and the business models. Yet technology evolves faster than governance and business, leading to shorter development cycles. Thus, technologies might need to be changed or renewed within the same governance and business cycle.

To manage the evolution of technology together with the evolution of governance and business, organisations need to develop a roadmap for technology. The roadmap can be developed by asking the following questions:

- How does policy need to be changed to exploit technological developments, such as digitisation?
- How can we manage cybersecurity?
- How can we improve the quality of data to enable correct decision-making?
- How can we deploy new technologies to enhance analytics?

11.5   DATA-DRIVEN APPROACH IN PRODUCTION: SIX IMPLEMENTATION STAGES AND FAILURE FACTORS

The data-driven approach is simple: management decisions are based on objective data analysis. The larger the production company, the more processes and data it has. They are more difficult to collect, bring into accordance, analyse, and draw correct conclusions. As a result, some data-driven experiments fail (Subbotin, 2020). However, a data-driven approach, when properly used, leads to well-grounded production forecasts.

A simplified schematic of the approach is shown in Figure 11.5.

Advantages of using the data-driven approach in production include the following

1. The cost of production is reduced in many aspects, from predicting equipment failures to modelling future product demand. For example, analysing time-series data from IoT sensors can be used to predict equipment failure and identify the causes. As a result, downtime is reduced, and the necessary adjustments eliminate the problem in the future. Sensors inform workers in different departments about the need for components. The speed of the reaction helps to avoid downtime.
2. The quality of products and processes is improved. Big Data analysis allows organisations to track failure, identify the causes, and eliminate them.
3. The production rate is increased, with improvements in inventory and supply chain management.

11.5.1   Six Implementation Steps

These are the six steps to implementing the data-driven approach in production (Subbotin, 2020):

1. Data collection: This includes the machine collection of available data.
2. Data storage: There should be a unified system to store large amounts of data.

FIGURE 11.5   Simplified scheme of well-grounded forecasts for use of data (Subbotin, 2020).

3. Data cleaning: Data must be put into a common format, eliminating unnecessary data and selecting comparable fragments. This is the most problematic point for production companies, along with the integration of information into a single whole.
4. Data comparison and analysis: This includes unifying data and defining dependencies, patterns, and identifying potential bottlenecks.
5. Data visualisation: This simplifies people's understanding of numbers and makes information available at any time, for example, in a chatbot.
6. Data-based forecasting: This is the planning step, based on the analysis of the data.

11.5.2 FACTORS OF FAILURE

If they are not considered, certain factors could lead to failure:

1. Data analysis is an important part of the approach. But not all data are equally useful. Data should be allocated at an early stage to avoid wasting time collecting and working with insignificant factors.
2. The business goals should be clear, and they should be adhered to in all ways.
3. At the initial stages of creating industrial AI systems, it is more important to make such pilots successful, than rather looking for speedy ROI. The result should provide an understanding of data handling methodologies and give the necessary impetus to the working group.
4. The internal leader who determines the area of data handling is critical (Subbotin, 2020).

11.6 DATA-DRIVEN POLICYMAKING

Data-driven approaches are to be successfully implemented; policymakers need to create a regulatory framework to address the following critical challenges:

- The regulatory framework needs a business model. It should encourage and facilitate investment from private actors for data acquisition and data processing. The framework should include a trade, incentive, and payment model for data usage.
- The regulatory framework should provide open public access to data and solutions, thus facilitating innovation.
- The regulatory framework should include well-defined guidelines and regulations for acquiring and storing data.
- The regulatory framework should provide quality assurance of information and information logistics.
- The framework should provide a security mechanism for accessing and consuming data, i.e. cybersecurity.
- The regulatory framework should include guidelines and instructions for investment and provisioning for operation and maintenance in digital infrastructures.
- The regulatory framework should facilitate availability and accessibility on equal terms for all stakeholders, i.e. data democratisation.
- The regulatory framework should provide data transparency; all stakeholders should have equal access to data on the same terms and conditions.
- The regulatory framework should include a mechanism to prohibit people and enterprises from manipulating data, thus ensuring an ethical, data-driven eco-system (Karim & Kumar, 2021).

11.6.1 INNOVATIONS IN DATA-DRIVEN POLICYMAKING

Data-driven policymaking draws on new sources of data, such as RT sensor data, and new techniques for processing these data to realise the co-creation of policies across relevant stakeholders. This section identifies some innovations of data-driven policymaking (Veenstra & Kotterink, 2017).

11.6.1.1 Use of New Data Sources in Policymaking

The use of new data sources will offer organisations greater operational efficiency and effectiveness and lead to the development of new products, services, and business models. There are more data, and data come from different sources and in different formats. These can lead to issues of interoperability. Data must be captured and integrated before they can be applied. Table 11.2 shows the main opportunities, challenges, and innovations involved in drawing on new data sources for policymaking (Veenstra & Kotterink, 2017).

1. Capturing data: Data can be physical, derived from sensor monitoring, or virtual, such as social media data. Data must be of sufficient quality, reliable, and secure to be of use to the policymaking process. Innovations in capturing data include crowdsourcing and nowcasting, i.e. the capturing of search engine data.
2. Integrating data: To use Big Data and open data in organisational processes, cross-boundary information integration (between organisations and/or within organisations) is necessary. The integration of data is crucial, but there are many challenges: lack of interoperability of data and lack of standardisation, architectures, and portals. Legacy systems may negatively influence this linking. Innovations in data integration include sentiment analysis, location mapping, and social network analysis.
3. Applying data: In this step, the integrated data are put to use. Innovations in data application include visualisation tools and computer simulations (Veenstra & Kotterink, 2017).

11.6.1.2 Co-Creation of Policy

Co-creation of policy refers to the exchange of ideas and information between relevant actors, such as governments, businesses, and civil society, that leads to the development of policies. This can include consulting or actually participating in decision-making and policy implementation. Table 11.3 summarises the stages in the co-creation of policies and shows the main innovations, impacts, and challenges at each stage (Veenstra & Kotterink, 2017).

1. Prediction and problem definition: RT sensor data are used in this phase of policymaking. Innovative approaches, such as crowdsourcing and nowcasting, are used to identify current problems and predict future ones. This leads to the development of RT information that allows more precise predictions than expert-based information. That said, experts are still important, as they can provide context for the trends spotted by technology. Main challenges are the availability, quality, reliability, representativeness, and security of the data.
2. Design and experimentation: The second phase of policymaking should ensure collaboration between all stakeholders in the decision-making process. This will include the use

---

TABLE 11.2

Opportunities, Challenges, and Innovations of New Data Sources for Policymaking (Veenstra & Kotterink, 2017)

Steps of Data Use	Opportunities	Challenges	Innovations
Capturing data	Availability of (real-time) sensor data, open data, and social media data.	Variety in data, data quality, reliability of data, and security of data.	Crowdsourcing; nowcasting.
Integrating data	Cross-organisational collaboration; linking new data sources to traditional statistics.	Interoperability; lack of standardisation, architectures, and portals; legacy systems.	Sentiment analysis, location mapping, and advanced social network analysis.
Application of data	Real-time monitoring of policy; transparency and accountability.	Sense-making and interpretation.	Visualisation techniques; computer simulation.

TABLE 11.3

Innovations and Challenges to Co-Creation of Policy (Veenstra & Kotterink, 2017)

Policy Cycle Phase	Innovations	Impact	Challenges
Predictive and problem definition	Use of (real-time) sensor data from citizens (e.g. social media data, crowdsourcing), business and government for problem definition and prediction.	Problem definition based on (real-time) data from different actors, rather than merely expert-based.	Capturing different data sources and ensuring data quality reliability and security as well as representativeness of the data.
Design & experimentation	Using advanced analyses such as sentiment analysis, location mapping, social network analysis, visualisation, computer simulation and serious games for decision-making.	Cross-organisational collaboration and involvement of citizens require more advanced analyses to be able to select policy options.	Creating an infrastructure ensuring interoperability and allowing the integration of data in the form of standards and architectures.
Evaluation & implementation	Collaborative data-driven policy implementation by governments, citizens, and businesses, allowing for agility of processes.	Public value creation, improved transparency and accountability, but may lead to more surveillance.	Accuracy of data and data models, ensuring privacy and security. Citizens' skills and motivation and culture of the government agency need to be sufficient.

of more advanced analytical approaches, such as sentiment analysis, visualisation techniques, location mapping, and computer simulation. A major challenge is setting up an infrastructure that allows data interoperability and integration.

3. Evaluation and implementation: The third phase comprises the collaborative co-creation and implementation of policy, as well as its ongoing evaluation. Today's technologies allow short cycles of decision-making and implementation. Although increased collaboration may result in greater transparency and accountability, issues of data security may arise. Accuracy of data and data models and ensuring privacy and security are major challenges.

These innovations are challenging, however, and organisations often use new technologies to enrich their traditional statistical data. New methodologies need to be developed to make use of these new data sources and technologies. Using a design science approach, Veenstra and Kotterink (2017) developed the Policy Lab approach to guide innovations in data-driven policymaking, allowing for experimentation with new policies and developing new data-driven methodologies at the same time. Figure 11.6 depicts the Policy Lab approach.

The figure consists of two circles. The inner circle represents the policymaking process, with phases of agenda setting, policy formulation, decision-making, implementation, and evaluation. The outer circle represents the development of data-driven methodologies and co-creation. The circles are separate, but they mutually influence each other: policy experiments can be used to develop and test new methodologies, and these, in turn can be used to develop and evaluate policies (Veenstra & Kotterink, 2017).

11.6.1.3   Government Policymaking in the Transport Sector

Governments are involved in policymaking in most industrial sectors. In this section, we focus on infrastructure in the transport sector, where government agencies play the following roles:

- Governments can act as infrastructure managers and, as such, will be responsible for the strategic maintenance of the infrastructure. They also provide maintenance budgets.

FIGURE 11.6 The policy lab approach for data-driven policymaking (Veenstra & Kotterink, 2017).

- Governments may privatise the infrastructure investment and the related decisions on maintenance; they maintain their influence over maintenance strategies through contracts, licences, and concessions.
- Governments also act as regulators; they regulate the transport sectors, including the way data can be shared. Their role is to guarantee safe, secure, and effective transport and data governance systems.

Note that there can be trade-offs between the different roles and interests of governments. The job of policymakers is to find an appropriate balance in the context of these trade-offs.

Data-driven approaches to transport infrastructure maintenance have considerable potential advantages. They provide more accurate insights into the actual state of the asset than more traditional maintenance methods like regular physical inspections. The extent to which data-driven approaches are implemented and the timeline for each might differ according to the sector, place, and context. For example, new technologies can be adopted when their value is known, whereas experimentation might be more suitable when it is unclear how new technologies can be leveraged for more effective maintenance.

Policy makers should take into account good practices related to data governance when introducing initiatives for data-driven approaches. They should make sure that data-driven approaches comply with privacy protection regulations. Data should be anonymised and encrypted. Policy makers should develop and endorse non-disclosure agreements, involve only trusted third parties, and develop approaches in which only query results are exchanged, not raw data.

Data-driven approaches to transport infrastructure maintenance may call for different, more flexible regulations and guidelines. Current regulations and guidelines that apply to condition-based maintenance strategies may not fit with the new approaches. Thus, policy makers will likely need to update transport infrastructure maintenance regulations and guidelines (ITF, 2021).

11.7   SUSTAINABILITY: THE TRIPLE BOTTOM LINE

The triple bottom line (TBL) is an accounting framework that incorporates three dimensions of performance: social, environmental, and financial. This differs from traditional reporting frameworks as it includes environmental (or ecological) and social aspects that can be difficult to measure. The TBL dimensions are also commonly called the three Ps: people, planet, and profits.

TBL addresses sustainability (Slaper & Hall, 2011). The nested spheres model, or the Venn diagram explanation is commonly used to describe sustainability and TBL. The model is shown in Figure 11.7. Sustainability can be considered the place where the three dimensions overlap. However, the model does not show levels of hierarchy between the three dimensions. Consequently, some consider it a "weak approach" to sustainability and suggest a "strong approach" should include a wider environmental (ecological) system where both the economic and the social domains have a limit. The model shown in Figure 11.8, often called the Russian doll model, is considered a stronger sustainability model (Correia, 2019).

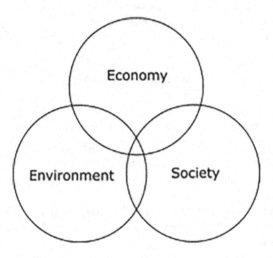

FIGURE 11.7   The nested spheres model (Correia, 2019).

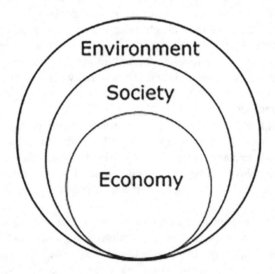

FIGURE 11.8   The overlapping spheres model (Correia, 2019).

11.7.1 ECONOMIC DIMENSION

The economic dimension of TBL goes beyond the organisation's financial performance to include the economic and operational impact it has on society. It also includes the organisation's efficient management of its strategic capabilities, for example, its core competencies and shareholder value creation. Economic sustainability has been of greater concern since the 2008 Great Recession (Correia, 2019).

11.7.2 SOCIAL DIMENSION

The social dimension of TBL includes the impact an organisation has on human welfare, not just for its employees but also for the wider community; for example, organisations may provide education assistance or give money to charitable causes. Today, the concept of Corporate Social Responsibility (CSR), whereby the corporation is understood to hold responsibility in the community, is an expected part of the business world. Consequently, CSR initiatives are affecting corporate strategies and operations (Correia, 2019).

11.7.3 ENVIRONMENTAL DIMENSION

The environmental dimension relates to the organisation's attempts to minimise environmental impact, including its use of energy and methods of waste disposal to reduce its ecological footprint. ISO 14001 certification addresses this dimension. Some consider the environmental dimension is the most important aspect of TBL because everything depends on the Earth's resources, limits, and systems (Correia, 2019).

11.7.4 OTHER SUSTAINABILITY DIMENSIONS

Some additional sustainability dimensions have been suggested beyond the three basic ones. For example, a fourth dimension could comprise human values, ethics, and worldviews. Other proposed dimensions are institutional, cultural, ethical, and technological (Correia, 2019).

11.7.5 THE TRIPLE BOTTOM LINE IMPLEMENTATION

There are five stages of sustainability integration:

1. Pre-compliance,
2. Compliance,
3. Beyond compliance,
4. Integrated strategy,
5. Purpose and passion.

Although most organisations understand the importance of TBL, very few have achieved the fourth stage, integrated strategy. Many are in the third stage, beyond compliance, cutting costs through more efficient use of resources and waste reduction, leading to financial gains.

Sustainable behaviour is expected to continue to grow, as research shows sustainable behaviour can contribute to an organisation's profits by increasing revenue and employee productivity, reducing energy, water, waste, and materials expenses, reducing turn-over, and decreasing strategic and operational risks.

Sustainable behaviour also leads to less volatility of stock prices and positive financial returns through increased market value and customer satisfaction. In other words, image is important. By the same token, a poor reputation for sustainability may have negative economic consequences.

Customers react negatively to poor company sustainability, and they value an organisation that shares their concern for social causes (Correia, 2019).

11.7.6 MEASURING SUSTAINABILITY

Despite the growing knowledge of how to integrate sustainability into business, it remains a challenge for many organisations, given the lack of measures for sustainability performance.

Many indexes and frameworks have been developed to measure private and public organisations' sustainability performance. There is also a growing number of evaluative rankings and related key performance indicators (KPIs) on sustainability. Examples include the Dow Jones Sustainability Stoxx Index, Global Reporting Initiative index, and EDIE's Sustainability Leaders Awards.

Sustainability indices include ecosystem-based indices (e.g., Ecological Footprint); investment, ratings, and asset management indices (e.g., Dow Jones sustainability group indices, FTSE Good Index); product-based sustainability indices (e.g. Life Cycle Index); and social and quality of life-based indices. The ISO 14000 series is a standard way to consider the environmental dimension of the management of a product or service and is widely adopted by organisations around the world.

Today, many organisations are drawing on sustainability and are reporting their environmental, social corporate governance initiatives, and KPIs (Correia, 2019). Yet these are still three different things. The application of TBL is motivated by the principles of economic, environmental, and social sustainability, and these are measured differently. While finding a common unit of measurement is challenging, researchers argue that the three categories need to be integrated to see the complete picture of the consequences that a regulation, policy, or economic development project may have and to assess policy options and analyse trade-offs.

The challenge is to make an index that is both comprehensive and meaningful and to identify suitable data for the variables in the index. The Genuine Progress Indicator (GPI), for example, consists of 25 variables encompassing economic, social, and environmental factors. Those variables are converted into monetary units and summed into a single, dollar-denominated measure (Slaper & Hall, 2011).

REFERENCES

Arcot, R. V. (2021). Cyber-physical systems: The core of Industry 4.0. ISA Interchange. https://blog.isa.org/cyber-physical-systems-the-core-of-industry-4.0

Correia, M. S. (2019). Sustainability: An overview of the triple bottom line and sustainability implementation. *International Journal of Strategic Engineering*, 2(1), 29–38. https://www.igi-global.com/article/sustainability/219322

Dickson, B. (2020). Understanding the AI factory. *TechTalks*. https://bdtechtalks.com/2020/12/02/competing-in-the-age-of-ai/

Dragomir, O. E., Gouriveau, R., Dragomir, F., Minca, E., & Zerhouni, N. (2009). Review of prognostic problem in condition-based maintenance. *2009 European Control Conference (ECC)*, 1587–1592. https://www.researchgate.net/publication/29597907_Review_of_prognostic_problem_in_condition-based_maintenance

Iansiti, M., & Lakhani, K. R. (2020). *Competing in the age of AI: Strategy and leadership when algorithms and networks run the world*. Harvard Business Press.

Intellipaat. (2022). Pros & cons of artificial intelligence – Insights from AI experts. https://intellipaat.com/blog/pros-and-cons-of-ai/

ITF. (2021). Data-driven transport infrastructure maintenance. International Transport Forum (ITF) Policy Papers, No. 95, OECD Publishing. https://www.itf-oecd.org/sites/default/files/docs/data-driven-transport-infrastructure-maintenance.pdf

Jain, S., Shao, G., & Shin, S. J. (2017). Manufacturing data analytics using a virtual factory representation. *International Journal of Production Research*, 55(18), 5450–5464. https://doi.org/10.1080/00207543.2017.1321799

Karim, R. (2008). *A service-oriented approach to e-maintenance of complex technical systems*. Doctoral Dissertation, Luleå tekniska universitet. http://epubl.ltu.se/1402-1544/2008/58/LTU-DT-0858-SE.pdf

Karim, R., Dersin, P., Galar, D., Kumar, U., & Jarl, H. (2021). AI factory – a framework for digital asset management. *Proceedings of the 31st European Safety and Reliability Conference*, 1160–1167. https://doi.org/10.3850/978-981-18-2016-8_767-cd

Karim & Kumar (2021).

Karim, R., Westerberg, J., Galar, D., & Kumar, U. (2016). Maintenance analytics: The new know in maintenance. *IFAC-PapersOnLine*, *49*(28), 214–219. https://doi.org/10.1016/j.ifacol.2016.11.037

Kour, R., Thaduri, A., & Karim, R. (2020). Predictive model for multistage cyber-attack simulation. *International Journal of Systems Assurance Engineering and Management*, *11*(3), 600–613. https://doi.org/10.1007/s13198-020-00952-5

Kumari, J., Karim, R., Karim, K., & Arenbro, M. (2022). Metaanalyser: A concept and toolkit for enablement of digital twin. *IFAC-PapersOnLine*, *55*(2), 199–204. DOI: 10.1016/j.ifacol.2022.04.193

Locke, S. (2020). Mastering AI in manufacturing: The three levels of competency. NightingaleHQ. https://nightingalehq.ai/blog/from-apprentice-to-master-attaining-competency-in-ai-for-manufacturing/

Patwardhan, A., Thaduri, A., & Karim, R. (2021). Distributed ledger for cybersecurity: Issues and challenges in railways. *Sustainability*, *13*(18), 10176. https://doi.org/10.3390/su131810176

Pressley, A. (2021). The role of artificial intelligence in manufacturing. *Intelligent CIO Europe*. https://www.intelligentcio.com/eu/2021/10/29/the-role-of-artificial-intelligence-in-manufacturing/#

Seidelson, C. E. (2021). Is artificial intelligence (AI) ready to run a factory? *International Journal on Engineering, Science and Technology*, *3*(2), 126–132. https://doi.org/10.46328/ijonest.52

Slaper, T. F., & Hall, T. J. (2011). The triple bottom line: What is it and how does it work? *Indiana Business Review*, *86*(1), 4–8. https://www.ibrc.indiana.edu/ibr/2011/spring/article2.html

Subbotin, V. (2020). Data-driven approach in industry: 6 implementation stages and failure factors. *ASRP. Tech: AI technologies*. https://medium.com/asrp-ai-technologies/data-driven-approach-in-industry-6-implementation-stages-and-failure-factors-c7e30daae96b

Veenstra, A. F., & Kotterink, B. (2017). Data-driven policy making: The policy lab approach. In *Electronic participation. ePart 2017. Lecture notes in computer science*, vol. 10429. Springer. https://doi.org/10.1007/978-3-319-64322-9

12 In Industrial AI We Believe

12.1 INDUSTRIAL AI

Industrial AI (IAI) is the application of AI to industrial use cases like the movement and storage of goods, supply chain management, advanced analytics, and automation and robotics in manufacturing. It is often differentiated from other types of AI because it focuses on the application of AI technologies, not the development of human-like systems.

IAI is especially appropriate for process plants because the huge amount of data generated today and the quickly changing circumstances are too complex for manual or even digital management (Precognize, 2022).

Industrial organisations need the capabilities from IAI applications to facilitate their transition to the new business models that will be necessary to stay competitive in the 21st century. IAI can be of significant value because it combines data science and machine learning (ML) with domain expertise to deliver industrial applications that will drive and sustain operational value (Aspentech, 2022a).

The important points about IAI are the following:

- IAI requires real-time (RT) processing capabilities, industrial-grade reliability, high security, and interconnectivity.
- IAI requires large-volume, high-velocity data from various sources; the datasets for IAI tend to be larger but potentially lower in quality than those for general AI.
- IAI requires the integration of physical, digital, and heuristic knowledge.
- IAI has a low tolerance for error, and the handling of uncertainty is a key concern; IAI also has zero tolerance for false positives or negatives, delayed insights, or unreliable predictions.
- IAI is concerned with concrete value creation through a combination of factors such as improved quality and augmented operator performance.
- IAI is able to find connections between seemingly disparate pieces of information.
- IAI can incorporate market information to optimise the value chain based on evolving prices of inputs and outputs. The ML software can keep information from many levels of an organisation close by; for example, market and sales data may inform maintenance scheduling (Aspentech, 2022a).
- In a nutshell, IAI is focused on helping an organisation monitor, optimise, or control the behaviour of its physical operations and systems to improve both efficiency and performance (Figure 12.1).

12.1.1 INDUSTRIAL AI VERSUS OTHER AI APPLICATIONS

IAI is different from other AI-enabled business and consumer applications. IAI includes applications relating to the manufacture of physical products, to supply chains and warehouses where physical items are stored and moved, to the operation of building HVAC systems, and so on (Charrington, 2017).

Figure 12.2 compares IAI use cases with other AI-enabled business applications.

Because IAI relates to the physical systems of an enterprise, access to training and test data is more difficult, the reliance on subject matter expertise is larger, the AI models are harder to develop, train, and test, and the costs associated with their failure are greater.

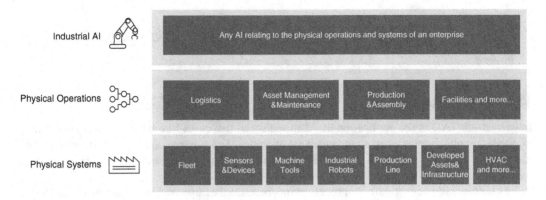

FIGURE 12.1   Defining IAI (Charrington, 2017).

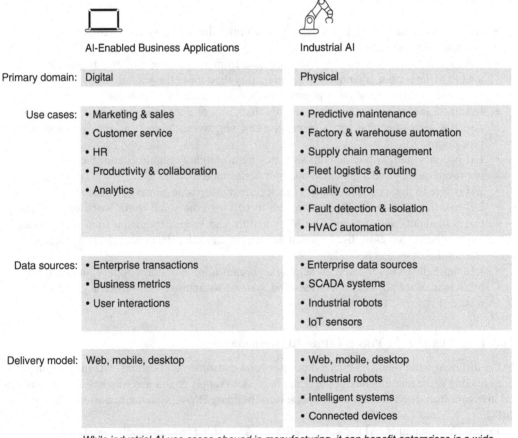

FIGURE 12.2   AI use cases (Charrington, 2017).

IAI thus presents several challenges that differentiate it from other applications of AI:

1. Difficulties in data acquisition and storage: IAI systems often rely on data captured from sensors, and this results in noisy and voluminous data. Acquiring these data and storing them for analysis can be very complex.
2. Cost of training: While it can be difficult in any domain to collect the amount of labelled training data required to train ML models, this can be even more challenging in industrial scenarios, increasing the complexity of training and raising the overall cost of developing the ML system.
3. Cost of simulation: Testing AI systems on actual operating production lines, industrial equipment, and other industrial systems is expensive and disruptive. Thus, IAI systems are often trained and tested using simulation. Digital twins (DTs) can be very effective, but can be difficult to create and maintain and computationally expensive to run.
4. Cost of regulatory requirements: Industrial environments are subject to technical, legal, and corporate requirements and government regulations. Compliance requirements range from product safety to public and employee health and safety, environmental impact, and workplace safety. They can also specify controls for automation systems. Regulatory controls often require that changes to industrial processes are extensively validated and verified, and this process can conflict with the overall goals of automation, i.e. the rapid adaptation of processes.
5. High cost of failure and change: In industrial scenarios, the cost of failure can be very high, as can the cost of change.
6. Problems of complexity: Modern industrial systems are extremely complex, offering myriad inputs that ML algorithms can optimise. This leads to complex development and training processes in terms of time and cost. Sophisticated techniques are required to ensure convergence to a solution.
7. Cost of talent: Data scientists, data engineers, programmers, and subject matter experts are all required to implement AI solutions. These skill sets are expensive (Charrington, 2017).

Other unique challenges of applying AI to industrial applications are the following: industrial data are often inaccurate; AI runs on the edge, not on the cloud; a single prediction can cost over $1,000; and complex models must be interpretable (Yao, 2017).

12.1.2 INDUSTRIAL AI AND LEVELS OF AUTONOMY

Autonomy is a key concern of IAI. IAI is an interdisciplinary area of research, encompassing fields such as robotics, ML, and natural language processing (NLP). The combination of these fields gives systems the ability to adapt and solve problems within pre-defined system boundaries through a certain degree of autonomous action (Peres et al., 2020). A taxonomy of system autonomy based on AI defining a six-level model of automated decision-making on the basis of industrial processes is shown in Figure 12.3, contextualised with industrial scenarios for each level.

IAI can be seen as a core technology driving the pursuit of higher levels of autonomy in industrial systems. However, IAI is mainly leveraged to augment human performance; it is not intended to fully replace humans. This is likely to be the case in more autonomous scenarios in the future (Peres et al., 2020).

12.1.3 DATA AND TRAINING

IAI requires a large amount of data to train its algorithms. These data should be as complete as possible. Relevant data may include such diverse information as maintenance records, current and historical operating conditions, delivery reports, and market conditions.

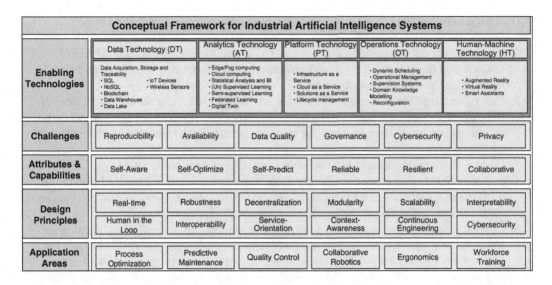

FIGURE 12.3 Taxonomy of system autonomy based on AI, defining a six-level model of automated decision-making for industrial processes (Peres et al., 2020).

Once the data are collected, human operators make decisions about what they want the ML algorithm to work on. Priorities range from value chain optimisation to production optimisation, emission reduction, and margin maximisation. The human operator sets the priorities by writing the values directly into the computer code or by using a software interface that presents the options and then does the back-end coding. The IAI then trains itself in a trial-and-error approach by:

1. making guesses about how the data are related,
2. testing the guesses, and
3. refining the guesses to match the actual observations.

This process occurs entirely on a computer, either on local computing resources or in the cloud. Later, changes are made in the relevant area. For example, the experimentation required to optimise a production line does not need to take place in production. Thus, there is no risk of disruption in the production processes (Aspentech, 2022a).

12.1.4 Using Trained Industrial AI

Once the IAI has been trained, how it is deployed depends on many factors, including the organisation's decision-making structure.

The changes suggested by an IAI application may constitute advice that goes against conventional wisdom. However, IAI can cut through old ways of thinking. It can produce a list of variables and adjustments or simply articulate a relationship or connection that previously escaped human attention. If a company uses process simulator software, the proposed changes can be tested in a simulation before being deployed. Alternatively, an organisation that empowers data-driven decisions across its entire hierarchy will be able to rapidly implement the recommendations by delegating control of the assets in question to the IAI system itself (Aspentech, 2022a).

12.1.5 Conceptual Framework for Industrial AI

A conceptual framework for IAI is shown in Figure 12.4 and explained below (Peres et al., 2020).

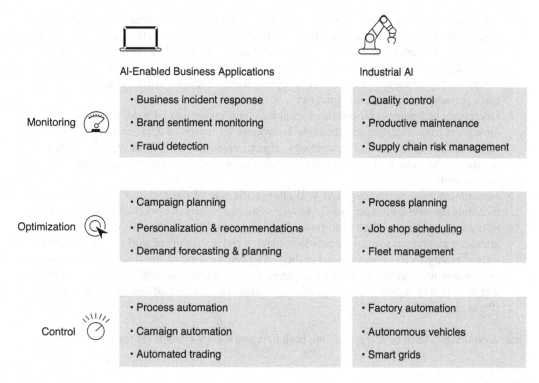

FIGURE 12.4 Conceptual framework for IAI systems (Peres et al., 2020).

The proposed conceptual framework highlights the capabilities and attributes systems should incorporate to meet the requirements of manufacturing environments in Industry 4.0. These capabilities include:

- self-awareness and self-optimisation for continuous improvement, and
- resilience and reliability.

With these capabilities, systems can handle equipment failures and unexpected disturbances and quickly restore the normal operating state.

As discussed in Table 12.1, with additional autonomy, a system's intelligent entities will collaboratively resume normal operation by dynamically rescheduling and implementing new plans in a coordinated manner (Peres et al., 2020).

IAI's enabling technologies can be broadly categorised as: data, analytics, platform, operations, and human-machine technology:

1. Data technology: With digitalisation, larger volumes of data are generated. These data can be structured, unstructured, or mixed, and they come from multiple sources at different levels of abstraction, such as the component level, the machine level, or the organisational unit level. It is important to understand the context, therefore, and to be able to standardise data acquisition and data exchange.
2. Analytics technology: Analytics technology transforms the raw data into knowledge, thus providing added value for organisations. This includes data processing at different levels, for example, the edge or the cloud. It also includes leveraging RT data streams and ML to enable continuous improvement through self-learning mechanisms and self-optimisation. New methods include federated learning and semi-supervised learning approaches.

3. Platform technology: Platform technology acts as an enabler of the remaining technologies (operations and human-machine), thus facilitating the interconnection between various elements, for example, at the edge, fog, or cloud levels. As added flexibility and agility are required, platform technology must also support self-reconfiguration and self-organisation. Given the higher degree of connectivity, cybersecurity becomes critical to ensure the system's privacy, availability, and integrity.
4. Operations technology: Operations technology is a major part of value creation, with a movement from analytics to actionable knowledge by means of decision-making support systems. Through operations technology, organisations can shift from experience-driven production to data-driven production and optimise both operational maintenance and management.
5. Human–machine technology: IAI will change the role of the human in manufacturing, including the interactions between industrial systems and human workers. Human–machine technology can be exploited to empower human stakeholders to effectively and seamlessly interact with systems to reap the benefits of IAI. It can assist human workers – for example, virtual reality (VR) or augmented reality (AR) can be used to improve operations such as maintenance and assembly or to diagnose system health remotely. Organisations must invest in proper training and acquisition of talent to take full advantage of AI systems (Peres et al., 2020).

These technologies must be integrated into both new and legacy systems (Peres et al., 2020).

12.1.6   Categories of Industrial AI

IAI has the potential to contribute to product and service innovation, process improvement, and insight discovery (Wikipedia, 2022). We discuss each of these in the following sections.

12.1.6.1   Product Applications

IAI can be embedded into existing products or services to make them more effective, reliable, safe, and longer-living. The automotive industry, for example, uses computer vision to avoid accidents and enable vehicles to stay in lane, facilitating safer driving (Wikipedia, 2021).

12.1.6.2   Process Applications

IAI technologies boost the performance and expand the capability of conventional AI applications. An example is the collaborative robot. Collaborative robots can learn the motion and path of human operators and perform the same tasks. AI also automates processes previously requiring human participation. An example is the Hong Kong subway where an AI program determines the distribution and job scheduling of engineers with more efficiency and reliability than humans.

Another advantage of process applications is the ability to model large-scale systems. Cyber manufacturing systems are networked and become resilient to faults through the use of evidence-based modelling and data-driven deep learning (DL). They can deal with large and geographically distributed assets; this is important because such assets cannot easily be modelled using a conventional physics-based model. Using ML and optimisation algorithms, a framework considering machine health can leverage large samples of assets to automate operations, spare parts management, and maintenance scheduling (Wikipedia, 2022).

12.1.6.3   Insight Applications

IAI can be used for knowledge discovery by identifying insights in engineering systems, for example, in aviation and aeronautics systems. AI can play a vital role in safety assurance and root cause analysis (RCA). Analysing why certain faults happened in the past will facilitate predictions of similar incidents in the future and proactively prevent problems.

Predictive and preventive maintenance through data-driven ML is another important application of IAI. For example, prognostics and health management (PHM) programs model equipment health degradation, thus facilitating prediction of failure (Wikipedia, 2022).

12.1.7 WHY INDUSTRIAL AI?

From a macroeconomic perspective, organisations are facing tremendous competitive pressure. Accordingly, they are looking for opportunities to reduce costs, increase efficiency, and create innovative business models using digital transformation. AI is an important tool for achieving all these things.

IAI can deliver enhanced and predictive situational awareness, better planning and decision-making, and greater efficiency and productivity. Organisations can improve their operational and business performance, while simultaneously increasing agility and innovation (Charrington, 2017).

12.1.8 CHALLENGES AND OPPORTUNITIES

IAI challenges can be categorised on three fronts:

1. Data: Ensuring data are easily findable, accessible, interoperable, and reusable (FAIR) is crucial.
2. Models: Models should be reliably found and re-used when appropriate, using identifiers linked to Big Data represented in common, standardised and secure formats.
3. Cyber-infrastructures: Proper infrastructures are crucial to ensure the level of quality, security, and reliability required to improve the adoption of IAI solutions.

The following sections address some of the challenges within these three major areas of concern (Peres et al., 2020).

12.1.8.1 Data Availability

Data availability remains a major challenge; sufficient and appropriate data must be available to train and validate models.

ML and DL require large amounts of labelled data to achieve proper generalisation and avoid overfitting. However, in real manufacturing environments, data from different settings, conditions, and configurations can be scarce, as these typically represent undesired states of the system, and acquiring these data tends to be economically and operationally unfeasible. In addition, labelling raw data is a time-consuming and costly process requiring both expertise and domain knowledge.

This challenge is being addressed by research in two areas:

1. Data synthesis. Synthetic data closely resemble data from real operational environments; thus, IAI solutions based on them can be generalised to real scenarios.
2. Transfer learning. Humans can apply previous knowledge to solve new problems either faster or with better solutions. In IAI, transfer learning represents learning in a new problem for which data are scarce through the transfer of knowledge from a related task in a given source domain for which sufficient data are available. Transfer learning in manufacturing can be applied to the transfer between:
   i different working conditions,
   ii different machines/stations, and
   iii different types of machine faults or product defects (Peres et al., 2020).

12.1.8.2 Data Quality

IAI models, especially ML models, rely on accurate, clean, and labelled training data to produce useful results. Thus, data quality is a critical concern. Data quality can be analysed along four main dimensions:

1. Intrinsic: This refers to the characteristics inherent to the data themselves. Relevant intrinsic features include timeliness, completeness, accuracy, and consistency.
2. Contextual: This refers to the attributes of the data that depend on the context of the task at hand. Important contextual features are relevance and quantity.
3. Representational: This refers to the need for systems to present data in a way that is interpretable. Data must be represented concisely and consistently.
4. Accessible: Systems must store data in a way that is accessible but also reliable, secure, and privacy-preserving (Peres et al., 2020).

The assessment of these dimensions has historically relied on self-report surveys and user questionnaires because of their association with subjective and situational human judgement for quantification. Further research is needed to improve the way the dimensions of data quality are monitored and optimised; this will improve the performance of the IAI applications leveraging these data (Peres et al., 2020).

12.1.8.3 Cybersecurity and Privacy

The typical Industry 4.0 combination of multiple data sources and emerging technologies such as IoT, cloud computing, AI, and blockchain enhance the operation efficiency of entire manufacturing processes. Yet this opens the door to cybersecurity threats, especially in the context of collecting large volumes of data for centralised processing. This can lead to strong concerns about privacy.

Federated learning approaches constitute a possible way to mitigate privacy and scalability issues by distributing the training process across multiple nodes. Through federated learning, the nodes can collaboratively build a model without sharing sensitive private data samples, using only local parameters.

It is imperative that research continues to study privacy constructs for IAI (Peres et al., 2020).

12.1.9 Industrial AI Application Case Examples

A framework for thinking about different types of IAI scenarios is helpful to identify the areas in which to apply it. We categorise IAI applications as performing the functions of monitoring, optimisation, or control based on the degree of automation that they provide. This framework applies to both digital-domain and physical-domain use cases.

Figure 12.5 compares these three categories for AI-enabled business applications and IAI applications (Charrington, 2017).

In the following sections, we discuss these categories and present representative IAI use cases for each.

12.1.9.1 Monitoring

In industrial scenarios, there is an ongoing need to monitor the performance of systems and processes to identify or predict faults or potential failure. Using ML, models can be trained on available data to learn the health state of a complex system. These models can be used to predict the system's future health state (Charrington, 2017).

The following monitoring applications benefit from an AI-based approach:

• Quality control: A common manufacturing use case for AI is for machines to visually inspect items on a production line. Quality control can be automated, and fewer defects

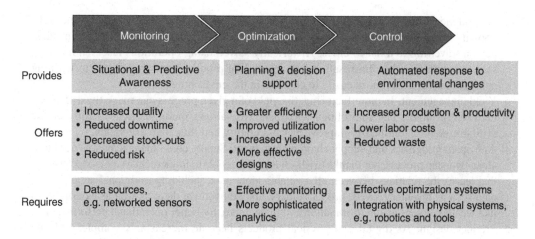

FIGURE 12.5   AI applications landscape (Charrington, 2017).

reach customers than when traditional statistical sampling methods are used. AI-based visual inspection systems can also validate many product attributes, such as surface finish, product classification, packaging, colour, and texture.

- Fault detection and isolation: By monitoring a variety of system operational factors, AI can be used in the detection, diagnosis, and prediction of undesirable operating conditions in industrial systems. Automated process surveillance helps prevent or minimise system downtime and hazardous conditions.
- Predictive maintenance: Predictive maintenance predicts the failure of industrial systems before the actual failure leads to undesirable downtime. Sensors produce large volumes of performance data. Based on these data, failures can be predicted before they happen, repairs can be proactively scheduled, and replacement parts can be ordered.
- Inventory monitoring: AI powers a wide variety of inventory management and supply chain use cases, allowing industries to avoid costly stock-outs. Autonomous mobile robots can use on-board computer vision systems to detect misplaced and out-of-stock inventory. Another possibility is to use a drone-based approach.
- Supply chain risk management: Managing a complex, global supply chain demands the ability to identify and mitigate potential disruptions before they cause delays or shortages. IAI can be used to predict supply disturbances even before they happen, thus providing early warning for enterprise supply chains (Charrington, 2017).

12.1.9.2 Optimisation

AI-based planning and decision support systems allow industry users to design a plan to reach a desired system state and optimise a target set of business metrics. Optimisation activities that can benefit from the application of AI and ML include the following:

1. Process planning: Many industrial scenarios involve complex sequences of work. How these sequences are ordered can significantly impact many different factors, including cost, time, quality, labour input, materials, equipment life, and waste. A wide variety of optimisation problems can be been solved using ML techniques, including genetic algorithms and neural networks.
2. Job shop scheduling: The job shop scheduling problem is actually a specific type of process planning problem. It models the allocation of jobs of varying processing times to a set of machines with varying processing power. In fact, many different types of problems can

be modelled using the general job shop scheduling approach and AI, including the well-known "travelling salesperson problem", which seeks to optimise the routing of a salesperson travelling to a list of cities. Historically solved using operations research methods such as combinatorial optimisation, job scheduling problems are well-suited to learning approaches that adapt more easily to changes in the environment.

3. Yield management: In manufacturing, the yield of a given process can mean the difference between profitable and unprofitable products. ML allows manufacturers to fully utilise available data to continually improve process quality and thus increase yields.

4. Anticipatory logistics and supply chain management: Supply chain management is traditionally a two-step process, but thanks to ML, it is now possible to implement a single-step process that learns the relations between all available input data, including traditional supply chain data such as inventory levels, product orders, and competitive data, as well as external data like weather, social media information and many more, for better operational performance.

5. Product design: As digital and physical products become increasingly complex, AI can be applied to speed up the design process. Designers can use an ML algorithm to produce design alternatives that optimise qualities such as weight or performance. ML can be used to ensure designed products can actually be manufactured. It can also be used in conjunction with product testing data to identify product deficiencies and suggest alternative designs.

6. Facilities location: ML systems can be used to direct the placement of many different types of physical facilities within an environment. This includes, for example, the placement of circuits and components within a semiconductor. It also includes the location of conference rooms and other facilities within an office building, the placement of roads and power sub-stations within residential areas, and the positioning of wireless and other sensors within a factory (Charrington, 2017).

12.1.9.3 Control

Control systems are at the centre of any modern industrial operation and their optimisation is necessary to gain the full benefits of automation. Many control applications benefit from AI and ML. These include the following:

1. Robotics: Robots are used in many different industrial scenarios, as they are suitable for diverse applications, including pick and place, sorting, assembly, painting, welding, storage, and retrieval. Another application is machine tending, in which robots load or operate other machines. Traditionally, robots were explicitly programmed; they were directed to move through a series of points in two- or three-dimensional space and perform specific actions at those points. Newer approaches such as collaborative robots (co-robots) simplify programming by allowing the points to be captured by physically positioning the robot. AI, coupled with computer vision techniques, allows robots to avoid potential interference from humans or other robots and to accommodate randomly positioned or incorrectly positioned items without operator intervention.

2. Autonomous vehicles: Autonomous mobile robots are deployed in warehouses and factories to support material transport and pick-and-pack applications. Autonomous robots and flying drones are also used to support inventory management applications in warehouses. When AI is coupled with computer vision technology, autonomous robots can complete these tasks more effectively; they can better understand, map, and navigate their environments and are safer around humans.

3. Factory automation: Industry 4.0 and smart factory refer to a vision of the plant or warehouse that is data-driven, intelligent, and automated. Robots and autonomous vehicles move materials and assemble goods, AI-based computer vision detects faults and defects, and smart systems coordinate and optimise the workflow.

4. HVAC automation: ML can help building owners maximise comfort, reduce energy costs, eliminate system faults, and extend the life of HVAC equipment.
5. Smart grids: Smart grids enhance traditional power distribution systems with data and offer connectivity to and from devices like smart metres, storage and charging systems, and distributed generation infrastructure. With AI, the smart grid can predict demands and faults in the power network, respond to changing conditions, and improve power consistency and quality (Charrington, 2017).

12.1.10 MONITORING, OPTIMISATION, AND CONTROL AS AN AI MATURITY MODEL

Monitoring, optimisation, and control are related, in that each stage depends on the previous one, and each requires more user trust. Consequently, these three often form a progression, or in other words, a maturity model:

1. First, organisations deploy monitoring systems to help them understand the current state of their operations and predict faults.
2. Second, as trust grows, they employ AI-based planning and decision support systems (DSS) to tell them what to do given a current state.
3. Third, with the requisite controls in place, AI-based control systems automatically take the actions required to achieve a desired end-state using robotics or other technologies.

Figure 12.6 shows this process.

12.2 INDUSTRIAL AI IN ACTION

Capital-intensive industries can leverage IAI to overcome barriers of digitalisation with the view of accomplishing increased productivity, efficiency, and reliability in their operations (Aspentech, 2022b). The following are a few examples of different industries' uses of IAI. Of course, there are many more. Our goal is simply to suggest how pervasive, innovative, and broadly applicable IAI is to industry in general.

1. Refinery industry: A refinery could use IAI to access a diverse set of data to evaluate hundreds, possibly even thousands, of oil production scenarios simultaneously to quickly identify optimal processing possibilities. The enterprise-wide insights would greatly improve executive decision-making (Aspentech, 2022b).
2. Chemical industry: A chemical plant could gain RT insights from rich, integrated data, thus enabling organisation-wide, agile decision-making. Supply chain and operations technologies (OTs) can be seamlessly linked to detect changes in market conditions and automatically adjust operations accordingly (Aspentech, 2022b).
3. Process industry: A process plant might build and deploy an advanced class of IAI-enabled hybrid models. Created through the collaboration of domain experts and data scientists, ML, and first principles, these models would be more comprehensive, more accurate, and better performing. They could be used to optimally design, operate, and maintain plant assets across the assets' lifecycles (Aspentech, 2022b). They could spot anomalies quickly, thus reducing unplanned downtime and fine-tuning maintenance scheduling. Smart equipment would measure performance to generate alerts when degradation reaches a critical point, or performance is reduced. Robotics and automation on the production floor could replace human involvement, thereby increasing efficiency and boosting production while improving human safety. Faster RCA could investigate, understand, and resolve issues quickly (Precognize, 2022).

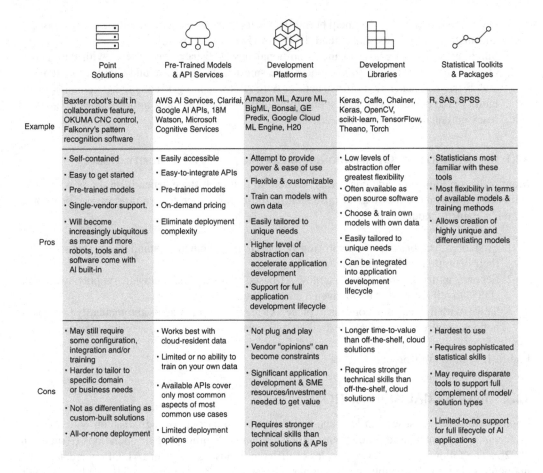

	Point Solutions	Pre-Trained Models & API Services	Development Platforms	Development Libraries	Statistical Toolkits & Packages
Example	Baxter robot's built in collaborative feature, OKUMA CNC control, Falkonry's pattern recognition software	AWS AI Services, Clarifai, Google AI APIs, 18M Watson, Microsoft Cognitive Services	Amazon ML, Azure ML, BigML, Bonsai, GE Predix, Google Cloud ML Engine, H20	Keras, Caffe, Chainer, Keras, OpenCV, scikit-learn, TensorFlow, Theano, Torch	R, SAS, SPSS
Pros	• Self-contained • Easy to get started • Pre-trained models • Single-vendor support. • Will become increasingly ubiquitous as more and more robots, tools and software come with AI built-in	• Easily accessible • Easy-to-integrate APIs • Pre-trained models • On-demand pricing • Eliminate deployment complexity	• Attempt to provide power & ease of use • Flexible & customizable • Train can models with own data • Easily tailored to unique needs • Higher level of abstraction can accelerate application development • Support for full application development lifecycle	• Low levels of abstraction offer greatest flexibility • Often available as open source software • Choose & train own models with own data • Easily tailored to unique needs • Can be integrated into application development lifecycle	• Statisticians most familiar with these tools • Most flexibility in terms of available models & training methods • Allows creation of highly unique and differentiating models
Cons	• May still require some configuration, integration and/or training • Harder to tailor to specific domain or business needs • Not as differentiating as custom-built solutions • All-or-none deployment	• Works best with cloud-resident data • Limited or no ability to train on your own data • Available APIs cover only most common aspects of most common use cases • Limited deployment options	• Not plug and play • Vendor "opinions" can become constraints • Significant application development & SME resources/investment needed to get value • Requires stronger technical skills than point solutions & APIs	• Longer time-to-value than off-the-shelf, cloud solutions • Requires stronger technical skills than off-the-shelf, cloud solutions	• Hardest to use • Requires sophisticated statistical skills • May require disparate tools to support full complement of model/solution types • Limited-to-no support for full lifecycle of AI applications

FIGURE 12.6   Trends driving AI advancement (Charrington, 2017).

4. Next-generation IAI: A next-generation industrial facility could "hire" IAI as a "virtual assistant" in RT and use its new assistant to validate the quality and efficiency of a production plan. AI-enabled cognitive guidance would reduce the facility's reliance on individual domain experts for complex decision-making (Aspentech, 2022b).

12.2.1   THE FUTURE OF INDUSTRY: THE SELF-OPTIMISING PLANT

Industries are hoping digital transformation will help them stay relevant and competitive. IAI is a major part of their transformation. Basically stated, IAI brings domain-specific know-how into conversation with the latest AI and ML to create context-specific AI-enabled applications. This, in turn, enables and accelerates the autonomous and semi-autonomous processes that run those operations. The end product is what Aspentech calls the "self-optimising plant" (Aspentech, 2022b).

Aspentech defines a self-optimising plant as "a self-adapting, self-learning, and self-sustaining set of industrial software technologies that work together to anticipate future conditions and act accordingly, adjusting operations within the digital enterprise" (Aspentech, 2022b). This is not simply an abstract vision of the future; it represents the real-world potential of IAI.

Because it enjoys a combination of RT data access and embedded IAI applications, the self-optimising plant can practice self-improvement. It has access to domain knowledge, can generate easy-to-execute recommendations, and is able to automate mission-critical workflows. The self-optimising organisation is able to:

- Meet environmental sustainability goals, for example, by curbing the carbon emissions caused by process upsets, unplanned shutdowns, and/or unplanned start-ups. This reduces both production waste and the organisation's carbon footprint.
- Enhance overall safety by dramatically reducing dangerous site conditions and reallocating staff to safer roles.
- Benefit from new production efficiencies for greater profitability by tapping into new areas of margin optimisation and production stability, even during economic downturns.

Thus, the self-optimising organisation meets important goals related to the environment, safety, and the economic bottom line. By democratising the application of AI, tomorrow's digital plant drives greater levels of safety, sustainability, and profitability and empowers the next generation of the digital workforce (Aspentech, 2022b).

12.3   APPLYING INDUSTRIAL AI

A variety of approaches, products, and services is already available to organisations hoping to apply IAI. In this section, we touch on some basic requirements for IAI solutions and discuss what is available in the market.

12.3.1   INDUSTRIAL AI REQUIREMENTS

Effective IAI offerings must help enterprises overcome the challenges and impediments previously discussed. To do so, offerings must exhibit a variety of attributes, such as:

1. Trainability on limited examples: To overcome the training challenges of IAI problems, AI tools must use sophisticated techniques to allow training to be performed and models to be developed using only a few examples of the most interesting and relevant behaviours such as defects, faults, or failure conditions. Care must be taken during training to preserve the statistical distribution of faults to avoid creating biased AI systems (Charrington, 2017).
2. Algorithmic fairness and bias: The topic of algorithmic fairness and bias is particularly challenging as there is no universally accepted notion of fairness. Bias can originate from many different sources other than the data themselves, including the data pipeline, data preprocessing steps, and the humans involved and their actions. The mitigation of unfairness and bias includes collecting additional data and adapting data processing and postprocessing (e.g. thresholding). One of the first steps should be auditing. Efforts to facilitate this process include the creation of the Aequitas open-source library to empower both practitioners and policymakers to audit ML models for discrimination and bias. This will help them make equitable decisions about the development and deployment of predictive solutions.

   In many scenarios, there can be a trade-off between fairness and performance. Models that are fairer or less discriminatory across different subsets of the population may do so at the cost of global performance. It is important to determine the application contexts in which the trade-off is worth it (Peres et al., 2020).
3. Simulation-based training: To be effective, IAI tools must work seamlessly with simulation environments to help organisations address the common problem of limited training examples and the need to train models without taking industrial systems out of service and thus incurring the loss of both time and money (Charrington, 2017).

4. Explainability: One of the biggest barriers to AI's acceptance is trust. The demystification of AI solutions is crucial to enable stakeholders to understand and appreciate the technology and facilitate its widespread industrial adoption. It is considerably easier to convince stakeholders that a given solution should be adopted to improve the bottom line if it can be easily broken down and its processes validated by domain experts (Peres et al., 2020).

  Different ML approaches have differing degrees of explainability. Systems based on neural networks are notoriously opaque (Charrington, 2017), but approaches based on model-agnostic methods are useful in this regard. These include local interpretable model-agnostic explanations (LIME) and Shapley additive explanations. Model-agnostic methods provide increased model flexibility because the interpretation method can work with most ML models. The modularity of model-agnostic interpretation methods makes them highly desirable, particularly for the automation of interpretability at scale. Since interpretations are decoupled from the underlying ML model, replacing either side of the process is easier, following the trend of automated feature engineering, hyper-parameter optimisation, model selection, and model interpretation (Peres et al., 2020).

5. Provable safety: In regulated industries and in situations where people might be injured, the burden is on the users and the vendors of IAI systems to prove the safety of their systems. By the same token, systems controlling significant company assets must be fireproof – in other words, impervious to failure. AI systems in these high-risk environments must have multiple levels of safeguards (Charrington, 2017).

6. Ability to leverage subject matter expertise: Effective training in and operation of IAI systems requires their ability to capture and incorporate institutional (i.e. contextual) knowledge from both people and industrial processes. This knowledge provides critical constraints to AI models, but the models remain easier to implement and maintain than rule-based systems. IAI systems should facilitate the capture of subject matter expertise and incorporate this knowledge into the generated models (Charrington, 2017).

7. Ease and speed of use: AI tools must be useable and understandable by both enterprise developers and the relevant employees of individual organisations. To promote innovation, the tools used by implementation teams must allow them to rapidly experiment and iterate quickly. Tools operating at the correct level of abstraction will enhance productivity and understandability, while still providing the flexibility to tackle real-world problems (Charrington, 2017).

8. Deployment flexibility: While some industrial systems exist in highly controlled environments, others are exposed to the elements and other demanding conditions. Still others are highly distributed or mobile. For this reason, IAI solutions must support a variety of deployment options, including cloud computing, on-premises deployment, and embedded or ruggedised systems (Charrington, 2017).

9. Context trumps fairness: Interpretability, fairness, and bias are key concerns, but this does not mean algorithms and models should always be fully interpretable or fair. We need to consider the context: the domain and the intended application. Moreover, the potential trade-off with other important metrics must be considered. Would improving the interpretability or fairness of the solution significantly impact its performance, security, or privacy in a negative manner? These questions do not necessarily have an immediate answer, thus making it imperative for the future research agenda on IAI to include ways to assess, quantify, and audit such characteristics in a continuous way, ensuring that stakeholders have all the knowledge required to take informed and conscious business actions (Peres et al., 2020).

12.3.2 Industrial AI Solutions Landscape

Enterprises have a variety of technology options at their disposal to help them on their IAI journey. Again, context is key. Ultimately, the only way to select the best technology is to understand the

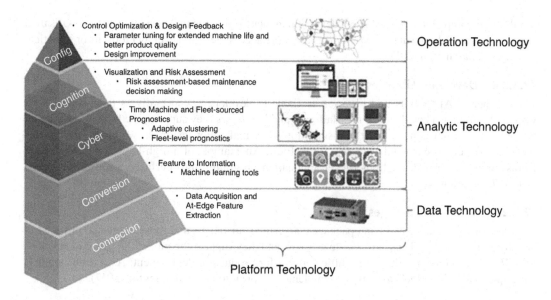

FIGURE 12.7 AI solutions landscape (Charrington, 2017).

various options – their upsides and their negatives – and apply these to the specific requirements of a given use-case scenario.

Five general categories of technology are available for IAI projects, as shown in Figure 12.7 and discussed below. We should note, however, that the distinction between categories is a bit blurry, and some tools span multiple categories (Charrington, 2017).

12.3.2.1 Point Solutions

Point solutions do not provide a platform for IAI that can be applied across multiple use cases, and customising point solutions to meet the requirements of a given organisation's real-world needs can be challenging. The effort required to do so could reduce or even eliminate its time-to-market advantage (Charrington, 2017).

12.3.2.2 Pre-Trained AI Models and Services

Today, the major cloud computing providers all offer pre-trained ML services that are run in their clouds. These application programming interfaces (APIs) can eliminate much of the complexity of training and deploying ML models. However, they are frequently limited in the depth of the models they support, in their ability to train using an organisation's own data, and in their supported deployment options (Charrington, 2017).

12.3.2.3 Development Platforms

AI rests on both data science and statistics. Not surprisingly, then, building enterprise-ready IAI systems is both a software engineering exercise and a data science one. AI-centric software development platforms are advantageous in that they can help deliver scalable, production-ready AI systems quickly. They also provide support for the entire lifecycle of an AI system, including:

- training models,
- deploying models,
- integrating models with downstream applications and systems, and
- monitoring models' performance over time.

Finally, while implementing IAI using development platforms calls for stronger technical skills than point or pre-trained offerings, the platforms are more accessible than developer toolkits or statistical packages (Charrington, 2017).

12.3.2.4   Developer Libraries

The number of AI toolkits and libraries available to developers, especially as open-source software, is exploding. They differ in the platforms and languages they support, the level of abstraction they provide for developers, and the assumptions they make. For instance, two low-level libraries are Python's sci-kit-learn and Google's TensorFlow. An example of a high-level application is the Keras library; it provides a higher-level application programming interface, specifically for DL tasks (Charrington, 2017).

12.3.2.5   Statistical Packages

A variety of statistical toolkits and packages targeting statisticians and those interested in statistics are currently available. These are low-level tools, and they support the modelling phase of developing ML applications. Yet they offer little support for production deployment. As a result, models developed using these tools are often re-implemented prior to use (Charrington, 2017).

12.4   THE IMS ARCHITECTURE FOR INDUSTRIAL AI

As we have discussed throughout this chapter, IAI can realise smart and resilient industrial systems and enable them to be fault-tolerant, on-demand, and self-organising. The IMS Global Learning Consortium's 5C-CPPS architecture (www.imsglobal.org), shown in Figure 12.8, sums up what we have been talking about over the past pages (see Section 13.1.5 for a similar but four-step architecture). This architecture provides a comprehensive step-by-step strategy for incorporating IAI from the initial data collection to the final value creation (Lee et al., 2019). It divides the enabling technologies into data technology, analytic technology, operation technology, and platform technology.

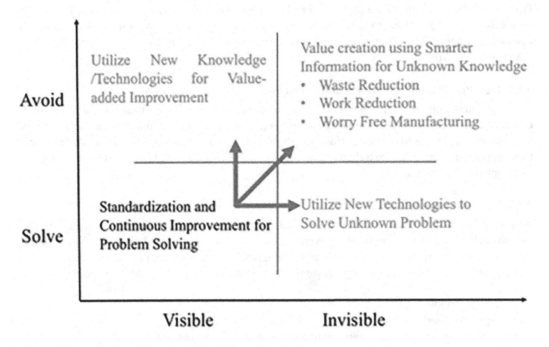

FIGURE 12.8   IAI-enabling technologies (Lee et al., 2019).

12.4.1 DATA TECHNOLOGY

Data, or more precisely actionable data, are required to yield information, knowledge, and insights. The more data we analyse, the smarter our decisions become.

The use of sensors gives a more complete view of the performance of assets including equipment, inventory, and people. Various types of signals can be captured from equipment, such as vibration, temperature, pressure, and oil particulates. The data can be static background information, such as machine IDs or process parameters, or they can be dynamic, such as asset health condition and use or inventory levels. Data can be generated at a component level, a machine level, or the shop-floor level and can be broadly divided into structured and unstructured data.

The role of data technology is to track, document, and control huge and varied data arriving at high speed in real time. The data technology must also be able to communicate these data and manage them. The communication technology, a subset of data technology, should feature security, fast data transfer, low latency, high reliability, traceability, and scalability (Lee et al., 2019).

12.4.2 ANALYTIC TECHNOLOGIES

It is one thing to have Big Data. It is another to know what to do with them. This is where analytics steps in. Analytics refers to the application of statistics and other mathematical tools to Big Data to assess and improve practices. Analytics can enable organisations to investigate tiny variations in production processes. The larger production process can be divided into very specific tasks or activities to identify any processes/components that are underperforming.

Using data-driven modelling, organisations can discover hitherto hidden patterns and unknown correlations, along with other useful information and integrate the obtained information with other technologies to improve both productivity and innovation.

Data visualisation tools are an essential element of analytic technologies. These tools allow the results of analysis to be communicated clearly and effectively to the people who are supposed to follow up on them. Easy-to-interpret and user-friendly graphs, charts, and reports enable stakeholders to understand the analysed data, track the most important metrics, and see where they are with respect to their goals (Lee et al., 2019).

12.4.3 PLATFORM TECHNOLOGIES

Platforms are a central aspect of IAI, providing the tools and flexibility required to develop application-centric functions unique to each industry and each organisation. Platform technologies help in coordinating, integrating, deploying, and supporting technologies, such as DT, connectivity, edge intelligence, data storage, and robotics integration.

Three major types of platform configurations are stand-alone, fog/edge, and cloud. The differentiating factor is the location where analytics are deployed.

12.4.3.1 Operations Technologies

Based on the information derived from the analytics, OT, in conjunction with the three other technologies, aims to achieve organisational control and optimisation through, for example, product lifecycle management, enterprise resource planning (ERP), manufacturing execution systems, customer relationship management, and supply chain management.

Outcomes of the analytics can be fed back to the equipment designer for closed-loop lifecycle redesign.

Supervisory control and feedback to the physical space are managed through the OT level. The advanced OT is used to form a closed-loop management system whereby tasks are generated and executed via intelligent agents running in a distributed and autonomous fashion. OT enables characteristics like self-configuration, self-adjustment, and self-optimisation within the industrial

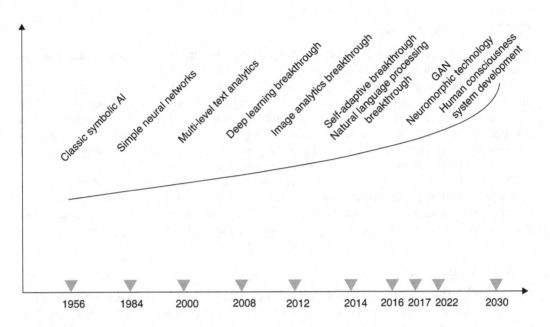

FIGURE 12.9   Impact of IAI: from solving visible problems to avoiding invisible ones (Lee et al., 2019).

ecosystem, enhancing flexibility and resilience throughout the whole system, improving efficiency, and saving money (Lee et al., 2019).

12.5   VISIBLE AND INVISIBLE ISSUES

Manufacturing issues can be mapped into two spaces: visible and invisible. This is visualised in Figure 12.9.

Visible issues include equipment breakdown, reduced yield, and loss of product quality, among many others. Invisible issues include asset degradation, component wear, and lack of lubrication, among others. Well-defined problems such as breakdowns, quality, and productivity are usually solved through continuous improvement based on a traditional manufacturing approach (lower left space in the figure).

Today, more organisations are using AI algorithms to design, produce, and deliver high-quality products faster than the competition (upper left space). Their efforts have led to the development of new techniques to address the invisible issues (lower right space). The adoption of an IAI-based approach will help produce new value-creation opportunities for smart manufacturing in a dynamic and uncertain environment (upper right space).

In brief, the unified implementation of the key elements of IAI help solve the visible problems while avoiding the invisible ones (Lee et al., 2019).

IAI can help achieve the "3Ws" in smart manufacturing:

1. Work reduction,
2. Waste reduction, and
3. Worry-free manufacturing.

Worry is an invisible concern and could be triggered by things like a product's bad quality, customer dissatisfaction, or business decline. It can be addressed by using advanced AI tools and taking a systematic approach. Work and waste reduction can be achieved by identifying visible problems in those areas and addressing them through AI applications (Lee et al., 2019).

12.6 BUILDING THE FUTURE WITH AI

IAI lets organisations better monitor, optimise, and control their physical operations and systems. This, in turn, leads to greater visibility and situational awareness, improved planning and decision-making, and increased efficiency and productivity.

The implications are significant and certainly cannot be underestimated. AI's quickly growing capability and maturity, combined with the high levels of automation in modern industrial environments, has created an ideal opportunity for forward-thinking organisations to beat out their competitors (Charrington, 2017).

12.6.1 AI in Industry 4.0

The most significant transformation in industry is digitalisation with the arrival of Industry 4.0 and the fourth Industrial Revolution. In a nutshell, Industry 4.0 aims to develop smart equipment with access to more data, thus allowing the equipment to become more efficient and productive by making RT decisions (Sharabov & Tsochev, 2020).

Critical thinking, problem-solving, communication, and teamwork have a significant impact on the development of innovations in the era of AI. Industry 4.0 puts the focus on the following innovations:

- Cyber-physical systems (CPS): These are mechanical devices manipulated by computer-based algorithms.
- Internet of things (IoT): The IoT is an interconnected network of devices embedded with computerised sensing, scanning, and monitoring capabilities.
- Cloud computing: This refers to offsite network hosting and data backup.
- Cognitive computing: This refers to technological platforms based on AI.

The successful integration of new technology relies on well-designed systems based on the following principles:

- Interoperability: Interoperability allows different systems, devices, or applications to communicate without involving the end user.
- Virtualisation: Virtualisation allows the CPS to monitor physical processes using sensors; the obtained data are used to build virtual and simulation models by providing a virtual copy of the physical world.
- Decentralisation: The decentralisation principle means CPS make decisions on their own to perform tasks as autonomously as possible.
- RT capability: The RT capability principle demands that data be collected and analysed in RT to provide the ability to react quickly in cases of failure and make the proper decisions.
- Service orientation: The key design principle of Industry 4.0 is service orientation. It enables the services of companies, CPS, and humans to be made available. It also enables new types of services to be created. In most cases, this is realised by service-oriented architecture (SOA) where the software services play small roles.
- Modularity: The design of modular systems enables flexible adaptation to changing user requirements by replacing some modules. The modular systems can be adjusted easily when changing some functions or product characteristics. With standardised software and hardware interfaces, the new modules can be automatically identified and utilised via the Internet of Services (IoS) (Sharabov & Tsochev, 2020).

The basic engine of Industry 4.0 is digitalisation, and the basis of digitalisation is AI. The development of AI is shown in Figure 12.10 (Sharabov & Tsochev, 2020).

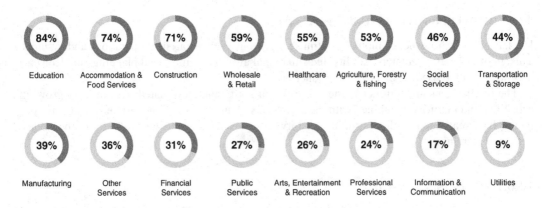

FIGURE 12.10 History of AI development (Sharabov & Tsochev, 2020).

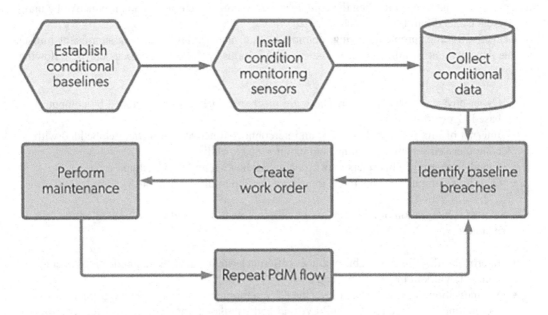

FIGURE 12.11 Top ten industries benefiting from AI (Sharabov & Tsochev, 2020).

The top ten industry types that benefit from AI are shown in Figure 12.11. AI has many industrial applications. It is particularly valuable for:

- Predictive analytics,
- Predictive maintenance,
- Industrial robotics,
- Computer vision, and
- Inventory management (Sharabov & Tsochev, 2020).

Each of these use cases is discussed at greater length in the following sections.

12.6.1.1 Predictive Analytics

The basic idea of predictive analytics is to work through a lot of data using AI. The analysis of the data generates different patterns that give information about what could happen based on what has happened before.

The first step is to acquire data from files, databases, sensors, and so on. In the next step, the data are pre-processed. They are reduced and transformed so that they can actually be used. When this is done, the features of interest can be extracted. The next step is to develop a predictive mode using ML; the parameters are optimised so the error rate is kept to a minimum. At the point, the model is validated through various tests and simulations. The final step is to integrate this analytics with the system in the whole workflow. This is done by integrating it with desktop apps, enterprise-scale systems like MATLAB, Excel, Java, C/C++,.exe, .NET,.dll, Python, and embedded devices and hardware (Sharabov & Tsochev, 2020).

Models for predictive analytics can be one of the following:

1. Predictive model: The predictive model is used to study the connection between a few samples of the examined unit and could involve conditions under uncertainty. Some predictive models can integrate optimisation techniques to determine the proper decisions.
2. Descriptive model: The descriptive model measures the relations in data and is used to classify data in groups.
3. Decision model: The decision model describes the relations between all the segments of the known data, including the results from the predictive models.

Predictive analytics uses regression and ML techniques, but the core of predictive analytics is the use of regression techniques (models). The key is to create a mathematical equation as a representation of the interactions between the different variables under consideration (Sharabov & Tsochev, 2020).

The models that can be used for predictive analytics are:

- Linear regression models,
- Discrete choice models,
- Logistic regression models,
- Probit regression models,
- Multinomial logistic regression models,
- Logit versus probit models,
- Time series models,
- Survival or duration analysis models,
- Classification and regression tree (CART) models,
- Multivariate adaptive regression spline models.

12.6.1.2   Predictive Maintenance

Predictive maintenance is often considered part of predictive analytics, but the two differ in one key area – how they use the collected data. Predictive analytics can be used for the whole workflow (see Figure 12.12), but predictive maintenance only gives an assessment when equipment has a defect (Sharabov & Tsochev, 2020).

ML is used in predictive maintenance. For this, we need to have the right quantity of the right data available; we need to frame the problem appropriately, and ultimately, we must evaluate the predictions properly.

First, we need to build a failure model; for this, we need enough historical data to capture information about events leading to failure. Other key components are the mechanical properties, average use, and operating conditions. When collecting data for creating a failure model, we must consider:

1. What types of failure can occur?
2. What does the failure process look like?
3. Which parts of the system can be related to each type of failure (Sharabov & Tsochev, 2020)?

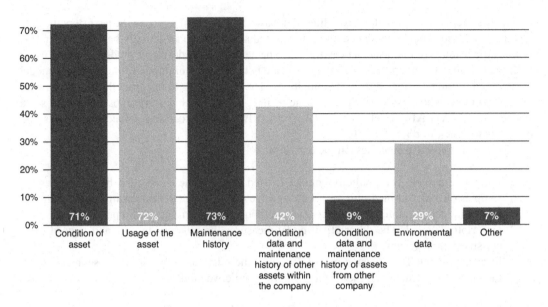

FIGURE 12.12 Predictive maintenance workflow (Sharabov & Tsochev, 2020).

When framing a problem, we need to answer a few methodological questions. In general, we need to know what kind of result we want, how long in advance the model should be able to indicate that a failure will occur, and what the performance target is.

Many strategies are used in ML. Not every strategy can be used everywhere, and the context must be considered in predictive maintenance. There are two ways to approach predictive maintenance:

1. Classification approach and
2. Regression approach.

The former approach only gives a Boolean answer but can offer greater accuracy with less data. The latter needs more data although it provides more information about when the failure will happen. Two additional strategies for predictive maintenance are:

1. Flagging anomalous behaviour and
2. Survival models for the prediction of failure probability over time.

The former is often used when a failure is not allowed or there is no failure, and the latter is used when we are interested in the degradation process itself (Sharabov & Tsochev, 2020).

The data types used for predictive maintenance are shown in Figure 12.13.

12.6.2 Industrial Robotics

Industrial robotics powered by AI are designed to work with people on the assembly line. In fact, industrial robotics and predictive maintenance go hand-in-hand. With current technology, a robot can monitor its own accuracy and performance, signalling when maintenance is required to avoid expensive downtime.

AI also allows a new way for a robot to be programmed. For example, a particular task is presented; then, the robot attempts to do it with varying levels of success. It learns from its mistakes until it can perform the task successfully with a high degree of repeatability.

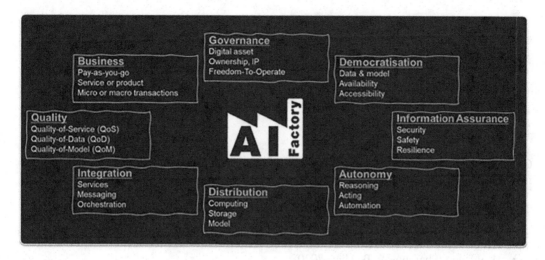

FIGURE 12.13 Types of data for predictive maintenance (Sharabov & Tsochev, 2020).

Additional benefits of robotics are related to increased operating and reduced programming time and higher efficiency using intuitionistic fuzzy techniques to control robotic motion or using speech applications for human-robot interaction systems.

Some key benefits of industrial robotics powered by AI include the following:

1. Vision system: There is improved depth and image recognition thanks to the integration of ML, semantic segmentation, and scene understanding;
2. Scalability: Thanks to DL, a 3D computer-aided design (CAD) model is no longer required, and the artificial neural network (ANN) can automatically identify the object in the image after training;
3. Intelligent placement.

12.6.2.1 Computer Vision

Computer vision is a fundamental use case of AI. Computer vision basically replicates the complexity of human vision and enables computers to identify and process objects in images like humans would. Thanks to neural networks and AI, the field has evolved in recent years and can surpass humans in some tasks related to detecting and labelling objects.

In general, the driving force is the amount of data used to train the vision. An image is then broken into individual pixels, and the trained computer vision tries to make sense of it. Although this sounds simple, interpreting information from pixels is a complicated process.

ML is the core of computer vision and is integrated into both manufacturing systems and things we use every day. Certain "features" can detect specific patterns in images. Fundamental algorithms like logistic and linear regression and decision trees are used to classify images and detect objects in them.

Before AI, machines could not be trained, and manual coding was required to achieve even remotely accurate results. This methodology has three main steps:

1. Create a database,
2. Annotate images, and
3. Capture new images.

Thanks to ML, the process has become dramatically more efficient and easier. Now it can be done in a matter of seconds. In most cases, this kind of computing is done on the cloud, because of the cloud's more powerful hardware (Sharabov & Tsochev, 2020).

In sequential order, the six steps in the workflow of computer vision are:

1. Object classification,
2. Identification,
3. Verification,
4. Detection,
5. Segmentation, and
6. Recognition.

Computer vision has a range of use scenarios from personal cameras to the identification of defects in products in manufacturing. Some use cases for computer vision are the following:

- Self-driving cars,
- Facial recognition,
- AR and mixed reality (MR), and
- Healthcare (Sharabov & Tsochev, 2020).

12.6.2.2 Inventory Management

An important use of AI in the industrial context is inventory management. If the inventory is managed perfectly, the workflow will be dramatically optimised. This can be achieved through AI, thanks to its computing power and its ability to work with databases in terms of both speed and reliability.

When an AI system is integrated correctly, it can provide information on when to order supplies, thanks to the data it has collected and the use of ML to process those data. The process is similar to predictive analytics but is concentrated on managing the inventory. The system looks for patterns in previous years and gives results based on the data collected (Sharabov & Tsochev, 2020).

12.7   WE BELIEVE IN INDUSTRIAL AI

We believe in AI as a transforming technology for both society and industry!

Why? Let's recap some of the aspects and characteristics of AI and digital technologies. As we discussed earlier, AI and digitalisation are changing both society and industry. In industry, IAI and digitalisation assist transformation by enabling the following capabilities:

1. Autonomy: Emerging technologies such as AI and digitalisation facilitate autonomy in industry. The enhanced analytics empowered by AI and digitalisation supports decision-making by providing artefacts to enable a *data-to-decision* approach. Data-to-decision refers to a semi-automated, human-centric decision-making process. However, AI and digitalisation can also be utilised to implement a *data-to-action* approach, referring to a fully automated decision process in which human intervention is not necessarily required.
2. Nowcasting and forecasting: Analytics for nowcasting and forecasting aims to yield insight into various industrial processes such as asset management, operation, and maintenance. It is expected to facilitate decision-making processes by providing capabilities to perceive "what is happening" or descriptive analytics, "why things are happening" or diagnostics, "what will happen in the future" or predictive analytics, and finally "whats need to be done next" or prescriptive analytics.
3. Health and function management: Asset health and function management deals with the management of risks identified through nowcasting and forecasting. Health and function management focuses on utilising forecasting in decision-making related to business, safety, security, maintenance, asset management, and asset life.
4. Safety: AI and digital technologies can be used to better identify, assess, and manage risks to humans in industrial contexts by augmenting human senses and their interaction

with the system. They can also be combined with robotics to replace humans in high-risk situations.

5. Security: Information assurance, including data and information security, i.e. cybersecurity, is an important aspect of business today. AI and digitalisation can be used to predict and prevent cybersecurity-related errors and failures. These technologies can also be utilised to assess the robustness and resilience of a system with respect to its digital components.

All these transformative enablers indicate that AI and digitalisation are both necessary and fundamental to achieve operational excellence in industry.

However, a number of challenges need to be addressed first. During the development of the AI Factory in various industrial domains, including railway, aviation, mining, and construction, we identified the following areas of concern (Figure 12.14):

1. Governance: It is challenging to implement AI and digital technologies in industries that are managing, operating, and maintaining complex technical systems. In many industrial contexts, the business, operation, and maintenance processes are distributed over several

Level	Industrial Scenario	
Level 0 - No autonomy: Human operators have full control without any assistance from the AI system		A robot performing pick and place operations in pre-defined, fixed positions within fixed system boundaries. The robot is programmed with a pre-set behaviour by humans, who select and prioritise its rules
Level 1 - Assistance with respect to select functions: Human operators have full responsibility and make all decisions		The robot functions similarly to Level 0. However, at autonomy level 1, a robot assistance system programmed using AI can suggest goal-oriented improvements, such as process optimizations concerning cost, energy or time. These suggestion require the approval of a human supervisor to take effect.
Level 2 - Partial autonomy: in clearly defined areas, human operators have full responsibility and define (some) goals		At level 2 the robot is still predominantly programmed in pre-set manner by humans. However, the self-improvements go beyond level 1, with the AI programming allowing the robot to improve its behaviour within specified system boundaries and goals. An example of this behaviour would be the robot being capable of recognising and picking parts which are not in the exact pre-set position. Humans retain decision-making power and intervene when/if necessary.
Level 3 - Delimited autonomy: In larger sub-areas, the AI system warns if problems occur, human beings validate the solutions recommended by the system		The robot is only partially programmed in a pre-set manner by humans. On top of being capable of adjusting its own behavior, the robot can make and implement plans within the specified system boundaries, including for instance autonomous path control. This can be done in collaboratively with other entities in its environment. For this purpose the robotic system should is equipped with sensors necessary to perceive the environment, its context and to learn skills. Humans oversee the system's decisions, assist in resolving unforeseen disturbances and intervene in case of emergency.
Level 4 - System is adaptable and functions autonomously: Within defined system boundaries, human operators can supervise or intervene in emergency situations		At this level the system behaves as an adaptive, autonomous system in larger sub-areas within known system boundaries. Self-optimization within these boundaries is enabled through continuous learning phases and defined (partial) goals, leading to improved predictions and problem-solving capability. Humans relinquish control of a specific part of the system, shifting to a monitoring role and intervening only in emergency cases. If the human fails to intervene, the robotic system is capable of handling some situations according to its own perception of adequate corrective action.
Level 5 - Full autonomy: The AI system operates autonomously in all areas, including in cooperation and in fluctuating system boundaries. Human operators do not need to be present		At level 5 the robotic system acts with full autonomy and in collaboration with other autonomous systems within system boundaries specified by humans. In case of disturbances or fluctuating working parameters, the system is capable of dynamically adapting the plan and communicate it to other autonomous entities. In emergency cases, the system independently puts itself in secure mode.

FIGURE 12.14 AI Factory's challenges.

organisational units (internal or external). These distributed processes cross organisation boundaries and are governed by heterogenous rules, regulations, requirement models, and incentive models. As such, they require an over-arching governance model for the provision and acceptance of diverse agreements and conventions. The management of digital assets, e.g. data and algorithms, requires a digital governance model to ensure that the existing and new agreements and conventions comply with stakeholders' internal and external requirements and incentives.

2. Business: Using AI to support business processes is vital. However, enabling appropriate business models to support an AI solution is equally essential. Business models aimed at supporting AI solutions need to adapt to the constraints of digital governance, but they also need to develop and provide incentive models to stimulate and facilitate the implementation of AI solutions. These incentives should encourage data and model sharing, ownership of digital assets, co-sharing, openness, confidentiality, protection of intellectual property rights, freedom-to-operate, and so on.

3. Democratisation: Digitalisation in industry generates a vast amount of data. These Big Data are used in AI algorithms to enable enhanced analytics, including, for example, now-casting and forecasting. In a digitalised industrial environment, democratisation refers to the availability and accessibility of data and models to "digital citizens", i.e. individuals and organisations that have agreed on and are committed to the defined digital governance model. A data democratisation model needs to be considered and agreed upon as part of the governance model when AI solutions are implemented in industry. The deployed AI solution then needs to develop, implement, and deploy mechanisms that comply with the agreed democratisation model to meet the needs and requirements of the various digital citizens.

4. Information assurance: When AI solutions are being designed, developed, implemented, and deployed, information assurance is very important for the solution's fidelity and resilience. Information assurance deals with the processing and logistics, i.e. storing and transmitting, of information between involved actors, i.e. people and systems. Information assurance needs to be considered at a strategic level when designing the architecture of the AI solution, as it is related to the overall risk management of digital solutions in industry. Information assurance strategies must be supported by a cybersecurity mechanism.

5. Autonomy: When developing AI solutions for enhanced analytics of autonomous, complex technical systems in industry, the level of autonomy of the solution is as important as the technical system it aims to support. The autonomy level of an AI solution can be related to capabilities such as data collection services, data quality assessment services, cybersecurity services, data processing services, and decision-making services. When the architecture of an AI solution is designed, the level of autonomy needs to be defined, and the necessary technologies for automation must be selected.

6. Distribution: Distribution and decomposition of computing are necessary to achieve reliability, scalability, maintainability, and resilience of any software solution. AI solutions are software-intensive by nature. Any AI solution requires a framework, i.e. a meta-model, through which a range of concepts, models, techniques, technologies, and methodologies can be clarified and integrated to enable distributed computing.

7. Integration: The use of a distributed model to decompose an AI solution into micro-services will impact the whole architecture of the solution, including the analytics algorithms. This means that the analytics algorithms need to be designed and developed to enable distributed execution. At the same time, decomposition of a solution requires appropriate integration models to orchestrate the various micro-services. The integration models can be based on SOA or event-oriented approaches. The integration model is part of the overall framework developed for an AI solution.

8. Quality: Quality is essential for the trustworthiness and fidelity of any AI solution in industry. Quality can be related to aspects of data, information, algorithms, and services. Quality of data has an obvious impact when implementing learning mechanisms, based on ML or DL. It also has an impact on the fidelity of the analytics services and the trustworthiness of the whole solution. Various aspects of quality must be considered when defining and designing a framework for an AI solution. It is also necessary to define quality indicators and develop mechanisms aimed at continuous monitoring and assessment of a highly autonomous AI solution.

REFERENCES

Aspentech. (2022a). Industrial AI. https://www.aspentech.com/en/apm-resources/industrial-ai

Aspentech. (2022b). The future starts with industrial AI. *MIT Technology Review*. https://www.technologyreview.com/2021/06/28/1026960/the-future-starts-with-industrial-ai

Charrington, S. (2017). Artificial intelligence for industrial applications. *Cloudpulse Strategias*.

Lee, J., Singh, J., & Azamfar, M. (2019). *Industrial Artificial Intelligence*. https://doi.org/10.48550/arxiv.1908.02150

Peres, R. S., Jia, X., Lee, J., Sun, K., Colombo, A. W., & Barata, J. (2020). Industrial artificial intelligence in industry 4.0-systematic review, challenges and outlook. *IEEE Access, 8*, 121–139.

Precognize. (2022). *What is Industrial AI?* https://www.precog.co/glossary/industrial-ai/

Sharabov, M., & Tsochev, G. (2020). The use of artificial intelligence in Industry 4.0. *Problems Engineering Cybernetics Robotics, 72*, 17–29.

Wikipedia. (2022). *Artificial Intelligence in Industry*. https://en.wikipedia.org/wiki/Artificial_intelligence_in_industry

Yao, M. (2017). *Unique Challenges of Industrial Artificial Intelligence*. https://www.forbes.com/sites/mariyayao/2017/04/14/unique-challenges-of-industrial-artificial-intelligence-general-electric/?sh=4f1b516e1305

Index

Printed in the United States
by Baker & Taylor Publisher Services